3 EDITION

The Landscape of Qualitative Research

Norman K. Denzin
University of Illinois at Urbana-Champaign

Yvonna S. Lincoln
Texas A&M University

Editors

SAGE Publications
Los Angeles • London • New Delhi • Singapore

For information:

Sage Publications, Inc.
2455 Teller Road
Thousand Oaks, California 91320
E-mail: order@sagepub.com

Sage Publications Ltd.
1 Oliver's Yard
55 City Road
London EC1Y 1SP
United Kingdom

Sage Publications India Pvt. Ltd.
B 1/I 1 Mohan Cooperative Industrial Area
Mathura Road, New Delhi 110 044
India

Sage Publications Asia-Pacific Pte. Ltd.
33 Pekin Street #02-01
Far East Square
Singapore 048763

Printed in the United States of America

Library of Congress Cataloging-in-Publication Data

The landscape of qualitative research/Norman K. Denzin, Yvonna S. Lincoln [editors]. — 3rd ed.
p. cm.
Includes bibliographical references and index.
ISBN 978-1-4129-5758-8 (pbk.: alk. paper)
1. Social sciences—Research. 2. Qualitative research. 3. Qualitative reasoning. I. Denzin, Norman K. II. Lincoln, Yvonna S.
H62.L274 2008
300.72—dc22 2007031744
This book is printed on acid-free paper.

07 08 09 10 11 10 9 8 7 6 5 4 3 2 1

Acquisitions Editor: Vicki Knight
Associate Editor: Sean Connelly
Editorial Assistant: Lauren Habib
Production Editor: Astrid Virding
Copy Editor: Gillian Dickens
Typesetter: C&M Digitals (P) Ltd.
Proofreader: Tracy Marcynzsyn
Indexer: Juniee Oneida
Cover Designer: Candice Harman
Marketing Manager: Stephanie Adams
Cover Photograph: C. A. Hoffman

CONTENTS

PREFACE

For nearly four decades, a quiet methodological revolution has been taking place in the social sciences. A blurring of disciplinary boundaries has occurred. The social sciences and humanities have drawn closer together in a mutual focus on an interpretive, qualitative approach to inquiry, research, and theory. Although these trends are not new, the extent to which the "qualitative revolution" has overtaken the social sciences and related professional fields continues to be nothing short of amazing.

Reflecting this revolution, a host of textbooks, journals, research monographs, and readers have been published in recent years. In 1994, we published the first edition of the *Handbook of Qualitative Research* in an attempt to represent the field in its entirety, to take stock of how far it had come and how far it might yet go. The immediate success of the first edition suggested the need to offer the *Handbook* in terms of three separate volumes. So in 1998, we published a three-volume set, *The Landscape of Qualitative Research: Theories and Issues; Strategies of Inquiry;* and *Collecting and Interpreting Qualitative Materials.* In 2003, we offered a new three-volume set, based on the second edition of the handbook.

By 2005, when we published the third edition of the *Handbook,* it was abundantly clear, as had been in 2000, when we published the second edition of the *Handbook,* that the "field" of qualitative research was still defined primarily by tensions, contradictions, and hesitations. These tensions exist in a less-than-unified arena. We have always believed that the handbook, in its first, second, and third editions, could and would be valuable for solidifying, interpreting, and organizing the field despite the essential differences that characterize it.

The first edition attempted to define the field of qualitative research. The second edition went one step further. Building on themes in the first edition, we asked how the practices of qualitative inquiry could be used to address issues equity and of social justice. The third edition continues where the second edition ended. The transformations that were taking place in the 1990s continue to gain momentum in the first decade of this new century.

Not surprisingly, this quiet revolution has been met by resistance. In many quarters, a resurgent, scientifically based research paradigm has gained the upper hand. Borrowing from the field of biomedical research, the National Research Council (NRC) has appropriated neo-positivist, evidence-based epistemologies. Calls for mixed-method designs are now common. Interpretive methods are read as being unscientific and unsuitable for use by those who legislate social policy.

Still, the days of a value-free inquiry based on a God's-eye view of reality are judged by many to be over. Today, many agree that all inquiry is moral and political. Experimental, reflexive ways of writing first-person ethnographic texts are now commonplace. There continues to be a pressing need to show how the practices of qualitative research can help change the world in positive ways. So, at the beginning of the 21st century, it is necessary to reengage the promise of qualitative research as a form of radical democratic practice.

We have been enormously gratified and heartened by the response to the *Handbook* since its publication. Especially gratifying has been that it has been used and adapted by such a wide variety of scholars and graduate students in precisely the way we had hoped: as a starting point, a springboard for new thought and new work.

The Paperback Project

The third edition of *The Landscape of Qualitative Research* of the *Handbook of Qualitative Research* is virtually a new volume. Indeed, in the third edition of the *Handbook,* there are 42 new chapters, authors, and/or coauthors. There are 16 totally new chapter topics, including contributions on indigenous inquiry, decolonizing methodologies, critical ethnography, critical humanism and queer theory, performance ethnography, narrative inquiry, arts-based inquiry, online ethnography, analytic methodologies, Foucault's methodologies, talk and text, focus groups and critical pedagogy, relativism, criteria and politics, the poetics of place, cultural and investigative poetics, qualitative evaluation and social policy, social science inquiry in the new millennium, and anthropology of the contemporary. All returning authors have substantially revised their original contributions, in many cases producing totally new and different chapters.

The third edition of the *Handbook of Qualitative Research* continues where the second edition ended. It takes as its theme the necessity to reengage the promise of qualitative research as a generative form of radical democratic practice. This is the agenda of the third edition of the *Landscape* series, as it is for the third edition of the *Handbook*—namely, to show how the discourses of qualitative research can be used to help create and imagine a free democratic society. Each of the chapters in the three-volume set takes up this project, in one way or another.

A handbook, we were told by our publisher, should ideally represent the distillation of knowledge of a field, a benchmark volume that synthesizes an existing literature, helping to define and shape the present and future of that discipline. This mandate organized the third edition. In metaphoric terms, if you were to take one book on qualitative research with you to a desert island or a mountaintop (or for a comprehensive graduate examination), a handbook would be the book.

It was again decided that the part structure of the *Handbook* could serve as useful point of departure for the organization of the paperbacks. Thus, Volume 1, titled *The Landscape of Qualitative Research: Theories and Issues,* takes a look at the field from a broadly theoretical perspective and is composed of the *Handbook*'s Parts I ("Locating the Field"), II ("Paradigms and Perspectives in Contention"), and VI ("The Future of Qualitative Research"). Volume 2, titled *Strategies of Qualitative Inquiry,* focuses on just that and consists of Part III of the *Handbook.* Volume 3, titled *Collecting and Interpreting Qualitative Materials,* considers the tasks of collecting, analyzing, and interpreting empirical materials and comprises the *Handbook*'s Parts IV ("Methods of Collecting and Analyzing Empirical Materials") and V ("The Art and Practices of Interpretation, Evaluation, and Presentation").

As with the first and second editions of the *Landscape* series, we decided that nothing should be cut from the original *Handbook.* Nearly everyone we spoke to who used the *Handbook* had his or her own way of using it, leaning heavily on certain chapters and skipping others altogether. But there was consensus that this reorganization made a great deal of sense both pedagogically and economically. We and Sage are committed to making this iteration of the *Handbook* accessible for classroom use. This commitment is reflected in the size, organization, and price of the paperbacks, as well as in the addition of end-of-book bibliographies.

It also became clear in our conversations with colleagues who used the *Handbook* that the single-volume, hardcover version has a distinct place and value, and Sage will keep the original version available until a revised edition is published.

▣ Organization of This Volume

The Landscape of Qualitative Research attempts to put the field of qualitative research in context. Part I locates the field, starting with action research and the academy, turning next to compositional studies and critical action inquiry, then to indigenous research, concluding with the ethics and politics of qualitative research. Part II isolates what we regard as the major historical and contemporary paradigms now structuring and influencing qualitative research in the human disciplines. The chapters move from competing paradigms (positivist, postpositivist, constructivist, critical theory) to specific interpretive perspectives, feminisms, racialized discourses, cultural studies, sexualities, and queer theory. Part III considers the future of qualitative research.

Acknowledgments

Of course, this book would not exist without its authors or the editorial board members for the *Handbook* on which it is based. These individuals were able to offer both long-term, sustained commitments to the project and short-term emergency assistance.

In addition, we would like to thank the following individuals and institutions for their assistance, support, insights, and patience: our respective universities and departments, as well as Aisha Durham, Grant Kien, Li Xiong, James Salvo, David Monje, and our respective graduate students. Without them, we could never have kept this project on course. There are also several people to thank at Sage Publications. We thank Lisa Cuevas Shaw, our editor. This three-volume version of the *Handbook* would not have been possible without Lisa's wisdom, support, humor, and grasp of the field in all its current diversity.

As always, we appreciate the efforts of Chris Klein, vice president of Books Acquisitions and Books Marketing at Sage, along with his staff, for their indefatigable efforts in getting the word out about the *Handbook* to teachers, researchers, and methodologists around the world. We thank Christina Ceisel for her excellent work in the production phase of all three volumes of this project. Astrid Virding was essential in moving this project through production; we are also grateful to the copy editor, Judy Selhorst, and to those whose proofreading and indexing skills were so central to the publication of the *Handbook* on which these volumes are based. Finally, as ever, we thank our spouses, Katherine Ryan and Egon Guba, for their forbearance and constant support.

The idea for this three-volume paperback version of the *Handbook* did not arise in a vacuum, and we are grateful for the feedback we received from countless teachers and students, both informally and in response to our formal survey. We wish especially to thank the following individuals: Bryant Alexander, Tom Barone, Jack Z. Bratich, Susan Chase, Shing-Ling Sarina Chen, Nadine Dolby, Susan Finley, Andrea Fontana, Jaber Gubrium, Stephen Hartnett, Stacy Holman Jones, Steve Jones, Ruthellen Josselson, Luis Miron, Ronald J. Pelias, John Prosser, Johnny Saldaña, Paula Saukko, Thomas Schwandt, Patrick Slattery, and Linda Tuhiwai Smith.

Norman K. Denzin
University of Illinois at Urbana-Champaign

Yvonna S. Lincoln
Texas A&M University

1

INTRODUCTION

The Discipline and Practice of Qualitative Research

Norman K. Denzin and Yvonna S. Lincoln

Writing about scientific research, including qualitative research, from the vantage point of the colonized, a position that she chooses to privilege, Linda Tuhiwai Smith (1999) states that "the term 'research' is inextricably linked to European imperialism and colonialism." She continues, "The word itself is probably one of the dirtiest words in the indigenous world's vocabulary. . . . It is implicated in the worst excesses of colonialism," with the ways in which "knowledge about indigenous peoples was collected, classified, and then represented back to the West" (p. 1). This dirty word stirs up anger, silence, distrust. "It is so powerful that indigenous people even write poetry about research" (p. 1). It is one of colonialism's most sordid legacies.

Sadly, qualitative research, in many if not all of its forms (observation, participation, interviewing, ethnography), serves as a metaphor for colonial knowledge, for power, and for truth. The metaphor works this way. Research, quantitative and qualitative, is scientific. Research provides the foundation for reports about and representations of "the Other." In the colonial context, research becomes an objective way of representing the dark-skinned Other to the white world.

Colonizing nations relied on the human disciplines, especially sociology and anthropology, to produce knowledge about strange and foreign worlds. This close

Authors' Note. We are grateful to many who have helped with this chapter, including Egon Guba, Mitch Allen, David Monje, and Katherine E. Ryan.

involvement with the colonial project contributed, in significant ways, to qualitative research's long and anguished history and to its becoming a dirty word (for reviews, see Foley & Valenzuela, Chapter 9, this volume; Tedlock, Volume 2, Chapter 5). In sociology, the work of the "Chicago school" in the 1920s and 1930s established the importance of qualitative inquiry for the study of human group life. In anthropology during the same period, the discipline-defining studies of Boas, Mead, Benedict, Bateson, Evans-Pritchard, Radcliffe-Brown, and Malinowski charted the outlines of the fieldwork method (see Gupta & Ferguson, 1997; Stocking, 1986, 1989).

The agenda was clear-cut: The observer went to a foreign setting to study the culture, customs, and habits of another human group. Often this was a group that stood in the way of white settlers. Ethnographic reports of these groups where incorporated into colonizing strategies, ways of controlling the foreign, deviant, or troublesome Other. Soon qualitative research would be employed in other social and behavioral science disciplines, including education (especially the work of Dewey), history, political science, business, medicine, nursing, social work, and communications (for criticisms of this tradition, see Smith, 1999; Vidich & Lyman, 2000; see also Rosaldo, 1989, pp. 25–45; Tedlock, Volume 2, Chapter 5).

By the 1960s, battle lines were drawn within the quantitative and qualitative camps. Quantitative scholars relegated qualitative research to a subordinate status in the scientific arena. In response, qualitative researchers extolled the humanistic virtues of their subjective, interpretive approach to the study of human group life. In the meantime, indigenous peoples found themselves subjected to the indignities of both approaches, as each methodology was used in the name of colonizing powers (see Battiste, 2000; Semali & Kincheloe, 1999).

Vidich and Lyman (1994, 2000) have charted many key features of this painful history. In their now-classic analysis they note, with some irony, that qualitative research in sociology and anthropology was "born out of concern to understand the 'other'" (Vidich & Lyman, 2000, p. 38). Furthermore, this "other" was the exotic Other, a primitive, nonwhite person from a foreign culture judged to be less civilized than ours. Of course, there were colonialists long before there were anthropologists and ethnographers. Nonetheless, there would be no colonial, and now no neocolonial, history were it not for this investigative mentality that turned the dark-skinned Other into the object of the ethnographer's gaze. From the very beginning, qualitative research was implicated in a racist project.[1]

In this introductory chapter, we define the field of qualitative research, then navigate, chart, and review the history of qualitative research in the human disciplines. This will allow us to locate this volume and its contents within their historical moments. (These historical moments are somewhat artificial; they are socially constructed, quasi-historical, and overlapping conventions. Nevertheless, they permit a "performance" of developing ideas. They also facilitate an increasing sensitivity to and sophistication about the pitfalls and promises of ethnography and qualitative research.) We also present a conceptual framework for reading the qualitative research act as a multicultural, gendered process and then provide a brief introduction to the chapters that follow. Returning to the observations of Vidich and Lyman as well as those of hooks, we conclude with a brief discussion of qualitative research and critical race theory (see also Ladson-Billings & Donnor, Chapter 11, this volume). We also discuss the threats to qualitative, human subject research from the methodological conservatism movement mentioned briefly in our preface. As we note in the preface, we use the metaphor of the bridge to structure what follows. This volume is intended to serve as a bridge connecting historical moments, politics, the decolonization project, research methods, paradigms, and communities of interpretive scholars.

Definitional Issues

Qualitative research is a field of inquiry in its own right. It crosscuts disciplines, fields, and subject matters.[2] A complex, interconnected family of terms, concepts, and assumptions surround the term *qualitative research.* These include the traditions associated with foundationalism, positivism, postfoundationalism, postpositivism, poststructuralism, and the many qualitative research perspectives, and/or methods connected to cultural and interpretive studies (the chapters in Part II, this volume, take up these paradigms).[3] There are separate and detailed literatures on the many methods and approaches that fall under the category of qualitative research, such as case study, politics and ethics, participatory inquiry, interviewing, participant observation, visual methods, and interpretive analysis.

In North America, qualitative research operates in a complex historical field that crosscuts at least eight historical moments. (We discuss these moments in detail below.) These moments overlap and simultaneously operate in the present.[4] We define them as the *traditional* (1900–1950); the *modernist*, or golden age (1950–1970); *blurred genres* (1970–1986); the *crisis of representation* (1986–1990); the *postmodern*, a period of experimental and new ethnographies (1990–1995); *postexperimental inquiry* (1995–2000); the *methodologically contested present* (2000–2004); and the *fractured future,* which is now (2005–). The future, the eighth moment, confronts the methodological backlash associated with the evidence-based social movement. It is concerned with moral discourse, with the development of sacred textualities. The eighth moment asks that the social sciences and the humanities become sites for critical conversations about democracy, race, gender, class, nation-states, globalization, freedom, and community.[5]

The postmodern and postexperimental moments were defined in part by a concern for literary and rhetorical tropes and the narrative turn, a concern for storytelling, for composing ethnographies in new ways (Bochner & Ellis, 2002; Ellis, 2004; Goodall, 2000; Pelias, 2004; Richardson & Lockridge, 2004; Trujillo, 2004). Laurel

Richardson (1997) observes that this moment was shaped by a new sensibility, by doubt, by a refusal to privilege any method or theory (p. 173). But now at the dawn of this new century we struggle to connect qualitative research to the hopes, needs, goals, and promises of a free democratic society.

Successive waves of epistemological theorizing move across these eight moments. The traditional period is associated with the positivist, foundational paradigm. The modernist or golden age and blurred genres moments are connected to the appearance of postpositivist arguments. At the same time, a variety of new interpretive, qualitative perspectives were taken up, including hermeneutics, structuralism, semiotics, phenomenology, cultural studies, and feminism.[6] In the blurred genres phase, the humanities became central resources for critical, interpretive theory, and the qualitative research project broadly conceived. The researcher became a *bricoleur* (see below), learning how to borrow from many different disciplines.

The blurred genres phase produced the next stage, the crisis of representation. Here researchers struggled with how to locate themselves and their subjects in reflexive texts. A kind of methodological diaspora took place, a two-way exodus. Humanists migrated to the social sciences, searching for new social theory, new ways to study popular culture and its local, ethnographic contexts. Social scientists turned to the humanities, hoping to learn how to do complex structural and poststructural readings of social texts. From the humanities, social scientists also learned how to produce texts that refused to be read in simplistic, linear, incontrovertible terms. The line between text and context blurred. In the postmodern, experimental moment, researchers continued to move away from foundational and quasi-foundational criteria (see Smith & Hodkinson, Volume 3, Chapter 13; Richardson & St. Pierre, Volume 3, Chapter 15). Alternative evaluative criteria were sought, criteria that might prove evocative, moral, critical, and rooted in local understandings.

Any definition of qualitative research must work within this complex historical field. *Qualitative research* means different things in each of these moments. Nonetheless, an initial, generic definition can be offered: Qualitative research is a situated activity that locates the observer in the world. It consists of a set of interpretive, material practices that make the world visible. These practices transform the world. They turn the world into a series of representations, including field notes, interviews, conversations, photographs, recordings, and memos to the self. At this level, qualitative research involves an interpretive, naturalistic approach to the world. This means that qualitative researchers study things in their natural settings, attempting to make sense of, or interpret, phenomena in terms of the meanings people bring to them.[7]

Qualitative research involves the studied use and collection of a variety of empirical materials—case study; personal experience; introspection; life story; interview; artifacts; cultural texts and productions; observational, historical, interactional, and visual texts—that describe routine and problematic moments and meanings in individuals' lives. Accordingly, qualitative researchers deploy a wide range of interconnected interpretive practices, hoping always to get a better understanding of the subject matter at hand. It is understood, however, that each practice makes the world visible in a different way. Hence there is frequently a commitment to using more than one interpretive practice in any study.

The Qualitative Researcher as *Bricoleur* and Quilt Maker

The qualitative researcher may be described using multiple and gendered images: scientist, naturalist, field-worker, journalist, social critic, artist, performer, jazz musician, filmmaker, quilt maker, essayist. The many methodological practices of qualitative research may be viewed as soft science, journalism, ethnography, bricolage, quilt making, or montage. The researcher, in turn, may be seen as a *bricoleur,* as a maker of quilts, or, as in filmmaking, a person who assembles images into montages. (On montage, see Cook, 1981, pp. 171–177; Monaco, 1981, pp. 322–328; and the discussion below. On quilting, see hooks, 1990, pp. 115–122; Wolcott, 1995, pp. 31–33.)

Harper (1987, pp. 9, 74–75, 92), de Certeau (1984, p. xv), Nelson, Treichler, and Grossberg (1992, p. 2), Lévi-Strauss (1966, p. 17), Weinstein and Weinstein (1991, p. 161), and Kincheloe (2001) clarify the meanings of *bricolage* and *bricoleur.*[8] A *bricoleur* makes do by "adapting the *bricoles* of the world. *Bricolage* is 'the poetic making do'" (de Certeau, 1984, p. xv) with "such bricoles—the odds and ends, the bits left over" (Harper, 1987, p. 74). The *bricoleur* is a "Jack of all trades, a kind of professional do-it-yourself" (Lévi-Strauss, 1966, p. 17). In their work, *bricoleurs* define and extend themselves (Harper, 1987, p. 75). Indeed, the *bricoleur's* life story, or biography, "may be thought of as bricolage" (Harper, 1987, p. 92).

There are many kinds of *bricoleurs*—interpretive, narrative, theoretical, political, methodological (see below). The interpretive *bricoleur* produces a bricolage—that is, a pieced-together set of representations that is fitted to the specifics of a complex situation. "The solution (bricolage) which is the result of the *bricoleur's* method is an [emergent] construction" (Weinstein & Weinstein, 1991, p. 161) that changes and takes new forms as the *bricoleur* adds different tools, methods, and techniques of representation and interpretation to the puzzle. Nelson et al. (1992) describe the methodology of cultural studies as "a bricolage. Its choice of practice, that is, is pragmatic, strategic and self-reflexive" (p. 2). This understanding can be applied, with qualifications, to qualitative research.

The qualitative researcher as *bricoleur,* or maker of quilts, uses the aesthetic and material tools of his or her craft, deploying whatever strategies, methods, and empirical materials are at hand (Becker, 1998, p. 2). If the researcher needs to invent, or piece together, new tools or techniques, he or she will do so. Choices regarding which interpretive practices to employ are not necessarily made in advance. As Nelson et al. (1992) note, the "choice of research practices depends upon the questions that are asked, and the questions depend on their context" (p. 2), what is available in the context, and what the researcher can do in that setting.

These interpretive practices involve aesthetic issues, an aesthetics of representation that goes beyond the pragmatic or the practical. Here the concept of *montage* is useful (see Cook, 1981, p. 323; Monaco, 1981, pp. 171–172). Montage is a method of editing cinematic images. In the history of cinematography, montage is most closely associated with the work of Sergei Eisenstein, especially his film *The Battleship Potemkin* (1925). In montage, several different images are juxtaposed to or superimposed on one another to create a picture. In a sense, montage is like *pentimento,* in which something that has been painted out of a picture (an image the painter "repented," or denied) becomes visible again, creating something new. What is new is what had been obscured by a previous image.

Montage and pentimento, like jazz, which is improvisation, create the sense that images, sounds, and understandings are blending together, overlapping, forming a composite, a new creation. The images seem to shape and define one another, and an emotional, gestalt effect is produced. In film montage, images are often combined in a swiftly run sequence that produces a dizzily revolving collection of several images around a central or focused picture or sequence; directors often use such effects to signify the passage of time.

Perhaps the most famous instance of montage in film is the Odessa Steps sequence in *The Battleship Potemkin*. In the climax of the film, the citizens of Odessa are being massacred by czarist troops on the stone steps leading down to the harbor. Eisenstein cuts to a young mother as she pushes her baby in a carriage across the landing in front of the firing troops.[9] Citizens rush past her, jolting the carriage, which she is afraid to push down to the next flight of stairs. The troops are above her, firing at the citizens. She is trapped between the troops and the steps. She screams. A line of rifles points to the sky, the rifle barrels erupting in smoke. The mother's head sways back. The wheels of the carriage teeter on the edge of the steps. The mother's hand clutches the silver buckle of her belt. Below her, people are being beaten by soldiers. Blood drips over the mother's white gloves. The baby's hand reaches out of the carriage. The mother sways back and forth. The troops advance. The mother falls back against the carriage. A woman watches in horror as the rear wheels of the carriage roll off the edge of the landing. With accelerating speed, the carriage bounces down the steps, past dead citizens. The baby is jostled from side to side inside the carriage. The soldiers fire their rifles into a group of wounded citizens. A student screams as the carriage leaps across the steps, tilts, and overturns (Cook, 1981, p. 167).[10]

Montage uses brief images to create a clearly defined sense of urgency and complexity. It invites viewers to construct interpretations that build on one another as a scene unfolds. These interpretations are based on associations among the contrasting images that blend into one another. The underlying assumption of montage is that viewers perceive and interpret the shots in a "montage sequence not *sequentially,* or one at a time, but rather *simultaneously*" (Cook, 1981, p. 172). The viewer puts the sequences together into a meaningful emotional whole, as if at a glance, all at once.

The qualitative researcher who uses montage is like a quilt maker or a jazz improviser. The quilter stitches, edits, and puts slices of reality together. This process creates and brings psychological and emotional unity—a pattern—to an interpretive experience. There are many examples of montage in current qualitative research (see Diversi, 1998; Holman Jones, 1999; Lather & Smithies, 1997; Ronai, 1998; see also Holman Jones, Volume 3, Chapter 7). Using multiple voices, different textual formats, and various typefaces, Lather and Smithies (1997) weave a complex text about AIDS and women who are HIV-positive. Holman Jones (1999) creates a performance text using lyrics from the blues songs sung by Billie Holiday.

In texts based on the metaphors of montage, quilt making, and jazz improvisation, many different things are going on at the same time—different voices, different perspectives, points of views, angles of vision. Like autoethnographic performance texts, works that use montage simultaneously create and enact moral meaning. They move from the personal to the political, from the local to the historical and the cultural. These are dialogical texts. They presume an active audience. They create spaces for give-and-take between reader and writer. They do more than turn the Other into the object of the social science gaze (see Alexander, Volume 2, Chapter 3; Holman Jones, Volume 3, Chapter 7).

Qualitative research is inherently multimethod in focus (Flick, 2002, pp. 226–227). However, the use of multiple methods, or triangulation, reflects an attempt to secure an in-depth understanding of the phenomenon in question. Objective reality can never be captured. We know a thing only through its representations. Triangulation is not a tool or a strategy of validation, but an alternative to validation (Flick, 2002, p. 227). The combination of multiple methodological practices, empirical materials, perspectives, and observers in a single study is best understood, then, as a strategy that adds rigor, breadth, complexity, richness, and depth to any inquiry (see Flick, 2002, p. 229).

In Chapter 15 of Volume 3, Richardson and St. Pierre dispute the usefulness of the concept of triangulation, asserting that the central image for qualitative inquiry should be the crystal, not the triangle. Mixed-genre texts in the postexperimental moment have more than three sides. Like crystals, Eisenstein's montage, the jazz solo, or the pieces in a quilt, the mixed-genre text "combines symmetry and substance with an infinite variety of shapes, substances, transmutations. . . . Crystals grow, change, alter. . . . Crystals are prisms that reflect externalities and refract within themselves, creating different colors, patterns, arrays, casting off in different directions" (Richardson, 2000, p. 934).

In the crystallization process, the writer tells the same tale from different points of view. For example, in *A Thrice-Told Tale* (1992), Margery Wolf uses fiction, field notes, and a scientific article to give three different accounts of the same set of experiences in a native village. Similarly, in her play *Fires in the Mirror* (1993), Anna Deavere Smith presents a series of performance pieces based on interviews with people who were involved in a racial conflict in Crown Heights, Brooklyn, on August 19, 1991. The play has multiple speaking parts, including conversations with gang members, police officers, and anonymous young girls and boys. There is no one "correct" telling of this event. Each telling, like light hitting a crystal, reflects a different perspective on this incident.

Viewed as a crystalline form, as a montage, or as a creative performance around a central theme, triangulation as a form of, or alternative to, validity thus can be extended. Triangulation is the simultaneous display of multiple, refracted realities. Each of the metaphors "works" to create simultaneity rather than the sequential or linear. Readers and audiences are then invited to explore competing visions of the context, to become immersed in and merge with new realities to comprehend.

The methodological *bricoleur* is adept at performing a large number of diverse tasks, ranging from interviewing to intensive self-reflection and introspection. The theoretical *bricoleur* reads widely and is knowledgeable about the many interpretive paradigms (feminism, Marxism, cultural studies, constructivism, queer theory) that can be brought to any particular problem. He or she may not, however, feel that paradigms can be mingled or synthesized. That is, one cannot easily move between paradigms as overarching philosophical systems denoting particular ontologies, epistemologies, and methodologies. They represent belief systems that attach users to particular worldviews. Perspectives, in contrast, are less well-developed systems, and one can move between them more easily. The researcher as *bricoleur*-theorist works between and within competing and overlapping perspectives and paradigms.

The interpretive *bricoleur* understands that research is an interactive process shaped by his or her own personal history, biography, gender, social class, race, and ethnicity, and by those of the people in the setting. The critical *bricoleur* stresses the dialectical and hermeneutic nature of interdisciplinary inquiry, knowing that the boundaries that previously separated traditional disciplines no longer hold (Kincheloe, 2001, p. 683). The political *bricoleur* knows that science is power, for all research findings have political implications. There is no value-free science. This researcher seeks a civic social science based on a politics of hope (Lincoln, 1999). The gendered, narrative *bricoleur* also knows that researchers all tell stories about the worlds they have studied. Thus the narratives, or stories, scientists tell are accounts couched and framed within specific storytelling traditions, often defined as paradigms (e.g., positivism, postpositivism, constructivism).

The product of the interpretive *bricoleur*'s labor is a complex, quiltlike bricolage, a reflexive collage or montage—a set of fluid, interconnected images and representations. This interpretive structure is like a quilt, a performance text, a sequence of representations connecting the parts to the whole.

Qualitative Research as a Site of Multiple Interpretive Practices

Qualitative research, as a set of interpretive activities, privileges no single methodological practice over another. As a site of discussion, or discourse, qualitative research is difficult to define clearly. It has no theory or paradigm that is distinctly its own. As the contributions to Part II of this volume reveal, multiple theoretical paradigms claim use of qualitative research methods and strategies, from constructivist to cultural studies, feminism, Marxism, and ethnic models of study. Qualitative research is used in many separate disciplines, as we will discuss below. It does not belong to a single discipline.

Nor does qualitative research have a distinct set of methods or practices that are entirely its own. Qualitative researchers use semiotics, narrative, content, discourse, archival and phonemic analysis, even statistics, tables, graphs, and numbers. They also draw on and utilize the approaches, methods, and techniques of ethnomethodology, phenomenology, hermeneutics, feminism, rhizomatics, deconstructionism, ethnography, interviewing, psychoanalysis, cultural studies, survey research, and participant observation, among others.[11] All of these research practices "can provide important insights and knowledge" (Nelson et al., 1992, p. 2). No specific method or practice can be privileged over any other.

Many of these methods, or research practices, are used in other contexts in the human disciplines. Each bears the traces of its own disciplinary history. Thus there is an extensive history of the uses and meanings of ethnography and ethnology in education (see in this volume Ladson-Billings & Donnor, Chapter 11; Kincheloe & McLaren, Chapter 12); of participant observation and ethnography in anthropology (see Foley & Valenzuela, Chaper 9, this volume; Tedlock, Volume 2, Chapter 5; Brady, Volume 3, Chapter 16), sociology (see Holstein & Gubrium, Volume 2, Chapter 6; Fontana & Frey, Volume 3, Chapter 4; Harper, Volume 3, Chapter 6), communications (see Alexander, Volume 2, Chapter 3; Holman Jones, Volume 3, Chapter 7), and cultural studies (see Saukko, Volume 3, Chapter 13); of textual, hermeneutic, feminist, psychoanalytic, arts-based, semiotic, and narrative analysis in cinema and literary studies (see Olesen, Chapter 10, this volume 1; Finley, Volume 3, Chapter 3; Brady, Volume 3, Chapter 16); and of narrative, discourse, and conversational analysis in sociology, medicine, communications, and education (see Miller & Crabtree, Volume 2, Chapter 11; Chase, Volume 3, Chapter 2; Peräkylä, Volume 3, Chapter 11).

The many histories that surround each method or research strategy reveal how multiple uses and meanings are brought to each practice. Textual analyses in literary studies, for example, often treat texts as self-contained systems. On the other hand, a researcher working from a cultural studies or feminist perspective reads a text in terms of its location within a historical moment marked by a particular gender, race, or class ideology. A cultural studies use of ethnography would bring a set of understandings from feminism, postmodernism, and poststructuralism to the project. These understandings would not be shared by mainstream postpositivist sociologists. Similarly, postpositivist and poststructural historians bring different understandings and uses to the methods and findings of historical research (see Tierney, 2000). These tensions and contradictions are all evident in the chapters in this volume.

These separate and multiple uses and meanings of the methods of qualitative research make it difficult for scholars to agree on any essential definition of the field, for it is never just one thing.[12] Still, we must establish a definition for purposes of this discussion. We borrow from, and paraphrase, Nelson et al.'s (1992, p. 4) attempt to define cultural studies:

> Qualitative research is an interdisciplinary, transdisciplinary, and sometimes counterdisciplinary field. It crosscuts the humanities and the social and physical sciences. Qualitative research is many things at the same time. It is multiparadigmatic in focus. Its practitioners are sensitive to the value of the multimethod approach. They are committed to the naturalistic perspective and to the interpretive understanding of human experience. At the same time, the field is inherently political and shaped by multiple ethical and political positions.
>
> Qualitative research embraces two tensions at the same time. On the one hand, it is drawn to a broad, interpretive, postexperimental, postmodern, feminist, and critical sensibility. On the other hand, it is drawn to more narrowly defined positivist, postpositivist, humanistic, and naturalistic conceptions of human experience and its analysis. Further, these tensions can be combined in the same project, bringing both postmodern and naturalistic, or both critical and humanistic, perspectives to bear.

This rather awkward statement means that qualitative research, as a set of practices, embraces within its own multiple disciplinary histories constant tensions and contradictions over the project itself, including its methods and the forms its findings and interpretations take. The field sprawls between and cuts across all of the human disciplines, even including, in some cases, the physical sciences. Its practitioners are variously committed to modern, postmodern, and postexperimental sensibilities and the approaches to social research that these sensibilities imply.

Resistances to Qualitative Studies

The academic and disciplinary resistances to qualitative research illustrate the politics embedded in this field of discourse. The challenges to qualitative research are many. As Seale, Gobo, Gubrium, and Silverman (2004) observe, we can best understand these criticisms by "distinguish[ing] analytically the political (or external) role of [qualitative] methodology from the procedural (or internal) one" (p. 7). Politics situate methodology within and outside the academy. Procedural issues define how qualitative methodology is used to produce knowledge about the world.

Often, the political and the procedural intersect. Politicians and "hard" scientists sometimes call qualitative researchers journalists or soft scientists. The work of qualitative scholars is termed unscientific, or only exploratory, or subjective. It is called criticism rather than theory or science, or it is interpreted politically, as a disguised version of Marxism or secular humanism (see Huber, 1995; see also Denzin, 1997, pp. 258–261).

These political and procedural resistances reflect an uneasy awareness that the interpretive traditions of qualitative research commit the researcher to a critique of the positivist or postpositivist project. But the positivist resistance to qualitative research goes beyond the "ever-present desire to maintain a distinction between hard science and soft scholarship" (Carey, 1989, p. 99; see also Smith & Hodkinson,

Volume 3, Chapter 13). The experimental (positivist) sciences (physics, chemistry, economics, and psychology, for example) are often seen as the crowning achievements of Western civilization, and in their practices it is assumed that "truth" can transcend opinion and personal bias (Carey, 1989, p. 99; Schwandt, 1997b, p. 309). Qualitative research is seen as an assault on this tradition, whose adherents often retreat into a "value-free objectivist science" (Carey, 1989, p. 104) model to defend their position. They seldom attempt to make explicit, or to critique, the "moral and political commitments in their own contingent work" (Carey, 1989, p. 104; see also Guba & Lincoln, Chapter 8, this volume).

Positivists further allege that the so-called new experimental qualitative researchers write fiction, not science, and that these researchers have no way of verifying their truth statements. Ethnographic poetry and fiction signal the death of empirical science, and there is little to be gained by attempting to engage in moral criticism. These critics presume a stable, unchanging reality that can be studied using the empirical methods of objective social science (see Huber, 1995). The province of qualitative research, accordingly, is the world of lived experience, for this is where individual belief and action intersect with culture. Under this model there is no preoccupation with discourse and method as material interpretive practices that constitute representation and description. Thus is the textual, narrative turn rejected by the positivists.

The opposition to positive science by the poststructuralists is seen, then, as an attack on reason and truth. At the same time, the positivist science attack on qualitative research is regarded as an attempt to legislate one version of truth over another.

Politics and Reemergent Scientism

The scientifically based research (SBR) movement initiated in recent years by the National Research Council (NRC) has created a hostile political environment for qualitative research. Connected to the federal legislation known as the No Child Left Behind Act of 2001, SBR embodies a reemergent scientism (Maxwell, 2004), a positivist, evidence-based epistemology. The movement encourages researchers to employ "rigorous, systematic, and objective methodology to obtain reliable and valid knowledge " (Ryan & Hood, 2004, p. 80). The preferred methodology employs well-defined causal models and independent and dependent variables. Researchers examine causal models in the context of randomized controlled experiments, which allow for replication and generalization of their results (Ryan & Hood, 2004, p. 81).

Under such a framework, qualitative research becomes suspect. Qualitative research does not require well-defined variables or causal models. The observations and measurements of qualitative scholars are not based on subjects' random assignment to experimental groups. Qualitative researchers do not generate "hard evidence" using such methods. At best, through case study, interview, and ethnographic methods, researchers can gather descriptive materials that can be tested with experimental methods. The epistemologies of critical race, queer, postcolonial, feminist, and postmodern theories are rendered useless by the SBR perspective, relegated at best to the category of scholarship, not science (Ryan & Hood, 2004, p. 81; St. Pierre, 2004, p. 132).

Critics of the SBR movement are united on the following points. "Bush science" (Lather, 2004, p. 19) and its experimental, evidence-based methodologies represent a racialized, masculinist backlash to the proliferation of qualitative inquiry methods over the past two decades. The movement endorses a narrow view of science (Maxwell, 2004) that celebrates a "neoclassical experimentalism that is a throwback to the Campbell-Stanley era and its dogmatic adherence to an exclusive reliance on quantitative methods" (Howe, 2004, p. 42). The movement represents "nostalgia for a simple and ordered universe of science that never was" (Popkewitz, 2004, p. 62). With its emphasis on only one form of scientific rigor, the NRC ignores the value of using complex historical, contextual, and political criteria to evaluate inquiry (Bloch, 2004).

As Howe (2004) observes, neoclassical experimentalists extol evidence-based "medical research as the model for educational research, particularly the random clinical trial" (p. 48). But dispensing a pill in a random clinical trial is quite unlike "dispensing a curriculum," and the "effects" of an educational experiment cannot be easily measured, unlike a "10-point reduction in diastolic blood pressure" (p. 48; see also Miller & Crabtree, Volume 2, Chapter 11).

Qualitative researchers must learn to think outside the box as they critique the NRC and its methodological guidelines (Atkinson, 2004). They must apply their imaginations and find new ways to define such terms as *randomized design, causal model, policy studies,* and *public science* (Cannella & Lincoln, 2004a, 2004b; Lincoln & Cannella, 2004a, 2004b; Lincoln & Tierney, 2004; Weinstein, 2004). More deeply, qualitative researchers must resist conservative attempts to discredit qualitative inquiry by placing it back inside the box of positivism.

Mixed-Methods Experimentalism

As Howe (2004) notes, the SBR movement finds a place for qualitative methods in mixed-methods experimental designs. In such designs, qualitative methods may be "employed either singly or in combination with quantitative methods, including the use of randomized experimental designs" (p. 49). Mixed-methods designs are direct descendants of classical experimentalism. They presume a methodological hierarchy in which quantitative methods are at the top and qualitative methods are relegated to "a largely auxiliary role in pursuit of the *technocratic* aim of accumulating knowledge of 'what works'" (pp. 53–54).

The mixed-methods movement takes qualitative methods out of their natural home, which is within the critical, interpretive framework (Howe, 2004, p. 54; but see Teddlie & Tashakkori, 2003, p. 15). It divides inquiry into dichotomous categories: exploration versus confirmation. Qualitative work is assigned to the first category, quantitative research to the second (Teddlie & Tashakkori, 2003, p. 15). Like the classic experimental model, it excludes stakeholders from dialogue and active participation in the research process. This weakens its democratic and dialogical dimensions and decreases the likelihood that previously silenced voices will be heard (Howe, 2004, pp. 56–57). As Howe (2004) cautions, it is not just the "'methodological fundamentalists' who have bought into [this] approach. A sizable number of rather influential . . . educational researchers . . . have also signed on. This might be a compromise to the current political climate; it might be a backlash against the perceived excesses of postmodernism; it might be both. It is an ominous development, whatever the explanation" (p. 57).

Pragmatic Criticisms of Antifoundationalism

Seale et al. (2004) contest what they regard as the excesses of an antimethodological, "anything goes," romantic postmodernism that is associated with our project. They assert that too often the approach we value produces "low quality qualitative research and research results that are quite stereotypical and close to common sense" (p. 2). In contrast, they propose a practice-based, pragmatic approach that places research practice at the center. They note that research involves an engagement "with a variety of things and people: research materials . . . social theories, philosophical debates, values, methods, tests . . . research participants" (p. 2). (Actually, this approach is quite close to our own, especially our view of the *bricoleur* and bricolage.) Seale et al.'s situated methodology rejects the antifoundational claim that there are only partial truths, that the dividing line between fact and fiction has broken down (p. 3). These scholars believe that this dividing line has not collapsed, and that qualitative researchers should not accept stories if they do not accord with the best available facts (p. 6).

Oddly, these pragmatic procedural arguments reproduce a variant of the evidence-based model and its criticisms of poststructural, performative sensibilities. They can be used to provide political support for the methodological marginalization of the positions advanced by many of the contributors to this volume.

▣ ▣ ▣

The complex political terrain described above defines the many traditions and strands of qualitative research: the British tradition and its presence in other national contexts; the American pragmatic, naturalistic, and interpretive traditions in sociology, anthropology, communications, and education; the German and French phenomenological, hermeneutic, semiotic, Marxist, structural, and poststructural perspectives; feminist studies, African American studies, Latino studies, queer studies, studies of indigenous and aboriginal cultures. The politics of qualitative research creates a tension that informs each of these traditions. This tension itself is constantly being reexamined and interrogated as qualitative research confronts a changing historical world, new intellectual positions, and its own institutional and academic conditions.

To summarize: Qualitative research is many things to many people. Its essence is twofold: a commitment to some version of the naturalistic, interpretive approach to its subject matter and an ongoing critique of the politics and methods of postpositivism. We turn now to a brief discussion of the major differences between qualitative and quantitative approaches to research. We then discuss ongoing differences and tensions within qualitative inquiry.

▣ Qualitative Versus Quantitative Research

The word *qualitative* implies an emphasis on the qualities of entities and on processes and meanings that are not experimentally examined or measured (if measured at all) in terms of quantity, amount, intensity, or frequency. Qualitative researchers stress the socially constructed nature of reality, the intimate relationship between the researcher and what is studied, and the situational constraints that shape inquiry. Such researchers emphasize the value-laden nature of inquiry. They seek answers to questions that stress *how* social experience is created and given meaning. In contrast, quantitative studies emphasize the measurement and analysis of causal relationships between variables, not processes. Proponents of such studies claim that their work is done from within a value-free framework.

Research Styles: Doing the Same Things Differently?

Of course, both qualitative and quantitative researchers "think they know something about society worth telling to others, and they use a variety of forms, media and means to communicate their ideas and findings" (Becker, 1986, p. 122). Qualitative research differs from quantitative research in five significant ways (Becker, 1996). These points of difference, discussed in turn below, all involve different ways of addressing the same set of issues. They return always to the politics of research and to who has the power to legislate correct solutions to social problems.

Uses of positivism and postpositivism. First, both perspectives are shaped by the positivist and postpositivist traditions in the physical and social sciences (see the discussion below). These two positivist science traditions hold to naïve and critical realist positions concerning reality and its perception. In the positivist version it is contended that there is a reality out there to be studied, captured, and understood, whereas the postpositivists argue that reality can never be fully apprehended, only approximated (Guba, 1990, p. 22). Postpositivism relies on multiple methods as a way of capturing as much of reality as possible. At the same time, it emphasizes the discovery and verification of theories. Traditional evaluation criteria, such as internal and external validity, are stressed, as is the use of qualitative procedures that lend themselves to structured (sometimes statistical) analysis. Computer-assisted methods of analysis that permit frequency counts, tabulations, and low-level statistical analyses may also be employed.

The positivist and postpositivist traditions linger like long shadows over the qualitative research project. Historically, qualitative research was defined within the positivist paradigm, where qualitative researchers attempted to do good positivist research with less rigorous methods and procedures. Some mid-20th-century qualitative researchers reported participant observation findings in terms of quasi-statistics (e.g., Becker, Geer, Hughes, & Strauss, 1961). As recently as 1998, Strauss and Corbin, two leading proponents of the grounded theory approach to qualitative research, attempted to modify the usual canons of good (positivist) science to fit their own postpositivist conception of rigorous research (but see Charmaz, Volume 2, Chapter 7; see also Glaser, 1992). Some applied researchers, while claiming to be atheoretical, often fit within the positivist or postpositivist framework by default.

Flick (2002) usefully summarizes the differences between these two approaches to inquiry, noting that the quantitative approach has been used for purposes of isolating "causes and effects . . . operationalizing theoretical relations . . . [and] measuring and . . . quantifying phenomena . . . allowing the generalization of findings" (p. 3). But today doubt is cast on such projects: "Rapid social change and the resulting diversification of life worlds are increasingly confronting social researchers with new social contexts and perspectives. . . . traditional deductive methodologies . . . are failing. . . . thus research is increasingly forced to make use of inductive strategies instead of starting from theories and testing them. . . . knowledge and practice are studied as *local* knowledge and practice" (p. 2).

Spindler and Spindler (1992) summarize their qualitative approach to quantitative materials: "Instrumentation and quantification are simply procedures employed to extend and reinforce certain kinds of data, interpretations and test hypotheses across samples. Both must be kept in their place. One must avoid their premature or overly extensive use as a security mechanism" (p. 69).

Although many qualitative researchers in the postpositivist tradition use statistical measures, methods, and documents as a way of locating a group of subjects within a larger population, they seldom report their findings in terms of the kinds of complex statistical measures or methods to which quantitative researchers are drawn (e.g., path, regression, and log-linear analyses).

Acceptance of postmodern sensibilities. The use of quantitative, positivist methods and assumptions has been rejected by a new generation of qualitative researchers who are attached to poststructural and/or postmodern sensibilities. These researchers argue that positivist methods are but one way of telling stories about societies or social worlds. These methods may be no better or no worse than any other methods; they just tell different kinds of stories.

This tolerant view is not shared by all qualitative researchers (Huber, 1995). Many members of the critical theory, constructivist, poststructural, and postmodern schools of thought reject positivist and postpositivist criteria when evaluating their own work. They see these criteria as irrelevant to their work and contend that such criteria reproduce only a certain kind of science, a science that silences too many voices. These researchers seek alternative methods for evaluating their work, including verisimilitude, emotionality, personal responsibility, an ethic of caring, political praxis, multivoiced texts, and dialogues with subjects. In response, positivists and postpositivists argue that what they do is good science, free of individual bias and subjectivity. As noted above, they see postmodernism and poststructuralism as attacks on reason and truth.

Capturing the individual's point of view. Both qualitative and quantitative researchers are concerned with the individual's point of view. However, qualitative investigators think they can get closer to the actor's perspective through detailed interviewing and observation. They argue that quantitative researchers are seldom able to capture their subjects' perspectives because they have to rely on more remote, inferential empirical methods and materials. Many quantitative researchers regard the empirical materials produced by interpretive methods as unreliable, impressionistic, and not objective.

Examining the constraints of everyday life. Qualitative researchers are more likely to confront and come up against the constraints of the everyday social world. They see this world in action and embed their findings in it. Quantitative researchers abstract from this world and seldom study it directly. They seek a nomothetic or etic science based on probabilities derived from the study of large numbers of randomly selected cases. These kinds of statements stand above and outside the constraints of everyday life. Qualitative researchers, on the other hand, are committed to an emic, idiographic, case-based position that directs attention to the specifics of particular cases.

Securing rich descriptions. Qualitative researchers believe that rich descriptions of the social world are valuable, whereas quantitative researchers, with their etic, nomothetic commitments, are less concerned with such detail. Quantitative researchers are deliberately unconcerned with rich descriptions because such detail interrupts the process of developing generalizations.

▣ ▣ ▣

The five points of difference described above reflect qualitative and quantitative scholars' commitments to different styles of research, different epistemologies, and different forms of representation. Each work tradition is governed by a different set of genres; each has its own classics, its own preferred forms of representation, interpretation, trustworthiness, and textual evaluation (see Becker, 1986, pp. 134–135). Qualitative researchers use ethnographic prose, historical narratives, first-person accounts, still photographs, life histories, fictionalized "facts," and biographical and autobiographical materials, among others. Quantitative researchers use mathematical models, statistical tables, and graphs, and they usually write about their research in impersonal, third-person prose.

Tensions Within Qualitative Research

It is erroneous to presume that all qualitative researchers share the same assumptions about the five points of difference described above. As the following discussion reveals, positivist, postpositivist, and poststructural differences define and shape the discourses of qualitative research. Realists and postpositivists within the interpretive, qualitative research tradition criticize poststructuralists for taking the textual, narrative turn. These critics contend that such work is navel gazing. It produces the conditions "for a dialogue of the deaf between itself and the community" (Silverman, 1997, p. 240). Critics accuse those who attempt to capture the point of view of the interacting subject in the world of naïve humanism, of reproducing "a Romantic impulse which elevates the experiential to the level of the authentic" (Silverman, 1997, p. 248).

Still others assert that those who take the textual, performance turn ignore lived experience. Snow and Morrill (1995) argue that "this performance turn, like the preoccupation with discourse and storytelling, will take us further from the field of social action and the real dramas of everyday life and thus signal the death knell of ethnography as an empirically grounded enterprise" (p. 361). Of course, we disagree.

Critical Realism

For some, there is a third stream, between naïve positivism and poststructuralism. Critical realism is an antipositivist movement in the social sciences closely associated with the works of Roy Bhaskar and Rom Harré (Danermark, Ekström, Jakobsen, & Karlsson, 2002). Critical realists use the word *critical* in a particular way. This is not "Frankfurt school" critical theory, although there are traces of social criticism here and there (see Danermark et al., 2002, p. 201). Instead, *critical* in this context refers to a transcendental realism that rejects methodological individualism and universal claims to truth. Critical realists oppose logical positivist, relativist, and antifoundational epistemologies. Critical realists agree with the positivists that there is a world of events out there that is observable and independent of human consciousness. They hold that knowledge about this world is socially constructed. Society is made up of feeling, thinking human beings, and their interpretations of the world must be studied (Danermark et al., 2002, p. 200). Critical realists reject a correspondence theory of truth. They believe that reality is arranged in levels and that scientific work must go beyond statements of regularity to analysis of the mechanisms, processes, and structures that account for the patterns that are observed.

Still, as postempiricist, antifoundational, critical theorists, we reject much of what the critical realists advocate. Throughout the past century, social science and philosophy have been continually tangled up with one another. Various "isms" and philosophical movements have crisscrossed sociological and educational discourses, from positivism to postpositivism, to analytic and linguistic philosophy, to hermeneutics, structuralism, poststructuralism, Marxism, feminism, and current post-post versions of all of the above. Some have said that the logical positivists steered the social sciences on a rigorous course of self-destruction.

We do not think that critical realism will keep the social science ship afloat. The social sciences are normative disciplines, always already embedded in issues of value, ideology, power, desire, sexism, racism, domination, repression, and control. We want a social science that is committed up front to issues of social justice, equity, nonviolence, peace, and universal human rights. We do not want a social science that says it can address these issues if it wants to. For us, that is no longer an option.

With these differences within and between interpretive traditions in hand, we must now briefly discuss the history of qualitative research. We break this history into eight historical moments, mindful that any history is always somewhat arbitrary and always at least partially a social construction.

The History of Qualitative Research

The history of qualitative research reveals that the modern social science disciplines have taken as their mission "the analysis and understanding of the patterned conduct and social processes of society" (Vidich & Lyman, 2000, p. 37). The notion that social scientists could carry out this task presupposed that they had the ability to observe this world objectively. Qualitative methods were a major tool of such observations.[13]

Throughout the history of qualitative research, qualitative investigators have defined their work in terms of hopes and values, "religious faiths, occupational and professional ideologies" (Vidich & Lyman, 2000, p. 39). Qualitative research (like all research) has always been judged on the "standard of whether the work communicates or 'says' something to us" (Vidich & Lyman, 2000, p. 39), based on how we conceptualize our reality and our images of the world. *Epistemology* is the word that has historically defined these standards of evaluation. In the contemporary period, as we have argued above, many received discourses on epistemology are now being reevaluated.

Vidich and Lyman's (2000) work on the history of qualitative research covers the following (somewhat) overlapping stages: early ethnography (to the 17th century), colonial ethnography (17th-, 18th-, and 19th-century explorers), the ethnography of the American Indian as "Other" (late-19th- and early 20th-century anthropology), community studies and ethnographies of American immigrants (early 20th century through the 1960s), studies of ethnicity and assimilation (midcentury through the 1980s), and the present, which we call the *eighth moment.*

In each of these eras, researchers were and have been influenced by their political hopes and ideologies, discovering findings in their research that confirmed their prior theories or beliefs. Early ethnographers confirmed the racial and cultural diversity of peoples throughout the globe and attempted to fit this diversity into a theory about the origins of history, the races, and civilizations. Colonial ethnographers, before the professionalization of ethnography in the 20th century, fostered a colonial pluralism that left natives on their own as long as their leaders could be co-opted by the colonial administration.

European ethnographers studied Africans, Asians, and other Third World peoples of color. Early American ethnographers studied the American Indian from the perspective of the conqueror, who saw the lifeworld of the primitive as a window to the prehistoric past. The Calvinist mission to save the Indian was soon transferred to the mission of saving the "hordes" of immigrants who entered the United States with the beginnings of industrialization. Qualitative community studies of the ethnic Other proliferated from the early 1900s to the 1960s and included the work of E. Franklin Frazier, Robert Park, and Robert Redfield and their students, as well as William Foote Whyte, the Lynds, August Hollingshead, Herbert Gans, Stanford Lyman, Arthur Vidich, and Joseph Bensman. The post-1960 ethnicity studies challenged the "melting pot" hypotheses of Park and his followers and corresponded to the emergence of ethnic studies programs that saw Native Americans, Latinos, Asian Americans, and African Americans attempting to take control over the study of their own peoples.

The postmodern and poststructural challenge emerged in the mid-1980s. It questioned the assumptions that had organized this earlier history in each of its colonizing moments. Qualitative research that crosses the "postmodern divide" requires the scholar, Vidich and Lyman (2000) argue, to "abandon all established and preconceived values, theories, perspectives . . . and prejudices as resources for ethnographic study" (p. 60). In this new era the qualitative researcher does more than observe history; he or she plays a part in it. New tales from the field will now be written, and they will reflect the researchers' direct and personal engagement with this historical period.

Vidich and Lyman's analysis covers the full sweep of ethnographic history. Ours is confined to the 20th and 21st centuries and complements many of their divisions. We begin with the early foundational work of the British and French as well as the Chicago, Columbia, Harvard, Berkeley, and British schools of sociology and anthropology. This early foundational period established the norms of classical qualitative and ethnographic research (see Gupta & Ferguson, 1997; Rosaldo, 1989; Stocking, 1989).

The Eight Moments of Qualitative Research

As we have noted above, we divide our history of qualitative research in North America in the 20th century and beyond into eight phases, which we describe in turn below.

The Traditional Period

We call the first moment the traditional period (this covers the second and third phases discussed by Vidich & Lyman, 2000). It begins in the early 1900s and continues until World War II. In this period, qualitative researchers wrote "objective," colonizing accounts of field experiences that were reflective of the positivist scientist paradigm. They were concerned with offering valid, reliable, and objective interpretations in their writings. The "Other" whom they studied was alien, foreign, and strange.

Here is Malinowski (1967) discussing his field experiences in New Guinea and the Trobriand Islands in the years 1914–1915 and 1917–1918. He is bartering his way into field data:

> Nothing whatever draws me to ethnographic studies. . . . On the whole the village struck me rather unfavorably. There is a certain disorganization . . . the rowdiness and persistence of the people who laugh and stare and lie discouraged me somewhat. . . . Went to the village hoping to photograph a few stages of the *bara* dance. I handed out half-sticks of tobacco, then watched a few dances; then took pictures—but results were poor. . . . they would not pose long enough for time exposures. At moments I was furious at them, particularly because after I gave them their portions of tobacco they all went away. (quoted in Geertz, 1988, pp. 73–74)

In another work, this lonely, frustrated, isolated field-worker describes his methods in the following words:

> In the field one has to face a chaos of facts. . . . in this crude form they are not scientific facts at all; they are absolutely elusive, and can only be fixed by interpretation. . . . *Only laws and generalizations are scientific facts,* and field work consists only and exclusively in the interpretation of the chaotic social reality, in subordinating it to general rules. (Malinowski, 1916/1948, p. 328; quoted in Geertz, 1988, p. 81)

Malinowski's remarks are provocative. On the one hand they disparage fieldwork, but on the other they speak of it within the glorified language of science, with laws and generalizations fashioned out of this selfsame experience.

During this period the field-worker was lionized, made into a larger-than-life figure who went into the field and returned with stories about strange peoples. Rosaldo (1989) describes this as the period of the Lone Ethnographer, the story of the man-scientist who went off in search of his native in a distant land. There this figure "encountered the object of his quest . . . [and] underwent his rite of passage by enduring the ultimate ordeal of 'fieldwork'" (p. 30). Returning home with his data, the Lone Ethnographer wrote up an objective account of the culture studied. This account was structured by the norms of classical ethnography. This sacred bundle of terms (Rosaldo, 1989, p. 31) organized ethnographic texts around four beliefs and commitments: a commitment to objectivism, a complicity with imperialism, a belief in monumentalism (the ethnography would create a museumlike picture of the culture studied), and a belief in timelessness (what was studied would never change). The Other was an "object" to be archived. This model of the researcher, who could also write complex, dense theories about what was studied, holds to the present day.

The myth of the Lone Ethnographer depicts the birth of classic ethnography. The texts of Malinowski, Radcliffe-Brown, Margaret Mead, and Gregory Bateson are still carefully studied for what they can tell the novice about fieldwork, taking field notes, and writing theory. But today the image of the Lone Ethnographer has been shattered. Many scholars see the works of the classic ethnographers as relics from the colonial past (Rosaldo, 1989, p. 44). Whereas some feel nostalgia for this past, others celebrate its passing. Rosaldo (1989) quotes Cora Du Bois, a retired Harvard anthropology professor, who lamented this passing at a conference in 1980, reflecting on the crisis in anthropology: "[I feel a distance] from the complexity and disarray of what I once found a justifiable and challenging discipline. . . . It has been like moving from a distinguished art museum into a garage sale" (p. 44).

Du Bois regards the classic ethnographies as pieces of timeless artwork contained in a museum. She feels uncomfortable in the chaos of the garage sale. In contrast, Rosaldo (1989) is drawn to this metaphor because "it provides a precise image of the postcolonial situation where cultural artifacts flow between unlikely places, and nothing is sacred, permanent, or sealed off. The image of anthropology as a garage sale depicts our present global situation" (p. 44). Indeed, many valuable treasures may be found in unexpected places, if one is willing to look long and hard. Old standards no longer hold. Ethnographies do not produce timeless truths. The commitment to objectivism is now in doubt. The complicity with imperialism is openly challenged today, and the belief in monumentalism is a thing of the past.

The legacies of this first period begin at the end of the 19th century, when the novel and the social sciences had become distinguished as separate systems of discourse (Clough, 1998, pp. 21–22). However, the Chicago school, with its emphasis on the life story and the "slice-of-life" approach to ethnographic materials, sought to develop an interpretive methodology that maintained the centrality of the narrated-life-history approach. This led to the production of texts that gave the researcher-as-author the power to represent the subject's story. Written under the mantle of straightforward, sentiment-free social realism, these texts used the language of ordinary people. They articulated a social science version of literary naturalism, which often produced the sympathetic illusion that a solution to a social problem had been found. Like the Depression-era juvenile delinquent and other "social problems" films (Roffman & Purdy, 1981), these accounts romanticized the subject. They turned the deviant into a sociological version of a screen hero. These sociological stories, like their film counterparts, usually had happy endings, as they followed individuals through the three stages of the classic morality tale: being in a state of grace, being seduced by evil and falling, and finally achieving redemption through suffering.

Modernist Phase

The modernist phase, or second moment, builds on the canonical works from the traditional period. Social realism, naturalism, and slice-of-life ethnographies are still valued. This phase extended through the postwar years to the 1970s and is still present in the work of many (for reviews, see Wolcott, 1990, 1992, 1995; see also Tedlock, Volume 2, Chapter 5). In this period many texts sought to formalize qualitative methods (see, e.g., Bogdan & Taylor, 1975; Cicourel, 1964; Filstead, 1970; Glaser & Strauss, 1967; Lofland, 1971, 1995; Lofland & Lofland, 1984, 1995; Taylor & Bogdan, 1998).[14] The modernist ethnographer and sociological participant observer attempted rigorous qualitative studies of important social processes, including deviance and social control in the classroom and society. This was a moment of creative ferment.

A new generation of graduate students across the human disciplines encountered new interpretive theories (ethnomethodology, phenomenology, critical theory, feminism). They were drawn to qualitative research practices that would let them give a voice to society's underclass. Postpositivism functioned as a powerful epistemological paradigm. Researchers attempted to fit Campbell and Stanley's (1963) model of internal and external validity to constructionist and interactionist conceptions of the research act. They returned to the texts of the Chicago school as sources of inspiration (see Denzin, 1970, 1978).

A canonical text from this moment remains *Boys in White* (Becker et al., 1961; see also Becker, 1998). Firmly entrenched in mid-20th-century methodological discourse, this work attempted to make qualitative research as rigorous as its quantitative counterpart. Causal narratives were central to this project. This multimethod work combined open-ended and quasi-structured interviewing with participant observation and the careful analysis of such materials in standardized, statistical form. In his classic article "Problems of Inference and Proof in Participant Observation," Howard S. Becker (1958/1970) describes the use of quasi-statistics:

> Participant observations have occasionally been gathered in standardized form capable of being transformed into legitimate statistical data. But the exigencies of the field usually prevent the collection of data in such a form to meet the assumptions of statistical tests, so that the observer deals in what have been called "quasi-statistics." His conclusions, while implicitly numerical, do not require precise quantification. (p. 31)

In the analysis of data, Becker notes, the qualitative researcher takes a cue from more quantitatively oriented colleagues. The researcher looks for probabilities or support for arguments concerning the likelihood that, or frequency with which, a conclusion in fact applies in a specific situation (see also Becker, 1998, pp. 166–170). Thus did work in the modernist period clothe itself in the language and rhetoric of positivist and postpositivist discourse.

This was the golden age of rigorous qualitative analysis, bracketed in sociology by *Boys in White* (Becker et al., 1961) at one end and *The Discovery of Grounded Theory*

(Glaser & Strauss, 1967) at the other. In education, qualitative research in this period was defined by George and Louise Spindler, Jules Henry, Harry Wolcott, and John Singleton. This form of qualitative research is still present in the work of scholars such as Strauss and Corbin (1998) and Ryan and Bernard (2000).

The "golden age" reinforced the picture of qualitative researchers as cultural romantics. Imbued with Promethean human powers, they valorized villains and outsiders as heroes to mainstream society. They embodied a belief in the contingency of self and society, and held to emancipatory ideals for "which one lives and dies." They put in place a tragic and often ironic view of society and self, and joined a long line of leftist cultural romantics that included Emerson, Marx, James, Dewey, Gramsci, and Martin Luther King, Jr. (West, 1989, chap. 6).

As this moment came to an end, the Vietnam War was everywhere present in American society. In 1969, alongside these political currents, Herbert Blumer and Everett Hughes met with a group of young sociologists called the "Chicago Irregulars" at the American Sociological Association meetings held in San Francisco and shared their memories of the "Chicago years." Lyn Lofland (1980) describes this time as a

> moment of creative ferment—scholarly and political. The San Francisco meetings witnessed not simply the Blumer-Hughes event but a "counter-revolution." . . . a group first came to . . . talk about the problems of being a sociologist and a female. . . . the discipline seemed literally to be bursting with new . . . ideas: labelling theory, ethnomethodology, conflict theory, phenomenology, dramaturgical analysis. (p. 253)

Thus did the modernist phase come to an end.

Blurred Genres

By the beginning of the third phase (1970–1986), which we call the moment of blurred genres, qualitative researchers had a full complement of paradigms, methods, and strategies to employ in their research. Theories ranged from symbolic interactionism to constructivism, naturalistic inquiry, positivism and postpositivism, phenomenology, ethnomethodology, critical theory, neo-Marxist theory, semiotics, structuralism, feminism, and various racial/ethnic paradigms. Applied qualitative research was gaining in stature, and the politics and ethics of qualitative research—implicated as they were in various applications of this work—were topics of considerable concern. Research strategies and formats for reporting research ranged from grounded theory to the case study, to methods of historical, biographical, ethnographic, action, and clinical research. Diverse ways of collecting and analyzing empirical materials were also available, including qualitative interviewing (open-ended and quasi-structured) and observational, visual, personal experience, and documentary methods. Computers were entering the situation, to be fully developed as aids in the analysis of qualitative data in the next decade, along with narrative, content, and semiotic methods of reading interviews and cultural texts.

Two books by Clifford Geertz, *The Interpretation of Cultures* (1973) and *Local Knowledge* (1983), defined the beginning and the end of this moment. In these two works, Geertz argued that the old functional, positivist, behavioral, totalizing approaches to the human disciplines were giving way to a more pluralistic, interpretive, open-ended perspective. This new perspective took cultural representations and their meanings as its points of departure. Calling for "thick description" of particular events, rituals, and customs, Geertz suggested that all anthropological writings are interpretations of interpretations.[15] The observer has no privileged voice in the interpretations that are written. The central task of theory is to make sense out of a local situation.

Geertz went on to propose that the boundaries between the social sciences and the humanities had become blurred. Social scientists were now turning to the humanities for models, theories, and methods of analysis (semiotics, hermeneutics). A form of genre diaspora was occurring: documentaries that read like fiction (Mailer), parables posing as ethnographies (Castañeda), theoretical treatises that look like travelogues (Lévi-Strauss). At the same time, other new approaches were emerging: poststructuralism (Barthes), neopositivism (Philips), neo-Marxism (Althusser), micro-macro descriptivism (Geertz), ritual theories of drama and culture (V. Turner), deconstructionism (Derrida), ethnomethodology (Garfinkel). The golden age of the social sciences was over, and a new age of blurred, interpretive genres was upon us. The essay as an art form was replacing the scientific article. At issue now was the author's presence in the interpretive text (Geertz, 1988). How can the researcher speak with authority in an age when there are no longer any firm rules concerning the text, including the author's place in it, its standards of evaluation, and its subject matter?

The naturalistic, postpositivist, and constructionist paradigms gained power in this period, especially in education, in the works of Harry Wolcott, Frederick Erickson, Egon Guba, Yvonna Lincoln, Robert Stake, and Elliot Eisner. By the end of the 1970s, several qualitative journals were in place, including *Urban Life and Culture* (now *Journal of Contemporary Ethnography*), *Cultural Anthropology, Anthropology and Education Quarterly, Qualitative Sociology,* and *Symbolic Interaction,* as well as the book series *Studies in Symbolic Interaction*.

Crisis of Representation

A profound rupture occurred in the mid-1980s. What we call the fourth moment, or the crisis of representation, appeared with *Anthropology as Cultural Critique* (Marcus & Fischer, 1986), *The Anthropology of Experience* (Turner & Bruner, 1986), *Writing Culture* (Clifford & Marcus, 1986), *Works and Lives* (Geertz, 1988), and *The Predicament of Culture* (Clifford, 1988). These works made research and writing more reflexive and called into question the issues of gender, class, and race. They articulated the consequences of Geertz's "blurred genres" interpretation of the field in the early 1980s.[16]

Qualitative researchers sought new models of truth, method, and representation (Rosaldo, 1989). The erosion of classic norms in anthropology (objectivism, complicity with colonialism, social life structured by fixed rituals and customs, ethnographies as monuments to a culture) was complete (Rosaldo, 1989, pp. 44–45; see also Jackson, 1998, pp. 7–8). Critical theory, feminist theory, and epistemologies of color now competed for attention in this arena. Issues such as validity, reliability, and objectivity, previously believed settled, were once more problematic. Pattern and interpretive theories, as opposed to causal, linear theories, were now more common, as writers continued to challenge older models of truth and meaning (Rosaldo, 1989).

Stoller and Olkes (1987, pp. 227–229) describe how they felt the crisis of representation in their fieldwork among the Songhay of Niger. Stoller observes: "When I began to write anthropological texts, I followed the conventions of my training. I 'gathered data,' and once the 'data' were arranged in neat piles, I 'wrote them up.' In one case I reduced Songhay insults to a series of neat logical formulas" (p. 227). Stoller became dissatisfied with this form of writing, in part because he learned "everyone had lied to me and . . . the data I has so painstakingly collected were worthless. I learned a lesson: Informants routinely lie to their anthropologists" (Stoller & Olkes, 1987, p. 9). This discovery led to a second—that he had, in following the conventions of ethnographic realism, edited himself out of his text. This led Stoller to produce a different type of text, a memoir, in which he became a central character in the story he told. This story, an account of his experiences in the Songhay world, became an analysis of the clash between his world and the world of Songhay sorcery. Thus Stoller's journey represents an attempt to confront the crisis of representation in the fourth moment.

Clough (1998) elaborates this crisis and criticizes those who would argue that new forms of writing represent a way out of the crisis. She argues:

> While many sociologists now commenting on the criticism of ethnography view writing as "downright central to the ethnographic enterprise" [Van Maanen, 1988, p. xi], the problems of writing are still viewed as different from the problems of method or fieldwork itself. Thus the solution usually offered is experiments in writing, that is a self-consciousness about writing. (p. 136)

It is this insistence on the difference between writing and fieldwork that must be analyzed. (Richardson & St. Pierre are quite articulate about this issue in Volume 3, Chapter 15).

In writing, the field-worker makes a claim to moral and scientific authority. This claim allows the realist and experimental ethnographic texts to function as sources of validation for an empirical science. They show that the world of real lived experience can still be captured, if only in the writer's memoirs, or fictional experimentations, or dramatic readings. But these works have the danger of directing attention away from the ways in which the text constructs sexually situated individuals in a field of social difference. They also perpetuate "empirical science's hegemony" (Clough, 1998, p. 8), for these new writing technologies of the subject become the site "for the production of knowledge/power . . . [aligned] with . . . the capital/state axis" (Aronowitz, 1988, p. 300; quoted in Clough, 1998, p. 8). Such experiments come up against, and then back away from, the difference between empirical science and social criticism. Too often they fail to engage fully a new politics of textuality that would "refuse the identity of empirical science" (Clough, 1998, p. 135). This new social criticism "would intervene in the relationship of information economics, nation-state politics, and technologies of mass communication, especially in terms of the empirical sciences" (Clough, 1998, p. 16). This, of course, is the terrain occupied by cultural studies.

In Chapter 15 of Volume 3, Richardson and St. Pierre develop the above arguments, viewing writing as a method of inquiry that moves through successive stages of self-reflection. As a series of written representations, the field-worker's texts flow from the field experience, through intermediate works, to later work, and finally to the research text, which is the public presentation of the ethnographic and narrative experience. Thus fieldwork and writing blur into one another. There is, in the final analysis, no difference between writing and fieldwork. These two perspectives inform one another throughout every chapter in this volume. In these ways the crisis of representation moves qualitative research in new and critical directions.

A Triple Crisis

The ethnographer's authority remains under assault today (Behar, 1995, p. 3; Gupta & Ferguson, 1997, p. 16; Jackson, 1998; Ortner, 1997, p. 2). A triple crisis of representation, legitimation, and praxis confronts qualitative researchers in the human disciplines. Embedded in the discourses of poststructuralism and postmodernism (Vidich & Lyman, 2000; see also Richardson & St. Pierre, Volume 3, Chapter 15), these three crises are coded in multiple terms, variously called and associated with the *critical, interpretive, linguistic, feminist,* and *rhetorical* turns in social theory. These new turns make problematic two key assumptions of qualitative research. The first is that qualitative researchers can no longer directly capture lived experience. Such experience, it is argued, is created in the social text written by the researcher. This is the representational crisis. It confronts the inescapable problem of representation, but does so within a framework that makes the direct link between experience and text problematic.

The second assumption makes problematic the traditional criteria for evaluating and interpreting qualitative research. This is the legitimation crisis. It involves a serious rethinking of such terms as *validity, generalizability,* and *reliability,* terms already retheorized in postpositivist (Hammersley, 1992), constructionist-naturalistic (Guba & Lincoln, 1989, pp. 163–183), feminist (Olesen, Chapter 10, this volume), interpretive and performative (Denzin, 1997, 2003), poststructural (Lather, 1993; Lather & Smithies, 1997), and critical discourses (Kincheloe & McLaren, Chapter 12, this volume). This crisis asks, How are qualitative studies to be evaluated in the contemporary, poststructural moment? The first two crises shape the third, which asks,

Is it possible to effect change in the world if society is only and always a text? Clearly these crises intersect and blur, as do the answers to the questions they generate (see Ladson-Billings, 2000; Schwandt, 2000; Smith & Deemer, 2000).

The fifth moment, the postmodern period of experimental ethnographic writing, struggled to make sense of these crises. New ways of composing ethnography were explored (Ellis & Bochner, 1996). Theories were read as tales from the field. Writers struggled with different ways to represent the "Other," although they were now joined by new representational concerns (Fine, Weis, Weseen, & Wong, 2000; see also Fine & Weis, Chapter 3, this volume). Epistemologies from previously silenced groups emerged to offer solutions to these problems. The concept of the aloof observer was abandoned. More action, participatory, and activist-oriented research was on the horizon. The search for grand narratives was being replaced by more local, small-scale theories fitted to specific problems and specific situations.

The sixth moment, postexperimental inquiry (1995–2000), was a period of great excitement, with AltaMira Press, under the direction of Mitch Allen, taking the lead. AltaMira's book series titled *Ethnographic Alternatives*, for which Carolyn Ellis and Arthur Bochner served as series editors, captured this new excitement and brought a host of new authors into the interpretive community. The following description of the series from the publisher reflects its experimental tone: "Ethnographic Alternatives publishes experimental forms of qualitative writing that blur the boundaries between social sciences and humanities. Some volumes in the series . . . experiment with novel forms of expressing lived experience, including literary, poetic, autobiographical, multivoiced, conversational, critical, visual, performative and co-constructed representations."

During this same period, two major new qualitative journals began publication: *Qualitative Inquiry* and *Qualitative Research*. The editors of these journals were committed to publishing the very best new work. The success of these ventures framed the seventh moment, what we are calling the methodologically contested present (2000–2004). As discussed above, this is a period of conflict, great tension, and, in some quarters, retrenchment.

The eighth moment is now, the future (2005–). In this moment scholars, as reviewed above, are confronting the methodological backlash associated with "Bush science" and the evidence-based social movement.

Reading History

We draw several conclusions from this brief history, noting that it is, like all histories, somewhat arbitrary. First, each of the earlier historical moments is still operating in the present, either as legacy or as a set of practices that researchers continue to follow or argue against. The multiple and fractured histories of qualitative research now make it possible for any given researcher to attach a project to a canonical text from any of the above-described historical moments. Multiple criteria of evaluation compete for attention in this field. Second, an embarrassment of choices now characterizes the field of qualitative research. Researchers have never before had so many paradigms, strategies of inquiry, and methods of analysis to draw upon and utilize. Third, we are in a moment of discovery and rediscovery, as new ways of looking, interpreting, arguing, and writing are debated and discussed. Fourth, the qualitative research act can no longer be viewed from within a neutral or objective positivist perspective. Class, race, gender, and ethnicity shape inquiry, making research a multicultural process. Fifth, we are clearly not implying a progress narrative with our history. We are not saying that the cutting edge is located in the present. We are saying that the present is a politically charged space. Complex pressures both within and outside of the qualitative community are working to erase the positive developments of the past 30 years.

▣ Qualitative Research as Process

Three interconnected, generic activities define the qualitative research process. They go by a variety of different labels, including *theory, analysis, ontology, epistemology,* and *methodology.* Behind these terms stands the personal biography of the researcher, who speaks from a particular class, gender, racial, cultural, and ethnic community perspective. The gendered, multiculturally situated researcher approaches the world with a set of ideas, a framework (theory, ontology) that specifies a set of questions (epistemology) that he or she then examines in specific ways (methodology, analysis). That is, the researcher collects empirical materials bearing on the question and then analyzes and writes about those materials. Every researcher speaks from within a distinct interpretive community that configures, in its special way, the multicultural, gendered components of the research act.

In this volume we treat these generic activities under five headings, or phases: the researcher and the researched as multicultural subjects, major paradigms and interpretive perspectives, research strategies, methods of collecting and analyzing empirical materials, and the art of interpretation. Behind and within each of these phases stands the biographically situated researcher. This individual enters the research process from inside an interpretive community. This community has its own historical research traditions, which constitute a distinct point of view. This perspective leads the researcher to adopt particular views of the "Other" who is studied. At the same time, the politics and the ethics of research must also be considered, for these concerns permeate every phase of the research process.

▣ The Other as Research Subject

Since its early 20th-century birth in modern, interpretive form, qualitative research has been haunted by a double-faced ghost. On the one hand, qualitative researchers have assumed that qualified, competent observers can, with objectivity, clarity, and precision, report on their own observations of the social world, including the experiences of others. Second, researchers have held to the belief in a real subject, or real individual, who is present in the world and able, in some form, to report on his or her experiences. So armed, researchers could blend their own observations with the self-reports provided by subjects through interviews and life story, personal experience, and case study documents.

These two beliefs have led qualitative researchers across disciplines to seek a method that will allow them to record accurately their own observations while also uncovering the meanings their subjects bring to their life experiences. Such a method would rely on the subjective verbal and written expressions of meaning given by the individuals studied as windows into the inner lives of these persons. Since Dilthey (1900/1976), this search for a method has led to a perennial focus in the human disciplines on qualitative, interpretive methods.

Recently, as noted above, this position and its beliefs have come under assault. Poststructuralists and postmodernists have contributed to the understanding that there is no clear window into the inner life of an individual. Any gaze is always filtered through the lenses of language, gender, social class, race, and ethnicity. There are no objective observations, only observations socially situated in the worlds of—and between—the observer and the observed. Subjects, or individuals, are seldom able to give full explanations of their actions or intentions; all they can offer are accounts, or stories, about what they have done and why. No single method can grasp all the subtle variations in ongoing human experience. Consequently, qualitative researchers deploy a wide range of interconnected interpretive methods, always seeking better ways to make more understandable the worlds of experience they have studied.

Table 1.1 depicts the relationships we see among the five phases that define the research process. Behind all but one of these phases stands the biographically situated researcher. These five levels of activity, or practice, work their way through the biography of the researcher. We take them up briefly in order here; we discuss these phases more fully in our introductions to the individual parts of this volume.

Phase 1: The Researcher

Our remarks above indicate the depth and complexity of the traditional and applied qualitative research perspectives into which a socially situated researcher enters. These traditions locate the researcher in history, simultaneously guiding and constraining the work that is done in any specific study. This field has always been characterized by diversity and conflict, and these are its most enduring traditions (see Greenwood & Levin, Chapter 2, this volume). As a carrier of this complex and contradictory history, the researcher must also confront the ethics and politics of research (see in this volume Fine & Weis, Chapter 3; Smith, Chapter 4; Bishop, Chapter 5; Christians, Chapter 6). Researching the native, the indigenous Other, while claiming to engage in value-free inquiry for the human disciplines is over. Today researchers

Table 1.1. The Research Process

Phase 1: The Researcher as a Multicultural Subject
History and research traditions Conceptions of self and the Other The ethics and politics of research
Phase 2: Theoretical Paradigms and Perspectives
Positivism, postpositivism Interpretivism, constructivism, hermeneutics Feminism(s) Racialized discourses Critical theory and Marxist models Cultural studies models Queer theory
Phase 3: Research Strategies
Design Case study Ethnography, participant observation, performance ethnography Phenomenology, ethnomethodology Grounded theory Life history, *testimonio* Historical method Action and applied research Clinical research
Phase 4: Methods of Collection and Analysis
Interviewing Observing Artifacts, documents, and records Visual methods Autoethnography Data management methods Computer-assisted analysis Textual analysis Focus groups Applied ethnography
Phase 5: The Art, Practices, and Politics of Interpretation and Evaluation
Criteria for judging adequacy Practices and politics of interpretation Writing as interpretation Policy analysis Evaluation traditions Applied research

struggle to develop situational and trans-situational ethics that apply to all forms of the research act and its human-to-human relationships. We no longer have the option of deferring the decolonization project.

Phase 2: Interpretive Paradigms

All qualitative researchers are philosophers in that "universal sense in which all human beings . . . are guided by highly abstract principles" (Bateson, 1972, p. 320). These principles combine beliefs about ontology (What kind of being is the human being? What is the nature of reality?), epistemology (What is the relationship between the inquirer and the known?), and methodology (How do we know the world, or gain knowledge of it?) (see Guba, 1990, p. 18; Lincoln & Guba, 1985, pp. 14–15; see also Guba & Lincoln, Chapter 8, this volume). These beliefs shape how the qualitative researcher sees the world and acts in it. The researcher is "bound within a net of epistemological and ontological premises which—regardless of ultimate truth or falsity—become partially self-validating" (Bateson, 1972, p. 314).

The net that contains the researcher's epistemological, ontological, and methodological premises may be termed a *paradigm*, or an interpretive framework, a "basic set of beliefs that guides action" (Guba, 1990, p. 17). All research is interpretive; it is guided by the researcher's set of beliefs and feelings about the world and how it should be understood and studied. Some beliefs may be taken for granted, invisible, only assumed, whereas others are highly problematic and controversial. Each interpretive paradigm makes particular demands on the researcher, including the questions the researcher asks and the interpretations he or she brings to them.

At the most general level, four major interpretive paradigms structure qualitative research: positivist and postpositivist, constructivist-interpretive, critical (Marxist, emancipatory), and feminist-poststructural. These four abstract paradigms become more complicated at the level of concrete specific interpretive communities. At this level it is possible to identify not only the constructivist, but also multiple versions of feminism (Afrocentric and poststructural),[17] as well as specific ethnic, Marxist, and cultural studies paradigms. These perspectives, or paradigms, are examined in Part II of this volume.

The paradigms examined in Part II work against and alongside (and some within) the positivist and postpositivist models. They all work within relativist ontologies (multiple constructed realities), interpretive epistemologies (the knower and known interact and shape one another), and interpretive, naturalistic methods.

Table 1.2 presents these paradigms and their assumptions, including their criteria for evaluating research, and the typical form that an interpretive or theoretical statement assumes in each paradigm.[18] These paradigms are explored in considerable detail in the chapters in Part II by Guba and Lincoln (Chapter 8), Olesen (Chapter 10), Ladson-Billings and Donnor (Chapter 11), Kincheloe and McLaren (Chapter 12), Saukko (Chapter 13), and Plummer (Chapter 14). We have discussed the positivist and

Table 1.2. Interpretive Paradigms

Paradigm/Theory	*Criteria*	*Form of Theory*	*Type of Narration*
Positivist/ postpositivist	Internal, external validity	Logical-deductive, grounded	Scientific report
Constructivist	Trustworthiness, credibility, transferability, confirmability	Substantive-formal	Interpretive case studies, ethnographic fiction
Feminist	Afrocentric, lived experience, dialogue, caring, accountability, race, class, gender, reflexivity, praxis, emotion, concrete grounding	Critical, standpoint	Essays, stories, experimental writing
Ethnic	Afrocentric, lived experience, dialogue, caring, accountability, race, class, gender	Standpoint, critical, historical	Essays, fables, dramas
Marxist	Emancipatory theory, falsifiability dialogical, race, class, gender	Critical, historical, economic	Historical, economic, sociocultural analyses
Cultural studies	Cultural practices, praxis, social texts, subjectivities	Social criticism	Cultural theory as criticism
Queer theory	Reflexivity, deconstruction	Social criticism, historical analysis	Theory as criticism, autobiography

postpositivist paradigms above. They work from within a realist and critical realist ontology and objective epistemologies, and they rely on experimental, quasi-experimental, survey, and rigorously defined qualitative methodologies. Ryan and Bernard (2000) have developed elements of this paradigm.

The constructivist paradigm assumes a relativist ontology (there are multiple realities), a subjectivist epistemology (knower and respondent cocreate understandings), and a naturalistic (in the natural world) set of methodological procedures. Findings are usually presented in terms of the criteria of grounded theory or pattern theories (see Guba & Lincoln, Chapter 8, this volume; Charmaz, Volume 2, Chapter 7; see also Ryan & Bernard, 2000). Terms such as *credibility, transferability, dependability,* and *confirmability* replace the usual positivist criteria of internal and external validity, reliability, and objectivity.

Feminist, ethnic, Marxist, cultural studies, and queer theory models privilege a materialist-realist ontology; that is, the real world makes a material difference in terms of race, class, and gender. Subjectivist epistemologies and naturalistic methodologies (usually ethnographies) are also employed. Empirical materials and theoretical arguments are evaluated in terms of their emancipatory implications. Criteria from gender and racial communities (e.g., African American) may be applied (emotionality and feeling, caring, personal accountability, dialogue).

Poststructural feminist theories emphasize problems with the social text, its logic, and its inability ever to represent the world of lived experience fully. Positivist and postpositivist criteria of evaluation are replaced by other criteria, including the reflexive, multivoiced text that is grounded in the experiences of oppressed peoples.

The cultural studies and queer theory paradigms are multifocused, with many different strands drawing from Marxism, feminism, and the postmodern sensibility (see in this volume Saukko, Chapter 13; Plummer, Chapter 14; Richardson & St. Pierre, Volume 3, Chapter 15). There is a tension between a humanistic cultural studies, which stresses lived experiences (meaning), and a more structural cultural studies project, which stresses the structural and material determinants (race, class, gender) and effects of experience. Of course, there are two sides to every coin, and both sides are needed—indeed, both are critical. The cultural studies and queer theory paradigms use methods strategically—that is, as resources for understanding and for producing resistances to local structures of domination. Scholars may do close textual readings and discourse analyses of cultural texts (see Olesen, Chapter 10, this volume; Saukko, Chapter 13; Chase, Volume 3, Chapter 2) as well as local, online, reflexive, and critical ethnographies, open-ended interviewing, and participant observation. The focus is on how race, class, and gender are produced and enacted in historically specific situations.

Paradigm and personal history in hand, focused on a concrete empirical problem to examine, the researcher now moves to the next stage of the research process—namely, working with a specific strategy of inquiry.

Phase 3: Strategies of Inquiry and Interpretive Paradigms

Table 1.1 presents some of the major strategies of inquiry a researcher may use. Phase 3 begins with research design, which, broadly conceived, involves a clear focus on the research question, the purposes of the study, and "what information most appropriately will answer specific research questions, and which strategies are most effective for obtaining it" (LeCompte & Preissle, 1993, p. 30; see also Cheek, Volume 2, Chapter 2). A research design describes a flexible set of guidelines that connect theoretical paradigms first to strategies of inquiry and second to methods for collecting empirical materials. A research design situates the researcher in the empirical world and connects him or her to specific sites, persons, groups, institutions, and bodies of relevant interpretive material, including documents and archives. A research design also specifies how the investigator will address the two critical issues of representation and legitimation.

A strategy of inquiry comprises a bundle of skills, assumptions, and practices that the researcher employs as he or she moves from paradigm to the empirical world. Strategies of inquiry put paradigms of interpretation into motion. At the same time, strategies of inquiry also connect the researcher to specific methods of collecting and analyzing empirical materials. For example, the case study strategy relies on interviewing, observing, and document analysis. Research strategies implement and anchor paradigms in specific empirical sites or in specific methodological practices, such as making a case an object of study. These strategies include the case study, phenomenological and ethnomethodological techniques, and the use of grounded theory, as well as biographical, autoethnographic, historical, action, and clinical methods. Each of these strategies is connected to a complex literature, and each has a separate history, exemplary works, and preferred ways of putting the strategy into motion.

Phase 4: Methods of Collecting and Analyzing Empirical Materials

Qualitative researchers employ several methods for collecting empirical materials.[19] These methods, which are taken up in Volume 3, Part I (Part IV in the *Handbook*), include interviewing; direct observation; the analysis of artifacts, documents, and cultural records; the use of visual materials; and the use of personal experience. The researcher may also read and analyze interviews or cultural texts in a variety of different ways, including content, narrative, and semiotic strategies. Faced with large amounts of qualitative materials, the investigator seeks ways of managing and interpreting these documents, and here data management methods and computer-assisted models of analysis may be of use.

Phase 5: The Art and Politics of Interpretation and Evaluation

Qualitative research is endlessly creative and interpretive. The researcher does not just leave the field with mountains of empirical materials and then easily write up his or her findings. Qualitative interpretations are constructed. The researcher first creates a field text consisting of field notes and documents from the field, what Roger Sanjek (1990, p. 386) calls "indexing" and David Plath (1990, p. 374) calls "filework." The writer-as-interpreter moves from this text to a research text: notes and interpretations based on the field text. This text is then re-created as a working interpretive document that contains the writer's initial attempts to make sense of what he or she has learned. Finally, the writer produces the public text that comes to the reader. This final tale from the field may assume several forms: confessional, realist, impressionistic, critical, formal, literary, analytic, grounded theory, and so on (see Van Maanen, 1988).

The interpretive practice of making sense of one's findings is both artistic and political. Multiple criteria for evaluating qualitative research now exist, and those that we emphasize stress the situated, relational, and textual structures of the ethnographic experience. There is no single interpretive truth. As we argued earlier, there are multiple interpretive communities, each with its own criteria for evaluating interpretations.

Program evaluation is a major site of qualitative research, and qualitative researchers can influence social policy in important ways. The chapters in this volume by Greenwood and Levin (Chapter 2), Kemmis and McTaggart (Volume 2, Chapter 10), Miller and Crabtree (Volume 2, Chapter 11), Tedlock (Volume 2, Chapter 5), Smith and Hodkinson (Volume 3, Chapter 13), and House (Volume 3, Chapter 19) trace and discuss the rich history of applied qualitative research in the social sciences. This is the critical site where theory, method, praxis, action, and policy all come together. Qualitative researchers can isolate target populations, show the immediate effects of certain programs on such groups, and isolate the constraints that operate against policy changes in such settings. Action-oriented and clinically oriented qualitative researchers can also create spaces where those who are studied (the Other) can speak. The evaluator becomes the conduit for making such voices heard.

Bridging the Historical Moments: What Comes Next?

In Chapter 15 of Volume 3, Richardson and St. Pierre argue that we are already in the post-"post" period—post-poststructuralism, post-postmodernism, post-postexperimentalism. What this means for interpretive ethnographic practices is still not clear, but it is certain that things will never again be the same. We are in a new age where messy, uncertain, multivoiced texts, cultural criticism, and new experimental works will become more common, as will more reflexive forms of fieldwork, analysis, and intertextual representation. The subject of our final essays in Volume 3 is these sixth, seventh, eighth, and ninth moments. It is true that, as the poet said, the center no longer holds. We can reflect on what should be at the new center.

Thus we come full circle. Returning to our bridge metaphor, the chapters that follow take the researcher back and forth through every phase of the research act. Like a good bridge, the chapters provide for two-way traffic, coming and going between moments, formations, and interpretive communities. Each chapter examines the relevant histories, controversies, and current practices that are associated with each paradigm, strategy, and method. Each chapter also offers projections for the future, where a specific paradigm, strategy, or method will be 10 years from now, deep into the formative years of the 21st century.

In reading the chapters that follow, it is important to remember that the field of qualitative research is defined by a series of tensions, contradictions, and hesitations. These tensions work back and forth between and among the broad, doubting postmodern sensibility; the more certain, more traditional positivist, postpositivist, and naturalistic conceptions of this project; and an increasingly conservative, neoliberal global environment. All of the chapters that follow are caught in and articulate these tensions.

Notes

1. Recall bell hooks's (1990, p. 127) reading of the famous photo of Stephen Tyler doing fieldwork in India that appears on the cover of *Writing Culture* (Clifford & Marcus, 1986). In the picture, Tyler is seated at some distance from three dark-skinned persons. One, a child, is poking his or her head out of a basket. A woman is hidden in the shadows of the hut. A man, a checkered white-and-black shawl across his shoulder, elbow propped on his knee, hand resting along the side of his face, is staring at Tyler. Tyler is writing in a field journal. A piece of white cloth is attached to his glasses, perhaps shielding him from the sun. This patch of whiteness marks Tyler as the white male writer studying these passive brown and black persons. Indeed, the brown male's gaze signals some desire, or some attachment to Tyler. In contrast, the female's gaze is completely hidden by the shadows and by the words of the book's title, which are printed across her face.

2. Qualitative research has separate and distinguished histories in education, social work, communications, psychology, history, organizational studies, medical science, anthropology, and sociology.

3. Some definitions are in order here. *Positivism* asserts that objective accounts of the real world can be given. *Postpositivism* holds that only partially objective accounts of the world can be produced, for all methods for examining such accounts are flawed. According to *foundationalism,* we can have an ultimate grounding for our knowledge claims about the world, and this involves the use of empiricist and positivist epistemologies (Schwandt, 1997a, p. 103). *Nonfoundationalism* holds that we can make statements about the world without "recourse to ultimate proof or foundations for that knowing" (Schwandt, 1997a, p. 102). *Quasi-foundationalism* holds that we can make certain knowledge claims about the world based on neorealist criteria, including the correspondence concept of truth; there is an independent reality that can be mapped (see Smith & Hodkinson, Volume 3, Chapter 13).

4. Jameson (1991, pp. 3–4) reminds us that any periodization hypothesis is always suspect, even one that rejects linear, stagelike models. It is never clear to what reality a stage refers, and what divides one stage from another is always debatable. Our eight moments are meant to mark discernible shifts in style, genre, epistemology, ethics, politics, and aesthetics.

5. Several scholars have termed this model a *progress narrative* (Alasuutari, 2004, pp. 599–600; Seale, Gobo, Gubrium, & Silverman, 2004, p. 2). Critics assert that we believe that the most recent moment is the most up-to-date, the avant-garde, the cutting edge (Alasuutari, 2004, p. 601). Naturally, we dispute this reading. Teddlie and Tashakkori (2003, pp. 5–8) have modified our historical periods to fit their historical analysis of the major moments in the emergence of the use of mixed methods in social science research in the past century.

6. Some additional definitions are needed here. *Structuralism* holds that any system is made up of a set of oppositional categories embedded in language. *Semiotics* is the science of signs or sign systems—a structuralist project. According to *poststructuralism,* language is an unstable system of referents, thus it is impossible ever to capture completely the meaning of an

action, text, or intention. *Postmodernism* is a contemporary sensibility, developing since World War II, that privileges no single authority, method, or paradigm. *Hermeneutics* is an approach to the analysis of texts that stresses how prior understandings and prejudices shape the interpretive process. *Phenomenology* is a complex system of ideas associated with the works of Husserl, Heidegger, Sartre, Merleau-Ponty, and Alfred Schutz. *Cultural studies* is a complex, interdisciplinary field that merges critical theory, feminism, and poststructuralism.

7. Of course, all settings are natural—that is, places where everyday experiences take place. Qualitative researchers study people doing things together in the places where these things are done (Becker, 1986). There is no field site or natural place where one goes to do this kind of work (see also Gupta & Ferguson, 1997, p. 8). The site is constituted through the researcher's interpretive practices. Historically, analysts have distinguished between experimental (laboratory) and field (natural) research settings, hence the argument that qualitative research is naturalistic. Activity theory erases this distinction (Keller & Keller, 1996, p. 20; Vygotsky, 1978).

8. According to Weinstein and Weinstein (1991), "The meaning of *bricoleur* in French popular speech is 'someone who works with his (or her) hands and uses devious means compared to those of the craftsman.' . . . the *bricoleur* is practical and gets the job done" (p. 161). These authors provide a history of the term, connecting it to the works of the German sociologist and social theorist Georg Simmel and, by implication, Baudelaire. Hammersley (1999) disputes our use of this term. Following Lévi-Strauss, he reads the *bricoleur* as a mythmaker. He suggests that the term be replaced with the notion of the boatbuilder. Hammersley also quarrels with our "moments" model of the history of qualitative research, contending that it implies some sense of progress.

9. Brian De Palma reproduced this baby carriage scene in his 1987 film *The Untouchables*.

10. In the harbor, the muzzles of the *Potemkin*'s two huge guns swing slowly toward the camera. Words on the screen inform us, "The brutal military power answered by guns of the battleship." A final famous three-shot montage sequence shows first a sculpture of a sleeping lion, then a lion rising from his sleep, and finally the lion roaring, symbolizing the rage of the Russian people (Cook, 1981, p. 167). In this sequence Eisenstein uses montage to expand time, creating a psychological duration for this horrible event. By drawing out this sequence, by showing the baby in the carriage, the soldiers firing on the citizens, the blood on the mother's glove, the descending carriage on the steps, he suggests a level of destruction of great magnitude.

11. Here it is relevant to make a distinction between techniques that are used across disciplines and methods that are used within disciplines. Ethnomethodologists, for example, employ their approach as a method, whereas others selectively borrow that method as a technique for their own applications. Harry Wolcott (personal communication, 1993) suggests this distinction. It is also relevant to make distinctions among topic, method, and resource. Methods can be studied as topics of inquiry; that is how a case study gets done. In this ironic, ethnomethodological sense, method is both a resource and a topic of inquiry.

12. Indeed, any attempt to give an essential definition of qualitative research requires a qualitative analysis of the circumstances that produce such a definition.

13. In this sense all research is qualitative, because "the observer is at the center of the research process" (Vidich & Lyman, 2000, p. 39).

14. See Lincoln and Guba (1985) for an extension and elaboration of this tradition in the mid-1980s, and for more recent extensions see Taylor and Bogdan (1998) and Creswell (1998).

15. Greenblatt (1997, pp. 15–18) offers a useful deconstructive reading of the many meanings and practices Geertz brings to the term *thick description.*

16. These works marginalized and minimized the contributions of standpoint feminist theory and research to this discourse (see Behar, 1995, p. 3; Gordon, 1995, p. 432).

17. Olesen (Chapter 10, this volume) identifies three strands of feminist research: mainstream empirical, standpoint and cultural studies, and poststructural, postmodern. She places Afrocentric and other models of color under the cultural studies and postmodern categories.

18. These, of course, are our interpretations of these paradigms and interpretive styles.

19. *Empirical materials* is the preferred term for what traditionally have been described as data.

References

Alasuutari, P. (2004). The globalization of qualitative research. In C. Seale, G. Gobo, J. F. Gubrium, & D. Silverman (Eds.), *Qualitative research practice* (pp. 595–608). London: Sage.

Aronowitz, S. (1988). *Science as power: Discourse and ideology in modern society.* Minneapolis: University of Minnesota Press.

Atkinson, E. (2004). Thinking outside the box: An exercise in heresy. *Qualitative Inquiry, 10,* 111–129.

Bateson, G. (1972). *Steps to an ecology of mind.* New York: Ballantine.

Battiste, M. (2000). Introduction: Unfolding lessons of colonization. In M. Battiste (Ed.), *Reclaiming indigenous voice and vision* (pp. xvi–xxx). Vancouver: University of British Columbia Press.

Becker, H. S. (1970). Problems of inference and proof in participant observation. In H. S. Becker, *Sociological work: Method and substance.* Chicago: Aldine. (Reprinted from *American Sociological Review,* 1958, *23,* 652–660)

Becker, H. S. (1986). *Doing things together.* Evanston, IL: Northwestern University Press.

Becker, H. S. (1996). The epistemology of qualitative research. In R. Jessor, A. Colby, & R. A. Shweder (Eds.), *Ethnography and human development: Context and meaning in social inquiry* (pp. 53–71). Chicago: University of Chicago Press.

Becker, H. S. (1998). *Tricks of the trade: How to think about your research while you're doing it.* Chicago: University of Chicago Press.

Becker, H. S., Geer, B., Hughes, E. C., & Strauss, A. L. (1961). *Boys in white: Student culture in medical school.* Chicago: University of Chicago Press.

Behar, R. (1995). Introduction: Out of exile. In R. Behar & D. A. Gordon (Eds.), *Women writing culture* (pp. 1–29). Berkeley: University of California Press.

Bloch, M. (2004). A discourse that disciplines, governs, and regulates: The National Research Council's report on scientific research in education. *Qualitative Inquiry, 10,* 96–110.

Bochner, A. P., & Ellis, C. (Eds.). (2002). *Ethnographically speaking: Autoethnography, literature, and aesthetics.* Walnut Creek, CA: AltaMira.

Bogdan, R., & Taylor, S. J. (1975). *Introduction to qualitative research methods: A phenomenological approach to the social sciences.* New York: John Wiley.

Campbell, D. T., & Stanley, J. C. (1963). *Experimental and quasi-experimental designs for research.* Chicago: Rand McNally.

Cannella, G. S., & Lincoln, Y. S. (2004a). Dangerous discourses II: Comprehending and countering the redeployment of discourses (and resources) in the generation of liberatory inquiry. *Qualitative Inquiry, 10,* 165–174.

Cannella, G. S., & Lincoln, Y. S. (2004b). Epilogue: Claiming a critical public social science—reconceptualizing and redeploying research. *Qualitative Inquiry, 10,* 298–309.

Carey, J. W. (1989). *Communication as culture: Essays on media and society.* Boston: Unwin Hyman.

Cicourel, A. V. (1964). *Method and measurement in sociology.* New York: Free Press.

Clifford, J. (1988). *The predicament of culture: Twentieth-century ethnography, literature, and art.* Cambridge, MA: Harvard University Press.

Clifford, J., & Marcus, G. E. (Eds.). (1986). *Writing culture: The poetics and politics of ethnography.* Berkeley: University of California Press.

Clough, P. T. (1998). *The end(s) of ethnography: From realism to social criticism* (2nd ed.). New York: Peter Lang.

Cook, D. A. (1981). *A history of narrative film.* New York: W. W. Norton.

Creswell, J. W. (1998). *Qualitative inquiry and research design: Choosing among five traditions.* Thousand Oaks, CA: Sage.

Danermark, B., Ekström, M., Jakobsen, L., & Karlsson, J. C. (2002). *Explaining society: Critical realism in the social sciences.* London: Routledge.

de Certeau, M. (1984). *The practice of everyday life.* Berkeley: University of California Press.

Denzin, N. K. (1970). *The research act.* Chicago: Aldine.

Denzin, N. K. (1978). *The research act: A theoretical introduction to sociological methods* (2nd ed.). New York: McGraw-Hill.

Denzin, N. K. (1997). *Interpretive ethnography: Ethnographic practices for the 21st century.* Thousand Oaks, CA: Sage.

Denzin, N. K. (2003). *Performance ethnography: Critical pedagogy and the politics of culture.* Thousand Oaks, CA: Sage.

Dilthey, W. L. (1976). *Selected writings.* Cambridge: Cambridge University Press. (Original work published 1900)

Diversi, M. (1998). Glimpses of street life: Representing lived experience through short stories. *Qualitative Inquiry, 4,* 131–137.

Ellis, C. (2004). *The ethnographic I: A methodological novel about autoethnography.* Walnut Creek, CA: AltaMira.

Ellis, C., & Bochner, A. P. (Eds.). (1996). *Composing ethnography: Alternative forms of qualitative writing.* Walnut Creek, CA: AltaMira.

Filstead, W. J. (Ed.). (1970). *Qualitative methodology.* Chicago: Markham.

Fine, M., Weis, L., Weseen, S., & Wong, L. (2000). For whom? Qualitative research, representations, and social responsibilities. In N. K. Denzin & Y. S. Lincoln (Eds.), *Handbook of qualitative research* (2nd ed., pp. 107–131). Thousand Oaks, CA: Sage.

Flick, U. (2002). *An introduction to qualitative research* (2nd ed.). London: Sage.

Geertz, C. (1973). *The interpretation of cultures: Selected essays.* New York: Basic Books.

Geertz, C. (1983). *Local knowledge: Further essays in interpretive anthropology.* New York: Basic Books.

Geertz, C. (1988). *Works and lives: The anthropologist as author.* Stanford, CA: Stanford University Press.

Glaser, B. G. (1992). *Emergence vs. forcing: Basics of grounded theory.* Mill Valley, CA: Sociology Press.

Glaser, B. G., & Strauss, A. L. (1967). *The discovery of grounded theory: Strategies for qualitative research.* Chicago: Aldine.

Goodall, H. L., Jr. (2000). *Writing the new ethnography.* Walnut Creek, CA: AltaMira.

Gordon, D. A. (1995). Culture writing women: Inscribing feminist anthropology. In R. Behar & D. A. Gordon (Eds.), *Women writing culture* (pp. 429–441). Berkeley: University of California Press.

Greenblatt, S. (1997). The touch of the real. In S. B. Ortner (Ed.), The fate of "culture": Geertz and beyond [Special issue]. *Representations, 59,* 14–29.

Guba, E. G. (1990). The alternative paradigm dialog. In E. G. Guba (Ed.), *The paradigm dialog* (pp. 17–30). Newbury Park, CA: Sage.

Guba, E. G., & Lincoln, Y. S. (1989). *Fourth generation evaluation.* Newbury Park, CA: Sage.

Gupta, A., & Ferguson, J. (Eds.). (1997). Discipline and practice: "The field" as site, method, and location in anthropology. In A. Gupta & J. Ferguson (Eds.), *Anthropological locations: Boundaries and grounds of a field science* (pp. 1–46). Berkeley: University of California Press.

Hammersley, M. (1992). *What's wrong with ethnography? Methodological explorations.* London: Routledge.

Hammersley, M. (1999). Not bricolage but boatbuilding: Exploring two metaphors for thinking about ethnography. *Journal of Contemporary Ethnography, 28,* 574–585.

Harper, D. (1987). *Working knowledge: Skill and community in a small shop.* Chicago: University of Chicago Press.

Holman Jones, S. (1999). Torch. *Qualitative Inquiry, 5,* 235–250.

hooks, b. (1990). *Yearning: Race, gender, and cultural politics.* Boston: South End.

Howe, K. R. (2004). A critique of experimentalism. *Qualitative Inquiry, 10,* 42–61.

Huber, J. (1995). Centennial essay: Institutional perspectives on sociology. *American Journal of Sociology, 101,* 194–216.

Jackson, M. (1998). *Minima ethnographica: Intersubjectivity and the anthropological project.* Chicago: University of Chicago Press.

Jameson, F. (1991). *Postmodernism; or, The cultural logic of late capitalism.* Durham, NC: Duke University Press.

Keller, C. M., & Keller, J. D. (1996). *Cognition and tool use: The blacksmith at work.* New York: Cambridge University Press.

Kincheloe, J. L. (2001). Describing the bricolage: Conceptualizing a new rigor in qualitative research. *Qualitative Inquiry, 7,* 679–692.

Ladson-Billings, G. (2000). Socialized discourses and ethnic epistemologies. In N. K. Denzin & Y. S. Lincoln (Eds.), *Handbook of qualitative research* (2nd ed., pp. 257–277). Thousand Oaks, CA: Sage.

Lather, P. (1993). Fertile obsession: Validity after poststructuralism. *Sociological Quarterly, 35,* 673–694.

Lather, P. (2004). This *is* your father's paradigm: Government intrusion and the case of qualitative research in education. *Qualitative Inquiry, 10,* 15–34.

Lather, P., & Smithies, C. (1997). *Troubling the angels: Women living with HIV/AIDS.* Boulder, CO: Westview.

LeCompte, M. D., & Preissle, J. (with Tesch, R.). (1993). *Ethnography and qualitative design in educational research* (2nd ed.). New York: Academic Press.

Lévi-Strauss, C. (1966). *The savage mind* (2nd ed.). Chicago: University of Chicago Press.

Lincoln, Y. S. (1999, June). *Courage, vulnerability and truth.* Keynote address delivered at the conference "Reclaiming Voice II: Ethnographic Inquiry and Qualitative Research in a Postmodern Age," University of California, Irvine.

Lincoln, Y. S., & Cannella, G. S. (2004a). Dangerous discourses: Methodological conservatism and governmental regimes of truth. *Qualitative Inquiry, 10,* 5–14.

Lincoln, Y. S., & Cannella, G. S. (2004b). Qualitative research, power, and the radical Right. *Qualitative Inquiry, 10,* 175–201.

Lincoln, Y. S., & Guba, E. G. (1985). *Naturalistic inquiry.* Beverly Hills, CA: Sage.

Lincoln, Y. S., & Tierney, W. G. (2004). Qualitative research and institutional review boards. *Qualitative Inquiry, 10,* 219–234.

Lofland, J. (1971). *Analyzing social settings.* Belmont, CA: Wadsworth.

Lofland, J. (1995). Analytic ethnography: Features, failings, and futures. *Journal of Contemporary Ethnography, 24,* 30–67.

Lofland, J., & Lofland, L. H. (1984). *Analyzing social settings: A guide to qualitative observation and analysis* (2nd ed.). Belmont, CA: Wadsworth.

Lofland, J., & Lofland, L. H. (1995). *Analyzing social settings: A guide to qualitative observation and analysis* (3rd ed.). Belmont, CA: Wadsworth.

Lofland, L. H. (1980). The 1969 Blumer-Hughes Talk. *Urban Life and Culture, 8,* 248–260.

Malinowski, B. (1948). *Magic, science and religion, and other essays.* New York: Natural History Press. (Original work published 1916)

Malinowski, B. (1967). *A diary in the strict sense of the term* (N. Guterman, Trans.). New York: Harcourt, Brace & World.

Marcus, G. E., & Fischer, M. M. J. (1986). *Anthropology as cultural critique: An experimental moment in the human sciences.* Chicago: University of Chicago Press.

Maxwell, J. A. (2004). Reemergent scientism, postmodernism, and dialogue across differences. *Qualitative Inquiry, 10,* 35–41.

Monaco, J. (1981). *How to read a film: The art, technology, language, history and theory of film* (Rev. ed.). New York: Oxford University Press.

Nelson, C., Treichler, P. A., & Grossberg, L. (1992). Cultural studies: An introduction. In L. Grossberg, C. Nelson, & P. A. Treichler (Eds.), *Cultural studies* (pp. 1–16). New York: Routledge.

Ortner, S. B. (1997). Introduction. In S. B. Ortner (Ed.), The fate of "culture": Geertz and beyond [Special issue]. *Representations, 59,* 1–13.

Pelias, R. J. (2004). *A methodology of the heart: Evoking academic and daily life.* Walnut Creek, CA: AltaMira.

Plath, D. W. (1990). Fieldnotes, filed notes, and the conferring of note. In R. Sanjek (Ed.), *Fieldnotes: The makings of anthropology* (pp. 371–384). Ithaca, NY: Cornell University Press.

Popkewitz, T. S. (2004). Is the National Research Council committee's report on scientific research in education scientific? On trusting the manifesto. *Qualitative Inquiry, 10,* 62–78.

Richardson, L. (1997). *Fields of play: Constructing an academic life.* New Brunswick, NJ: Rutgers University Press.

Richardson, L. (2000). Writing: A method of inquiry. In N. K. Denzin & Y. S. Lincoln (Eds.), *Handbook of qualitative research* (2nd ed., pp. 923–948). Thousand Oaks, CA: Sage.

Richardson, L., & Lockridge, E. (2004). *Travels with Ernest: Crossing the literary/sociological divide.* Walnut Creek, CA: AltaMira.

Roffman, P., & Purdy, J. (1981). *The Hollywood social problem film.* Bloomington: Indiana University Press.

Ronai, C. R. (1998). Sketching with Derrida: An ethnography of a researcher/erotic dancer. *Qualitative Inquiry, 4,* 405–420.

Rosaldo, R. (1989). *Culture and truth: The remaking of social analysis.* Boston: Beacon.

Ryan, G. W., & Bernard, H. R. (2000). Data management and analysis methods. In N. K. Denzin & Y. S. Lincoln (Eds.), *Handbook of qualitative research* (2nd ed., pp. 769–802). Thousand Oaks, CA: Sage.

Ryan, K. E., & Hood, L. K. (2004). Guarding the castle and opening the gates. *Qualitative Inquiry, 10,* 79–95.

St. Pierre, E. A. (2004). Refusing alternatives: A science of contestation. *Qualitative Inquiry, 10,* 130–139.

Sanjek, R. (1990). On ethnographic validity. In R. Sanjek (Ed.), *Fieldnotes: The makings of anthropology* (pp. 385–418). Ithaca, NY: Cornell University Press.

Schwandt, T. A. (1997a). *Qualitative inquiry: A dictionary of terms.* Thousand Oaks, CA: Sage.

Schwandt, T. A. (1997b). Textual gymnastics, ethics and angst. In W. G. Tierney & Y. S. Lincoln (Eds.), *Representation and the text: Re-framing the narrative voice* (pp. 305–311). Albany: State University of New York Press.

Schwandt, T. A. (2000). Three epistemological stances for qualitative inquiry: Interpretivism, hermeneutics, and social constructionism. In N. K. Denzin & Y. S. Lincoln (Eds.), *Handbook of qualitative research* (2nd ed., pp. 189–213). Thousand Oaks, CA: Sage.

Seale, C., Gobo, G., Gubrium, J. F., & Silverman, D. (2004). Introduction: Inside qualitative research. In C. Seale, G. Gobo, J. F. Gubrium, & D. Silverman (Eds.), *Qualitative research practice* (pp. 1–11). London: Sage.

Semali, L. M., & Kincheloe, J. L. (1999). Introduction: What is indigenous knowledge and why should we study it? In L. M. Semali & J. L. Kincheloe (Eds.), *What is indigenous knowledge? Voices from the academy* (pp. 3–57). New York: Falmer.

Silverman, D. (1997). Towards an aesthetics of research. In D. Silverman (Ed.), *Qualitative research: Theory, method and practice* (pp. 239–253). London: Sage.

Smith, A. D. (1993). *Fires in the mirror: Crown Heights, Brooklyn, and other identities.* New York: Anchor.

Smith, J. K., & Deemer, D. K. (2000). The problem of criteria in the age of relativism. In N. K. Denzin & Y. S. Lincoln (Eds.), *Handbook of qualitative research* (2nd ed., pp. 877–896). Thousand Oaks, CA: Sage.

Smith, L. T. (1999). *Decolonizing methodologies: Research and indigenous peoples.* Dunedin, New Zealand: University of Otago Press.

Snow, D., & Morrill, C. (1995). Ironies, puzzles, and contradictions in Denzin and Lincoln's vision of qualitative research. *Journal of Contemporary Ethnography, 22,* 358–362.

Spindler, G., & Spindler, L. (1992). Cultural process and ethnography: An anthropological perspective. In M. D. LeCompte, W. L. Millroy, & J. Preissle (Eds.), *The handbook of qualitative research in education* (pp. 53–92). New York: Academic Press.

Stocking, G. W., Jr. (1986). Anthropology and the science of the irrational: Malinowski's encounter with Freudian psychoanalysis. In G. W. Stocking, Jr. (Ed.), *Malinowski, Rivers,*

Benedict and others: Essays on culture and personality (pp. 13–49). Madison: University of Wisconsin Press.

Stocking, G. W., Jr. (1989). The ethnographic sensibility of the 1920s and the dualism of the anthropological tradition. In G. W. Stocking, Jr. (Ed.), *Romantic motives: Essays on anthropological sensibility* (pp. 208–276). Madison: University of Wisconsin Press.

Stoller, P., & Olkes, C. (1987). *In sorcery's shadow: A memoir of apprenticeship among the Songhay of Niger.* Chicago: University of Chicago Press.

Strauss, A. L., & Corbin, J. (1998). *Basics of qualitative research: Techniques and procedures for developing grounded theory* (2nd ed.). Thousand Oaks, CA: Sage.

Taylor, S. J., & Bogdan, R. (1998). *Introduction to qualitative research methods: A guidebook and resource* (3rd ed.). New York: John Wiley.

Teddlie, C., & Tashakkori, A. (2003). Major issues and controversies in the use of mixed methods in the social and behavioral sciences. In A. Tashakkori & C. Teddlie (Eds.), *Handbook of mixed methods in social and behavioral research* (pp. 3–50). Thousand Oaks, CA: Sage.

Tierney, W. G. (2000). Undaunted courage: Life history and the postmodern challenge. In N. K. Denzin & Y. S. Lincoln (Eds.), *Handbook of qualitative research* (2nd ed., pp. 537–553). Thousand Oaks, CA: Sage.

Trujillo, N. (2004). *In search of Naunny's grave: Age, class, gender, and ethnicity in an American family.* Walnut Creek, CA: AltaMira.

Turner, V., & Bruner, E. (Eds.). (1986). *The anthropology of experience.* Urbana: University of Illinois Press.

Van Maanen, J. (1988). *Tales of the field: On writing ethnography.* Chicago: University of Chicago Press.

Vidich, A. J., & Lyman, S. M. (1994). Qualitative methods: Their history in sociology and anthropology. In N. K. Denzin & Y. S. Lincoln (Eds.), *Handbook of qualitative research* (pp. 23–59). Thousand Oaks, CA: Sage.

Vidich, A. J., & Lyman, S. M. (2000). Qualitative methods: Their history in sociology and anthropology. In N. K. Denzin & Y. S. Lincoln (Eds.), *Handbook of qualitative research* (2nd ed., pp. 37–84). Thousand Oaks, CA: Sage.

Vygotsky, L. S. (1978). *Mind in society: The development of higher psychological processes* (M. Cole, V. John-Steiner, S. Scribner, & E. Souberman, Eds.). Cambridge, MA: Harvard University Press.

Weinstein, D., & Weinstein, M. A. (1991). Georg Simmel: Sociological flaneur bricoleur. *Theory, Culture & Society, 8,* 151–168.

Weinstein, M. (2004). Randomized design and the myth of certain knowledge: Guinea pig narratives and cultural critique. *Qualitative Inquiry, 10,* 246–260.

West, C. (1989). *The American evasion of philosophy: A genealogy of pragmatism.* Madison: University of Wisconsin Press.

Wolf, M. A. (1992). *A thrice-told tale: Feminism, postmodernism, and ethnographic responsibility.* Stanford, CA: Stanford University Press.

Wolcott, H. F. (1990). *Writing up qualitative research.* Newbury Park, CA: Sage.

Wolcott, H. F. (1992). Posturing in qualitative inquiry. In M. D. LeCompte, W. L. Millroy, & J. Preissle (Eds.), *The handbook of qualitative research in education* (pp. 3–52). New York: Academic Press.

Wolcott, H. F. (1995). *The art of fieldwork.* Walnut Creek, CA: AltaMira.

Part I

Locating the Field

This volume, *The Landscape of Qualitative Research*, begins with the suggested reform of the social sciences and the academy through action research. It then moves to issues surrounding compositional studies and critical theorizing. Inquiry under neocolonial regimes is examined next. The discussion then turns to the social, political, and moral responsibilities of the researcher as well as the ethics and politics of qualitative inquiry.

History and the Participatory Action Tradition

The opening chapter, by Greenwood and Levin, reveals the depth and complexity of the traditional and applied qualitative research perspectives that are consciously and unconsciously inherited by the researcher-as-interpretive-bricoleur.[1] These traditions locate the investigator in a system of historical (and organizational) discourse. This system guides and constrains the interpretive work that is being done in any specific study.

In their monumental chapter ("Qualitative Methods: Their History in Sociology and Anthropology"), reprinted in the second edition of the *Handbook*, Vidich and Lyman (2000) show how the ethnographic tradition extends from the Greeks through the 15th- and 16th-century interests of Westerners in the origins of primitive cultures; to colonial ethnology connected to the empires of Spain, England, France, and Holland; to several 20th-century transformations in America and Europe. Throughout this history, the users of qualitative research have displayed commitments to a small set of beliefs, including objectivism, the desire to contextualize experience, and a willingness to interpret theoretically what has been observed.

These beliefs supplement the positivist tradition of complicity with colonialism, the commitments to monumentalism, and the production of timeless texts discussed in our introductory Chapter 1. The colonial model located qualitative inquiry in racial and sexual discourses that privileged white patriarchy. Of course, as indicated in our introductory chapter, recently these beliefs have come under considerable attack. Vidich and Lyman, as well as Smith (Chapter 4), Bishop (Chapter 5), and Ladson-Billings and Donnor (Chapter 11), document the extent to which early as well as contemporary qualitative researchers were (and remain) implicated in these systems of oppression.

Greenwood and Levin expand and extend this line of criticism. They are quite explicit that scholars have a responsibility to do work that is socially meaningful and socially responsible. The relationship between researchers, universities, and society must change. Politically informed action research, inquiry committed to praxis and social change, is the vehicle for accomplishing this transformation.

Action researchers are committed to a set of disciplined, material practices that produce radical, democratizing transformations in the civic sphere. These practices involve collaborative dialogue, participatory decision making, inclusive democratic deliberation, and the maximal participation and representation of all relevant parties (Ryan & Destefano, 2000, p. 1). Action researchers literally help transform inquiry into praxis, or action. Research subjects become coparticipants and stakeholders in the process of inquiry. Research becomes praxis—practical, reflective, pragmatic action—directed to solving problems in the world.

These problems originate in the lives of the research coparticipants—they do not come down from on high, by way of grand theory. Together, stakeholders and action researchers co-create knowledge that is pragmatically useful and is grounded in local knowledge. In the process, they jointly define research objectives and political goals, co-construct research questions, pool knowledge, hone shared research skills, fashion interpretations and performance texts that implement specific strategies for social change, and measure validity and credibility by the willingness of local stakeholders to act on the basis of the results of the action research.

Academic science has a history in the past century of not being able to accomplish consistently goals such as these. According to Greenwood and Levin, there are several reasons for this failure, including the inability of a so-called positivistic, value-free social science to produce useful social research; the increasing tendency of outside corporations to define the needs and values of the university; the loss of research funds to entrepreneurial and private sector research organizations; and bloated, inefficient internal administrative infrastructures.

Greenwood and Levin are not renouncing the practices of science; rather, they are calling for a reformulation of what science and the academy are all about. Their model of pragmatically grounded action research is not a retreat from disciplined scientific inquiry.[2] This form of inquiry reconceptualizes science as a collaborative, communicative, communitarian, context-centered, moral project. They want to locate action research at the center of the contemporary university. Their chapter is a call for a civic social science, a pragmatic science that will lead to the radical reconstruction of the university's relationships with society, state, and community in this new century.

Critical Theorizing, Social Responsibility, Decolonizing Research, and the Ethics of Inquiry

The contributions of Michelle Fine and Lois Weis (Chapter 3), Linda Tuhiwai Smith (Chapter 4), Russell Bishop (Chapter 5), Clifford Christians (Chapter 6), and Yvonna Lincoln (Chapter 7) extend this call for a committed, civic moral social science. Fine and Weis offer a theory of method, a new approach to ethnography, a new way of reading and writing this complex, fragmented, and fractured social puzzle we call America. Compositional studies are contextual, relational, and sensitive to the fluidity of social identities. Fine and Weis seek to create compositional works that place race, class, gender, and ethnicity in relation to one another, in ways that work back and forth among history, economy, and politics. Their chapter offers brief looks at two compositional designs: Weis's long-term study of white working-class men and women, and Fine's participatory action project involving youth as critical researchers of desegregation. Each of these ethnographic projects is designed to understand how "global and national formations, as well as relational interactions, seep through the lives, identities, relations, and communities of youth and adults, ultimately refracting back on the larger formations that give rise to them to begin with" (p. 69). They offer a series of stories that reveal a set of knotty, emergent ethical and rhetorical dilemmas that were encountered as they attempted to write for, with, and about poor and working-class stakeholders.

These are the problems of qualitative inquiry in the current historical moment. They turn on the issues of voice, reflexivity, "race," informed consent, good and bad stories, and "coming clean at the hyphen." Voice and reflexivity are primary. Fine and Weis struggled with how to locate themselves and their stakeholders in the text. They also struggled with how to write about "race," a floating, unstable fiction that is also an inerasable aspect of the self and its personal history. With them, we take heart in the observations of Nikoury, a youth researcher from the Lower East Side of Manhattan who stunned an audience with these words: "I used to see flat. No more . . . now I know things are much deeper than they appear. And it's my job to find out what's behind the so-called facts. I can't see flat anymore" (p. 80).

Fine and Weis are hopeful that compositional studies can "provide a scholarly mirror of urgency, refracting back on a nation . . . [asking] us to re-view the very structures of power upon which the country, the economy, our schools, and our fragile sense of selves . . . are premised, and to imagine, alternatively, what could be" (p. 80).

Linda Tuhiwai Smith, a Mâori scholar, discusses research in and on indigenous communities—those who have witnessed, have been excluded from, and have survived modernity and imperialism. She analyses how indigenous peoples, the native Other, historically have been vulnerable to neocolonial research. Recently, as part of the decolonization process, indigenous communities have begin to resist hegemonic research and to invent new research methodologies. Mâori scholars have developed a research approach known as Kaupapa Mâori. Smith (Chapter 4) and Bishop (Chapter 5) outline this approach, which makes research a highly political activity.

In indigenous communities, research ethics involves both establishing and maintaining nurturing reciprocal and respectful relationships. This ethical framework is very much at odds with the Western, Institutional Review Board type of apparatus, with its informed consent forms. Indigenous research activity offers genuine utopian hope for creating and living in a more just and humane social world.

Russell Bishop shows how a Kaupapa Mâori position can be used by the Mâori to get free of neocolonial domination. Kaupapa Mâori creates the conditions for self-determination. It emphasizes five issues of power that become criteria for evaluating research: initiation, benefits, representation, legitimation, and accountability. Indigenous researchers should initiate research, not be the subject of someone else's research agenda. The community should benefit from the research, which should represent the voices of indigenous peoples. The indigenous community should have the power to legitimate and produce the research texts that are written, as well as the power to hold researchers accountable for what is written. When these five criteria are addressed in the affirmative, empowering knowledge is created, allowing indigenous persons to free themselves from neocolonial domination.

A Feminist, Communitarian Ethical Framework

Clifford Christians (Chapter 6) locates the ethics and politics of qualitative inquiry within a broader historical and intellectual framework. He first examines the Enlightenment model of positivism, value-free inquiry, utilitarianism, and utilitarian ethics. In a value-free social science, codes of ethics for professional societies become the conventional format for moral principles. By the 1980s, each of the major social science associations (contemporaneous with passage of federal laws and promulgation of national guidelines) had developed its own ethical code, with an emphasis on several guidelines: informed consent, nondeception, the absence of psychological or physical harm, privacy and confidentiality, and a commitment to collecting and presenting reliable and valid empirical materials. Institutional Review Boards (IRBs) implemented these guidelines, including ensuring that informed consent is always obtained in human subject research. However, Christians notes, as do Smith and Bishop, that in reality IRBs protect institutions and not individuals.

Several events challenged the Enlightenment model, including the Nazi medical experiments, the Tuskegee Syphilis Study, Project Camelot in the 1960s, Milgram's deception of subjects in his psychology experiments, Humphrey's deceptive study of homosexuals, and the complicity of social scientists with military initiatives in Vietnam. In addition, charges of fraud, plagiarism, data tampering, and misrepresentation continue to the present day.

Christians details the poverty of this model. It creates the conditions for deception, for the invasion of private spaces, for duping subjects, and for challenges to the subjects' moral worth and dignity (see also Angrosino, Volume 3, Chapter 5; Guba & Lincoln, 1989, pp. 120–141). Christians calls for its replacement with an ethics based on the values of feminist communitarianism.

This is an evolving, emerging ethical framework that serves as a powerful antidote to the deception-based, utilitarian IRB system. It presumes a community that is ontologically and axiologically prior to the person. This community has common moral values, and research is rooted in a concept of care, of shared governance, of neighborliness, and of love, kindness, and the moral good. Accounts of social life should display these values and be based on interpretive sufficiency. They should have sufficient depth to allow the reader to form a critical understanding about the world studied. These texts should exhibit an absence of racial, class, and gender stereotyping. These texts should generate social criticism and should lead to resistance, empowerment, and social action—to positive change in the social world.

In the feminist communitarian model, as with the model of participatory action research advocated by Greenwood and Levin; Fine and Weis; Smith, Bishop, and Kemmis and McTaggart; participants have a co-equal say in how research should be conducted, what should be studied, which methods should be used, which findings are valid and acceptable, how the findings are to be implemented, and how the consequences of such action are to be assessed. Spaces for disagreement are recognized, and discourse aims for mutual understanding and for the honoring of moral commitments.

A sacred, existential epistemology places us in a noncompetitive, nonhierarchical relationship to the earth, to nature, and to the larger world (Bateson, 1972, p. 335). This sacred epistemology stresses the values of empowerment, shared governance, care, solidarity, love, community, covenant, morally involved observers, and civic transformation. As Christians observes, this ethical epistemology recovers the moral values that were excluded by the rational, Enlightenment science project. This sacred epistemology is based on a philosophical anthropology which declares that "all humans are worthy of dignity and sacred status without exception for class or ethnicity" (Christians, 1995, p. 129). A universal human ethic, stressing the sacredness of life, human dignity, truth-telling, and nonviolence derives from this position (Christians, 1997, pp. 12–15). This ethic is based on locally experienced, culturally prescribed protonorms (Christians, 1995, p. 129). These primal norms provide a defensible "conception of good rooted in universal human solidarity" (Christians, 1995, p. 129; see also Christians, 1997, 1998). This sacred epistemology recognizes and interrogates the ways in which race, class, and gender operate as important systems of oppression in the world today.

Thus does Christians outline a radical ethical path for the future. In so doing, he transcends the usual middle-of-the-road ethical models that focus on the problems associated with betrayal, deception, and harm in qualitative research. Christians's call for a collaborative social science research model makes the researcher responsible not to a removed discipline (or institution) but rather to those studied. This implements critical, action, and feminist traditions that forcefully align the ethics of research with a politics of the oppressed. Christians's framework reorganizes existing discourses on ethics and the social sciences.[3]

The Biomedical Model of Ethics[4]

Christians reviews the criticisms of the biomedical model of ethics, the apparatus of the Institutional Review Board, and Common Rule understandings. Criticisms center on four key terms and their definitions: human subjects, human subject research, harm, and ethical conduct.

A note on the relationship between science and ethics is in order. As Christians notes in Chapter 6, the Common Rule principles reiterate the basic themes of "value-neutral experimentalism—individual autonomy, maximum benefits with minimal risks, and ethical ends exterior to scientific means" (p. 146). These principles "dominate the codes of ethics: informed consent, protection of privacy, and nondeception" (p. 146). These rules do not conceptualize research in participatory or collaborative formats. Christians observes that in reality the guidelines do not stop other ethical violations, including plagiarism, falsification, fabrication, and violations of confidentiality.

Pritchard (2002, pp. 8–9) notes that there is room for ethical conflict as well. The three principles contained in the Common Rule rest on three different ethical traditions: respect, from Kant; beneficence, from Mill and the utilitarians; and justice as a distributive ideal, from Aristotle. These ethical traditions are not compatible: They rest on different moral, ontological, and political assumptions, as well as on different understandings of what is right, just, and respectful. The Kantian principle of respect may contradict the utilitarian principle of beneficence, for instance.

Respect, *beneficence*, and *justice* are problematic terms. Surely there is more to respect than informed consent—more, that is, than getting people to agree to be participants in a study. Respect involves caring for others, honoring them, and treating them with dignity. An informed consent form does not do this, and it does not confer respect on another person.

Beneficence, including risks and benefits, cannot be quantified, nor can a clear meaning be given to acceptable risk or to benefits that clearly serve a larger cause. Smith (Chapter 4) and Bishop (Chapter 5), for instance, both argue that the collectivity must determine collectively what are the costs and benefits for participating in research. Furthermore, individuals may not have the individual right to allow particular forms of research to be done if the research has negative effects for the greater social whole. A cost-benefit model of society and inquiry does injustice to the empowering, participatory model of research that many peoples are now advocating.

Justice extends beyond implementing fair selection procedures or unfairly distributing the benefits of research across a population. Justice involves principles of care, love, kindness, and fairness, as well as commitments to shared responsibility and to honesty, truth, balance, and harmony. Taken out of their Western utilitarian framework, respect, beneficence, and justice must be seen as principles that are felt as they are performed; that is, they can serve as performative guidelines to a moral way of being in the world with others. As currently enforced by IRBs, however, they serve as coldly calculating devices that may position persons against one another.

Regarding research, Pritchard (2002) contends that the biomedical model's concept of research does not adequately deal with procedural changes in research projects and with unforeseen contingencies that lead to changes in purpose and intent. Often, anonymity cannot be maintained, nor is it always desirable; for example, participatory action inquiry presumes full community participation in a research project.

Staffing presents another level of difficulty. IRBs often are understaffed or have members who either reject or are uninformed about the newer, critical qualitative research tradition. Many IRBs lack proper appeal procedures or methods for expediting research that should be exempted.

Recent summaries by the American Association of University Professors (AAUP) (2001, 2002) raise additional reservations, which also center on the five issues discussed above. These reservations involve the following topics.

Research and Human Subjects

- A failure by IRBs to be aware of new interpretive and qualitative developments in the social sciences, including participant observation, ethnography, autoethnography, and oral history research
- The application of a concept of research and science that privileges the biomedical model of science and not the model of trust, negotiation, and respect that must be established in ethnographic or historical inquiry, where research is not *on*, but is rather *with*, other human beings
- An event-based and not a process-based conception of research and the consent process

Ethics

- A failure to see human beings as social creatures located in complex historical, political, and cultural spaces
- Infringements on academic freedom resulting from failure to allow certain types of inquiry to go forward

- Inappropriate applications of the "Common Rule" in assessing potential harm
- Overly restrictive applications of the informed consent rule

IRBs as Institutional Structures

- A failure to have an adequate appeal system in place
- The need to ensure that IRBs have members from the newer interpretive paradigms

Academic Freedom

- First Amendment and academic freedom infringements
- Policing of inquiry in the humanities, including oral history research
- Policing and obstruction of research seminars and dissertation projects
- Constraints on critical inquiry, including historical or journalistic work that contributes to the public knowledge of the past, while incriminating, or passing negative judgment on, persons and institutions
- A failure to consider or incorporate existing forms of regulation into the Common Rule, including laws and rules regarding libel, copyright, and intellectual property rights
- The general extension of IRB powers across disciplines, creating a negative effect on what will, or will not, be studied
- Vastly different applications of the Common Rule across campus communities

Important Topics Not Regulated

- The conduct of research with indigenous peoples (see below)
- The regulation of unorthodox or problematic conduct in the field (e.g., sexual relations)
- Relations between IRBs and ethical codes involving universal human rights
- Disciplinary codes of ethics and IRBs, and new codes of ethics and moral perspectives coming from the standpoints of feminist, queer, and racialized epistemologies
- Appeal mechanisms for any human subject who needs to grieve and who seeks some form of restorative justice as a result of harm experienced as a research subject
- Indigenous discourses and alternative views of research, science, and human beings

Disciplining and Constraining Ethical Conduct

The consequence of these restrictions is a disciplining of qualitative inquiry, with the discipline process extending from oversight by granting agencies to the policing of qualitative research seminars and even the conduct of qualitative dissertations (Lincoln & Cannella, 2004a, 2004b). In some cases, lines of critical inquiry have not been funded and have not gone forward because of criticisms from local IRBs. Pressures from the political right discredit critical interpretive inquiry. From the federal to the local levels, a trend seems to be emerging. In too many instances, there seems to be a move away from protecting human subjects and toward increased monitoring, censuring, and policing of projects that are critical of conservative politics.

Lincoln and Tierney (2004) observe that these policing activities have at least five important implications for critical, social justice inquiry. First, the widespread rejection of alternative forms of research means that qualitative inquiry will be heard less and less in federal and state policy forums. Second, it appears that qualitative researchers are being deliberately excluded from this national dialogue. Consequently, third, young researchers trained in the critical tradition are not being listened to. Fourth, the definition of research has not changed to fit newer models of inquiry. Fifth, in rejecting qualitative inquiry, traditional researchers are endorsing a more distanced form of research that is compatible with existing stereotypes concerning persons of color.

Lincoln extends this analysis in Chapter 7, underscoring the negative effects of these recent developments on academic freedom, graduate student training, and qualitative inquiry. These developments threaten academic freedom in four ways: (a) They lead to increased scrutiny of human subject research, as well as (b) new scrutiny of classroom research and training in qualitative research involving human subjects; (c) they connect to evidence-based discourses, which define qualitative research as being unscientific; and (d) by endorsing methodological conservatism, they reinforce the status quo on many campuses. This conservatism produces new constraints on graduate training, leads to the improper review of faculty research, and creates conditions for politicizing the IRB review process, while protecting institutions and not individuals from risk and harm.

These constraints must be resisted, and the local IRB is a good place to start.

Conclusions

As does Christians, we endorse a *feminist, communitarian ethic* that calls, after Smith and Bishop, for collaborative, trusting, nonoppressive relationships between researchers and those studied. Such an ethic presumes that investigators are committed to stressing personal accountability, caring, the value of individual expressiveness, the capacity for empathy, and the sharing of emotionality (Collins, 1990, p. 216).

Notes

1. Any distinction between applied and non-applied qualitative research traditions is somewhat arbitrary. Both traditions are scholarly. Each has a long history, and each carries basic implications for theory and social change. Good theoretical research should also have applied relevance and implications. On occasion, it is argued that applied and action research

are nontheoretical, but even this conclusion can be disputed, as Kemmis and McTaggart (Volume 2, Chapter 10) demonstrate.

2. We will develop a notion of a sacred science below and in our concluding chapter (Epilogue).

3. Given Christians's framework, there are two primary ethical models: utilitarian and non-utilitarian. Historically and most recently, however, one of five ethical stances (absolutist, consequentialist, feminist, relativist, deceptive) has been followed, and often these stances merge with one another. The *absolutist* position argues that any method that contributes to a society's self-understanding is acceptable, but only conduct in the public sphere should be studied. The *deception* model says that any method, including the use of lies and misrepresentation, is justified in the name of truth. The *relativist* stance says that researchers have absolute freedom to study what they want and that ethical standards are a matter of individual conscience. Christians's feminist-communitarian framework elaborates a *contextual-consequential framework* that stresses mutual respect, noncoercion, nonmanipulation, and the support of democratic values (see Guba & Lincoln, 1989, pp. 120–141; Smith, 1990; also Collins,1990, p. 216; Mitchell, 1993).

4. This section draws from Denzin (2003, pp. 248–257).

▣ References

American Association of University Professors. (2001). Protecting human beings: Institutional Review Boards and social science research. *Academe, 87*(3), 55–67.

American Association of University Professors. (2002). Should all disciplines be subject to the Common Rule? Human subjects of social science research. *Academe, 88*(1), 1–15.

Bateson, G. (1972). *Steps to an ecology of mind.* New York: Ballantine.

Christians, G. C. (1995). The naturalistic fallacy in contemporary interactionist-interpretive research. *Studies in Symbolic Interaction, 19,* 125–130.

Christians, G. C. (1997). The ethics of being in a communications context. In C. Christians & M. Traber (Eds.), *Communication ethics and universal values* (pp. 3–23). Thousand Oaks, CA: Sage.

Christians, G. C. (1998). The sacredness of life. *Media Development, 2,* 3–7.

Collins, P. H. (1990). *Black feminist thought.* New York: Routledge.

Guba, E. G., & Lincoln, Y. S. (1989). *Fourth generation evaluation.* Newbury Park, CA: Sage.

Lincoln, Y. S., & Cannella, G. S. (2004a). Dangerous discourses: Methodological conservatism and governmental regimes of truth. *Qualitative Inquiry, 10*(1), 5–14.

Lincoln, Y. S., & Cannella, G. S. (2004b). Qualitative research, power, and the radical right. *Qualitative Inquiry, 10*(2), 175–201.

Lincoln, Y. S., & Tierney, W. G. (2004). Qualitative research and Institutional Review Boards. *Qualitative Inquiry, 10*(2), 219–234.

Mitchell, R. J., Jr. (1993). *Secrecy and fieldwork.* Newbury Park, CA: Sage.

Pritchard, I. A. (2002). Travelers and trolls: Practitioner research and Institutional Review Boards. *Educational Researcher, 31,* 3–13.

Ryan, K., & Destefano, L. (2000). Introduction. In K. Ryan & L. Destefano (Eds.), *Evaluation in a democratic society: Deliberation, dialogue and inclusion* (pp. 1–20). San Francisco: Jossey-Bass.

Smith, L. M. (1990). Ethics, field studies, and the paradigm crisis. In E. G. Guba (Ed.), *The paradigm dialog* (pp. 137–157). Newbury Park, CA: Sage.

Vidich, A. J., & Lyman, S. M. (2000). Qualitative methods: Their history in sociology and anthropology. In N. K. Denzin & Y. S. Lincoln (Eds.), *Handbook of qualitative research* (2nd ed., pp. 37–84). Thousand Oaks, CA: Sage.

2

REFORM OF THE SOCIAL SCIENCES AND OF UNIVERSITIES THROUGH ACTION RESEARCH

Davydd J. Greenwood and Morten Levin

When dissatisfied practitioners seek to explain why important, innovative, transdisciplinary developments such as feminism, grounded theory, cultural studies, social studies of science, naturalistic inquiry, and action research have difficulty gaining a foothold and then surviving in universities, the analysis focuses on the organizational structures created by the disciplines and their aggregations into centrifugal colleges (Messer-Davidow, 2002). Most critics account for the conservative behavior of which they do not approve by referring to academic "politics," to the maintenance of mini-cartels and disciplinary monopolies that control publication, promotion, research funding, and similar processes. The apparent cause is the political power of the owners of the various disciplinary bunkers on campuses.

As "political" as this behavior seems, it is obvious worldwide that the relationship between what is done in universities—especially what we do in the social sciences—and what the rest of society (on which we depend) wants is not being handled with much political skill. In our opinion, university relationships to key external constituencies (e.g., taxpayers, national and state government funders, private foundations, our surrounding communities, and public and private sector organizations) embody politically (and economically) self-destructive behavior.

A great number of university social scientists write about each other and for each other, purposely engaging as little as possible in public debates and in issues that are socially salient. Often, their research is written up in a language and with concepts that are incomprehensible to the people who are the "subjects" of research and to those outside the university who might want to use the findings. That philosophers, mathematicians, or musicologists do this fits their image as humanists conserving and enhancing ideas and productions of human value, regardless of their direct applicability. That social scientists do this as well, despite their claims to study and comprehend the workings of society, is more problematic.

Put more bluntly, most social science disciplines have excused themselves from social engagement by defining doing "social science" as separate from the application of their insights. The remaining gestures toward social engagement are left mainly to the social science associations' mission statements. The cost of this disengagement to the social sciences is visible in the small state and federal research allocations for academic social science research.[1]

These observations raise the following questions: How can social scientists be at once so "political" on campus and so impolitic in relation to society at large? Why is it that the knowledge created by social science research seldom leads to solutions to major societal problems? Why is it that social disengagement is more typical than atypical for social scientists? This chapter is our effort to sort out these issues. We seek to account for the disconnection between the internal politics of professional practice and the external constituencies of the conventional social sciences (e.g., sociology, anthropology, political science, and many branches of economics) in view of the fact that those external constituencies provide the financial and institutional support needed for the survival of the social sciences. We then present an alternative approach to social science and action research, because we believe that action research is key to the needed fundamental transformation of the behaviors engaged in by social scientists.

▣ Why Is There Such a Disconnection Between the Social Sciences and Society at Large?

There is no one right way to conceptualize and understand the relationship between social science work at universities and society at large, and different perspectives lead to different insights. What we offer is simply our view, based on the use of three elements: Marxism, the sociology of the professions, and historical/developmental perspectives.

Marxist or Neo-Marxist Views

These analytical frameworks stress the impact of the larger political economy on institutions and ideologies, including those of the academy (Silva & Slaughter, 1984;

Slaughter & Leslie, 1997). From this perspective, the principal function of universities is the reproduction of social class differences through teaching, research, and the provision of new generations with access to key positions of power within the class system. From a Marxist perspective, universities contain a complex mix of elements that involve both promoting and demoting the claims of aspirants to social mobility.

Universities emphasize respect for the past and its structuring value schemes while simultaneously engaging in research designed to change the human condition. Much of this research is externally funded, placing universities in a service relationship to existing structures of power. Furthermore, most universities are both tax exempt and tax subsidized, placing them in a relationship of subordination to the state and to the public. Despite this, it is quite typical for many of those employed in universities to forget that they are beneficiaries of public subsidies.

As work organizations, universities are characterized by strong hierarchical structures and a number of superimposed networks. They are divided into colleges, with further division of the colleges into disciplinary departments and the departments into subdisciplines, with nationally and internationally networked sets of relationships linking individual researchers to each other. Teaching is strongly controlled bureaucratically, but the organization of research is more entrepreneurial and more determined by the researchers themselves. Despite the recruitment of some senior faculty into administrative roles, universities increasingly are run by managers who often have strongly Tayloristic visions of work organization and who operate at a great distance from the site of value production.

As in feudalism, administrative power is wielded by enforcing competitiveness among the units. Academic management philosophies and schemes generally mimic those of the private sector, but with a time delay measured in years. As a result, most of the recent efforts to become more "businesslike" in universities involve the application of management strategies already tried and discarded by the private sector (Birnbaum, 2000).

Ideologically, universities claim to serve the "public good" by educating the young for good jobs and conducting research that is in society's interest or that directly creates value for society. Internal management ideologies stress cost-effectiveness, encouragement of entrepreneurial activity in university operations, competitiveness in student admissions and support services, and entrepreneurialism in attracting research money and alumni gifts.

The Tayloristic and economistic ideologies of cost-effectiveness and market tests, increasingly used by university administrators and boards of trustees to discipline campus activities, have to deal with the crippling inconvenience that there are few true "market tests" for academic activity. As a result, administrative "impressions" and beliefs often substitute for market tests, and framing them in "market" language serves mainly to obscure the constant shifts of power within the system, including shifts in the structures of patron-client relationships, changes in favoritisms, and the ongoing consolidation of administrative power. This situation is basically the same in most industrial societies, even if the university forms part of the public administrative system, as it does in many European countries.

At the level of work organization, universities are characterized by intensely hierarchical relationships between senior and junior faculty; between faculty and staff; and among faculty, students, and staff. The same contradictions between public political expressions of prosocial values and privately competitive and entrepreneurial behaviors that characterize major corporations and political parties are visible within university structures at all levels. The notion of egalitarian collegiality, often used to describe relationships between "disciplinary" peers, rarely is visible and arises usually when a disciplinary peer group is under threat or is trying to wrest resources from other such groups. Most people involved in the workings of universities—faculty, students, administrators, and staff—experience them as profoundly authoritarian workplaces.

Sociology of the Professions Views

Perhaps the most abundant literature on the issues discussed in this chapter is found in the many variants of the sociology of the professions. These approaches range among Marxist, functionalist, and intepretivist strategies and resist easy summary (see Abbott, 1988; Brint, 1996; Freidson, 1986; Krause, 1996). What they share is a more "internalist" perspective than is commonly found in the more comprehensive Marxist/neo-Marxist framings of these issues. The sociology of the professions focuses on the multiple structurings of professional powers. These structurings involve centrally the development of boundary maintenance mechanisms that serve to include, exclude, certify, and decertify practitioners and groups of practitioners. This literature also emphasizes the development of internal professional power structures that set agendas for work, that define the "discipline" of which the profession is an embodiment, and that establish the genealogies of some of the most powerful subgroups of practitioners and turn these partisan genealogies into a "history" of the profession (Madoo Lengermann & Niebrugge-Brantley, 1998).

In these approaches, the self-interest of the established academic practitioners is central. Essential to professionalism is that a strong boundary exist between what is inside and what is outside the profession. This is key to the development of academic professional structures and also directly requires that groups of professional colleagues engage in numerous transactions with superordinate systems of power in order to be certified by them. To function, the academic professions must be accepted and accredited by those in power at universities, yet members of the profession owe principal allegiance to their professional peers, not to their universities.

Within the university structure, disciplinary department chairs—no matter how important their discipline might be—are subordinate to deans, provosts, and presidents. Thus, a department chair who might be a major player in the national and international disciplinary associations in his or her field is, on campus, a relatively low-level functionary. This situation often leads to a double strategy. Ambitious department chairs work on the ranking of their departments in various national schemes in order to acquire and control university resources. Deans, provosts, and vice-chancellors must pay attention to these rankings because declines in the rankings of the units in their charge are part of the pseudo-market test of their abilities as academic administrators.

Such professional strategies have some advantages for senior academic administrators or public higher education officials because they encourage the faculty and the departments to compete mainly with each other. In this way, the disciplines "discipline" each other and permit higher administrators to behave like referees in a contest. Clearly, organizations structured this way are generally passive in relation to central power and are relatively easy to control. These campus controls are backed up by national ranking schemes that encourage further competitiveness and by state and national funding schemes that set the terms of the competition within groups and that privilege and punish professional groups according to extradisciplinary criteria.

Students and junior colleagues are socialized into these structures through required curricula, examinations, ideological pressures, and threats to their ability to continue in the profession. Their attention is driven inward and away from the external relations or social roles/responsibilities of their professions, and certainly away from issuing any challenges to higher authorities.

These structures, of course, are highly sensitive to the larger management schemes into which they fit and to the larger political economy. As a result, there are quite dramatic national differences in the composition, mission, and ranking of different professions, as Elliott Krause has shown (1996), but pursuing this topic would take us beyond the scope of this chapter.

Historical/Developmental Views

Perhaps the best-developed literature on these topics comes from history. Scholars such as Mary Furner (1975), Ellen Messer-Davidow (2002), Dorothy Ross (1991), and George Stocking, Jr. (1968) have documented and analyzed the long-run transitions in the social sciences and the humanities. There are also scores of self-promoting and self-protective professional association histories (i.e., the "official stories"). We ignore this latter set here, finding them useful as ethnographic documents but not as explanations of the processes involved. There is an advantage in having a long time perspective because large-scale changes in the disciplines often become sharply visible only when viewed as they develop over several decades.

The literature on the history of the social sciences in the United States suggests something like the following narrative. It begins with the founding of the American Social Science Association in 1865 as an association of senior academics who would study and debate major issues of public policy and provide governments and corporate leaders with supposedly balanced advice. By the 1880s, this approach began to wane, and the various social science disciplinary associations emerged, beginning with economics. The link between the founding of these associations and the emergence of disciplinary departments in PhD-granting institutions was a sea change in the trajectory of the social sciences and resulted in many of the structures that exist today.

The works of Mary Furner (1975), Patricia Madoo Lengermann and Jill Niebrugge-Brantley (1998), Ellen Messer-Davidow (2002), and Edward Silva and Sheila Slaughter (1984) amplify this larger picture by showing how the institutionalization of the disciplines and their professional associations was achieved through homogenizing the intellectual and political agendas of each field, ejecting the reformers, and creating the self-regulating and self-regarding disciplinary structures that are so powerful in universities today.

These histories also show that these outcomes were human products, were context dependent, and were fought over for decades at a time. Despite differences in the disciplines and in timing, the overall trajectory from "advocacy to objectivity" (as Furner [1975] phrased it) seems to be overdetermined. One of the sobering apparent lessons of these histories is that the prospect of rebuilding a socially connected or, less likely, a socially reformist agenda in the conventional social sciences not only faces negative odds but also runs directly counter to the course of 120 years of disciplinary histories.

Just how this process of disciplinarization and domestication applies to the newer social sciences (e.g., policy studies, management studies, organizational behavior) is not clear, as there is little critical historical work available. Impressionistically, it seems to us that these newer social sciences are beginning to repeat the process undergone in conventional social sciences, a process that resulted in their current disciplinarization and separation from engagement in the everyday world of social practice.

The consistent divergence between theory and practice in all the social science fields is especially notable. How this develops in a group of disciplines explicitly founded to inform social practice should puzzle everyone. Even the great national differences that appear in these trajectories and their organizational contexts do not overcome the global dynamics of disciplinarization and the segregation of theory from practice in academic work. Whatever the causes of these consistent phenomena, they must be both powerful and global. There appear to be direct links among disciplinarization, the purging of reformers, and the splitting of theory and practice, with theory becoming the focus of the academic social sciences. Having better understandings of these dynamics obviously is crucial to the future of the social sciences.

The above, highly selective, survey suggests a few things about this subject. There is ample reason to agree with Pierre Bourdieu's (1994) observation that academics resist being self-reflective about their professional practice. As interesting as the materials we have cited are, they are a very small window into a largely unstudied world. We social scientists generally do not apply our own social science frameworks to the study of our professional behavior. Instead, we permit ourselves to inhabit positions and espouse ideologies often in direct conflict with the very theories and methods we claim to have created (Bourdieu, 1994). For example, Greenwood has pointed out repeatedly that when threatened, anthropologists—who for generations assiduously have deconstructed the notion of the homogeneity and stability of notions like "tradition"—often refer to the "traditions" of anthropology as an ideological prop to defend their professional interests.

It is also striking how little academics reflect upon and understand the idea that they are members of a larger work organization in which relationships both to colleagues and to management have important effects on their capacity to do academic work. "Social" scientists regularly conceptualize themselves as solo entrepreneurs, leaving aside their professional knowledge of social structures and power relations, as if these were only disguises they wear while making their way into the "discipline."

The Political Economy Within Institutions of Higher Education

Whatever else one concludes from the above, it should be clear that what happens on university campuses is not isolated from what happens in society at large. The notion of the "ivory tower" notwithstanding, universities are both "in" and "of" their societies, but it is important to understand that these external forces do not apply across a smooth, undifferentiated internal academic surface. Universities show a high degree of internal differentiation, and this differentiation matters a great deal to our topic of university reform.

The internal political economy of universities is heterogeneous. In the United States and in other industrialized societies, one of the strongly emergent features of university life is the highly entrepreneurial behavior in the sciences and in engineering. Driven by the governmental and private sector markets and by explicit higher education policy designs, these fields have become expert in and structurally organized to capture, manage, and recapture the governmental and private sector funds that keep their research operations going. A complex web of interpenetrated interests links governments, businesses, and university scientists and engineers in a collaborative activity in which senior scientists and engineers basically become entrepreneurs who manage large laboratories and research projects, with the assistance of large numbers of graduate assistants, lab technicians, and grants administrators.

Social scientists, except those in the relatively rare environments of major contract research shops (such as the University of Michigan's Survey Research Center), are not so organized. Groups of economists, some psychologists, and some sociologists occasionally manage to mount multiperson projects, found institutes, support some graduate students, and bring some resources into the university. In this regard, from a university budgetary point of view, they are scientist-like, with the virtue that their research does not require the large infrastructural investments typical of much scientific research. The activities of even the most successful economists, psychologists, and sociologists, however, appear minuscule financially when compared to the scale of what goes on in the natural sciences and engineering.

Generally speaking, in political science, anthropology, and the qualitative branches of sociology and psychology, the funding sources brought in for external research are derisory. As a consequence, from the point of view of a central financial officer at a university, large proportions of the budgets for the social sciences and the humanities in the U.S. context represent calls on the university's resources that are not matched by an external revenue source. Instead, the social sciences and humanities, focused as they are on issues of social critique, interdisciplinary research, gender, and positionality, provide a kind of prestige to universities. They are part of the university "offering" that makes an institution seem appropriately academic, but their activities are maintained by cross-subsidies, justified in ideological rather than economic terms, and always in danger of being cut off.

Because self-justification in terms of financial revenues in excess of costs is not possible, the social sciences generally focus on being highly ranked nationally among their competitor departments at other universities. That is, they substitute one kind of market test for another. These national rankings follow a variety of reputational and accountancy schemes and are the subject of both strong critique and constant attention in the United States, the United Kingdom, and, increasingly, elsewhere.

Explaining how these ranking systems were generated and are maintained would take us beyond the scope of this chapter, but such an explanation must be provided. Suffice it to say that the disciplinary departments need to do well in national rankings in order to carry clout on campus, to recruit bright faculty, and to attract good undergraduate and graduate students. A great deal of energy goes into assessing, managing, and debating these rankings.

These dynamics create a heterogeneous surface within universities. The sciences, engineering, parts of economics, psychology (mainly laboratory work) and sociology (mainly quantitative), the applied fields of management, and law all generate significant revenues. Most are either organized as profit centers or are understood to be self-financing and to be good investments. By contrast, the rest of the social sciences (including all those practicing qualitative methods) and the humanities depend for their survival on redistributions from these "profitable" units and on subsidies from tuition, the general fund, alumni giving, and earnings on university investments. That is to say, a competitive, market-based research economy—in which the deans, individual entrepreneurial academics, and others seek to minimize costs and maximize earnings—coexists with a redistributive economy in which those who generate expenses without revenues are the net beneficiaries of the profits of others.

Whatever else this means, it suggests that a university "economy" is a complex organization in which a variety of economic principles are at work and in which the relationships among the sciences, engineering, the social sciences, and the humanities are negotiated through the central administration. Counterintuitively, there currently exists no overall management model that explicitly conceptualizes these conditions or provides guidance about how to manage them effectively for the ongoing growth of the organization. Rather, given the hierarchical structure of decision making described above, senior administrators are faced with attempting to keep a complex system afloat while not being able to operate most of the units in an "economic" way. To put it more bluntly, the complexity of university "economies" is such that neither faculty nor senior administrators have relevant understandings to guide them in making choices. No one can turn to well-argued visions about the principles that should be used to operate a university, about how much entrepreneurial activity is compatible with university life, and about what happens when and if tuition revenues, research contracts, patent income, and alumni gifts start oscillating wildly. Neither social democratic nor neoliberal models are adequate to the task. In the absence of intelligently structured models, simplistic neoliberal fiscal fantasies take over, to the detriment of everyone (Rhind, 2003).

This is the internal "political economy" of the contemporary research university. Because its structures are neither widely understood nor carefully studied, most university administrators and public authorities apply less differentiated, monodimensional management models to universities, succumbing often to the temptation of attempting to view whole universities as for-profit businesses and thereby making both "irrational" and counterproductive decisions, engaging in anti-economic behavior, and supporting unjustified and highly politicized cross-subsidies while not guaranteeing the survival of their institutions.

▣ What Counts as Knowledge in Contemporary Universities?

If, among other things, one of the key missions of universities is the production and transmission of knowledge, then what counts as knowledge is central to any definition and proposed reform of universities. Within this, what counts as social science knowledge is quite problematic.

Just because universities are, among other things, knowledge producing systems, it is not necessarily the case that universities have a very clear idea about what constitutes relevant knowledge. There are some conventional views of knowledge in the sciences and engineering that at least keep their enterprises funded, but the views of knowledge in current circulation are not much help when we try to think about the social sciences.

The conventional understanding of knowledge tends to be grounded in its explicit forms: what can be recorded in words, numbers, and figures and thus is explicitly accessible for humans. Based on this understanding, knowledge tends to be treated as an individualistic, cognitive phenomenon formed by the ability to capture insights (Fuller, 2002). This conception of knowledge is of very little use in the social sciences and the humanities, and challenging this view is necessary to our argument.

Social Science Knowledge

If we attempt to conceptualize social science knowledge, consistent with its origins, as the knowledge that is necessary to create a bridge between social research and the knowledge needs of society at large, then the disconnection between what currently counts as social science knowledge and what serves society's needs is nearly complete. In what follows, we intend to create a different picture by expanding the understanding of what counts as knowledge to include bridging concrete practical intelligence and reflective and value-based reflectivity.

Knowing

Very limited organizational and administrative meanings attach to knowledge concepts at universities. Contemporary debates about what constitutes knowledge can add three important dimensions to commonsense notions, dimensions that have the potential for shifting the way universities generate and apply knowledge.

Tacit Knowing

Much of our knowing is tacit; it expresses itself in our actions. We focus on the verb *knowing* instead of the noun *knowledge* because knowing emphasizes the point that knowledge is linked to people's actions. Tacit knowing is a term generally attributed to Michael Polanyi (1974), and Polanyi's argument is partially built on the arguments in *The Concept of Mind* written by Oxford philosopher Gilbert Ryle (1949). In Polanyi's view, tacit knowing connotes the "hidden" understandings that guide our actions without our ability to explicitly communicate what the knowledge is.

Knowing How

Although Polanyi's work is more recent, in our view, Ryle created a more fruitful concept than Polanyi's "tacit knowing" by introducing the notion of "knowing how." "Knowing how" grounds knowledge in actions and, because this is precisely how we are able to identify tacit knowing, knowing how seems a more direct anchor to use.

Collective Knowing

Knowledge is also inherently collective. Work by Berger and Luckmann (1967) and Schutz (1967/1972) on the social construction of social realities paved the road for a deeper understanding of knowing as a socially constructed and socially distributed phenomenon. People working together develop and share knowledge as a collective effort and collective product, the petty commodity view of knowledge production notwithstanding (Greenwood, 1991).

Bent Flyvbjerg (2001) follows a somewhat different path but ends up making some of the same distinctions. He refers to the work of Aristotle in making a taxonomy based on *episteme* (theoretical knowledge), *techne* (pragmatic and context-dependent practical rationality[2]), and *phronesis* (practical and context-dependent deliberation about values).

He seeks a solution to the current dilemmas of the social sciences by advocating a closer link to *phronesis.*[3] The argument is that *techne* and *phronesis* constitute the necessary "know-how" for organizational change, social reform, and regional economic development. Neither we nor Flyvbjerg assign any special priority to *episteme*, the conventional and favored form of explicit and theoretical knowledge and the form that currently dominates the academic social sciences.

The Aristotelian distinctions between *episteme*, *techne*, and *phronesis* center on distinguishing three kinds of knowledge. One is not superior to the other; all are equally valid forms of knowing in particular contexts. The key here is the equal validity of these forms of knowing when they are properly contextualized and deployed.

Episteme centers fundamentally on contemplative ways of knowing aimed at understanding the eternal and unchangeable operations of the world. The sources of *episteme* are multiple—speculative, analytical, logical, and experiential—but the focus is always on eternal truths beyond their materialization in concrete situations. Typically, the kinds of complexity found in *episteme* take the form of definitional statements, logical connections, and building of models and analogies. *Episteme* is highly self-contained because it is deployed mainly in theoretical discourses themselves. Although *episteme* obviously is not a self-contained activity, it aims to remove as many concrete empirical referents as possible in order to achieve the status of general truth.

If this meaning of *episteme* accords rather closely to everyday usage of the term *theory*, this is not the case with *techne* and *phronesis. Techne* is one of two other kinds of knowledge beyond *episteme. Techne* arises from Aristotle's poetical episteme. It is a form of knowledge that is inherently action oriented and inherently productive. *Techne* engages in the analysis of what should be done in the world in order to increase human happiness. The sources of *techne* are multiple. They necessarily involve sufficient experiential engagement in the world to permit the analysis of "what should be done." It is a mode of knowing and acting of its own. To quote Flyvbjerg, "*Techne* is thus craft and art, and as an activity it is concrete, variable, and context-dependent. The objective of *techne* is application of technical knowledge and skills according to a pragmatic instrumental rationality, what Foucault calls 'a practical rationality governed by a conscious goal'" (Flyvbjerg, 2001, p. 56).

The development of *techne* involves, first and foremost, the creation of that conscious goal, the generation of ideas of better designs for living that will increase human happiness. The types of complexity involved in *techne* arise around the debate among ideal ends, the complex contextualization of these ends, and the instrumental design of activities to enhance the human condition. *Techne* is not the application of *episteme* and, indeed, its link to *episteme* is tenuous in many situations. *Techne* arises from its own sources in moral/ethical debate and visions of an ideal society.

Techne is evaluated primarily by impact measures developed by the professional experts themselves who decide whether or not their projects have enhanced human happiness and, if not, why not. Practitioners of *techne* do engage with local stakeholders, power holders, and other experts, often being contracted by those in power to attempt to achieve positive social changes. Their relationship to the subjects of their work is often close and collaborative, but they are first and foremost professional experts who do things "for," not "with," the local stakeholders. They bring general designs and habits of work to the local case and privilege their own knowledge over that of the local stakeholders.

Phronesis is a less well-known idea. Formally defined by Aristotle as internally consistent reasoning that deals with all possible particulars, *phronesis* is best understood as the design of action through collaborative knowledge construction with the legitimate stakeholders in a problematic situation.

The sources of *phronesis* are collaborative arenas for knowledge development in which the professional researcher's knowledge is combined with the local knowledge of the stakeholders in defining the problem to be addressed. Together, they design and implement the research that needs to be done to understand the problem. They then design the actions to improve the situation together, and they evaluate the adequacy of what was done. If they are not satisfied, they cycle through the process again until the results are satisfactory to all the parties.

The types of complexity involved in *phronesis* are at once intellectual, contextual, and social, as *phronesis* involves the creation of a new space for collaborative reflection, the contrast and integration of many kinds of knowledge systems, the linking of the general and the particular through action and analysis, and the collaborative design of both the goals and the actions aimed at achieving them.

Phronesis is a practice that is deployed in groups in which all the stakeholders—both research experts and local collaborators—have legitimate knowledge claims and rights to determine the outcome. It is evaluated by the collaborators diversely according to their interests, but all share an interest in the adequacy of the outcomes achieved in relation to the goals they collaboratively developed. Thus, *phronesis* involves an egalitarian engagement across knowledge systems and diverse experiences.

This praxis-oriented knowing, which is collective, develops out of communities of practice, to use the wording of Brown and Duguid (1991) and Wenger (1998). This literature pinpoints how people, through working together, develop and cultivate knowledge that enables the participants to take the appropriate actions to achieve the goals they seek. The core perspective is a conceptualization of knowledge as inscribed in actions that are collectively developed and shared by people working together. Explicit knowledge is present and necessary but not dominant.

This kind of knowing linked to action inherently has physical and technological dimensions. Theoretical capability is necessary, but no results ever will be achieved unless local actors learn how to act in appropriate and effective ways and use suitable tools and methods. Thus technique, technology, and knowledge merge in an understanding of *knowing how to act* to reach certain desired goals. Knowledge is not a passive form of reflection but emerges through actively struggling to know how to act in real-world contexts with real-world materials.

When knowledge is understood as *knowing how to act*, skillful actions are always highly contextual. It is impossible to conceptualize action as taking place in a "generalized" environment. To act is to contextualize behavior, and being able to act skillfully implies that actions are appropriate to the given context. The actor needs to make sense of the context to enable appropriate actions. "Knowing how" thus implies knowing how in a given context in which appropriate actions emerge from contextual knowing. The conventional understanding of general knowledge that treats it as supracontextual and thus universally applicable is of very little interest to us because we do not believe that what constitutes knowledge in the social sciences can be addressed usefully from the hothouse of armchair intellectual debate.

Why Knowledge Matters to Universities

Universities increasingly view themselves as knowledge generation and knowledge management organizations, and they attempt to profit from knowledge generation efforts and gain or retain control over knowledge products that have a value in the marketplace (Fuller, 2002). In this regard, scientific and engineering knowledge has led the way, creating patentable discoveries and processes that, at least in the United States, make significant contributions to the financial well-being of research universities. There are pressures for the expansion of this commodity production notion of knowledge into broader spheres, pressures that go along with increasing emphasis on cost-benefit models in decision making by higher education managers.

Just how this struggle over the university generation, management, and sale of knowledge will turn out is not clear. On one hand, research universities increasingly act to commoditize knowledge production to create regular revenue flows (as well as academic prestige in the commodity production–based ranking systems). In the sciences, this has led to a spate of applied research and a de-emphasis on basic research. In the social sciences, the bulk of the external research money available to university social science is for positivistic research on economic issues, demographic trends, and public attitudes.

Whatever else it does, the current academic fiscal regime does not support unequivocally *episteme*-centered views of social science knowledge. However, it is also clear that few universities support "knowing how" work either, because such work focuses attention on fundamental needs for social and economic reform and thus often irritates public and private sector constituencies and wealthy donors. There is almost no indication that existing research funding patterns support more linked efforts between multiple academic partners and relevant non-university stakeholders.

The "Humpty Dumpty" Problem

Another difficulty in the way universities, most particularly in the social sciences, organize knowledge production activities has been called the "Humpty Dumpty" problem by Waddock and Spangler:

> Specialization in professions today resembles all the king's horses and all the king's men tackling the puzzle created by the fragments of Humpty Dumpty's broken body. Professionals . . . are tackling problems with only some of the knowledge needed to solve the problems. . . . Despite the fragmentation into professional specialties, professionals and managers are expected to somehow put their—and only their—pieces of Humpty Dumpty back together again. Further, they are to accomplish this task without really understanding what Humpty looked like in the first place, or what the other professions can do to make him whole again. Clearly, this model does not work. In addition to their traditional areas of expertise, professionals must be able to see society holistically, thorough lenses capable of integrating multiple perspectives simultaneously. (Waddock & Spangler, 2000, p. 211)

The Humpty Dumpty problem is relevant because the world does not issue problems in neat disciplinary packages. Problems come up as complex, multidimensional, and often confusing congeries of issues. To deal with them, their multiple dimensions must be understood, as well as what holds them together as problems. Only a university work organization that moves easily across boundaries between forms of expertise and between insider and outsider knowledges can deal with such problems.

Action Research as "Science"[4]

We reject arguments for separating praxis and theory in social research. Either social research is collaboratively applied or we do not believe that it deserves to be called research. It should simply be called what it is: speculation. The terms "pure" and "applied" research, current everywhere in university life, imply that a division of labor between the "pure" and the "applied" can exist. We believe that this division makes social research impossible. Thus, for us, the world divides into action research, which we support and practice, and conventional social research (subdivided into pure and applied social research and organized into professional subgroupings) that we reject on combined epistemological, methodological, and ethical/political grounds (Greenwood & Levin, 1998a, 1998b, 2000a, 2000b, 2001a, 2001b; Levin & Greenwood, 1998).

Because of the dominance of positivistic frameworks and *episteme* in the organization of the conventional social sciences, our view automatically is heard as a retreat from the scientific method into "activism." To hard-line interpretivists, we are seen as so epistemologically naïve as not to understand that it is impossible to commit ourselves to any course of action on the basis of any kind of social research, since all knowledge is contingent and positional—the ultimate form of self-justifying inaction. The operating assumptions in the conventional social sciences are that greater relevance and engagement automatically involves a loss of scientific validity or a loss of courage in the face of the yawning abyss of endless subjectivity.

Pragmatism

A different grounding for social research can be found in pragmatic philosophy. Dewey, James, Pierce, and others (Diggins, 1994) offer an interesting and fruitful foundation for ontological and epistemological questions inherent in social research that is action relevant. Pragmatism links theory and praxis. The core reflection process is connected to action outcomes that involve manipulating material and social factors in a given context. Experience emerges in a continual interaction between people and their environment; accordingly, this process constitutes both the subjects and objects of inquiry. The actions taken are purposeful and aim at creating desired outcomes. Hence, the knowledge creation process is based on the inquirers' norms, values, and interests.

Validity claims are identified as "warranted" assertions resulting from an inquiry process in which an indeterminate situation is made determinate through concrete actions in an actual context. The research logic is constituted in the inquiry process itself, and it guides the knowledge generation process.

Although it seems paradoxical to positivists, with their *episteme*-based views of knowledge, as action researchers we strongly advocate the use of scientific methods and emphasize the importance and possibility of the creation of valid knowledge in social research (see Greenwood & Levin, 1998b). Furthermore, we believe that this kind of inquiry is a foundational element in democratic processes in society and is the core mission of the "social" sciences.

These general characteristics of the pragmatist position ground the action research approach. Two central parameters stand out clearly: knowledge generation through action and experimentation in context, and participative democracy as both a method and a goal. Neither of these is routinely found in the current academic social sciences.

The Action Research Practice of Science

Everyone is supposed to know by now that social research is different from the study of atoms, molecules, rocks, tigers, slime molds, and other physical objects. Yet one can only be amazed by the emphasis that so many conventional social scientists still place on the claim that being "scientific" requires researchers to sever all relations with the observed. Though epistemologically and methodologically indefensible, this view is still largely dominant in social science practice, most particularly in the fields gaining the bulk of social science research money and dominating the world of social science publications: economics, sociology, and political science. This positivistic credo obviously is wrong, and it leads away from producing reliable information, meaningful interpretations, and social actions in social research. It has been subjected to generations of critique, even from within the conventional social sciences.[5] Yet it persists, suggesting that its social embeddedness itself deserves attention.

We believe that strong interventions in the organization of universities and the academic professions are required to root it out. Put more simply, the epistemological ideas underlying action research are not new ideas; they simply have been purged as conventional social researchers (and the social interests they serve—consciously or unconsciously) have rejected university engagement in social reform.

Cogenerative Inquiry

Action research aims to solve pertinent problems in a given context through democratic inquiry in which professional researchers collaborate with local stakeholders to seek and enact solutions to problems of major importance to the stakeholders. We refer to this as cogenerative inquiry because it is built on professional researcher–stakeholder collaboration and aims to solve real-life problems in context. Cogenerative inquiry processes involve trained professional researchers and knowledgeable local stakeholders who work together to define the problems to be addressed, to gather and organize relevant knowledge and data, to analyze the resulting information, and to design social change interventions. The relationship between the professional researcher and the local stakeholders is based on bringing the diverse bases of their knowledge and their distinctive social locations to bear on a problem collaboratively. The professional researcher often brings knowledge of other relevant cases and of relevant research methods, and he or she often has experience in organizing research processes. The insiders have extensive and long-term knowledge of the problems at hand and the contexts in which they occur, as well as knowledge about how and from whom to get additional information. They also contribute urgency and focus to the process, because it centers on problems they are eager to solve. Together, these partners create a powerful research team.

Local Knowledge and Professional Knowledge

For cogenerative inquiry to occur, the collaboration must be based on an interaction between local knowledge and professional knowledge. Whereas conventional social research and consulting privileges professional knowledge over local knowledge, action research does not. Given the complexity of the problems addressed, only local stakeholders, with their years of experience in a particular situation, have sufficient information and knowledge about the situation to design effective social change processes. We do not, however, romanticize local knowledge and denigrate professional knowledge. Both forms of knowledge are essential to cogenerative inquiry.

Validity, Credibility, and Reliability

Validity, credibility, and reliability in action research are measured by the willingness of local stakeholders to act on the results of the action research, thereby risking their welfare on the "validity" of their ideas and the degree to which the outcomes meet their expectations. Thus, cogenerated contextual knowledge is deemed valid if it generates warrants for action. The core validity claim centers on the workability of the actual social change activity engaged in, and the test is whether or not the actual solution to a problem arrived at solves the problem.

Dealing With Context-Centered Knowledge

Communicating context-centered knowledge effectively to academics and to other potential users is a complex process. The action research inquiry process is linked intimately to action in context. This means considerable challenges in communicating and abstracting results in a way that others who did not participate in a particular project, including other stakeholder groups facing comparable but not identical situations, will understand. Precisely because the knowledge is cogenerated, includes local knowledge and analyses, and is built deeply into the local context, comparison of results across cases and the creation of generalizations is a challenge.[6]

Comparison and Generalization

We do not think that these complexities justify having handed over the territory of comparative generalization and abstract theorization to conventional social researchers working in an *episteme* mode only. The approach of positivistic research to generalization has been to abstract from context, average out cases, lose sight of the world as lived in by human beings, and generally make the knowledge gained impossible to apply (which, for us, means that it is not "knowledge" at all). Despite the vast sums of money and huge numbers of person-hours put into this kind of research, we find the theoretical harvest scanty. On the other side, the rejection of the possibility of learning and generalizing at all, typical of much interpretivism, constructivism, and vulgar postmodernism, strikes us as an equally open invitation to intellectual posturing without any sense of social or moral responsibility.

Central to the action research view of generalization is that any single case that runs counter to a generalization invalidates it (Lewin, 1948) and requires the generalization to be reformulated. In contrast, positivist research often approaches exceptional cases by attempting to disqualify them, in order to preserve the existing generalization. Rather than welcoming the opportunity to revise the generalization, the reaction often is to find a way to ignore it.

Greenwood became particularly well aware of this during his period of action research in the labor-managed cooperatives of Mondragón, Spain, the most successful labor-managed industrial cooperatives anywhere (see Greenwood, González Santos, et al., 1992). Because the "official story" is that cooperatives cannot succeed, that Spaniards are religious fanatics, and that they are not good at working hard or at making money, the bulk of the literature on Mondragón in the 1960s and 1970s attempted to explain the case away as a mere oddity. Basque cultural predispositions, charismatic leadership, and solidarity were all tried as ways of making this exception one that could be ignored, letting the celebration of the supposed greater competitiveness of the standard capitalist firm go on unaffected by this, and other, glaring exceptions. Positivist theorists did not want to learn from the case, in direct contravention of the requirements of scientific thinking that view important exceptions as the most potentially valuable sources of new knowledge.

William Foote Whyte (1982) captured the idea of the productivity of exceptions in his concept of "social inventions." He proposed that all forms of business organizations could learn from this Basque case by trying to figure out how the unique social inventions they had made helped explain their success. Having identified these inventions, researchers could then begin the process of figuring out which of them could be generalized and diffused to other contexts where their utility could be tested, again in collaborative action. Of course, the key to this approach is that the validity of the comparison is also tested in action and not treated as a thought experiment.

If we readdress generalizations in light of what we have argued above, we reframe generalization in action research terms as necessitating a process of reflective action rather than as being based on structures of rule-based interpretation. Given our position that knowledge is context bound, the key to utilizing this knowledge in a different setting is to follow a two-step model. First, it is important to understand the contextual conditions under which the knowledge has been created. This recognizes the inherent contextualization of the knowledge itself. Second, the transfer of this knowledge to another setting implies understanding the contextual conditions of the new setting, how these differ from the setting in which the knowledge was produced, and it involves a reflection on what consequences this has for applying the actual knowledge in the new context. Hence, generalization becomes an active process of reflection in which involved actors must make up their minds whether the previous knowledge makes sense in the new context or not and begin working on ways of acting in the new context.

Although it would take much more space to make the full case (see Greenwood & Levin, 1998b), we have said enough to make it clear that action research is not some kind of a social science dead end. It is a disciplined way of developing valid knowledge and theory while promoting positive social change.

Reconstructing the Relationships Between Universities and Social Stakeholders

We believe that the proper response to the epistemological, methodological, political economic, and ethical issues we have been raising is to reconstruct the relationships between the universities and the multiple stakeholders in society. We believe that a significant part of the answer is to make action research *the* central strategy in social research and organizational development. This is because action research, as we have explained above, involves research efforts in which the users (such as governments, social service agencies, corporations large and small, communities, and nongovernmental organizations) have a definite stake in the problems under study and in which the research process integrates collaborative teaching/learning among multiple disciplines with groups of these non-university partners. We know that this kind of university-based action research is possible because a number of successful examples exist. We will end this chapter by providing an account of two such examples, drawn from a much larger set.

Social Science–Engineering Research Relationships and University-Industry Cooperation: The "Offshore Yard"[7]

This project began when the Norwegian Research Council awarded a major research and development contract to SINTEF, a Norwegian research organization located in Trondheim and closely linked to the Norwegian University of Science and Technology. This contract focused on what is called "enterprise modeling," an information systems–centered technique for developing models of complex organizational processes, both to improve efficiency and to restructure organizational behavior. SINTEF received the contract for this work as part of a major national initiative to support applied research and organizational development in manufacturing industries.

A key National Research Council requirement for this program was that engineering research on enterprise modeling had to be linked to social science research on organization and leadership. This required the collaboration of engineers and social scientists within SINTEF of a more intensive sort than usual. The National Research Council argued that enterprise modeling could not be reduced to a technical effort and that the enterprise models themselves had to deal with organizational issues as well, because their deployment would depend on the employees' ability to use the models as "tools" in everyday work.

The research focus of this activity was not clear at the outset. The instrumental goal for the national research organization was to create a useful enterprise model rather than one that would be only a nice puzzle for information technologists to solve. The research focus emerged in the form of an engineering focus on enterprise models as learning opportunities for all employees and a social science focus on participatory change processes.

The Offshore Yard agreed to be a partner in this effort, and the project was launched in early 1996. The Yard employs approximately 1,000 persons and is located a 90-minute drive north of Trondheim on the Trondheim fjord. The yard has a long history of specializing in the design and construction of the large and complex offshore installations used in North Sea oil exploration.

The project was to be comanaged by a joint group of engineers and social scientists. The key researchers were Ivar Blikø, Terje Skarlo, Johan Elvemo, and Ida Munkeby, two engineers and two social scientists, all employed at SINTEF. The expectation was that cooperation across professional boundaries would somehow arise as an automatic feature of their being engaged in the same project.

The process was by no means so simple. Throughout the initial phase of the project, the only cooperation seen meant merely that team members were present at the company site at the same time. In part, this was because the two engineers on the team had a long history with the company. They had many years of contact with the company as consulting researchers, and, before that, they worked as engineers on the staff in the Yard. As a result, the engineers took the lead in the early project activity.[8] They were running the project, and the social scientists seemed fairly passive. The engineers were working concretely on computer-based mockups of enterprise models and, because this was a strong focus of planning interest in the company, they accordingly received a great deal of attention from the senior management of the Yard.

While this was going on, the social scientists were devoting their attention to a general survey of the company and making an ethnographic effort to learn about the organization and social realities of the company. This was considered important to give the social scientists a grasp of what the company was like. This research-based knowledge generation meant little to company people, as this work was neither understood nor valued by the company or by the engineering members of the team.

The first opening for social science knowledge came when the social researchers organized a search conference[9] to address the problems of the organization of work at the shop floor level. This search conference produced results that captured the attention of both the local union and management and made it clear locally that the social scientists had skills that offered significant opportunities for learning and collaborative planning in the company. This was also the first time the researchers managed to include a fairly large number of employees from different layers of the organization in the same knowledge production process.

As a consequence of this experience, cooperation between the university and Offshore Yard began to deepen. At the time, the company was developing a leadership training program. Through the social scientists, company officials learned about other experiences in running such programs, and this helped them plan locally. They were better able to plan their overall organizational development activity in their own training program because knowing about other programs helped them with their design. In addition, they felt it would be an advantage to them if company participants in the training also could get official university credits for their involvement. Thus, the resulting program was designed through a university-company dialogue and, in the end, one of the social scientists on the team ran it. The program also gave official university-based credits to those participants who decided to take a formal exam. The leadership program became an effort that enhanced the formal skill level of the participants, and the university credits gave them recognition outside the context of the Yard.

The program was very successful, making evident how close collaboration between the company and the university could be mutually rewarding. The university people could experiment professionally and pedagogically in real-life contexts, while the company got access to cutting-edge knowledge both from the university and from other companies, through the university's contacts. As an interesting side effect, the Yard decided to invite managers from neighboring plants to participate. The Yard recognized that its own future depended on its having good relations with its neighbors and suppliers. Company officials decided that one way to improve this cooperation was to share their program, as a gesture symbolizing the interdependent relationships they have and the mutual stakes in each other's success.

During the course of the project, the cooperation between engineers and social scientists began to grow and create new insights. A key first move in this direction was a redesign of the tube manufacturing facility in the Yard. The reorganization of work processes that was cogeneratively developed through workers' participation meant that shop floor workers gained direct access to the computer-based production planning and scheduling the company engineers used. Instead of having information from the system filtered through the foreman, workers at the shop floor level could utilize the information system and decide for themselves how to manage the production process. This form of organizational leveling probably would not have come about had it not been for the increased mutual understanding between the SINTEF engineers and social scientists and their company partners that emerged through their working together on the same concrete problems as a team.

Gradually, based on these experiences, a reconceptualization emerged of the whole way to develop enterprise models. The conventional engineering take on enterprise models was that the experts (the engineers) collected information, made an analysis, and then made expert decisions regarding what the model should look like. A new approach to enterprise modeling in the Yard was developed in which the involved employees actually have a direct say. Although this is a modest step in the direction of participation, it is potentially a very important one. It is fair to say that this changed focus toward participation would not have occurred unless the social scientists had presented substantive knowledge on issues of organization and leadership that were testable through participatory processes.

As more mutual trust developed between company people and researchers, the marginalized position of the social scientists gradually changed, and the company came to count on the social scientists as well. For example, one of the major challenges for the company in the future will be how to manage with a significant reduction in the number of employees humanely and without destroying company morale. These changes originate both from restructuring of the corporation the Yard is part of and from new engineering and production processes that led to a reduced need for laborers. The Yard has invited the researchers to take a serious role in this process by asking them to draw, from all over the world, knowledge and diverse perspectives on this difficult subject. The researchers have been able to support new and often critical knowledge that has changed or extended the company's understanding of its downsizing challenge.

The research team also has been asked to assist in working on the learning atmosphere in the Yard. This has involved extensive interviewing of a broad spectrum of employees to build a view about how to improve the Yard's capacity for ongoing learning. The results of these interviews were fed back to the involved employees, and the researchers shaped dialogues with them that aimed both at presenting the results and at examining the inferences made by the researchers through comparison with the local knowledge of the workers. Again, we can see how models of learning with an origin in social science circles can be applied to the local learning process, and the results are important factors in the researchers' assessments of the strength and value of their academic findings.

Perhaps the most interesting overall development in this project is how the company–university relationship developed. The senior executive officer is now a strong supporter of the fruitfulness of the company's relationship with the university. In public presentations, he credits the researchers with bringing relevant and important knowledge to the company and explains that he can see how this relationship can become increasingly important. It took him several years of cooperation to see these possibilities, but now he does, and the university is glad to respond. Although there is no reason to romanticize the relationship, because differences of opinion and interest do emerge, the relationship seems so robust that further developments are likely.

In the end, only through multidisciplinary action research over a sustained period of time were these results possible. The research values and the action values in the process have both been respected, and all the partners in the process have benefited.

Collaborative Research for Organizational Transformation Within the Walls of the University

Here we report on an example of an action research initiative that occurred at Cornell University, resulting in reform of a major, required university course: introductory physics. The protagonist of this effort was Michael Reynolds, who wrote this work up as a doctoral dissertation in science education at Cornell (Reynolds, 1994).[10] Because universities are redoubts of hierarchical and territorial behavior, changes initiated by students or by graduate assistants and lecturers are rare, making this case particularly interesting.

At the time the project began, Reynolds was employed as a teaching assistant in an introductory physics course that is one of the requirements for students wishing to go to medical school. This makes the course a key gatekeeping mechanism in the very competitive process of acquiring access to the medical profession and makes the stake the students have in doing well high and the power of the faculty and university over their lives considerable. It also means that the course has a guaranteed clientele, almost no matter how badly it is taught.

Although there is more than one physics course, this particular one is crucial in completing premedical requirements. Because of a comprehensive reform undertaken in the late 1960s, this course was and is delivered in what is called an "auto-tutorial" format. This means that students work through the course materials at their own pace (within limits), doing experiments and studying in a learning center, asking for advice there, and taking examinations on each unit (often many times) until they have achieved the mastery of the material and grade they seek. Despite the inviting and apparently flexible format, the course had become notoriously unpopular among students. Performance on standardized national exams was poor, morale among the students and staff was relatively low, and the Physics Department was concerned.

The staff structure included a professor in charge, a senior lecturer who was the de facto principal course manager, and some graduate assistants. Among these, Reynolds was working as a teaching assistant in the course to support himself while he worked on his PhD in Education. Having heard about action research and finding it consistent with his view of the world, he proposed to the professor and lecturer in charge that they attempt an action research evaluation and reform of the course. With Greenwood's help, they got funding from the office of the Vice President for Academic Programs to support the reform effort.

There followed a long and complex process that was skillfully guided by Reynolds. It involved the undergraduate students, teaching assistants, lecturers, professor, and members of Reynolds's PhD committee in a long-term process. It began with an evaluation of the main difficulties students had with the course, then involved the selection of a new text and piloting the revised course. Reynolds guided this process patiently and consistently. Ultimately, the professor, the lecturer, instructors, teaching assistants, and students collaborated in redesigning the course through intensive meetings and debates.

One of the things they discovered was that the course had become unworkable in part because of its very nature. As new concepts and theories were developed in physics, they were added to the course, but there was no overall system for examining what materials should be eliminated or consolidated to make room for the new ones. The result was an increasingly overstuffed course that the students found increasingly difficult to deal with. In bringing the whole course before all the stakeholders and in examining the choice of a possible new textbook, it was possible for the group to confront these issues.

There were many conflicts on issues of substance and authority during the process, which was stressful for all involved, yet they stayed together and kept at the process until they had completely redesigned the course. It was then piloted, and the results were a dramatic improvement in student performance on national tests and a considerable increase in student satisfaction with the course.

Reynolds then wrote the process up from his detailed field notes and journals and drafted his dissertation. He submitted the draft to his collaborators for comment and revision, then explained to them the revisions he would make. He also offered them the option to add their own written comments in a late chapter of the dissertation, using either their real names or pseudonyms.

This iteration of the process produced some significant changes in the dissertation and solidified the group's own learning process. Eventually, many of the collaborators attended Reynolds's dissertation defense and were engaged in the discussion, the first time we know of that such a "collaborative" defense occurred at Cornell. Subsequently, that kind of defense, with collaborators present, has been repeated with other PhD candidates (Boser, 2001; Grudens-Schuck, 1998).

Interestingly, though the process was extremely stressful for the participants, the results were phenomenally good for the students. A proposal was made to extend this approach to curriculum reform to other courses at Cornell, but the university administration was unprepared to underwrite the process, despite its obvious great success in this case.

Perhaps the reform of a single course does not seem like much of a social change, but we think it has powerful implications. This case demonstrates the possibility of an action research–based reform being initiated from a position of little power within a profoundly bureaucratic and hierarchical organization, the university. The value of the knowledge of each category of stakeholder was patent throughout, and the shared interests of all in a good outcome for the students helped hold the process together. That such reform is possible and successful means that those who write off the possibility of significant university reforms are simply wrong. Of course, it also shows that an isolated success does not add up to ongoing institutional change without a broader strategy to back it up. Thus, it was a success, but an isolated one.

Although this is a very modest amount of case material to present in support of our contentions, we believe that the cases at least give the reader a general sense of the kind of vision of social research we advocate.

Institutionalizing AR in Academic Environments

One of the major challenges facing modern universities that are funded with private or public money lies in making visible their contribution to important social and technological challenges in the larger society. This cannot be done unless research and teaching are clearly aligned to extra-university needs.

Although such an argument is often heard in the current debates about the social obligations of universities, little progress has been made at mediating university–society relationships because of the profound differences between what is considered appropriate research and teaching by academics and what the public wants and expects. Few processes are in place to work toward creating a shared understanding of what a desired focus of collaboration should be. The parties operate in two different worlds, with very limited cross-boundary communication and learning, and they operate with the inconvenience that the public has the power to make decisions affecting future university budgets.

Action research meets the need for this kind of mediated communication and action. It deals with real-life problems in context, and it is built on participation by the non-university problem owners. It creates mutual learning opportunities for researchers and participants, it produces tangible results. Hence, action research, if managed skillfully, can respond in a positive way to the changing and increasingly interventionist public and private sector environments in which universities must operate.

How, then, do we envisage a university operating within the frame of reference of action research? Given what we have already said about how research would have to be organized, it is clear that problem definition must be accomplished cooperatively with the actors who experience the actual problem situations. Thus, research will have to be conducted in "natural" settings without trying to create a university-centered substitute experimental situation.

Conducting research this way guarantees that research foci will not emerge from reading about the latest fashionable theory within an academic profession, but rather as a negotiated joint understanding of what the problem in focus should be, an understanding in which both professionals and problem owners have a say in setting the issue the group will deal with. For academic researchers, this places a premium on the ability and willingness to frame researchable questions in concrete problem situations, a process that certainly forces the researchers to adopt perspectives that often are not central or even well known within their own disciplines.

One way to create this potential is to train researchers who are capable of embracing perspectives beyond those of single, constrained professional disciplinary territories. Another possibility is to create teams that contain enough varieties of expertise relevant to the problem at hand so that the internal capacity to mobilize the needed forms of knowledge exists. In both situations, the centerpiece is the requirement that academic researchers be able to operate in a transdisciplinary environment, where the challenges center on actively transforming their own perspectives in order to accommodate and help build the necessary knowledge platform needed for working through the problem. They would also have to understand their accountability to the extra-university stakeholders' evaluation of the results through action. Thus, team-based research and breaking down boundaries between different professional positions are central features of the deployment of action research in universities.

Teaching would have to change in much the same way. In fact, it is possible to envisage a teaching process that mirrors the action research process we have articulated above. The obvious starting point would be use of concrete problem situations in classrooms, probably accomplished by use of real cases. Starting here, the development of learning foci (e.g., problem definitions) would have to emerge from the concrete problem situations, a position that is the centerpiece of John Dewey's pedagogy.

In this regard, this teaching situation is parallel to an action research project. The main difference is that there are three types of principal actors in the classroom: the problem owners, the students, and the teachers. As in action research, they will all be linked in a mutual learning process. Even though students might themselves be participants, without many of the necessary skills and insights, they will discover that, as students, they bring a different set of experiences and points of view into the collaborative learning arena and can make important contributions as they gain confidence in their own abilities. Thus, all three parties will be teachers and colearners.

The professional academics will have a special obligation to structure the learning situation effectively and to provide necessary substantive knowledge to the participants in the learning process. As is generally the case in teaching, the professors would start the course using their conception of what are key substantive issues in the situation under examination. Because this kind of teaching is problem driven, however, all predetermined plans will have to be adjusted to the concrete teaching situation as new, cogenerated understandings emerge from the learning group.

Focusing on real-life problems also forces the different disciplines to cooperate because relevant knowledge must be sought from any and all sources. No single discipline or strand of thinking can dominate action research because real-world problems are not tailored to match disciplinary structures and standards of academic popularity. The valuable academic professional thus is not the world's leading expert in discipline "X" or theory "Y" but instead is the person who can bring relevant knowledge for solving the problem to the table.

Through such pedagogical processes, whatever else they do, it is certain that students will learn how to apply what they know and how to learn from each other, from the professors, and from the problem owners. What they will not develop is a narrow allegiance to a particular discipline or to a university world separated from life in society at large. And together, the professors and students will be of service to the world outside the academy. Thus, universities that focus their teaching on action research will be able to supply practical results and insights to the surrounding society.

Is This Possible?

The question is not whether action research can be accommodated in contemporary universities, but how to create experimental situations to make it happen. We can find examples of this in undergraduate education, in professional degree courses, and in PhD programs. Programs in action research at both of the authors' institutions (Cornell and the Norwegian University of Science and Technology) have shown that such programs are possible, albeit on a very small scale at present.

The biggest obstacle is how to integrate this type of alternative educational process fully in the current structures of universities. Everything we have said above constitutes a challenge to the current division of labor and to the disciplinary and administrative structures of universities. Pursuing this would weaken the hegemony of separate professional and disciplinary structures, would force professional activity to move toward meeting social needs, and would limit the self-serving and self-regarding academic professionalism that is the hallmark of contemporary universities.

Despite how difficult it appears to be, there are reasons to think that progress can be made along these lines. The increasing public and fiscal pressure on universities to justify themselves and their activities creates a risky but promising situation in which experimenting with action research approaches may be the only possible solution for universities that wish to survive into the next generation.

There is a choice. One strategy some universities have adopted is that, as the public financial support for universities drops, they consider themselves even less accountable to the public. Another is to try to renegotiate this relationship and reverse the negative trend. We believe in using action research to try to repair the deeply compromised relationships universities have with their publics and governments.

NOTES

1. The exceptions to this poverty are positivistic, policy-oriented economic research and bits of policy-relevant social science research anchored primarily in schools of business, planning, and public policy.

2. *Techne* can also be interpreted as the technical rationality that is in the heads and the hands of experts, but, in the context of this essay, it denotes the kind of knowing necessary for making skilled transformation processes and therefore is not connected to the experts' power position.

3. These arguments have been made in much more detail and with a much more comprehensive understanding of their Greek origins by Olav Eikeland (1997).

4. A version of this section was delivered by Greenwood as a paper titled *La antropología "inaplicable": El divorcio entre la teoría y la práctica y el declive de la antropología universitaria* (Inapplicable Anthropology: The Divorce Between Theory and Practice and the Decline of University Anthropology) at the conference of Sociedad Española de Antropología Aplicada in Granada, Spain, in November of 2002.

5. A critique of this kind of blind positivism was central to the ideas of the major social thinkers who gave rise to the social sciences in the first place (Adam Smith, Karl Marx, Max Weber, Emile Durkheim, and John Dewey, among others). A good source of current critiques is James Scheurich (1997).

6. For a full discussion of these issues, see Robert Stake (1995).

7. This is a pseudonym.

8. Levin observed much of this process because he served as a member of the local steering committee for the project. He recollects how little linkage there was at the outset between engineering and the social sciences.

9. A search conference is a democratically organized action research means for bringing a group of problem owners together for an intensive process of reflection, analysis, and action planning. For a more detailed description, see Greenwood and Levin (1998b).

10. Greenwood served as a member of Reynolds's PhD committee and worked with him throughout this research. However, the ideas, processes, and interpretations offered here are those Reynolds generated, not Greenwood's. Because Reynolds is now hard at work in secondary school reform, he has not made a further write-up of his work, so we encourage the interested reader to consult his dissertation directly.

References

Abbott, A. (1988). *The system of professions.* Chicago: University of Chicago Press.

Berger, P., & Luckmann, T. (1967). *The social construction of reality: A treatise in the sociology of knowledge.* New York: Anchor.

Birnbaum, R. (2000). *Management fads in higher education.* San Francisco: Jossey-Bass.

Boser, S. (2001). *An action research approach to reforming rural health and human services administration through Medicaid managed care: Implication for the policy sciences.* Unpublished doctoral dissertation, Cornell University.

Bourdieu, P. (1994). *Homo academicus* (Peter Collier, Trans.). Stanford, CA: Stanford University Press.

Brint, S. (1996). *In an age of experts: The changing roles of professionals in politics and public life.* Princeton, NJ: Princeton University Press.

Brown, J. S., & Duguid, P. (1991). Organizational learning and communities-of-practice: Toward a unified view of working, learning, and innovation. *Organization Science, 2,* 40–57.

Diggins, J. (1994). *The promise of pragmatism.* Chicago: University of Chicago Press.

Eikeland, O. (1997). *Erfaring, dialogikk og politickk.* Oslo: Acta Humaniora, Scandinavian University Press.

Flyvbjerg, B. (2001). *Making social science matter: Why social inquiry fails and how it can succeed again.* Cambridge, UK: Cambridge University Press.

Freidson, E. (1986). *Professional powers: A study of the institutionalization of formal knowledge.* Chicago: University of Chicago Press.

Fuller, S. (2002). *Knowledge management foundations.* Boston: Butterworth/Heinemann.

Furner, M. (1975). *From advocacy to objectivity.* Lexington: University of Kentucky Press.

Greenwood, D. J. (1991). Collective reflective practice through participatory action research: A case study from the Fagor cooperatives of Mondragón. In D. A. Schön (Ed.), *The reflective turn: Case studies in and on educational practice* (pp. 84–107). New York: Teachers College Press.

Greenwood, D. J., & González Santos, J. L., with Cantón Alonso, J., Galparsoro Markaide, I., Goiricelaya Arruza, A., Legarreta Ruin, I., & Salaberría Amesti, K. (1992). *Industrial democracy as process: Participatory action research in the Fagor cooperative group of Mondragón.* Assen-Maastricht, Netherlands: Van Gorcum.

Greenwood, D., & Levin, M. (1998a). Action research, science, and the co-optation of social research. *Studies in Cultures, Organizations and Societies, 4*(2), 237–261.

Greenwood, D. J., & Levin, M. (1998b). *Introduction to action research: Social research for social change.* Thousand Oaks, CA: Sage.

Greenwood, D. J., & Levin, M. (2000a). Reconstructing the relationships between universities and society through action research. In N. K. Denzin & Y. S. Lincoln (Eds.), *Handbook of qualitative research* (2nd ed., pp. 85–106). Thousand Oaks, CA: Sage.

Greenwood, D. J., & Levin, M. (2000b). Recreating university-society relationships: Action research versus academic Taylorism. In O. N. Babüroglu, M. Emery, and Associates (Eds.), *Educational futures: Shifting paradigms of universities and education* (pp. 19–30). Istanbul: Fred Emery Memorial Book, Sabanci University.

Greenwood, D. J., & Levin, M. (2001a). Pragmatic action research and the struggle to transform universities into learning communities. In P. Reason & H. Bradbury (Eds.), *Handbook of action research* (pp. 103–113). London: Sage.

Greenwood, D. J., & Levin, M. (2001b). Re-organizing universities and "knowing how": University restructuring and knowledge creation for the twenty-first century. *Organization, 8*(2), 433–440.

Grudens-Schuck, N. (1998). *When farmers design curriculum: Participatory education for sustainable agriculture in Ontario, Canada.* Unpublished doctoral dissertation, Cornell University.

Krause, E. (1996). *The death of the guilds.* New Haven, CT: Yale University Press.

Levin, M., & Greenwood, D. (1998). The reconstruction of universities: Seeking a different integration into knowledge development processes. *Concepts and Transformation, 2*(2), 145–163.

Lewin, K. (1948). The conflict between Aristotelian and Galilean modes of thought in contemporary psychology. In *A dynamic theory of personality* (pp. 1–42). New York: McGraw-Hill.

Madoo Lengermann, P., & Niebrugge-Brantley, J. (1998). *The women founders.* Boston: McGraw-Hill.

Messer-Davidow, E. (2002). *Disciplining feminism: From social activism to academic discourse.* Durham, NC: Duke University Press.

Polanyi, M. (1974). *Personal knowledge: Toward a post-critical philosophy.* Chicago: University of Chicago Press.

Reynolds, M. (1994). *Democracy in higher education: Participatory action research in the Physics 101–102 curriculum revision project at Cornell University.* Unpublished doctoral dissertation, Cornell University.

Rhind, D. (2003). *Great expectations: The social sciences in Britain.* London: Commission on the Social Sciences.

Ross, D. (1991). *The origin of American social science.* Cambridge, UK: Cambridge University Press.

Ryle, G. (1949). *The concept of mind.* Chicago: University of Chicago Press.

Scheurich, J. (1997). *Research method in the postmodern.* London: Falmer.

Schutz, A. (1972). *The phenomenology of the social world.* Chicago: Northwestern University Press. (Original work published 1967)

Silva, E., & Slaughter, S. (1984). *Serving power: The making of a modern social science expert.* Westport, CT: Greenwood.

Slaughter, S., & Leslie, L. (1997). *Academic capitalism: Politics, policies, and the entrepreneurial university.* Baltimore: Johns Hopkins University Press.

Stake, R. (1995). *The art of case study research.* Thousand Oaks, CA: Sage.

Stocking, G., Jr. (1968). *Race, culture, and evolution: Essays in the history of anthropology.* Chicago: University of Chicago Press.

Waddock, S. A., & Spangler, E. (2000). Action learning in leadership for change: Partnership, pedagogy, and projects for responsible management development. In F. Sherman & W. Torbert (Eds.), *Transforming social inquiry, transforming social action: New paradigms for crossing the theory/ practice divide in universities and communities* (pp. 207–228). Boston: Kluwer.

Wenger, E. (1998). *Communities of practice: Learning, meaning, and identity.* Cambridge, UK: Cambridge University Press.

Whyte, W. F. (1982). Social inventions for solving human problems. *American Sociological Review, 47,* 1–13.

3

COMPOSITIONAL STUDIES, IN TWO PARTS

Critical Theorizing and Analysis on Social (In)Justice

Michelle Fine and Lois Weis

Like the artist, we explicitly explore the negative bridging spaces within the composition; we intentionally explore the relationship between "negative" and "positive" spaces and understand that no "positive" exists except in relation to the "negative."

—Fine and Weis, from this chapter

We offer here a detailed explanation of what we are putting forward as "compositional studies," in which analyses of public and private institutions, groups, and lives are lodged in relation to key social and economic structures. We draw on what some have described as oscillation (Alford, 1998; Deleuze, 1990; Farmer, 2001; Hitchcock, 1999), a deliberate movement between theory "in the clouds" and empirical materials "on the ground." In this chapter, we articulate our theory of method, offering a critical look at compositional studies as frame and a serious elaboration as to how we oscillate from local to structural, how we analyze in ways that reveal what photographers call the "varied depths of field," and how we try

Authors' Note. Our continued thanks to Craig Centrie, who offered great insight into our artistic metaphor. Craig, a visual artist in his own right, prompted us to think through the relationship between the visual arts and what we do as ethnographers.

to position the work to "have legs," that is, to be useful to struggles for social justice. We write to name the assumptions of our compositional studies, reflect upon its possibilities for theory and activism, and consider the limits of this work.

We write as well-educated and influenced by ethnographers who have written powerful "oscillating" works (see Anzaldúa, 1999; Crenshaw, 1995; Fanon, 1967; hooks, 1984; Ladson-Billings, 2000; Matsuda, 1995). Paul Willis (1977) and Valerie Walkerdine (e.g., Walkerdine, Lacey, & Melody, 2001), for instance, have crafted analyses of white working-class youth situated explicitly in historical and class politics, with a keen eye toward development and identity. Patricia Hill Collins (1991), Mari Matsuda (1995), Gloria Ladson-Billings (2000), and Patricia Williams (1992) have crafted Critical Race Theory to speak explicitly back to the webbed relations of history, the political economy, and everyday lives of women and men of color. Barrie Thorne (1993) has boldly broadened our understandings of gender, arguing fervently against "sex difference" research, insisting instead that gender be analyzed as relational performance. Paul Farmer (2001) moves from biography of individuals living in Haiti who suffer tuberculosis to the international politics of epidemiology, illness, and health care, while Angela Valenzuela (1999) skillfully helps us come to know Mexican American youth across contexts in the school, home, and community. These scholars produce writings centered on the rich complexity within a given group, offering complex, detailed, and sophisticated analyses of a slice of the social matrix and theorizing its relation to the whole (see also Bourgois, 2002; Duneier, 1994; Foley, 1990; Rubin, 1976; Scheper-Hughes & Sargent, 1998; Stepick, Stepick, Eugene, & Teed 2001; Stack, 1997; Twine, 2000; Waters, 1999).

In compositional studies, we take up a companion project, writing through the perspectives of multiple groups of this social puzzle we call America, fractured by jagged lines of power, so as to theorize carefully this relationality and, at the same time, recompose the institution, community, and nation as a series of fissures and connections. Although there is always a risk that the in-group depth may be compromised in the pursuit of cross-group analysis, we try, in this chapter, to articulate how this method responds to questions of social critique and imagination, social justice theory, and advocacy.

To be more specific, in *The Unknown City* (Fine & Weis, 1998) and in *Working Class Without Work* (Weis, 1990), analytically speaking, we have argued that white working-class men (at least in the urban Northeast of the United States) can be understood only in relation to a constructed African American "other," with the most powerful refraction occurring in relation to African American men. These white working-class men must be theorized about and their words analyzed, then, in relation to "bordering" groups—white women, African American men and women, gay men across racial/ethnic groups, and so forth. Although their narrations rarely reference history or the global economy explicitly, we have had to situate these men, as they move through their daily lives and narrate their social relations, in the shifting historic sands of social, economic, and political conditions.

The key point here is that social theory and analyses can no longer afford to isolate a "group," or to re-present their stories as "transparent," as though that group were coherent and bounded; instead, we must theorize explicitly—that is, "connect the dots"—to render visible relations to other "groups" and to larger sociopolitical formations. The emergent montage of groups must simultaneously be positioned within historically shifting social and economic relations in the United States and across the globe. Although the specific "bordering" groups are uncovered ethnographically and may vary by site, deep theorizing and deep analysis are required to join these seemingly separate and isolated groups and to link them institutionally and ideologically. More broadly speaking, our notion and practice of qualitative work suggests that *no* one group can be understood as if outside the relational and structural aspects of identity formation.

At the heart of compositional studies lie three analytic moves we seek to make explicit. The first is the deliberate placement of ethnographic and narrative material into a contextual and historic understanding of economic and racial formations (see Sartre, 1968). Without presuming a simple determinism of economics to identity, we nevertheless take as foundational the idea that individuals navigate lives in what Martín-Baró (1994) and Freire (1982) would call "limit situations," within historic moments, unequal power relations, and the everyday activities of life. As Jean-Paul Sartre articulated in 1968, weaving a method between Marxism and existentialism, "If one wants to grant to Marxist thought its full complexity, one would have to say that man [*sic*] in a period of exploitation is at once both the product of his own product and a historical agent who can under no circumstances be taken as a product. This contradiction is not fixed; it must be grasped in the very movement of *praxis*" (1968, p. 87).

Yet when we engage ethnographically, speak to people, collect survey data, or conduct a focus group, it is most unusual for individuals to connect the dots between their "personal lives" and the historic, economic, and racial relations within which they exist (Mills, 1959). History appears as a "foreign force"; people do not recognize the "meaning of their enterprise . . . in the total, objective result" (Sartre, 1968, p. 89). That is, indeed, the insidious victory of neoliberal ideology: People speak as if they are self-consciously immune and independent, disconnected and insulated from history, the state, the economic context, and "others." As social theorists, we know well that the webs that connect structures, relations, and lives are essential to understanding the rhythm of daily life, possibilities for social change, and the ways in which individuals take form in, and transform, social relations. Thus, we work hard to situate our analyses of communities, schools, and lives, positioning them historically, economically, and socially so that the material context within which individuals are "making sense" can be linked to their very efforts to reflect upon and transform these conditions.

Second, in our work we rely more on categories of social identity than do many of our poststructural scholar-friends. That is, while we refuse essentialism, resisting the mantra-like-categories of social life—race, ethnicity, class, gender—as coherent, in the body, "real," consistent, or homogeneous, we also take very seriously the notion that these categories become "real" inside institutional life, yielding dire political and economic consequences. Even if resisted, they come to be foundational to social identities. Even as performed, multiple, shifting, and fluid, the technologies of surveillance ensure partial penetration of the politics of social identities (Butler, 1999; Foucault, 1977; Scott, 1990). You simply can't hang out in poor and working-class communities, a suburban mall, a prison, or an elite suburban golf course and come away believing that race, ethnicity, and class are simply inventions. Thus, with theoretical ambivalence and political commitment, we analytically embrace these categories of identity as social, porous, flexible, and yet profoundly political ways of organizing the world. By so doing, we seek to understand how individuals make sense of, resist, embrace, and embody social categories, and, just as dramatically, how they situate "others," at times even essentializing and reifying "other" categories, in relation to themselves. This is, we argue, what demands a relational method.

Third, as a corollary to our interest in categories as fluid sites for meaning making, we seek to elaborate the textured variations of identities that can be found within any single category. Thus, as you will read, our method enables us to search explicitly for variety, dissent within, outliers who stand (by "choice" or otherwise) at the dejected or radical margins, those who deny category membership, and those who challenge the existence of categories at all. Analytically, it is crucial to resist searching for in-group coherence or consensus as anything other than a hegemonic construction, although, as we argue, the search for modal forms is exceedingly useful. Nevertheless, it is critical to theorize how variation and outliers in relation to such modality re-present the larger group (Bhavnani, 1994).

These three moves—contextual, relational, and potentially focusing on and through individual variation while seeking modal forms—are crucial to what we are calling our "theory of method." Indeed, we would argue that this "theory of method" is conceptually akin to what an artist does, and this leads us to call our articulated method "compositional studies." A visual artist can have no composition without paying explicit attention to both the positive and the negative spaces of a composition. Positive space (the main object) must have a negative referent, and the negative referent, visually speaking, is as important as the positive to the composition as a whole. It is these "blank" or "black" spaces in relation to "color" or "white" that we pay attention to in our work. Like the artist, we explicitly explore the negative bridging spaces within the composition; we intentionally explore the relationship between "negative" and "positive" spaces and understand that no "positive" exists except in relation to the "negative." Again, this is an artistic metaphor, but it is one that offers great power as we reflect upon and name our ethnographic practice. Under our theory and practice of method, then, relevant bordering groups (those groups that border the primary subject of interest in the ethnography) are as essential to the ethnographic composition as any primary group under consideration. Thus, our specific genre of ethnographic practice historically implies a particular analytic method, one that considers the in-between, the gauze that glues groups together, even as it is narrated to distinguish "them." The in-between, like DuBois's color line, grows to be as theoretically and politically critical as that group which initially captures our ethnographic attention. Like the Black arts movement in the 1960s and 1970s, then, we intentionally and self-consciously politicize our artistic/compositional metaphor, arguing that our ethnographic compositions sit at the nexus of structural forces and individual lives/agency.[1]

Extending our notion of "compositional studies," we also argue that no group, even as in relation to other bordering groups, can be understood without reference to the larger economic and racial formations within which interactions take place. Given kaleidoscopic changes in the world economy in the past several decades, for instance, Lois Weis's follow-up study of individuals who initially were the subjects in *Working Class Without Work* (Weis, 1990) drives home the point that none of this is static and that it is important to watch the ways in which this all plays out over time. Identities are constructed in relation to the constructed identities of others, as well as dialectically in relation to the broader economy and culture. But none of this remains unchanged. Long-term ethnographic investigations enable us to track this set of interactions and relationships over time. Here is the unique contribution of Weis's *Class Reunion* (2004); she uses data gathered in 1985 in a working-class high school and then re-interviews students from that school 15 years later. This form of ethnographic longitudinality enables us to shift our eye from pieces drawn at one point in time to those drawn at another, opening ever further the spectrum of compositional ethnography. We thus begin here—with a clear(ish) focus as to what the economic and racial formations look like over time, and as to what the field of relational interactions is within this broader, evolving context.

Importantly, our notion of compositional studies invites a rotating position for the writer/researcher; that is, compositional studies affords researchers the opportunity and obligation to be at once grounded and analytically oscillating between engagement and distance; explicitly committed to deep situatedness yet able to embrace shifting perspectives as to the full composition. Our theory of method, then, extends an invitation to the researcher as multiply positioned: grounded, engaged, reflective, well versed in scholarly discourse, knowledgeable as to external circumstances, and able to move between theory and life "on the ground." Whether in a school, a prison, a neighborhood, a cultural arts center, a community center, a religious institution, or wherever, we invite researchers/writers to travel between theory "in the clouds," so to speak, and the everyday practices of individuals living in communities as they (and we) negotiate, make sense of, and change their/our positionalities and circumstance. This method suggests, then, an articulate, intellectually and personally flexible, and engaged individual who really does enjoy and respect what others have to say. The responsibility of placing these interactions/narrations and all that we have come to refer to as "data," then, lies largely with us.

We offer, in this chapter, a brief look at two compositional designs, both of which will be elaborated elsewhere (Fine et al., 2004; Weis, 2004): a longitudinal analysis of white working-class men and women, followed by Lois Weis after 15 years as their lives, stories, and homes carry the seams of the economic and racial formations in contemporary white working-class America, and a participatory action research project that Michelle Fine has coordinated, in which youth across suburban and urban districts learn to be critical researchers of "desegregation" through an analysis of race, ethnicity, class, and opportunity in their own schools and in the New York metropolitan region. In putting these two pieces forward, we argue that both projects are fundamentally rooted in what we call compositional studies—ethnographic inquiry designed to understand how global and national formations, as well as relational interactions, seep through the lives, identities, relations, and communities of youth and adults, ultimately refracting back on the larger formations that give rise to them to begin with.

Class Reunion

Amid cries of "farewell to the working class" (Gorz, 1982) and the assertion of the complete eclipse of this class given the lack of "direct representations of the interaction among workers on American television" (Aronowitz, 1992), I (Lois) offer *Class Reunion* (2004)—a volume aimed at targeting and explicating the remaking of the American white working class in the latter quarter of the 20th century. Arguing that we cannot write off the white working class simply because white men no longer have access to well-paying laboring jobs in the primary labor market (Edwards, 1979), jobs that created a distinctive place for labor in the capital-labor accord (Apple, 2001; Hunter, 1987), and that we cannot assume that this class can be understood only as a tapestry that seamlessly integrates people across ethnicity, race, and gender (Bettie, 2003), I explore empirically and longitudinally the remaking of this class both discursively and behaviorally inside radical, globally based economic restructuring (Reich, 1991, 2002).

Beginning in 1985 with my ethnographic investigation of Freeway High (*Working Class Without Work: High School Students in a De-Industrializing Economy*; Weis, 1990) and culminating with intensive follow-up interviews with these same students in 2000–2001, I track a group of the sons and daughters of the workers of "Freeway Steel" over a 15-year time period. The original volume, *Working Class Without Work* (1990), explores identity formation among white working-class male and female students in relation to the school, economy, and family of origin, capturing the complex relations among secondary schooling, human agency, and the formation of collective consciousness within a radically changing economic and social context.

I suggest in the volume that young women exhibit a "glimmer of critique" regarding traditional gender roles in the working-class family and that young men are ripe for New Right consciousness given their strident racism and male-dominant stance in an economy that, like the ones immortalized in the justly celebrated films *The Full Monty* and *The Missing Postman* (Walkerdine et al., 2001), offers them little.

Fifteen years later, I return to these same students as they (and we) meet in *Class Reunion*, a study lodged firmly in our theory of method as outlined earlier. Through a careful look at the high school and young adult years (ages 18–31) of the sons and daughters of the industrial proletariat in the northeastern "Rust Belt" of the United States, I capture and theorize the reshaping of this class under a wholly restructured global economy. Traversing the lives of these men and women in line with our larger working method of compositional ethnography, I argue that the remaking of this class can be understood only through careful and explicit attention to issues that swirl around theories of whiteness, masculinity, violence, representations, and the economy. Reflective of the triplet of theoretical and analytic moves that we put forward here as signature of our work—deep work within one group (over a 15-year time period in this case); serious relational analyses between and among relevant bordering groups; and broad structural connections to social, economic, and political arrangements—I argue that the remaking of the white working class can be understood only in relation to gendered constructions within that group and the construction of relevant "others" outside itself—in this case, African Americans and Yemenites, particularly men—as well as deep shifts in large social formations, particularly the global economy.

▣ Changing Economies, Changing Gender

In this chapter, I (Lois) probe varying ways in which white working-class men remake class and masculinity in the context of massive changes in the global economy, changes that most specifically target the former industrial proletariat. Stretching to situate themselves within the postindustrial world, young white working-class Freeway men take their selves as forged in relation to the three primary definitional axes that are defining characteristics of their youth identity: (a) an emerging contradictory code of respect toward school knowledge and culture not in evidence in key previous studies of this group conducted when the economy was kinder to the white working class, (b) a set of virulently patriarchal constructions of home/family life that position future wives in particular kinds of subordinate relationships, and (c) constructed notions of racial "others" (Weis, 1990). Through careful engagement with data collected in 2000–2001, I argue here that it is the ways in which individual white working-class men simultaneously position themselves and are positioned vis-à-vis these three major axes that determine, to some extent at least, both where they individually land 15 years later *and* the broader contours of white working-class culture. Specifically, in the case of the men, it is in the pulling away from what are defined within peer groups in high school as normative or perhaps hegemonic masculine cultural forms that we begin to see young people, in this case young men, move toward adulthood. Tracing the push and pull of hegemonic cultural forms as defined in high school, I suggest here that it is within this push and pull, as lived inside the new global economy and accompanying tighter sorting mechanisms, that we can begin to understand both the generalized shape of the new working class and the individual positions within this class as well as potentially outside it.

In this section, we meet, for illustrative purposes, Jerry and Bob, both of whom were in the honors bubble in high school (constituting 20 students out of a class of 300—the only students specifically pursuing college prep work in high school) and thus already were outside, to some extent at least, the dominant white working-class male culture as described in *Working Class Without Work* (Weis, 1990). Jerry, a star athlete, in high school lived mainly inside the honors group. Bob, on the other hand, did not. When I first met him, when he was 16 years old, Bob loved heavy metal bands and wore their T-shirts. He often got into fights, and he frequently got stoned and drunk. He exhibited a set of attitudes and behaviors that placed him squarely within the hegemonic working-class masculinity exhibited during the high school years of Freeway students. Most of his friends were in the non-honors classes, leaving him little time or interest for his peers in the honors bubble. Ultimately, however, both men distanced themselves from the normative male white working-class youth culture—Jerry is now a middle school math teacher, and Bob is completing his degree in veterinary medicine at what is arguably the most prestigious veterinary school in the country.

Jerry: I grew up in the second ward which is, so the first ward is definitely the lower class, lower than most of Freeway, but it's [where] I live now, it's similar to where I grew up, I'd say a little bit more, you know, where I may have grown up in a lower-middle class neighborhood, I'd say maybe where I live now it's middle class. And so it's a little step above. . . . My dad was definitely proud of me; he got to expect that of me and always congratulated me, and I think I made him very proud of me. All my siblings went to college. None of them were scored as well academically. I'm a little bit more serious than the rest of them. . . . Yeah, it is weird that our close immediate five to ten group of people [not including Bob] that were in that advanced group together all had a lot of similar beliefs and goals and we all wanted to go to college, wanted to succeed. And that's the minority. If you look overall at that class [Freeway High], you wouldn't find as much success, but in that group, I don't know. We were all competitive with each other, and yet still friends.

Lois: What do you think happened to some of the rest of the kids that were not in that [advanced] class?

Jerry: I don't know. Probably just went out to work wherever they found a job and maybe they'd have high goals for themselves, but a lot of them are still living in Freeway.

Lois: [Fifteen years ago] We talked about your parents, what kind of work they did. You said your mom is not educated past 8th Grade. How does she talk about her work? Does she work now?

Jerry: No. She's retired also [like his dad]. She actually made envelopes. She worked full-time and then there were times when she worked part-time when the kids were really young, and I remember once for a few years, when I was very young, she worked on the night shift and she stayed home with the kids during the day. Then my dad came home and she went to work at night. I remember going with my dad to go pick her up late at night. How did she talk about it? I never once heard her say, "I hate my job." I never heard her say she loved her job. She never really talked about it a whole lot. . . . Except when she was happy when she brought a box of envelopes home that she got at work.

Lois: You're describing [earlier he did so] your dad as a pretty traditional Italian man. Sometimes those men are not real happy when their wives work outside the home. How did that play out in your household?

Jerry: I never sensed that he might feel that. We needed . . . with all the kids [five kids] we needed two incomes in the family . . . I don't know, it was pretty, like I said, traditional, what I think of back to the 1950s, how when my mom cooked, my dad expected a meal when he came home. You look back now at how silly it was. But that's how they grew up and that's how it was.

Lois: Can you describe a typical weekday in your house [now]?

Jerry: Typical weekday, yeah. From morning, getting up and coming to school here, extra early, always having kids here before school. Giving, really giving of what I have as I teach. I kind of work very hard until the school day is over. Then I'm involved with extracurricular activities, whether it be running the fitness program after school, or when softball season comes, coaching the teams, which involves practice every day. But then, coming home and cooking dinner. I like to cook dinner . . . I do it more because I like to, and so she'll [his wife] do more of the cleanup work, which I hate to do. So, we share that responsibility. And then, whether it be working out or just relaxing watching TV or going to a sporting event or coming back to school to watch a sporting event, watch the kids play. . . . So, that's a typical day. . . . Weekend? Sundays are pretty typical of going to Mom's at one and having a big dinner and staying there for a couple of hours. And then coming home, doing the laundry, grocery shopping and planning for the next school week. But Saturdays are the ones that are

> changing. Usually we'll do more fun things. That would be going to a movie or something.

Jerry had several things going for him that enabled him to stake out a nonhegemonic form of white working-class masculinity as far back as middle school. Although solidly in the white manual-laboring working class, his parents worked to instill a strong work ethic in their children. This, though, is not enough to explain Jerry's class repositioning. Many, but certainly not all, of the Freeway parents had a strong work ethic tied to manual labor, and many in the 1980s desired that their children go on to school (Weis, 1990), feeling strongly that schooling was their only chance to secure an economic future. Jerry's break came when his measured intelligence (whatever "measured intelligence" is, it can have serious consequences) placed him in the honors classes in middle school, classes that he took seriously for the next 6 years. By his own admission, and that of most of the honors students whom I interviewed in the mid-1980s, he associated only with this group of students, the majority of them holding together as a group formed in relation to the non-honors students. For the men, this meant elaborating a form of masculinity forged centrally around academic achievement rather than physical prowess, sexism, and racism, as I suggested earlier were the valued norms in Freeway High. This does not mean that Jerry did not have in mind marrying a girl like his mother, who could take care of him. Indeed, evidence suggests that he did have such a girl in mind whom he dated throughout high school. But as he grew into his twenties, he changed that opinion and now participates in family life wherein he does a good portion of the domestic activity. He does all of the cooking, for example—something unheard of in his father's generation—while she "cleans up." The honors bubble encouraged the formation of a different kind of working-class masculinity, one exempt in many respects from that outlined above as hegemonic within this class faction. The majority of the 20 students in the honors bubble socialized and learned only with one another over a 6-year period. The young men thus could stand squarely on the space of a different kind of masculinity, and virtually every one of them (all but two) did so in the mid-1980s, when I engaged in the original work. The honors bubble, in fact, enabled and encouraged young working-class men to forge a masculinity different from that embedded in the broader class and gendered culture. Significantly, the honors bubble had no African American students or Puerto Rican students (unlike the broader school) and only two Yemenites, one male and one female, in spite of the much larger representation of students of color in the school as a whole. The just-mentioned woman is of mixed heritage (Yemenite and Vietnamese), and she grew up on the "white" side of town. Thus, core masculinist culture in the honors bubble was not formed in relation to people of color, women who were positioned as "less than" in precisely the same way as occurred in the larger class cultural configuration, or the contradictory code of respect outlined earlier. Rather, like the men from professional families whom Bob Connell talks about (1993, 1995), the men in this tiny segment of the working class have a dominant masculinity etched around academics, offering a distinct alternative to the blasting hegemonic masculinity that permeated the 1980s white youth in Freeway and the broader class cultural relations at the time. Jerry's hard work, parental support, connection to athletics, winning personality, and sheer smarts allowed him to move off the class space into which he was born. Jerry is now married to a young woman from an affluent suburban family, and his class background is now largely invisible.

Space does not permit an intensive analysis of Bob, who, in contrast to Jerry, lived a hegemonic form of white working-class masculinity in high school despite being placed in the honors bubble. Suffice it to say that Bob moved off that space as he embarked on a trajectory that ultimately led to the near completion of a highly valued veterinary school program. Working against and with the image of his father—a ne'er-do-well who had a distant relationship with his son—Bob never wants to "stagnate." Living in a church-owned house rented for a small sum of money to an obviously poor family, Bob's mother augmented family income, which could never be counted on, by taking in one foster child after another. As a youth and teenager, Bob walked between the cracks of the foster care system, listening to his music, frequently getting drunk and stoned, engaging in physical fights, and impregnating his 17-year-old girlfriend when he was 18. Working at Home Depot, earning the minimum wage, and eventually entering the service, Bob appeared to have a clear life trajectory, in that he would play off of and live out deeply rooted and well-articulated hegemonic working-class masculinist forms in the early 21-century economy. Ironically, Bob's Army service interrupted this, offering space within which his marriage was brutally severed, he was mentored by his platoon sergeant, and ultimately he found God (Weis, 2004). Now desirous of a male-female relationship in which he takes seriously his role as protector, he claims that his wife, although highly educated and the daughter of a university faculty member, would like to bake pies, make quilts, and ultimately "open a Christian bookstore." Whether or not his wife would agree with this or not is open to debate, but I would argue that for many reasons, her agreement is irrelevant for the purpose of the current discussion. Bob has been catapulted, or has catapulted himself, across whatever class border may exist for a man from his social class background. Whatever fantasies Bob may or may not have about his wife's future pie-making activity, the fact is that his wife, born into a professional family, is highly educated, possessing a research-based master's degree and working toward a PhD in the sciences; she has a job and, by Bob's own admission, they share on a day-to-day basis all household tasks. He is, in fact, almost totally responsible for his two teenage sons when they come to visit, which is often (the entire summer and two weekends per month in spite of the fact that he lives 3 hours from them). Bob has moved far from his high school enactment of working-class core white male masculinity. He, like Jerry, is headed for a new space within the economy, one very different from that occupied by their parents and substantially different from the majority of their peers. Significantly, both men are physically distanced from Freeway, although Jerry lives, for the moment at least, in a bordering inner-ring white working-class suburb. Nevertheless, both men metaphorically and actually crossed the bridge that links working-class Freeway with the wider society. Jerry is a well-respected middle school teacher and, by the time of this writing, Bob will have become a veterinarian, having graduated from one of the top vet schools in the world.

In terms of our theory and method of compositional studies, *Class Reunion* allows us to interrogate the relation of large-scale economic and social relations on individual and group identities—to excavate the social psychological relations "between" genders and races, as narrated by white men, and to explore the nuanced variations among these men. We come to see identities carved in relation, in solidarity, and in opposition to other marked groups and, importantly, in relation to what the economy "offers up" over time. It is in the push and pull of these men, both within hegemonic high school masculinist forms *and* the currency of such forms in the restructured economy, that we can begin to understand the remaking of the white working class. Significantly, for white working-class males, struggles to ensure symbolic dominance in an ever-fragile economy sit perched on the unsteady fulcrum of racial and gender hierarchy (Weis, 2004).

For an alternative construction of compositional studies, designed with some of the same epistemological commitments, we turn now to a broad-based qualitative study of racial justice and public education, conducted by Michelle Fine and colleagues through a participatory design with youth. In this case, we witness compositional design in the critical study of race-, ethnicity-, and class-based academic opportunities within and across the New York City (NYC) metropolitan area, investigating in particular the ways in which white, African American, Latino, Afro-Caribbean, and Asian American youth conceptualize themselves and their opportunities, their "place" in the United States and in their schools, at the very revealing fractures of social hierarchies.

Compositional Studies on the Fault Lines of Racial Justice and Public Education

Almost 50 years after *Brown v. Board of Education*, we continue to confront what is problematically coined an "achievement gap" between African Americans and Latinos, on one hand, and whites and Asian Americans, on the other; a similar gap appears between middle-class and poor children (Anyon, 1997; Bowles & Gintis, 1976; Ferguson, 1998; Fine, 1991; Fordham, 1996; Hochschild, 2003; New York Association of Community Organizations for Reform Now [ACORN], 2000; Orfield & Easton, 1996; Wilson, 1987; Woodson, 1972).[2] In 2001, a series of school districts within the New York metropolitan area, in suburban New York and New Jersey, joined to form a consortium to take up this question of the "gap" and invited Michelle and students from the Graduate Center, City University of New York, to collaborate on critical research into the production of, performance of, and resistance to the "gap." Drawing on Ron Hayduk's (1999) call for regional analyses (rather than urban or suburban analyses in isolation), we conceptualized an ethnographic analysis of the political economy of schooling as lived by youth in and around the NYC metropolitan area.

By crossing the lines separating suburbs and urban areas, we designed the work to reveal similarities across county lines and identify important contrasts. We sought to document the codependent growth of the suburbs and the defunding of urban America, as well as to reveal the fractures of inequity that echo within "desegregated" suburban communities and schools. We hoped, finally, to capture some of the magic of those spaces in which rich, engaging education flourishes for youth across lines of race, ethnicity, class, geography, and "track." With graduate students Maria Elena Torre, Janice Bloom, April Burns, Lori Chajet, Monique Guishard, Yasser Payne, and Kersha Smith, Michelle undertook this work committed to a textured, multimethod critical ethnographic analysis of urban and suburban schooling with youth, designed to speak back to questions of racial, ethnic, and class (in)justice in American education (see Torre & Fine, 2003, for design). To reach deep into the varied standpoints that constitute these schools, we created a participatory action research design with youth representing the full ensemble of standpoints within these urban and suburban desegregated settings (Anand, Fine, Perkins, Surrey, & the graduating class of 2000; Renaissance Middle School, 2001; Fals-Borda, 1979; Fine, Torre, et al., 2001, 2002; Freire, 1982; Hartsock, 1983).

The Design, in Brief

We have, over the past 18 months, been collaborating with more than 70 diverse youth from 11 racially integrated suburban school districts and 3 New York City high schools, crossing racial, ethnic, class, gender, academic, geographic, and sexuality lines. We designed a series of research camps in schools, on college campuses, and in communities ranging from wealthy Westchester suburbs to the South Bronx of New York City.

At the first research camp, a 2-day overnight at a New Jersey college, youth participated in "methods training," learning about qualitative design, critical race theory, and a series of methods including interview, focus group, observation, and survey design (e.g., we read with them Collins, 1991, and Harding, 1983). Urban and suburban students and those of us from the Graduate Center crafted a survey of questions to be distributed across districts, focusing on youth views of distributive (in)justice in the nation and their schools. The youth insisted that the survey *not* look like a test, so they creatively subverted the representations of "science" by including photos, cartoons for respondents to interpret, a chart of the achievement gap, and open-ended questions such as "What is the most powerful thing a teacher has ever said to you?" Available in English, French, Spanish, and Braille, as well as on tape, the survey was administered to nearly 5,000 9th and 12th graders in 13 urban and suburban districts. Within 6 weeks, we received 3,799 surveys—brimming with rich qualitative and quantitative data that could be disaggregated by race, ethnicity, gender, and "track." Beyond the surveys, over the past year we have engaged in participant observations within four suburban and two urban schools, arranged for four cross-school visitations, and conducted more than 20 focus group interviews. In addition, five school "teams" and one community-based activist group pursued their own inquiry crafted under the larger "opportunity gap" umbrella.

We offer here a slice into our material on racial, ethnic, and class justice in public education, to understand how differently positioned youth, like the men in *Class Reunion*, spin meaningful identities as students, researchers, and activists when they "discover" how deeply historic inequities are woven into the fabric of U.S. public education. The empirical material presented has been carved out of the larger project, at a key fracture point where youth confront structures, policies, practices, and relations that organize, naturalize, and ensure persistent inequity. We enter through this crack because we find it to be a compelling window into how privileged and marginalized youth negotiate political and intellectual identities, dreams, and imaginations in a (national and local) Grand Hall of mirrors in which privilege comes to be read as merit and in which being poor and/or of color gets read as worth-less.

Separate and Unequal? The Interior Life of "Desegregated" Schools

As we visited and worked with a number of desegregated suburban schools, 49 years after *Brown v. Board of Education*, we couldn't help but notice that diverse bodies indeed pass through the integrated school doors of historic victory but then funnel into classes largely segregated by race, ethnicity, and social class. Compared to urban schools, these schools are indeed well resourced. However, within these schools, we were struck by the persistence of "separate and unequal" access to educational rigor and quality. Unlike most students in U.S. schools, youth in desegregated schools must theorize their own identities relationally all the time and every day, because they are making selves in spaces where "difference" matters. That is, they are learning, claiming, and negotiating their places in a microcosmic racial/classed hierarchy on a daily basis.

To understand how youth make sense of their positions in these global/local race, ethnic, and class hierarchies, we enter a focus group composed of diverse youth from across schools, zip codes, and tracks who have come together to discuss academic tracking within their schools. These students attend desegregated schools in which almost 70% of whites and Asians are in advanced placement (AP) and/or honors classes, but only about 35% of African American and Latino students are. We listen now as students justify and challenge the America in which they are being educated, the space of the racial dream of integration, about which they know far too much.

Charles: My thoughts? When we just had [one group in a class] . . . you really don't get the full perspective of everything. You know what I mean? If they were in tracked classes, they wouldn't get to interact. And like . . . when you're in class with like all white people, because I know the same thing happens at [my school] like sometimes *I'm the only black male in class, and you do feel sort of inferior, or you do like sort of draw back a little bit* [authors' emphasis] because you have nobody else to relate with, you know. If it's more integrated, like, you know, you feel more comfortable and the learning environment is better . . . you just get more sides of it because, I don't know, it's hard to, even with math, everybody learns the same thing in math, but if it's all white people, you know what I mean? They're going to learn it somewhat different. *It's not that they don't get the same education, but they're going to miss that one little thing that a Latino person or a black person could add to the class. . . .* [authors' emphasis]

▣ ▣ ▣

Jack: [I don't think we should detrack entirely], maybe not in like all classes, but that really like what they, like maybe if they just had all freshman classes like that, you know, it would help out a lot . . . [to change it all] . . . you know the *kids that might not have achieved so much in the past could see like, you know, like "I do have a chance"* [authors' emphasis]. And you know, "I don't . . . I just don't have to stop. I can keep going and keep learning more stuff." So I don't know, maybe not like every class should be tracked, but *they* [authors' emphasis] should definitely be exposed.

▣ ▣ ▣

Tarik: It starts from when you graduate eighth grade. In eighth grade they ask you, "would you want to be in [top track]?" It depends on your grades. If your grades are good enough to be in top, then you can, but if not, you have to *choose* [authors' emphasis] the [regular] level.

▣ ▣ ▣

Jane: Because, like you know, some people even say that, you know, *the smart kids* [authors' emphasis] should be in a class by themselves because it's more conductive to their learning. But then the other people would say like well the special education kids . . . they need to be *with their kind so they'll learn better* [authors' emphasis].

Charles (African American, high- and medium-track classes) opens by revealing his discomfort with racial stratifications in his school. In one sweep, he poses a critique of the school, and he smuggles in the possibility that African American or Latino students may have "one little thing" to contribute. Jack (white, high-achieving boy) quickly navigates the "presenting problem" away from school structure or black/Latino contributions. Reverting to a discourse of pity, he detours the group's focus onto the students' presumed (lack of) motivation. Tarik, who sits at the top of an underresourced school composed entirely of students of color, lengthens Jack's line of analysis by foregrounding individual motivation and "choice." Jane, a white girl in top tracks, returns the conversation to school structure, but now—given that low motivation and bad grades are "in the room"—she justifies tracks as responsive to, indeed "needed" by, students at the top and at the bottom.

In less than 2 minutes, race has been evacuated from the conversation, replaced by the tropes of "smart" and "special education." Collectively performing a "color-blind" exchange, the group has evacuated the politics of race. Black and Latino students have degenerated from potential contributors to needy. Tracks have been resuscitated from racist to responsive. Melanie and Emily (both biracial, high-achieving young women) try to reassert questions of race and racism by introducing aspects of racializing by educators (Deleuze, 1990):

Melanie: Like tracking has been in the whole school system that I've been going to like from beginning, and if you grow up in a tracking system, that's all you can know. So if you grow up and the whole time I've been in honors classes, and a lot of the time, and I'm mixed so a lot of the time when, if you want to hang out with different people and you're forced, and the other students in your classes and you're kind of forced to hang out with some people that you don't normally, wouldn't normally like hang around with. And at the same time, it's like a lot of emphasis is put on by the parents and teacher, I remember a lot of the time, like "You're a good" . . . like teachers would tell me, "You're a good student, but you need to watch out who you hang out with, because they're going to have a bad influence on you." They didn't see me doing anything. I was just walking down the hallway talking to somebody. It wasn't like, you know, we were out doing whatever. But a lot of times it is the teachers and the parents' first impressions of their ideas that come off . . .

▣ ▣ ▣

Emily: But I want to say like . . . Melanie and I are a lot alike because we're both interracial and we were both in like honors classes. But with her, a lot of her friends are black and with me a lot of my friends are white. And *I get really tired of being the only . . . one of the very few people in my class to actually speak up* [authors' emphasis] if I see something that's like . . . or if I hear

> something that's not . . . that bothers me. And then I feel like *I'm all of a sudden the black voice* [authors' emphasis], you know. Like I'm all black people. And it's not true at all. I . . . lots of people have different kinds of opinions and I want to hear them. It's just that I think a lot of the time, like Charles was saying, when you're the only person in the class, you do get intimidated. And voices aren't heard any more then because of everyone else overpowering.

Across this focus group, we hear youth identities constructed in relation to state school practices that reify and stratify race, as well as in relation to "others" (whites, blacks, teachers, parents, "them," unmotivated students, students with bad grades). These youths sculpt themselves in a nation, in a community, and in local school buildings in which racial signifiers have come to be the organizational mortar with which intellectual hierarchies are built, sustained, and resisted. Although stratified schools, and perhaps focus groups, undoubtedly invite a set of essentialized performances (Butler, 1999; Phoenix, Frosh, & Pattman, 2003), these youth, like the men in *Class Reunion*, scaffold identities through the thick (and sometimes toxic) fog of national and local policies, and within local representations of themselves as value-ful or worth-less. Note that Jack, Tarik, and Jane frame the problem (and their worth) as one of lacks in "others." Charles, Melanie, and Emily try to insert critique of racial formations within the school building. All these youth are growing selves amid social and academic relations stinging with power, privilege, and inequity. All define themselves, and are defined, in relation and in hierarchy; fortunately, they are also defined in flux and in complexity. Although their personal selves may be fluid and performed wildly differently across sites, "others" are fixed, in ways that legitimate existing structures, buttress their own position within, and anesthetize themselves to their anxieties about inequity.

April Burns (2004) argues powerfully that privileged (primarily but not solely white) students are indeed discomforted with their advantage within the tight quarters of internal segregation. In a close discursive analysis of high achiever focus groups, she documents the reversals, critiques, and momentary interruptions that students offer as they reflect on the racialized hierarchies within their presumably integrated schools. More expressly, we hear African American, biracial, and Latino students—like Charles, Emily, and Melanie—struggling with the hall of mirrors in which they attend school—mirrors that typically represent them in ways discrepant from how they see themselves. Students of color traverse and negotiate social policies and practices of symbolic and material violence as they survive a torrent of everyday representations within their desegregated schools. Some do beautifully; others fall. To this task they all import DuBois's "double consciousness" by which the "seventh son" watches through a veil.

> The Negro is a sort of seventh son, born with a veil and gifted with second sight in this American world—a world which yields him no true self consciousness but only lets him see himself through the revelation of the other world. It is a peculiar sensation, this double-consciousness, this sense of always looking at one's self through the eyes of

> others, of measuring one's soul by the tape of a world that looks on in amused contempt and pity. One ever feels his two-ness—an American, a Negro; two souls, two thoughts, two unreconciled strivings; two warring ideals in one dark body, whose dogged strength alone keeps it from being torn asunder. (DuBois, 1990, p. 9)

The veil is critical to compositional studies because it is the lens that, at once, connects and separates. It is gauze, a way of seeing, shifty. It is not a tattoo, an inoculation, a stain on the soul. And yet the veil is, itself, work, both intellectual and psychological. We heard about the veil in various forms, from sons and daughters, beneficiaries of *Brown v. Board of Education*. With access to suburban schools of material wealth and opportunity, African American and Latino youth, compared to white and Asian American youth, offer vastly different responses to survey items related to alienation: Does your teacher know you? Understand you? Give you a second chance?

Black and Latino students score much higher on alienation, and lower on being known—even and especially those in high-track courses—than white and Asian American students. When asked "What was the most powerful thing a teacher has ever said to you—positively or negatively?," Black and Latino students, in sharp and biting contrast to their white and Asian American peers, were far more likely to write such words as "No effect" or "No teacher ever said anything to me that affected me."

The veil doubles. A prophylactic against engagement, it also facilitates other forms of connection. As a shield of protection, it is a way to view the world without assault. It also fills a moat of alienation. The veil, like the color line, constitutes a relational analysis; it recognizes the ironies of walls that at once separate and connect. Through the veil, youth of color witness all. Some narrate pain, some pleasure, and a significant group claims they do not allow the words to penetrate. This is not to say that youth internalize fully the blaring messages, nor that they are fully inoculated by the wisdom of their critical analysis. The veil is the social psychological texture through which the gap is produced, lived, witnessed, and embodied.

The "gap" is a trope for the most penetrating fissures that have formed America. Urban/suburban finance inequities guarantee the gap; academic tracks vivify and produce an embodiment of the gap. The "gap" is neither inevitable nor natural. Schools do not have to reproduce social formations; many of the small, detracked urban schools in our study were designed, indeed, to resist.[3] But broadly conceived, the structures and praxis of class and racial formations constitute public schooling (Noguera, 2003; Payne, 1995). Inequitable state financing, school organization, school size, and classed and racialized access to rigor, as well as deep-pocket private supports that privileged students enjoy—rather than the "bodies" or "cultures" of race/ethnicity—produce consistent differential outcomes within and across schools (Gramsci, 1971). The "gap" is overdetermined but not fully inhaled by all.

Although social analysis may reveal the effects of the long arm of the state, the economy, and racial formations on the lives of youth and young adults, it is interesting, for a moment, to consider who does, and who doesn't, acknowledge the presence (and stranglehold) of the arm. As in the focus group narrative and our survey material, we see that youth of privilege and success largely (for critical re-examination see Burns, 2004) re-present themselves "as if" untouched by these structural forces, "as if" they are gracefully moving forward simply on the basis of merit, hard work, good luck, and/or committed parenting. In contrast, youth of color and/or poverty—never immune to hegemonic discourse—season their words with critique, outrage, and the twinned relations of structural and personal responsibility. Like the men in *Class Reunion* (and maybe even more so), these young women and men speak through a relational, comparative sense of the "other." But in their formulations, they are saddened to realize that they have become the "other."

All lives are formed in history, power inequities, institutional arrangements, and relational negotiations. Compositional studies are well suited to reveal these relations. Youth of color and in poverty know these relations and consistently narrate them for us all.

This project, like *Class Reunion*, reveals the complexity and, we believe, the power of compositional studies. Across and within institutions of public education, we come to see how finance inequities tattoo shame and lack on the intellectually hungry souls of poor and working-class urban youth, as well as how, within racially desegregated high schools, the theater of tracking organizes and produces differences associated with race, ethnicity, and class within buildings, radically differentiating students' access to rigorous curriculum and teaching. The interior politics of these schools have been linked theoretically and systematically to the economic, racial, and policy environments in the states; the production of the "gap" has been empirically tied to the production of privilege-as-merit; and the identity formations of "high-track" and "low-track" youth are interrogated as they define themselves with and against one another. Then—better developed elsewhere—we enter the vast variation within groups: the struggles of low-achieving Asian American students confronting the "model minority myth" (Lee, 1996), the high-track African American students who report loyalty oaths and mixed messages from faculty, and the high-achieving white students who recognize and are discomforted by the structural props and private supports that enable segregation and assure their advantage (Burns, 2004). It is this compositional capacity to move, theoretically and empirically, between structures, groups, and lives and behind the scenes, that enables us to produce work that speaks back to larger struggles for social and educational justice.

A Note on Social Justice and Compositional Studies

Compositional studies responds to the question of social research for social justice in varied ways. In its largest sense, compositional studies makes explicit a mapping of economic, racial, and political formations inside the structures, relations, and identities of youth and young adults. Our invitation toward method asks researchers to render visible the long arms of the state, capital, and racial formations as they saturate communities, homes, schools, souls, identities, and dreams of poor and working-class, middle and upper middle-class America. As Lois's work reveals, the trajectory of young white working-class men and women can be understood only in relation to the economy, gendered constructions and relations, and the constructions and benefits of whiteness—all of which will be occluded in the typical narrative and, as such, must be instantiated through theory. The tracking of the remaking of the white working class in the last quarter of the 20th century speaks volumes about economic justice and injustice, the ways in which groups and individuals at one and the same time refuse to be "slotted" even as they are "slotted" into "appropriate" and predetermined positions. The white working-class men and women have, in fact, fought back in the past 15 years, demanding cultural and economic space within the new economy, but, as Lois suggests in the larger project, this is not without contradictory impulses and outcomes. Surely this "fighting back" is not simply around white male demands expressed through union activities, as was largely the case in the past. The desire to reposition and maintain relative privilege in relation to groups of color continues—a set of struggles that revolves around reconstituted notions of appropriate gender relations and roles. It is the pain and delight of these understandings through which we gain a deeper sense of social and economic injustice. We can also witness the contradictory impulses embedded within narrow identity movements. Here, "compositional studies" reveals the power of what could be a class-based movement across working people, as well as the political shortsightedness and divisiveness of organizing exclusively for white males.

So, too, in Michelle's work, youth across race/ethnic groups, rich and poor, yearn for schools and societies "not yet" (Greene, 1995). We hear discomfort from all with the current states of finance inequities and tracking; we hear the dire price, paid most dearly by urban youth of color, but also suburban youth, of inequitable state policies, tracking systems, and perverse local (mis)representations. Yet we see the power of youth standing together—across lines of race, ethnicity, class, geography, and "academic level"—to speak back to educators and to America.

We leave you with a scene of ambivalence from a recent "speak back." Youth researchers in a suburban school were presenting their "findings" to the faculty. Quite critical of racial and ethnic stratification in his school's academics and disciplinary policies, Derrick explained to the almost-all-white teacher group that he, as an African American male, spends "lots of time in the suspension room . . . and you notice it's mostly black, right?" Hesitant nods were erased rapidly by awkward discursive gymnastics, "Well, no, actually in June it gets whiter when the kids who haven't shown up for detention have to come in," followed by "Sometimes there are white students, maybe when you're not there." But Derrick persists, with the courage of speaking his mind to educators who may or may not listen; standing with peers across racial and ethnic groups and a few adults willing to bear witness as he speaks truth to power.

Derrick is no more optimistic than we that in his school, at this moment, his critique will transform local policy. In our research camps, we rehearse the presentation, expecting engagement and resistance. In the folded arms of disbelieving faculty, the institution declares, "We are coherent, we are integrated, we are fair, it's not about race." But now, skillfully able to slice the school-based analyses by race, ethnicity, and track, able to read the tables and the discursive analyses, Derrick knows he stands not alone. He insists, "I don't speak just for me. I'm speaking for 1,179 other Black and Latino students who completed the survey and report high rates of suspensions." Suddenly his dismissible, personal "anecdote" transforms into fact. He stands tall and represents the concerns of hundreds of African American and Latino students in his school, and from more than a dozen other schools, who report that suspensions, and access to rigor, are unevenly distributed, and opportunities are denied or discouraged. Flanked by white, African American, and biracial students—allies—together they have a job to do. He writes, after his presentation, that he will not "walk away, to swagger to the policies of life . . ." He will, instead, continue to deepen his analysis and outrage, surrounded by allies and representing hundreds, with the critical skills of participatory research directed toward social justice.

When asked, "Do you think it's fair to teach students of color about racism and critical consciousness and involve them in this work? Doesn't it depress you?" Jeneusse, a youth researcher from the South Bronx, assured an audience at Columbia University, "We've long known about racism; that's not news. What I know now, though, is that I can study it, speak about it, and we need to do something to change it." Nikoury, a youth researcher from the Lower East Side of Manhattan, stunned an audience with her astute reflection on participatory action research and its benefits: "I used to see flat. No more . . . now I know things are much deeper than they appear. And it's my job to find out what's behind the so-called facts. I can't see flat anymore." These young women and men have, indeed, come to appreciate the complexity of the composition, the shape of the fractures, and their own capacity to repaint the canvas of the future.

Compositional studies will require scholars willing to dip into the waters of history and political economy, while sharpening the skills of case study, ethnography, and autoethnography. We may witness a delicate, perhaps clumsy, choreography balancing over the waters of structural and cultural explanations, as Sartre wrote, through both Marxism and existentialism (1968; see O'Connor, 2001). The costs may be overtheorizing and underattending to the material before us, or losing the fine-grained analyses of what Geertz calls "thick description" inside a group, a space, a fraction of the nation. Yet we are hopeful that compositional studies can provide a scholarly mirror of urgency, refracting back on a nation, constructed and represented as if we were simply individuals flourishing or languishing in parallel lives, as we move toward conquering chunks of the globe in our own frightening image.

In both instances, *Class Reunion* and critical analysis of the "gap," compositional studies speak back to our nation and ask us to re-view the very fractures of power upon which the country, the economy, our schools, and our fragile sense of selves/comfort/leisure are premised, and to imagine, alternatively, what could be.

Notes

1. We are indebted to Norman Denzin for stretching our thinking on this point. See Maulana Karenga (1982), a theorist of the Black arts movement, as a reaction to "high" European art.

2. Race-, ethnicity-, and class-based inequities in educational opportunities and outcomes persist despite struggles for finance equity (Hochschild, 2003; Kozol, 1991), teacher quality in poor urban districts (Darling-Hammond, 2000; Education Trust, 1998; Iatarola, 2001), school integration (see Cross, 1991; Fine, Anand, Jordan, & Sherman, 2000; Fullilove, 2000), affirmative action (Bok & Bowen, 1998), small schools (Wasley et al., 1999), special education and bilingual reform (Nieto, 1996; Rousso & Wehmeyer, 2001; Stanton-Salazar, 1997), and parent organizing (Fruchter, Galletta, & White, 1992), as well as struggles against high-stakes standardized testing (Haney, Russell, & Jackson, 1997) and tracking (Dauber, Alexander, & Entwisle, 1996; Hurtado, Haney, & Garcia, 1998; New York ACORN, 2000; Noguera, 2003; Oakes, Wells, Yonezawa, & Ray, 1997; Useem, 1990; Wheelock,1992).

3. The youth researchers attend East Side Community High School, a small, detracked urban school on the Lower East Side of New York City. Most of the students come from poor and working-class families, many are recent immigrants from Central and South America, and resources are low and academic expectations high. They are, indeed, neighborhood kids who were lucky enough to find an "alternative" school committed to rigorous education for all.

References

Alford, R. (1998). *The craft of inquiry: Theories, methods, evidence.* New York: Oxford University Press.

Anand, B., Fine, M., Perkins, T., Surrey, D., & the graduating class of 2000 Renaissance School. (2001). *The struggle never ends: An oral history of desegregation in a northern community.* New York: Teachers College Press.

Anyon, J. (1997). *Ghetto schooling.* New York: Teachers College Press.

Anzaldúa, G. (1999). *Borderlands/La Frontera.* San Francisco: Aunt Lute Publishers.

Apple, M. (2001). *Educating the "right" way: Markets, standards, God and inequality.* New York: Routledge.

Aronowitz, S. (1992). *False promises: The shaping of American working class consciousness* (2nd ed.). Durham, NC: Duke University Press.

Bettie, J. (2003). *Women without class.* Berkeley: University of California Press.

Bhavnani, K. (1994). Tracing the contours: Feminist research and objectivity. In H. Afshar & M. Maynard (Eds.), *The dynamics of "race" and gender: Some feminist interventions.* London: Taylor & Francis.

Bok, W., & Bowen, D. (1998). *The shape of the river: Long-term consequences of considering race in college and university admissions.* Princeton, NJ: Princeton University Press.

Bourgois, P. (2002). *In search of respect: Selling crack in El Barrio.* Cambridge, UK: Cambridge University Press.

Bowles, S., & Gintis, H. (1976). *Schooling in capitalist society.* New York: Basic Books.

Burns, A. (2004). The racing of capability and the culpability in desegregated schools: Discourses of merit and responsibility. In M. Fine, L. Weis, L. Pruitt, & A. Burns (Eds.), *Off white: Readings on power, privilege and resistance* (2nd ed.). New York: Routledge.

Butler, J. (1999). *Gender trouble: Tenth anniversary.* New York: Routledge.

Collins, P. H. (1991). *Black feminist thought: Knowledge, consciousness, and the politics of empowerment.* New York: Routledge.

Connell, R. W. (1993). Disruptions: Improper masculinities and schooling. In L. Weis & M. Fine (Eds.), *Beyond silenced voices.* Albany: SUNY Press.

Connell, R. W. (1995). *Masculinities.* Cambridge, UK: Polity.

Crenshaw, K. (1995). Mapping the margins: Intersectionality, identity politics, and violence against women of colour. In K. Crenshaw, N. Gotanda, G. Peller, & K. Thomas (Eds.), *Critical race theory: The key writings that formed the movement.* New York: New Press.

Cross, W. E., Jr. (1991). *Shades of black: Diversity in African-American identity.* Philadelphia: Temple University Press.

Darling-Hammond, L. (2000). Teaching quality and student achievement. *Education Policy Analysis Archives, 8*(1), 27–54.

Dauber, S., Alexander, K. L., & Entwisle, D. R. (1996). Tracking and transitions through the middle grades: Channeling educational trajectories. *Sociology of Education, 69*(3), 290–307.

Deleuze, G. (1990, May). Postscript on societies of control. *L'Autre Journal, 1.*

DuBois, W. E. B. (1990). *Souls of black folks.* New York: First Vintage Books.

Duneier, M. (1994). *Slim's table: Race, respectability, and masculinity.* Chicago: University of Chicago Press.

Education Trust. (1998). Good teaching matters: How well-qualified teachers can close the gap. *Thinking K–16, 3*(2), 1–14.

Edwards, R. (1979). *Contested terrain.* New York: Basic Books.

Fals-Borda, O. (1979). Investigating the reality in order to transform it: The Colombian experience. *Dialectical Anthropology, 4,* 33–55.

Fanon, F. (1967). *Black skin, white masks.* New York: Grove.

Farmer, P. (2001). *Infections and inequalities: The modern plagues.* Berkeley: University of California Press.

Ferguson, R. (1998). Can schools narrow the Black-White test score gap? In C. Jencks & M. Phillips (Eds.), *The Black-White test score gap.* Washington, DC: Brookings Institution.

Fine, M. (1991). *Framing dropouts: Notes on the politics of an urban high school.* Albany: SUNY Press.

Fine, M., Anand, B., Jordan, C., & Sherman, D. (2000). Before the bleach gets us all. In L. Weis & M. Fine (Eds.), *Construction sites: Spaces for urban youth to reimagine race, class, gender and sexuality.* New York: Teachers College Press.

Fine, M., Roberts, R., Torre, M., Bloom, J., Burns, A., Chajet, L., et al. (2004). *Echoes of Brown: Youth documenting and performing the legacy of* Brown v. Board of Education. New York: Teachers College Press.

Fine, M., Torre, M., Boudin, K., Bowen, I., Clark, J., Hylton, D., et al. (2001). *Changing minds: The impact of college in a maximum security prison.* New York: The Graduate Center, City University of New York.

Fine, M., Torre, M., Boudin, K., Bowen, I., Clark, J., Hylton, D., et al. (2002). Participatory action research: From within and beyond prison bars. In P. Camic, J. E. Rhodes, & L. Yardley

(Eds.), *Qualitative research in psychology: Expanding perspectives in methodology and design.* Washington, DC: American Psychological Association.

Fine, M., & Weis, L. (1998). *The unknown city.* Boston: Beacon Press.

Foley, D. (1990). *Learning capitalist culture: Deep in the heart of Texas.* Philadelphia: University of Pennsylvania Press.

Fordham, S. (1996). *Black out: Dilemmas of race, identity and success at Capital High School.* Chicago: University of Chicago Press.

Foucault, M. (1977). *Discipline and punish: The birth of the prison.* New York: Pantheon.

Freire, P. (1982). Creating alternative research methods. Learning to do it by doing it. In B. Hall, A. Gillette, & R. Tandon (Eds.), *Creating knowledge: A monopoly.* New Delhi: Society for Participatory Research in Asia.

Fruchter, N., Galletta, A., & White, J. (1992). *New directions in parent involvement.* Washington, DC: Academy for Educational Development.

Fullilove, M. (2000). The house of Joshua. In L. Weis & M. Fine (Eds.), *Construction sites.* New York: Teachers College Press.

Gorz, A. (1982). *Farewell to the working class.* London: Pluto.

Gramsci, A. (1971). *Selections from prison notebooks.* New York: International.

Greene, M. (1995). *Releasing the imagination: Essays on education, the arts, and social change.* San Francisco: Jossey-Bass.

Haney, W., Russell, M., & Jackson, L. (1997). *Using drawings to study and change education.* Boston: Center for the Study of Testing, Evaluation and Educational Policy at Boston College.

Harding, S. (1983). *Discovering reality: Feminist perspectives on epistemology, metaphysics, methodology, and philosophy of science.* Dordrecht, Holland: D. Reidel.

Hartstock, N.C.M. (1983). *Money, sex, and power: Toward a feminist historical materialism.* New York: Longman.

Hayduk, R. (1999). *Regional analyses and structural racism.* Aspen, CO: Aspen Roundtable on Comprehensive Community Reform.

Hitchcock, P. (1999). *Oscillate wildly.* Minneapolis: University of Minnesota Press.

Hochschild, J. (2003). Social class meets the American dream in public schools. *Journal of Social Issues, 59*(4), 821–840.

hooks, b. (1984). *Feminist theory from margin to center.* Boston: South End.

Hunter, A. (1987). The role of liberal political culture in the construction of middle America. *University of Miami Law Review, 42*(1).

Hurtado, A., Haney, C., & Garcia, E. (1998). Becoming the mainstream: Merit, changing demographics and higher education in California. *La Raza Law Journal, 10*(2), 645–690.

Iatarola, P. (2001). *Distributing teacher quality equitably: The case of New York City* [Policy brief]. New York: Institute for Education and Social Policy.

Karenga, M. (1982). *Introduction to black studies.* Inglewood, CA: Kawaida.

Kozol, J. (1991). *Savage inequalities.* New York: Crown.

Ladson-Billings, G. (2000). Racialized discourses and ethnic epistemologies. In N. K. Denzin & Y. S. Lincoln (Eds.), *Handbook of qualitative research* (2nd ed.). Thousand Oaks, CA: Sage.

Lee, S. J. (1996). *Unraveling the "model minority" stereotype: Listening to Asian American youth.* New York: Teachers College Press.

Martín-Baró, I. (1994). *Writings for a liberation psychology.* Cambridge, MA: Harvard University Press.

Matsuda, M. (1995). Looking to the bottom: Critical legal studies and reparations. In K. Crenshaw, N. Gotanda, G. Peller, & K. Thomas (Eds.), *Critical race theory: The key writings that formed the movement.* New York: New Press.

Mills, C. W. (1959). *The sociological imagination.* London: Oxford University Press.

New York Association of Community Organizations for Reform Now. (2000). *The secret apartheid.* New York: ACORN Organizing Project.

Nieto, S. (1996). *Affirming diversity: The sociopolitical context of multicultural education* (2nd ed.). New York: Longman.

Noguera, P. (2003). *City schools and the American dream: Fulfilling the promise of public education.* New York: Teachers College Press.

Oakes, J., Wells, A., Yonezawa, S., & Ray, K. (1997). Equity lessons from detracking schools. In A. Hargreaves (Ed.), *Rethinking educational change with heart and mind.* Alexandria, VA: Association for Supervision and Curriculum Development.

O'Connor, C. (2001). Making sense of the complexity of social identity in relation to achievement: A sociological challenge in the new millennium. *Sociology of Education, 74,* 159–169.

Orfield, G., & Easton, S. (1996). *Dismantling desegregation.* New York: New Press.

Payne, C. (1995). *I've got the light of freedom: The organizing tradition and the Mississippi freedom struggle.* Berkeley: University of California Press.

Phoenix, A., Frosh, S., & Pattman, R. (2003). Producing contradictory masculine subject positions: Narrative of threat, homophobia and bullying in 11-14-year-old boys. *Journal of Social Issues, 59*(1), 179–196.

Reich, R. (1991). *The work of nations.* London: Simon and Schuster.

Reich, R. (2002). *The future of success.* New York: Alfred Knopf.

Rousso, H., & Wehmeyer, M. (2001). *Double jeopardy: Addressing gender equity in special education.* Albany: SUNY Press.

Rubin, L. (1976). *Worlds of pain: Life in the working-class family.* New York: Basic Books.

Sartre, J.-P. (1968). *Search for method.* New York: Vintage.

Scheper-Hughes, N., & Sargent, N. (1998). *Small wars: The cultural politics of childhood.* Berkeley: University of California Press.

Scott, J. (1990). *Domination and the art of resistance: Hidden transcripts.* New Haven, CT: Yale University Press.

Stack, C. B. (1997). *All our kin.* New York: Basic Books.

Stanton-Salazar, R. (1997). A social capital framework for understanding the socialization of racial minority children and youths. *Harvard Educational Review, 67,* 1–38.

Stepick, A., Stepick, C., Eugene, E., & Teed, D. (2001). Shifting identities. In A. Portes & R. Rumbaut (Eds.), *Ethnicities: Coming of age in immigrant America.* Berkeley: University of California Press.

Thorne, B. (1993). *Gender play: Girls and boys in school.* New Brunswick, NJ: Rutgers University Press.

Torre, M. E., & Fine, M. (2003). Critical perspectives on the "gap": Participatory action research with youth in "integrated" and segregated school settings. *Harvard Evaluation Exchange Newsletter.*

Twine, F. (2000). Racial ideologies and racial methodologies. In F. Twine & J. Warren (Eds.), *Racing research, researching race: Methodological dilemmas in the critical race studies.* New York: New York University Press.

Useem, E. (1990). Tracking students out of advanced mathematics. *American Educator, 14,* 24–46.

Valenzuela, A. (1999). *Subtractive schooling.* Albany: SUNY Press.

Walkerdine, V., Lacey, H., & Melody, J. (2001). *Growing up girl.* New York: New York University Press.

Wasley, P., Fine, M., King, S., Powell, L., Holland, N., & Gladden, M. (1999). *Small schools: Great strides.* New York: Bank Street College of Education.

Waters, M. (1999). *Black identities: West Indian immigrant dreams and American realities.* New York: Russell Sage Foundation.

Weis, L. (1990). *Working class without work: High school students in a de-industrializing economy.* New York: Routledge.

Weis, L. (2004). *Class reunion: The new working class.* New York: Routledge.

Wheelock, A. (1992). *Crossing the tracks.* New York: New Press.

Williams, P. (1992). *The alchemy of race and rights.* Cambridge, MA: Harvard University Press.

Willis, P. (1977). *Learning to labour.* Farnborough, UK: Saxon House.

Wilson, W. J. (1987). *The truly disadvantaged: The inner city, the underclass and public policy.* Chicago: University of Chicago Press.

Woodson, C. G. (1972). *The mis-education of the Negro.* New York: AMS Press. (Original work published 1933)

4

ON TRICKY GROUND

Researching the Native in the Age of Uncertainty

Linda Tuhiwai Smith

Introduction

In the spaces between research methodologies, ethical principles, institutional regulations, and human subjects as individuals and as socially organized actors and communities is tricky ground. The ground is tricky because it is complicated and changeable, and it is tricky also because it can play tricks on research and researchers. Qualitative researchers generally learn to recognize and negotiate this ground in a number of ways, such as through their graduate studies, their acquisition of deep theoretical and methodological understandings, apprenticeships, experiences and practices, conversations with colleagues, peer reviews, their teaching of others. The epistemological challenges to research—to its paradigms, practices, and impacts—play a significant role in making those spaces richly nuanced in terms of the diverse interests that occupy such spaces and at the same time much more dangerous for the unsuspecting qualitative traveler. For it is not just the noisy communities of difference "out there" in the margins of society who are moving into the research domain with new methodologies, epistemological approaches, and challenges to the way research is conducted. The neighbors are misbehaving as well. The pursuit of new scientific and technological knowledge, with biomedical research as a specific example, has presented new challenges to our understandings of what is scientifically possible and ethically acceptable. The turn back to the modernist and imperialist discourse of discovery, "hunting, racing, and gathering" across the globe to map the human genome or curing disease through the new science of genetic engineering, has an impact on the work of qualitative social science researchers. The discourse of discovery speaks through globalization and the marketplace of knowledge. "Hunting, racing, and gathering" is without doubt about winning. But wait—there is more. Also lurking around the corners are countervailing conservative forces that seek to disrupt any agenda of social justice that may form on such tricky ground. These forces have little tolerance for public debate, have little patience for alternative views, and have no interest in qualitative richness or complexity. Rather, they are nostalgic for a return to a research paradigm that, like life in general, should be simple.

It is often at the level of specific communities in the margins of a society that these complex currents intersect and are experienced. Some indigenous communities are examples of groups that have been historically vulnerable to research and remain vulnerable in many ways, but also have been able to resist as a group and to attempt to reshape and engage in research around their own interests. This chapter applies indigenous perspectives to examine the intersecting challenges of methodologies, ethics, institutions, and communities. It is a chapter about arriving at and often departing from commonly accepted understandings about the relationships between methodology, ethics, institutional demands, and the communities in which we live and with whom we research. Rather than a story of how complex the world is and how powerless we are to change it, this chapter is framed within a sense of the possible, of what indigenous communities have struggled for, have tried to assert and have achieved.

Indigenous Research and the Spaces From Which It Speaks

Indigenous peoples can be defined as the assembly of those who have witnessed, been excluded from, and have survived modernity and imperialism. They are peoples who have experienced the imperialism and colonialism of the modern historical period beginning with the Enlightenment. They remain culturally distinct, some with their native languages and belief systems still alive. They are minorities in territories and states over which they once held sovereignty. Some indigenous peoples do hold sovereignty, but of such small states that they wield little power over their own lives because they are subject to the whims and anxieties of large and powerful states. Some indigenous communities survive outside their traditional lands because they were forcibly removed from their lands and connections. They carry many names and labels, being referred to as natives, indigenous, autochthonous, tribal peoples, or ethnic minorities. Many indigenous peoples come together at regional and international levels to argue for rights and recognition. In some countries, such as China, there are many different indigenous groups and languages. In other places, such as New Zealand, there is one indigenous group, known as Māori, with one common language but multiple ways of defining themselves.

There are, of course, other definitions of indigenous or native peoples, stemming in part from international agreements and understandings, national laws and regulations, popular discourses, and the self-defining identities of the peoples who have been colonized and oppressed (Burger, 1987; Pritchard, 1998; Wilmer, 1993). The category of the native Other is one that Fanon (1961/1963) and Memmi (1957/1967) have argued is implicated in the same category as the settler and the colonizer. As opposing identities, they constitute each other as much as they constitute themselves. Rey Chow (1993) reminds us, however, that the native did exist before the "gaze" of the settler and before the image of "native" came to be constituted by imperialism, and that the native does have an existence outside and predating the settler/native identity. Chow refers to the "fascination" with the native as a "labor with endangered authenticities." The identity of "the native" is regarded as complicated, ambiguous, and therefore troubling even for those who live the realities and contradictions of being native and of being a member of a colonized and minority community that still remembers other ways of being, of knowing, and of relating to the world. What is troubling to the dominant cultural group about the definition of "native" is not what necessarily troubles the "native" community. The desire for "pure," uncontaminated, and simple definitions of the native by the settler is often a desire to continue to know and define the Other, whereas the desire by the native to be self-defining and self-naming can be read as a desire to be free, to escape definition, to be complicated, to develop and change, and to be regarded as fully human. In between such desires are multiple and shifting identities and hybridities with much more nuanced positions about what constitutes native identities, native communities, and native knowledge in anti/postcolonial times. There are also the not-insignificant matters of disproportionately high levels of poverty and underdevelopment, high levels of sickness and early death from preventable illnesses, disproportionate levels of incarceration, and other indices of social marginalization experienced by most indigenous communities.

There are some cautionary notes to these definitions, as native communities are not homogeneous, do not agree on the same issues, and do not live in splendid isolation from the world. There are internal relations of power, as in any society, that exclude, marginalize, and silence some while empowering others. Issues of gender, economic class, age, language, and religion are also struggled over in contemporary indigenous communities. There are native indigenous communities in the developed and in the developing world, and although material conditions even for those who live in rich countries are often horrendous, people in those countries are still better off than those in developing countries. There are, however, still many native and indigenous families and communities who possess the ancient memories of another way of knowing that informs many of their contemporary practices. When the foundations of those memories are disturbed, space sometimes is created for alternative imaginings to be voiced, to be sung, and to be heard (again).

The genealogy of indigenous approaches to research and the fact that they can be reviewed in this chapter is important because they have not simply appeared overnight, nor do they exist—as with other critical research approaches—without a politics of support around them or a history of ideas. This chapter speaks from particular historical, political, and moral spaces, along with a set of relationships and connections between indigenous aspirations, political activism, scholarship, and other social justice movements and scholarly work. Indigenous communities and researchers from different parts of the globe have long and often voiced concern about the "problem of research" and represented themselves to be among the "most researched" peoples of the world. The critique of research came to be voiced in the public domain in the 1970s, when indigenous political activism was also reasserting itself (Eidheim, 1997; Humphery, 2000; Langton, 1981; L. T. Smith, 1999). The history of research from many indigenous perspectives is so deeply embedded in colonization that it has been regarded as a tool only of colonization and not as a potential tool for self-determination and development. For indigenous peoples, research has a significance that is embedded in our history as natives under the gaze of Western science and colonialism. It is framed by indigenous attempts to escape the penetration and surveillance of that gaze while simultaneously reordering, reconstituting, and redefining ourselves as peoples and communities in a state of ongoing crisis. Research is a site of contestation not simply at the level of epistemology or methodology but also in its broadest sense as an organized scholarly activity that is deeply connected to power. That resistance to research, however, is changing ever so slightly as more indigenous and minority scholars have engaged in research methodologies and debates about research with communities (Bishop, 1998; Cram, Keefe, Ormsby, & Ormsby, 1998; Humphery, 2000; Pidgeon & Hardy, 2002; Smith, 1985; Worby & Rigney, 2002). It is also changing as indigenous communities and nations have mobilized internationally and have engaged with issues related to globalization, education systems, sovereignty, and the development of new technologies.

Indigenous peoples are used to being studied by outsiders; indeed, many of the basic disciplines of knowledge are implicated in studying the Other and creating expert knowledge of the Other (Helu Thaman, 2003; Said, 1978; Minh-ha, 1989; Vidich & Lyman, 2000). More recently, however, indigenous researchers have been active in seeking ways to disrupt the "history of exploitation, suspicion, misunderstanding, and prejudice" of indigenous peoples in order to develop methodologies and approaches to research that privilege indigenous knowledges, voices, experiences, reflections, and analyses of their social, material, and spiritual conditions (Rigney, 1999, p. 117). This shift in position, from seeing ourselves as passive victims of all research to seeing ourselves as activists engaging in a counterhegemonic struggle over research, is significant. The story of that progression has been told elsewhere in more depth and is not unique to indigenous peoples; women, gay and lesbian communities, ethnic minorities, and other marginalized communities have made similar journeys of critical discovery of the role of research in their lives (Hill Collins, 1991; Ladson-Billings, 2000; Mies, 1983; Moraga & Anzaldúa, 1983; Sedgwick, 1991). There have been multiple challenges to the epistemic basis of the dominant scientific paradigm of research, and these have led to the development of approaches that have offered a promise of counterhegemonic work. Some broad examples of these include oral history as stories of the working class, the range of feminist methodologies in both quantitative and qualitative research, the development of cultural and anti/postcolonial studies, critical race theory, and other critical approaches within disciplines (Beverley, 2000; Ladson-Billings, 2000; McLaren, 1993; Mohanty, 1984; Reinharz, 1992; Spivak, 1987; Stanley & Wise, 1983). Critical theorists have held out the hope that research could lead to emancipation and social justice for oppressed groups if research understood and addressed unequal relations of power. Feminism has challenged the deep patriarchy of Western knowledge and opened up new spaces for the examination of epistemological difference. Third World women, African American women, black women, Chicanas, and other minority group women have added immensely to our understandings of the intersections of gender, race, class, and imperialism and have attempted to describe what that means for themselves as researchers choosing to research in the margins (Aldama, 2001; Elabor-Idemudia, 2002; Hill Collins, 1991; Ladson-Billings, 2000; Mohanty, 1984; Moraga & Anzaldúa, 1983; Te Awekotuku, 1999). Indigenous women have played important roles in exploring the intersections of gender, race, class, and difference through the lens of native people and against the frame of colonization and oppression (K. Anderson, 2000; Maracle, 1996; Moreton-Robinson, 2000; L. T. Smith, 1992; Te Awekotuku, 1991; Trask, 1986).

The decolonization project in research engages in multiple layers of struggle across multiple sites. It involves the unmasking and deconstruction of imperialism, and its aspect of colonialism, in its old and new formations alongside a search for sovereignty; for reclamation of knowledge, language, and culture; and for the social transformation of the colonial relations between the native and the settler. It has been argued elsewhere that indigenous research needs an agenda that situates approaches and programs of research in the decolonization politics of the indigenous peoples movement (L. T. Smith, 1999). I would emphasize the importance of retaining the connections between the academy of researchers, the diverse indigenous communities, and the larger political struggle of decolonization because the disconnection of that relationship reinforces the colonial approach to education as divisive and destructive. This is not to suggest that such a relationship is, has been, or ever will be harmonious and idyllic; rather, it suggests that the connections, for all their turbulence, offer the best possibility for a transformative agenda that moves indigenous communities to someplace better than where they are now. Research is not just a highly moral and civilized search for knowledge; it is a set of very human activities that reproduce particular social relations of power. Decolonizing research, then, is not simply about challenging or making refinements to qualitative research. It is a much broader but still purposeful agenda for transforming the institution of research, the deep underlying structures and taken-for-granted ways of organizing, conducting, and disseminating research and knowledge. To borrow from

Edward Said (1978), research can also be described as "a corporate institution" that has made statements about indigenous peoples, "authorising views" of us, "describing [us], teaching about [us], settling [us] and ruling over [us]." It is the corporate institution of research, as well as the epistemological foundations from which it springs, that needs to be decolonized.

> *I name this research methodology as Indigenist.*
>
> —Lester Rigney (1999, p. 118)

Becoming an indigenous researcher is somewhat like Maxine Green's (2000) description of how artists from the margins come to re-imagine public spaces. "Through resistance in the course of their becoming—through naming what stood in their way, through coming together in efforts to overcome—people are likely to find out the kinds of selves they are creating" (p. 301). Indigenous researchers are "becoming" a research community. They have connected with each other across borders and have sought dialogue and conversations with each other. They write in ways that deeply resonate shared histories and struggles. They also write about what indigenous research ought to be. Australian Aborigine scholar Lester Rigney (1999), emphasizing Ward Churchill's (1993) earlier declarations of indigenist positioning, has argued for an indigenist approach to research that is formed around the three principles of

Table 4.1. Corporate Layers of Research

- Foundations, genealogies, and disciplines of knowledge that define its methodologies and its systems of classification and representation
- Historical embeddedness in imperialism, the production of knowledge, and the development of science
- Cultures and subcultures of its institutions and infrastructures
- Communities of like-minded or trained scholars, disciplinary bodies, and research associations
- Ways in which research is regulated and inscribed through notions of ethics, ethical review boards, and codes of conduct
- Practices of reporting and publishing
- National and international funding agencies and their links to particular agendas
- Ways in which some forms of research legitimate dominant forms of knowledge and maintain hegemony or dominant myths
- Chain and distribution of benefits from research
- Intersection of research with policy and the design and implementation of interventions

resistance, *political integrity*, and *privileging* indigenous voices. He, like other indigenous researchers, connects research to liberation and to the history of oppression and racism. Rigney argues that research must serve and inform the political liberation struggle of indigenous peoples. It is also a struggle for development, for rebuilding leadership and governance structures, for strengthening social and cultural institutions, for protecting and restoring environments, and for revitalizing language and culture. Some indigenous writers would argue that indigenous research is research that is carried out by indigenous researchers with indigenous communities for indigenous communities (Cram, 2001; Rigney, 1999). Implicit in such a definition is that indigenous researchers are committed to a platform for changing the status quo and see the engagement by indigenous researchers as an important lever for transforming institutions, communities, and society. Other writers state that purpose more explicitly in that they define indigenous research as being a transformative project that is active in pursuit of social and institutional change, that makes space for indigenous knowledge, and that has a critical view of power relations and inequality (Bishop, 1998; Brady, 1999; Pihama, 2001; L. T. Smith, 1991). Others emphasize the critical role of research in enabling peoples and communities to reclaim and tell their stories in their own ways and to give *testimonio* to their collective herstories and struggles (Battiste, 2000; Beverley, 2000; The Latina Feminist Group, 2001). Embedded in these stories are the ways of knowing, deep metaphors, and motivational drivers that inspire the transformative praxis that many indigenous researchers identify as a powerful agent for resistance and change. These approaches connect and draw from indigenous knowledge and privilege indigenous pedagogies in their practices, relationships, and methodologies. Most indigenous researchers would claim that their research validates an ethical and culturally defined approach that enables indigenous communities to theorize their own lives and that connects their past histories with their future lives (Marker, 2003). Indigenous approaches are also mindful of and sensitive to the audiences of research and therefore of the accountabilities of researchers as storytellers, documenters of culture, and witnesses of the realities of indigenous lives, of their ceremonies, their aspirations, their incarcerations, their deaths. (Pihama, 1994; Steinhauer, 2003; Te Hennepe, 1993; Warrior, 1995).

In New Zealand, Māori scholars have coined their research approach as Kaupapa Māori or Māori research rather than employing the term "indigenist." There are strong reasons for such a naming, as the struggle has been seen as one over Māori language and the ability by Māori as Māori to name the world, to theorize the world, and to research back to power. The genealogy of indigenous research for Māori has one of its beginnings in the development of alternative Māori immersion-based schooling (Pihama, Cram, & Walker, 2002; G. H. Smith, 1990; L. T. Smith, 2000). Graham Smith (1990) has argued that the struggle to develop alternative schools known as Kura Kaupapa Māori helped produce a series of educational strategies that engaged with multiple levels of colonization and social inequality. These strategies included engagement with theory and research in new ways. Kaupapa Māori research has developed its own life, and as an approach or theory of research methodology, it has been applied across different disciplinary fields, including the sciences. It can be argued that researchers who employ a Kaupapa Māori approach are employing quite consciously a set of arguments, principles, and frameworks that relate to the purpose, ethics, analyses, and outcomes of research (Bishop & Glynn, 1999; Durie, 1992; Johnston, 2003; Pihama, 1993; L. T. Smith, 1991; Tomlins-Jahnke, 1997). It is a particular approach that sets out to make a positive difference for Māori, that incorporates a model of social change or transformation, that privileges Māori knowledge and ways of being, that sees the engagement in theory as well as empirical research as a significant task, and that sets out a framework for organizing, conducting, and evaluating Māori research (Jahnke & Taiapa, 1999; Pihama et al., 2002). It is also an approach that is active in building capacity and research infrastructure in order to sustain a sovereign research agenda that supports community aspirations and development (L. T. Smith, 1999). Those who work within this approach would argue that Kaupapa Māori research comes out of the practices, value systems, and social relations that are evident in the taken-for-granted ways that Māori people live their lives.

Indigenist research also includes a critique of the "rules of practice" regarding research, the way research projects are funded, and the development of strategies that address community concerns about the assumptions, ethics, purposes, procedures, and outcomes of research. These strategies often have led to innovative research questions, new methodologies, new research relationships, deep analyses of the researcher in context, and analyses, interpretations, and the making of meanings that have been enriched by indigenous concepts and language. To an extent, these strategies have encouraged nonindigenous researchers into a dialogue about research and, on occasion, to a reformulated and more constructive and collaborative research relationship with indigenous communities (Cram, 1997; Haig-Brown & Archibald, 1996; Simon & Smith, 2001; G. H. Smith, 1992). Critical and social justice approaches to qualitative research have provided academic space for much of the early work of indigenous research. Denzin and Lincoln (2000) describe a moment in the history of qualitative research (1970–1986) as the moment of "blurred genres" when local knowledge and lived realities became important, when a diversity of paradigms and methods developed, and when a theoretical and methodological blurring across boundaries occurred. Arguably, an indigenist research voice emerged in that blurred and liminal space as it paralleled the rise in indigenous political activism, especially in places like Australia, New Zealand, Norway, and North America. For indigenous activists, this moment was also one of recognition that decolonization needed a positive and more inclusive social vision and needed more tools for development and self-determination (as an alternative to violent campaigns of resistance). Research, like schooling, once the tool of colonization and oppression, is very gradually coming to be seen as a potential means to reclaim languages, histories, and knowledge, to find solutions to the negative impacts of colonialism and to give voice to an alternative way of knowing and of being.

Indigenous research focuses and situates the broader indigenous agenda in the research domain. This domain is dominated by a history, by institutional practices, and by particular paradigms and approaches to research held by academic communities and disciplines. The spaces within the research domain through which indigenous research can operate are small spaces on a shifting ground. Negotiating and transforming institutional practices and research frameworks is as significant as the carrying out of actual research programs. This makes indigenous research a highly political activity that can be perceived as threatening, destabilizing, and privileging of indigeneity over the interests and experiences of other diverse groups. Decolonization is political and disruptive even when the strategies employed are pacifist because anything that requires a major change of worldview, that forces a society to confront its past and address it at a structural and institutional level that challenges the systems of power, is indeed political. Indigenous research presents a challenge to the corporate institution of research to change its worldview, to confront its past and make changes.

Indigenous research approaches, like feminist methodologies, have not emerged into a neutral context, although their arrival has been predicted by those working with silenced and marginalized communities. As Lincoln (1993) forewarned, however, social sciences cannot simply develop grand narratives of the silenced without including the voices and understandings of marginalized and silenced communities. There continues to be vigorous critique of indigenous approaches and claims to knowledge, and, indeed, the indigenous presence in the academy. In some cases, this critique is framed by the discourses of anti–affirmative action, such as calls for "color- and race-free" policies. In other cases, the critique is a very focused attack on the possibility that indigenous people have a knowledge that can be differentiated from dogma and witchcraft or is a very focused and personal attack on an individual (Trask, 1993). In other examples, the critique does reflect attempts by nonindigenous scholars to engage seriously with indigenous scholarship and understand its implications for the practices of nonindigenous scholars and their disciplines. In a limited sense, there has been an attempt at dialogue between indigenous and nonindigenous scholars, usually occurring after indigenous scholars have provided a critique of the discipline—for example Vine Deloria's (1995) critique of anthropology and Ngugi wa Thiong'o's (1981/1987) critique of what counted as African literature. Kenyan writer Ngugi wa Thiong'o viewed the language of the settler/colonizer as being implicated in the "colonization of the mind" and came to the decision that he would not write in the language of the colonizer but instead would write in his own language of Gikuyu or Ki-Swahili. Ngugi's stance helped create further space for debate about "postcolonial" literature and the role of literature in colonial education systems (Ashcroft, Griffiths, & Tiffin, 1989). Vine Deloria's sustained political critique of the place of the American Indian in the American system has created space for the further development of American Indian Studies and a dialogue with other disciplines (Biolsi & Zimmerman, 1997). Unfortunately, dialogue is often the solution to fractures created through lack of dialogue between those with power and marginalized groups. Similar debates have occurred and continue to occur in other fields, including literature (Cook-Lynn, 1996; Harjo & Bird, 1997; Womack, 1999), feminist studies (Maracle, 1996; Moraga & Anzaldúa, 1983; Moreton-Robinson, 2000), and multicultural and ethnic studies (Mihesuah, 1998). Some debates are very public media campaigns that invoke the prejudices and attitudes toward indigenous peoples held by the dominant social group.[1] In some of these campaigns, the ethnicity of the dominant group is masked behind such social categories as "the public," "the taxpayers," or "the rest of society." The fears and attitudes of the dominant social group, and of other minority social groups, are employed quite purposefully in public debates about indigenous knowledge as the arbiters of what indigenous people are permitted to do, of what they are allowed to know, and indeed of who they are.

An important task of indigenous research in "becoming" a community of researchers is about capacity building, developing and mentoring researchers, and creating the space and support for new approaches to research and new examinations of indigenous knowledge. That activity can now be seen in a range of strategies that are being applied by diverse communities across the world to build research capability. Conversations about indigenous methodologies—albeit in different historical, disciplinary, and institutional spaces—are being discussed and applied by a diverse range of indigenous scholars across the globe. These include Sami scholars in northern Norway, Finland, Sweden, and Russia (Keskitalo, 1997) and native scholars in the Pacific Islands (Helu Thaman, 2003; Kaomea, 2003). Sami literary scholar Harald Gaski (1997), for example, argues that "Ever since the world's various indigenous peoples began turning their efforts to co-operative endeavours in the 1970s, the Sami have participated actively in the struggle to make these peoples' and their own voice heard. Art and literature have always played an important role in this endeavour. Therefore, the time for Sami literature to join world literature is past due" (p. 6). Jan Henri Keskitalo (1997) points to a research agenda for Sami people that is "based on the freedom to define, initiate and organize research, and the possibility to prioritise what kind of research should be defined as Sami research, at least when using public funding" (p. 169). All these discussions represent cross-border conversations and activism, as the territorial boundaries of many indigenous communities have been intersected and overlaid by the formation of modern states. Some discussions occur through specific indigenous forums, or through feminist or environmentalist networks, and others occur through the diaspora of the Third World, the "developing world," and regional gatherings (Alexander & Mohanty, 1997; Saunders, 2002; Shiva, 1993; Spivak, 1987).

Researching the Native in the Knowledge Economy

Knowledge is a key commodity in the 21st century. We understand this at a commonsense level simply as an effect of living in the era of globalization, although it is also expressed as the consequences of life in the postindustrial age, the age of information and postmodernity. Knowledge as a commodity is a conception of knowledge (and curriculum) that is situated in the intersection of different visions of and alliances

Table 4.2. Strategies for Building Indigenous Research Capability

- The training of indigenous people as researchers
- The employment of indigenous people as researchers
- Participation by indigenous people in a wide range of research projects employing different kinds of approaches and methodologies
- The generating of research questions by communities
- Developing indigenous research methodologies
- Developing research protocols for working with communities
- The support by various individuals and communities of research-based decision making
- The establishment of indigenous research organizations
- Presentation of their research by indigenous researchers to other indigenous researchers
- Engagements and dialogue between indigenous and nonindigenous researchers and communities

for globalization (Peters, 2003). Michael Apple (2001) refers to this alliance as one that brings together neoliberals, neoconservatives, authoritarian populists, and the new middle class. Apple defines neoliberals as those who are "deeply committed to markets and to freedom as 'individual choice,'" neoconservatives as ones who "want a return to discipline and traditional knowledge," authoritarian populists as ones who "want a return to (their) God in all of our institutions" (p. 11), and the new middle class as those who have created and stand to benefit most from this configuration of interests. The neoliberal economic vision of globalization is one in which the market shapes and determines most, if not all, human activities. Far from being simply an economic theory, neoliberal proponents have used their access to power to attempt to reform all aspects of society, including the relationships between the state and society. New Zealand is often used as a model, the "experiment" for how far this agenda can be pursued, because of the significant neoliberal reforms undertaken over the past 20 years (Kelsey, 1995). The reforms have included a "hollowing out" of the state; the reform and re-regulation of the welfare system—education, health, banking, and finance; and the removal of tariffs and other barriers to free trade (Moran, 1999). The reforms have been supported by a powerful ideological apparatus that has denied empirical evidence that groups were being marginalized further by policies and that the gaps between the rich and poor, the well and the sick, were widening under the reform regime. This ideological apparatus is most visible in its discursive strategies with rhetoric and slogans such as "user pays," privatization, increased competition, freedom of choice, and voucher education. It is also evident in the construction of new, idealized neoliberal subjects who are supposed to be "self-regulating selective choosers, highly competitive and autonomous individuals liberated from their locations in history, the economy, culture and community in order to become consumers in a global market"(L. T. Smith et al., 2002, p. 170).

The significance of the neoliberal agenda for social science research is that the "social," the "science," and the "research" have also been re-envisioned and re-regulated according to the neoliberal ideologies. One site where this re-envisioning and re-regulation of the social, the science, and the research intersects is in the economy of knowledge. As with other strategies of power, it is often the marginalized and silenced communities of society who experience the brunt and the cruelty of both the slogans and the material changes in their lives. The "knowledge economy" is a term used by businesspeople such as Thomas Stewart (1997) to define the ways in which changes in technology such as the Internet, the removal of barriers to travel and trade, and the shift to a postindustrial economy have created conditions in which the knowledge content of all goods and services will underpin wealth creation and determine competitive advantage. As a commodity, knowledge is produced under capitalist labor market conditions: it can be bought and sold, and it is private rather than public property. Researchers are knowledge workers who produce new knowledge. In this environment, new and unique knowledge products become highly prized objects of capitalist desire. Mapping the human genome and searching for cures to various diseases that will require the manufacturing of special products are just two examples of the "race" now on for "knowledge," the new El Dorado. Now, where can one discover new knowledge that is not already under private ownership? The laboratories? The rain forests? The human body? The knowledge and practices of those who have maintained their unique ways of living? The answer to all the above is "Yes," and there is more. Indigenous knowledge once denied by science as irrational and dogmatic is one of those new frontiers of knowledge. The efforts by indigenous peoples to reclaim and protect their traditional knowledge now coincides and converges with scientific interests in discovering how that knowledge can offer new possibilities for discovery (Stewart-Harawira, 1999).

One convergence of indigenous knowledge and science is in the field of ethnobotany, a field that has botanists and biologists working closely with indigenous communities in the collection and documentation of plants, medicinal remedies, and other practices. In doing science, ethnobotanists are also doing qualitative research, talking to community experts, observing practices, and developing word banks and other resources. The protocols that have been developed by the International Society of Ethnobotany will be discussed again later in this chapter. One use of the research that its members gather lies in the identification of medicinal properties that can be reproduced in the laboratory and developed for commercialization. The pharmaceutical industry has a keen hunger for such research, and there is real intensity in the hunt for new miracles to cure or alleviate both old and modern diseases. The search for new knowledge knows no borders. It is competitive and expensive, and only a few can participate. In the biomedical field, the rapid advances in knowledge and technology—for example, in reproductive birth technologies and in genetic engineering—present new challenges to what society thinks is ethically acceptable. Issues raised in relation to cloning a human being, new genetic therapies, and other remedies and practices stretch our understandings of what life is about. Although the science can develop the new knowledge, it is the *social* science that has an understanding of the nature of social change. Scientists, however, can also be powerful advocates of their own discoveries and fields of research, such that institutions and industries "buy into" the promise of new technologies and expect society to "catch up" to the ethical implications of the new knowledge. For qualitative research, new technologies present new vistas in a sense, new attitudes to examine and new dilemmas to resolve. For indigenous and other marginalized communities, the new vistas present new threats and risks in terms of their ability to protect their traditional knowledge and the likelihood of the benefits of research being distributed equitably to the poor rather than to the rich.

As Apple (2001) reminds, us, however, the neoliberal agenda also converges with the countervailing neoconservative and authoritarian tendencies that seek to protect and strengthen certain "traditional" forms of privilege. The "traditional" values and forms of knowledge being reified by these interest groups are not the same traditional values and ways of knowing that indigenous peoples speak of but are in fact the very antithesis of any form of non-Western, nonheterosexual, nonfeminist knowledge. Graham Hingangaroa Smith (1994) argues that there are new types of colonization in the neoliberal version of globalization that enable dominant interests in society to be maintained. Smith further contends that in the global marketplace, where everything can be commodified, local communities, cultures, practices, and values are put at accelerated risk, with little room to maneuver or develop resistance. One analogy of how the global marketplace works to put local communities and knowledge at risk is the impact of the large multinational or national company that sets up its store or its mall in a town that has small and struggling businesses. There are powerful driving forces that shape the ways in which individual interests come to be either aligned with or marginalized from the new development. For example, some people may need employment and others may need access to cheaper products; some people need to retain their businesses or see their community as being defined by the "Main Street," not the Mall. Young people may see the Mall as presenting new social possibilities that would cater more to their tastes by providing access to more global brands. In the end, the community becomes divided by economic interests, although all may ultimately wish for a united community. In the end, the Mall wins: The small businesses either collapse or struggle on; Main Street looks even more depressing, driving more people to the Mall; and everyone in town begins wearing the global brands, just like the people on television and the people who live in the next community, the next state, the next country. Local products, if they are made, find their way to a boot sale or a market day, basically consigned to the margins of the economy and community consciousness. Some local or native products are selected as marketable in the Mall, such as native medicine wheels and small hanging crystals. These products are not produced locally, because that would cost too much, so the *image* is reproduced at a cheaper price in countries with poor labor market conditions and then sold in every mall in the world. Imagine this as a global process having an impact in every little community of the world. It is a very seductive process, but something gets lost, in this process, for the community. For indigenous communities, the "something lost" has been defined as indigenous knowledge and culture. In biological terms, the "something lost" is our diversity; in sociolinguistics, it is the diversity of minority languages; culturally, it is our uniqueness of stories and experiences and how they are expressed. These are the "endangered authenticities" of which Rey Chow (1993) speaks, ones that are being erased through the homogenization of culture.

The knowledge economy, as one theme of globalization, constitutes the new identities of the self-regulating and selective chooser, the consumer of knowledge products, the knowledge worker and knowledge manager, and the clients of knowledge organizations. McLaren (1993, p. 215) calls these *market identities* that reflect the corporate model of market education and educational consumption. One might think that this makes for a very educated and knowledgeable society—not so. The knowledge economy is about creating and processing knowledge, trading and using knowledge for competitive advantage—it is not about knowing or knowledge for its own sake, it is not about the pursuit of knowledge but about "creating" knowledge by turning knowledge into a commodity or product. Research plays an important role in the creation of knowledge and, as argued by Steven Jordan (2003) in an article he entitled "Who stole my methodology?," even the most participatory research models are being subjected to the processes of commodification "for the purposes of supporting and reproducing the social relations of accumulation in their multifarious forms" (p. 195). Jordan further suggests that the methodology of participatory research is being appropriated and reconstituted by neoliberal discourses of participation "in ways that are antithetical to both its founding principles and traditions" (p. 195).

The neoliberal version of globalization is not, however, the only ideology at work across the globe. There are other interests at work, some repressive and others progressive. Trafficking in drugs and people, catering to pedophilia, and other organized criminal activities also have gone global. More recently, global terrorism (recognizing that some communities have been terrorized for hundreds of years by various forms of colonialism) has heightened the impulses and fears of neoconservatives and authoritarian populists and simultaneously has created threats to the free operations of the global marketplace. The powerful nostalgia of neoconservatives and authoritarian populists for a curriculum of the right (Apple, 2001), a curriculum of simple "facts," and a reification of what Denzin (1991) refers to as "ancient narratives" augurs dangers for education, for educational research, and for any social justice research. Neoconservative and authoritarian interest groups seek to disrupt any agenda for social justice and already have been effective in peeling back gains in social justice programs, although Roman and Eyre (1997) caution us to see the dangers of "applying 'backlash' exclusively to Right-wing political reactions [that] fail to draw attention to reactionary and defensive politics within and across left-wing/progressive groups—whether feminist, critical multicultural/anti-racist, or anti-heterosexist" (p. 3). The neoliberal agenda crosses the left and right of the political spectrum, and to some extent the fellow travelers of neoliberalism manage to infiltrate a wide spectrum of politics.

Other, more progressive groups also have managed to go global and make use of knowledge in the pursuit of a social justice agenda. Nongovernmental organizations and communities of interest have managed to put up resistance to the powerful interests of wealthy nations and corporations. Some of these coalitions have brought together diverse interests and unusual bedfellows to contest free trade; others have organized important consciousness-raising activities to keep information about injustice in the public eye. Small communities still cling to their own schools and identities as they attempt to build democratic community consensus. One of the perspectives that indigenous research brings to an understanding of this moment in the history of globalization is that it is simply another historical moment (one of many that indigenous communities have survived) that reinscribes imperialism with new versions of old colonialisms. This is not as cynical as it may sound; rather, it comes from the wisdom of survival on the margins. This moment can be analyzed, understood, and disrupted by holding onto and rearticulating an alternative vision of life and society. It is also not the only defining moment: Other changes have occurred that make communities somewhat more prepared to act or resist. For example, more indigenous researchers are choosing to research alongside their own communities. There are more allies. There also are other imperatives that have driven an agenda of transformation; among them is language regeneration. Language regeneration programs have created a momentum, especially in New Zealand, that neoliberal reforms have not been able or willing to subvert, as these programs have a strong hold on the community's aspirations. Indigenous development is optimistic despite what often appear to be huge barriers.

The new subjectivities of the free market and the knowledge economy also include the re-envisioning and re-regulation of new native subjects, a reworked Other, still raced and gendered, idealized and demonized, but now in possession of "market potential." Some of these new subjectivities resonate with the global market, where evoking of "the image" is a powerful mechanism for distancing the material conditions of the people from the image itself. Other subjectivities are "turning the gaze" back onto the dominant settler society, reflecting the momentum of political, educational, and economic change that already has occurred in many indigenous communities. These identities are formed "in translation," in the constant negotiation for meaning in a changing context. New identities form and re-form in response to or as a consequence of other changes and other identities. New voices are expressed, new leaders emerge, new organizations form, and new narratives of identity get told.

One newly worked native identity is that of the native intellectual as scientist. This is a small, emerging group of native scientists with strong connections to their native knowledge and practices. These scientists represent a new type of translator or interlocutor, one who bridges different knowledge traditions in ways that Western scientists find difficult to dismiss and indigenous communities find acceptable (Little Bear, 2000; Thomas, 2001). The native scientist not only is the native healer, herbalist, or spiritual expert but also is someone who understands the philosophies, knowledge, and histories that underpin cultural practices and beliefs and who generates his or her science from these foundations. As Basso (1996) and Marker (2003) have suggested, these people are not in the academy to "play word and idea games" but intend to contribute to change for the benefit of communities, to ensure that science listens to, acknowledges, and benefits indigenous communities. The role of these indigenous professionals is similar to the role played by the first generation of indigenous teachers and nurses and by the first generation of medical doctors and social workers in native communities, a difficult role of translating, mediating, and negotiating values, beliefs, and practices from different worldviews in difficult political contexts.

Ethics and Research

One area of research being vigorously contested by indigenous communities is that of research ethics and the definitions and practices that exemplify ethical and respectful research. Indigenous researchers often situate discussions about ethics in the context of indigenous knowledge and values and in the context of imperialism, colonialism, and racism (Cram, 1993, 2001; Menzies, 2001; Rigney, 1999). Indigenous understandings of research ethics have often been informed by indigenous scholars' broad experience of research and other interactions with the media, health system, museums, schools, and government agencies. Increasingly, however, research ethics has come to be a focus of indigenous efforts to transform research and institutions (Worby & Rigney, 2002). Research ethics is often much more about institutional and professional regulations and codes of conduct than it is about the needs, aspirations, or worldviews of "marginalized and vulnerable" communities. Institutions are bound by ethical regulations designed to govern conduct within well-defined principles that have been embedded in international agreements and national laws. The Nuremberg Code (1949) was the first major international expression of principles that set out to protect the rights of people from research abuse, but there are other significant agreements, such as the World Medical Association Declaration of Helsinki Agreement of 1964 and the Belmont Report of 1979. National jurisdictions and professional societies have their own regulations that govern ethical conduct of research with human subjects. Increasingly, the challenges of new biotechnologies—for example, new birth technologies, genetic engineering, and issues related to cloning—also have given rise to ethical concerns, reviews, and revised guidelines.

For indigenous and other marginalized communities, research ethics is at a very basic level about establishing, maintaining, and nurturing reciprocal and respectful relationships, not just among people as individuals but also with people as individuals, as collectives, and as members of communities, and with humans who live in and with other entities in the environment. The abilities to enter preexisting relationships; to build, maintain, and nurture relationships; and to strengthen connectivity are important research skills in the indigenous arena. They require critical sensitivity and reciprocity of spirit by a researcher. Bishop (1998) refers to an example of relationship building in the Māori context as *whakawhanaungatanga*, "the process of establishing family (*whânau*) relationships, literally by means of identifying, through culturally appropriate means, your bodily linkage, your engagement, your connectedness, and therefore, an unspoken but implicit commitment to other people" (p. 203). Worby and Rigney (2002) refer to the "Five Rs: Resources, Reputations, Relationships, Reconciliation and Research" (pp. 27–28) as informing the process of gaining ethical consent. They argue that "The dynamic relationship between givers and receivers of knowledge is a reminder that dealing with indigenous issues is one of the most sensitive and complex tasks facing teachers, learners and researchers at all levels . . ." (p. 27). Bishop and Glynn (1992) also make the point that relationships are not simply about making friends. They argue that researchers must be self-aware of their position within the relationship and aware of their need for engagement in power-sharing processes.

In *Decolonizing Methodologies* (L. T. Smith, 1999), I also gave some examples of the ways in which my communities may describe respect, respectful conduct, trustworthiness, and integrity at a day-to-day level of practice and community assessment. My concern was to show that community people, like everyone else, make assessments of character at every interaction. They assess people from the first time they see them, hear them, and engage with them. They assess them by the tone of a letter that is sent, as well as by the way they eat, dress, and speak. These are applied to strangers as well as insiders. We all do it. Different cultures, societies, and groups have ways of masking, revealing, and managing how much of the assessment is actually conveyed to the other person and, when it is communicated, in what form and for what purpose. A colleague, Fiona Cram (2001), has translated how the selected value statements in *Decolonizing Methodologies* could be applied by researchers to reflect on their own codes of conduct. This could be described as an exercise of "bottom-up" or "community-up" defining of ethical behaviors that create opportunities to discuss and negotiate what is meant by the term "respect." Other colleagues have elaborated on the values, adding more and reframing some to incorporate other cultural expressions. One point to make is that most ethical codes are top down, in the sense of "moral" philosophy framing the meanings of ethics and in the sense that the powerful still make decisions for the powerless. The discussions, dialogues, and conversations about what ethical research conduct looks like are conducted in the meeting rooms of the powerful.

No one would dispute the principle of *respect*; indeed, it is embedded in all the major ethical protocols for researching with human subjects. However, what is *respect*, and how do we know when researchers are behaving respectfully? What does *respect* entail at a

Table 4.3. "Community-Up" Approach to Defining Researcher Conduct

Cultural Values (Smith, 1999)	*Researcher Guideline (Cram, 2001)*
Aroha ki te tangata	A respect for people—allow people to define their own space and meet on their own terms.
He kanohi kitea	It is important to meet people face to face, especially when introducing the idea of the research, "fronting up" to the community before sending out long, complicated letters and materials.
Titiro, whakarongo . . . kôrero	Looking and listening (and then maybe speaking). This value emphasizes the importance of looking/observing and listening in order to develop understandings and find a place from which to speak.
Manaaki ki te tangata	Sharing, hosting, being generous. This is a value that underpins a collaborative approach to research, one that enables knowledge to flow both ways and that acknowledges the researcher as a learner and not just a data gatherer or observer. It also facilitates the process of "giving back," of sharing results, and of bringing closure if that is required for a project but not to a relationship.
Kia tupato	Be cautious. This suggests that researchers need to be politically astute, culturally safe, and reflective about their insider/outsider status. It is also a caution to insiders and outsiders that in community research, things can come undone without the researcher being aware or being told directly.
Kaua e takahia te mana o te tangata	Do not trample on the "mana" or dignity of a person. This is about informing people and guarding against being paternalistic or impatient because people do not know what the researcher may know. It is also about simple things like the way Westerners use wit, sarcasm, and irony as discursive strategies or where one sits down. For example, Māori people are offended when someone sits on a table designed and used for food.
Kaua e mahaki	Do not flaunt your knowledge. This is about finding ways to share knowledge, to be generous with knowledge without being a "show-off" or being arrogant. Sharing knowledge is about empowering a process, but the community has to empower itself.

day-to-day level of interaction? To be respectful, what else does a researcher need to understand? It is when we ask questions about the apparently universal value of respect that things come undone, because the basic premise of that value is quintessentially Euro-American. What at first appears a simple matter of *respect* can end up as a complicated matter of cultural protocols, languages of respect, rituals of respect, dress codes: in short, the "p's and q's" of etiquette specific to cultural, gender, and class groups and subgroups. *Respect*, like other social values, embraces quite complex social norms, behaviors, and meanings, as one of many competing and active values in any given social situation. As an ethical principle, *respect* is constructed as universal partly through the process of defining what it means in philosophical and moral terms, partly through a process of distancing the social value and practice of *respect* from the messiness of any particular set of social interactions, and partly through a process of wrapping up the principle in a legal and procedural framework. The practice of *respect* in research is interpreted and expressed in very different ways on the basis of methodology, theoretical paradigms, institutional preparation, and individual idiosyncrasies and "manners."

Similarly, the principle and practice of *informed consent* presents real-world problems for researchers and for the researched. Fine, Weis, Weseen, and Wong (2000) already have discussed the ways in which "the consent form sits at the contradictory base of the institutionalisation of research" (p. 113). The form itself can be, as they argue, a "crude tool—a conscience—to remind us of our accountability and position" (p. 113). They argue that a consent form makes the power relations between researchers and researched concrete, and this can present challenges to researchers and researched alike, with some participants *wanting* to share their stories while others may feel *compelled* to share. The form itself can be the basis of dialogue and mediation, but the individual person who is participating in the research still must sign it. The principle of *informed consent* is based on the right of individuals to give consent to participation once they have been informed about the project and believe that they understand the project. In some jurisdictions, this right does not necessarily apply to children, prisoners, or people who have a mental illness. Nevertheless, the right is an individual one. However, what if participating in a research project, unwittingly or wittingly, reveals collective information to researchers—for example, providing DNA, sharing the making of a medicine, or revealing secret women's or men's business as may occur in societies like Aboriginal Australian communities, where men's knowledge and women's knowledge is strictly differentiated? Researching with children already has opened up the possibility that family secrets, especially stories of abuse, require actions to be taken beyond the simple gathering of data. One concern of indigenous communities about the *informed consent* principle is about the bleeding of knowledge away from collective protection through individual participation in research, with knowledge moving to scientists and organizations in the world at large. This process weakens indigenous collectively shared knowledge and is especially risky in an era of knowledge hunting and gathering. Another concern is about the nature of what it really means to be informed for people who may not be literate or well educated, who may not speak the language of the researcher, and who may not be able to differentiate the *invitation* to participate in research from the enforced compliance in signing official forms for welfare and social service agencies.

The claim to universal principles is one of the difficulties with ethical codes of conduct for research. It is not just that the concepts of respect, beneficence, and justice have been defined through Western eyes; there are other principles that inform ethical codes that can be problematic under certain conditions. In some indigenous contexts, the issue is framed more around the concept of *human rights* rather than principles or values. However, whether it is about principles, values, or rights, there is a common underpinning. Ethics codes are for the most part about protecting the individual, not the collective. Individuals can be "picked off" by researchers even when a community signals it does not approve of a project. Similarly, the claim to beneficence, the "save mankind" claim made even before research has been completed, is used to provide a moral imperative that certain forms of research must be supported at the expense of either individual or community consent. Research is often assumed to be beneficial simply because it is framed as research; its benefits are regarded as "self-evident" because the intentions of the researcher are "good." In a review of health research literature reporting on research involving indigenous Australians, I. Anderson, Griew, and McAullay (2003) suggest that very little attention is paid to the concept of benefit by researchers, and even less attention is paid to the assessment of research benefit. A consequence of the lack of guidelines in this area, they argue, is that "in the absence of any other guidelines the values that guide such a judgement will reflect those of the ethics committee as opposed to those of the Indigenous community in which research is proposed" (p. 26).

A more significant difficulty, already alluded to, can be expressed more in terms of "who" governs, regulates, interprets, sanctions, and monitors ethical codes of conduct." "Who" is responsible if things go terribly wrong? And "who" really governs and regulates the behaviors of scientists outside institutions and voluntary professional societies? For example, rogue scientists and quirky religious groups are already competing for the glory of cloning human beings with those whose research is at least held to an acceptable standard because of their employment in recognized institutions. From an indigenous perspective, the "who" on ethical review boards is representative of narrow class, religious, academic, and ethnic groups rather than reflecting the diversity of society. Because these boards are fundamentally supportive of research for advancing knowledge and other high-level aims, their main task is to advance research, not to limit it. In other words, their purpose is not neutral; it is to assist institutions to undertake research—within acceptable standards. These boards are not where larger questions about society's interests in research ought to be discussed; they generally are the place where already determined views about research are processed, primarily to protect institutions. Marginalized and vulnerable groups are not, by and large, represented on such boards. If a marginalized group is represented, its voice is muted as one of many voices of equal weight but not of equal power. Hence, even if a representative of a marginalized group is included on a review board, the individual may not have the support, the knowledge, or the language to debate the issue among those who accept the dominant Western view of ethics and society. These are difficult concerns to resolve but need to be discussed in an ongoing way, as ethical challenges will always exist in societies.

King, Henderson, and Stein (1999) suggest that there are two paradigms of ethics, the one we know as principalist and a potentially new one in process that is about relationships. King, Henderson, and Stein argue that the ethics regulations that researchers currently work under are based on three factors:

- Balancing principles: autonomy, beneficence, justice, informed consent, and confidentiality
- Ethical universalism (not moral relativism): truth (not stories)
- Atomistic focus: small frame, centered on individuals.

In the case of the International Society of Ethnobiology (ISE), a society of scientists whose work involves indigenous communities, the Code of Ethics that was developed with indigenous participation identifies 15 principles upon which ethical conduct rests. These principles include such things as the principles of self-determination, inalienability, traditional guardianship, and active participation. The ISE Code of Ethics suggests that research needs to be built on meaningful partnerships and collaboration with indigenous communities. Similarly, the Australian Institute of Aboriginal and Torres Strait Islander Studies published the *Guidelines for Ethical Research in Indigenous Studies* (2000) after conducting workshops with indigenous studies researchers. The *Guidelines* connect the notion of ethical principles with human rights and seek to "embody the best standards of ethical research and human rights" (p. 4). The *Guidelines* propose three major principles, inside of which are fuller explanations of the principles and practical applications. The three main principles are

- Consultation, negotiation, and mutual understanding
- Respect, recognition, and involvement
- Benefits, outcomes, and agreement.

Within the principles of the *Guidelines* are further subprinciples, such as respect for indigenous knowledge systems and processes, recognition of the diversity and uniqueness of peoples and individuals, and respect for intellectual and cultural property rights and involvement of indigenous individuals and communities as research collaborators.

Principles are balancing factors that still rest upon the assumption that the principles are understood as meaning the same thing to all people under all circumstances.

As Denzin (2003) argues, this approach implies a singular approach to all forms of inquiry that oversimplifies and dehumanizes the human subject. Indigenous communities and other marginalized groups may not understand the history of the ethical code of conduct or its basis in Western moral philosophy, but they do understand breaches of respect and negative impacts from research such as the removal of their rights and lands. Qualitative researchers also know that emerging methodologies and emerging researchers have a difficult time making their way through the review process to gain approval. Kathleen M. Cumiskey (1998) narrates her experiences in dealing with her institutional review board as ones that came down to a reminder that graduate students would not be indemnified if she happened to be arrested or her work subpoenaed. The emphasis on procedural issues, including the balancing of risks and benefits, inhibits or limits the potential for institutions and society to examine ethics against a much broader social and epistemological framework.

What does an indigenous approach to research contribute to a discussion about ethical standards? Indigenous perspectives challenge researchers to reflect upon two significant contributions. In the first instance, indigenous communities share with other marginalized and vulnerable communities a collective and historically sustained experience of research as the Object. They also share the use of a "research as expert" representation of who they are. It is an experience indigenous communities associate with colonialism and racism, with inequality and injustice. More important, indigenous communities hold an alternative way of knowing about themselves and the environment that has managed to survive the assaults of colonization and its impacts. This alternative way of knowing may be different from what was known several hundred years ago by a community, but it is still a way of knowing that provides access to a different epistemology, an alternative vision of society, an alternative ethics for human conduct. It is not, therefore, a question of whether the knowledge is "pure" and authentic but whether it has been the means through which people have made sense of their lives and circumstances, that has sustained them and their cultural practices over time, that forms the basis for their understanding of human conduct, that enriches their creative spirit and fuels their determination to be free. The first contribution of an indigenous perspective to any discussion about research ethics is one that challenges those of us who teach about research ethics, who participate in approving and monitoring ethics proposals, to understand the historical development of research as a corporate, deeply colonial institution that is structurally embedded in society and its institutions. It is not just about training and then policing individual researchers, nor about ensuring that research with human subjects is an ethical activity. One thing we must have learned from the past is that when research subjects are not regarded as human to begin with, when they have been dehumanized, when they have been marginalized from "normal" human society, the human researcher does not see human subjects. To unravel the story of research ethics with human subjects, teachers and students must understand that research ethics is not just a body of historical "hiccups" and their legal solutions. It is a study of how societies, institutions, disciplines, and individuals *authorize, describe, settle, and rule.* It is a study of historical imperialism, racism, and patriarchy and the new formations of these systems in contemporary relations of power. It is a study of how humans fail and succeed at treating each other with respect.

Just as important, the second contribution indigenous research offers is a rich, deep, and diverse resource of alternative ways of knowing and thinking about ethics, research relationships, personal conduct, and researcher integrity. There are other ways to think about ethics that are unique to each culture. There are other ways to guide researcher conduct and ensure the integrity of research and the pursuit of knowledge. In New Zealand, as one example, Māori are discussing ethics in relation to *tikanga*, defined briefly by Mead (2003) as "A body of knowledge and customary practices carried out characteristically by communities" (p. 15). Mead argues that Tikanga has three main aspects, of knowledge, practices, and actors, and that among other things, tikanga provides guidelines about moral and behavioral issues and informs ethical matters. He proposes five "tests" that can be applied to an ethical dilemma from a *tikanga Māori* perspective. These "tests" draw on Māori values to provide a framework for arriving at a Māori position on a specific ethical issue. The "tests" include the following:

- Applying cultural understandings of knowledge (for example applying *mauri*, the view that every living thing has a *mauri or life force*)
- Genealogical stories (such as those that explain how living things were created)
- Precedents in history
- Relationships
- Cultural values (such as the value of looking after people).

Mead suggests that examining an ethical issue against each of the five "tests" provides a framework that enables the dilemma created by new technologies to be thought through in a way that meets cultural and ethical scrutiny while remaining open to new possibilities. It is also a way to build a cultural and community body of knowledge about new discoveries, technologies, and research ethics.

It may be that these and other explorations connect with King, Henderson, and Stein's (1999) conception of a relationships paradigm that includes the following elements:

Layering of relevant relationships—individuals and groups

Context based—what are the relevant contexts? Culture, gender, race/ethnicity, community, place, others

Crosscutting issues, wider frame of reference

Narrative focus

Continuity—issues arise before and continue after projects

Change—in relationships over time

It may also be a way that connects with Denzin's (2003) call for a more inclusive and flexible model that would apply to all forms of inquiry. Also, as suggested by I. Anderson, Griew, and McAullay (2003), there is a tension between the regulations of practice and the development of ethical relationships. They argue that there is a need to develop at least two layers of responsiveness, one involving institutional collaborations with communities and the other involving researcher relationships with communities that are also mediated by reformed research structures. Indigenous research offers access to a range of epistemic alternatives. I would not want to suggest that such ways are simply out there waiting to be discovered, but certainly there are people and communities willing to engage in a meaningful dialogue, and there is much to talk about.

▣ Qualitative Travelers on Tricky Ground

Qualitative research in an age of terrorism, in a time of uncertainty, and in an era when knowledge as power is reinscribed through its value as a commodity in the global market place presents tricky ground for researchers. It is often at the local level of marginalized communities that these complex currents intersect and are experienced as material conditions of poverty, injustice, and oppression. It is also at this level that responses to such currents are created on the ground, for seemingly pragmatic reasons. Sometimes this approach may indeed be a reasonable solution, but at other times it draws into question the taken-for-granted understandings that are being applied to decisions made under pressure. What maps should qualitative researchers study before venturing onto such terrain? This is not a trick question but rather one that suggests that we do have some maps. We can begin with all the maps of qualitative research we currently have, then draw some new maps that enrich and extend the boundaries of our understandings beyond the margins. We need to draw on all our maps of understanding. Even those tired and retired maps of qualitative research may hold important clues such as the origin stories or genealogical beginnings of certain trends and sticking points in qualitative research.

Qualitative researchers, however, must be more than either travelers or cultural tourists. Qualitative research is an important tool for indigenous communities because it is the tool that seems most able to *wage the battle of representation* (Fine et al., 2000); to weave and unravel competing *storylines* (Bishop, 1998); to situate, place, and contextualize; to create spaces for decolonizing (Aldama, 2001; Tierney, 2000); to provide frameworks for hearing silence and listening to the voices of the silenced (LeCompte, 1993; L. T. Smith, 2001); to create spaces for dialogue across difference; to analyze and make sense of complex and shifting experiences, identities, and realities; and to understand little and big changes that affect our lives. Qualitative research approaches have the potential to respond to epistemic challenges and crises, to unravel and weave, to fold in and unmask the layers of the social life and depth of human experience. This is not an argument for reducing qualitative research to social activism, nor is it an argument that suggests that quantitative research cannot also do some of the same things, but rather an argument for the tools, strategies, insights, and expert knowledge that can come with having a focused mind trained on the qualitative experience of people.

Qualitative research has an expanding set of tools that enable finer-grained interpretations of social life. Expanding the understandings and tools of qualitative researchers is important in an era when the diversity of human experience in social groups and communities, with languages and epistemologies, is undergoing profound cultural and political shifts. Although it could be argued that this has always been the case because societies always are dynamic, there is an argument to be made about the rapid loss of languages and cultures, the homogenization of cultures through globalization, and the significance for many communities of the impact of human beings on the environment. Indigenous communities live with the urgency that these challenges present to the world and have sought, through international mobilization, to call attention to these concerns. It is considered a sign of success when the Western world, through one of its institutions, pauses even momentarily to consider an alternative possibility. Indigenous research actively seeks to extend that momentary pause into genuine engagement with indigenous communities and alternative ways of seeking to live with and in the world.

Note

1. For example, in January, 2004, a series of speeches was made in New Zealand by a conservative political leader that attacked the role of the Treaty of Waitangi in legislation, that claimed Māori had extra holiday entitlements, that Māori with academic qualifications had lower standards because of affirmative action entry practices, and that purported to represent a "race free" vision for New Zealand. The speeches were quickly taken up as a populist message even though they were based on information later found to be incorrect and exaggerated and were clearly underpinned by an understanding of race and ethnicity that resonated with the racist messages of Australia's One Nation Leader Pauline Hanson.

References

Aldama, A. J. (2001). *Disrupting savagism: Intersecting Chicana/o, Mexican immigrant, and Native American struggles for self-representation.* Durham, NC: Duke University Press.

Alexander, M. J., & Mohanty, C. T. (1997). *Feminist genealogies, colonial legacies, democratic futures.* New York: Routledge.

Anderson, I., Griew, R., & McAullay, D. (2003). Ethics guidelines, health research and indigenous Australians. *New Zealand Bioethics Journal, 4*(1), 20–29.

Anderson, K. (2000). *A recognition of being: Reconstructing native womanhood.* Toronto: Sumach Press.

Apple, M. (2001). *Educating the "right" way: Markets, standards, God, and inequality.* New York: RoutledgeFalmer.

Ashcroft, B., Griffiths, G., & Tiffin, H. (1989). *The empire writes back: Theory and practice in post-colonial literatures.* London: Routledge.

Australian Institute of Aboriginal and Torres Strait Islander Studies. (2000). *Guidelines for ethical research in indigenous studies.* Canberra: Author.

Basso, K. H. (1996). *Wisdom sits in places: Landscape and language among the Western Apache.* Albuquerque: University of New Mexico Press.

Battiste, M. (Ed.). (2000). *Reclaiming indigenous voice and vision.* Vancouver: University of British Columbia Press.

Beverley, J. (2000). Testimonio, subalternity, and narrative authority. In N. Denzin & Y. S. Lincoln (Eds.), *Handbook of qualitative research* (2nd ed., pp. 555–566). Thousand Oaks: Sage.

Biolsi, T., & Zimmerman, L. J. (Eds.). (1997). *Indians and anthropologists: Vine Deloria and the critique of anthropology.* Tucson: University of Arizona Press.

Bishop, R. (1998). Freeing ourselves from neo-colonial domination in research: A Māori approach to creating knowledge. *Qualitative Studies in Education, 11*(2), 199–219.

Bishop, R., & Glynn, T. (1992). He kanohi kitea: Conducting and evaluating educational research. *New Zealand Journal of Educational Studies, 27*(2), 125–135.

Bishop, R., & Glynn, T. (1999). Researching in Māori contexts: An interpretation of participatory consciousness. *Journal of Intercultural Studies,* 20(2), 167–182.

Brady, W. (1999). Observing the Other. *Eureka Street,* 9(1), 28–30.

Burger, J. (1987). *Report from the frontier: The state of the world's indigenous peoples.* London: Zed Books.

Chow, R. (1993). *Writing diaspora: Tactics of intervention in contemporary cultural studies.* Bloomington: Indiana University Press.

Churchill, W. (1993). I am indigenist. In W. Churchill (Ed.), *Struggle for the land: Indigenous resistance to genocide, ecocide, and expropriation in contemporary North America* (pp. 403–451). Monroe, ME: Common Courage Press.

Cook-Lynn, E. (1996). *Why I can't read Wallace Stegner and other essays: A tribal voice.* Madison: University of Wisconsin Press.

Cram, F. (1993). Ethics in Māori research. In L. Nikora (Ed.), *Cultural justice and ethics.* [Proceedings of the Cultural Justice and Ethics Symposium held as part of the New Zealand Psychological Society's annual conference]. Wellington, New Zealand: Victoria University.

Cram, F. (1997). Developing partnerships in research: Pâkehâ researchers and Māori research. *Sites, 35,* 44–63.

Cram, F. (2001). Rangahau Māori: Tona tika, tona pono—The validity and integrity of Māori research. In M. Tolich (Ed.), *Research ethics in Aotearoa New Zealand* (pp. 35–52). Auckland, New Zealand: Pearson Education.

Cram, F., Keefe, V., Ormsby, C., & Ormsby, W. (1998). Memorywork and Māori health research: Discussion of a qualitative method. *He Pukenga Kôrero: A Journal of Māori Studies,* 37–45.

Cumiskey, K. M. (1998). (De)facing the Institutional Review Board: Wrangling the fear and fantasy of ethical dilemmas and research on "at-risk" youth. In J. Ayala et al. (Eds.), *Speed bumps: Reflections on the politics and methods of qualitative work* (pp. 28–31). New York: State University of New York, Graduate School of Education.

Deloria, V., Jr. (1995). *Red earth, white lies: Native Americans and the myth of scientific fact.* New York: Scribner.

Denzin, N. (1991). *Images of postmodern society: Social theory and contemporary cinema.* Newbury Park, CA: Sage.

Denzin, N., & Lincoln, Y. S. (2000). The discipline and practice of qualitative research. In N. Denzin & Y. S. Lincoln (Eds.), *Handbook of qualitative research* (2nd ed., pp. 128). Thousand Oaks, CA: Sage.

Durie, A. (1992). *Whaia te Ara Tika: Research methodologies and Māori.* Seminar on Māori research at Massey University, Palmerston North, New Zealand.

Eidheim, H. (1997). Ethno-political development among the Sami after World War II: The invention of self-hood. In H. Gaski (Ed.), *Sami culture in a new era: The Norwegian Sami experience* (pp. 29–61). Kárásjohka, Norway: Davvi Girji.

Elabor-Idemudia, P. (2002). Participatory research: A tool in the production of knowledge in development discourse. In K. Saunders (Ed.), *Feminist development and thought: Rethinking modernity, post-colonialism and representation* (pp. 227–242). London: Zed Books.

Fanon, F. (1963). *Wretched of the earth* (C. Farrington, Trans.). New York: Grove Press. (Original work published 1961)

Fine, M., Weis, L., Weseen, S., & Wong, L. (2000). For whom? Qualitative research, representations, and social responsibilities. In N. Denzin & Y. S. Lincoln (Eds.), *Handbook of qualitative research* (2nd ed., pp. 107–132). Thousand Oaks, CA: Sage.

Gaski, H. (Ed.). (1997). *In the shadow of the midnight sun: Contemporary Sami prose and literature.* Kárásjohka, Norway: Davvi Girji.

Green, M. (2000). Lived spaces, shared spaces, public spaces. In L. Weis & M. Fine (Eds.), *Construction sites: Excavating race, class, and gender among urban youth* (pp. 293–304). New York: Teachers College Press.

Haig-Brown, C., & Archibald, J. (1996). Transforming First Nations research with respect and power. *Qualitative Studies in Education, 9*(3), 245–267.

Harjo, J., & Bird, G. (1997). *Reinventing the enemy's language. Contemporary native women's writing of North America.* New York: W. W. Norton and Company.

Helu Thaman, K. (2003). *Re-presenting and re-searching Oceania: A suggestion for synthesis.* Keynote address to the Pacific Health Research Fono, Health Research Council of New Zealand, Auckland.

Hill Colllins, P. (1991). Learning from the outsider within. In M. Fonow & J. A. Cook (Eds.), *Beyond methodology: Feminist scholarship as lived research* (pp. 35–57). Bloomington: Indiana University Press.

Humphery, K. (2000). *Indigenous health and "Western research"* (Discussion paper for VicHealth Koori Health Research and Community Development Unit). Melbourne: Centre for the Study of Health and Society, University of Melbourne.

Humphery, K. (2002). Dirty questions: Indigenous health and "Western research." *Australian and New Zealand Journal of Public Health, 25*(3), 197–202.

Jahnke, H., & Taiapa, J. (1999). Māori research. In C. Davidson & M. Tolich (Eds.), *Social science research in New Zealand: Many paths to understanding* (pp. 39–50). Auckland, New Zealand: Longman Pearson Education.

Johnston, P. M. (2003). Research in a bicultural context: The case in Aotearoa/New Zealand. In J. Swann & J. Pratt (Eds.), *Educational research practice: Making sense of methodology* (pp. 98–110). London: Continuum.

Jordan, S. (2003). Who stole my methodology? Co- opting PAR. *Globalisation, Societies and Education, 1*(2), 185–200.

Kaomea, J. (2003). Reading erasures and making the familiar strange: Defamiliarizing methods for research in formerly colonized and historically oppressed communities. *Educational Researcher, 32*(2), 14–25.

Kelsey, J. (1995). *The New Zealand experiment.* Auckland, New Zealand: Auckland University Press.

Keskitalo, J. H. (1997). Sami post-secondary education—Ideals and realities. In H. Gaski (Ed.), *Sami culture in a new era: The Norwegian Sami experience* (pp. 155–171). Kárásjohka, Norway: Davvi Girji.

King, N., Henderson, G. E., & Stein, J. E. (1999). *Beyond regulations. Ethics in human subjects research.* Chapel Hill: University of North Carolina Press.

Ladson-Billings, G. (2000). Racialized discourses and ethnic epistemologies. In N. K. Denzin & Y. S. Lincoln (Eds.), *Handbook of qualitative research* (2nd ed., pp. 257–278). Thousand Oaks, CA: Sage.

Langton, M. (1981). Anthropologists must change. *Identity, 4*(4), 11.

The Latina Feminist Group. (2001). *Telling to live: Latina feminist testimonios.* Durham, NC: Duke University Press.

LeCompte, M. (1993). A framework for hearing silence: What does telling stories mean when we are supposed to be doing science? In D. McLaughlin & W. G. Tierney (Eds.), *Naming silenced lives* (pp. 9–28). New York: Routledge.

Lincoln, Y. S. (1993). I and thou: Method, voice, and roles in research with the silenced. In D. McLaughlin & W. G. Tierney (Eds.), *Naming silenced lives* (pp. 29–50). New York: Routledge.

Little Bear, L. (2000). Jagged worldviews colliding. In M. Battiste (Ed.), *Reclaiming indigenous voice and vision* (pp. 77–85). Vancouver: University of British Columbia Press.

Maracle, L. (1996). *I am woman: A native perspective on sociology and feminism.* Vancouver: Press Gang Publishers.

Marker, M. (2003). Indigenous voice, community, and epistemic violence: The ethnographer's "interests" and what "interests" the ethnographer. *Qualitative Studies in Education, 16*(3), 361–375.

McLaren, P. (1993). Border disputes: Multicultural narrative, identity formation, and critical pedagogy in postmodern America. In D. McLaughlin & W. G. Tierney (Eds.), *Naming silenced lives* (pp. 201–236). New York: Routledge.

Mead, H. M. (2003). *Tikanga Māori: Living by Māori values.* Wellington, New Zealand: Huia Publications and Te Whare Wananga o Awanuiarangi Press.

Memmi, A. (1967). *The colonizer and the colonized.* Boston: Beacon Press. (Original work published 1957)

Menzies, C. (2001). Researching with, for and among indigenous peoples. *Canadian Journal of Native Education, 25*(1), 19–36.

Mies, M. (1983). Towards a methodology for feminist research. In G. Bowles & R. D. Klein (Eds.), *Theories of women's studies* (pp. 117–139). New York: Routledge.

Minh-ha, T. T. (1989). *Woman, native, other: Writing, postcoloniality and feminism.* Bloomington: Indiana University Press.

Mohanty, C. (1984). Under Western eyes: Feminist scholarship and colonial discourses. *Boundary, 12*(3) and *13*(1), 338–358.

Moraga, C., & Anzaldúa, G. (Eds.). (1983). *This bridge called my back.* New York: Kitchen Table Press.

Moran, W. (1999). Democracy and geography in the reregulation of New Zealand. In D. B. Knight & A. E. Joseph (Eds.), *Restructuring societies: Insights from the social sciences* (pp. 33–58). Ottawa: Carleton University Press.

Moreton-Robinson, A. (2000). *Talkin' up to the white woman: Indigenous women and feminism.* St. Lucia: University of Queensland Press.

Ngugi Wa Thiong'o. (1997). *Writers in politics: A re-engagement with issues of literature and society.* Oxford, UK: James Currey. (Original work published 1981)

Peters, M. A. (2003). Classical political economy and the role of universities in the new knowledge economy. *Globalization, Societies and Education, 1*(2), 153–168.

Pidgeon, M., & Hardy, C. (2002). Researching with Aboriginal peoples: Practices and principles. *Canadian Journal of Native Education, 26*(2), 96–106.

Pihama, L. (1993). *Tungia te ururua kia tupu whakarirorito te tupu o te harakeke.* Unpublished master's thesis, University of Auckland.

Pihama, L. (1994). Are films dangerous?: A Māori woman's perspective on *The Piano. Hecate, 20*(2), 239–242.

Pihama, L. (2001). *Tihei Mauriora: Honouring our voices—mana wahine as a kaupapa Māori theoretical framework.* Unpublished doctoral thesis, University of Auckland.

Pihama, L., Cram, F., & Walker, S. (2002). Creating methodological space: A literature review of Kaupapa Māori research. *Canadian Journal of Native Education, 26*(1), 30–43.

Pritchard, S. (Ed.). (1998). *Indigenous peoples, the United Nations and human rights.* London: Zed Books.

Reinharz, S. (1992). *Feminist methods in social research.* New York: Oxford University Press.

Rigney, L. (1999). Internationalization of an indigenous anticolonial cultural critique of research methodologies. A guide to indigenist research methodology and its principles. *Wicazo SA Journal of Native American Studies Review, 14*(2), 109–121.

Roman, L. G., & Eyre, L. (1997). *Dangerous territories: Struggles for difference and equality in education.* New York: Routledge.

Said, E. (1978). *Orientalism.* London: Vintage Books.

Saunders, K. (Ed.). (2002). *Feminist development and thought: Rethinking modernity, post-colonialism and representation.* London. Zed Books.

Sedgwick, E. K. (1991). *Epistemology of the closet.* New York: Harvester Wheatsheaf.

Shiva, V. (1993). *Monocultures of the mind.* London: Zed Books.

Simon, J., & Smith, L. T. (Eds.). (2001). *A civilising mission? Perceptions and representations of the New Zealand Native Schools system.* Auckland, New Zealand: Auckland University Press.

Smith, G. H. (1990).The politics of reforming Māori education: The transforming potential of kura kaupapa Māori. In H. Lauder & C. Wylie (Eds.), *Towards successful schooling* (pp. 73–89). Basingstoke: Falmer.

Smith, G. H. (1992). *Research issues related to Māori education.* Auckland, New Zealand: Research Unit for Māori Education, The University of Auckland.

Smith, G. H. (1994). For sale: Indigenous language, knowledge and culture. *Polemic: A Journal of the University of Sydney Law School, 4*(3).

Smith, L. T. (1991). Te rapunga i te ao marama (the search for the world of light): Māori perspectives on research in education. In T. Linzey & J. Morss (Eds.), *Growing up: The politics of human learning* (pp. 46–55). Auckland, New Zealand: Longman Paul.

Smith, L. T. (1992). Māori women: Discourses, projects and mana wahine. In S. Middleton & A. Jones (Eds.), *Women and education in Aotearoa 2* (pp. 33–51). Wellington, New Zealand Bridget Williams Books.

Smith, L. T. (1999). *Decolonizing methodologies: Research and indigenous peoples.* London: Zed Books.

Smith, L. T. (2000). Kaupapa Māori research. In M. Battiste (Ed.), *Reclaiming indigenous voice and vision* (pp. 225–247). Vancouver: University of British Columbia Press.

Smith, L. T. (2001). Troubling spaces. *Journal of Critical Psychology, 4,* 175–182.

Smith, L. T., Smith, G. H., Boler, M., Kempton, M., Ormond, A., Chueh, H. C., et al. (2002). "Do you guys hate Aucklanders too?" Youth: Voicing difference from the rural heartland. *Journal of Rural Studies, 18,* 169–178.

Spivak, G. (1987). *In other worlds: Essays in cultural politics.* New York: Methuen.

Stanley, L., & Wise, S. (1983). *Breaking out: Feminist consciousness and feminist research.* London: Routledge & Kegan Paul.

Steinhauer, E. (2003). Thoughts on an indigenous research methodology. *Canadian Journal of Native Education, 26*(2), 69–81.

Stewart, T. A. (1997). *Intellectual capital: The new wealth of organizations.* New York. Doubleday/Currency.

Stewart-Harawira, M. (1999, October). Neo-imperialism and the (mis)appropriation of indigenousness. *Pacific World, 54,* pp. 10–15.

Te Awekotuku, N. (1991). *Mana wahine Māori.* Auckland, New Zealand: New Women's Press.

Te Awekotuku, N. (1999). Māori women and research: Researching ourselves. In *Māori psychology: Research and practice* (pp. 57–63) [Proceedings of a symposium sponsored by the Māori and Psychology Research Unit, University of Waikato]. Hamilton, New Zealand: University of Waikato.

Te Hennepe, S. (1993). Issues of respect: Reflections of First Nations students' experiences in post- secondary anthropology classrooms. *Canadian Journal of Native Education, 20,* 193–260.

Thomas, G. (2001). The value of scientific engineering training for Indian communities. In K. James (Ed.), *Science and Native American communities* (pp. 149–154). Lincoln: University of Nebraska Press.

Thompson, P. (1978). *The voices of the past.* London: Oxford University Press.

Tierney, W. G. (2000). Undaunted courage: Life history and the postmodern challenge. In N. K. Denzin & Y. S. Lincoln (Eds.), *Handbook of qualitative research* (2nd ed., pp. 537–554). Thousand Oaks, CA: Sage.

Tomlins-Jahnke, H. (1997). Towards a theory of mana wahine. *He Pukenga Kôrero: A Journal of Māori Studies, 3*(1), 27–36.

Trask, H.-K. (1986). *Eros and power: The promise of feminist theory.* Philadelphia: University of Pennsylvania Press.

Trask, H.-K. (1993). *From a native daughter: Colonialism and sovereignty in Hawai'i.* Monroe, ME: Common Courage Press.

Vidich, A. J., & Lyman, S. M. (2000). Qualitative methods: Their history in sociology and anthropology. In N. K. Denzin & Y. S. Lincoln (Eds.), *Handbook of qualitative research* (pp. 37–84). Thousand Oaks, CA: Sage.

Warrior, R. A. (1995). *Tribal secrets: Recovering American Indian intellectual traditions.* Minneapolis: University of Minnesota Press.

Wilmer, F. (1993). *The indigenous voice in world politics.* Newbury Park, CA: Sage.

Womack, C. S. (1999). *Red on red: Native American literary separatism.* Minneapolis: University of Minnesota Press.

Worby, G., & Rigney, D. (2002). Approaching ethical issues: Institutional management of indigenous research. *Australian Universities Review, 45*(1), 24–33.

5

FREEING OURSELVES FROM NEOCOLONIAL DOMINATION IN RESEARCH

A Kaupapa Māori Approach to Creating Knowledge[1]

Russell Bishop

One of the challenges for Māori researchers . . . has been to retrieve some space—first, some space to convince Māori people of the value of research for Māori; second, to convince the various, fragmented but powerful research communities of the need for greater Māori involvement in research; and third, to develop approaches and ways of carrying out research which take into account, without being limited by, the legacies of previous research, and the parameters of both previous and current approaches. What is now referred to as Kaupapa Māori approaches

Author's Note. I am very grateful to Lous Heshusius, Norman Denzin, and Donna Deyhle for their careful consideration of earlier drafts of this chapter. I am also grateful to Susan Sandretto for her thoughtful assistance in preparing this chapter. To those of my family and friends who have worked on this and other research projects over the years, I want to express my gratitude. Ma te Runga Rawa koutou, e tiaki, e manaaki.

to research . . . is an attempt to retrieve that space and to achieve those general aims.

—L. T. Smith (1999, p. 183)

This chapter seeks to identify how issues of power, including initiation, benefits, representation, legitimation, and accountability, are addressed in practice within an indigenous Kaupapa Māori approach in such a way as to promote the self-determination of the research participants. In addition, this chapter questions how such considerations may affect Western-trained and -positioned researchers.

Māori people, along with many other minoritized peoples, are concerned that educational researchers have been slow to acknowledge the importance of culture and cultural differences as key components in successful research practice and understandings. As a result, key research issues of power relations, initiation, benefits, representation, legitimization, and accountability continue to be addressed in terms of the researchers' own cultural agendas, concerns, and interests. This chapter seeks to identify how such domination can be addressed by both Māori and non-Māori educational researchers through their conscious participation within the cultural aspirations, preferences, and practices of the research participants.

It is important to position this chapter within the growing body of literature that questions traditional approaches to researching on/for/with minoritized peoples by placing the culture of "an ethnic group at the center of the inquiry" (Tillman, 2002, p. 4). Notable among these authors are Frances Rains, Jo-Ann Archibald, and Donna Deyhle (2000), who, in editing and introducing a special edition of the *International Journal of Qualitative Studies in Education* (*QSE*) titled *Through Our Eyes and in Our Own Words—The Voices of Indigenous Scholars*, featured examples of "American-Indian/Native American intellectualism, culture, culture-based curriculum, and indigenous epistemologies and paradigms" (Tillman, 2002, p. 5). K. Tsianina Lomawaima's (2000) analysis of the history of power struggles between academic researchers and those whom they study identified how the history of scholarly research (including education) in Native America "has been deeply implicated in the larger history of the domination and oppression of Native American communities" (p. 14). On a positive note, however, she identified how the development of new research protocols by various tribes shows the way toward more respectful and responsible scholarship. Similarly, Verna Kirkness, Carl Urion, and Jo-Anne Archibald in Canada and their work with the *Canadian Journal of Native Education* have brought issues of researching with respect to the fore. In addition, Donna Deyhle and Karen Swisher (1997) have examined the growth of self-determination approaches among indigenous peoples of North America. Others involved in such scholarship include African American scholars (Ladson-Billings, 1995, 2000; Stanfield, 1994; Tillman, 2002) and Chicana and Chicano scholars (González, 2001; Moll, 1992; Reyes, Scribner, & Scribner, 1999; Villegas &

Lucas, 2002) who are calling for greater attention to power relations and the role of culture in the research process.

While drawing on the work of these scholars and others to illustrate some of the arguments in this chapter, however, this discussion of culturally responsive research will focus on Māori people's experiences of research as an example of the wider argument.

Māori People's Concerns About Research: Issues of Power

Despite the guarantees of the Treaty of Waitangi,[2] the colonization of Aotearoa/New Zealand and the subsequent neocolonial dominance of majority interests in social and educational research have continued. The result has been the development of a tradition of research[3] into Māori people's lives that addresses concerns and interests of the predominantly non-Māori researchers' own making, as defined and made accountable in terms of the researchers' own cultural worldview(s).

Researchers in Aotearoa/New Zealand have developed a tradition of research that has perpetuated colonial power imbalances, thereby undervaluing and belittling Māori knowledge and learning practices and processes in order to enhance those of the colonizers and adherents of colonial paradigms. A social pathology research approach has developed in Aotearoa/New Zealand that has become implied in all phases of the research process: the "inability" of Māori culture to cope with human problems and propositions that Māori culture was and is inferior to that of the colonizers in human terms. Furthermore, such practices have perpetuated an ideology of cultural superiority that precludes the development of power-sharing processes and the legitimization of diverse cultural epistemologies and cosmologies.

Furthermore, traditional research has misrepresented Māori understandings and ways of knowing by simplifying, conglomerating, and commodifying Māori knowledge for "consumption" by the colonizers. These processes have consequently misrepresented Māori experiences, thereby denying Māori authenticity and voice. Such research has displaced Māori lived experiences and the meanings that these experiences have with the "authoritative" voice of the methodological "expert," appropriating Māori lived experience in terms defined and determined by the "expert." Moreover, many misconstrued Māori cultural practices and meanings are now part of our everyday myths of Aotearoa/New Zealand, believed by Māori and non-Māori alike, and traditional social and educational research has contributed to this situation. As a result, Māori people are deeply concerned about the issue of to whom researchers are accountable. Who has control over the initiation, procedures, evaluations, construction, and distribution of newly defined knowledge? Analyses by myself (Bishop, 1996, 1998b) and Linda Tuhiwai Smith (1999) have concluded that control over legitimization and representation is maintained within the domain of the colonial and neocolonial paradigms and that locales of initiation and accountability are situated within Western cultural frameworks, thus precluding Māori cultural forms and processes of initiation and accountability.

Traditional research epistemologies have developed methods of initiating research and accessing research participants that are located within the cultural preferences and practices of the Western world, as opposed to the cultural preferences and practices of Māori people themselves. For example, the preoccupation with neutrality, objectivity, and distance by educational researchers has emphasized these concepts as criteria for authority, representation, and accountability and, thus, has distanced Māori people from participation in the construction, validation, and legitimization of knowledge. As a result, Māori people are increasingly becoming concerned about who will directly gain from the research. Traditionally, research has established an approach in which the research has served to advance the interests, concerns, and methods of the researcher and to locate the benefits of the research at least in part with the researcher, other benefits being of lesser concern.

Table 5.1 summarizes these concerns, noting that this analysis of Māori people's concerns about research reveals five crises that affect indigenous peoples.

▣ Insiders/Outsiders: Who Can Conduct Research in Indigenous Settings?

The concerns about initiation, benefits, representation, legitimacy, and accountability raise a number of questions about how research with Māori and indigenous peoples should be conducted, but perhaps initially it is important to consider by whom that research should be conducted.

One answer to this question might well be to take an essentializing position and suggest that cultural "insiders" might well undertake research in a more sensitive and responsive manner than "outsiders." As Merriam et al. (2001) suggest, it has "commonly been assumed that being an insider means easy access, the ability to ask more meaningful questions and read non-verbal cues, and most importantly be able to project a more truthful, authentic understanding of the culture under study" (p. 411). On the other hand, of course, there are concerns that insiders are inherently biased, or that they are too close to the culture to ask critical questions.

Whatever the case, such understandings assume a homogeneity that is far from the reality of the diversity and complexity that characterizes indigenous peoples' lives and that ignores the impacts that age, class, gender, education, and color, among other variables, might have upon the research relationship. Such understandings might arise even among researchers who might consider themselves to be "insiders." A number of studies by researchers who had initially considered themselves to be "insiders" (Brayboy & Deyhle, 2000; Johnson-Bailey, 1999; Merriam et al., 2001; L. T. Smith, 1999) attest to this problem. Further, as Linda Tuhiwai Smith (1999) argues, even Western-trained indigenous researchers who are intimately involved with community members

Table 5.1. Māori People's Concerns About Research Focuses on the Locus of Power Over Issues of Initiation, Benefits, Representation, Legitimacy, and Accountability Being With the Researcher

Initiation	This concern focuses on how the research process begins and whose concerns, interests, and methods of approach determine/define the outcomes. Traditional research has developed methods of initiating research and accessing research participants that are located within the cultural concerns, preferences, and practices of the Western world.
Benefits	The question of benefits concerns who will directly gain from the research, and whether anyone actually will be disadvantaged. Māori people are increasingly becoming concerned about this important political aspect because traditional research has established an approach to research in which the benefits of the research serve to advance the interests, concerns, and methods of the researcher and that locates the benefits of the research at least in part with the researcher, others being of lesser concern.
Representation	Whose research constitutes an adequate depiction of social reality? Traditional research has misrepresented, that is, simplified/conglomerated and commodified, Māori knowledge for "consumption" by the colonizers and denied the authenticity of Māori experiences and voice. Such research has displaced Māori lived experiences with the "authoritative" voice of the "expert" voiced in terms defined/determined by the "expert." Furthermore, many misconstrued Māori cultural practices and meanings are now part of our everyday myths of Aotearoa/New Zealand, believed by Māori and non-Māori alike.
Legitimacy	This issue concerns what authority we claim for our texts. Traditional research has undervalued and belittled Māori knowledge and learning practices and processes in order to enhance those of the colonizers, and adherents of neocolonial paradigms. Such research has developed a social pathology research approach that has focused on the "inability" of Māori culture to cope with human problems, and it has proposed that Māori culture was inferior to that of the colonizers in human terms. Such practices have perpetuated an ideology of cultural superiority that precludes the development of power-sharing processes and the legitimation of diverse cultural epistemologies and cosmologies.
Accountability	This concern questions researchers' accountability. Who has control over the initiation, procedures, evaluations, text constructions, and distribution of newly defined knowledge? Traditional research has claimed that all people have an inalienable right to utilize all knowledge and has maintained that research findings be expressed in term of criteria located within the epistemological framework of traditional research, thus creating locales of accountability that are situated within Western cultural frameworks.

typically will employ research techniques and methodologies that will likely marginalize the communities' contribution to the investigation. This suggests that indigenous researchers will not automatically conduct research in a culturally appropriate manner even when researching their own communities.

However, as Native American scholar Karen Swisher (1998) argues, the dilemma remains, for despite developments in research that attempt to listen to the voices and the stories of the people under study and present them in ways "to encourage readers to see through a different lens . . . much research still is presented from an outsider's perspective" (p. 191). Nevertheless, despite the problems that indigenous researchers might well face, she argues that American Indian scholars need to become involved in leading research rather than being the subjects or consumers of research. She suggests that this involvement will assist in keeping control over the research in the hands of those involved. She cites (among other sources) a 1989 report of regional dialogues, *Our Voices, Our Vision: American Indians Speak Out for Educational Excellence*, as an example of research that addressed the self-determination of the people involved because from the "conception of the dialogue format to formulation of data and publication, Indian people were in charge of and guided the project; and the voices and concerns of the people were clearly evident" (p. 192).

Swisher (1998) argues that what is missing from the plethora of books, journals, and articles produced by non-Indians about Indians is "the passion from within and the authority to ask new and different questions based on histories and experiences as indigenous people" (p. 193). Furthermore, she argues that the difference involves more than just diverse ways of knowing; it concerns "knowing that what we think is grounded in principles of sovereignty and self-determination; and that it has credibility" (p. 193). In this way, Swisher is clear that "Indian people also believe that they have the answers for improving Indian education and feel they must speak for themselves" (p. 192). If we were to extrapolate this argument to other indigenous settings, we could see this as a call for the power of definition over issues of research, with initiation, benefits, representation, legitimation, and accountability being with indigenous peoples. Swisher identifies an attitude of "we can and must do it ourselves," yet it is also clear that nonindigenous people must help, but not in the impositional ways of the past. Of course, this raises the question of just what are the new positions on offer to nonindigenous researchers—and to indigenous researchers, for that matter.

Tillman (2002), when considering who should conduct research in African American communities, suggests that it is not simply a matter of saying that the researcher must be African American, but "[r]ather it is important to consider whether the researcher has the cultural knowledge to accurately interpret and validate the experiences of African-Americans within the context of the phenomenon under study" (p. 4). Margie Maaka, at the 2003 joint conference of the New Zealand Association for Research in Education and Australian Association for Research in Education, extended this understanding of where nonindigenous peoples should be positioned by stating that Māori must be in control of the research agenda and must be the ones who set the parameters; however, others can participate at the invitation of the indigenous people. In other words, it is Māori research by Māori, for Māori with the help of invited others.

For native scholars, Jacobs-Huey (2002) and L. T. Smith (1999) emphasize the power of critical reflexivity. The former states that "critical reflexivity in both writing and identification as a native researcher may act to resist charges of having played the 'native card' via a non-critical privileging of one's insider status" (Jacobs-Huey, 2002, p. 799). Smith emphasizes that "at a general level insider researchers have to have ways of thinking critically about their processes, their relationships and the quality and richness of their data and analysis. So too do outsiders . . ." (Smith, 1999, p. 137).

Researchers such as Narayan (1993), Griffiths (1998), and Bridges (2001) explain that it is no longer useful to think of researchers as insiders or outsiders; instead, researchers might be positioned "in terms of shifting identifications amid a field of interpenetrating communities and power relations" (Narayan, 1993, p. 671). Narayan proposes that instead of trying to define insider or outsider status,

> what we must focus our attention on is the quality of relations with the people we seek to represent in our texts: are they viewed as mere fodder for professionally self-serving statements about a generalized Other, or are they accepted as subjects with voices, views, and dilemmas—people to whom we are bonded through ties of reciprocity . . . ? (1993, p. 672)

This chapter suggests how these concerns and aspirations might be met by invoking a discursive repositioning of all researchers into those positions that operationalize self-determination for indigenous peoples.

Kaupapa[4] Māori Research

Out of the discontent with traditional research and its disruption of Māori life, an indigenous approach to research has emerged in Aotearoa/New Zealand. This approach, termed *Kaupapa Māori research*, is challenging the dominance of the Pâkehâ worldview in research. Kaupapa Māori research emerged from within the wider ethnic revitalization movement that developed in New Zealand following the rapid Māori urbanization of the post–World War II period. This revitalization movement blossomed in the 1970s and 1980s with the intensifying of a political consciousness among Māori communities. More recently, in the late 1980s and the early 1990s, this consciousness has featured the revitalization of Māori cultural aspirations, preferences, and practices as a philosophical and productive educational stance, along with a resistance to the hegemony[5] of the dominant discourse.[6] In effect, therefore, Kaupapa Māori presupposes positions that are committed to a critical analysis of the existing unequal power relations within the wider New Zealand society that were created with the signing of the Treaty of Waitangi in 1840, those structures that work to oppress Māori people. These include rejection of hegemonic, belittling "Māori can't cope" discourses, together with a commitment to the power of conscientization and politicization through struggle for wider community and social freedoms (G. H. Smith, 1997).

A number of significant dimensions to Kaupapa Māori research serve to set it apart from traditional research. One main focus of a Kaupapa Māori approach to research is the operationalization of self-determination (*tino rangatiratanga*) by Māori people (Bishop, 1996; Durie, 1994, 1995,1998; Pihama, Cram, & Walker, 2002; G. H. Smith, 1997; L. T. Smith, 1999). Self-determination in Durie's (1995) terms "captures a sense of Māori ownership and active control over the future" (p. 16). Such a position is consistent with the Treaty of Waitangi, in which Māori people are able "to determine their own policies, to actively participate in the development and interpretation of the law, to assume responsibility for their own affairs and to plan for the needs of future generations" (Durie, 1995, p. 16). In addition, the promotion of self-determination has benefits beyond these aspects. A 10-year study of Māori households conducted by Durie (1998) shows that the development of a secure identity offers Māori people advantages that may

> afford some protection against poor health; it is more likely to be associated with active educational participation and with positive employment profiles. The corollary is that reduced access to the Māori resources, and the wider Māori world, may be associated with cultural, social and economic disadvantage. (pp. 58–59)

Such an approach challenges the locus of power and control over the research issues of initiation, benefits, representation, legitimation, and accountability as outlined above, being located in another cultural frame of reference/worldview. Kaupapa Māori is, therefore, challenging the dominance of traditional, individualistic research that primarily, at least in its present form, benefits the researchers and their agenda. In contrast, Kaupapa Māori research is collectivistic and is oriented toward benefiting all the research participants and their collectively determined agendas, defining and acknowledging Māori aspirations for research, while developing and implementing Māori theoretical and methodological preferences and practices for research.

Kaupapa Māori is a discourse that has emerged from and is legitimized from within the Māori community. Māori educationalist Graham Hingangaroa Smith (1992) describes Kaupapa Māori as "the philosophy and practice of being and acting Māori" (p. 1). It assumes the taken-for-granted social, political, historical, intellectual, and cultural legitimacy of Māori people, in that it is an orientation in which "Māori language, culture, knowledge and values are accepted in their own right" (p. 13). Linda Tuhiwai Smith (1999), another leading Māori exponent of this approach, argues that such naming provides a means whereby communities of the researched and the researchers can "engage in a dialogue about setting directions for the priorities, policies, and practices of research for, by, and with Māori" (p. 183).

One fundamental understanding of a Kaupapa Māori approach to research is that it is the discursive practice that is Kaupapa Māori that positions researchers in such a way as to operationalize self-determination in terms of agentic positioning and behavior for research participants. This understanding challenges the essentializing dichotomization of the insider/outsider debate by offering a discursive position for researchers, irrespective of ethnicity. This positioning occurs because the cultural aspirations, understandings, and practices of Māori people are used both literally and figuratively to implement and organize the research process. Furthermore, the associated research issues of initiation, benefits, representation, legitimization, and accountability are addressed and understood in practice by practitioners of Kaupapa Māori research within the cultural context of the research participants.

Such understandings challenge traditional ways of defining, accessing, and constructing knowledge about indigenous peoples and the process of self-critique, sometimes termed "paradigm shifting," that is used by Western scholars as a means of "cleansing" thought and attaining what becomes their version of the "truth." Indigenous peoples are challenging this process because it maintains control over the research agenda within the cultural domain of the researchers or their institutions.

A Kaupapa Māori position is predicated on the understanding that Māori means of accessing, defining, and protecting knowledge existed before European arrival in New Zealand. Such Māori cultural processes were protected by the Treaty of Waitangi then subsequently marginalized; however, they have always been legitimate within Māori cultural discourses. As with other Kaupapa Māori initiatives in education, health, and welfare, Kaupapa Māori research practice is, as Irwin (1994) explains, epistemologically based within Māori cultural specificities, preferences, and practices.[7] In Olssen' s (1993) terms, Māori initiatives are "epistemologically productive where in constructing a vision of the world and positioning people in relation to its classifications, it takes its shape from its interrelations with an infinitely proliferating series of other elements within a particular social field" (p. 4).

However, this is not to suggest that such an analysis promotes an essentialist view of Māori in which all Māori must act in prescribed ways, for Māori are just as diverse a people as any other. One of the main outcomes of Durie's (1998) longitudinal study of Māori families, Te Hoe Nuku Roa, is the identification of this very diversity within Māori peoples. To Pihama et al. (2002), this means that Kaupapa Māori analysis must take this diversity of Māori peoples into account. They argue that Kaupapa Māori analysis is for all Māori, "not for select groups or individuals. Kaupapa Māori is not owned by any group, nor can it be defined in ways that deny Māori people access to its articulation" (p. 8). In other words, Kaupapa Māori analysis must benefit Māori people in principle and in practice in such a way that the current realities of marginalization and the heritage of colonialism and neocolonialism are addressed.

Examples of Culturally Responsive Research Practices

This analysis is based on a number of studies conducted by the author using Kaupapa Māori research. The first study, *Collaborative Research Stories: Whakawhanaungatanga*

(1996; also see Bishop, 1998b), was a collaborative meta-study of five projects that addressed Māori agendas in research in order to ascertain the ways in which a group of researchers were addressing Māori people's concerns about research and what the researchers' experiences of these projects meant to them individually. The experiences of the various researchers and their understandings of their experiences were investigated by co-constructing collaborative research stories. The objective was to engage in a process of critical reflection and build a discourse based on the formal and informal meetings that were part of each of the projects in order to connect epistemological questions to indigenous ways of knowing by way of descriptions of actual research projects. The meta-study examined how a group of researchers addressed the importance of devolving power and control in the research exercise in order to promote *tino Rangatiratanga* of Māori people—that is, to act as educational professionals in ways consistent with Article Two of the Treaty of Waitangi.[8] I talked with other researchers who had accepted the challenge of being repositioned by and within the discursive practice that is Kaupapa Māori.

The meta-study in effect sought to investigate my own position as a researcher within a conjoint reflection on shared experiences and conjoint construction of meanings about these experiences, a position where the stories of the other research participants merged with my own to create new stories. Such *collaborative stories* go beyond an approach that simply focuses on the cooperative sharing of experiences and focuses on connectedness, engagement, and involvement with the other research participants within the cultural worldview/discursive practice within which they function. This study sought to identify what constitutes this engagement and what implications this constitution has for promoting self-determination/agency/voice in the research participants by examining concepts of *participatory and cultural consciousness* and *connectedness* within Māori discursive practice.

The second study, *Te Toi Huarewa: Teaching and Learning in Total Immersion Māori Language Educational Settings* (Bishop, Berryman, & Richardson, 2002), sought to identify effective teaching and learning strategies, effective teaching and learning materials, and the ways in which teachers assess and monitor the effectiveness of their teaching in Māori-medium reading and writing programs for students aged 5 to 9 years. Following a period of establishing relationships and developing a joint agenda for the research to identify what effective teachers do in their classrooms and why they teach in a particular manner, the researchers sought to operationalize Kaupapa Māori concerns that the self-determination of the research participants over issues of representation and legitimation be paramount. The strategy consisted of conducting interviews and directed observations, followed by facilitated teacher reflections on what had been observed by using stimulated recall interviews (Calderhead, 1981). The stimulated recall interviews that followed the observation sessions focused on specific interactions observed in the classrooms. In the stimulated recall interviews, the teachers were encouraged to reflect upon what had been observed and to bring their own sense-making processes to the discussions in order to co-construct a "rich" descriptive picture of their classroom practices. In other words, they were encouraged to reflect upon and explain why they did what they did, in their own terms. Through the use of this process, they explained for us that they all placed the culture of the child at the center of learning relationships by developing in their classrooms what we later termed (after Gay, 2000; Villegas & Lucas, 2002) a *culturally appropriate and responsive context for learning.*

The third study, *Te Kotahitanga: The Experiences of Year 9 and 10 Māori Students in Mainstream Classrooms* (Bishop, Berryman, & Richardson, 2003), is a work-in-progress, a research/professional development project that is now entering its third phase of implementation in 12 schools with some 360 teachers. The project commenced in 2001, seeking to address the self-determination of Māori secondary school students by talking with them and other participants in their education about just what is involved in limiting and/or improving their educational achievement. The project commenced with the gathering of a number of narratives of students' classroom experience from a range of engaged and non-engaged Māori students (as defined by their schools), in five non–structurally modified mainstream secondary schools using the process of collaborative storying. This approach is very similar to that termed *testimonio*, in that it is the intention of the direct narrator (research participant) to use an interlocutor (the researcher) to bring their situation to the attention of an audience "to which he or she would normally not have access because of their very condition of subalternity to which the *testimonio* bears witness" (Beverley, 2000, p. 556). In this research project, the students were able to share their narratives about their experiences of schooling, so that teachers who otherwise might not have had access to the narratives could reflect upon them in terms of their own experiences and understandings.

It was from these amazing stories that the rest of this project developed. In their narratives, the students clearly identified the main influences on their educational achievement by articulating the impacts and consequences of their living in a marginalized space. That is, they explained how they were perceived in pathological terms by their teachers and how this perception has had negative effects on their lives. In addition, the students told the research team how teachers, in changing how they related to and interacted with Māori students in their classrooms, could create a context for learning wherein Māori students' educational achievement could improve, again by placing the self-determination of Māori students at the center of classroom relationships.

Such an approach is consistent with Ryan (1999), who suggests that a solution to the one-sidedness of representations that are promoted by the dominance of the powerful—in this case, pathologizing discourses—is to portray events as was done in the collaborative stories of the Māori students, in terms of "competing discourses rather than as simply the projection of inappropriate images" (p. 187). He suggests that this approach, rather than seeking the truth or "real pictures," allows for previously marginalized discourses "to emerge and compete on equal terms with previously dominant discourses" (p. 187).

On the basis of the suggestions from Year 9 and Year 10 (ages 14–16) Māori students, the research team developed an "Effective Teaching Profile." Together with other information from narratives of experiences from those parenting the students, from their principals and their teachers, and from the literature, this Effective Teaching Profile has formed the basis of a professional development program that, when implemented with a group of teachers in four schools, was associated with improved learning, behavior, and attendance outcomes for Māori students in the classrooms of those teachers who had been able to participate fully in the professional development program (Bishop, Berryman, et al., 2003).

▣ Addressing Issues of Self-Determination

Western approaches to operationalizing self-determination (agentic positioning and behavior) in others are, according to Noddings (1986) and B. Davies (1990), best addressed by those who position themselves within empowering relationships. Authors such as Oakley (1981), Tripp (1983), Burgess (1984), Lather (1986, 1991), Patton (1990), Delamont (1992), Eisner (1991), Reinharz (1992), and Sprague and Hayes (2000) suggest that an "empowering" relationship could be attained by developing what could be termed an "enhanced research relationship," in which there occurs a long-term development of mutual purpose and intent between the researcher and the researched. To facilitate this development of mutuality, the research must recognize the need for personal investment in the form of self-disclosure and openness. Sprague and Hayes (2000) explain that such relationships are mutual

> [to] the degree to which each party negotiates a balance between commitment to the other's and to one's own journey of self-determination. In mutual relationships each strives to recognize the other's unique and changing needs and abilities, [and] takes the other's perspectives and interests into account. (p. 684)

In the practice of Kaupapa Māori research, however, there develops a degree of involvement on the part of the researcher, constituted as a way of knowing, that is fundamentally different from the concepts of personal investment and collaboration suggested by the above authors. Although it appears that "personal investment" is essential, this personal investment is not on terms determined by the "investor." Instead, the investment is made on terms of mutual understanding and control by all participants, so that the investment is reciprocal and could not be otherwise. In other words, the "personal investment" by the researcher is not an act by an individual agent but instead emerges out of the context within which the research is constituted.

Traditional conceptualizations of knowing do not adequately explain this understanding. Elbow (1986, as cited in Connelly & Clandinin, 1990) identifies a different form of reciprocity, one he terms "connected knowing," in which the "knower is attached to the known" (p. 4). In other words, there is common understanding and a common basis for such an understanding, where the concerns, interests, and agendas of the researcher become the concerns, interests, and agendas of the researched and vice versa. Hogan (as cited in Connelly & Clandinin, 1990, p. 4) refers to this as a "feeling of connectedness." Heshusius (1994, 2002) transforms this notion by suggesting the need to move from an alienated mode of consciousness that sees the knower as separate from the known to a *participatory mode of consciousness.* Such a mode of consciousness addresses a fundamental reordering of understandings of the relationship "between self and other (and therefore of reality), and indeed between self and the world, in a manner where such a reordering not only includes connectedness but necessitates letting go of the focus on self" (Heshusius, 1994, p. 15).

Heshusius (1994) identifies this form of knowing as involving, that which Polanyi (1966) calls "tacit knowing," which Harman calls "compassionate consciousness" (as cited in Heshusius, 1994), and which Berman calls "somatic" or "bodily" knowing (as cited in Heshusius, 1994). Barbara Thayer-Bacon (1997) describes a relational epistemology that views "knowledge as something that is socially constructed by embedded, embodied people who are in relation with each other" (p. 245). Each of these authors is referring to an embodied way of being and of a knowing that is a nonaccountable, nondescribable way of knowing. Heshusius (1994) suggests that "the act of coming to know is not a subjectivity that one can explicitly account for," but rather it is of a "direct participatory nature one cannot account for" (p. 17). Heshusius (1996) also suggests that

> In a participatory mode of consciousness the *quality* of attentiveness is characterised by an absence of the need to separate, distance and to insert predetermined thought patterns, methods and formulas between self and other. It is characterised by an absence of the need to be in charge. (p. 627)

Heshusius (1994) identifies the ground from which a participatory mode of knowing emerges as "the recognition of the deeper kinship between ourselves and other" (p. 17). This form of knowing speaks in a very real sense to Māori ways of knowing, for the Māori term for connectedness and engagement by kinship is *whanaungatanga.* This concept is one of the most fundamental ideas within Māori culture, both as a value and as a social process.[9] Whanaungatanga literally consists of kin relationships between ourselves and others, and it is constituted in ways determined by the Māori cultural context.

Whakawhanaungatanga as a Kaupapa Māori Research Approach

Whakawhanaungatanga is the process of establishing *whânau* (extended family) relationships, literally by means of identifying, through culturally appropriate means, your bodily linkage, your engagement, your connectedness, and, therefore, an unspoken but implicit commitment to other people. For example, a *mihimihi* (formal ritualized introduction) at a *hui* (Māori ceremonial gathering) involves stating your own *whakapapa* in order to establish relationships with the hosts/others/visitors. A mihimihi does not identify you in terms of your work, in terms of your academic rank or title, for example. Rather, a mihimihi is a statement of where you are from and of how you can be related and connected to these other people and the land, in both the past and the present.

For Māori people, the process of whakawhanaungatanga identifies how our identity comes from our whakapapa and how our whakapapa and its associated *raranga kôrero* (those stories that explain the people and events of a whakapapa) link us to all other living and inanimate creatures and to the very earth we inhabit. Our mountain, our river, our island are us. We are part of them, and they are part of us. We know this in a bodily way, more than in a recitation of names. More than in the actual linking of names, we know it because we are related by blood and body. We are of the same bones (*iwi*) and of the same people (iwi). We are from the same pregnancies (*hapû*) and of the same subtribe (hapû). We are of the same family (*whânau*), the family into which we were born (whânau). We were nurtured by the same land (*whenua*), by the same placenta (whenua). In this way, the language reminds us that we are part of each other.

So when Māori people introduce ourselves as *whanaunga* (relatives), whether it be to engage in research or not, we are introducing part of one to another part of the same oneness. Knowing who we are is a somatic acknowledgment of our connectedness with and commitment to our surroundings, human and nonhuman. For example, from this positioning it would be very difficult to undertake research in a "nonsomatic," distanced manner. To invoke "distance" in a Māori research project would be to deny that it is a Māori project. It would have different goals, not Māori goals.

Establishing and maintaining whânau relationships, which can be either literal or metaphoric within the discursive practice that is Kaupapa Māori, is an integral and ongoing constitutive element of a Kaupapa Māori approach to research. Establishing a research group as if it were an extended family is one form of embodying the process of whakawhanaungatanga as a research strategy.

In a Kaupapa Māori approach to research, research groups constituted as whânau attempt to develop relationships and organizations based on similar principles to those that order a traditional or literal whânau. Metge (1990) explains that to use the term *whânau* is to identify a series of rights and responsibilities, commitments and obligations, and supports that are fundamental to the collectivity. These are the *tikanga* (customs) of the whânau: warm interpersonal interactions, group solidarity, shared responsibility for one another, cheerful cooperation for group ends, corporate responsibility for group property, and material or nonmaterial (e.g., knowledge) items and issues. These attributes can be summed up in the words *aroha* (love in the broadest sense, also mutuality), *awhi* (helpfulness), *manaaki* (hospitality), and *tiaki* (guidance).

The whânau is a location for communication, for sharing outcomes, and for constructing shared common understandings and meanings. Individuals have responsibilities to care for and to nurture other members of the group, while still adhering to the kaupapa of the group. The group will operate to avoid singling out particular individuals for comment and attention and to avoid embarrassing individuals who are not yet succeeding within the group. Group products and achievement frequently take the form of group performances, not individual performances.[10] The group typically will begin and end each session with prayer and also will typically share food together. The group will make major decisions as a group and then refer those decisions to kaumâtua (respected elders of either gender) for approval, and the group will seek to operate with the support and encouragement of kaumâtua. This feature acknowledges the multigenerational constitution of a whânau with associated hierarchically determined rights, responsibilities, and obligations.[11]

Determining Benefits: Identifying Lines of Accountability Using Māori Metaphor

Determining who benefits from the research and to whom the researchers are accountable also can be understood in terms of Māori discursive practices. What non-Māori people would refer to as management or control mechanisms are traditionally constituted in a whânau as *taonga tuku iho*—literally, those treasures passed down to us from the ancestors, those customs that guide our behavior. In this manner, the structure and function of a whânau describes and constitutes the relationship among research participants—in traditional research terminology, between the researcher and the researched—within Kaupapa Māori research practice. Research thus cannot proceed unless whânau support is obtained, unless kaumâtua provide guidance, and unless there is aroha between the participants, evidenced by an overriding feeling of tolerance, hospitality, and respect for others, their aspirations, and their preferences and practices. The research process is participatory as well as *participant driven* in the sense that the concerns, interests, and preferences of the whânau are what guide and drive the research processes. The research itself is driven by the participants in terms of setting the research questions, ascertaining the likely benefits, outlining the design of the work, undertaking the work that had to be done, distributing rewards, providing access to research findings, controlling the distribution of the knowledge, and deciding to whom the researcher is accountable.

This approach has much in common with that described by Kemmis and McTaggart (2000) as participatory and collaborative action research, which emerged "more or less deliberately as forms of resistance to conventional research practices that were perceived by particular kinds of participants as acts of colonization" (p. 572). To Esposito and Murphy (2000), participatory action research emphasizes the political nature of knowledge production and places a premium on self-emancipation (p. 180), where

> [s]uch research groups are typically comprised of both professionals and ordinary people, all of whom are regarded as authoritative sources of knowledge. By making minorities the

> authorized representatives of the knowledge produced, their experiences and concerns are brought to the forefront of the research. The resulting information is applied to resolving the problems they define collectively as significant. As a result, the integrity of distinct racial groups is not annihilated or subsumed within dominant narratives that portray them as peripheral members of society. (p. 181)

For researchers, this approach means that they are not information gatherers, data processors, and sense-makers of other people's lives; rather, they are expected to be able to communicate with individuals and groups, to participate in appropriate cultural processes and practices, and to interact in a dialogic manner with the research participants. Esposito and Murphy (2000) explain that research "methods are geared to offer opportunities for discussion. After all, information is not transmitted between researchers and individuals; instead, information is cocreated, . . . data are coproduced intersubjectively in a manner that preserves the existential nature of the information" (p. 182).

Esposito and Murphy (2000) also suggest that such an approach may facilitate the development of the kind of research that Lomawaima (2000) and Fine and Weis (1996) describe, a type in which investigators are more attuned to "locally meaningful expectations and concerns" (Lomawaima, 2000, p. 15). In addition, they suggest that researchers become actively involved in the solutions and promote the well-being of communities, instead of merely using locations as sites for data collection. As Lomawaima (2000) suggests, researchers should thus open up the "possibilities for directly meaningful research—research that is as informative and useful to tribes as it is to academic professionals and disciplinary theories" (p. 15).

What is crucial to an understanding of what it means to be a researcher in a Kaupapa Māori approach is that it is through the development of a participatory mode of consciousness that a researcher becomes part of this process. He or she does not start from a position outside the group and then choose to invest or reposition himself or herself. Rather, the (re)positioning is part of participation. The researcher cannot "position" himself or herself or "empower" the other. Instead, through entering a participatory mode of consciousness, the individual agent of the "I" of the researcher is released in order to enter a consciousness larger than the self.

One example of how whânau processes in action affect the position of the researcher is the way in which different individuals take on differing discursive positionings within the collective. These positionings fulfill different functions oriented toward the collaborative concerns, interests, and benefits of the whânau as a group, rather than toward the benefit of any one member—a member with a distanced research agenda, for example. Such positionings are constituted in ways that are generated by Māori cultural practices and preferences. For example, the leader of a research whânau, here termed a *whânau of interest* to identify it as a metaphoric whânau, will not necessarily be the researcher. Kaumâtua, which is a Māori-defined and -apportioned position (which can be singular or plural), will be the leader. Leadership in a whânau of interest, however, is not in the sense of making all the decisions, but instead in the sense of being a guide to *kawa* (culturally appropriate procedures) for decision making and a listener to the voices of all members of the whânau. The kaumâtua are the consensus seekers for the collective and are the producers of the collaborative voice of the members. By developing research within such existing culturally constituted practices, concerns about voice and agency can be addressed.

This emphasis on positionings within a group constituted as a whânau also addresses concerns about accountability, authority, and control. A Māori collective whânau contains a variety of discursively determined positions, some of which are open to the researcher and some of which are not. The extent to which researchers can be positioned within a whânau of interest is therefore tied very closely to *who* they are, often more so than to *what* they are. Therefore, positioning is not simply a matter of the researchers' choice, because this would further researcher imposition. That is, researchers are not free to assume any position that they think the whânau of interest needs in order for the whânau to function. The researchers' choice of positions is generated by the structure of the whânau and the customary ways of behaving constituted within the whânau. The clear implication is that researchers are required to locate themselves within new "story lines" that address the contradictory nature of the traditional researcher/researched relationship.

The language used by researchers working in Kaupapa Māori contexts in research reported by Bishop (1996, 1998b), for example, contains the key to the new story lines. The metaphors and imagery these researchers used to explain their participation in the research were those located within the research participants' domains, and the researchers either were moved or needed to move to become part of this domain. Researchers were positioned within the discursive practices of Kaupapa Māori by the use of contextually constituted metaphor within the domain where others constituted themselves as agentic. Furthermore, within this domain existed discursive practices that provided the researchers with positions that enabled them to carry through their negotiated lines of action whether they were insiders or outsiders. As a result of these negotiations, they had differing positions and expectations/tasks offered to them.

From this analysis, it can be seen that through developing a research group by using Māori customary sociopolitical processes, the research participants become members of a research whânau of interest, which, as a metaphoric whânau, is a group constituted in terms understandable and controllable by Māori cultural practices. These whânau of interest determine the research questions and the methods of research, and they use Māori cultural processes for addressing and acknowledging the construction and validation/legitimization of knowledge. Furthermore, the whânau of interest develops a collaborative approach to processing and constructing meaning/theorizing about the information, again by culturally constituted means. It is also important to recognize that whânau of interest are not isolated groups but rather are constituted and conduct their endeavors in terms of the wider cultural aspirations, preferences, and practices of Māori cultural revitalization within which their projects are composed.

Spiral Discourse

Whanâu of interest are developed by and use a Māori cultural process in both its literal and its metaphoric senses. This process is termed here *spiral discourse*, a culturally constituted discursive practice found in many Māori cultural practices associated, for example, with hui. A hui generally commences with a *pôwhiri* (formal welcome), a welcome rich in cultural meaning, imagery, and practices that fulfill the enormously important task of recognizing the relative *tapu* (specialness; being with potentiality for power) and *mana* (power) of the two sides, the hosts and the visitors (Salmond, 1975; Shirres, 1982). Once the formal welcome is complete and once the participants have been ritually joined together by the process of the welcoming ceremony, hui participants move on to the discussion of the matter under consideration (the kaupapa of the hui). This usually takes place within the meeting house, a place designated for this very purpose, free of distractions and interruptions. This house is symbolically the embodiment of an ancestor, which further emphasizes the normality of a somatic approach to knowing in such a setting and within these processes.

The participants address the matters under consideration, under the guidance of respected and authoritative elders (kaumâtua), whose primary function is to provide and monitor the correct spiritual and procedural framework within which the participants can discuss the issues before them. People get a chance to address the issue without fear of being interrupted. Generally, the procedure is for people to speak one after another, in sequence of left to right. People get a chance to state and restate their meanings, to revisit their meanings, and to modify, delete, and adapt their meanings according to *tikanga* (customary practices).

The discourse spirals, in that the flow of talk may seem circuitous and opinions may vary and waver, but the seeking of a collaboratively constructed story is central. The controls over proceedings are temporal and spiritual, as in all Māori cultural practices. The procedures are steeped in metaphoric meanings, richly abstract allusions being made constantly to cultural messages, stories, events of the past, and aspirations for the future. Such procedures are time proven and to the participants are highly effective in dealing with contemporary issues and concerns of all kinds.[12] The aim of a hui is to reach a consensus, to arrive at a jointly constructed meaning. This takes time, days if need be, or sometimes a series of hui will be held in order that the elders monitoring proceedings can tell when a constructed "voice" has been found.

Initiating Research Using Māori Metaphor: Rejecting Empowerment

Addressing the self-determination of participants is embedded within many Māori cultural practices and understandings. For example, during the proceedings of a hui, one visible manifestation of this reality is seen in the ways that visitors make contributions toward the cost of the meeting. This contribution is termed a *koha.* In the past, this koha was often a gift of food to contribute to the running of the hui; nowadays, it is usually money that is laid down on the ground, by the last speaker of the visitors' side, between the two groups of people who are coming together at the welcoming ceremony. The koha remains an important ritualized part of a ceremony that generally proceeds without too much trouble. What must not be forgotten, however, is that the reception of the koha is up to the hosts. The koha, as a gift or an offering of assistance toward the cost of running the hui, goes with the full mana of the group so offering. It is placed in a position, such as laying it on the ground between the two groups coming together, so as to be able to be considered by the hosts. It is not often given into the hands of the hosts, but whatever the specific details of the protocol, the process of "laying down" is a very powerful recognition of the right of others to self-determination, that is, to choose whether to pick it up or not.

The koha generally precedes the final coming together of the two sides. The placing of the koha comes at a crucial stage in the ceremony, at which the hosts can refuse to accept the mana of the visitors, the hosts can display their ultimate control over events, and the hosts can choose whether they want to become one with the *manuhiri* (visitors) by the process of the *hôngi* and *haruru* (pressing noses and shaking hands). Symbolically, with the koha, the hosts are taking on the kaupapa of the guests by accepting that which the manuhiri are bringing for debate and mediation. Overall, however, it is important that the kaupapa the guests laid down at the hui is now the "property" of the whole whânau. It is now the task of the whole whânau to deliberate the issues and to own the problems, concerns, and ideas in a way that is real and meaningful, the way of *whakakotahitanga* (developing unity), where all will work for the betterment of the idea.

By invoking these processes in their metaphoric sense, Kaupapa Māori research is conducted within the discursive practices of Māori culture. Figuratively, laying down a koha as a means of initiating research, for example, or of offering solutions to a problem challenges notions of empowerment, which is a major concern within contemporary Western-defined research. It also challenges what constitutes "self" and "other" in Western thought. Rather than figuratively saying "I am giving you power" or "I intend to empower you," the laying down of a koha and stepping away for the others to consider your gift means that your mana is intact, as is theirs, and that you are acknowledging their power of self-determination. The three research projects referred to above all saw the researchers either laying out their potential contributions as researchers, or asking research participants to explain what has been observed in their classrooms or seeking the meaning that participants construct about their experiences as young people in secondary schools. In each of these cases, the researchers indicated that they did not have the power to make sense of the events or experiences alone and, indeed, did not want anything from the relationship that was not a product of the relationship. In this way, it is up to the others to exert agency, to decide if they wish to "pick it up," to explain the meanings of their own experiences on their own terms. Whatever they do, both sides have power throughout the process. Both sides have tapu that is being acknowledged.

In this sense, researchers in Kaupapa Māori contexts are repositioned in such a way that they no longer need to seek to *give voice to others*, to *empower* others, to *emancipate* others, or to refer to others as *subjugated voices*. Instead, they are able to listen to and participate with those traditionally "othered" as constructors of meanings of their own experiences and agents of knowledge. Not wanting anything from the experience for one's "self" is characteristic of what Schachtel (as cited in Heshusius, 1994) calls "allocentric knowing." It is only when nothing is desired for the self, not even the desire to empower someone, that complete attention and participation in "kinship" terms is possible.

In such ways, researchers can participate in a process that facilitates the development in people of a sense of themselves as agentic and of having an authoritative voice. This is not a result of the researcher "allowing" this to happen or "empowering" participants; it is the function of the cultural context within which the research participants are positioned, negotiate, and conduct the research.[13] In effect, the cultural context positions the participants by constructing the story lines, and with them the cultural metaphors and images, as well as the "thinking as usual," the talk/language through which research participants are constituted and researcher/researched relationships are organized. Thus, the joint development of new story lines is a collaborative effort. The researcher and the researched together rewrite the constitutive metaphors of the relationship. What makes it Māori is that it is done using Māori metaphor within a Māori cultural context.[14]

Such approaches are essential to move the power dynamics of research relationships because, as was mentioned earlier, differential power relations among participants, while construed and understood as collaborative by the researcher, may still enable researcher concerns and interests to dominate how understandings are constructed. This can happen even within relations constructed as reciprocal, if the research outcome remains one determined by the researcher as a data-gathering exercise (Goldstein, 2000; Tripp, 1983). When attempts at developing dialogue move beyond efforts to gather "data" and move toward mutual, symmetrical, dialogic construction of meaning within appropriate culturally constituted contexts, as is illustrated in the three examples introduced earlier, then the voice of the research participants is heard and their agency is facilitated.

Such understandings seek to address the self/other relationship by examining how researchers shift themselves from a "speaking for" position to a situation that Michelle Fine (1994) describes as *taking place* "when we construct texts collaboratively, self-consciously examining our relations with/for/despite those who have been contained as Others, we move against, we enable resistance to, Othering" (p. 74). Fine (1994) attempts to

> unravel, critically, the blurred boundaries in our relation, and in our texts; to understand the political work of our narratives; to decipher how the traditions of social science serve to inscribe; and to imagine how our practice can be transformed to resist, self-consciously, acts of othering. (p. 57)

Fine and her colleagues Lois Weis, Susan Weseen, and Loonmun Wong (2000) stress "that questions of responsibility-for-whom will, and should, forever be paramount" (p. 125). Reciprocity in indigenous research, however, is not just a political understanding, an individual act, or a matter of refining and/or challenging the paradigms within which researchers work. Instead, every worldview within which the researcher becomes immersed holds the key to knowing. For example, establishing relationships and developing research whânau by invoking the processes of whakawhanaungatanga establishes interconnectedness, commitment, and engagement, within culturally constituted research practices, by means of constitutive metaphor from within the discursive practice of Kaupapa Māori. It is the use of such metaphor that reorders the relationship of the researcher/researched from within, from one focused on the researcher as "self" and on the researched as "other" to one of a common consciousness of all research participants.

Similarly, a Kaupapa Māori approach suggests that concepts of "distance," "detachment," and "separation," epistemological and methodological concerns on which researchers have spent much time in the recent past (Acker, Barry, & Esseveld, 1991; Stacey, 1991; Troyna, 1992, personal communication), do not characterize these research relationships in any way. Rather, Kaupapa Māori research experiences insist that the focus on "self" is blurred and that the focus turns to what Heshusius (1994) describes as a situation where "reality is no longer understood as truth to be interpreted but as mutually evolving" (p. 18). In an operational sense, it is suggested that researchers address the concerns and issues of the participants in ways that are understandable and able to be controlled by the research participants so that these concerns and issues also are, or become, those of the researchers. In other words, spiral discourse provides a means of effecting a qualitative shift in how participants relate to one another.

Sidorkin (2002) suggests that such understandings have major implications for how we understand the "self" and "invites us to think about the possibilities of a relational self" (p. 96), one in which "only analysis of specific relations in their interaction can provide a glimpse of the meaning of the self" (p. 97). To this end, Fitzsimons and Smith (2000) describe Kaupapa Māori philosophy as that which is "call[ing] for a relational identity through an interpretation of kinship and genealogy and current day events, but not a de-contextualised retreat to a romantic past" (p. 39).

This reordering of what constitutes the research relationship, with its implications and challenges to the essential enlightenment-generated self, is not on terms or within understandings constructed by the researcher, however well-intentioned contemporary impulses to "empower" the "other" might be. From an indigenous perspective, such impulses are misguided and perpetuate neocolonial sentiments. In other words, rather than using researcher-determined criteria for participation in a research process, whakawhanaungatanga uses Māori cultural practices, such as those found in hui, to set the pattern for research relationships, collaborative storying being but one example of this principle in practice. Whakawhanaungatanga as a research process uses methods and principles similar to those used to establish relationships among Māori people. These principles are invoked to address the means of research initiation, to establish the research questions, to facilitate participation in the work of the project, to address issues of representation and accountability, and to legitimate the ownership of knowledge that is defined and created.

Kincheloe and McLaren (2000) demonstrate how developments in critical ethnography, as one example, have benefited from such new understandings of culture and cultural practices and processes, used in both literal and figurative senses, to identify "possibilities for cultural critique, that have been opened up by the current blurring and mixing of disciplinary genres—those that emphasize experience, subjectivity, reflexivity and dialogical understanding" (p. 302). One major benefit from such analysis is that social life is "not viewed as preontologically available for the researcher to study" (p. 302). Kincheloe and McLaren suggest that this is a major breakthrough in the domain of critical theory, which previously remained rooted in the Western-based dialectic of binary analysis of oppositional pairings that viewed emancipation in terms of emancipating "others" (Kincheloe & McLaren, 2000) and, in many cases, conflated economic marginalization with ethnicity and gender and other axes of domination (see Bishop & Glynn, 1999, Chap. 2, for a detailed critique of this approach in New Zealand).

▣ Addressing Issues of Representation and Legitimation: A Narrative Approach

Interviewing as collaborative storying (Bishop, 1997), as used in the three studies identified earlier, addresses what Lincoln and Denzin (1994) identify as the twin crises of qualitative research—representation and legitimation. It does so by suggesting that rather than there being distinct stages in the research, from gaining access to data gathering to data processing, there is a process of continually revisiting the agenda and the sense-making processes of the research participants within the interview. In this way, meanings are negotiated and co-constructed between the research participants within the cultural frameworks of the discourses within which they are positioned. This process is captured by the image of a spiral. The concept of the spiral not only speaks in culturally preferred terms, the fern or koru,[15] but also indicates that the accumulation is always reflexive. This means that the discourse always returns to the original initiators, where control lies.

Mishler (1986) and Ryan (1999) explain these ideas further by suggesting that in order to construct meaning, it is necessary to appreciate how meaning is grounded in, and constructed through, discourse. Discursive practice is contextually, culturally, and individually related. Meanings in discourse are neither singular nor fixed. Terms take on "specific and contextually grounded meanings within and through the discourse as it develops and is shaped by speakers" (Mishler, 1986, p. 65). To put it another way, "meaning is constructed in the dialogue between individuals and the images and symbols they perceive" (Ryan, 1999, p. 11). A "community of interest" between researchers and participants (call them what you will) cannot be created unless the interview, as one example, is constructed so that interviewers and respondents strive to arrive together at meanings that both can understand. The relevance and appropriateness of questions and responses emerge through and are realized in the discourse itself. The standard process of analysis of interviews abstracts both questions and responses from this process. By suppressing the discourse and by assuming shared and standard meanings, this approach short-circuits the problem of obtaining meaning (Mishler, 1986).

This analysis suggests that when interviewing—one of the most commonly used qualitative methods—there needs to be a trade-off between two extremes. The first position claims "the words of an interview are the most accurate data and that the transcript of those words carries that accuracy with negligible loss" (Tripp, 1983, p. 40). In other words, what people say should be presented unaltered and not analyzed in any way beyond that which the respondent undertook. The second position maximizes researcher interpretation, editorial control, and ownership by introducing researcher coding and analysis in the form often referred to as "grounded theory" (after Glaser & Strauss, 1967). This chapter suggests there is a third position, in which the "coding" procedure is established and developed by the research participants as a process of storying and restorying, that is the co-joint construction of further meaning within a sequence of interviews. In other words, there is an attempt within the interview, or rather, within a series of in-depth, semistructured interviews as "conversations" (see Bishop, 1996, 1997), to actually co-construct a mutual understanding by means of sharing experiences and meanings.

The three examples of research outlined at the start of this chapter all used research approaches associated with the process of collaborative storying so that the research participants were able to recollect, to reflect on, and to make sense of their experiences within their own cultural context and, in particular, in their own language, hence being able to position themselves within those discourses wherein explanations/meanings lie. In such ways, their interpretations and analyses became "normal" and "accepted," as opposed to those of the researcher being what is legitimate.

Indeed, when indigenous cultural ways of knowing and aspirations—in this case, for self-determination—are central to the creation of the research context, then the situation goes beyond empowerment to one in which sense making, decision making, and theorizing take place in situations that are "normal" to the research participants rather than constructed by the researcher. Of course, the major implication for researchers is that they should be able to participate in these sense-making contexts rather than expecting the research participants to engage in theirs, emphasizing, as Tillman (2002, p. 3) suggests, the centrality of culture to the research process and "the multi-dimensional aspects of African-American cultures(s) and the possibilities for the resonance of the cultural knowledge of African-Americans in educational research" (p. 4).

This is not to suggest that only interviews as collaborative stories are able to address Māori concerns and aspirations for self-determination. Indeed, Sleeter (2001) has even argued that "quantitative research can be used for liberatory as well as oppressive ends" (p. 240). My own experiences when researching within secondary schools demonstrate that when spiral discourse occurs "with full regard for local complexities, power relations and previously ignored life experiences" (Sleeter, 2001, p. 241), then powerful outcomes are possible using a variety of research approaches. What is fundamental is not the approach per se, but rather establishing and maintaining relationships that address the power of the participants for self-determination.

The considerations above demonstrate the usefulness of the notion of collaborative storying as a generic approach, not just as a research method that speaks of a reordering of the relationships between researchers and research participants. Sidorkin (2002) suggests that this understanding addresses power imbalances because "[r]elations cannot belong to one thing: they are the joint property of at least two things" (p. 94). Scheurich and Young (1997) describe this as deconstructing research practices that arise out of the "social history and culture of the dominant race" and that "reflect and reinforce that social history and the controlling position of that racial group" (p. 13). Such practices are, as a result, epistemologically racist in that they deny the relational constructedness of the world in order to promote and maintain the hegemony of one of the supposed partners.

Approaches to Authority and Validity

Many of the problems identified above arise from researchers positioning themselves within modernist discourses. It is essential to challenge modernist discourses, with their concomitant concerns regarding validity that are addressed by such strategies as objectivity/subjectivity, replicability, and external measures for validity. These discourses are so pervasive that Māori/indigenous researchers may automatically revert to using such means of establishing validity for their texts, but problematically so because these measures of validity are all positioned/defined within another worldview. As bell hooks (1993) explains, the Black Power movement in the United States in the 1960s was influenced by the modernist discourses on race, gender, and class that were current at the time. As a result of not addressing these discourses and the ways they affected the condition of black people, issues such as patriarchy were left unaddressed within the Black Liberation movement. Unless black people address these issues themselves, hooks insists, others will do so for them, in ways determined by the concerns and interests of others rather than those that "women of color" would prefer.[16] Indeed, Linda Tillman (2002) promotes a culturally sensitive research approach for African Americans that focuses on "how African Americans understand and experience the world" (p. 4) and that advocates the use of an approach to qualitative research wherein "interpretative paradigms offer greater possibilities for the use of alternative frameworks, co-construction of multiple realities and experiences, and knowledge that can lead to improved educational opportunities for African Americans" (p. 5).

Yet historically, traditional forms of nonreflective research conducted within what Lincoln and Denzin (1994) term as positivist and post-positivist frames of reference perpetuate problems of outsiders determining what is valid for Māori. This occurs by the very process of employing non-Māori methodological frameworks and conventions for writing about such research processes and outcomes. For example, Lincoln and Denzin (1994) argue that terms such as "logical, construct, internal, ethnographic, and external validity, text-based data, triangulation, trustworthiness, credibility, grounding, naturalistic indicators, fit, coherence, comprehensiveness, plausibility, truth and relevance . . . [are] all attempts to reauthorize a text's authority in the post-positivist moment" (Lincoln & Denzin, 1994, p. 579).

These concepts, and the methodological frameworks within which they exist, represent attempts to contextualize the grounding of a text in the external, empirical world. "They represent efforts to develop a set of transcendent rules and procedures that lie outside any specific research project" (Lincoln & Denzin, 1994, p. 579). These externalized rules are the criteria by which the validity of a text is then judged. The author of the text is thus able to present the text to the reader as valid, replacing the sense making, meaning construction, and voice of the researched person with that of the researcher by representing the text as an authoritative re-presentation of the experiences of others by using a system of researcher-determined and -dominated coding and analytical tools.

Ballard (1994), referring to Donmoyer's work, suggests that formulaic research procedures are rarely in fact useful as "prescriptions for practice" because people use their own knowledge, experience, feelings, and intuitions "when putting new ideas into practice or when working in new settings" (pp. 301–302). Furthermore, personal knowledge and personal experience can be seen as crucial in the application of new knowledge and/or working in new settings. This means that the application of research findings is filtered through the prior knowledge, feelings, and intuitions we already have. Donmoyer (as cited in Ballard, 1994) proposes that experience compounds, and this compounded knowledge/experience, when brought to a new task, provides for the occurrence of an even more complex process of understandings. Experience builds on and compounds experience, and, as Ballard suggests, this is why there is such value placed on colleagues with experience in the Pâkehâ world and on kaumâtua (elders) in the Māori world.

A related, and somewhat more complex, danger of referring to an existing methodology of participation is that there may be a tendency to construct a set of rules and procedures that lie outside any one research project. In doing so, researchers might take control over what constitutes legitimacy and validity, that is, what authority is claimed for the text will be removed from the participants. With such recipes comes the danger of outsiders controlling what constitutes reality for other people.

It is important to note, though, that the Kaupapa Māori approach does not suggest that all knowledge is completely relative. Instead, as Heshusius (1996) states,

> the self of the knower and the larger self of the community of inquiry are, from the very starting point, intimately woven into the very fabric of that which we claim as knowledge and of what we agree to be the proper ways by which we make knowledge claims. It is to say that the knower and the known are one movement. Moreover, any inquiry is an expression of a particular other-self relatedness. (p. 658)

Kaupapa Māori research, based in a different worldview from that of the dominant discourse, makes this political statement while at the same time rejecting a meaningless relativism by acknowledging the need to recognize and address the ongoing effects of racism and colonialism in the wider society.

Kaupapa Māori rejects outside control over what constitutes the text's call for authority and truth. A Kaupapa Māori position promotes what Lincoln and Denzin (1994) term an epistemological version of validity, one in which the authority of the text is "established through recourse to a set of rules concerning knowledge, its production and representation" (p. 578). Such an approach to validity locates the power within Māori cultural practices, where what are acceptable and what are not acceptable research, text, and/or processes is determined and defined by the research community itself in reference to the cultural context within which it operates.

As was explained above, Māori people have always had criteria for evaluating whether a process or a product is valid for them. *Taonga tuku iho* are literally the "treasures from the ancestors." These treasures are the collected wisdom of ages, the means that have been established over a long period of time that guide and monitor people's very lives, today and in the future. Within these treasures are the messages of kawa,[17] those principles that, for example, guide the process of establishing relationships. Whakawhanaungatanga is not a haphazard process, decided on an ad hoc basis, but rather is based on time-honored and proven principles. How each of these principles is addressed in particular circumstances varies from tribe to tribe and hapu to hapu. Nevertheless, it is important that these principles are addressed.

For example, as described earlier, the meeting of two groups of people at a hui on a *marae* (ceremonial meeting place) involves acknowledgment of the tapu of each individual and of each group, by means of addressing and acknowledging the sacredness, specialness, genealogy, and connectedness of the guests with the hosts. Much time will be spent establishing this linkage, a connectedness between the people involved. How this actually is done is the subject of local customs, which are the correct ways to address these principles of kawa. *Tikanga* are an ongoing fertile ground for debate, but all participants know that if the kawa is not observed, then the event is "invalid": It does not have authority.

Just as Māori practices are epistemologically validated within Māori cultural contexts, so are Kaupapa Māori research practices and texts. Research conducted within a Kaupapa Māori framework has rules established as taonga tuku iho that are protected and maintained by the tapu of Māori cultural practices, such as the multiplicity of rituals within the hui and within the central cultural processes of whanaungatanga. Furthermore, the use of these concepts as constitutive research metaphors is subject to the same culturally determined processes of validation, and the same rules concerning knowledge, its production, and its representation, as are the literal phenomena. Therefore, the verification of a text, the authority of a text, and the quality of its representation of the experiences and its perspective of the participants are judged by criteria constructed and constituted within the culture.

By using such Māori concepts as *whânau*, *hui*, and *whakawhanaungatanga* as metaphors for the research process itself, Kaupapa Māori research invokes and claims authority for the processes and for the texts that are produced in terms of the principles, processes, and practices that govern such events in their literal sense. Metaphoric whânau are governed by the same principles and processes that govern a literal whânau and, as such, are understandable to and controllable by Māori people. Literal whânau have means of addressing contentious issues, resolving conflicts, constructing narratives, telling stories, raising children, and addressing economic and political issues, and, contrary to popular non-Māori opinion, such practices change over time to reflect changes going on in the wider world. Research whânau-of-interest also conduct their deliberations in a whânau style. Kaumâtua preside, others get their say according to who they are, and positions are defined in terms of how the definitions will benefit the whânau.

Subjectivities/Objectivities

As was discussed above, an indigenous Kaupapa Māori approach to research challenges colonial and neocolonial discourses that inscribe "otherness." Much quantitative research has dismissed, marginalized, or maintained control over the voice of others by insistence on the imposition of researcher-determined positivist and neopositivist evaluative criteria, internal and external validity, reliability, and objectivity. Nonetheless, a paradigm shift to qualitative research does not necessarily obviate this problem. Much qualitative research has also maintained a colonizing discourse of the "other" by seeking to hide the researcher/writer under a veil of neutrality or of objectivity or subjectivity, a situation in which the interests, concerns, and power of the researcher to determine the outcome of the research remain hidden in the text (B. Davies & Harré, 1990).

Objectivity, "that pathology of cognition that entails silence about the speaker, about [his or her] interests and [his or her] desires, and how these are socially situated and structurally maintained" (Gouldner, as cited in Tripp, 1983, p. 32), is a denial of identity. Just as identity to Māori people is tied up with being part of a whânau, a hapu, and an iwi, in the research relationship, membership in a metaphoric whânau of interest also provides its members with identity and hence the ability to participate. In Thayer-Bacon's (1997) view, "we develop a sense of 'self' through our relationships with others" (p. 241). For Māori researchers to stand aside from involvement in such a sociopolitical organization is to stand aside from their identity. This would signal the ultimate victory of colonization. For non-Māori researchers, denial of membership of the research whânau of interest is, similarly, to deny them a means of identification and hence participation within the projects. Furthermore, for non-Māori researchers to stand aside from participation in these terms is to promote colonization, albeit participation in ways defined by indigenous peoples may well pose difficulties for them. What is certain is that merely shifting one's position within the Western-dominated research domain need not address questions of interest to Māori people, because paradigm shifting is really a concern from another worldview. Non-Māori researchers need to seek inclusion on Māori terms, in terms of kin/metaphoric kin relationships and obligations—that is, within Māori-constituted practices and understandings—in order to establish their identity within research projects.

This does not mean, however, that researchers need to try to control their subjectivities. Heshusius (1994) suggests that managing subjectivity is just as problematic for qualitative researchers as managing objectivity is for the positivists. Esposito and Murphy (2000) similarly raise this problem of the preoccupation of many researchers who, while ostensibly locating themselves within critical race theory, for example, remain focused "strictly on subjectivity" and employ analytic tools "to interpret the discursive exchanges that, in the end, silence the study participants . . . [because] the investigator's subjectivity replaces the co-produced knowledge her research presumably represents" (p. 180).

This problem is epistemic in that the development of objectivity, through borrowing methodology from the natural sciences, introduced the concept of distance into the research relationship. Heshusius (1994) argues that the displacement of "objective positivism" by qualitative concerns about managing and controlling subjectivities perpetuates the fundamental notion that knowing is possible through constructing and regulating distance, a belief that presumes that the knower is separable from the known, a belief that is anathema to many indigenous people's ways of knowing. Heshusius suggests that the preoccupation with "managing subjectivity" is a "subtle form of empiricist thought" (p. 16) in that it assumes that if one can know subjectivity, then one can control it. Intellectualizing "the other's impact on self" perpetuates the notion of distance; validates the notions of "false consciousness" in others, emancipation as a project, and "othering" as a process; and reduces the self-other relationship to one that is mechanistic and methodological.

Operationally, Heshusius (1994) questions what we as researchers do after being confronted with "subjectivities": "Does one evaluate them and try to manage and to restrain them? And then believe one has the research process once again under control?" (p. 15). Both these positions address "meaningful" epistemological and methodological questions of the researcher's own choosing. Instead, Heshusius suggests that researchers need to address those questions that would address moral issues, such as "what kind of society do we have or are we constructing?" (p. 20). For example, how can racism be addressed unless those who perpetuate it become aware, through a participatory consciousness, of the lived reality of those who suffer? How can researchers become aware of the meaning of Māori schooling experiences if they perpetuate an artificial "distance" and objectify the "subject," dealing with issues in a manner that is of interest to the researchers rather than of concern to the subjects? The message is that you have to "live" the context in which schooling experiences occur. For example, the third study referred to before, *Te Kotahitanga* (Bishop, Berryman, et al., 2003), commenced by providing teachers with *testimonios* of students' experiences as a means of critically reflecting on the teachers' positioning in respect to deficit thinking and racism.

Preoccupations with managing and controlling one's subjectivities also stand in contrast with Berman's historical analysis, which suggests that "before the scientific revolution (and presumably the enlightenment) the act of knowing had always been understood as a form of participation and enchantment" (cited in Heshusius, 1994, p. 16). Berman states that "for most of human history, man [*sic*] saw himself as an integral part of it" (cited in Heshusius, 1994, p. 16). The very act of participation was knowing. Participation was direct, somatic (bodily), psychic, spiritual, and emotional involvement. "The belief that one can actually distance oneself, and then regulate that distance in order to come to know [has] left us alienated from each other, from nature and from ourselves" (Heshusius, 1994, p. 16).

Heshusius (1994) suggests that instead of addressing distance, researchers need to acknowledge their participation and attempt to develop a "participatory consciousness." This means becoming involved in a "somatic, non-verbal quality of attention that necessitates letting go of the focus of self" (p. 15). The three examples of Kaupapa Māori research projects identified earlier demonstrate that the researchers understand themselves to be involved somatically in a group process, a process whereby the researcher becomes part of a research whânau, limiting the development of insider/outsider dualisms. To be involved somatically means to be involved bodily—that is, physically, ethically, morally, and spiritually, not just in one's capacity as a "researcher" concerned with methodology. Such involvement is constituted as a way of knowing that is fundamentally different from the concepts of personal investment and collaboration that are suggested in traditional approaches to research. Although it appears that "personal investment" is essential, this personal investment is not on terms determined by the "investor." Instead, the investment is on terms mutually understandable and controllable by all participants, so that the investment is reciprocal and could not be otherwise. The "personal investment" by the researcher is not an act by an individual agent but instead emerges out of the context within which the research is constituted.

The process of colonization developed an alienated and alienating mode of consciousness and, thus, has tried to take a fundamental principle of life away from Māori people—that we do not objectify nature, nor do we subjectify nature. As we learn our whakapapa, we learn of our total integration, connectedness, and commitment to the world and the need to let go of the focus on self. We know that there is a way of knowing that is different from that which was taught to those colonized into the Western way of thought. We know about a way that is born of time, connectedness, kinship, commitment, and participation.

▣ Epilogue: A Means of Evaluating Researcher Positioning

This chapter has concluded that researchers and research participants need a means whereby they can critically reflect upon the five issues of power that are identified in Figure 5.1. Figure 5.1 provides a series of critical questions that can be used by researchers and research participants to evaluate power relations prior to and during research activity. The outer circle shows some of the metaphors that might constitute a discursive position within which researchers can be positioned.

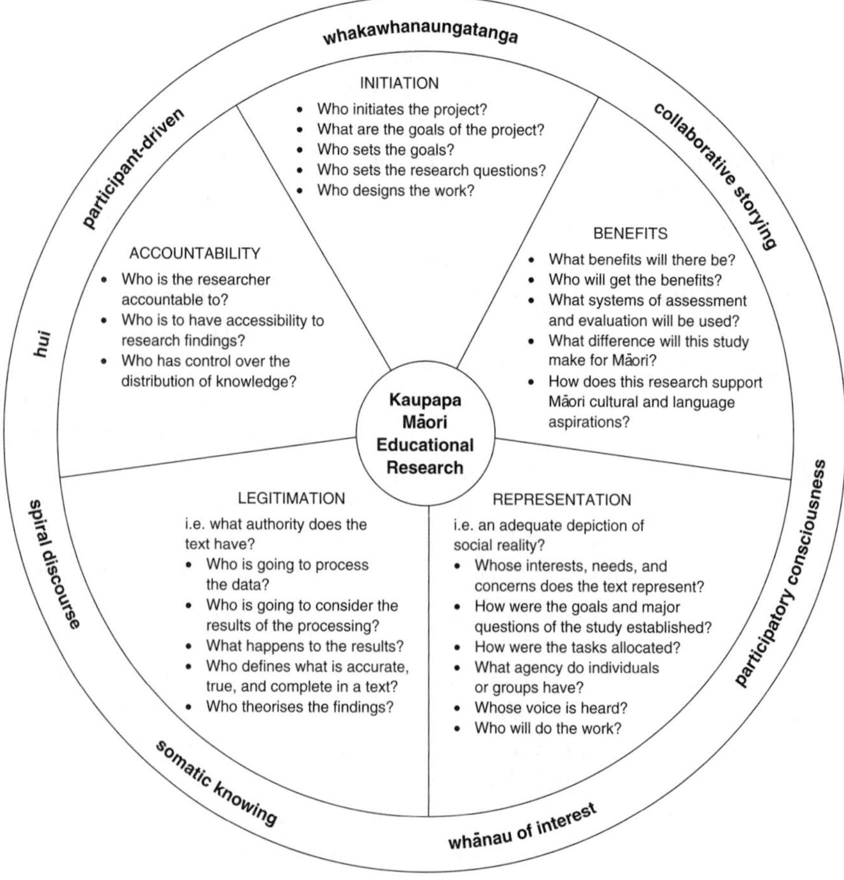

Figure 5.1. A Means of Evaluating Researcher Positioning

Source: Reproduced with permission from Bishop and Glynn (1999, p. 129).

Appendix: Glossary of Māori Terms

aroha	love in its broadest sense; mutuality
awhi	helpfulness
hapu	subtribe, usually linked to a common ancestor; pregnant
haruru	greeting others by shaking hands and performing a hôngi
hôngi	greeting another person by pressing noses together, to share the breath of life
hui	ceremonial, ritualized meeting
iwi	tribe; bones
kaumâtua	respected elder
kaupapa	agenda, philosophy
kawa	protocol
koha	gift
mana	power
manaaki	hospitality, caring
manuhiri	guest(s)
Māori	indigenous people of Aotearoa/New Zealand
marae	ceremonial meeting place
mihimihi	ritualized self-introduction
Pâkehâ	New Zealanders of European descent
pôwhiri	formal welcome
raranga kôrero	those stories that explain the people and events of a whakapapa
taonga	treasures, including physical, social, cultural, and intellectual
taonga tuku iho	treasures passed down to the present generation from the ancestors
tapu	sacred, to be treated with respect, a restriction, a being with potentiality for power, integrity, specialness
tiaki	to look after; guidance
tikanga	customs, values, beliefs, and attitudes
tino Rangatiratanga	self-determination
whakakotahitanga	developing unity
whakapapa	genealogy
whakawhanaungatanga	establishing relationships
whânau	extended family; to be born
whanaunga	relatives
whanaungatanga	kin relationships

▣ Notes

1. This chapter is based on Bishop (1998a, 1998b).

2. Two peoples created Aotearoa/New Zealand when, in 1840, lieutenant-governor Hobson and the chiefs of New Zealand signed the Treaty of Waitangi on behalf of the British Crown and the Māori descendants of New Zealand. The treaty is seen as a charter for power sharing in the decision-making processes of this country and for Māori determination of their own destiny as the indigenous people of New Zealand (Walker, 1990). The history of Māori and Pâkehâ relations since the signing of the treaty has not been one of partnership, of two peoples developing a nation, but instead one of domination by Pâkehâ and marginalization of the Māori people (Bishop, 1991b; Simon, 1990; Walker, 1990). This has created the myth of our nation being "one people" with equal opportunities (Hohepa, 1975; Simon, 1990; Walker, 1990). Results of this domination are evident today in the lack of equitable participation by Māori in all positive and beneficial aspects of life in New Zealand and by their overrepresentation in the negative aspects (Pomare, 1988; Simon, 1990). In education, for example, the central government's sequential policies of assimilation, integration, and multiculturalism (Irwin, 1989; Jones, McCulloch, Marshall, Smith, & Smith, 1990) and Taha Māori (Holmes, Bishop, & Glynn, 1993; G. H. Smith, 1990), while concerned for the welfare of Māori people, effectively stress the need for Māori people to subjugate their destiny to the needs of the nation-state, whose goals are determined by the Pâkehâ majority.

3. "Traditional" is used here to denote that "tradition" of research that has grown in New Zealand as a result of the dominance of the Western worldview in research institutions. Māori means of accessing, defining, and protecting knowledge, however, existed before European arrival. Such Māori cultural processes were protected by the Treaty of Waitangi, subsequently marginalized, but are today legitimized within Māori cultural discursive practice.

4. Please see the glossary of Māori terms for English translations.

5. The concept of hegemony is used here in the sense defined by Michel Foucault (Smart, 1986), who suggests that hegemony is an insidious process that is acquired most effectively through "practices, techniques, and methods which infiltrate minds and bodies, cultural practices which cultivate behaviors and beliefs, tastes, desires and needs as seemingly naturally occurring qualities and properties embodied in the psychic and physical reality of the human subject" (p. 159).

6. I am using the term "discourse" to mean language in social use or in action.

7. Irwin (1992a) argues that prior to the signing of the Treaty of Waitangi and the colonization of New Zealand, there existed a "complex, vibrant Māori education system" that had "Māori development [as] its vision, its educational processes and its measurable outcomes" (p. 9). Protection of this education system was guaranteed under Article Two of the Treaty of Waitangi, just as Article Three guaranteed Māori people, as citizens of New Zealand, the right to equitable educational outcomes. This promise had been negated by subsequent practice, and the outcome is the present educational crisis (L. Davies & Nicholl, 1993; Jones et al., 1990). The posttreaty education system that developed in New Zealand—the mission schools (Bishop, 1991a), the Native schools (Simon, 1990), and the present mainstream schools (Irwin, 1992a)—has been unable to "successfully validate matauranga Māori, leaving it marginalised and in a precarious state" (Irwin, 1992a, p. 10). Furthermore, while mainstream schooling does not serve Māori people well (L. Davies & Nicholl, 1993), the Māori schooling initiatives of Te Kohanga reo (Māori medium preschools), Kura Kaupapa Māori (Māori medium primary schools), Whare Kura (Māori

medium secondary schools), and Whare Waananga (Māori tertiary institutions), "which have developed from within Māori communities to intervene in Māori language, cultural, educational, social and economic crises *are successful in the eyes of the Māori people*" (G. H. Smith, 1992, p. 1, emphasis added).

8. Article Two of an English translation of the Māori version of the Treaty of Waitangi states: "The Queen of England agrees to protect the Chiefs, the sub-tribes and all the people of New Zealand in the unqualified exercise of their chieftainship over their lands, villages and all their treasures. But on the other hand the Chiefs of the Confederation and all the Chiefs will sell land to the Queen at a price agreed to by the person owning it and by the person buying it (the latter being) appointed by the Queen as her purchase agent" (Kawharu, as cited in Consedine & Consedine, 2001, p. 236). It is the first part of this article that has relevance to this argument, that is, the promise that Māori people were guaranteed chiefly control over that which they treasured.

9. Whânau is a primary concept (a cultural preference) that underlies narratives of Kaupapa Māori research practice. This concept contains both values (cultural aspirations) and social processes (cultural practices). The root word of "whânau" literally means "family" in its broad, "extended" sense. However, the word "whânau" is increasingly being used in a metaphoric sense (Metge, 1990). This generic concept of whânau subsumes other related concepts: whanaunga (relatives), whanaungatanga (relationships), whakawhanaungatanga (the process of establishing relationships), and whakapapa (literally, the means of establishing relationships). (The prefix "whaka" means "to make"; the suffix "tanga" has a naming function.)

10. This poses major challenges for assessment in education settings.

11. It is important to emphasize at this point that the use of Māori cultural practices (literally and/or metaphorically) in research might lead those not familiar with New Zealand to question how relevant such an analysis is to the lived realities of Māori people today. Because Māori people today are a Fourth World nation or nations—that is, within a larger entity—it is more a matter of degree as to who participates and when they participate. Therefore, rather than being able to quantify which portion of the Māori population still acts in this way, it is perhaps more realistic to say that most Māori do at some time. For some, it might be only at funerals or weddings; others, of course, (albeit a small proportion) live this way all the time, but increasingly more and more Māori people are participating in (for example) kaupapa Māori educational initiatives, and these are all run in a Māori manner. Thus, most people do sometimes, some all the time, and others not so often. What is perhaps more critical is that most Māori people are able to understand the processes and are able to participate. Much is said of the impact of urbanization on Māori people and the removal of young people from their tribal roots and the consequent decline in language abilities and cultural understandings. It is a measure of the strength of the whânau (the extended family) and the strength of genealogical linkages, however, that when Māori people gather, the hui (formal meetings) process is usually the one that is used, almost as a "default setting," despite more than a century of colonization. Indeed, it is a measure of the strength of these cultural practices and principles that they have survived the onslaught of the past 150 years. It is to these underlying strengths that I turn also as inspiration for developing an approach to Māori research. My argument, then, is not an attempt to identify "past practices" or reassemble a romantic past, but rather to examine what might constitute the emerging field of Kaupapa Māori research in reference to present Māori cultural practices that are guided by the messages from the past. Māori, along with many other indigenous people, are guided by the principle of guidance

from the ancestors. It is not a matter of studying how people did things in the past but more an ongoing dynamic interactive relationship between those of us alive today as the embodiment of all those who have gone before. It seems to me that, in practice, Māori cultural practices are alive and well and that, when used either literally or metaphorically, they enable Māori people to understand and control what is happening.

12. Eminent Māori scholar Rose Pere (1991) describes the key qualities of a hui as

> respect, consideration, patience, and cooperation. People need to feel that they have the right and the time to express their point of view. You may not always agree with the speakers, but it is considered bad form to interrupt their flow of speech while they are standing on their feet; one has to wait to make a comment. People may be as frank as they like about others at the hui, but usually state their case in such a way that the person being criticized can stand up with some dignity in his/her right of reply. Once everything has been fully discussed and the members come to some form of consensus, the hui concludes with a prayer and the partaking of food. (p. 44)

13. This may appear to be somewhat patronizing; however, our experience when conducting Kaupapa Māori research is that research participants are often surprised by our insistence that we wish to enter into a dialogue with them about the meaning they construct from their experiences. Our experience is that the traditional "speaking for" type of research is so pervasive and dominant that participants are initially surprised that they might have an authoritative voice in the process rather than just being a source of data for an outside researcher. What are truly heartening are the positive responses we have had from participants of all ages, once they realized that they were able to engage in a dialogue.

14. For further details of the use of Māori metaphor, see Bishop (1996) and Bishop and Glynn (1999).

15. In New Zealand, the koru represents growth, new beginnings, renewal, and hope for the future.

16. Donna Awatere (1981) and Kathie Irwin (1992b) are two Māori feminist scholars who have taken up this challenge in Aotearoa/New Zealand, in a way that has clearly delineated their stance as different from white feminisms. In operationalizing Māori feminisms, they have critiqued modernist issues from a Māori worldview in Māori ways. Awatere critiqued white modernist feminists for hegemonically voicing Māori feminist concerns as identical to their own. Kathie Irwin's (1992b) critique addressed a question that is vexatious to non-Māori modernist feminists: "Why don't women speak on a marae?" She responded with other questions, such as "What do you mean by speaking? . . . Is a karanga not speaking?" and "Who is defining what speaking is?" She asserts that rather than taking an essentialist position, the validity of a text written about Māori women "speaking" on a marae is understandable only in terms of the rules established within Māori cultural practices associated with marae protocols. In this, she is not only addressing a Māori issue but also is addressing modernist feminists in poststructural terms of epistemological validity.

17. People often use the term *kawa* to refer to marae protocols. For example, at the time of whaikorero (ritualized speechmaking), some tribes conduct this part of the pôwhiri by a tikanga known as *paeke*, where all the male speakers of the hosts' side will speak at one time, then turn the marae over to the visitors' speaker, who then follows. Other tribes prefer to follow a tikanga termed *utuutu*, where hosts and visitors alternate. Some tribes welcome visitors into their meeting house following a hôngi; others keep the hôngi until the end of the welcoming

time. It is clear that these various tikanga are practices that are correct in certain tribal or hapu contexts, but underneath is the practice of the kawa being handed down from those who have gone before, concerning the need to recognize the tapu of people, their mana, their wairua, and the mauri of the place and events. See Salmond (1975) for a detailed ethnographic study.

References

Acker, F., Barry, K., & Esseveld, J. (1991). Objectivity and truth problems in doing feminist research. In M. Fonow & J. Cook (Eds.), *Beyond methodology: Feminist scholarship as lived research* (pp. 133–154). Bloomington: Indiana University Press.

Awatere, D. (1981). *Māori sovereignty.* Auckland, New Zealand: Broadsheet.

Ballard, K. (Ed.). (1994). *Disability, family, whanau and society.* Palmerston North, New Zealand: Dunmore Press.

Beverley, J. (2000). Testimonio, subalternity, and narrative authority. In N. K. Denzin & Y. S. Lincoln (Eds.), *Handbook of qualitative research* (2nd ed., pp. 555–565). Thousand Oaks, CA: Sage.

Bishop, R. (1991a). *He whakawhanaungatanga tikanga rua. Establishing links: A bicultural experience.* Unpublished master's thesis, University of Otago, Dunedin, New Zealand.

Bishop, R. (1991b, December). *Te ropu rangahau tikanga rua: The need for emancipatory research under the control of the* Māori *people for the betterment of* Māori *people.* Paper presented at the 13th Annual New Zealand Association for Research in Education, Knox College, Dunedin, New Zealand.

Bishop, R. (1996). *Collaborative research stories: Whakawanaungatanga.* Palmerston North, New Zealand: Dunmore Press.

Bishop, R. (1997). Interviewing as collaborative storying. *Educational Research and Perspectives, 24*(1), 28–47.

Bishop, R. (1998a). Examples of culturally specific research practices: A response to Tillman and López. *Qualitative Studies in Education, 11*(3), 419–434.

Bishop, R. (1998b). Freeing ourselves from neo-colonial domination in research: A Māori approach to creating knowledge. *Qualitative Studies in Education, 11*(2), 199–219.

Bishop, R., Berryman, M., & Richardson, C. (2002). Te toi huarewa: Effective teaching and learning in total immersion Māori language educational settings. *Canadian Journal of Native Education, 26*(1), 44–61.

Bishop, R., Berryman, M., & Richardson, C. (2003). *Te Kotahitanga: The experiences of year 9 and 10 Māori students in mainstream classrooms.* Wellington, New Zealand: Ministry of Education. Retrieved from www.minedu.govt.nz/goto/tekotahitanga

Bishop, R., & Glynn, T. (1999). *Culture counts: Changing power relations in education.* Palmerston North, New Zealand: Dunmore Press.

Brayboy, B. M., & Deyhle, D. (2000). Insider-outsider: Researchers in American Indian communities. *Theory Into Practice, 39*(3), 163–169.

Bridges, D. (2001). The ethics of outsider research. *Journal of Philosophy of Education, 35*(3), 371–386.

Burgess, R. G. (1984). *In the field: An introduction to field research.* New York: Falmer.

Calderhead, J. (1981). Stimulated recall: A method for research on teaching. *British Journal of Educational Psychology, 51,* 211–217.

Connelly, F. M., & Clandinin, D. J. (1990). Stories of experience and narrative inquiry. *Educational Researcher, 19*(5), 2–14.

Consedine, R., & Consedine, J. (2001). *Healing our history: The challenge of the Treaty of Waitangi.* Auckland, New Zealand: Penguin Books.

Davies, B. (1990). Agency as a form of discursive practice: A classroom observed. *British Journal of Sociology of Education, 11*(3), 341–361.

Davies, B., & Harré, R. (1990). Positioning: The discursive production of selves. *Journal of the Theory of Social Behaviour, 20,* 43–65.

Davies, L., & Nicholl, K. (1993). *Te Māori i roto i nga mahi whakaakoranga: Māori in education.* Wellington, New Zealand: Ministry of Education.

Delamont, S. (1992). *Fieldwork in educational settings: Methods, pitfalls and perspectives.* London: Falmer.

Deyhle, D., & Swisher, K. (1997). Research in American Indian and Alaska Native education: From assimilation to self-determination. In M. W. Apple (Ed.), *Review of Research in Education* (Vol. 22, pp. 113–194). Washington, DC: American Educational Research Association.

Durie, M. (1994). *Whaiora: Māori health development.* Auckland, New Zealand: Oxford University Press.

Durie, M. (1995). *Principles for the development of Māori policy.* Paper presented at the *Māori* Policy Development, Māori Policy Development Conference, Wellington, New Zealand.

Durie, M. (1998). *Te mana, te kawanatonga: The politics of Māori self-determination.* Auckland, New Zealand: Oxford University Press.

Eisner, E. W. (1991). *The enlightened eye: Qualitative inquiry and the enhancement of educational practice.* New York: Teachers College Press.

Esposito, L., & Murphy, J. W. (2000). Another step in the study of race relations. *The Sociological Quarterly, 41*(2), 171–187.

Fine, M. (1994). Working the hyphens: Reinventing the self and other in qualitative research. In N. K. Denzin & Y. S. Lincoln (Eds.), *Handbook of qualitative research* (pp. 70–82). Thousand Oaks, CA: Sage.

Fine, M., & Weis, L. (1996). Writing the "wrongs" of fieldwork: Confronting our own research/writing dilemmas in urban ethnographies. *Qualitative Inquiry, 2*(3), 251–274.

Fine, M., Weis, L., Weseen, S., & Wong, L. (2000). For whom? Qualitative research, representations, and social responsibilities. In N. K. Denzin & Y. S. Lincoln (Eds.), *Handbook of qualitative research* (2nd ed., pp. 107–131). Thousand Oaks, CA: Sage.

Fitzsimons, P., & Smith, G. H. (2000). Philosophy and indigenous cultural transformation. *Educational Philosophy and Theory, 32*(1), 25–41.

Gay, G. (2000). *Culturally responsive teaching: Theory, research and practice.* New York: Teachers College Press.

Glaser, B. G., & Strauss, A. L. (1967). *The discovery of grounded theory: Strategies for qualitative research.* London: Weidenfeld and Nicolson.

Goldstein, L. S. (2000). Ethical dilemmas in designing collaborative research: Lessons learned the hard way. *Qualitative Studies in Education, 13*(5), 517–530.

González, F. E. (2001). *Haciendo que hacer*—cultivating a Mestiz worldview and academic achievement: Braiding cultural knowledge into educational research, policy, practice. *International Journal of Qualitative Studies in Education, 14*(5), 641–656.

Griffiths, M. (1998). *Educational research for social justice: Getting off the fence.* Buckingham, UK: Open University Press.

Heshusius, L. (1994). Freeing ourselves from objectivity: Managing subjectivity or turning toward a participatory mode of consciousness? *Educational Researcher, 23*(3), 15–22.

Heshusius, L. (1996). Modes of consciousness and the self in learning disabilities research: Considering past and future. In D. K. Reid, W. P. Hresko, & H. L. Swanson (Eds.), *Cognitive approaches to learning disabilities* (3rd ed., pp. 651–671). Austin, TX: PRO-ED.

Heshusius, L. (2002). More than the (merely) rational: Imagining inquiry for ability diversity. An essay response to Jim Paul. *Disability, Culture and Education, 1*(2), 95–118.

Hohepa, P. (1975). The one people myth. In M. King (Ed.), *Te ao hurihuri: The world moves on: Aspects of Māoritanga* (pp. 98–111). Auckland, New Zealand: Hicks Smith.

Holmes, H., Bishop, R., & Glynn, T. (1993). *Tu mai kia tu ake: Impact of taha Māori in Otago and Southland schools* (Te Ropu Rangahau Tikanga Rua Monograph No. 4). Dunedin, New Zealand: Department of Education, University of Otago.

hooks, b. (1993). Postmodern blackness. *Postmodern Culture, 1*(1). Retrieved from http://muse .jhu.edu/journals/pmc/index.html

Irwin, K. (1989). Multicultural education: the New Zealand response. *New Zealand Journal of Educational Studies, 24*(1), 3–18.

Irwin, K. (1992a). *Māori research methods and processes: An exploration and discussion.* Paper presented at the Joint New Zealand Association for Research in Education/Australian Association for Research in Education Conference, Geelong, Australia.

Irwin, K. (1992b). Towards theories of Māori feminisms. In R. Du Plessis (Ed.), *Feminist voices: Women's studies texts for Aotearoa/New Zealand* (pp. 1–21). Auckland, New Zealand: Oxford University Press.

Irwin, K. (1994). Māori research methods and processes: An exploration. *Sites: A Journal for Radical Perspectives on Culture, 28,* 25–43.

Jacobs-Huey, L. (2002). The natives are gazing and talking back: Review the problematics of positionality, voice and accountability among "Native" anthropologists. *American Anthropologist, 104*(3), 791–804.

Johnson-Bailey, J. (1999). The ties that bind and the shackles that separate: Race, gender, class, and color in a research process. *Qualitative Studies in Education, 12*(6), 659–670.

Jones, A., McCulloch, G., Marshall, J. D., Smith, G. H., & Smith, L. T. (1990). *Myths and realities: Schooling in New Zealand.* Palmerston North, New Zealand: Dunmore Press.

Kemmis, S., & McTaggart, R. (2000). Participatory action research. In N. K. Denzin & Y. S. Lincoln (Eds.), *Handbook of qualitative research* (2nd ed., pp. 567–605). Thousand Oaks, CA: Sage.

Kincheloe, J. L., & McLaren, P. (2000). Rethinking critical theory and qualitative research. In N. K. Denzin & Y. S. Lincoln (Eds.), *Handbook of qualitative research* (2nd ed., pp. 279–313). Thousand Oaks, CA: Sage.

Ladson-Billings, G. (1995). Toward a theory of culturally relevant pedagogy. *American Educational Research Journal, 32*(3), 465–491.

Ladson-Billings, G. (2000). Racialized discourses and ethnic epistemologies. In N. K. Denzin & Y. S. Lincoln (Eds.), *Handbook of qualitative research* (2nd ed., pp. 257–277). Thousand Oaks, CA: Sage.

Lather, P. (1986). Research as praxis. *Harvard Educational Review, 56*(3), 257–274.

Lather, P. (1991). *Getting smart: Feminist research and pedagogy with/in the postmodern.* New York: Routledge.

Lincoln, Y. S., & Denzin, N. K. (1994). The fifth moment. In N. K. Denzin & Y. S. Lincoln (Eds.), *Handbook of qualitative research* (pp. 575–586). Thousand Oaks, CA: Sage.

Lomawaima, K. T. (2000). Tribal sovereigns: Reframing research in American Indian education. *Harvard Educational Review, 70*(1), 1–21.

Merriam, S. B., Johnson-Bailey, J., Lee, M.-Y., Kee, Y., Ntseane, G., & Muhamad, M. (2001). Power and positionality: Negotiating insider/outsider status within and across cultures. *International Journal of Lifelong Education, 20*(5), 405–416.

Metge, J. (1990). Te rito o te harakeke: Conceptions of the Whaanau. *Journal of the Polynesian Society, 99*(1), 55–91.

Mishler, E. G. (1986). *Research interviewing: Context and narrative.* Cambridge, MA: Harvard University Press.

Moll, L. C. (1992). Bilingual classroom studies and community analysis: Some recent trends. *Educational Researcher, 21,* 20–24.

Narayan, K. (1993). How native is a "native" anthropologist? *American Anthropologist, 95,* 671–686.

Noddings, N. (1986). Fidelity in teaching, teacher education, and research for teaching. *Harvard Educational Review, 56*(4), 496–510.

Oakley, A. (1981). Interviewing women: A contradiction in terms. In H. Roberts (Ed.), *Doing feminist research* (pp. 30–61). London: Routledge.

Olssen, M. (1993, April). *Habermas, post-modernism and the science question for education.* Paper presented at the Staff Seminar, University of Otago, Dunedin, New Zealand.

Patton, M. (1990). *Qualitative evaluation and research methods* (2nd ed.). Newbury Park, CA: Sage.

Pere, R. (1991). *Te wheke: A celebration of infinite wisdom.* Gisborne, New Zealand: Ao Ako.

Pihama, L., Cram, F., & Walker, S. (2002). Creating a methodological space: A literature review of Kaupapa Māori research. *Canadian Journal of Native Education, 26*(1), 30–43.

Polanyi, M. (1966). *The tacit dimension.* New York: Doubleday.

Pomare, E. (1988). *Hauora: Māori standards of health.* Wellington, New Zealand: Department of Health.

Rains, F. V., Archibald, J.-A., & Deyhle, D. (2000). Introduction: Through our eyes and in our own words. *International Journal of Qualitative Studies in Education, 13*(4), 337–342.

Reinharz, S. (1992). *Feminist methods in social research.* New York: Oxford University Press.

Reyes, P., Scribner, J., & Scribner, A. P. (Eds.). (1999). *Lessons from high-performing Hispanic schools: Greater learning communities.* New York: Teachers College Press.

Ryan, J. (1999). *Race and ethnicity in multi-ethnic schools: A critical case study.* Clevedon, UK: Multilingual Matters.

Salmond, A. (1975). *Hui: A study of Māori ceremonial greetings.* Auckland, New Zealand: Reed & Methuen.

Scheurich, J. J., & Young, M. D. (1997). Coloring epistemologies: Are our research epistemologies racially biased? *Educational Researcher, 26*(4), 4–16.

Shirres, M. (1982). Tapu. *Journal of the Polynesian Society, 91*(1), 29–52.

Sidorkin, A. M. (2002). *Learning relations: Impure education, deschooled schools, and dialogue with evil.* New York: Peter Lang.

Simon, J. A. (1990). *The role of schooling in Māori-Pâkehâ relations.* Unpublished doctoral dissertation, Auckland University, Auckland, New Zealand.

Sleeter, C. E. (2001). Epistemological diversity in research on preservice teacher preparation for historically underserved children. In W. G. Secada (Ed.), *Review of Research in Education* (Vol. 6, pp. 209–250). Washington, DC: American Educational Research Association.

Smart, B. (1986). The politics of truth and the problems of hegemony. In D. C. Hoy (Ed.), *Foucault: A critical reader* (pp. 157–173). Oxford, UK: Basil Blackwell.

Smith, G. H. (1990). Taha Māori: Pâkehâ capture. In J. Codd, R. Harker & R. Nash (Eds.), *Political issues in New Zealand education* (pp. 183–197). Palmerston North, New Zealand: Dunmore Press.

Smith, G. H. (1992, November). *Tane-nui-a-rangi's legacy: Propping up the sky: Kaupapa Māori as resistance and intervention.* Paper presented at the New Zealand Association for Research in Education/Australian Association for Research in Education Joint Conference, Deakin University, Australia. Retrieved from www.swin.edu/.au/aare/conf92/SMITG92.384

Smith, G. H. (1997). *Kaupapa Māori as transformative praxis.* Unpublished doctoral dissertation, University of Auckland, Auckland.

Smith, L. T. (1999). *Decolonizing methodologies: Research and indigenous peoples.* London: Zed Books.

Sprague, J., & Hayes, J. (2000). Self-determination and empowerment: A feminist standpoint analysis of talk about disability. *American Journal of Community Psychology, 28*(5), 671–695.

Stacey, J. (1991). Can there be a feminist ethnography? In S. B. Gluck & D. Patai (Eds.), *Women's words: The feminist practice of oral history* (pp. 111–119). New York: Routledge.

Stanfield, J. H. (1994). Ethnic modeling in qualitative research. In N. K. Denzin & Y. S. Lincoln (Eds.), *Handbook of qualitative research* (pp. 175–188). Thousand Oaks, CA: Sage.

Swisher, K. G. (1998). Why Indian people should be the ones to write about Indian education. In D. A. Mihesuah (Ed.), *Natives and academics: Researching and writing about American Indians* (pp. 190–200). Lincoln: University of Nebraska Press.

Thayer-Bacon, B. (1997). The nurturing of a relational epistemology. *Educational Theory, 47*(2), 239–260.

Tillman, L. C. (2002). Culturally sensitive research approaches: An African-American perspective. *Educational Researcher, 31*(9), 3–12.

Tripp, D. H. (1983). Co-authorship and negotiation: The interview as act of creation. *Interchange, 14*(3), 32–45.

Villegas, A. M., & Lucas, T. (2002). *Educating culturally responsive teachers: A coherent approach.* New York: State University of New York Press.

Walker, R. (1990). *Ka whawhai tonu matou: Struggle without end.* Auckland, New Zealand: Penguin.

6

ETHICS AND POLITICS IN QUALITATIVE RESEARCH

Clifford G. Christians

The Enlightenment mind clustered around an extraordinary dichotomy. Intellectual historians usually summarize this split in terms of subject/object, fact/value, or material/spiritual dualisms. All three of these are legitimate interpretations of the cosmology inherited from Galileo, Descartes, and Newton. None of them, however, puts the Enlightenment into its sharpest focus. Its deepest root was a pervasive autonomy. The cult of human personality prevailed in all its freedom. Human beings were declared a law unto themselves, set loose from every faith that claimed their allegiance. Proudly self-conscious of human autonomy, the 18th-century mind saw nature as an arena of limitless possibilities in which the sovereignty of human personality was demonstrated by its mastery over the natural order. Release from nature spawned autonomous individuals who considered themselves independent of any authority. The freedom motif was the deepest driving force, first released by the Renaissance and achieving maturity during the Enlightenment.[1]

Obviously, one can reach autonomy by starting with the subject/object dualism. In constructing the Enlightenment worldview, the prestige of natural science played a key role in setting people free. Achievements in mathematics, physics, and astronomy allowed humans to dominate nature, which formerly had dominated them. Science provided unmistakable evidence that by applying reason to nature and to human beings in fairly obvious ways, people could live progressively happier lives. Crime and insanity, for example, no longer needed repressive theological explanations, but instead were deemed capable of mundane empirical solutions.

Likewise, one can get to the autonomous self by casting the question in terms of a radical discontinuity between hard facts and subjective values. The Enlightenment did push values to the fringe through its disjunction between knowledge of what is and what ought to be, and Enlightenment materialism in all its forms isolated reason from faith, and knowledge from belief. As Robert Hooke insisted in 1663, when he helped found London's Royal Society, "To improve the knowledge of natural things, this Society will not meddle with Divinity, Metaphysics, Morals, Politics and Rhetoric" (Lyons, 1944, p. 41). With factuality gaining a stranglehold on the Enlightenment mind, those regions of human interest that implied oughts, constraints, and imperatives simply ceased to appear. Certainly those who see the Enlightenment as separating facts and values have identified a cardinal difficulty. Likewise, the realm of the spirit can easily dissolve into mystery and intuition. If the spiritual world contains no binding force, it is surrendered to speculation by the divines, many of whom accepted the Enlightenment belief that their pursuit was ephemeral.

But the Enlightenment's autonomy doctrine created the greatest mischief. Individual self-determination stands as the centerpiece, bequeathing to us the universal problem of integrating human freedom with moral order. In struggling with the complexities and conundrums of this relationship, the Enlightenment, in effect, refused to sacrifice personal freedom. Even though the problem had a particular urgency in the 18th century, its response was not resolution but a categorical insistence on autonomy. Given the despotic political regimes and oppressive ecclesiastical systems of the period, such an uncompromising stance for freedom at this juncture is understandable. The Enlightenment began and ended with the assumption that human liberty ought to be cut away from the moral order, never integrated meaningfully with it.

Jean-Jacques Rousseau was the most outspoken advocate of this radical freedom. He gave intellectual substance to free self-determination of the human personality as the highest good. Rousseau is a complicated figure. He refused to be co-opted by Descartes's rationalism, Newton's mechanistic cosmology, or Locke's egoistic selves. He was not merely content to isolate and sacralize freedom, either, at least not in his *Discourse on Inequality* or in the *Social Contract*, where he answers Hobbes.

Rousseau represented the romantic wing of the Enlightenment, revolting against its rationalism. He won a wide following well into the 19th century for advocating immanent and emergent values rather than transcendent and given ones. While admitting that humans were finite and limited, he nonetheless promoted a freedom of breathtaking scope—not just disengagement from God or the Church, but freedom from culture and from any authority. Autonomy became the core of the human being and the center of the universe. Rousseau's understanding of equality, social systems, axiology, and language were anchored in it. He recognized the consequences more astutely than those comfortable with a shrunken negative freedom. The only solution that he found tolerable, however, was a noble human nature that enjoyed freedom beneficently and, therefore, one could presume, lived compatibly in some vague sense with a moral order.

Value-Free Experimentalism

Typically, debates over the character of the social sciences revolve around the theory and methodology of the natural sciences. However, the argument here is not how they resemble natural science, but rather their inscription into the dominant Enlightenment worldview. In political theory, the liberal state as it emerged in 17th- and 18th-century Europe left citizens free to lead their own lives without obeisance to the Church or the feudal order. Psychology, sociology, and economics—known as the human or moral sciences in the 18th and 19th centuries—were conceived as "liberal arts" that opened minds and freed the imagination. As the social sciences and liberal state emerged and overlapped historically, Enlightenment thinkers in Europe advocated the "facts, skills, and techniques" of experimental reasoning to support the state and citizenry (Root, 1993, pp. 14–15).

Consistent with the presumed priority of individual liberty over the moral order, the basic institutions of society were designed to ensure "neutrality between different conceptions of the good" (Root, 1993, p. 12). The state was prohibited "from requiring or even encouraging citizens to subscribe to one religious tradition, form of family life, or manner of personal or artistic expression over another" (Root, 1993, p. 12). Given the historical circumstances in which shared conceptions of the good were no longer broad and deeply entrenched, taking sides on moral issues and insisting on social ideals were considered counterproductive. Value neutrality appeared to be the logical alternative "for a society whose members practiced many religions, pursued many different occupations, and identified with many different customs and traditions" (Root, 1993, p. 11). The theory and practice of mainstream social science reflect liberal Enlightenment philosophy, as do education, science, and politics. Only a reintegration of autonomy and the moral order provides an alternative paradigm for the social sciences today.[2]

Mill's Philosophy of Social Science

For John Stuart Mill, "neutrality is necessary in order to promote autonomy. . . . A person cannot be forced to be good, and the state should not dictate the kind of life a citizen should lead; it would be better for citizens to choose badly than for them to be forced by the state to choose well" (Root, 1993, pp. 12–13). Planning our lives according to our own ideas and purposes is sine qua non for autonomous beings in Mill's *On Liberty* (1859/1978): "The free development of individuality is one of the principal ingredients of human happiness, and quite the chief ingredient of individual and social progress" (p. 50; see also Copleston, 1966, p. 303, n. 32). This neutrality, based on the supremacy of individual autonomy, is the foundational principle in his *Utilitarianism* (1861/1957) and in *A System of Logic, Ratiocinative and Inductive* (1843/1893) as well. For Mill, "the principle of utility demands that the individual should enjoy full liberty, except the liberty to harm others" (Copleston, 1966, p. 54). In addition to bringing classical utilitarianism to its maximum development and establishing with Locke the liberal state, Mill delineated the foundations of inductive inquiry as social scientific method. In terms of the principles of empiricism, he perfected the inductive techniques of Francis Bacon as a problem-solving methodology to replace Aristotelian deductive logic.

According to Mill, syllogisms contribute nothing new to human knowledge. If we conclude that because "all men are mortal" the Duke of Wellington is mortal by virtue of his manhood, then the conclusion does not advance the premise (see Mill, 1843/1893, II, 3, 2, p. 140). The crucial issue is not reordering the conceptual world but discriminating genuine knowledge from superstition. In the pursuit of truth, generalizing and synthesizing are necessary to advance inductively from the known to the unknown. Mill seeks to establish this function of logic as inference from the known, rather than certifying the rules for formal consistency in reasoning (Mill, 1843/1893, Bk. 3). Scientific certitude can be approximated when induction is followed rigorously, with propositions empirically derived and the material of all our knowledge provided by experience.[3] For the physical sciences, he establishes four modes of experimental inquiry: agreement, disagreement, residues, and the principle of concomitant variations (Mill, 1843/1893, III, 8, pp. 278–288). He considers them the only possible methods of proof for experimentation, as long as one presumes the realist position that nature is structured by uniformities.[4]

In Book 6 of *A System of Logic,* "On the Logic of the Moral Sciences," Mill (1843/1893) develops an inductive experimentalism as the scientific method for studying "the various phenomena which constitute social life" (VI, 6, 1, p. 606). Although he conceived of social science as explaining human behavior in terms of causal laws, he warned against the fatalism of full predictability. "Social laws are hypothetical, and statistically-based generalizations by their very nature admit of exceptions" (Copleston, 1966, p. 101; see also Mill, 1843/1893, VI, 5, 1, p. 596). Empirically confirmed instrumental knowledge about human behavior has greater predictive power when it deals with collective masses than when we are dealing with individual agents.

Mill's positivism is obvious throughout his work on experimental inquiry.[5] Based on the work of Auguste Comte, he defined matter as the "permanent possibility of sensation" (Mill, 1865, p. 198) and believed that nothing else can be said about metaphysical substances.[6] With Hume and Comte, Mill insisted that metaphysical substances are not real and that only the facts of sense phenomena exist. There are no essences or ultimate reality behind sensations; therefore, Mill (1865/1907, 1865) and Comte (1848/1910) argued that social scientists should limit themselves to particular data as a factual source out of which experimentally valid laws can be derived. For both, this is the only kind of knowledge that yields practical benefits (Mill, 1865, p. 242); in fact, society's salvation is contingent upon such scientific knowledge (p. 241).[7]

As with his consequentialist ethics, Mill's philosophy of social science is built on a dualism of means and ends. Citizens and politicians are responsible for articulating ends in a free society, and science is responsible for the know-how to achieve them.

Science is amoral, speaking to questions of means but with no wherewithal or authority to dictate ends. Methods in the social sciences must be disinterested regarding substance and content, and rigorously limited to the risks and benefits of possible courses of action. Protocols for practicing liberal science "should be prescriptive, but not morally or politically prescriptive and should direct against bad science but not bad conduct" (Root, 1993, p. 129). Research cannot be judged right or wrong, only true or false. "Science is political only in its applications" (Root, 1993, p. 213). Given his democratic liberalism, Mill advocates neutrality "out of concern for the autonomy of the individuals or groups" social science seeks to serve. It should "treat them as thinking, willing, active beings who bear responsibility for their choices and are free to choose" their own conception of the good life by majority rule (Root, 1993, p. 19).

Value Neutrality in Max Weber

When 20th-century mainstream social scientists contended that ethics is not their business, they typically invoked Weber's essays written between 1904 and 1917. Given Weber's importance, methodologically and theoretically, for sociology and economics, his distinction between political judgments and scientific neutrality is given canonical status.

Weber distinguishes between value freedom and value relevance. He recognizes that in the discovery phase, "personal, cultural, moral, or political values cannot be eliminated; . . . what social scientists choose to investigate . . . they choose on the basis of the values" they expect their research to advance (Root, 1993, p. 33). But he insists that social science be value-free in the presentation phase. Findings ought not to express any judgments of a moral or political character. Professors should hang up their values along with their coats as they enter their lecture halls.

"An attitude of moral indifference," Weber (1904/1949b) writes, "has no connection with scientific objectivity" (p. 60). His meaning is clear from the value-freedom/value-relevance distinction. For the social sciences to be purposeful and rational, they must serve the "values of relevance."

> The problems of the social sciences are selected by the value relevance of the phenomena treated. . . . The expression "relevance to values" refers simply to the philosophical interpretation of that specifically scientific "interest" which determines the selection of a given subject matter and problems of empirical analysis. (Weber, 1917/1949a, pp. 21–22)

> In the social sciences the stimulus to the posing of scientific problems is in actuality always given by practical "questions." Hence, the very recognition of the existence of a scientific problem coincides personally with the possession of specifically oriented motives and values. . . . (Weber, 1904/1949b, p. 61)

> Without the investigator's evaluative ideas, there would be no principle of selection of subject matter and no meaningful knowledge of the concrete reality. Without the investigator's

> conviction regarding the significance of particular cultural facts, every attempt to analyze concrete reality is absolutely meaningless. (Weber, 1904/1949b, p. 82)

Whereas the natural sciences, in Weber's (1904/1949b, p. 72) view, seek general laws that govern all empirical phenomena, the social sciences study those realities that our values consider significant. Whereas the natural world itself indicates what reality to investigate, the infinite possibilities of the social world are ordered in terms of "the cultural values with which we approach reality" (1904/1949b, p. 78).[8] However, even though value relevance directs the social sciences, as with the natural sciences, Weber considers the former value-free. The subject matter in natural science makes value judgments unnecessary, and social scientists by a conscious decision can exclude judgments of "desirability or undesirability" from their publications and lectures (1904/1949b, p. 52). "What is really at issue is the intrinsically simple demand that the investigator and teacher should keep unconditionally separate the establishment of empirical facts . . . and his own political evaluations" (Weber, 1917/1949a, p. 11).

Weber's opposition to value judgments in the social sciences was driven by practical circumstances. Academic freedom for the universities of Prussia was more likely if professors limited their professional work to scientific know-how. With university hiring controlled by political officials, only if the faculty refrained from policy commitments and criticism would officials relinquish their control.

Few of the offices in government or industry in Germany were held by people who were well trained to solve questions of means. Weber thought that the best way to increase the power and economic prosperity of Germany was to train a new managerial class learned about means and silent about ends. The mission of the university, in Weber's view, should be to offer such training (Root, 1993, p. 41; see also Weber, 1973, pp. 4–8).[9]

Weber's practical argument for value freedom and his apparent limitation of it to the reporting phase have made his version of value neutrality attractive to 21st-century social science. He is not a positivist such as Comte or a thoroughgoing empiricist in the tradition of Mill. He disavowed the positivists' overwrought disjunction between discovery and justification, and he developed no systematic epistemology comparable to Mill's. His nationalism was partisan compared to Mill's liberal political philosophy. Nevertheless, Weber's value neutrality reflects Enlightenment autonomy in a fundamentally similar fashion. In the process of maintaining his distinction between value relevance and value freedom, he separates facts from values and means from ends. He appeals to empirical evidence and logical reasoning rooted in human rationality. "The validity of a practical imperative as a norm," he writes, "and the truth-value of an empirical proposition are absolutely heterogeneous in character" (Weber, 1904/1949b, p. 52). "A systematically correct scientific proof in the social sciences" may not be completely attainable, but that is most likely "due to faulty data," not because it is conceptually impossible (1904/1949b, p. 58).[10] For Weber, as with Mill, empirical science deals with questions of means, and his warning against inculcating political and moral values presumes a means-ends dichotomy (see Weber, 1917/1949a, pp. 18–19; 1904/1949b, p. 52).

As Michael Root (1993) concludes, "John Stuart Mill's call for neutrality in the social sciences is based on his belief" that the language of science "takes cognizance of a phenomenon and endeavors to discover its laws" (p. 205). Max Weber likewise "takes it for granted that there can be a language of science—a collection of truths—that excludes all value-judgments, rules, or directions for conduct" (Root, 1993, p. 205). In both cases, scientific knowledge exists for its own sake as morally neutral. For both, neutrality is desirable "because questions of value are not rationally resolvable" and neutrality in the social sciences is presumed to contribute "to political and personal autonomy" (Root, 1993, p. 229). In Weber's argument for value relevance in social science, he did not contradict the larger Enlightenment ideal of scientific neutrality between competing conceptions of the good.

Utilitarian Ethics

In addition to its this-worldly humanism, utilitarian ethics was attractive for its compatibility with scientific thought. It fit the canons of rational calculation as they were nourished by the Enlightenment's intellectual culture.

> In the utilitarian perspective, one validated an ethical position by hard evidence. You count the consequences for human happiness of one or another course, and you go with the one with the highest favorable total. What counts as human happiness was thought to be something conceptually unproblematic, a scientifically establishable domain of facts. One could abandon all the metaphysical or theological factors which made ethical questions scientifically undecidable. (Taylor, 1982, p. 129)

Utilitarian ethics replaces metaphysical distinctions with the calculation of empirical quantities. It follows the procedural demand that if "the happiness of each agent counts for one . . . the right course of action should be what satisfies all, or the largest number possible" (Taylor, 1982, p. 131). Autonomous reason is the arbiter of moral disputes.

With moral reasoning equivalent to calculating consequences for human happiness, utilitarianism presumes there is "a single consistent domain of the moral, that there is one set of considerations which determines what we ought morally to do." This "epistemologically-motivated reduction and homogenization of the moral" marginalizes the qualitative languages of admiration and contempt—integrity, healing, liberation, conviction, dishonesty, and self-indulgence, for example (Taylor, 1982, pp. 132–133). In utilitarian terms, these languages designate subjective factors that "correspond to nothing in reality. . . . They express the way we feel, not the way things are" (Taylor, 1982, p. 141). This single-consideration theory not only demands that we maximize general happiness but also considers irrelevant other moral imperatives that conflict with it, such as equal distribution. One-factor models appeal to the "epistemological squeamishness" of value-neutral social science, which "dislikes contrastive languages." Moreover, utilitarianism appealingly offers "the prospect of exact calculation of policy through . . . rational choice theory" (Taylor, 1982, p. 143). "It portrays all moral issues as discrete problems amenable to largely technical solutions" (Euben, 1981, p. 117). However, to its critics, this kind of exactness represents "a semblance of validity" by leaving out whatever cannot be calculated (Taylor, 1982, p. 143).[11]

Given the dualism of means and ends in utilitarian theory, the domain of the good in utilitarianism is extrinsic. All that is worth valuing is a function of its consequences. Prima facie duties are literally inconceivable. The degree to which one's actions and statements truly express what is important to someone does not count. Ethical and political thinking in consequentialist terms legislates intrinsic valuing out of existence (Taylor, 1982, p. 144). The exteriority of ethics is seen to guarantee the value neutrality of experimental procedures.[12]

▣ Codes of Ethics

In value-free social science, codes of ethics for professional and academic associations are the conventional format for moral principles. By the 1980s, each of the major scholarly associations had adopted its own code, with an overlapping emphasis on four guidelines for directing an inductive science of means toward majoritarian ends.

1. *Informed consent.* Consistent with its commitment to individual autonomy, social science in the Mill and Weber tradition insists that research subjects have the right to be informed about the nature and consequences of experiments in which they are involved. Proper respect for human freedom generally includes two necessary conditions. First, subjects must agree voluntarily to participate—that is, without physical or psychological coercion. Second, their agreement must be based on full and open information. "The Articles of the Nuremberg Tribunal and the Declaration of Helsinki both state that subjects must be told the duration, methods, possible risks, and the purpose or aim of the experiment" (Soble, 1978, p. 40; see also Veatch, 1996).

The self-evident character of this principle is not disputed in rationalist ethics. Meaningful application, however, generates ongoing disputes. As Punch (1994) observes, "In much fieldwork there seems to be no way around the predicament that informed consent—divulging one's identity and research purpose to all and sundry—will kill many a project stone dead" (p. 90). True to the privileging of means in a means-ends model, Punch reflects the general conclusion that codes of ethics should serve as a guideline prior to fieldwork but not intrude on full participation. "A strict application of codes" may "restrain and restrict" a great deal of "innocuous" and "unproblematic" research (p. 90).

2. *Deception.* In emphasizing informed consent, social science codes of ethics uniformly oppose deception. Even paternalistic arguments for possible deception of criminals, children in elementary schools, or the mentally incapacitated are no longer credible. The ongoing exposé of deceptive practices since Stanley Milgram's experiments have given this moral principle special status—deliberate misrepresentation is forbidden. Bulmer (1982) is typical of hard-liners who conclude with the codes that deception is "neither ethically justified nor practically necessary, nor in the best interest of sociology as an academic pursuit" (p. 217; see also Punch, 1994, p. 92).

The straightforward application of this principle suggests that researchers design different experiments free of active deception. But with ethical constructions exterior to the scientific enterprise, no unambiguous application is possible. Given that the search for knowledge is obligatory and deception is codified as morally unacceptable, in some situations both criteria cannot be satisfied. Within both psychology and medicine, some information cannot be obtained without at least deception by omission. The standard resolution for this dilemma is to permit a modicum of deception when there are explicit utilitarian reasons for doing so. Opposition to deception in the codes is de facto redefined in these terms: If "the knowledge to be gained from deceptive experiments" is clearly valuable to society, it is "only a minor defect that persons must be deceived in the process" (Soble, 1978, p. 40).

3. *Privacy and confidentiality.* Codes of ethics insist on safeguards to protect people's identities and those of the research locations. Confidentiality must be assured as the primary safeguard against unwanted exposure. All personal data ought to be secured or concealed and made public only behind a shield of anonymity. Professional etiquette uniformly concurs that no one deserves harm or embarrassment as a result of insensitive research practices. "The single most likely source of harm in social science inquiry" is the disclosure of private knowledge considered damaging by experimental subjects (Reiss, 1979, p. 73; see also Punch, 1994, p. 93).

As Enlightenment autonomy was developed in philosophical anthropology, a sacred innermost self became essential to the construction of unique personhood. Already in John Locke, this private domain received nonnegotiable status. Democratic life was articulated outside these atomistic units, a secondary domain of negotiated contracts and problematic communication. In the logic of social science inquiry revolving around the same autonomy inscribed in being, invading persons' fragile but distinctive privacy is intolerable.

Despite the signature status of privacy protection, watertight confidentiality has proved to be impossible. Pseudonyms and disguised locations often are recognized by insiders. What researchers consider innocent is perceived by participants as misleading or even betrayal. What appears neutral on paper is often conflictual in practice. When government agencies or educational institutions or health organizations are studied, what private parts ought not be exposed? And who is blameworthy if aggressive media carry the research further? Encoding privacy protection is meaningless when "there is no consensus or unanimity on what is public and private" (Punch, 1994, p. 94).

4. *Accuracy.* Ensuring that data are accurate is a cardinal principle in social science codes as well. Fabrications, fraudulent materials, omissions, and contrivances are both nonscientific and unethical. Data that are internally and externally valid are the coin of the realm, experimentally and morally. In an instrumentalist, value-neutral social science, the definitions entailed by the procedures themselves establish the ends by which they are evaluated as moral.

Institutional Review Boards

As a condition of funding, government agencies in various countries have insisted that review and monitoring bodies be established by institutions engaged in research involving human subjects. Institutional Review Boards (IRBs) embody the utilitarian agenda in terms of scope, assumptions, and procedural guidelines.

In 1978, the U.S. National Commission for the Protection of Human Subjects in Biomedical and Behavioral Research was established. As a result, three principles, published in what became known as the Belmont Report, were developed as the moral standards for research involving human subjects: respect for persons, beneficence, and justice.

1. The section on respect for persons reiterates the codes' demands that subjects enter the research voluntarily and with adequate information about the experiment's procedures and possible consequences. On a deeper level, respect for persons incorporates two basic ethical tenets: "First, that individuals should be treated as autonomous agents, and second, that persons with diminished autonomy [the immature and incapacitated] are entitled to protection" (University of Illinois at Urbana-Champaign, 2003).

2. Under the principle of beneficence, researchers are enjoined to secure the well-being of their subjects. Beneficent actions are understood in a double sense as avoiding harm altogether and, if risks are involved for achieving substantial benefits, minimizing as much harm as possible:

> In the case of particular projects, investigators and members of their institutions are obliged to give forethought to the maximization of benefits and the reduction of risks that might occur from the research investigation. In the case of scientific research in general, members of the larger society are obliged to recognize the longer term benefits and risks that may result from the improvement of knowledge and from the development of novel medical, psychotherapeutic, and social procedures. (University of Illinois at Urbana-Champaign, 2003)

3. The principle of justice insists on fair distribution of both the benefits and the burdens of research. An injustice occurs when some groups (e.g., welfare recipients, the institutionalized, or particular ethnic minorities) are overused as research subjects because of easy manipulation or their availability. And when research supported by public funds leads to "therapeutic devices and procedures, justice demands that these not provide advantages only to those who can afford them" (University of Illinois at Urbana-Champaign, 2003).

These principles reiterate the basic themes of value-neutral experimentalism—individual autonomy, maximum benefits with minimal risks, and ethical ends exterior to scientific means. The policy procedures based on them reflect the same guidelines as dominate the codes of ethics: informed consent, protection of privacy, and nondeception. The authority of IRBs was enhanced in 1989 when Congress passed the NIH Revitalization Act and formed the Commission on Research Integrity. The emphasis at that point was on the invention, fudging, and distortion of data. Falsification, fabrication, and plagiarism continue as federal categories of misconduct, with a new report in 1996 adding warnings against unauthorized use of confidential information, omission of important data, and interference (that is, physical damage to the materials of others).

With IRBs, the legacy of Mill, Comte, and Weber comes into its own. Value-neutral science is accountable to ethical standards through rational procedures controlled by value-neutral academic institutions in the service of an impartial government. Consistent with the way anonymous bureaucratic regimes become refined and streamlined toward greater efficiency, the regulations rooted in scientific and medical experiments now extend to humanistic inquiry. Protecting subjects from physical harm in laboratories has grown to encompass human behavior, history, and ethnography in natural settings. In Jonathon Church's metaphor, "a biomedical paradigm is used like some threshing machine with ethnographic research the resulting chaff" (2002, p. 2). Whereas Title 45/Part 46 of the Code of Federal Regulations (45 CFR 46) designed protocols for research funded by 17 federal agencies, at present most universities have multiple project agreements that consign all research to a campus IRB under the terms of 45 CFR 46 (Shopes, 2000, pp. 1–2).

While this bureaucratic expansion has gone on unremittingly, most IRBs have not changed the composition of their membership. Medical and behavioral scientists under the aegis of value-free neutrality continue to dominate, and the changes in procedures generally have stayed within the biomedical model. Expedited review under the Common Rule, for social research with no risk of physical or psychological harm, depends on enlightened IRB chairs and organizational flexibility. Informed consent, mandatory before medical experiments, is simply incongruent with interpretive research that interacts with human beings in their natural settings, rather than analyzing human subjects in a laboratory (Shopes, 2000, p. 5).[13] Despite technical improvements, "Intellectual curiosity remains actively discouraged by the IRB. Research projects must ask only surface questions and must not deviate from a path approved by a remote group of people. . . . Often the review process seems to be more about gamesmanship than anything else. A better formula for stultifying research could not be imagined" (Blanchard, 2002, p. 11).

In its conceptual structure, IRB policy is designed to produce the best ratio of benefits to costs. IRBs ostensibly protect the subjects who fall under the protocols they approve. However, given the interlocking utilitarian functions of social science, the academy, and the state that Mill identified and promoted, IRBs in reality protect their own institutions rather than subject populations in society at large (see Vanderpool, 1996, chaps. 2–6). Only if professional associations like the American Anthropological Association could create their own best practices for ethnographic research would IRBs take a significant step in the right direction. Such renovations are contrary to the centralizing homogeneity of closed systems such as the IRBs.[14]

The Current Crisis

Mill and Comte, each in his own way, presumed that experimental social science benefited society by uncovering facts about the human condition. Durkheim and Weber believed that a scientific study of society could help people come to grips with "the development of capitalism and the industrial revolution" (Jennings & Callahan, 1983, p. 3). The American Social Science Association was created in 1865 to link "real elements of the truth" with "the great social problems of the day" (Lazarsfeld & Reitz, 1975, p. 1). This myth of beneficence was destroyed with "the revelations at the Nuremberg trials (recounting the Nazis' 'medical experiments' on concentration camp inmates) and with the role of leading scientists in the Manhattan Project" (Punch, 1994, p. 88).

The crisis of confidence multiplied with the exposure to actual physical harm in the Tuskegee Syphilis Study and the Willowbrook Hepatitis Experiment. In the 1960s, Project Camelot, a U.S. Army attempt to use social science to measure and forecast revolutions and insurgency, was bitterly opposed around the world and had to be canceled. Stanley Milgram's (1974) deception of unwitting subjects and Laud Humphreys's (1970, 1972) deceptive research on homosexuals in a public toilet, and later in their homes, were considered scandalous for psychologically abusing research subjects. Noam Chomsky exposed the complicity of social scientists with military initiatives in Vietnam.

Vigorous concern for research ethics since the 1980s, support from foundations, and the development of ethics codes and the IRB apparatus are credited by their advocates with curbing outrageous abuses. However, the charges of fraud, plagiarism, and misrepresentation continue on a lesser scale, with dilemmas, conundrums, and controversies unabated over the meaning and application of ethical guidelines. Entrepreneurial faculty competing for scarce research dollars are generally compliant with institutional control, but the vastness of social science activity in universities and research entities makes full supervision impossible.

Underneath the pros and cons of administering a responsible social science, the structural deficiencies in its epistemology have become transparent (Jennings, 1983, pp. 4–7). A positivistic philosophy of social inquiry insists on neutrality regarding definitions of the good, and this worldview has been discredited. The Enlightenment model setting human freedom at odds with the moral order is bankrupt. Even Weber's weaker version of contrastive languages rather than oppositional entities is not up to the task. Reworking the ethics codes so that they are more explicit and less hortatory will make no fundamental difference. Requiring ethics workshops for graduate students and strengthening government policy are desirable but of marginal significance. Refining the IRB process and exhorting IRBs to account for the pluralistic nature of academic research are insufficient.

In utilitarianism, moral thinking and experimental procedures are homogenized into a unidimensional model of rational validation. Autonomous human beings are clairvoyant about aligning means and goals, presuming that they can objectify the mechanisms for understanding themselves and the social world surrounding them (see Taylor, 1982, p. 133). This restrictive definition of ethics accounts for some of the goods we seek, such as minimal harm, but those outside a utility calculus are excluded. "Emotionality and intuition" are relegated "to a secondary position" in the decision-making process, for example, and no attention is paid to an "ethics of caring" grounded in "concrete particularities" (Denzin, 1997, p. 273; see also Ryan, 1995, p. 147). The way power and ideology influence social and political institutions is largely ignored. Under a rhetorical patina of deliberate choice and the illusion of autonomous creativity, a means-ends system operates in fundamentally its own terms.

This constricted environment no longer addresses adequately the complicated issues we face in studying the social world. Celebrity social scientists generate status and prestige—McGeorge Bundy in the Kennedy years, political scientist Henry Kissinger, Daniel Moynihan while in the Senate. But failure in the War on Poverty, contradictions over welfare, and ill-fated studies of urban housing have dramatized the limitations of a utility calculus that occupies the entire moral domain.[15]

Certainly, levels of success and failure are open to dispute even within the social science disciplines themselves. More unsettling and threatening to the empirical mainstream than disappointing performance is the recognition that neutrality is not pluralistic but imperialistic. Reflecting on past experience, disinterested research under presumed conditions of value freedom is increasingly seen as de facto reinscribing the agenda in its own terms. Empiricism is procedurally committed to equal reckoning, regardless of how research subjects may constitute the substantive ends of life. But experimentalism is not a neutral meeting ground for all ideas; rather, it is a "fighting creed" that imposes its own ideas on others while uncritically assuming the very "superiority that powers this imposition."[16] In Foucault's (1979, pp. 170–195) more decisive terms, social science is a regime of power that helps maintain social order by normalizing subjects into categories designed by political authorities (see Root, 1993, chap. 7). A liberalism of equality is not neutral but represents only one range of ideals, and it is itself incompatible with other goods.

This noncontextual, nonsituational model that assumes that "a morally neutral, objective observer will get the facts right" ignores "the situatedness of power relations associated with gender, sexual orientation, class, ethnicity, race, and nationality." It is hierarchical (scientist-subject) and biased toward patriarchy. "It glosses the ways in which the observer-ethnographer is implicated and embedded in the 'ruling apparatus' of the society and the culture." Scientists "carry the mantle" of university-based authority as they venture out into "local community to do research" (Denzin, 1997, p. 272; see also Ryan, 1995, pp. 144–145).[17] There is no sustained questioning of expertise itself in democratic societies that belong in principle to citizens who do not share this specialized knowledge (see Euben, 1981, p. 120).

▣ Feminist Communitarianism

Social Ethics

Over the past decade, social and feminist ethics have made a radical break with the individual autonomy and rationalist presumption of canonical ethics (see Koehn, 1998). The social ethics of Agnes Heller (1988, 1990, 1996, 1999), Charles Taylor (1989, 1991, 1995; Taylor et al., 1994), Carole Pateman (1985, 1988, 1989), Edith Wyschogrod (1974, 1985, 1990, 1998), Kwasi Wiredu (1996), and Cornel West (1989, 1991, 1993) and the feminist ethics of Carol Gilligan (1982, 1983; Gilligan, Ward, & Taylor, 1988), Nel Noddings (1984, 1989, 1990), Virginia Held (1993), and Seyla Benhabib (1992) are fundamentally reconstructing ethical theory (see Code, 1991). Rather than searching for neutral principles to which all parties can appeal, social ethics rests on a complex view of moral judgments as integrating into an organic whole various perspectives—everyday experience, beliefs about the good, and feelings of approval and shame—in terms of human relations and social structures. This is a philosophical approach that situates the moral domain within the general purposes of human life that people share contextually and across cultural, racial, and historical boundaries. Ideally, it engenders a new occupational role and normative core for social science research (White, 1995).

Carol Gilligan (1982, 1983; Gilligan et al., 1988) characterizes the female moral voice as an ethic of care. This dimension of moral development is rooted in the primacy of human relationships. Compassion and nurturance resolve conflicting responsibilities among people, and as such these standards are totally the opposite of merely avoiding harm.[18] In *Caring,* Nel Noddings (1984) rejects outright the "ethics of principle as ambiguous and unstable" (p. 5), insisting that human care should play the central role in moral decision making. For Julia Wood (1994), "an interdependent sense of self" undergirds the ethic of care, wherein we are comfortable acting independently while "acting cooperatively . . . in relationship with others" (pp. 108, 110). Feminism in Linda Steiner's work critiques the conventions of impartiality and formality in ethics while giving precision to affection, intimacy, nurturing, egalitarian and collaborative processes, and empathy. Feminists' ethical self-consciousness also identifies subtle forms of oppression and imbalance, and it teaches us to "address questions about whose interests are regarded as worthy of debate" (Steiner, 1991, p. 158; see also Steiner, 1997).

While sharing in the turn away from an abstract ethics of calculation, Charlene Seigfried (1996) argues against the Gilligan-Noddings tradition. Linking feminism to pragmatism, in which gender is socially constructed, she contradicts "the simplistic equation of women with care and nurturance and men with justice and autonomy" (p. 206). Gender-based moralities de facto make one gender subservient to another. In her social ethics, gender is replaced with engendering: "To be female or male is not to instantiate an unchangeable nature but to participate in an ongoing process of negotiating cultural expectations of femininity and masculinity" (p. 206). Seigfried challenges us to a social morality in which caring values are central but contextualized in webs of relationships and constructed toward communities with "more autonomy for women and more connectedness for men" (p. 219). Agnes Heller and Edith Wyschogrod are two promising examples of proponents of social ethics that meet Seigfried's challenge while confronting forthrightly today's contingency, mass murder, conceptual upheavals in ethics, and hyperreality.

Heller, a former student of Georg Lukács and a dissident in Hungary, is the Hannah Arendt Professor of Philosophy at the New School for Social Research. Her trilogy developing a contemporary theory of social ethics (Heller, 1988, 1990, 1996) revolves around what she calls the one decisive question: "Good persons exist—how are they possible?" (1988, p. 7). She disavows an ethics of norms, rules, and ideals external to human beings. Only exceptional acts of responsibility under duress and predicaments, each in their own way, are "worthy of theoretical interest" (1996, p. 3). Accumulated wisdom, moral meaning from our own choices of decency, and the ongoing summons of the Other together reintroduce love, happiness, sympathy, and beauty into a modern, nonabsolutist, but principled theory of morals.

In *Saints and Postmodernism*, Edith Wyschogrod (1990) asserts that antiauthority struggles are possible without assuming that our choices are voluntary. She represents a social ethics of self and Other in the tradition of Emmanuel Levinas (see Wyschogrod, 1974).[19] "The other person opens the venue of ethics, the place where ethical existence occurs." The Other, "the touchstone of moral existence, is not a conceptual anchorage but a living force." Others function "as a critical solvent." Their existence carries "compelling moral weight" (Wyschogrod, 1990, p. xxi). As a professor of philosophy and religious thought at Rice University, with a commitment to moral narrative, Wyschogrod believes that one venue for Otherness is the saintly life, defined as one in "which compassion for the Other, irrespective of cost to the saint, is the primary trait." Saints put their own "bodies and material goods at the disposal of the Other. . . . Not only do saints contest the practices and beliefs of institutions, but in a more subtle way they contest the order of narrativity itself" (1990, pp. xxii–xxiii).

In addition to the Other-directed across a broad spectrum of belief systems who have "lived, suffered, and worked in actuality," Wyschogrod (1990, p. 7) examines historical narratives for illustrations of how the Other's self-manifestation is depicted. Her primary concern is the way communities shape shared experience in the face of cataclysms and calamities, arguing for historians who situate themselves "in dynamic relationship to them" (1998, p. 218). The overriding challenge for ethics, in Wyschogrod's view, is how historians enter into communities that create and sustain hope in terms of immediacy—"a presence here and now" but "a presence that must be deferred" to the future (1998, p. 248). Unless it is tangible and actionable, hope serves those in control. Hope that merely projects a future redemption obscures abuses of power and human need in the present.

Martin Buber (1958) calls the human relation a primal notion in his famous lines, "in the beginning is the relation" (p. 69) and "the relation is the cradle of life" (p. 60). Social relationships are preeminent. "The one primary word is the combination I-Thou" (p. 3). This irreducible phenomenon—the relational reality, the in-between, the reciprocal bond, the interpersonal—cannot be decomposed into simpler elements without destroying it. Given the primacy of relationships, unless we use our freedom to help others flourish, we deny our own well-being.

Rather than privileging an abstract rationalism, the moral order is positioned close to the bone, in the creaturely and corporeal rather than the conceptual. "In this way, ethics . . . is as old as creation. Being ethical is a primordial movement in the beckoning force of life itself" (Olthuis, 1997, p. 141). The ethics of Levinas is one example:

> The human face is the epiphany of the nakedness of the Other, a visitation, a meeting, a saying which comes in the passivity of the face, not threatening, but obligating. My world is ruptured, my contentment interrupted. I am already obligated. Here is an appeal from which there is no escape, a responsibility, a state of being hostage. It is looking into the face of the Other that reveals the call to a responsibility that is before any beginning, decision or initiative on my part. (Olthuis, 1997, p. 139)

Humans are defined as communicative beings within the fabric of everyday life. Through dialogic encounter, subjects create life together and nurture one another's moral obligation to it. Levinas's ethics presumes and articulates a radical ontology of social beings in relation (see, e.g., Levinas, 1985, 1991).

Moreover, in Levinasian terms, when I turn to the face of the Other, I not only see flesh and blood, but a third party also arrives—the whole of humanity. In responding to the Other's need, a baseline is established across the human race. For Benhabib (1992), this is interactive universalism.[20] Our universal solidarity is rooted in the principle that "we have inescapable claims on one another which cannot be renounced except at the cost of our humanity" (Peukert, 1981, p. 11).

A Feminist Communitarian Model

Feminist communitarianism is Denzin's (1997, pp. 274–287; 2003, pp. 242–258) label for the ethical theory to lead us forward at this juncture.[21] This is a normative model that serves as an antidote to individualist utilitarianism. It presumes that the community is ontologically and axiologically prior to persons. Human identity is constituted through the social realm. We are born into a sociocultural universe where values, moral commitments, and existential meanings are negotiated dialogically. Fulfillment is never achieved in isolation, but only through human bonding at the epicenter of social formation.

For communitarians, the liberalism of Locke and Mill confuses an aggregate of individual pursuits with the common good. Moral agents need a context of social commitments and community ties for assessing what is valuable. What is worth preserving as a good cannot be self-determined in isolation, but can be ascertained only within specific social situations where human identity is nurtured. The public sphere is conceived as a mosaic of particular communities, a pluralism of ethnic identities and worldviews intersecting to form a social bond but each seriously held and competitive as well. Rather than pay lip service to the social nature of the self while presuming a dualism of two orders, communitarianism interlocks personal autonomy with communal well-being. Morally appropriate action intends community. Common moral values are intrinsic to a community's ongoing existence and identity.

Therefore, the mission of social science research is enabling community life to prosper—equipping people to come to mutually held conclusions. The aim is not fulsome data per se, but community transformation. The received view assumes that research advances society's interests by feeding our individual capacity to reason and make calculated decisions. Research is intended to be collaborative in its design and participatory in its execution. Rather than ethics codes in the files of academic offices and research reports prepared for clients, the participants themselves are given a forum to activate the polis mutually. In contrast to utilitarian experimentalism, the substantive conceptions of the good that drive the problems reflect the conceptions of the community rather than the expertise of researchers or funding agencies.

In the feminist communitarian model, participants have a say in how the research should be conducted and a hand in actually conducting it, "including a voice or hand in deciding which problems should be studied, what methods should be used to study them, whether the findings are valid or acceptable, and how the findings are to be used or implemented" (Root, 1993, p. 245). This research is rooted in "community, shared governance . . . and neighborliness." Given its cooperative mutuality, it serves "the community in which it is carried out, rather than the community of knowledge producers and policymakers" (Lincoln, 1995, pp. 280, 287; see also Denzin, 1997, p. 275). It finds its genius in the maxim that "persons are arbitrators of their own presence in the world" (Denzin, 1989, p. 81).

For feminist communitarians, humans have the discursive power "to articulate situated moral rules that are grounded in local community and group understanding." Moral reasoning goes forward because people are "able to share one another's point of view in the social situation." Reciprocal care and understanding, rooted in emotional experience and not in formal consensus, are the basis on which moral discourse is possible (Denzin, 1997, p. 277; see also Denzin, 1984, p. 145; Reinharz, 1993).

Multiple moral and social spaces exist within the local community, and "every moral act is a contingent accomplishment" measured against the ideals of a universal respect for the dignity of every human being regardless of gender, age, race, or religion (Denzin, 1997, p. 274; see also Benhabib, 1992, p. 6). Through a moral order, we resist those social values that are divisive and exclusivist.

Interpretive Sufficiency

Within a feminist communitarian model, the mission of social science research is interpretive sufficiency. In contrast to an experimentalism of instrumental efficiency, this paradigm seeks to open up the social world in all its dynamic dimensions. The thick notion of sufficiency supplants the thinness of the technical, exterior, and statistically precise received view. Rather than reducing social issues to financial and administrative problems for politicians, social science research enables people to come to terms with their everyday experience themselves.

Interpretive sufficiency means taking seriously lives that are loaded with multiple interpretations and grounded in cultural complexity (Denzin, 1989, pp. 77, 81). Ethnographic accounts "should possess that amount of depth, detail, emotionality, nuance, and coherence that will permit a critical consciousness to be formed by the reader. Such texts should also exhibit representational adequacy, including the absence of racial, class, and gender stereotyping" (Denzin, 1997, p. 283; see also Christians et al., 1993, pp. 120–122).

From the perspective of a feminist communitarian ethics, interpretive discourse is authentically sufficient when it fulfills three conditions: it represents multiple voices, enhances moral discernment, and promotes social transformation. Consistent with the community-based norms advocated here, the focus is not on professional ethics per se but on the general morality.[22]

Multivocal and Cross-Cultural Representation

Within social and political entities are multiple spaces that exist as ongoing constructions of everyday life. The dialogical self is situated and articulated within these decisive contexts of gender, race, class, and religion. In contrast to contractarianism, where tacit consent or obligation is given to the state, people make and sustain the promises to one another. Research narratives reflect a community's multiple voices through which promise keeping takes place.

In Carole Pateman's communitarian philosophy, sociopolitical entities are not to be understood first of all in terms of contracts. Making promises is one of the basic ways in which consenting human beings "freely create their own social relationships" (Pateman, 1989, p. 61; see also Pateman, 1985, pp. 26–29). We assume an obligation by making a promise. When individuals promise, they are obliged to act accordingly. But promises are made not primarily to authorities through political contracts, but to fellow citizens. If obligations are rooted in promises, obligations are owed to other colleagues in institutions and to participants in community practices. Therefore, only under conditions of participatory democracy can there be self-assumed moral obligation.

Pateman understands the nature of moral agency. We know ourselves primarily in relation, and derivatively as thinkers withdrawn from action. Only by overcoming the traditional dualisms between thinker and agent, mind and body, reason and will, can we conceive of being as "the mutuality of personal relationships" (MacMurray, 1961a, p. 38). Moral commitments arise out of action and return to action for their incarnation and verification. From a dialogical perspective, promise keeping through action and everyday language is not a supercilious pursuit, because our way of being is not inwardly generated but socially derived.

> We become full human agents, capable of understanding ourselves, and hence of defining our identity, through . . . rich modes of expression we learn through exchange with others. . . .
>
> My discovering my own identity doesn't mean that I work it out in isolation, but that I negotiate it through dialogue, partly overt, partly internal, with others. My own identity crucially depends on my dialogical relations with others. . . .
>
> In the culture of authenticity, relationships are seen as the key loci of self discovery and self- affirmation. (Taylor et al., 1994, pp. 32, 34, 36)

If moral bondedness flows horizontally and obligation is reciprocal in character, the affirming and sustaining of promises occur cross-culturally. But the contemporary challenge of cultural diversity has raised the stakes and made easy solutions impossible. One of the most urgent and vexing issues on the democratic agenda at present is not just the moral obligation to treat ethnic differences with fairness, but how to recognize explicit cultural groups politically.

Communitarianism as the basis for ethnic plurality rejects melting pot homogeneity and replaces it with the politics of recognition. The basic issue is whether democracies are discriminating against their citizens in an unethical manner, when major institutions fail to account for the identities of their members (Taylor et al., 1994, p. 3). In what sense should the specific cultural and social features of African Americans, Asian Americans, Native Americans, Buddhists, Jews, the physically disabled, or children publicly matter? Should not public institutions insure only that democratic citizens share an equal right to political liberties and due process without regard to race, gender, or religion? Beneath the rhetoric is a fundamental philosophical dispute that Taylor calls the "politics of recognition." As he puts it, "Nonrecognition or miscrecognition can inflict harm, can be a form of oppression, imprisoning someone in a false, distorted, and reduced mode of being. Due recognition is not just a courtesy we owe people. It is a vital human need" (Taylor et al., 1994, p. 26). This foundational issue regarding the character of cultural identity needs to be resolved for cultural pluralism to come into its own. Feminist communitarianism is a non-assimilationist framework in which such resolution can occur.

However, liberal proceduralism cannot meet this vital human need. Emphasizing equal rights with no particular substantive view of the good life "gives only a very restricted acknowledgement of distinct cultural identities" (Taylor et al., 1994, p. 52). Insisting on neutrality, and without collective goals, produces at best personal freedom, safety, and economic security understood homogeneously. As Bunge (1996) puts it: "Contractualism is a code of behavior for the powerful and the hard—those who write contracts, not those who sign on the dotted line" (p. 230). However, in promise-based communal formation, the flourishing of particular cultures, religions, and ethnic groups is the substantive goal to which we are morally committed as human beings.

Norman Denzin (2002) demonstrates how multicultural representation ought to operate in the media's construction of the American racial order. An ethnic cinema that honors racial difference is not assimilationist, nor does it "celebrate exceptional blackness" supporting white values; and it refuses to pit "the ethnic other against a mainstream white America" as well as "dark skin against dark skin" (p. 6). Rather than "a didactic film aesthetic based on social problems realism"—one that is "trapped by the modernist agenda"—Denzin follows Hal Foster and bell hooks in arguing for an anti-aesthetic or postmodern aesthetic that is cross-disciplinary, oriented to the vernacular, and denies "the idea of a privileged aesthetic realm" (pp. 11, 180). A "feminist, Chicana/o and black performance-based aesthetic" creates "a critical counter-hegemonic race consciousness" and implements critical race theory (p. 180).

In feminist communitarian terms, this aesthetic is simultaneously political and ethical. Racial difference is imbricated in social theories and in conceptions of the human being, of justice, and of the common good. It requires an aesthetic that "in generating social criticism . . . also engenders resistance" (Denzin, 2002, p. 181). It is not a "protest or integrationist initiative" aimed at "informing a white audience of racial injustice," but instead "offers new forms of representation that create the space for new forms of critical race consciousness" (p. 182). The overarching standard made possible by this aesthetic is enhancing moral agency, that is, serving as a catalyst for moral discernment (Christians, 2002a, p. 409).

With the starting hypothesis that all human cultures have something important to say, social science research recognizes particular cultural values consistent with universal human dignity (Christians, 1997a, pp. 11–14). Interpretive sufficiency in its multicultural dimension "locates persons in a non-competitive, non-hierarchical relationship to the larger moral universe." It helps persons "imagine how things could be different in the everyday world. It imagines new forms of human transformation and emancipation. It enacts those transformations through dialogue" (Denzin, 2002, p. 181).

Moral Discernment

Societies are embodiments of institutions, practices, and structures recognized internally as legitimate. Without allegiance to a web of ordering relations, society becomes, as a matter of fact, inconceivable. Communities not only are linguistic entities but also require at least a minimal moral commitment to the common good. Because social entities are moral orders and not merely functional arrangements, moral commitment constitutes the self-in-relation. Our identity is defined by what we consider good or worth opposing. Only through the moral dimension can we make sense of human agency. As Mulhall and Swift (1996) write:

> Developing, maintaining and articulating [our moral intuitions and reactions] is not something humans could easily or even conceivably dispense with. . . . We can no more imagine a human life that fails to address the matter of its bearings in moral space than we can imagine one in which developing a sense of up and down, right and left is regarded as an optional human task. . . . A moral orientation is inescapable because the questions to which the framework provides answers are themselves inescapable. (pp. 106–108; see also Taylor, 1989, pp. 27–29)

A self exists only within "webs of interlocution," and all self-interpretation implicitly or explicitly "acknowledges the necessarily social origin of any and all their conceptions of the good and so of themselves" (Mulhall & Swift, 1996, pp. 112–113). Moral frameworks are as fundamental for orienting us in social space as the need to establish ourselves in physical space. The moral dimension must, therefore, be considered intrinsic to human beings, not a system of rules, norms, and ideals external to society. Moral duty is nurtured by the demands of social linkage and not produced by abstract theory.

The core of a society's common morality is pretheoretical agreement. However, "what counts as common morality is not only imprecise but variable . . . and a difficult practical problem" (Bok, 1995, p. 99). Moral obligation must be articulated within the fallible and irresolute voices of everyday life. Among disagreements and uncertainty, we look for criteria and wisdom in settling disputes and clarifying confusions; and normative theories of an interactive sort can invigorate our common moral discourse. But generally accepted theories are not necessary for the common good to prosper. The common good is not "the complete morality of every participant . . . but a set of agreements among people who typically hold other, less widely shared ethical beliefs" (Bok, 1995, p. 99). Instead of expecting more theoretical coherence than history warrants, Reinhold Niebuhr inspires us to work through inevitable social conflicts while maintaining "an untheoretical jumble of agreements" called here the common good (Barry, 1967, pp. 190–191). Through a common morality, we can approximate consensus on issues and settle disputes interactively. In Jürgen Habermas's (1993) terms, discourse in the public sphere must be oriented "toward mutual understanding" while allowing participants "the communicative freedom to take positions" on claims to final validity (p. 66; see also Habermas, 1990).

Communitarians challenge researchers to participate in a community's ongoing process of moral articulation. In fact, culture's continued existence depends on the identification and defense of its normative base. Therefore, ethnographic texts must enable us "to discover moral truths about ourselves"; narratives ought to "bring a moral compass into readers' lives" by accounting for things that matter to them (Denzin, 1997, p. 284). Feminist communitarianism seeks to engender moral reasoning internally. Communities are woven together by narratives that invigorate their common understanding of good and evil, happiness and reward, the meaning of life and death. Recovering and refashioning moral vocabulary help to amplify our deepest humanness. Researchers are not constituted as ethical selves antecedently, but moral discernment unfolds dialectically between researchers and the researched who collaborate with them.

Our widely shared moral convictions are developed through discourse within a community. These communities, where moral discourse is nurtured and shared, are a radical alternative to the utilitarian individualism of modernity. But in feminist communitarianism, communities are entered from the universal. The total opposite of an ethics of individual autonomy is universal human solidarity. Our obligation to sustain one another defines our existence. The primal sacredness of all without exception is the heart of the moral order and the new starting point for our theorizing (Christians, 1997b, 1998).

The rationale for human action is reverence for life on Earth. Living nature reproduces itself as its very character. Embedded in the animate world is the purposiveness of bringing forth life. Therefore, within the natural order is a moral claim on us for its own sake and in its own right. Nurturing life has a taken-for-granted character outside subjective preferences. Reverence for life on Earth is a pretheoretical given that makes the moral order possible. The sacredness of life is not an abstract imperative but the ground of human action.[23] It is a primordial generality that underlies reification into ethical principles, an organic bond that everyone shares inescapably. In our systematic reflection on this protonorm, we recognize that it entails such basic ethical principles as human dignity and nonviolence.

Reverence for life on Earth establishes a level playing floor for cross-cultural collaboration in ethics. It represents a universalism from the ground up. Various societies articulate this protonorm in different terms and illustrate it locally, but every culture can bring to the table this fundamental norm for ordering political relationships and social institutions. We live out our values in a community setting where the moral life is experienced and a moral vocabulary articulated. Such protonorms as reverence for life can be recovered only locally. Language situates them in history. The sacredness of life reflects our common condition as a species, but we act on it through the immediate reality of geography, ethnicity, and ideology. But according to feminist communitarianism, if we enter this communal arena not from individual decision making but from a universal commonness, we have the basis for believing that researchers and the researched can collaborate on the moral domain. Researchers do not bring a set of prescriptions into which they school their subjects. Instead, they find ways interactively to bring the sacredness of life into its own—each culture and all circumstances providing an abundance of meaning and application.

How the moral order works itself out in community formation is the issue, not first of all what researchers consider virtuous. The challenge for those writing culture is not to limit their moral perspectives to their own generic and neutral principles, but to engage the same moral space as the people they study. In this perspective, research strategies are not assessed first of all in terms of "experimental robustness," but for their "vitality and vigor in illuminating how we can create human flourishing" (Lincoln & Denzin, 2000, p. 1062).

Politics of Resistance

Ethics in the feminist communitarian mode generates social criticism, leads to resistance, and empowers to action those who are interacting (see Habermas, 1971, pp. 301–317). Thus, a basic norm for interpretive research is enabling the humane transformation of the multiple spheres of community life, such as religion, politics, ethnicity, and gender.

From his own dialogic perspective, Paulo Freire speaks of the need to reinvent the meaning of power:

> For me the principal, real transformation, the radical transformation of society in this part of the century demands not getting power from those who have it today, or merely to make some reforms, some changes in it. . . . The question, from my point of view, is not just to take power but to reinvent it. That is, to create a different kind of power, to deny the need power has as if it were metaphysics, bureaucratized, anti-democratic. (quoted in Evans, Evans, & Kennedy, 1987, p. 229)

Certainly oppressive power blocs and monopolies—economic, technological, and political—need the scrutiny of researchers and their collaborators. Given Freire's political-institutional bearing, power for him is a central notion in social analysis. But, in concert with him, feminist communitarian research refuses to deal with power in cognitive terms only. The issue is how people can empower themselves instead.

The dominant understanding of power is grounded in nonmutuality; it is interventionist power, exercised competitively and seeking control. In the communitarian alternative, power is relational, characterized by mutuality rather than sovereignty. Power from this perspective is reciprocity between two subjects, a relationship not of domination, but of intimacy and vulnerability—power akin to that of Alcoholics Anonymous, in which surrender to the community enables the individual to gain mastery. As understood so clearly in the indigenous Kaupapa Māori approach to research, "the researcher is led by the members of the community and does not presume to be a leader, or to have any power that he or she can relinquish" (Denzin, 2003, p. 243).

Dialogue is the key element in an emancipatory strategy that liberates rather than imprisons us in manipulation or antagonistic relationships. Although the control version of power considers mutuality weakness, the empowerment mode maximizes our humanity and thereby banishes powerlessness. In the research process, power is unmasked and engaged through solidarity as a researched-researcher team. There is certainly no monologic "assumption that the researcher is giving the group power" (Denzin, 2003, p. 243). Rather than play semantic games with power, researchers themselves are willing to march against the barricades. As Freire insists, only with everyone filling his or her own political space, to the point of civil disobedience as necessary, will empowerment mean anything revolutionary (see, e.g., Freire, 1970b, p. 129).

What is nonnegotiable in Freire's theory of power is participation of the oppressed in directing cultural formation. If an important social issue needs resolution, the most vulnerable will have to lead the way: "Revolutionary praxis cannot tolerate an absurd dichotomy in which the praxis of the people is merely that of following the [dominant elite's] decisions" (Freire, 1970a, p. 120; see also Freire, 1978, pp. 17ff.).[24] Arrogant politicians—supported by a bevy of accountants, lawyers, economists, and social science researchers—trivialize the nonexpert's voice as irrelevant to the problem or its solution. On the contrary, transformative action from the inside out is impossible unless the oppressed are active participants rather than being a leader's objects of action. "Only power that springs from the weakness of the oppressed will be sufficiently strong to free both" (Freire, 1970b, p. 28).[25]

In Freire's (1973) terms, the goal is conscientization, that is, a critical consciousness that directs the ongoing flow of praxis and reflection in everyday life. In a culture of silence, the oppressor's language and way of being are fatalistically accepted without contradiction. But a critical consciousness enables us to exercise the uniquely human capacity of "speaking a true word" (Freire, 1970b, p. 75). Under conditions of sociopolitical control, "the vanquished are dispossessed of their word, their expressiveness, their culture" (1970b, p. 134). Through conscientization, the oppressed gain their own voice and collaborate in transforming their culture (1970a, pp. 212–213). Therefore, research is not the transmission of specialized data but, in style and content, a catalyst for critical consciousness. Without what Freire (1970b, p. 47) calls "a critical comprehension of reality" (that is, the oppressed "grasping with their minds the truth of their reality"), there is only acquiescence in the status quo.

The resistance of the empowered is more productive at the interstices—at the fissures in social institutions where authentic action is possible. Effective resistance is nurtured in the backyards, the open spaces, and voluntary associations, and among neighborhoods, schools, and interactive settings of mutual struggle without elites. Because only nonviolence is morally acceptable for sociopolitical change, there is no other option except an educational one—having people movements gain their own voice, and nurturing a critical conscience through dialogic means. People-based development from below is not merely an end in itself but a fundamental condition of social transformation.

Transforming the IRB

Interpretive sufficiency as a philosophy of social science fundamentally transforms the IRB system in form and content. As with IRBs, it emphasizes relentless accuracy but understands it as the researcher's authentic resonance with the context and the subject's self-reflection as a moral agent. In an indigenous Māori approach to knowledge, for example, "concrete experience is the criterion of meaning and truth" and researchers are "led by the members of the community to discover them" (Denzin, 2003, p. 243). However, because the research-subject relation is reciprocal, the IRB's invasion of privacy, informed consent, and deception are nonissues. In communitarianism, conceptions of the good are shared by the research subjects, and researchers collaborate in bringing these definitions into their own. "Participants have a co-equal say in how research should be conducted, what should be studied, which methods should be used, which findings are valid and acceptable, how the findings are to be implemented, and how the consequences of such actions are to be assessed" (Denzin, 2003, p. 257).

Interpretive sufficiency transcends the current regulatory system governing research on human subjects. Therefore, it recommends a policy of strict territorialism for the IRB regime. Given its historical roots in biomedicine, and with the explosion in both genetic research and privately funded biomedical research, 45 CFR 46 should be confined to medical, biological, and clinical studies, and the positivist and postpositivist social science that is epistemologically identical to them. Research methodologies that have broken down the walls between subjects and researchers ought to be excluded from IRB oversight. As Denzin observes:

> Performance autoethnography, for example, falls outside this [IRB] model, as do many forms of participatory action research, reflexive ethnography, and qualitative research involving testimonies, life stories, life-history inquiry, personal narrative inquiry, performance autobiography, conversation analysis, and ethnodrama. In all of these cases, subjects and researchers develop collaborative, public, pedagogical relationships. (2003, p. 249)

Because participation is voluntary, subjects do not need "to sign forms indicating that their consent is 'informed.'" . . . Confidentiality is not an issue, "for there is nothing to hide or protect." Participants are not subjected to preapproved procedures, but "acting together, researchers and subjects work to produce change in the world" (Denzin, 2003, pp. 249–250).

Given the different understandings of human inquiry, the review of research protocols ought to be given to peers in academic departments or units familiar with these methodologies. The Oral History Association, for example, has codified a set of principles and responsibilities for guiding work in oral history. These "Evaluation Guidelines," as they are commonly called, would serve as the framework for assessing research practice.[26] In her reference to oral history, Linda Shopes speaks for feminist communitarianism as a whole:

> The current regulatory system governing research on human subjects is simply incongruent with oral history interviewing. It has been used inappropriately to inhibit critical inquiry, and it is based on a definition of research far removed from historical practice. Moreover, historians are acutely aware of the ethical dimensions of our work and have well-developed professional standards governing oral history interviewing. I would like to see oral history recognized as lying outside the domain inscribed by the Common Rule. (Shopes, 2000, p. 8)

Denzin enriches feminist communitarian ethics by integrating it with an indigenous research ethic, particularly that of the Kaupapa Māori (2003, pp. 242–248, 257–258). The charters of various indigenous peoples are rooted in a participatory mode of knowing and presume collective, not individual, rights.

> These rights include control and ownership of the community's cultural property . . . and the rights of indigenous peoples to protect their culture's new knowledge and its dissemination. These charters embed codes of ethics within this larger perspective. They spell out specifically how researchers are to protect and respect the rights and interests of indigenous peoples, using the same protocols that regulate daily moral life in these cultures. (Denzin, 2003, p. 257)

This collaborative research model "makes the researcher responsible not to a removed discipline (or institution), but to those he or she studies." It aligns the ethics of research "with a politics of resistance, hope, and freedom" (Denzin, 2003, p. 258).

Conclusion

As Guba and Lincoln (1994) argue, the issues in social science ultimately must be engaged at the worldview level. "Questions of method are secondary to questions of paradigm, which we define as the basic belief system or worldview that guides the investigator, not only in choices of method but in ontologically and epistemologically fundamental ways" (p. 105). The conventional view, with its extrinsic ethics, gives us a truncated and unsophisticated paradigm that needs to be ontologically transformed.

This historical overview of theory and practice points to the need for an entirely new model of research ethics in which human action and conceptions of the good are interactive.

"Since the relation of persons constitutes their existence as persons, . . . morally right action is [one] which intends community" (MacMurray, 1961b, p. 119). In feminist communitarianism, personal being is cut into the very heart of the social universe. The common good is accessible to us only in personal form; it has its ground and inspiration in a social ontology of the human.[27] "Ontology must be rescued from submersion in things by being thought out entirely from the viewpoint of person and thus of Being" (Lotz, 1963, p. 294). "Ontology is truly itself only when it is personal and persons are truly themselves only as ontological" (Lotz, 1963, p. 297).

When rooted in a positivist worldview, explanations of social life are considered incompatible with the renderings offered by the participants themselves. In problematics, lingual form, and content, research production presumes greater mastery and clearer illumination than the nonexperts who are the targeted beneficiaries. Protecting and promoting individual autonomy have been the philosophical rationale for value neutrality since its origins in Mill. But the incoherence in that view of social science is now transparent. By limiting the active involvement of rational beings or judging their self-understanding to be false, empiricist models contradict the ideal of rational beings who "choose between competing conceptions of the good" and make choices "deserving of respect." The verification standards of an instrumentalist system "take away what neutrality aims to protect: a community of free and equal rational beings legislating their own principles of conduct" (Root, 1993, p. 198). The social ontology of feminist communitarianism escapes this contradiction by reintegrating human life with the moral order.

Notes

1. For greater detail regarding this argument than I can provide in the summary below, see Christians, Ferre, and Fackler (1993, pp. 18–32, 41–44).

2. Michael Root (1993) is unique among philosophers of the social sciences in linking social science to the ideals and practices of the liberal state on the grounds that both institutions "attempt to be neutral between competing conceptions of the good" (p. xv). As he elaborates:

> Though liberalism is primarily a theory of the state, its principles can be applied to any of the basic institutions of a society; for one can argue that the role of the clinic, the corporation, the scholarly associations, or professions is not to dictate or even recommend the kind of life a person should aim at. Neutrality can serve as an ideal for the operations of these institutions as much as it can for the state. Their role, one can argue, should be to facilitate whatever kind of life a student, patient, client, customer, or member is aiming at and not promote one kind of life over another. (p. 13)

Root's interpretations of Mill and Weber are crucial to my own formulation.

3. Although committed to what he called "the logic of the moral sciences" in delineating the canons or methods for induction, Mill shared with natural science a belief in the uniformity of nature and the presumption that all phenomena are subject to cause-and-effect relationships. His five principles of induction reflect a Newtonian cosmology.

4. Utilitarianism in John Stuart Mill's thought was essentially an amalgamation of Jeremy Bentham's greatest happiness principle, David Hume's empirical philosophy and concept of utility as a moral good, and Auguste Comte's positivist tenets that things-in-themselves cannot be known and knowledge is restricted to sensations. In his influential *A System of Logic,* Mill (1843/1893) typically is characterized as combining the principles of French positivism (as developed by Comte) and British empiricism into a single system.

5. For an elaboration of the complexities in positivism—including reference to its Millian connections—see Lincoln and Guba (1985, pp. 19–28).

6. Mill's realism is most explicitly developed in his *Examination of Sir William Hamilton's Philosophy* (1865). Our belief in a common external world, in his view, is rooted in the fact that our sensations of physical reality "belong as much to other human or sentient beings as to ourselves" (p. 196; see also Copleston, 1966, p. 306, n. 97).

7. Mill (1873/1969) specifically credits to Comte his use of the inverse deductive or historical method: "This was an idea entirely new to me when I found it in Comte; and but for him I might not soon (if ever) have arrived at it" (p. 126). Mill explicitly follows Comte in distinguishing social statics and social dynamics. He published two essays on Comte's influence in the *Westminster Review*, which were reprinted as *Auguste Comte and Positivism* (Mill, 1865/1907; see also Mill, 1873/1969, p. 165).

8. Emile Durkheim is more explicit and direct about causality in both the natural and the social worlds. Although he argued for sociological over psychological causes of behavior and did not believe intention could cause action, he unequivocally saw the task of social science as discovering the causal links between social facts and personal behavior (see, e.g., Durkheim, 1966, pp. 44, 297–306).

9. As one example of the abuse Weber resisted, Root (1993, pp. 41–42) refers to the appointment of Ludwig Bernhard to a professorship of economics at the University of Berlin. Though he had no academic credentials, the Ministry of Education gave Bernhard this position without a faculty vote (see Weber, 1973, pp. 4–30). In Shils's (1949) terms, "A mass of particular, concrete concerns underlies [his 1917] essay—his recurrent effort to penetrate to the postulates of economic theory, his ethical passion for academic freedom, his fervent nationalist political convictions and his own perpetual demand for intellectual integrity" (p. v).

10. The rationale for the creation of the Social Science Research Council in 1923 is multilayered, but in its attempt to link academic expertise with policy research, as well as in its preference for rigorous social scientific methodology, the SSRC reflects and implements Weber.

11. Often in professional ethics at present, we isolate consequentialism from a full-scale utilitarianism. We give up on the idea of maximizing happiness, but "still try to evaluate different courses of action purely in terms of their consequences, hoping to state everything worth considering in our consequence-descriptions." However, even this broad version of utilitarianism, in Taylor's terms, "still legislates certain goods out of existence" (Taylor, 1982, p. 144). It is likewise a restrictive definition of the good that favors the mode of reasoned

calculation and prevents us from taking seriously all facets of moral and normative political thinking (Taylor, 1982). As Yvonna Lincoln observes, utilitarianism's inescapable problem is that "in advocating the greatest good for the greatest number, small groups of people (all minority groups, for example) experience the political regime of the 'tyranny of the majority.'" She refers correctly to "liberalism's tendency to reinscribe oppression by virtue of the utilitarian principle" (personal communication, February 16, 1999).

12. Given the nature of positivist inquiry, Jennings and Callahan (1983) conclude that only a short list of ethical questions is considered and, these questions "tend to merge with the canons of professional scientific methodology. . . . Intellectual honesty, the suppression of personal bias, careful collection and accurate reporting of data, and candid admission of the limits of the scientific reliability of empirical studies—these were essentially the only questions that could arise. And, since these ethical responsibilities are not particularly controversial (at least in principle), it is not surprising that during this period [the 1960s] neither those concerned with ethics nor social scientists devoted much time to analyzing or discussing them" (p. 6).

13. Most biomedical research occurs in a laboratory. Researchers are obliged to inform participants of potential risk and obtain consent before the research takes place. Ethnographic research occurs in settings where subjects live, and informed consent is a process of "ongoing interaction between the researcher and the members of the community being studied. . . . One must establish bonds of trust and negotiate consent . . . taking place over weeks or months—not prior to a structured interview" (Church, 2002, p. 3).

14. For a sociological and epistemological critique of IRBs, see Denzin (2003, pp. 248–257).

15. As Taylor (1982) puts it, "The modern dispute about utilitarianism is not about whether it occupies some of the space of moral reason, but whether it fills the whole space." "Comfort the dying" is a moral imperative in contemporary Calcutta, even though "the dying are in an extremity that makes [utilitarian] calculation irrelevant" (p. 134).

16. This restates the well-known objection to a democratic liberalism of individual rights:

> Liberalism is not a possible meeting ground for all cultures, but is the political expression of one range of cultures, and quite incompatible with other ranges. Liberalism can't and shouldn't claim complete cultural neutrality. Liberalism is also a fighting creed. Multiculturalism as it is often debated today has a lot to do with the imposition of some cultures on others, and with the assumed superiority that powers this imposition. Western liberal societies are thought to be supremely guilty in this regard, partly because of their colonial past, and partly because of their marginalization of segments of their populations that stem from other cultures. (Taylor et al., 1994, pp. 62–63).

17. Denzin in this passage credits Smith (1987, p. 107) with the concept of a "ruling apparatus."

18. Gilligan's research methods and conclusions have been debated by a diverse range of scholars. For this debate and related issues, see Brabeck (1990), Card (1991), Tong (1989, pp. 161–168; 1993, pp. 80–157), Wood (1994), and Seigfried (1996).

19. Levinas (b. 1905) was a professor of philosophy at the University of Paris (Nanterre) and head of the Israelite Normal School in Paris. In Wyschogrod's (1974) terms, "He continues the tradition of Martin Buber and Franz Rosenweig" and was "the first to introduce Husserl's

work into . . . the French phenomenological school" (pp. vii-viii). Although Wyschogrod is a student of Heidegger, Hegel, and Husserl (see, e.g., Wyschogrod, 1985)—and engaged Derrida, Lyotard, Foucault, and Deleuze—her work on ethics appeals not to traditional philosophical discourse but to concrete expressions of self–Other transactions in the visual arts, literary narrative, historiography, and the normalization of death in the news.

20. Martha Nussbaum (1993) argues for a version of virtue ethics in these terms, contending for a model rooted in Aristotle that has cross-cultural application without being detached from particular forms of social life. In her model, various spheres of human experience that are found in all cultures represent questions to answer and choices to make—attitudes toward the ill or good fortune of others, how to treat strangers, management of property, control over bodily appetites, and so forth. Our experiences in these areas "fix a subject for further inquiry" (p. 247), and our reflection on each sphere will give us a "thin or nominal definition" of a virtue relevant to this sphere. On this basis, we can talk across cultures about behavior appropriate in each sphere (see Nussbaum, 1999).

21. Root (1993, chap. 10) also chooses a communitarian alternative to the dominant paradigm. In his version, critical theory, participatory research, and feminist social science are three examples of the communitarian approach. This chapter offers a more complex view of communitarianism developed in political philosophy and intellectual history, rather than limiting it to social theory and practical politics. Among the philosophical communitarians (Sandel, 1998; Taylor, 1989; Walzer, 1983, 1987), Carole Pateman (1985, 1989) is explicitly feminist, and her promise motif forms the axis for the principle of multivocal representation outlined below. In this chapter's feminist communitarian model, critical theory is integrated into the third ethical imperative—empowerment and resistance. In spite of that difference in emphasis, I agree with Root's (1993) conclusion: "Critical theories are always critical for a particular community, and the values they seek to advance are the values of that community. In that respect, critical theories are communitarian. . . . For critical theorists, the standard for choosing or accepting a social theory is the reflective acceptability of the theory by members of the community for whom the theory is critical" (pp. 233–234). For a review of communitarian motifs in terms of Foucault, see Olssen (2002).

22. For an elaboration of interpretive sufficiency in terms of news reporting, see Christians (2004, pp. 46–55).

23. The sacredness of life as a protonorm differs fundamentally from the Enlightenment's monocultural ethical rationalism, in which universal imperatives were considered obligatory for all nations and epochs. Cartesian foundationalism and Kant's formalism presumed noncontingent starting points. Universal human solidarity does not. Nor does it flow from Platonism, that is, the finite participating in the infinite and receiving its essence from it (see Christians, 1997b, pp. 3–6). In addition to the sacredness of life as a protonorm, there are other appeals to universals that neither are Western nor presume a Newtonian cosmology; for a summary, see Christians (2002b).

24. Mutuality is a cardinal feature of the feminist communitarian model generally, and therefore is crucial to the principle of empowerment. For this reason, critical theory is inscribed into the third principle here, rather than following Root (see note 18, above), allowing it to stand by itself as an illustration of communitarianism. Root (1993, p. 238) himself observes that critical theorists often fail to transfer the "ideals of expertise" to their research subjects or give them little say in the research design and interpretation. Without a fundamental shift to communitarian interactivity, research in all modes is prone to the distributive fallacy.

25. Because of his fundamental commitment to dialogue, empowering for Freire avoids the weaknesses of monologic concepts of empowerment in which researchers are seen to free up the weak and unfortunate (summarized by Denzin [2003, pp. 242–245] citing Bishop, 1998). Although Freire represents a radical perspective, he does not claim, "as more radical theorists" do, that "only they and their theories can lead" the researched into freedom (Denzin, 2003, p. 246; citing Bishop, 1998).

26. Thomas Puglisi (2001) contends that the Oral History Association's (OHA) "Evaluation Guidelines" are not incompatible with federal regulations. However, actual experience with IRBs from oral historians indicates their disjuncture in theory and practice.

27. Michael Theunissen (1984) argues that Buber's relational self (and therefore its legacy in Levinas, Freire, Heller, Wyschogrod, and Taylor) is distinct from the subjectivity of Continental existentialism. The subjective sphere of Husserl and Sartre, for example, "stands in no relation to a Thou and is not a member of a We" (p. 20; see also p. 276). "According to Heidegger the self can only come to itself in a voluntary separation from other selves; according to Buber, it has its being solely in the relation" (p. 284).

References

Barry, B. (1967). Justice and the common good. In A. Quinton (Ed.), *Political philosophy* (pp. 190–191). Oxford, UK: Oxford University Press.

Benhabib, S. (1992). *Situating the self: Gender, community and postmodernism in contemporary ethics.* Cambridge, UK: Polity.

Bishop, R. (1998). Freeing ourselves from neo-colonial domination in research: A Māori approach to creating knowledge. *International Journal of Qualitative Studies in Education, 11,* 199–219.

Blanchard, M. A. (2002, January). *Should all disciplines be subject to the Common Rule? Human subjects of social science research.* Panel, U.S. Department of Health and Human Services. Retrieved from www.aaup.org/publications/Academe/2002/02m/ 02mjftr.htm

Bok, S. (1995). *Common values.* Columbia: University of Missouri Press.

Brabeck, M. M. (Ed.). (1990). *Who cares? Theory, research, and educational implications of the ethic of care.* New York: Praeger.

Buber, M. (1958). *I and thou* (2nd ed.; R. G. Smith, Trans.). New York: Scribner's.

Bulmer, M. (1982). The merits and demerits of covert participant observation. In M. Bulmer (Ed.), *Social research ethics* (pp. 217–251). London: Macmillan.

Bunge, M. (1996). *Finding philosophy in social science.* New Haven, CT: Yale University Press.

Card, C. (Ed.). (1991). *Feminist ethics.* Lawrence: University of Kansas Press.

Christians, C. G. (1997a). The ethics of being. In C. G. Christians & M. Traber (Eds.), *Communication ethics and universal values* (pp. 3–23). Thousand Oaks, CA: Sage.

Christians, C. G. (1997b). Social ethics and mass media practice. In J. M. Makau & R. C. Arnett (Eds.), *Communication ethics in an age of diversity* (pp. 187–205). Urbana: University of Illinois Press.

Christians, C. G. (1998). The sacredness of life. *Media Development, 45*(2), 3–7.

Christians, C. G. (2002a). Ethical theorists and qualitative research. *Qualitative Inquiry, 8*(1), 407–410.

Christians, C. G. (2002b). The latest developments in world ethics. *Proceedings: Media ethics pre-conference, cross-cultural ethics in a digitalized age* (pp. 3–11). Gwangju City, Korea: Chonnam National University.

Christians, C. G. (2004). The changing news paradigm: From objectivity to interpretive sufficiency. In S. H. Iorio (Ed.), *Qualitative research in journalism: Taking it to the streets* (pp. 41–56). Mahwah, NJ: Lawrence Erlbaum.

Christians, C. G., Ferre, J. P., & Fackler, P. M. (1993). *Good news: Social ethics and the press.* New York: Oxford University Press.

Church, J. T. (2002, January). *Should all disciplines be subject to the Common Rule? Human subjects of social science research.* Panel, U. S. Department of Health and Human Services. Retrieved from www.aaup.org/publications/Academe/2002/02m/02mjftr.htm

Code, L. (1991). *What can she know? Feminist theory and the construction of knowledge.* Ithaca, NY: Cornell University Press.

Comte, A. (1910). *A general view of positivism* (J. H. Bridges, Trans.). London: Routledge. (Original work published 1848)

Copleston, F. (1966). *A history of philosophy: Vol. 8. Modern philosophy: Bentham to Russell.* Garden City, NY: Doubleday.

Denzin, N. K. (1984).*On understanding emotion.* San Francisco: Jossey-Bass.

Denzin, N. K. (1989). *Interpretive biography.* Newbury Park, CA: Sage.

Denzin, N. K. (1997). *Interpretive ethnography: Ethnographic practices for the 21st century.* Thousand Oaks, CA: Sage.

Denzin, N. K. (2002). *Reading race: Hollywood and the cinema of racial violence.* Thousand Oaks, CA: Sage.

Denzin, N. K. (2003). *Performance ethnography: Critical pedagogy and the politics of culture.* Thousand Oaks, CA: Sage.

Durkheim, E. (1966). *Suicide: A study of sociology.* New York: Free Press.

Euben, J. P. (1981). Philosophy and the professions. *Democracy, 1*(2), 112–127.

Evans, A. F., Evans, R. A., & Kennedy, W. B. (1987). *Pedagogies for the non-poor.* Maryknoll, NY: Orbis.

Foucault, M. (1979). *Discipline and punish: The birth of the prison* (A. Sheridan, Trans.). New York: Random House.

Freire, P. (1970a). *Education as the practice of freedom: Cultural action for freedom.* Cambridge, MA: Harvard Educational Review/Center for the Study of Development.

Freire, P. (1970b). *Pedagogy of the oppressed.* New York: Seabury.

Freire, P. (1973). *Education for critical consciousness.* New York: Seabury.

Freire, P. (1978). *Pedagogy in process: The letters of Guinea-Bissau.* New York: Seabury.

Gilligan, C. (1982). *In a different voice: Psychological theory and women's development.* Cambridge, MA: Harvard University Press.

Gilligan, C. (1983). Do the social sciences have an adequate theory of moral development? In N. Haan, R. N. Bellah, P. Rabinow, & W. M. Sullivan (Eds.), *Social science as moral inquiry* (pp. 33–51). New York: Columbia University Press.

Gilligan, C., Ward, J. V., & Taylor, J. M. (1988). *Mapping the moral domain.* Cambridge, MA: Harvard University, Graduate School of Education.

Guba, E. G., & Lincoln, Y. S. (1994). Competing paradigms in qualitative research. In N. K. Denzin & Y. S. Lincoln (Eds.), *Handbook of qualitative research* (pp. 105–117). Thousand Oaks, CA: Sage.

Habermas, J. (1971). *Knowledge and human interests* (J. J. Shapiro, Trans.). Boston: Beacon.

Habermas, J. (1990). *Moral consciousness and communicative action* (C. Lenhardt & S. W. Nicholson, Trans.). Cambridge: MIT Press.

Habermas, J. (1993). *Justification and application: Remarks on discourse ethics* (C. Cronin, Trans.). Cambridge: MIT Press.

Held, V. (1993). *Feminist morality: Transforming culture, society, and politics.* Chicago: University of Chicago Press.

Heller, A. (1988). *General ethics.* Oxford, UK: Blackwell.

Heller, A. (1990). *A philosophy of morals.* Oxford, UK: Blackwell.

Heller, A. (1996). *An ethics of personality.* Oxford, UK: Blackwell.

Heller, A. (1999). *A theory of modernity.* Oxford, UK: Blackwell.

Humphreys, L. (1970). *Tearoom trade: Impersonal sex in public places.* Chicago: Aldine.

Humphreys, L. (1972). *Out of the closet.* Englewood Cliffs, NJ: Prentice Hall.

Jennings, B. (1983). Interpretive social science and policy analysis. In D. Callahan & B. Jennings (Eds.), *Ethics, the social sciences, and policy analysis* (pp. 3–35). New York: Plenum.

Jennings, B., & Callahan, D. (1983, February). Social sciences and the policy-making process. *Hastings Center Report,* pp. 3–8.

Koehn, D. (1998). *Rethinking feminist ethics: Care, trust and empathy.* New York: Routledge.

Lazarsfeld, P., & Reitz, J. G. (1975). *An introduction to applied sociology.* New York: Elsevier.

Levinas, E. (1985). *Ethics and infinity* (R. A. Cohen, Trans.). Pittsburgh, PA: Duquesne University Press.

Levinas, E. (1991). *Otherwise than being or beyond essence* (A. Lingis, Trans.). Dordrecht, Netherlands: Kluwer Academe.

Lincoln, Y. S. (1995). Emerging criteria for quality in qualitative and interpretive inquiry. *Qualitative Inquiry, 1,* 275–289.

Lincoln, Y. S., & Denzin, N. K. (2000). The seventh moment: Out of the past. *Handbook of Qualitative Research* (2nd ed. pp. 1047–1065). Thousand Oaks, CA: Sage.

Lincoln, Y. S., & Guba, E. G. (1985). *Naturalistic inquiry.* Beverly Hills, CA: Sage.

Lotz, J. B. (1963). Person and ontology. *Philosophy Today, 7,* 294–297.

Lyons, H. (1944). *The Royal Society 1660–1940.* Cambridge, UK: Cambridge University Press.

MacMurray, J. (1961a). *The form of the personal: Vol. 1. The self as agent.* London: Faber & Faber.

MacMurray, J. (1961b). *The form of the personal: Vol. 2. Persons in relation.* London: Faber & Faber.

Milgram, S. (1974). *Obedience to authority.* New York: Harper & Row.

Mill, J. S. (1865). *Examination of Sir William Hamilton's philosophy and of the principal philosophical questions discussed in his writings.* London: Longman, Green, Roberts & Green.

Mill, J. S. (1893). *A system of logic, ratiocinative and inductive: Being a connected view of the principles of evidence and the methods of scientific investigation* (8th ed.). New York: Harper & Brothers. (Original work published 1843)

Mill, J. S. (1907). *Auguste Comte and positivism.* London: Kegan Paul, Trench, Trubner & Co. (Original work published 1865)

Mill, J. S. (1957). *Utilitarianism.* Indianapolis: Bobbs-Merrill. (Original work published 1861)

Mill, J. S. (1969). *Autobiography.* Boston: Houghton Mifflin. (Original work published 1873)

Mill, J. S. (1978). *On liberty.* Indianapolis: Hackett. (Original work published 1859)

Mulhall, S., & Swift, A. (1996). *Liberals and communitarians* (2nd ed.). Oxford, UK: Blackwell.

Noddings, N. (1984). *Caring: A feminine approach to ethics and moral education.* Berkeley: University of California Press.

Noddings, N. (1989). *Women and evil.* Berkeley: University of California Press.

Noddings, N. (1990). Ethics from the standpoint of women. In D. L. Rhode (Ed.), *Theoretical perspectives on sexual difference* (pp. 160–173). New Haven, CT: Yale University Press.

Nussbaum, M. (1993). Non-relative virtues: An Aristotelian approach. In M. Nussbaum & A. Sen, *The quality of life* (pp. 242–269). Oxford, UK: Clarendon.

Nussbaum, M. (1999). *Sex and social justice.* New York: Oxford University Press.

Olssen, M. (2002). Michel Foucault as "thin" communitarian: Difference, community, democracy. *Cultural Studies—Critical Methodologies, 2*(4), 483–513.

Olthuis, J. (1997). Face-to-face: Ethical asymmetry or the symmetry of mutuality? In J. Olthuis (Ed.), *Knowing other-wise* (pp. 134–164). New York: Fordham University Press.

Pateman, C. (1985). *The problem of political obligation: A critique of liberal theory.* Cambridge, UK: Polity.

Pateman, C. (1988). *The sexual contract.* Stanford, CA: Stanford University Press.

Pateman, C. (1989). *The disorder of women: Democracy, feminism and political theory.* Stanford, CA: Stanford University Press.

Peukert, H. (1981). Universal solidarity as the goal of ethics. *Media Development, 28*(4), 10–12.

Puglisi, T. (2001). IRB review: It helps to know the regulatory framework. *American Psychological Society Observer, 1*(May/June), 34–35.

Punch, M. (1994). Politics and ethics in qualitative research. In N. K. Denzin & Y. S. Lincoln (Eds.), *Handbook of qualitative research* (pp. 83–97). Thousand Oaks, CA: Sage.

Reinharz, S. (1993). *Social research methods: Feminist perspectives.* New York: Elsevier.

Reiss, A. J., Jr. (1979). Governmental regulation of scientific inquiry: Some paradoxical consequences. In C. B. Klockars & F. W. O'Connor (Eds.), *Deviance and decency: The ethics of research with human subjects* (pp. 61–95). Beverly Hills, CA: Sage.

Root, M. (1993). *Philosophy of social science: The methods, ideals, and politics of social inquiry.* Oxford, UK: Blackwell.

Ryan, K. E. (1995). Evaluation ethics and issues of social justice: Contributions from female moral thinking. In N. K. Denzin (Ed.), *Studies in symbolic interaction: A research annual* (Vol. 19, pp. 143–151). Greenwich, CT: JAI.

Sandel, M. J. (1998). *Liberalism and the limits of justice* (2nd ed.). Cambridge, UK: Cambridge University Press.

Seigfried, C. H. (1996). *Pragmatism and feminism: Reweaving the social fabric.* Chicago: University of Chicago Press.

Shils, E. A. (1949). Foreword. In M. Weber, *The methodology of the social sciences* (pp. iii–x). New York: Free Press.

Shopes, L. (2000). Institutional Review Boards have a chilling effect on oral history. *Perspectives online.* Retrieved from www.theaha.org/perspectives/ issues/2000/0009/0009vie1.cfm

Smith, D. E. (1987). *The everyday world as problematic: A feminist sociology.* Boston: Northeastern University Press.

Soble, A. (1978, October). Deception in social science research: Is informed consent possible? *Hastings Center Report,* pp. 40–46.

Steiner, L. (1991). Feminist theorizing and communication ethics. *Communication, 12*(3), 157–174.

Steiner, L. (1997). A feminist schema for analysis of ethical dilemmas. In F. L. Casmir (Ed.), *Ethics in intercultural and international communication* (pp. 59–88). Mahwah, NJ: Lawrence Erlbaum.

Taylor, C. (1982). The diversity of goods. In A. Sen & B. Williams (Eds.), *Utilitarianism and beyond* (pp. 129–144). Cambridge, UK: Cambridge University Press.

Taylor, C. (1989). *Sources of the self: The making of the modern identity.* Cambridge, MA: Harvard University Press.

Taylor, C. (1991). *The ethics of authenticity.* Cambridge, MA: Harvard University Press.

Taylor, C. (1995). *Philosophical arguments.* Cambridge, MA: Harvard University Press.

Taylor, C., Appiah, K. A., Habermas, J., Rockefeller, S. C., Walzer, M., & Wolf, S. (1994). *Multiculturalism: Examining the politics of recognition* (A. Gutmann, Ed.). Princeton, NJ: Princeton University Press.

Theunissen, M. (1984). *The other: Studies in the social ontology of Husserl, Heidegger, Sartre, and Buber* (C. Macann, Trans.). Cambridge: MIT Press.

Tong, R. (1989). *Feminist thought.* Boulder, CO: Westview.

Tong, R. (1993). *Feminine and feminist ethics.* Belmont, CA: Wadsworth.

University of Illinois at Urbana-Champaign, Institutional Review Board. (2003, January). Part I: Fundamental principles for the use of human subjects in research. In *Handbook for investigators: For the protection of human subjects in research.* Urbana: Author. (Available from www.irb.uiuc.edu)

Vanderpool, H. Y. (Ed.). (1996). *The ethics of research involving human subjects: Facing the 21st century.* Frederick, MD: University Publishing Group.

Veatch, R. M. (1996). From Nuremberg through the 1990s: The priority of autonomy. In H. Y. Vanderpool (Ed.), *The ethics of research involving human subjects: Facing the 21st century* (pp. 45–58). Frederick, MD: University Publishing Group.

Walzer, M. (1983). *Spheres of justice: A defense of pluralism and equality.* New York: Basic Books.

Walzer, M. (1987). *Interpretation and social criticism.* Cambridge, MA: Harvard University Press.

Weber, M. (1949a). The meaning of ethical neutrality in sociology and economics. In M. Weber, *The methodology of the social sciences* (E. A. Shils & H. A. Finch, Eds. & Trans., pp. 1–47). New York: Free Press. (Original work published 1917)

Weber, M. (1949b). Objectivity in social science and social policy. In M. Weber, *The methodology of the social sciences* (E. A. Shils & H. A. Finch, Eds. & Trans., pp. 50–112). New York: Free Press. (Original work published 1904)

Weber, M. (1973). *Max Weber on universities* (E. A. Shils, Ed. & Trans.). Chicago: University of Chicago Press.

West, C. (1989). *The American evasion of philosophy: A genealogy of pragmatism.* Madison: University of Wisconsin Press.

West, C. (1991). *The ethical dimensions of Marxist thought.* New York: Monthly Review Books.

West, C. (1993). *Race matters.* Boston: Beacon Press.

White, R. (1995). From codes of ethics to public cultural truth. *European Journal of Communication, 10,* 441–460.

Wiredu, K. (1996). *Cultural universals: An African perspective.* Bloomington: Indiana University Press.

Wood, J. (1994). *Who cares? Women, care, and culture.* Carbondale: Southern Illinois University Press.

Wyschogrod, E. (1974). *Emmanuel Levinas: The problem of ethical metaphysics.* The Hague: Martinus Nijhoff.

Wyschogrod, E. (1985). *Spirit in ashes: Hegel, Heidegger, and man-made death.* Chicago: University of Chicago Press.

Wyschogrod, E. (1990). *Saints and postmodernism: Revisioning moral philosophy.* Chicago: University of Chicago Press.

Wyschogrod, E. (1998). *An ethics of remembering: History, heterology, and the nameless others.* Chicago: University of Chicago Press.

7

INSTITUTIONAL REVIEW BOARDS AND METHODOLOGICAL CONSERVATISM

The Challenge to and From Phenomenological Paradigms

Yvonna S. Lincoln

Qualitative research, as exemplified by the *Handbook*, hundreds of other books, and perhaps thousands of journal articles, has not only gained a foothold but has established a small stronghold in education and the social and clinical sciences. The number of national and international conferences, small and large, devoted to qualitative research and its practitioners has grown geometrically in recent years, and several annual conferences are now in their second decade.

As the variety of qualitative methods has expanded and been refined, paradigms, theoretical perspectives, and epistemological stances have been elaborated (e.g., feminist theory, race/ethnic studies theories, subaltern and postcolonial epistemologies, queer theory), and interpretive lenses have been developed (postmodernism, poststructuralism), increasing numbers of practitioners and would-be practitioners have been attracted to the promise and democratic and pluralistic ethics of qualitative practices. The inclusionary bent (Mertens, 1998) and social justice orientation (see Denzin, Volume 3, Chapter 14; Lincoln & Denzin, 2000) of the new social science has drawn a fresh cadre of methodologists committed to seeing social science used for democratic and liberalizing social purposes.

The resurgence of "high modernism" (Giddens, 1990), however, carries with it a return to some presumed "golden age" of methodological purity (and innocence) when broad consensus on the constituent elements of science supposedly reigned. Voices in the biomedical community (the Campbell and Cochrane Collaborations) and in the educational research community bespeak a turn toward "methodological conservatism" (Cannella & Lincoln, 2004a, 2004b; Lincoln & Cannella, 2004a, 2004b).

A recent series of legislative actions and committee policy changes, however, may directly and indirectly influence paradigmatic and methodological issues in ways unforeseen a scant decade ago. In turn, qualitative research may be compromised or even threatened by the new methodological conservatism being propagated in the name of evidence-based research and "scientifically based educational research."

Currently, there appear to be four ways in which the work of qualitative researchers and scholars who teach qualitative research philosophies and methods is constrained by the manner in which new paradigms encounter institutional review board (IRB) regulation on campuses: (a) increased scrutiny surrounding research with human subjects (a response to failures in biomedical research), (b) new scrutiny of classroom research and training in qualitative methods involving human subjects, (c) new discourses regarding what constitutes "evidence-based research," and (d) the long-term effects of the recent National Research Council (NRC, 2002) report on what should be considered to be scientific inquiry. After presenting a brief history of IRBs, I offer below a set of suggestions to help scholars cope with these constraints in both qualitative research and the teaching of qualitative methods.

▣ A Brief History of Institutional Review Boards

As I have noted elsewhere, the "original impulse to regulate U.S. scientific research federally followed World War II and the Nuremberg trials," where testimony regarding medical and psychological experiments performed on prisoners of war and inmates in the Nazi death camps left the civilized world reeling with anguish and horror (Denzin & Lincoln, in press). The Helsinki Agreement was formulated in response to the nightmares uncovered during those trials.

Following closely on the Nuremberg trials, however, were public revelations about a series of medical and psychological experiments conducted in the United States. The publicity surrounding the scandals of the Tuskegee Syphilis Study, the Willowbrook Hepatitis Experiments, Project Camelot in the 1960s (a series of military and CIA experiments with psychotropic drugs, including LSD, involving enlisted U.S. Army recruits), Stanley Milgram's psychological deception studies involving deliberately delivered electroshock torture, and the work of social scientists directed toward military purposes in Vietnam, particularly covert espionage activities, prompted the federal government to undertake reexamination of its own policies and procedures around ethics in human subjects research. In 1974, the Belmont Report, which embodied a code for human subjects protections, was adopted as the standard for overseeing U.S. Public Health Service grants and contracts. Originally limited to use in decisions regarding PHS grants, the federal regulations and ethics guidelines were soon extended to cover all federally funded research with human subjects. Eventually, they came to be applied to all human subjects research, whether funded or not, undertaken by federal grantees, foundation researchers, biomedical researchers, and social science and educational researchers as well.

Although the four broad areas covered by the Belmont Report (and subsequent federal legislation, including, for example, the Buckley Amendment)—informed consent, deception, privacy of records, and confidentiality and protection of research participants' identities—were a strong start for a research ethics code, the guidelines as they are now deployed have failed to keep pace with developments in research methodologies, particularly qualitative and action research methodologies, with their high emphasis on collaboration between researchers and those researched, high levels of interactivity, and new mandates for a reformulated communitarian and democratic ethics in the field. In light of emergent epistemologies deeply rooted in cultural practices but divorced from federal concerns, federal standards for research ethics (as well as newer legislation such as the No Child Left Behind Act of 2001) "collide with other understandings circulating in the field of qualitative research" (Denzin & Lincoln, in press). In the face of this collision, a reexamination of the role of IRBs vis-à-vis qualitative research appears to be critical at this juncture (Denzin & Lincoln, in press; see also in Cheek, Volume 2, Chapter 2; Miller & Crabtree, Volume 2, Chapter 11).

The Challenges to Qualitative Research Posed by IRBs

Increased Scrutiny in Research With Human Subjects

New regulations regarding the protection of human subjects, created largely in response to tragic incidents involving biomedical and drug testing and informed consent, have acted to limit or severely constrain what teachers and students can do as part of classroom training as well as research (Gillespie, 1997). Two such incidents—one death resulting from an experimental procedure in a New York hospital and one from an experimental drug at Johns Hopkins—were sufficient to raise questions regarding whether participants in clinical and experimental trials of drugs and biomedical procedures receive enough information, and accurate information, on informed consent forms to understand fully the risks involved in their research participation. As a consequence, any and all research with human subjects, regardless of level of risk, has become the focus of increased regulation and oversight.

To be very clear: Classroom teachers have always gone to IRBs for approval of class activities and research training that involves human participants outside of class, including observation targets, potential interviewees, and survey respondents. But the arrangements between IRBs and researchers in the past were often much less formal than they are now, and they were assuredly not mandated by federal policies and procedures.

Today, the question of risk is rarely examined thoroughly (Gordon, Sugarman, & Kass, 1998) or taken into account in IRB deliberations. After conducting a series of nationwide hearings with social scientists, the American Association of University Professors (AAUP, 2001) recently concluded that IRBs are treating the level of risk in research with human subjects as though it were irrelevant, although information about risk level is clearly vital to considerations of what harm research is likely to do, if any. The AAUP report states that whereas biomedical and clinical trial research deserves maximum scrutiny for risk, many issues in social science and educational research may need only expedited review (p. 62). The recent federal policy decision, announced via the *Federal Register,* to remove oral history work from the list of the kinds of projects that must undergo IRB scrutiny is a tantalizing example of what may be a site-by-site battle around qualitative research methods.

An intriguing sidebar: Many of the individuals tapped for testimony because of their concerns about the new IRB regulations were oral historians who were worried that their inquiries might provoke levels of review not previously encountered in history departments or historical studies. In a somewhat stunning move, the federal government, on the recommendation of the National Research Council, has simply made oral history research permanently exempt from IRB review, imputing such little rigor to this work that it is not considered "social science" at all, but rather something else. I will have more to say about this later; for now, I simply want to note that this decision, in and of itself, although it frees historians who engage in oral history research from IRB review and therefore permits the broadest level of academic freedom in that research arena, can be seen as insulting and demeaning to those who do this kind of work.

The most prominent effects of increased IRB scrutiny cataloged so far have been the multiple rereviews of faculty proposals for qualitative research projects and in the rereviews and denials of proposed student research (particularly dissertation research) projects that utilize action research and participatory action research methods, research in the subjects' own settings (e.g., high schools), and/or research that is predominantly qualitative in nature (although not all researchers or their students have this problem; D. J. Greenwood, personal communication, 2003).[1] I have cited several examples of increased IRB scrutiny in my own previous work (Lincoln & Tierney, 2004), and scholars are collecting additional examples every month around the country. Qualitative researchers and doctoral students pursuing largely ethnographic and/or action research dissertations, however, are not the only researchers facing such additional scrutiny.

Increased Scrutiny in Qualitative Research Classroom Training and Course Work

The high-profile cases of failed medical protocols and ensuing deaths at two separate teaching hospitals mentioned earlier have led to renewed caution on the part of university IRBs and the researchers they serve. Increased attention to biomedical research has been accompanied by increased attention to regular course work and student training. One way in which this sharpened focus has been expressed has been in new requirements surrounding graduate teaching for qualitative research.

In the past, graduate course work in qualitative research required of a professor little more than an amicable visit with the IRB on some regular, but distant, basis—perhaps once every 5 to 10 years, unless a course was radically altered in substance or presentation. Formal procedures were rarely, if ever, followed, and IRB members were quite content to receive a complete course syllabus outlining the readings and assignments and describing the nature of the training students would undertake. In the past few years, however, the relationships between IRBs and professors have been seriously and profoundly restructured. Today, professors who teach qualitative methods, and whose assignments require students to move outside the classroom and begin practicing observational and interview skills on their own, are required to complete the entire IRB protocol, requesting permission even to teach courses in a manner that permits students to practice the skills they need to conduct research in a trained and ethical way.

The central point of much of graduate work is to prepare advanced students and college-trained scientists and intellectuals to undertake even more advanced intellectual and scientific exploration independent of their graduate advisers—as is the case in universities and laboratories around the world. The idea that graduate students may be trained in the use of nuclear reactors, the application of medical protocols, the techniques of electron microscopy, or any of the many other techniques they may need to continue scientific exploration on their own, largely without any IRB intervention at all, but students must seek IRB approval to interview professors on campus about their research in order to become familiar with interview techniques strikes many scholars as somewhat unreasonable. Although there has been some explication of the circumstances under which professors may use students, especially students in their own classrooms, as research subjects, particularly when the research concerns the classroom experience itself (DuBois, 2002; Hammack, 1997), little guidance is available about what experiences students themselves may have as part of their formal training.

I am not referring here to the kind of scrutiny that goes on as a result of the "political correctness" battles currently being waged between the political Right and much of academia based on the perception of members of the Right, or of the National Association of Scholars, that American colleges and universities are indoctrinating students with left-wing ideology (Burris & Diamond, 1991; Giroux, 1995). That form of scrutiny and reporting has far more to do with political agendas aimed at limiting academic freedom (Benjamin, Kurland, & Molotsky, 1985) than it does with research oversight. It is, furthermore, unofficial and intimidating in intent. As Giroux (1995) points out, "Many subordinate groups argue that the act of knowing is integrally related to the power of self-definition, which, in part, necessitates that more diverse histories and narratives be included in the curriculum. For many conservatives, however, such inclusiveness represents both a call to politicize the curriculum and a social practice that promotes national disunity and cultural decay" (p. 133).

Although academic freedom is deeply implicated in this set of arguments and, indeed, is being represented by political conservatives as a "casualty of this process" of politicization and the presumed lowering of academic standards, the reality is quite likely the reverse. Academic freedom is under assault from the Right's tactics of intimidation (e.g., public denunciation, Web sites that list the names of "ultraliberal" professors, Lynne Cheney's announced monitoring of specific professors who do not support the war in Iraq) and ongoing media assaults on "political correctness" (Devine, 1996; Diamond, 1991; Teller, 1988). In addition, students and other resident hecklers on campuses who shout down unpopular ideas represent a danger to academic freedom in the form of a "threat from within," as Trow (1985) aptly puts it.

Rather, I am referring in this chapter to scrutiny that represents increasing activism on the part of IRB structures. For example, when IRB review requirements were extended from public health research to all research involving human subjects under the National Research Act of 1974, "the original guidelines stated simply that informed consent must be obtained from subjects, [but] the present regulations contain a list of six specific topics which must be disclosed to subjects" (Gray, 1978, p. 35). The issue of research conducted within a classroom setting or, more specifically, as part of classroom assignments but *not* within the classroom or with class members themselves, is a critical one. Hecht (1995) labels this question "When is it teaching and when is it research?" (p. 9). He notes that his own institution arrived at a set of definitions and circumstances that many other institutions have now adopted:

> Within the confines of a class . . . there appears to be adequate provisions for protecting the rights of all individuals involved. Whether it happens within the physical classroom or outside, both faculty and students have an *academic* responsibility and obligation to behave in certain ways.
>
> Such protections, however, are not found when a faculty or student actively encounters individuals not enrolled in the class. An outsider is most likely unfamiliar with the requirements of the course, the particular assignment being accomplished, or the protections available through academic channels. Further, if the activity is a research activity—one where an [*sic*] systematic observation or interaction is made of human subjects in a naturally occurring or purposefully manipulated condition—those human subjects may be totally unaware of their participation. For these reasons, the . . . IRB has defined teaching as an activity that occurs between and among students and teachers. If the activity is to be a research activity (as defined above) but is to take place solely among the students and teachers as part of a recognized instructional process, where the students and teachers all know of the design and purpose (such as through a syllabus or handout), the activity is not considered research for IRB purposes. If, on the other hand, the activity is to involve individuals not students or faculty *in the course,* or is to involve activities where the students and/or teachers are unaware of their participation (such as a faculty systematically studying their students' responses to manipulated conditions) the activity would be considered research and subject to IRB review and approval. (pp. 9–10)

This set of principles—between teachers and students, where the syllabus serves as the learning contract, versus between students and those outside the classroom, where participants are unaware of the specific assignments, purposes, and so on—appears to be the one that guides most IRBs' reviews of even advanced graduate classes in qualitative research today. Although qualitative researchers across the United States have long engaged with IRBs in discussions of the kinds of exercises that students may carry out as part of their class assignments, until recent years such discussions have been rather informal. The paperwork associated with such discussions previously took the form of only class syllabi, which professors thoroughly discussed with IRB committee members in amicable and informal conversations prior to teaching their first classes.

One might argue that, at least on some campuses, the extended IRB review that is the norm today—often every time the same course is taught—has a chilling effect on qualitative methods teaching, especially given that no other courses in methods (e.g., statistics, practice teaching, medical internships) are subject to such rigorous oversight. Further, whereas the whole issue of inadequate protection of human subjects arose as a result of some profoundly questionable medical experiments (such as the Tuskegee Syphilis Study and the Willowbrook studies), it is difficult to find examples of such egregious research conduct in the human or social sciences. That is not to argue that such is not possible, only that it has thus far not happened, or is very rare.

Taking the opposite, and equally reasonable, side of this argument, Howe and Dougherty (1993) tactfully point out that "although moral abominations in social research are rare (but consider Milgram), other pressures—for instance, pressures to 'publish or perish'—are real and ubiquitous, and one need not be a bad person to be tempted to cut ethical corners in response to them, especially if cutting corners is the norm" (p. 16). Howe and Dougherty go on to argue that much of qualitative research should indeed be subject to review, for two reasons: the "open-ended and intimate" nature of qualitative research, especially as it puts researchers and research participants into face-to-face contact with each other; and the fact that its open-endedness requires that researchers and research participants negotiate meanings. These characteristics, they suggest, make qualitative research both more "ethically charged and unpredictable from the outset" (p. 19).

Although most qualitative researchers would strongly agree with Howe and Dougherty's description, many would also object that too often their research is subject to review by researchers who know nothing about qualitative research, who feel that it is not "good science," and/or who have no special sensitivity to social science research conducted using qualitative methods. Some IRBs go out of their way to ensure that proposals for qualitative research are reviewed by board members who have expertise in nonclinical, natural, and field settings; others make no such efforts. For qualitative researchers, the first type of review board rarely presents any problem for well-designed, strongly supervised student work. When the IRB is of the second kind, however, trying to secure approval is frequently a demoralizing endeavor.

New Discourses Around Evidence

IRBs are not always forces for methodological "purity" or conservatism on campuses, but they have been and they can be. When that is the case, qualitative researchers may find themselves subject to an additional set of pressures, as embodied in the NCR report *Scientific Research in Education* (2002) and new discourses emerging around the topic of what constitutes "scientific evidence."

As long ago as 1978, Gray recognized that it is "desirable for research to be considered from a variety of viewpoints" (p. 35). Gray was referring not only to research modes but also to research audiences, including individuals who themselves might be considered (at some point) research participants/subjects, and their participation in deliberations and debates regarding proposed research projects. Although the suggestion concerning increased participation on the part of "community members" (rather than simply other academic researchers) has not traveled very far in many institutions (but see Bauer, 2001), the discourse about modes of research has taken a decidedly alarming turn.

The rise of a neoconservative and neoliberal discourse (Baez & Slaughter, 2001; Messer-Davidow, 1993) regarding "political correctness" on campuses has been extended and reconfigured into a discourse around "standards" (Giroux, 1995), attaching to the criticisms of French political theories, feminist theories, critical theories, and gay, race/ethnic, border, postcolonial, and other emerging streams of thought that have been so prominent in the strident attacks on the "liberal campus" (Parenti, 1995). Although some have pointed out that it is a myth that campuses are liberal (Burris & Diamond, 1991), and Parenti (1995) has described "most college professors and students . . . [as] drearily conventional in their ideological proclivities" (p. 20), an emphasis on *standards for research* has arisen from the broader accusation that multiculturalism has watered down standards. The No Child Left Behind Act of 2001 and the more recent report of the National Research Council (2002) on scientific research in education amount to a manifesto concerning the standards for "true" scientific research, especially what should be considered meaningful "evidence" and what (in the case of No Child Left Behind) will be funded for research and evaluation purposes.

The NRC (2002) report in particular has sent shock waves through the educational research community, supporting as it does "evidence-based research" and randomized controlled experiments based on clinical field trial models. Although the report does not disallow qualitative research as a strategy or set of methods that may produce evidence for research purposes, its clear focus on objectivity and causal connections, as well as generalizability, indicates a distinctly modernist and experimental bent that acts to freeze out inquiry models that take explicit account of alternative epistemologies or the emergent critiques of contemporary science that make alternative epistemologies so compelling and socially trenchant.

The questions that have been raised regarding the NRC (2002) report have less to do with the "principles for scientific inquiry" (p. 52) it lays out than with the report's underlying assumptions regarding what constitutes "evidence." The report asserts that two characteristics of scientific inquiry are replication and generalizability (p. 74). It then takes two examples—Elliot Eisner's notion of educational *connoisseurship* and Sara Lawrence-Lightfoot's qualitative methodology for *portraiture*—and demonstrates, using the NRC's own criteria, why neither of these well-recognized methods in educational research constitutes scientific inquiry (pp. 74–77). For the NRC, evidence is apparently not what is produced through the processes that Cronbach and Suppes (1969) describe in their groundbreaking work: "The report of a disciplined inquiry has a texture that displays the raw materials entering the argument and the logical processes by which they were compressed and rearranged to make the conclusion credible" (p. 16). Cronbach and Suppes themselves were sufficiently sophisticated to avoid the particular traps the NRC sets in limiting what constitutes evidence (primarily quantitative, generated by experimental method, replicable—never mind that few studies are ever replicated unless they are in high-stakes biomedical or technology-oriented arenas—empirically verifiable). Rather, the NRC's standards concerning what constitutes scientific research are based in the criteria for establishing the rigor of conventional experimental research: internal validity, external validity (generalizability), replicability, and objectivity. These criteria have been criticized as inappropriate for phenomenological inquiry (see Guba & Lincoln, 1994; Lincoln & Guba, 2000; see also Lincoln & Guba, 1985), and race and ethnic studies theorists, feminist theorists, and postcolonial and border studies theorists have proposed new formulations more appropriate to their own inquiry concerns as well as criteria more meaningful to the communities with which they work (Collins, 2000; Reinharz, 1992; Sandoval, 2000; Smith, 1999; Stanfield & Dennis, 1993).

The claims advanced in the NRC report concerning what constitutes scientific inquiry function on multiple levels. First, these claims act to narrow the range of what is to be considered "scientific," effectively shutting out of the scientific community a wide range of critical and alternate epistemology researchers. By defining nonexperimentalists as "the Other" and therefore outsiders to the community of scientific research, the NRC undermines serious and indeed lethal criticisms of the very practices it proclaims as "true" science. Philosophers, feminist theorists, race and ethnic theorists, and alternative paradigm practitioners have mounted pointed critiques around two issues regarding the kind of "scientific inquiry" the NRC supports: its claims to knowledge hegemony (Cowen, 1995) and, indeed, scientific supremacy; and its claims that other forms of inquiry, while they may be "scholarship" (NRC, 2002, pp. 73–74), are not "science" because of their inability to achieve science's principal aims of generalizability, disinterestedness, objectivity, and replicability. Scholars of all stripes and political leanings, including such experimentalists as Lee J. Cronbach himself, have recognized the inherent shortcomings of conventional scientific inquiry and have rejected the neomodernist formulation as unachievable and likely impractical in the social sphere.

On a second level, the NRC report lends support to IRBs in their attempts to limit the range of activities that researchers can undertake with human subjects. As I have reported elsewhere (Lincoln & Tierney, 2004), IRBs are rarely favorably disposed toward emergent research methods, paradigms, and methodologies (e.g., action research, participatory action research, constructivist inquiries, qualitative studies), especially when these boards are constituted primarily of hard scientists and experimentalists, as they have traditionally been (although D. J. Greenwood provides evidence of the opposite situation; personal communication, 2003). In all fairness, as much of this can be blamed on board members' lack of knowledge of such methods or their intended usages as on scientific "sacerdotalism" and a desire to maintain a kind of secular priesthood of science. Whatever the source, however, the effects are the same. Just as alternative epistemologies and qualitative methods are beginning to gain a foothold in the social sciences and educational research, the NRC report threatens an academic lockout of paradigmatic dissidents and alternative epistemology practitioners. Indeed, some members of the community strongly supported by the NRC are sufficiently threatened by alternative paradigm practitioners to declare: "Theorists of educational evaluation such as [here several names are listed, including my own] . . . have explicitly rejected this method [random assignment]. . . . By now, they have influenced the practice of many generations of young educational evaluators and *are probably a major cause of the impoverished current state of knowledge about what reform initiatives in American education have actually achieved*" (Cook & Payne, 2002, pp. 150–151; emphasis added). Although it is unnerving to be blamed for impoverishing the "current state of knowledge" about what works in American education, it is also refreshing to see an admission from the "gold standard" side of the debate that a handful of solid theorists have been responsible for such a profound alteration in the scholarly landscape.

This imputation that certain specific individuals are "probably a major cause of the impoverished current state of knowledge" does nothing, however, to open the academy to its promise as a marketplace of ideas. Quite the opposite: By defining some social scientists as practitioners of scientific inquiry, some as merely scholars, and others as perhaps responsible for outright ignorance (Cook & Payne, 2002), the NRC and others who are vocal in their support of randomized field trials (the clinical model for educational research) have attempted to re-create a class system that acts to define some knowledge as worthy of being utilized to address serious and weighty issues, such as policy formulation, or for serious purposes such as evaluation funding, and other knowledge as merely the purview of a nonscientific minority whose findings should not enter into the political fray of policy and/or legislative action. Thus practitioners of alternative paradigm inquiry are obliquely defined as dilettantes, scholars of no consequence, or, as one scholar has acerbically put it, "not good enough to play with the Big Boys."

On a third level, the aggrandizement of the power to define what should be considered scientific and what should not to a rather small group of individuals represents precisely the reification of a number of substantial criticisms of the practices of conventional inquiry, including maintenance of status, power, and privilege for a few; maintenance of the status quo, particularly with regard to the counterclaims of knowledges and ways of knowing that are outside of the Eurocentric and frequently patriarchal "Western canon"; and a limiting of the diversity and openness that a pluralistic society needs to flourish. A community of specialized elites is reinscribed by the public assertion of a single, true way—the "gold standard"—of conducting scientific inquiry. As Trow (1985) describes it, from another and more political context:

> Membership in such communities is very comfortable and rewarding; it often gives one a sense of personal worth and security. . . . But the good teacher and effective university environment do not make life more comfortable, but on the contrary, make it less comfortable by challenging positions that students already hold. And by challenging political and social pieties, higher education always threatens to disrupt the communities of partisans that live by rhetoric, slogans, symbols of unity and *a claim to a monopoly on the truth.* (p. 64; emphasis added)

On a fourth level, such declarations must be taken seriously because of their ability, directly and indirectly, to *limit discussions on individual campuses* concerning what constitutes disciplined scientific inquiry and, therefore, what studies are approved by IRBs and which researchers find that their academic freedom to engage in significant research on social problems may be curtailed or abrogated altogether. The NRC report acts as a kind of political barometer, albeit one that masquerades as a disinterested and objective "scientific" barometer, that indicates the extent to which a given study may be classified as scientific or nonscientific and, therefore, even worthy of IRB review, federal funding (as in the No Child Left Behind Act), or federally supported research and evaluation activities.

Oral history is a case in point. As noted above, oral history is now classified as some other form of scholarly enterprise, so far removed from science that even though it deals exclusively with humans, it is automatically exempt from IRB review. Such classification—as sufficiently far removed from the scientific enterprise that scholars using this method needn't even bother with IRB review—is apt to make some important studies (e.g., the history of reform in a particular school as recounted by a former principal, a life history of practice in the teaching profession, the recounting of a scholar's experiences in entering and navigating the community of science or academia, an African American woman's experiences of growing up in the segregated South) fall outside the purview of meaningful or critical knowledge. Narrow definitions of scientific inquiry—and evidence—serve ultimately to circumscribe painfully and dangerously the range of what is considered useful knowledge and, consequently, to limit the kinds of studies supported by a range of administrative and managerial structures, including IRBs, funding agencies, foundations, and state governments and agencies. The long-term results are systemic constriction of academic freedom (for individual researchers) (Akker, 2002), a seeping loss of institutional autonomy (for institutions of higher education), and a loss of needed epistemological perspectives on persistent social justice issues.

Long-Term Effects of the NRC Report

The new discourse on "evidence-based research"—as well as "evidence-based teaching" (Pressley, Duke, & Boling, 2004), "evidence-based medicine," and other arenas where "evidence" is considered the "gold standard"—obscures the larger discourse of what evidence, which evidence, whose evidence, evidence gathered under what circumstances, evidence gathered for what uses, and for whom, shall be considered worthwhile, and thereby usable. No reasonable individual would argue that clinical field trials, or randomized experiments, do not have sound purposes under some conditions. Double-blind experiments have proven efficacy in testing pharmaceuticals, and some kinds of clinical trials of medical protocols have proven the effectiveness of revolutionary new therapies. But such randomized treatment procedures constitute a fairly narrow application of scientific method by themselves (see, e.g., Howe, 2004; Popkewitz, 2004; see also House, Volume 3, Chapter 19). Nevertheless, the NRC (2002) report comes rather closer to a "manifesto" on what constitutes scientific truth (Popkewitz, 2004) than it does to a reasoned argument that takes into account the many varieties of recognized epistemologies and methodologies abroad in the social sciences today. The many levels of unexamined assumptions in the NRC report itself—it is no misrepresentation to call it a manifesto—cast it clearly into the category of an ideological statement.

To take one example, consider the question of *knowledge for whom*. It is clear, on multiple readings of the report, that the NRC assumes that the major "consumers" of scientific research, particularly scientific research in education, are other scientists and the policy community. This assumption is true of others as well (Mosteller & Boruch, 2002). Although it is no doubt true that other scientists and academic researchers, as well as policy community members, are major consumers of educational and other social science research, it is not inappropriate to consider community members also as users and consumers of research. With an increasing amount of political and social action now emanating from local-level agencies and community organizations, it is not unreasonable to expect that communities themselves (broadly defined as neighborhoods, municipalities, organizations, and other coherent groups) will want to have access to information, data, knowledge, and interpretations regarding their own circumstances and possibilities for action. As communities acquire systematic information about themselves, they are empowered to participate in designing their own futures and to take action where it is meaningful: locally. If the assumption, however, is that scientific (or other systematic) social knowledge belongs to the knowledge-production community alone, then social action is curtailed in favor of official action. Democratic participation in social change, especially social change on behalf of social justice, is impaired or discouraged altogether. If methodological conservatism is not challenged, it can have the effect of undermining a democratic polity.

The NRC report's focus on "appropriate" inquiry methods (as opposed to those used by Eisner, Lawrence-Lightfoot, and many postmodern theorists, to name some of those whose work the NRC rejects from the panoply of acceptable "science"), especially when fortified with legislative intent to fund nothing but experimental and random assignment research and evaluation studies, creates a discourse that seeks to discipline, govern, and regulate (Bloch, 2004) the *practices* of research as well as the *practitioners* of research (Cannella & Lincoln, 2004a, 2004b; Lincoln & Cannella, 2004a, 2004b; Lincoln & Tierney, 2004). Such conservatism, especially when repeated and reinscribed in the practices of local institutional IRBs, disciplines scholars either by forcing them to use research designs that are inappropriate to the questions they raise (a matter of *fit;* see, for instance, Lincoln & Guba, 1985) or by subjecting them to multiple reviews in which they must define and redefine the nature of the "problems" proposed, often until the researchers simply give up and abandon those particular studies.

Methodological conservatism governs by prescribing a set of practices that are to be considered normative and standard, and relegating all others to subsidiary status, frequently with the threat of disapproval. Such conservatism also regulates by ensuring conformity to certain sets of practices and discouraging nonconformity by dismissing some forms of inquiry as "dangerous," "unscientific," or harmful to the institution. In one actual case of which I am personally aware, the chairman of the IRB made it quite clear, when challenged, that his first responsibility was to protect the institution from any untoward event. This is, of course, a complete perversion/inversion of what human subjects protection laws were created to do. Although the institution's reputation and integrity (as well as its standing with funding agencies) must be protected, the purposes of the IRB are to ensure freedom from harm for human subjects, to establish the likelihood of beneficence for a larger group (of similar research participants), and to ensure that subjects' consent to participate in the research is fully and authentically informed.

Meanwhile, some forms of dismissed or disapproved research might well be classified as "innovative . . . or novel nonvalidated practices" (Schaffner, 1997, p. 6) that have the potential to lead to new insights or theoretically advanced formulations, even by adherents of "gold standard" scientific method. The power of this methodologically conservative discourse to interrupt the pursuit of serious social insight cannot and should not be underestimated, for the discourse itself encodes a set of political assumptions regarding the nature of truth, the kinds of researchers who are able to deliver this "truth," and the kinds of findings that will be admitted into the policy arena. Conflicting, contradictory, and contested findings will not gain admission and will find few audiences. The emphasis on causal inference will short-circuit other forms of explanatory power and, consequently, lead to less, rather than more, deep understanding of social and educational microprocesses, especially the processes of oppression, injustice, economic and educational failure, and discrimination.

The "quick fix" focus on "what works," rather than on the patient and thorough work that leads to greater understanding of *what is at work,* will ultimately prove a chimera. "What works" is a mythical beast, and the search for this beast leads us farther and farther astray, away from research that addresses serious liberatory aims with a purpose-driven social science.

Potential Constraints on Qualitative Research From Methodological Conservatism

That the rising chorus of opinions from experimentalists and methodological conservatives has led to serious constraints on counterdiscourses is not in doubt. The outcry from the research community has been strong and steady (Cannella & Lincoln, 2004a, 2004b; Lincoln & Cannella, 2004a, 2004b; see also two entire issues of *Qualitative Inquiry*, vol. 10, nos. 1 and 2, 2004, for commentary from many segments of the educational research community). The stakes are high, especially for qualitative researchers. Further, the amount of influence on IRBs of statements such as the NRC report is, at present, unknown. The largely conservative bent of many local IRBs, however, particularly in their mistrust of action research, participatory action research, and other "experience-near" projects, suggests that methodological conservatism will reestablish itself firmly on some campuses unless opponents undertake proactive educative intervention. Some of this reestablishment can already be seen in contextual constraints that are currently in operation, as I describe below.

Constraint 1: Oversight of graduate training. For example, whereas academics who teach statistical research methods are not constrained in how or what they teach, professors who teach qualitative research methods now must undergo full IRB review of their proposed courses, limit (probably correctly) the populations with which students may work, and submit extensive paperwork verifying the studies to be done, the studies completed, and the populations sought both before and after they teach the courses. The slightest error in protocol can now have the effect of preventing a required graduate-level research preparation course from being taught at all. This may have a somewhat chilling effect on the issues that students can raise in their research and on the kinds of discussions that normally take place in classrooms around problems that students face in the communities outside of academia. Two issues are at stake here. First is the professors' ability to teach what they believe to be important and/or critical topic areas for students who will also join the academy. Second is the limitation placed on the nature of studies that students can do, for example, in schools, although a large number of students who go through education doctoral programs are likely to go back into schools, where they must conduct studies, assessments, testing, and other forms of research virtually on a daily basis. If they do not receive training in these arenas from teachers who are familiar with ethical and protocol issues, from whom will they receive appropriate socialization (Wolf, Croughan, & Lo, 2002)?

IRB approval processes now also act to limit the kinds of research, as well as the research methodologies, that students may employ in their doctoral dissertation work. The IRBs in some institutions often disapprove newer strategies such as action research, participatory action research, and research in, for example, a teacher's own district or school—even when such research is both desired and approved by the district-level IRB. In my own previous work, I have reported on a number of instances in which student work was turned down by campus-level IRBs even though the work was requested by school districts (Lincoln & Tierney, 2004).

Between federal imperatives for how research projects should be designed and IRB scrutiny and disapproval of nonconventional forms of inquiry, qualitative research is undergoing radical challenge. The stark politicization of research and its methods no doubt poses the gravest threat to qualitative researchers that has been seen in the past half century.

Concerned researchers can use several strategies to counter this problem. First, they must be active with their own institutional IRBs, whether by communicating with the boards on a regular basis or by agreeing to serve on them (Cannella, 2004), as some of my colleagues have done. Nothing appears to work so well as serving an educative function, not only to students but to colleagues as well. Those of us on campuses with large hard science, engineering, and agriculture complexes frequently find that IRBs are dominated by members from these units, most of whom know little about social scientific methods, processes, and questions, or about emerging paradigms in the social sciences. Efforts to enhance board members' awareness of competing paradigms for scientific inquiry are virtually always rewarded with increased sophistication. Active members who provide other members with opportunities to learn about alternative epistemologies, research methods, special problems in international research, and research with indigenous peoples (e.g., the American Anthropological Association has created a stunning database of thoughtful pieces on ethics in work with indigenous peoples) create IRBs that are educated about and responsive to multiple frameworks and multiple methods.

Constraint 2: Improper review of faculty research. Just as IRBs sometimes improperly review the proposals of students who wish to undertake research utilizing newer and more participatory methodologies—that is, the IRBs conduct their reviews with inappropriate criteria in mind—faculty research is likewise in jeopardy from IRB members who lack the training or sophistication to make appropriate scientific judgments. An underlying principle of academic freedom is that, in conducting research wherever they believe the critical questions lie, faculty will exercise care, thought, and due diligence in selecting the research models and methodologies they believe will best answer the critical questions. IRBs, however, sometimes dictate other research strategies that the researchers who are proposing the work believe to be inadequate or inappropriate. This happened prior to the publication of the NRC report, and there is some danger that it will happen with more frequency now that the NRC has created a discourse that serves to regulate and govern what is deemed "scientific" and what is not.

A critical principle of academic freedom is at stake in this discourse. If academics are no longer quite as free to utilize the models and methodologies they believe to be the most efficacious for answering critical social science questions, then a portion of the principle of academic freedom has been compromised. Vigilance on the part of concerned researchers, as well as some empirical studies examining which research projects are approved and which denied by IRBs from campus to campus, is necessary to determine whether this aspect of academic freedom is at risk and, if so, to what extent.

Constraint 3: Threats to institutional autonomy. The extent to which the NRC report will influence local IRBs is currently unknown and theoretically unknowable. Certainly, criticism of the report, which has issued from many quarters, is not likely to be dampened over time, especially as individual researchers see their options for conducting research and acquiring external funding limited by both the report and the No Child Left Behind legislation. It seems likely that on some campuses, IRBs will use the NRC report to support the kinds of decisions they have made all along—that is, to deny project approval for research that does not fit with experimental, quasi-experimental, or other conventional models.

The NRC report has the potential to politicize the IRB review process further if concerned researchers do nothing. The discourse around "standards" for research obscures the ideological persuasions of conventional inquiry, shrouding ideology as it does in the language of objectivity, disinterest, rationality, and random assignment (Lincoln & Cannella, 2004b; Weinstein, 2004). This discourse confronts liberatory social science with the *j'accuse* of "advocacy," a tactic that effectively disguises the particular and pernicious advocacies embedded in terms such as *rationality* and *objectivity* and the standpoints of those who evoke rationality and/or objectivity.

Although it has long been assumed that IRBs are strictly, or at least primarily, local oversight groups, and therefore a part of the local decision making that accrues to institutions as loci of knowledge creation, the NRC report jeopardizes that traditional institutional autonomy by "disciplining" (in a Foucauldian sense) what constitutes acceptable research and, therefore, who has the right to practice it. Consequently, whether they believe it is necessary now or not, institutions should give some thought to resisting the National Research Council's role in dictating research methodologies to those responsible for creating knowledge. At a minimum, institutions should be protesting as well as lobbying against the particularly narrow provisions of the No Child Left Behind Act, which prevents the use of federal funds for research that falls outside any but the most limiting criteria for inquiry.

To the extent that IRBs themselves resist the NRC's intellectually limited definition of scientific inquiry, institutions will have leverage in the fight to protect institutional autonomy. To the extent that IRBs are "captured" by this pinched and illiberal discursive strategy, institutions will have lost ground in the battle for autonomy and self-determination. Indeed, as Neave (1996) observes, there is "a growing chorus amongst political parties, anxious to rally a skeptical electorate to their flagging programmes, which holds academic freedom and institutional autonomy as examples of unjustified privilege wielded by the 'producers', i.e., by the academic estate" (p. 263). This description most assuredly fits with current neoconservative efforts to "tame liberal faculties" and rein in their presumed power. If institutions permit this to happen, they will surrender all pretense of intellectual freedom for faculty (Verbitskaya, 1996).

Constraint 4: Inappropriate decision making in the weighing of risks and benefits. One direct role of IRBs has always been, under current legislation, to weigh the risks and benefits of proposed research. Any risk to human research participants has to be outweighed, or at least counterbalanced, by potential benefits, not only to participants but also to a number of assumed and projected audiences (Amdur & Bankert, 1997; Howe & Dougherty, 1993; Oakes, 2002; Olivier, 2002; Pritchard, 2002; Wagner, 2003; Weijer, 1999). As noted above, in one case I have reported on previously, a professor who spoke with his institutional IRB on behalf of a student's dissertation research was told in no uncertain terms that the IRB sought to "protect" the institution before it protected the human participants who were supposedly at risk (Lincoln & Tierney, 2004). Nor were the board members ashamed or in any way embarrassed by this admission. Although it is surely the case that IRBs protect institutions (from lawsuits, from researchers who conduct haphazard or sloppy or unethical research)—and should do so—protection of the institution is assumed to be a *by-product* of the oversight and review process, not a primary goal. The weighing of risks and benefits is presumed to be directed toward research subjects and scientific findings. The intent of the law, one presumes, is to protect human subjects through this risk assessment process, not to ensure that the university's general counsel has a nice day.

Institutions can use several strategies to counter this kind of misguided decision making on the part of IRBs. Clear guidance for IRB members regarding the law and their roles in the review process from superordinate supervisors who are themselves well versed in the legal ramifications of research activities will help. Periodic training for board members—perhaps each time one group exits IRB service and another group enters—can counter the kind of groupthink that may lead them to believe their role is to act solely on behalf of the institution. Continuing education, perhaps in the form of workshops each semester, can help to keep IRB members informed of their proper roles. Institutions can also help to prevent IRBs from tilting in favor of institutional protectionism rather than human subject protection by assuring that IRB membership includes balanced numbers of representatives from the hard sciences, the social sciences, the humanities, and medical research units.

The Challenges of Qualitative Research to Ethics Regulations

At this moment in history, a concatenation of forces led by the "conservative cultural logics of neo-liberalism" (Denzin & Lincoln, in press) seeks to shape a definition of inquiry that precludes multiple paradigms, epistemologies, and theoretical perspectives from the policy arena. The constraints on qualitative scholars take several forms: constraints on what they may teach and on what classroom activities require IRB review, constraints on the kinds of research they may conduct, constraints on institutional autonomy, and constraints related to IRBs' weighing of risks and benefits, as concerns about protecting human subjects are subordinated to concerns about avoiding legal actions against the institution. These constraints on methodology are interactive, and all coalesce in a context in which federal initiatives aimed at regulating, governing, and/or disciplining the discourse around "what works" and definitions of "evidence" and "scientific inquiry" constitute genuine threats to academic freedom, to continued federal funding for research, to free and open inquiry, and to individual researcher integrity in determining best practices for pursuing research questions.

More important, these conservative discourses act to stamp out inquiry—particularly, but not exclusively, qualitative inquiry—aimed at democratic action and liberatory, antioppressive, social justice–oriented aims. They also act to silence voices that have only in the past quarter century begun to be heard in any great numbers—voices of the poor, of the members of underrepresented groups, of the disabled, the oppressed, and postcolonial peoples, among others. For conspiracy theorists, it is no large leap to see a connection between the rise of nonmajority scholarship and the current conservative backlash. Faludi (1991) has carefully explicated the backlash that women experienced when their gains in the job market and legal arenas threatened the status quo. The so-called culture wars, led by Lynne Cheney and members of the National Association of Scholars, among others, represents a backlash against challenges to the Eurocentric knowledge of the Western canon (D'Souza, 1991; Graff, 1992) and efforts to expand awareness of non-Western literatures and philosophies on campuses around the nation as a consequence of rapid globalization. Yet another backlash is currently taking place against the rights achieved by nonheterosexual individuals, as illustrated by the drive to "protect marriage" that has led to a proposal to amend the U.S. Constitution. In light of the startling gains in visibility and stature of alternative paradigm practices and practitioners in the past decade, it should neither surprise nor shock anyone that a backlash is taking place against qualitative and other alternative methodologies and epistemologies.

The current challenge for qualitative researchers is to work toward legal and policy changes that reflect the reconfigured relationships of qualitative research. These new relationships are cooperative, mutual, democratic, open-ended, communitarian. They are highly incompatible with the asymmetrical power, informed consent, risk-beneficence model of research ethics currently in force. Participatory, social justice–oriented social science demands a research ethics attuned to the postmodern, postfoundational, postcolonial, and globalized inquiry environment of alternative paradigms.

As the ground rules for trade, economics, diplomacy, and education shift, so should the ground rules for conducting research. As we move toward a postcolonial, globalized, "McDonaldized" (Ritzer, 1996), homogenized, corporatized world order, there is some danger that, for the purposes of rationalization and in the name of modernity, legislation regarding research ethics will become frozen where it now stands. The system that exists now in the United States, which is highly appropriate for the decade in which it was forged, was outgrown and inadequate once phenomenological philosophies began to permeate the inquiry environment and once qualitative researchers realized they were dealing with far more than a shift to a separate set of methods (Lincoln & Guba, 1989). Reformulated relationships between researcher and researched, the potential for trading and sharing roles between them, and the mandate to exercise moral discretion regarding the purposes and representations of social inquiry (Fine, Weis, Weseen, & Wong, 2000) re-created research in the image of democracy, care/caring, and social justice.

Clearly, the current system is not attuned to the needs, purposes, concerns, or relationships now being generated by postmodern and poststructural critical inquiry of a variety of paradigms, perspectives, and models. It seems unlikely, even with the reassertion of a modernist stance on the part of the National Research Council, that participatory, antihegemonic inquiry will quietly go away. Its practitioners and theoreticians deeply intuit the communitarian qualities of such inquiry, and, having switched epistemological communities from the academy to the communities they see themselves as serving, they will not readily readopt outmoded standards for research ethics.

The axiological challenge for this new epistemological community will be to find the means not only to influence their own IRBs (for instance, on how to present arguments to one's own IRB, see Cheek, Volume 2, Chapter 2) but also to effect a shift in legislation, policy, and legislative intent. That will be no easy task. It will require activism of a different sort: not in the field, but rather in the halls of power. In the current neoliberal pinched and conservative environment, it seems nearly impossible to begin such a conversation. Nevertheless, qualitative researchers must undertake it, because, as always—whether in technology, science, or social science—practice has far outstripped policy and civic dialogue. Concerned scholars are likely to find that thoughtful analysis of the issues, careful strategizing, and thinking globally while acting locally are the best strategies for countering these narrow, illiberal discourses. And local IRBs are good places to begin a mutually educative and liberalizing process.

Note

1. By *rereviews,* I mean multiple reviews that are conducted as the result of an IRB's denial of permission to conduct proposed research because of what the IRB believes to be inappropriate methodology. In such a case, the IRB tells the researcher to provide "additional clarification," which may range from primarily trivial changes to major revisions in the research plans.

REFERENCES

Akker, J. (2002). Protecting academic freedom worldwide. *Academe, 88*(3), 44–45.

Amdur, R. J., & Bankert, E. (1997). Continuing IRB review when research activity is limited to routine follow-up evaluations. *IRB: Ethics and Human Research, 19*(1), 7–11.

American Association of University Professors. (2001). Protecting human beings: Institutional review boards and social science research. *Academe, 87*(3), 55–67.

Baez, B., & Slaughter, S. (2001). Academic freedom and the federal courts in the 1990s: The legitimation of the conservative entrepreneurial state. In J. C Smart (Ed.), *Higher education: Handbook of theory and research* (Vol. 16, pp. 73–118). New York: Agathon.

Bauer, P. E. (2001). A few simple truths about your community IRB members. *IRB: Ethics and Human Research, 23*(1), 7–8.

Benjamin, E., Kurland, J. E., & Molotsky, I. F. (1985). On "accuracy in academia" and academic freedom. *Academe, 71*(5), 4.

Bloch, M. (2004). A discourse that disciplines, governs, and regulates: The National Research Council's report on scientific research in education. *Qualitative Inquiry, 10*(1), 96–110.

Burris, V., & Diamond, S. (1991). Academic freedom, conspicuous benevolence and the National Association of Scholars. *Critical Sociology, 18*(3), 125–142.

Cannella, G. S. (2004). Regulatory power: Can a feminist poststructuralist engage in research oversight? *Qualitative Inquiry, 10,* 235–245.

Cannella, G. S., & Lincoln, Y. S. (2004a). Dangerous discourses II: Comprehending and countering the redeployment of discourses (and resources) in the generation of liberatory inquiry. *Qualitative Inquiry, 10,* 165–174.

Cannella, G. S., & Lincoln, Y. S. (2004b). Epilogue: Claiming a critical public social science—reconceptualizing and redeploying research. *Qualitative Inquiry, 10,* 298–309.

Collins, P. H. (2000). *Black feminist thought: Knowledge, consciousness, and the politics of empowerment* (2nd ed.). New York: Routledge.

Cook, T. D., & Payne, M. R. (2002). Objecting to the objections to using random assignment in educational research. In F. Mosteller & R. Boruch (Eds.), *Evidence matters: Randomized trials in education research* (pp. 150–178). Washington, DC: Brookings Institution Press.

Cowen, R. C. (1995, June 20). Scientists rally to quell anti-science political movements. *Christian Science Monitor,* p. 13.

Cronbach, L. J., & Suppes, P. (1969). *Research for tomorrow's schools: Disciplined inquiry in education.* New York: Macmillan.

Denzin, N. K., & Lincoln, Y. S. (in press). Preface. In Y. S. Lincoln & N. K. Denzin (Eds.), *IRBs and qualitative research.* Walnut Creek, CA: AltaMira.

Devine, P. E. (1996). Academic freedom in the postmodern world. *Public Affairs Quarterly, 10,* 185–201.

Diamond, S. (1991, February). Readin', writin', and repressin'. *Z Magazine, 4,* 44–48.

D'Souza, D. (1991). *Illiberal education: The politics of race and sex on campus.* New York: Free Press.

DuBois, J. M. (2002). When is informed consent appropriate in educational research? Regulatory and ethical issues. *IRB: Ethics and Human Research, 24*(1), 1–8.

Faludi, S. (1991). *Backlash: The undeclared war against American women.* New York: Crown.

Fine, M., Weis, L., Weseen, S., & Wong, L. (2000). For whom? Qualitative research, representations, and social responsibilities. In N. K. Denzin & Y. S. Lincoln (Eds.), *Handbook of qualitative research* (2nd ed., pp. 107–131). Thousand Oaks, CA: Sage.

Giddens, A. (1990). *The consequences of modernity.* Stanford, CA: Stanford University Press.

Gillespie, J. F. (1997, August). *Institutional review boards and university student research learning opportunities.* Paper presented at the 105th Annual Meeting of the American Psychological Association, Chicago.

Giroux, H. A. (1995). Teaching in the age of "political correctness." *Educational Forum, 50*(2), 130–139.

Gordon, V. M., Sugarman, J., & Kass, N. (1998). Toward a more comprehensive approach to protecting human subjects. *IRB: Ethics and Human Research, 20*(1), 1–5.

Graff, G. (1992). *Beyond the culture wars: How teaching the conflicts can revitalize American education.* New York: W. W. Norton.

Gray, B. H. (1978, May). *Institutional review boards as an instrument of assessment: Research involving human subjects.* Paper presented at the U.S. Conference on the Social Assessment of Science, University of Bielefeld, West Germany.

Guba, E. G., & Lincoln, Y. S. (1994). Competing paradigms in qualitative research. In N. K. Denzin & Y. S. Lincoln (Eds.), *Handbook of qualitative research* (pp. 105–117). Thousand Oaks, CA: Sage.

Hammack, F. M. (1997). Ethical issues in teacher research. *Teachers College Record, 99,* 247–265.

Hecht, J. B. (1995, October). *The institutional review board in social science research.* Paper presented at the annual meeting of the Mid-Western Educational Research Association, Chicago.

Howe, K. R. (2004). A critique of experimentalism. *Qualitative Inquiry, 10,* 42–61.

Howe, K. R., & Dougherty, K. C. (1993). Ethics, institutional review boards, and the changing face of educational research. *Educational Researcher, 22*(9), 16–21.

Lincoln, Y. S., & Cannella, G. S. (2004a). Dangerous discourses: Methodological conservatism and governmental regimes of truth. *Qualitative Inquiry, 10,* 5–14.

Lincoln, Y. S, & Cannella, G. S. (2004b). Qualitative research, power, and the radical Right. *Qualitative Inquiry, 10,* 175–201.

Lincoln, Y. S., & Denzin, N. K. (2000). The seventh moment: Out of the past. In N. K. Denzin & Y. S. Lincoln (Eds.), *Handbook of qualitative research* (2nd ed., pp. 1047–1065). Thousand Oaks, CA: Sage.

Lincoln, Y. S., & Guba, E. G. (1985). *Naturalistic inquiry.* Beverly Hills, CA: Sage.

Lincoln, Y. S., & Guba, E. G. (1989). Ethics: The failure of positivist science. *Review of Higher Education, 12,* 221–240.

Lincoln, Y. S., & Guba, E. G. (2000). Paradigmatic controversies, contradictions, and emerging confluences. In N. K. Denzin & Y. S. Lincoln (Eds.), *Handbook of qualitative research* (2nd ed., pp. 163–188). Thousand Oaks, CA: Sage.

Lincoln, Y. S., & Tierney, W. G. (2004). Qualitative research and institutional review boards. *Qualitative Inquiry, 10,* 219–234.

Mertens, D. M. (1998). *Research methods in education and psychology: Integrating diversity with quantitative and qualitative approaches.* Thousand Oaks, CA: Sage.

Messer-Davidow, E. (1993, Autumn). Manufacturing the attack on liberalized higher education. *Social Text, 36*, 40–80.

Mosteller, F., & Boruch, R. (Eds.). (2002). *Evidence matters: Randomized trials in education research.* Washington, DC: Brookings Institution Press.

National Research Council. (2002). *Scientific research in education.* Committee on Scientific Principles for Education Research (R. J. Shavelson & L. Towne, Eds.). Center for Education, Division of Behavioral and Social Sciences and Education. Washington, DC: National Academy Press.

Neave, G. (1996). Academic freedom and university autonomy: An abiding concern. *Higher Education Policy, 9*, 263–266.

Oakes, J. M. (2002). Risks and wrongs in social science research: An evaluator's guide to the IRB. *Evaluation Review, 26*, 443–479.

Olivier, S. (2002). Ethics review of research projects involving human subjects. *Quest, 54*, 196–204.

Parenti, M. (1995). The myth of the liberal campus. *Humanist, 55*(5), 20–24.

Popkewitz, T. S. (2004). Is the National Research Council committee's report on scientific research in education scientific? On trusting the manifesto. *Qualitative Inquiry, 10*, 62–78.

Pressley, M., Duke, N. K., & Boling, E. C. (2004). The educational science and scientifically based instruction we need: Lessons from reading research and policymaking. *Harvard Educational Review, 74*, 30–61.

Pritchard, I. A. (2002). Travelers and trolls: Practitioner research and institutional review boards. *Educational Researcher, 31*(3), 3–13.

Reinharz, S. (1992). *Feminist methods in social research.* New York: Oxford University Press.

Ritzer, G. (1996). *The McDonaldization of society* (Rev. ed.). Thousand Oaks, CA: Pine Forge.

Sandoval, C. (2000). *Methodology of the oppressed.* Minneapolis: University of Minnesota Press.

Schaffner, K. F. (1997). Ethical considerations in human investigation involving paradigm shifts: Organ transplantation in the 1990s. *IRB: Ethics and Human Research, 19*(6), 5–11.

Smith, L. T. (1999). *Decolonizing methodologies: Research and indigenous peoples.* Dunedin, New Zealand: University of Otago Press.

Stanfield, J. H., II, & Dennis, R. M. (Eds.). (1993). *Race and ethnicity in research methods.* Newbury Park, CA: Sage.

Teller, E. (1988). Freedom of speech and advocacy in academia: The debate on "Star Wars." In L. Csorba III (Ed.), *Academic license: The war on academic freedom* (pp. 123–129). Evanston, IL: UCA.

Trow, M. (1985, September-October). The threat from within: Academic freedom and negative evidence. *Change, 17*, 8–9, 61–64.

Verbitskaya, L. A. (1996). Academic freedom and university autonomy: A variety of concepts. *Higher Education Policy, 9*, 289–294.

Wagner, R. M. (2003). Ethical review of research involving human subjects: When and why is IRB review necessary? *Muscle & Nerve, 28*, 27–39.

Weijer, C. (1999). Thinking clearly about research risk: Implications of the work of Benjamin Freedman. *IRB: Ethics and Human Research, 21*(6), 1–5.

Weinstein, M. (2004). Randomized design and the myth of certain knowledge: Guinea pig narratives and cultural critique. *Qualitative Inquiry, 10*, 246–260.

Wolf, L. W., Croughan, M., & Lo, B. (2002). The challenges of IRB review and human subjects protections in practice-based research. *Medical Care, 40*, 521–529.

Additional Resources

Hammerschmidt, D. E. (1997). "There is no substantive due process right to conduct human-subjects research": The saga of the Minnesota gamma hydroxybutyrate study. *IRB: Ethics and Human Research, 19*(3–4), 13–15.

Huer, J. (1991). *Tenure for Socrates: A study in the betrayal of the American professor.* New York: Bergin & Garvey.

Pinsker, S. (1998, August 20). Politicized academia? *Christian Science Monitor,* p. 11.

Rabban, D. M. (2001). Academic freedom, individual or institutional? *Academe, 87*(6), 16–20.

Rajagopal, B. (2003). Academic freedom as a human right: An internationalist perspective. *Academe, 89*(3), 25–28.

Reilly, P. K. (2001). Been there; done that (we've been there; they've done that). *IRB: Ethics and Human Research, 23*(1), 8–9.

Russell, C. (1993). *Academic freedom.* London: Routledge.

University of Illinois at Chicago Research Ethics Study Group. (2002). "Doing it right—together": Study groups and research agendas. *IRB: Ethics and Human Research, 24*(1), 9–10.

Part II

PARADIGMS AND PERSPECTIVES IN CONTENTION

In our introductory chapter, following Guba (1990, p. 17), we defined a paradigm as a basic set of beliefs that guide action. Paradigms deal with first principles, or ultimates. They are human constructions. They define the worldview of the researcher-as-interpretive-bricoleur. These beliefs can never be established in terms of their ultimate truthfulness. Perspectives, in contrast, are not as solidified, nor as well unified, as paradigms, although a perspective may share many elements with a paradigm—for example, a common set of methodological assumptions or a particular epistemology.

A paradigm encompasses four terms: ethics (axiology), epistemology, ontology, and methodology. *Ethics* asks, "How will I be as a moral person in the world?" *Epistemology* asks "How do I know the world?" "What is the relationship between the inquirer and the known?" Every epistemology, as Christians (Chapter 6, this volume) indicates, implies an ethical-moral stance toward the world and the self of the researcher. *Ontology* raises basic questions about the nature of reality and the nature of the human being in the world. *Methodology* focuses on the best means for acquiring knowledge about the world.

Part II of the *Handbook* examines the major paradigms and perspectives that now structure and organize qualitative research. These paradigms and perspectives are positivism, postpositivism, constructivism, and participatory action frameworks. Alongside these paradigms are the perspectives of feminism (in its multiple forms), critical race theory, queer theory, and cultural studies. Each of these perspectives has developed its own criteria, assumptions, and methodological practices. These practices are then applied to disciplined inquiry within that framework. (Tables 6.1 and 6.2 in Lincoln and Guba [2000, pp. 165–166] outline the major differences between the positivist, postpositivist, critical theory, constructivist, and participatory paradigms.)

We have provided a brief discussion of each paradigm and perspective in Chapter 1; here we elaborate them in somewhat more detail. However, before turning to this discussion, it is important to note three interconnected events. Within the past decade, the borders and boundary lines between these paradigms and perspectives have begun to blur. As Lincoln and Guba observe, the "pedigrees" of various paradigms are themselves beginning to "interbreed." However, though the borders have blurred, perceptions of differences between perspectives have hardened. Even as this occurs, the discourses of methodological conservatism, discussed in our Preface and in Chapter 1, threaten to narrow the range and effectiveness of qualitative research practices. Hence, the title of this section, "Paradigms and Perspectives in Contention."

Major Issues Confronting All Paradigms

Lincoln and Guba (2000) suggest that in the present moment, all paradigms must confront seven basic, critical issues. These issues involve axiology (ethics and values), accommodation and commensurability (can paradigms be fitted into one another?), action (what the researcher does in the world), control (who initiates inquiry, who asks questions), foundations of truth (foundationalism vs. anti- and nonfoundationalism), validity (traditional positivist models vs. poststructural-constructionist criteria), and voice, reflexivity, and postmodern representation (single- vs. multivoiced).

Each paradigm takes a different stance on these topics. Of course, the *positivist* and *postpositivist* paradigms provide the backdrop against which these other paradigms and perspectives operate. Lincoln and Guba analyze these two traditions in considerable detail, including their reliance on naïve realism; their dualistic epistemologies; their verificational approach to inquiry; and their emphasis on reliability, validity, prediction, control, and a building block approach to knowledge. Lincoln and Guba discuss the inability of these paradigms to address adequately issues surrounding voice, empowerment, and praxis. They also allude to the failure to satisfactorily address the theory- and value-laden nature of facts, the interactive nature of inquiry, and the fact that the same set of "facts" can support more than one theory.

Constructivism, Interpretivism, and Hermeneutics

According to Lincoln and Guba, *constructivism* adopts a relativist ontology (relativism), a transactional epistemology, and a hermeneutic, dialectical methodology. Users of this paradigm are oriented to the production of reconstructed understandings of the social world. The traditional positivist criteria of internal and external validity are replaced by such terms as *trustworthiness* and *authenticity*. Constructivists value transactional knowledge. Their work overlaps with the several different participatory action approaches discussed by Kemmis and McTaggart (Volume 2, Chapter 10). Constructivism connects action to praxis and builds on antifoundational arguments while encouraging experimental and multivoiced texts.

Critical Ethnography

Douglas Foley and Angela Valenzuela (Chapter 9, this volume) offer a history and analysis of critical ethnography, giving special attention to critical ethnographers who do applied policy studies and also involve themselves in political movements. They observe that post-1960s critical ethnographers began advocating cultural critiques of modern society. These scholars revolted against positivism and sought to pursue a politically progressive agenda using multiple standpoint epistemologies. Various approaches were taken up in this time period, including action anthropology; global, neo-Marxist, Marxist feminist, and critical ethnography; and participatory action research.

Their chapter presents two case studies, Foley's career as doing activist anthropology, including his involvement in the Chicano civil rights movement, and Valenzuela's activities as an activist sociologist working on educational policy studies within the Latina/o activist community in Texas. Foley experimented with an evolving research methodology involving collaborative relationships, dialogic interviewing, community review of what was written, and the use of an engaging narrative style. Valenzuela was involved directly in everyday struggles of Chicana/o legislators to craft new legislation, including calling for more humanizing assessment measures. She was both researcher and advocate.

In reflexively exploring their own careers as critical ethnographers, Foley and Valenzuela illustrate different forms of collaboration and different forms of activism. Foley joined the ideological struggle against scientism. Valenzuela formed a passionate moral bond with her ethnic group. She collaborated with her subjects in a deep psychological and political way. Both authors conclude that critical ethnography will truly serve the public only when the academy has been transformed, which would involve, Smith (Chapter 4, this volume) and Bishop (Chapter 5, this volume) remind us, embracing the complex process of decolonization.

The Feminisms

Virginia Olesen (Chapter 10, this volume) observes that feminist qualitative research, at the dawn of this new century, is a highly diversified and contested site. Already we see multiple articulations of gender, as well as its enactment in post-9/11 spaces.

Competing models, on a global scale, blur together. But beneath the fray and the debate, there is agreement that feminist inquiry in the new millennium is committed to action in the world. Feminists insist that a social justice agenda address the needs of men and women of color, because gender, class, and race are intimately interconnected. Olesen's is an impassioned feminism. "Rage is not enough," she exclaims. We need "incisive scholarship to frame, direct, and harness passion in the interests of redressing grievous problems in the many areas of women's health" (p. 236).

In 1994, Olesen identified three major strands of feminist inquiry (standpoint epistemology, empiricist, postmodernism-cultural studies). A decade later, these strands continue to multiply. There are today separate feminisms associated with specific disciplines; with the writings of women of color; women problematizing Whiteness; postcolonial discourse; decolonizing arguments of indigenous women; lesbian research and queer theory; disabled women; standpoint theory; and postmodern and deconstructive theory. This complexity has made the researcher-participant relationship more complicated. It has destabilized the insider-outsider model of inquiry. Within indigenous spaces, it has produced a call for the decolonization of the academy. This is linked to a deconstruction of such traditional terms as experience, difference, and gender.

A gendered decolonizing discourse focuses on the concepts of bias and objectivity, validity and trustworthiness, voice, and feminist ethics. On this last point, Olesen's masterful chapter elaborates the frameworks presented by Smith (Chapter 4), Bishop (Chapter 5), and Christians (Chapter 6) presented in Part I.

▣ Moral Activism and Critical Race Theory Scholarship

Gloria Ladson-Billings and Jamel Donnor (Chapter 11, this volume) move critical race theory directly into the fields of politics and qualitative inquiry. They advocate an activist, moral, and ethical epistemology committed to social justice and a revolutionary habitus. They focus their analysis on the meaning of the "call," an epiphanic moment when persons of color are reminded that they are locked into a hierarchical racial structure. The "N word" can be invoked at any time to hail a person of color. Racialized others occupy the liminal space of alterity in white society; they are forced to play the role of alter ego to the ideal self prescribed by the dominant cultural model. Critical race theory (CRT) "seeks to decloak the seemingly race-neutral, and color-blind ways . . . of constructing and administering race-based appraisals . . . of the law, administrative policy, electoral politics . . . political discourse [and education] in the USA" (Parker, Deyhle, Villenas, & Nebeker, 1998, p. 5). Critical race theory uses multiple interpretive methodologies—stories, plays, performances. Critical race theory enacts an ethnic and ethical epistemology, arguing that ways of knowing and being are shaped by one's standpoint, or position in the world. This standpoint undoes the cultural, ethical, and epistemological logic (and racism) of the Eurocentric, Enlightenment paradigm. At the same time, it contests positivism's hegemonic control over what is and what is not acceptable research. Thus do they criticize the National Research Council's report on Scientific Research in Education (Shavelson & Towne, 2003).

Drawing on recent work by African American, Asian Pacific Islander, Asian American, Latina/o, and Native American scholars, Ladson-Billings and Donnor introduce the concepts of multiple or double consciousness, mestiza consciousness, and tribal secrets. The analysis of these terms allows them to show how the dominant cultural paradigms have produced fractured, racialized identities and experiences of exclusion for minority scholars. American society, they observe, has been constructed as a nation of white people whose politics and culture are designed to serve the interests of whites. Critical race theorists experiment with multiple interpretive strategies, ranging from storytelling to autoethnography, case studies, textual and narrative analyses, traditional fieldwork, and, most important, collaborative, action-based inquiries and studies of race, gender, law, education, and racial oppression in daily life.

Using the construct of "political race," they call for street-level cross-racial coalitions and alliances involving grassroots workers seeking to invigorate democracy. Connections with the hip-hop generation are central to this project. Political race enlarges the critical race project. It is not color-blind. It proposes multitextured political strategies that go beyond traditional legal or economic solutions to issues of racial justice. Ladson-Billings and Donnor show, drawing from Patricia Hill Collins, how "political" race embodies a nonviolent visionary pragmatism that is "actualized in the hearts and minds of ordinary people" (p. 292). For this to happen, the academy must change; it must embrace the principles of decolonization outlined by Smith and Bishop. A reconstructed university will become a home for racialized others, a place where indigenous, liberating, empowering pedagogies have become commonplace. In such a place, Ladson-Billings and Donnor argue, a new version of the call will be answered.

▣ Critical Theory

Multiple *critical theories*, among them *Marxist* and *neo-Marxist models*, now circulate within the discourses of qualitative research (see Kincheloe & McLaren, Chapter 12, this volume). In Lincoln and Guba's framework, this paradigm, in its many formulations, articulates an ontology based on historical realism, an epistemology that is transactional, and a methodology that is both dialogic and dialectical. Kincheloe and McLaren trace the history of critical research (and Marxist theory), from the Frankfurt School through more recent transformations in poststructural, postmodern, feminist, critical pedagogy, and cultural studies theory.

They outline a critical theory, what they call critical humility, an evolving criticality for the new millennium, beginning with the assumption that the societies of the West are not unproblematically democratic and free. Their version of critical theory rejects economic determinism and focuses on the media, culture, language, power, desire, critical enlightenment, and critical emancipation. Their framework embraces a critical hermeneutics. They read instrumental rationality as one of the most repressive features of contemporary society. Building on Dewey and Gramsci, they present a critical, pragmatic approach to texts and their relationships to lived experience. This leads to a "resistance" version of critical theory, a version connected to critical ethnography, and partisan, critical inquiry committed to social criticism. Critical theorists, as bricoleurs, seek to produce practical, pragmatic knowledge, a bricolage that is cultural and structural, judged by its degree of historical situatedness and its ability to produce praxis, or action.

This chapter, like Olesen's and Ladson-Billings and Donnor's, is a call to arms. Getting mad no longer is enough. We must learn how to act in the world in ways that allow us to expose the workings of an invisible empire that has given us yet another Gulf War and another economic agenda that leaves even more children behind.

▣ Cultural Studies

Cultural studies cannot be contained within a single framework. There are multiple cultural studies projects, including those connected to the Birmingham school and to the work of Stuart Hall and his associates (see Hall, 1996). Cultural studies research is historically self-reflective, critical, interdisciplinary, conversant with high theory, and focused on the global and the local; it takes into account historical, political, economic, cultural, and everyday discourses. It focuses on questions of community, identity, agency, and change (Grossberg & Pollock, 1998).

In its generic form, cultural studies involves an examination of how the history people live is produced by structures that have been handed down from the past. Each version of cultural studies is joined by a threefold concern with cultural texts, lived experience, and the articulated relationship between texts and everyday life. Within the cultural text tradition, some scholars examine the mass media and popular culture as sites where history, ideology, and subjective experiences come together. These scholars produce critical ethnographies of the audience in relation to particular historical moments. Other scholars read texts as sites where hegemonic meanings are produced, distributed, and consumed. Within the ethnographic tradition, there is a postmodern concern for the social text and its production.

The open-ended nature of the cultural studies project leads to a perpetual resistance against attempts to impose a single definition over the entire project. There are critical-Marxist, constructionist, and postpositivist paradigmatic strands within the formation, as well as emergent feminist and ethnic models. Scholars within the cultural studies project are drawn to historical realism and relativism as their ontology, to transactional epistemologies, and to dialogic methodologies, while remaining committed to a historical and structural framework that is action oriented.

Paula Saukko (Chapter 13, this volume) outlines a critical materialist, hermeneutic, poststructural, contextualist cultural studies project. Drawing on her own research on testing for genetic thrombophilia, she outlines a methodological program in cultural studies that is defined by its interest in lived, discursive, and contextual dimensions of reality. Weaving back and forth between culturalist and realist agendas, she identifies three key methodological currents or strands in cultural studies today: hermeneutics, poststructuralism, and contextualism. She translates these three dimensions into three validities (contextual, dialogic, self-reflexive), focused, respectively, on historical reality, authenticity, and deconstruction. These strands yield critical analyses of postindustrialism, globalization, neoliberalism, postcolonialism, and the recent trend toward the corporatization of universities, a trend that threatens to erase cultural studies.

Contextualism and contextual validity move back and forth in time, from the particular and the situational to the general and the historical. It shows how each instance of a phenomenon is embedded in its historical space, a space marked by politics, culture, and biography. In moving back and forth in time, the researcher situates a subject's projects in time and space. Dialogic validity grounds interpretation in lived reality. Self-reflexive validity analyzes how social discourses shape or mediate experience.

Saukko's contextualism confronts the hard, lived local facts of life in a global economy. Discursively, her project shows how the real is mediated by systems of discourse, which are themselves embedded in socially mediated realities. Thus does she move back and forth between the local and the global, the cultural and the real, the personal and the political.

The disciplinary boundaries that define cultural studies keep shifting, and there is no agreed upon standard genealogy of its emergence as a serious academic discipline. Nonetheless, there are certain prevailing tendencies, including feminist understandings of the politics of the everyday and the personal; disputes between proponents of textualism, ethnography, and autoethnography; and continued debates surrounding the dreams of modern citizenship.

◘ Critical Humanism and Queer Theory

Critical race theory brought race and the concept of a complex racial subject squarely into qualitative inquiry. It remained for queer theory to do the same; namely, to question and deconstruct the concept of a unified sexual (and racialized) subject. Ken Plummer (Chapter 14, this volume) takes queer theory in a new direction. He writes from his own biography as a postgay humanist, a sort of feminist, a little queer, a critical humanist who wants to move on. He thinks that in the postmodern moment certain terms, like *family*, and much of our research methodology language are obsolete. He calls them zombie categories. They are no longer needed. They are dead.

With the arrival of queer theory, the social sciences are in a new space. This is the age of postmodern fragmentation, globalization, posthumanism. This is a time for new research styles, styles that take up the reflexive queer, polyphonic, narrative, ethical turn. Plummer's critical humanism, with its emphasis on symbolic interactionism, pragmatism, democratic thinking, storytelling, moral progress, and social justice, enters this space. It is committed to reducing human suffering, to an ethics of care and compassion, a politics of respect, and the importance of trust.

His queer theory is radical. It encourages the postmodernization of sexual and gender studies. It deconstructs all conventional categories of sexuality and gender. It is transgressive, gothic, and romantic. It challenges the heterosexual/homosexual binary; the deviance paradigm is abandoned. His queer methodology takes the textual turn seriously and endorses subversive ethnographies, scavenger methodologies, ethnographic performances, and queered case studies.

By troubling the place of the homo/heterosexual binary in everyday life, queer theory has created spaces for multiple discourses on transgendered, bisexual, lesbian, and gay subjects. This means that researchers must examine how any social arena is structured, in part by this homo/hetero dichotomy. They must ask how the epistemology of the closet is central to the sexual and material practices of everyday life. Queer theory challenges this epistemology, just as it deconstructs the notion of unified subjects. Queerness becomes a topic and a resource for investigating the way group boundaries are created, negotiated, and changed. Institutional and historical analyses are central to this project, for they shed light on how the self and its identities are embedded in institutional and cultural practices.

▣ In Conclusion

The researcher-as-interpretive-bricoleur cannot afford to be a stranger to any of the paradigms and perspectives discussed in Part II of the *Handbook*. The researcher must understand the basic ethical, ontological, epistemological, and methodological assumptions of each, and be able to engage them in dialogue. The differences between paradigms and perspectives have significant and important implications at the practical, material, everyday level. The blurring of paradigm differences is likely to continue as long as proponents continue to come together to discuss their differences while seeking to build on those areas where they are in agreement.

It is also clear that there is no single "truth." All truths are partial and incomplete. There will be no single conventional paradigm, as Lincoln and Guba (2000) argue, to which all social scientists might ascribe. We occupy a historical moment marked by multivocality, contested meanings, paradigmatic controversies, and new textual forms. This is an age of emancipation, freedom from the confines of a single regime of truth, emancipation from seeing the world in one color.

References

Grossberg, L., & Pollock, D. (1998). Editorial statement. *Cultural Studies, 12*(2), 114.

Guba, E. (1990). The alternative paradigm dialog. In E. Guba (Ed.), *The paradigm dialog* (pp. 17–30). Newbury Park, CA: Sage.

Hall, S. (1996). Gramsci's relevance for the study of race and ethnicity. In D. Morley & K.-H. Chen (Eds.), *Stuart Hall: Critical dialogues in cultural studies* (pp. 411–444). London: Routledge.

Lincoln, Y. S., & Guba, E. (2000). Paradigmatic controversies, contradictions, and emerging confluences. In N. K. Denzin & Y. S. Lincoln (Eds.), *Handbook of qualitative research* (2nd ed., pp. 163–188). Thousand Oaks, CA: Sage.

Olesen, V. (1994). Feminisms and models of qualitative research. In N. K. Denzin & Y. S. Lincoln (Eds.), *Handbook of qualitative research* (pp. 158–174). Thousand Oaks, CA: Sage.

Parker, L., Deyhle, D., Villenas, S., & Nebeker, K. C. (1998). Guest editor's introduction: Critical race theory and qualitative studies in education. *Qualitative Studies in Education, 11,* 5–6.

Shavelson, R., & Towne, L. (Eds.). (2003). *Scientific research in education.* Washington, DC: National Academies Press.

8

PARADIGMATIC CONTROVERSIES, CONTRADICTIONS, AND EMERGING CONFLUENCES

Egon G. Guba and Yvonna S. Lincoln

In our chapter for the first edition of the *Handbook of Qualitative Research,* we focused on the contention among various research paradigms for legitimacy and intellectual and paradigmatic hegemony (Guba & Lincoln, 1994). The postmodern paradigms that we discussed (postmodernist critical theory and constructivism)[1] were in contention with the received positivist and postpositivist paradigms for legitimacy, and with one another for intellectual legitimacy. In the more than 10 years that have elapsed since that chapter was published, substantial changes have occurred in the landscape of social scientific inquiry.

On the matter of legitimacy, we observe that readers familiar with the literature on methods and paradigms reflect a high interest in ontologies and epistemologies that differ sharply from those undergirding conventional social science. Second, even those established professionals trained in quantitative social science (including the two of us) want to learn more about qualitative approaches, because new young professionals being mentored in graduate schools are asking serious questions about and looking for guidance in qualitatively oriented studies and dissertations. Third, the number of qualitative texts, research papers, workshops, and training materials has exploded. Indeed, it would be difficult to miss the distinct turn of the social sciences toward more interpretive, postmodern, and criticalist practices and theorizing (Bloland, 1989, 1995). This nonpositivist orientation has created a context (surround) in which virtually no study can go unchallenged by proponents of contending paradigms. Further, it is obvious that the number of practitioners of new-paradigm inquiry is growing daily. There can be no question that the legitimacy of postmodern paradigms is well established and at least equal to the legitimacy of received and conventional paradigms (Denzin & Lincoln, 1994).

On the matter of hegemony, or supremacy, among postmodern paradigms, it is clear that Geertz's (1988, 1993) prophecy about the "blurring of genres" is rapidly being fulfilled. Inquiry methodology can no longer be treated as a set of universally applicable rules or abstractions. Methodology is inevitably interwoven with and emerges from the nature of particular disciplines (such as sociology and psychology) and particular perspectives (such as Marxism, feminist theory, and queer theory). So, for instance, we can read feminist critical theorists such as Olesen (2000) or queer theorists such as Gamson (2000), or we can follow arguments about teachers as researchers (Kincheloe, 1991) while we understand the secondary text to be teacher empowerment and democratization of schooling practices. Indeed, the various paradigms are beginning to "interbreed" such that two theorists previously thought to be in irreconcilable conflict may now appear, under a different theoretical rubric, to be informing one another's arguments. A personal example is our own work, which has been heavily influenced by action research practitioners and postmodern critical theorists. Consequently, to argue that it is paradigms that are in contention is probably less useful than to probe where and how paradigms exhibit confluence and where and how they exhibit differences, controversies, and contradictions.

▣ Major Issues Confronting All Paradigms

In our chapter in the first edition of the *Handbook*, we presented two tables that summarized our positions, first, on the axiomatic nature of paradigms (the paradigms we considered at that time were positivism, postpositivism, critical theory, and constructivism; Guba & Lincoln, 1994, p. 109, Table 6.1); and second, on the issues we believed were most fundamental to differentiating the four paradigms (p. 112, Table 6.2). These tables are reproduced here as a way of reminding our readers of our previous statements. The axioms defined the ontological, epistemological, and methodological bases for both established and emergent paradigms; these are shown here in Table 8.1. The issues most often in contention that we examined were inquiry aim, nature of knowledge, the way knowledge is accumulated, goodness (rigor and validity) or quality criteria, values, ethics, voice, training, accommodation, and hegemony; these are shown in Table 8.2. An examination of these two tables will reacquaint the reader with our original *Handbook* treatment; more detailed information is, of course, available in our original chapter.

Table 8.1. Basic Beliefs (Metaphysics) of Alternative Inquiry Paradigms

Item	*Positivism*	*Postpositivism*	*Critical Theory et al.*	*Constructivism*
Ontology	Naïve realism—"real" reality but apprehendible	Critical realism—"real" reality but only imperfectly and probabilistically apprehendible	Historical realism—virtual reality shaped by social, political, cultural, economic, ethnic, and gender values; crystallized over time	Relativism—local and specific constructed and co-constructed realities
Epistemology	Dualist/objectivist; findings true	Modified dualist/objectivist; critical tradition/community; findings probably true	Transactional/subjectivist; value-mediated findings	Transactional/subjectivist; created findings
Methodology	Experimental/manipulative; verification of hypotheses; chiefly quantitative methods	Modified experimental/manipulative; critical multiplism; falsification of hypotheses; may include qualitative methods	Dialogic/dialectical	Hermeneutical/dialectical

Table 8.2. Paradigm Positions on Selected Practical Issues

Item	*Positivism*	*Postpositivism*	*Critical Theory et al.*	*Constructivism*
Inquiry aim	Explanation: prediction and control		Critique and transformation; restitution and emancipation	Understanding; reconstruction
Nature of knowledge	Verified hypotheses established as facts or laws	Nonfalsified hypotheses that are probable facts or laws	Structural/historical insights	Individual or collective reconstructions coalescing around consensus
Knowledge accumulation	Accretion—"building blocks" adding to "edifice of knowledge"; generalizations and cause-effect linkages		Historical revisionism; generalization by similarity	More informed and sophisticated reconstructions; vicarious experience
Goodness or quality criteria	Conventional benchmarks of "rigor": internal and external validity, reliability, and objectivity		Historical situatedness; erosion of ignorance and misapprehension; action stimulus	Trustworthiness and authenticity, including catalyst for action
Values	Excluded—influence denied		Included—formative	Included—formative
Ethics	Extrinsic: tilt toward deception		Intrinsic: moral tilt toward revelation	Intrinsic: process tilt toward revelation; special problems
Voice	"Disinterested scientist" as informer of decision makers, policy makers, and change agents		"Transformative intellectual" as advocate and activist	"Passionate participant" as facilitator of multivoice reconstruction
Training	Technical and quantitative; substantive theories	Technical; quantitative and qualitative; substantive theories	Resocialization; qualitative and quantitative; history; values of altruism, empowerment, and liberation	
Accommodation	Commensurable		Incommensurable with previous two	
Hegemony	In control of publication, funding, promotion, and tenure		Seeking recognition and input; offering challenges to predecessor paradigms, aligned with postcolonial aspirations	

Since publication of that chapter, at least one set of authors, John Heron and Peter Reason, have elaborated on our tables to include the *participatory/cooperative* paradigm (Heron, 1996; Heron & Reason, 1997, pp. 289–290). Thus, in addition to the paradigms of positivism, postpositivism, critical theory, and constructivism, we add the participatory paradigm in the present chapter (this is an excellent example, we might add, of the hermeneutic elaboration so embedded in our own view, constructivism).

Our aim here is to extend the analysis further by building on Heron and Reason's additions and by rearranging the issues to reflect current thought. The issues we have chosen include our original formulations and the additions, revisions, and amplifications made by Heron and Reason (1997), and we have also chosen what we believe to be the issues most important today. We should note that *important* means several things to us. An important topic may be one that is widely debated (or even hotly contested)—validity is one such issue. An important issue may be one that bespeaks a new awareness (an issue such as recognition of the role of values). An important issue may be one that illustrates the influence of one paradigm on another (such as the influence of feminist, action research, critical theory, and participatory models on researcher conceptions of action within and with the community in which research is carried out). Or issues may be important because new or extended theoretical and/or field-oriented treatments for them are newly available—voice and reflexivity are two such issues.

Table 8.3 reprises the original Table 6.1 but adds the axioms of the participatory paradigm proposed by Heron and Reason (1997). Table 8.4 deals with seven issues and represents an update of selected issues first presented in the old Table 6.2. "Voice" in the 1994 version of Table 6.2 has been renamed "Inquirer Posture," and we have inserted a redefined "Voice" in the current Table 8.5. In all cases except "Inquirer Posture," the entries for the participatory paradigm are those proposed by Heron and Reason; in the one case not covered by them, we have added a notation that we believe captures their intention.

We make no attempt here to reprise the material well discussed in our earlier *Handbook* chapter. Instead, we focus solely on the issues in Table 8.5: axiology; accommodation and commensurability; action; control; foundations of truth and knowledge; validity; and voice, reflexivity, and postmodern textual representation. We believe these seven issues to be the most important at this time.

While we believe these issues to be the most contentious, we also believe they create the intellectual, theoretical, and practical space for dialogue, consensus, and confluence to occur. There is great potential for interweaving of viewpoints, for the incorporation of multiple perspectives, and for borrowing, or *bricolage,* where borrowing seems useful, richness enhancing, or theoretically heuristic. For instance, even though we are ourselves social constructivists/constructionists, our call to action embedded in the authenticity criteria we elaborated in *Fourth Generation Evaluation* (Guba & Lincoln, 1989) reflects strongly the bent to action embodied in critical

(Text continues on page 264)

Table 8.3. Basic Beliefs of Alternative Inquiry Paradigms—Updated

Issue	*Positivism*	*Postpositivism*	*Critical Theory et al.*	*Constructivism*	*Participatory*[a]
Ontology	Naïve realism—"real" reality but apprehendible	Critical realism—"real" reality but only imperfectly and probabilistically apprehendible	Historical realism—virtual reality shaped by social, political, cultural, economic, ethnic, and gender values; crystallized over time	Relativism—local and specific co-constructed realities	Participative reality—subjective-objective reality, co-created by mind and given cosmos
Epistemology	Dualist/objectivist; findings true	Modified dualist/objectivist; critical tradition/community; findings probably true	Transactional/subjectivist; value-mediated findings	Transactional/subjectivist; co-created findings	Critical subjectivity in participatory transaction with cosmos; extended epistemology of experiential, propositional, and practical knowing; co-created findings
Methodology	Experimental/manipulative; verification of hypotheses; chiefly quantitative methods	Modified experimental/manipulative; critical multiplism; falsification of hypotheses; may include qualitative methods	Dialogic/dialectical	Hermeneutical/dialectical	Political participation in collaborative action inquiry; primacy of the practical; use of language grounded in shared experiential context

a. Entries in this column are based on Heron and Reason (1997).

Table 8.4. Paradigm Positions on Selected Issues—Updated

Issue	*Positivism*	*Postpositivism*	*Critical Theories*	*Constructivism*	*Participatory*[a]
Nature of knowledge	Verified hypotheses established as facts or laws	Nonfalsified hypotheses that are probable facts or laws	Structural/ historical insights	Individual and collective reconstructions sometimes coalescing around consensus	Extended epistemology: primacy of practical knowing; critical subjectivity; living knowledge
Knowledge accumulation	Accretion—"building blocks" adding to "edifice of knowledge"; generalizations and cause-effect linkages		Historical revisionism; generalization by similarity	More informed and sophisticated reconstructions; vicarious experience	In communities of inquiry embedded in communities of practice
Goodness or quality criteria	Conventional benchmarks of "rigor": internal and external validity, reliability, and objectivity		Historical situatedness; erosion of ignorance and misapprehensions; action stimulus	Trustworthiness and authenticity including catalyst for action	Congruence of experiential, presentational, propositional, and practical knowing; leads to action to transform the world in the service of human flourishing
Values	Excluded—influence denied		Included—formative		
Ethics	Extrinsic—tilt toward deception		Intrinsic—moral tilt toward revelation	Intrinsic—process tilt toward revelation	
Inquirer posture	"Disinterested scientist" as informer of decision makers, policy makers, and change agents		"Transformative intellectual" as advocate and activist	"Passionate participant" as facilitator of multivoice reconstruction	Primary voice manifest through aware self-reflective action; secondary voices in illuminating theory, narrative, movement, song, dance, and other presentational forms
Training	Technical and quantitative; substantive theories	Technical; quantitative and qualitative; substantive theories	Resocialization; qualitative and quantitative; history; values of altruism, empowerment and liberation		Coresearchers are initiated into the inquiry process by facilitator/researcher and learn through active engagement in the process; facilitator/researcher requires emotional competence, democratic personality, and skills

a. Entries in this column are based on Heron and Reason (1997), except for "ethics" and "values."

Table 8.5. Critical Issues of the Time

Issue	*Positivism*	*Postpositivism*	*Critical Theory et al.*	*Constructivism*	*Participatory*
Axiology	Propositional knowing about the world is an end in itself, is intrinsically valuable		Propositional, transactional knowing is instrumentally valuable as a means to social emancipation, which is an end in itself, is intrinsically valuable		Practical knowing about how to flourish with a balance of autonomy, cooperation, and hierarchy in a culture is an end in itself, is intrinsically valuable
Accommodation and commensurability	Commensurable for all positivist forms		Incommensurable with positivist forms; some commensurability with constructivist, criticalist, and participatory approaches, especially as they merge in liberationist approaches outside the West		
Action	Not the responsibility of the researcher; viewed as "advocacy" or subjectivity, and therefore a threat to validity and objectivity		Found especially in the form of empowerment; emancipation anticipated and hoped for; social transformation, particularly toward more equity and justice, is end goal	Intertwined with validity; inquiry often incomplete without action on the part of participants; constructivist formulation mandates training in political action if participants do not understand political systems	
Control	Resides solely in researcher		Often resides in "transformative intellectual"; in new constructions, control returns to community	Shared between inquirer and participants	Shared to varying degrees
Relationship to foundations of truth and knowledge	Foundational	Foundational	Foundational within social critique	Antifoundational	Nonfoundational

Issue	*Positivism*	*Postpositivism*	*Critical Theory et al.*	*Constructivism*	*Participatory*
Extended considerations of validity (goodness criteria)	Traditional positivist constructions of validity; rigor, internal validity, external validity, reliability, objectivity		Action stimulus (see above); social transformation, equity, social justice	Extended constructions of validity: (a) crystalline validity (Richardson); (b) authenticity criteria (Guba & Lincoln); (c) catalytic, rhizomatic, voluptuous validities (Lather); (d) relational and ethics-centered criteria (Lincoln); (e) community-centered determinations of validity	See "action" above
Voice, reflexivity, postmodern textual representations	Voice of the researcher, principally; reflexivity may be considered a problem in objectivity; textual representation unproblematic and somewhat formulaic		Voices mixed between researcher and participants	Voices mixed, with participants' voices sometimes dominant; reflexivity serious and problematic; textual representation an extended issue	Voices mixed; textual representation rarely discussed but problematic; reflexivity relies on critical subjectivity and self-awareness
			Textual representation practices may be problematic—i.e., "fiction formulas" or unexamined "regimes of truth"		

theorists' perspectives. And although Heron and Reason have elaborated a model they call the *cooperative paradigm,* careful reading of their proposal reveals a form of inquiry that is post-postpositive, postmodern, and criticalist in orientation. As a result, the reader familiar with several theoretical and paradigmatic strands of research will find that echoes of many streams of thought come together in the extended table. What this means is that the categories, as Laurel Richardson (personal communication, September 12, 1998) has pointed out, "are fluid, indeed what should be a category keeps altering, enlarging." She notes that "even as [we] write, the boundaries between the paradigms are shifting." This is the paradigmatic equivalent of the Geertzian "blurring of genres" to which we referred earlier.

Our own position is that of the constructionist camp, loosely defined. We do not believe that criteria for judging either "reality" or validity are absolutist (Bradley & Schaefer, 1998); rather, they are derived from community consensus regarding what is "real," what is useful, and what has meaning (especially meaning for action and further steps). We believe that a goodly portion of social phenomena consists of the meaning-making activities of groups and individuals around those phenomena. The meaning-making activities themselves are of central interest to social constructionists/constructivists, simply because it is the meaning-making/sense-making/attributional activities that shape action (or inaction). The meaning-making activities themselves can be changed when they are found to be incomplete, faulty (e.g., discriminatory, oppressive, or nonliberatory), or malformed (created from data that can be shown to be false).

We have tried, however, to incorporate perspectives from other major nonpositivist paradigms. This is not a complete summation; space constraints prevent that. What we hope to do in this chapter is to acquaint readers with the larger currents, arguments, dialogues, and provocative writings and theorizing, the better to see perhaps what we ourselves do not even yet see: where and when confluence is possible, where constructive rapprochement might be negotiated, where voices are beginning to achieve some harmony.

▣ Axiology

Earlier, we placed values on the table as an "issue" on which positivists or phenomenologists might have a "posture" (Guba & Lincoln, 1989, 1994; Lincoln & Guba, 1985). Fortunately, we reserved for ourselves the right to either get smarter or just change our minds. We did both. Now, we suspect (although Table 8.5 does not yet reflect it) that "axiology" should be grouped with "basic beliefs." In *Naturalistic Inquiry* (Lincoln & Guba, 1985), we covered some of the ways in which values feed into the inquiry process: choice of the problem, choice of paradigm to guide the problem, choice of theoretical framework, choice of major data-gathering and data-analytic methods, choice of context, treatment of values already resident within the context, and choice of format(s) for presenting findings. We believed those were strong enough reasons to argue for the inclusion of values as a major point of departure between positivist, conventional modes of inquiry and interpretive forms of inquiry.

A second "reading" of the burgeoning literature and subsequent rethinking of our own rationale have led us to conclude that the issue is much larger than we first conceived. If we had it to do all over again, we would make values or, more correctly, axiology (the branch of philosophy dealing with ethics, aesthetics, and religion) a part of the basic foundational philosophical dimensions of paradigm proposal. Doing so would, in our opinion, begin to help us see the embeddedness of ethics within, not external to, paradigms (see, for instance, Christians, 2000) and would contribute to the consideration of and dialogue about the role of spirituality in human inquiry. Arguably, axiology has been "defined out of" scientific inquiry for no larger a reason than that it also concerns "religion." But defining "religion" broadly to encompass spirituality would move constructivists closer to participative inquirers and would move critical theorists closer to both (owing to their concern with liberation from oppression and freeing of the human spirit, both profoundly spiritual concerns). The expansion of basic issues to include axiology, then, is one way of achieving greater confluence among the various interpretivist inquiry models. This is the place, for example, where Peter Reason's profound concerns with "sacred science" and human functioning find legitimacy; it is a place where Laurel Richardson's "sacred spaces" become authoritative sites for human inquiry; it is a place—or *the* place—where the spiritual meets social inquiry, as Reason (1993), and later Lincoln and Denzin (1994), proposed some years earlier.

Accommodation and Commensurability

Positivists and postpositivists alike still occasionally argue that paradigms are, in some ways, commensurable; that is, they can be retrofitted to each other in ways that make the simultaneous practice of both possible. We have argued that at the paradigmatic, or philosophical, level, commensurability between positivist and postpositivist worldviews is not possible, but that within each paradigm, mixed methodologies (strategies) may make perfectly good sense (Guba & Lincoln, 1981, 1982, 1989, 1994; Lincoln & Guba, 1985). So, for instance, in *Effective Evaluation* we argued:

> The guiding inquiry paradigm most appropriate to responsive evaluation is . . . the naturalistic, phenomenological, or ethnographic paradigm. It will be seen that qualitative techniques are typically most appropriate to support this approach. There are times, however, when the issues and concerns voiced by audiences require information that is best generated by more conventional methods, especially quantitative methods. . . . In such cases, the responsive conventional evaluator will not shrink from the appropriate application. (Guba & Lincoln, 1981, p. 36)

As we tried to make clear, the "argument" arising in the social sciences was *not about method,* although many critics of the new naturalistic, ethnographic, phenomenological, and/or case study approaches assumed it was.[2] As late as 1998, Weiss could be found to claim that "some evaluation theorists, notably Guba and Lincoln (1989), hold that it is impossible to combine qualitative and quantitative approaches responsibly within an evaluation" (p. 268), even though we stated early on in *Fourth Generation Evaluation* (1989) that

> those claims, concerns, and issues that have *not* been resolved become the advance organizers for information collection by the evaluator. . . . *The information may be quantitative or qualitative.* Responsive evaluation does not rule out quantitative modes, as is mistakenly believed by many, but deals with whatever information is responsive to the unresolved claim, concern, or issue. (p. 43)

We had also strongly asserted earlier, in *Naturalistic Inquiry* (1985), that

> qualitative methods are stressed within the naturalistic paradigm not because the paradigm is antiquantitative but because qualitative methods come more easily to the human-as-instrument. *The reader should particularly note the absence of an antiquantitative stance,* precisely because the naturalistic and conventional paradigms are so often—mistakenly—equated with the qualitative and quantitative paradigms, respectively. Indeed, *there are many opportunities for the naturalistic investigator to utilize quantitative data—probably more than are appreciated.* (pp. 198–199; emphasis added)

Having demonstrated that we were not then (and are not now) talking about an antiquantitative posture or the exclusivity of *methods,* but rather about the philosophies of which paradigms are constructed, we can ask the question again regarding commensurability: Are paradigms commensurable? Is it possible to blend elements of one paradigm into another, so that one is engaging in research that represents the best of both worldviews? The answer, from our perspective, has to be a cautious *yes.* This is especially so if the models (paradigms) share axiomatic elements that are similar, or that resonate strongly between them. So, for instance, *positivism* and *postpositivism* are clearly commensurable. In the same vein, elements of *interpretivist/postmodern* critical theory, constructivist and participative inquiry, fit comfortably together. Commensurability is an issue only when researchers want to "pick and choose" among the axioms of positivist and interpretivist models, because the axioms are contradictory and mutually exclusive.

The Call to Action

One of the clearest ways in which the paradigmatic controversies can be demonstrated is to compare the positivist and postpositivist adherents, who view action as a form of contamination of research results and processes, and the interpretivists, who see action on research results as a meaningful and important outcome of inquiry processes. Positivist adherents believe action to be either a form of advocacy or a form of subjectivity, either or both of which undermine the aim of objectivity. Critical theorists, on the other hand, have always advocated varying degrees of social action, from the overturning of specific unjust practices to radical transformation of entire societies. The call for action—whether in terms of internal transformation, such as ridding oneself of false consciousness, or of external social transformation—differentiates between positivist and postmodern criticalist theorists (including feminist and queer theorists). The sharpest shift, however, has been in the constructivist and participatory phenomenological models, where a step beyond interpretation and *Verstehen,* or understanding, toward social action is probably one of the most conceptually interesting of the shifts (Lincoln, 1997, 1998a, 1998b). For some theorists, the shift toward action came in response to widespread nonutilization of evaluation findings and the desire to create forms of evaluation that would attract champions who might follow through on recommendations with meaningful action plans (Guba & Lincoln, 1981, 1989). For others, embracing action came as both a political and an ethical commitment (see, for instance, Carr & Kemmis, 1986; Christians, 2000; Greenwood & Levin, 2000; Schratz & Walker, 1995; Tierney, 2000).

Whatever the source of the problem to which inquirers were responding, the shift toward connecting research, policy analysis, evaluation, and/or social deconstruction (e.g., deconstruction of the patriarchal forms of oppression in social structures, which is the project informing much feminist theorizing, or deconstruction of the homophobia embedded in public policies) with action has come to characterize much new-paradigm inquiry work, both at the theoretical and at the practice and *praxis*-oriented levels. Action has become a major controversy that limns the ongoing debates among practitioners of the various paradigms. The mandate for social action, especially action designed and created by and for research participants with the aid and cooperation of researchers, can be most sharply delineated between positivist/postpositivist and new-paradigm inquirers. Many positivist and postpositivist inquirers still consider "action" the domain of communities other than researchers and research participants: those of policy personnel, legislators, and civic and political officials. Hard-line foundationalists presume that the taint of action will interfere with, or even negate, the objectivity that is a (presumed) characteristic of rigorous scientific method inquiry.

Control

Another controversy that has tended to become problematic centers on *control* of the study: Who initiates? Who determines salient questions? Who determines what constitutes findings? Who determines how data will be collected? Who determines in what forms the findings will be made public, if at all? Who determines what representations will be made of participants in the research? Let us be very clear: The issue of control is deeply embedded in the questions of voice, reflexivity, and issues of postmodern textual representation, which we shall take up later, *but only for new-paradigm inquirers.* For more conventional inquirers, the issue of control is effectively walled off from voice, reflexivity, and issues of textual representation, because each of those issues in some way threatens claims to rigor (particularly objectivity and validity). For new-paradigm inquirers who have seen the preeminent paradigm issues of ontology and epistemology effectively folded into one another, and who have watched as methodology and axiology logically folded into one another (Lincoln, 1995, 1997), control of an inquiry seems far less problematic, except insofar as inquirers seek to obtain participants' genuine participation (see, for instance, Guba & Lincoln, 1981, on contracting and attempts to get some stakeholding groups to do more than stand by while an evaluation is in progress).

Critical theorists, especially those who work in community organizing programs, are painfully aware of the necessity for members of the community, or research participants, to take control of their futures. Constructivists desire participants to take an increasingly active role in nominating questions of interest for any inquiry and in designing outlets for findings to be shared more widely within and outside the community. Participatory inquirers understand action controlled by the local context members to be the aim of inquiry within a community. For none of these paradigmatic adherents is control an issue of advocacy, a somewhat deceptive term usually used as a code within a larger metanarrative to attack an inquiry's rigor, objectivity, or fairness. Rather, for new-paradigm researchers control is a means of fostering emancipation, democracy, and community empowerment, and of redressing power imbalances such that those who were previously marginalized now achieve voice (Mertens, 1998) or "human flourishing" (Heron & Reason, 1997). Control as a controversy is an excellent place to observe the phenomenon that we have always termed "Catholic questions directed to a Methodist audience." We use this description—given to us by a workshop participant in the early 1980s—to refer to the ongoing problem of illegitimate questions: questions that have no meaning because the frames of reference are those for which they were never intended. (We could as well call these "Hindu questions to a Muslim," to give another sense of how paradigms, or overarching philosophies—or theologies—are incommensurable, and how questions in one framework make little, if any, sense in another.) Paradigmatic formulations interact such that control becomes inextricably intertwined with mandates for objectivity. Objectivity derives from the Enlightenment prescription for knowledge of the physical world, which is postulated to be separate and distinct from those who would know (Polkinghorne, 1989). But if knowledge of the social (as opposed to the physical) world resides in meaning-making mechanisms of the social, mental, and linguistic worlds that individuals inhabit, then knowledge cannot be separate from the knower, but rather is rooted in his or her mental or linguistic designations of that world (Polkinghorne, 1989; Salner, 1989).

▣ Foundations of Truth and Knowledge in Paradigms

Whether or not the world has a "real" existence outside of human experience of that world is an open question. For modernist (i.e., Enlightenment, scientific method, conventional, positivist) researchers, most assuredly there is a "real" reality "out there," apart from the flawed human apprehension of it. Further, that reality can be approached (approximated) only through the utilization of methods that prevent human contamination of its apprehension or comprehension. For foundationalists in the empiricist tradition, the foundations of scientific truth and knowledge about reality reside in rigorous application of testing phenomena against a template as much devoid of human bias, misperception, and other "idols" (Francis Bacon, cited in Polkinghorne, 1989) as instrumentally possible. As Polkinghorne (1989) makes clear:

> The idea that the objective realm is independent of the knower's subjective experiences of it can be found in Descartes's dual substance theory, with its distinction between the objective and subjective realms.... In the splitting of reality into subject and object realms, what can be known "objectively" is only the objective realm. True knowledge is limited to the objects and the relationships between them that exist in the realm of time and space. Human consciousness, which is subjective, is not accessible to science, and thus not truly knowable. (p. 23)

Now, templates of truth and knowledge can be defined in a variety of ways—as the end product of rational processes, as the result of experiential sensing, as the result of empirical observation, and others. In all cases, however, the referent is the physical or empirical world: rational engagement with it, experience of it, empirical observation of it. Realists, who work on the assumption that there is a "real" world "out there," may in individual cases also be foundationalists, taking the view that all of these ways of defining are rooted in phenomena existing outside the human mind. Although we can think about them, experience them, or observe them, they are nevertheless transcendent, referred to but beyond direct apprehension. Realism is an ontological question, whereas foundationalism is a criterial question. Some foundationalists argue that real phenomena necessarily imply certain final, ultimate criteria for testing them as truthful (although we may have great difficulty in determining what those criteria are); nonfoundationalists tend to argue that there are no such ultimate criteria, only those that we can agree upon at a certain time and under certain conditions. Foundational criteria are discovered; nonfoundational criteria are negotiated. It is the case, however, that most realists are also foundationalists, and many nonfoundationalists or antifoundationalists are relativists.

An ontological formulation that connects realism and foundationalism within the same "collapse" of categories that characterizes the ontological-epistemological collapse is one that exhibits good fit with the other assumptions of constructivism. That state of affairs suits new-paradigm inquirers well. Critical theorists, constructivists, and participatory/cooperative inquirers take their primary field of interest to be precisely that subjective and intersubjective social knowledge and the active construction and co-creation of such knowledge by human agents that is produced by human consciousness. Further, new-paradigm inquirers take to the social knowledge field with zest, informed by a variety of social, intellectual, and theoretical explorations. These theoretical excursions include Saussurian linguistic theory, which views all relationships between words and what those words signify as the function of an internal relationship within some linguistic system; literary theory's deconstructive contributions, which seek to disconnect texts from any *essentialist* or transcendental meaning and resituate them within both author and reader historical and social contexts (Hutcheon, 1989; Leitch, 1996); feminist (Addelson, 1993; Alpern, Antler, Perry, & Scobie, 1992; Babbitt, 1993; Harding, 1993), race and ethnic (Kondo, 1990, 1997; Trinh, 1991), and queer theorizing (Gamson, 2000), which seeks to uncover and explore varieties of oppression and historical colonizing between dominant and subaltern genders, identities, races, and social worlds; the postmodern historical moment (Michael, 1996), which problematizes truth as partial, identity as fluid, language as an unclear referent system, and method and criteria as potentially coercive (Ellis & Bochner, 1996); and criticalist theories of social change (Carspecken, 1996; Schratz & Walker, 1995). The realization of the richness of the mental, social, psychological, and linguistic worlds that individuals and social groups create and constantly re-create and cocreate gives rise, in the minds of new-paradigm postmodern and poststructural inquirers, to endlessly fertile fields of inquiry rigidly walled off from conventional inquirers. Unfettered from the pursuit of transcendental scientific truth, inquirers are now free to resituate themselves within texts, to reconstruct their relationships with research participants in less constricted fashions, and to create re-presentations (Tierney & Lincoln, 1997) that grapple openly with problems of inscription, reinscription, metanarratives, and other rhetorical devices that obscure the extent to which human action is locally and temporally shaped. The processes of uncovering forms of inscription and the rhetoric of metanarratives are *genealogical*—"expos[ing] the origins of the view that have become *sedimented and accepted as truths*" (Polkinghorne, 1989, p. 42; emphasis added)—or *archaeological* (Foucault, 1971; Scheurich, 1997).

New-paradigm inquirers engage the foundational controversy in quite different ways. Critical theorists, particularly critical theorists more positivist in orientation, who lean toward Marxian interpretations, tend toward foundational perspectives, with an important difference. Rather than locating foundational truth and knowledge in some external reality "out there," such critical theorists tend to locate the foundations of truth in specific historical, economic, racial, and social infrastructures of oppression, injustice, and marginalization. Knowers are not portrayed as *separate from* some objective reality, but may be cast as unaware actors in such historical realities ("false consciousness") or as aware of historical forms of oppression, but unable or unwilling, because of conflicts, to act on those historical forms to alter specific conditions in this historical moment ("divided consciousness"). Thus the "foundation" for critical theorists is a duality: social critique tied in turn to raised consciousness of the possibility of positive and liberating social change. Social critique may exist apart from social change, but both are necessary for criticalist perspectives.

Constructivists, on the other hand, tend toward the antifoundational (Lincoln, 1995, 1998b; Schwandt, 1996). *Antifoundational* is the term used to denote a refusal to adopt any permanent, unvarying (or "foundational") standards by which truth can be universally known. As one of us has argued, truth—and any agreement regarding what is valid knowledge—arises from the relationship between members of some stakeholding community (Lincoln, 1995). Agreements about truth may be the subject of community *negotiations* regarding what will be accepted as truth (although there are difficulties with that formulation as well; Guba & Lincoln, 1989). Or agreements may eventuate as the result of a *dialogue* that moves arguments about truth claims or validity past the warring camps of objectivity and relativity toward "a communal test of validity through the argumentation of the participants in a discourse" (Bernstein, 1983; Polkinghorne, 1989; Schwandt, 1996). This "communicative and pragmatic concept" of validity (Rorty, 1979) is never fixed or unvarying. Rather, it is created by means of a community narrative, itself subject to the temporal and historical conditions that gave rise to the community. Schwandt (1989) has also argued that these discourses, or community narratives, can and should be bounded by moral considerations, a premise grounded in the emancipatory narratives of the critical theorists, the philosophical pragmatism of Rorty, the democratic focus of constructivist inquiry, and the "human flourishing" goals of participatory and cooperative inquiry.

The controversies around foundationalism (and, to a lesser extent, essentialism) are not likely to be resolved through dialogue between paradigm adherents. The likelier event is that the "postmodern turn" (Best & Kellner, 1997), with its emphasis on the social construction of social reality, fluid as opposed to fixed identities of the self, and the partiality of all truths, will simply overtake modernist assumptions of an objective reality, as indeed, to some extent, it has already done in the physical sciences. We might predict that, if not in our lifetimes, at some later time the dualist idea of an objective reality suborned by limited human subjective realities will seem as quaint as flat-earth theories do to us today.

▣ Validity: An Extended Agenda

Nowhere can the conversation about paradigm differences be more fertile than in the extended controversy about validity (Howe & Eisenhart, 1990; Kvale, 1989, 1994; Ryan, Greene, Lincoln, Mathison, & Mertens, 1998; Scheurich, 1994, 1996). Validity is not like objectivity. There are fairly strong theoretical, philosophical, and pragmatic rationales for examining the concept of objectivity and finding it wanting. Even within positivist frameworks it is viewed as conceptually flawed. But validity is a more irritating construct, one neither easily dismissed nor readily configured by new-paradigm practitioners (Enerstvedt, 1989; Tschudi, 1989). Validity cannot be dismissed simply because it points to a question that has to be answered in one way or another: Are these findings sufficiently authentic (isomorphic to some reality, trustworthy, related to the way others construct their social worlds) that I may trust myself in acting on their implications? More to the point, would I feel sufficiently secure about these findings to construct social policy or legislation based on them? At the same time, radical reconfigurations of validity leave researchers with multiple, sometimes conflicting, mandates for what constitutes rigorous research.

One of the issues around validity is the conflation between method and interpretation. The postmodern turn suggests that no method can deliver on ultimate truth, and in fact "suspects all methods," the more so the larger their claims to delivering on truth (Richardson, 1994). Thus, although one might argue that some methods are more suited than others for conducting research on human construction of social realities (Lincoln & Guba, 1985), no one would argue that a single method—or collection of methods—is the royal road to ultimate knowledge. In new-paradigm inquiry, however, it is not merely method that promises to deliver on some set of local or context-grounded truths, it is also the processes of interpretation. Thus we have two arguments proceeding simultaneously. The first, borrowed from positivism, argues for a kind of rigor in the application of method, whereas the second argues for both a community consent and a form of rigor—defensible reasoning, plausible alongside some other reality that is known to author and reader—in ascribing salience to one interpretation over another and for framing and bounding an interpretive study itself. Prior to our understanding that there were, indeed, two forms of rigor, we assembled a set of methodological criteria, largely borrowed from an earlier generation of thoughtful anthropological and sociological methodological theorists. Those methodological criteria are still useful for a variety of reasons, not the least of which is that they ensure that such issues as prolonged engagement and persistent observation are attended to with some seriousness.

It is the second kind of rigor, however, that has received the most attention in recent writings: Are we *interpretively* rigorous? Can our cocreated constructions be trusted to provide some purchase on some important human phenomenon?

Human phenomena are themselves the subject of controversy. Classical social scientists would like to see "human phenomena" limited to those social experiences from which (scientific) generalizations may be drawn. New-paradigm inquirers, however, are increasingly concerned with the single experience, the individual crisis, the epiphany or moment of discovery, with that most powerful of all threats to conventional objectivity, feeling and emotion. Social scientists concerned with the expansion of what count as social data rely increasingly on the experiential, the embodied, the emotive qualities of human experience that contribute the narrative quality to a life. Sociologists such as Ellis and Bochner (2000) and Richardson (2000) and psychologists such as Michelle Fine (see Fine, Weis, Weseen, & Wong, 2000) concern themselves with various forms of autoethnography and personal experience methods, both to overcome the abstractions of a social science far gone with quantitative descriptions of human life and to capture those elements that make life conflictual, moving, problematic.

For purposes of this discussion, we believe the adoption of the most radical definitions of social science is appropriate, because the paradigmatic controversies are often taking place at the edges of those conversations. Those edges are where the border work is occurring, and, accordingly, they are the places that show the most promise for projecting where qualitative methods will be in the near and far future.

Whither and Whether Criteria

At those edges, several conversations are occurring around validity. The first—and most radical—is a conversation opened by Schwandt (1996), who suggests that we say "farewell to criteriology," or the "regulative norms for removing doubt and settling disputes about what is correct or incorrect, true or false" (p. 59), which have created a virtual cult around criteria. Schwandt does not, however, himself say farewell to criteria forever; rather, he resituates social inquiry, with other contemporary philosophical pragmatists, within a framework that transforms professional social inquiry into a form of practical philosophy, characterized by "aesthetic, prudential and moral considerations as well as more conventionally scientific ones" (p. 68). When social inquiry becomes the practice of a form of practical philosophy—a deep questioning about how we shall get on in the world and what we conceive to be the potentials and limits of human knowledge and functioning—then we have some preliminary understanding of what entirely different criteria might be for judging social inquiry.

Schwandt (1996) proposes three such criteria. First, he argues, we should search for a social inquiry that "generate[s] knowledge that complements or supplements rather than displac[ing] lay probing of social problems," a form of knowledge for which we do not yet have the *content,* but from which we might seek to understand the aims of practice from a variety of perspectives, or with different lenses. Second, he proposes a "social inquiry as practical philosophy" that has as its aim "enhancing or cultivating *critical* intelligence in parties to the research encounter," critical intelligence being defined as "the capacity to engage in moral critique." And finally, he proposes a third way in which we might judge social inquiry as practical philosophy: We might make judgments about the social inquirer-as-practical-philosopher. He or she might be "evaluated on the success to which his or her reports of the inquiry enable the training or calibration of human judgment" (p. 69) or "the capacity for practical wisdom" (p. 70).

Schwandt is not alone, however, in wishing to say "farewell to criteriology," at least as it has been previously conceived. Scheurich (1997) makes a similar plea, and in the same vein, Smith (1993) also argues that validity, if it is to survive at all, must be radically reformulated if it is ever to serve phenomenological research well (see also Smith & Deemer, 2000).

At issue here is not whether we shall have criteria, or whose criteria we as a scientific community might adopt, but rather what the nature of social inquiry ought to be, whether it ought to undergo a transformation, and what might be the basis for criteria within a projected transformation. Schwandt (1989; also personal communication, August 21, 1998) is quite clear that both the transformation and the criteria are rooted in dialogic efforts. These dialogic efforts are quite clearly themselves forms of "moral discourse." Through the specific connections of the dialogic, the idea of practical wisdom, and moral discourses, much of Schwandt's work can be seen to be related to, and reflective of, critical theorist and participatory paradigms, as well as constructivism, although Schwandt specifically denies the relativity of truth. (For a more sophisticated explication and critique of forms of constructivism, hermeneutics, and interpretivism, see Schwandt, 2000. In that chapter, Schwandt spells out distinctions between realists and nonrealists, and between foundationalists and nonfoundationalists, far more clearly than it is possible for us to do in this chapter.)

To return to the central question embedded in validity: How do we know when we have specific social inquiries that are faithful enough to some human construction that we may feel safe in acting on them, or, more important, that members of the community in which the research is conducted may act on them? To that question, there is no final answer. There are, however, several discussions of what we might use to make both professional and lay judgments regarding any piece of work. It is to those versions of validity that we now turn.

Validity as Authenticity

Perhaps the first nonfoundational criteria were those we developed in response to a challenge by John K. Smith (see Smith & Deemer, 2000). In those criteria, we attempted to locate criteria for judging the *processes* and *outcomes* of naturalistic or constructivist inquiries (rather than the application of methods; see Guba & Lincoln, 1989). We described five potential outcomes of a social constructionist inquiry (evaluation is one form of disciplined inquiry; see Guba & Lincoln, 1981), each grounded in concerns specific to the paradigm we had tried to describe and construct, and apart from any concerns carried over from the positivist legacy. The criteria were instead rooted in the axioms and assumptions of the constructivist paradigm, insofar as we could extrapolate and infer them.

Those authenticity criteria—so called because we believed them to be hallmarks of authentic, trustworthy, rigorous, or "valid" constructivist or phenomenological inquiry—were fairness, ontological authenticity, educative authenticity, catalytic authenticity, and tactical authenticity (Guba & Lincoln, 1989, pp. 245–251). *Fairness* was thought to be a quality of balance; that is, all stakeholder views, perspectives, claims, concerns, and voices should be apparent in the text. Omission of stakeholder or participant voices reflects, we believe, a form of bias. This bias, however, was and is not related directly to the concerns of objectivity that flow from positivist inquiry and that are reflective of inquirer blindness or subjectivity. Rather, this fairness was defined by deliberate attempts to prevent marginalization, to act affirmatively with respect to inclusion, and to act with energy to ensure that all voices in the inquiry effort had a chance to be represented in any texts and to have their stories treated fairly and with balance.

Ontological and educative authenticity were designated as criteria for determining a raised level of awareness, in the first instance, by individual research participants and, in the second, by individuals about those who surround them or with whom they come into contact for some social or organizational purpose. Although we failed to see it at that particular historical moment (1989), there is no reason these criteria cannot be—at this point in time, with many miles under our theoretic and practice feet—reflective also of Schwandt's (1996) "critical intelligence," or capacity to engage in moral critique. In fact, the authenticity criteria we originally proposed had strong moral and ethical overtones, a point to which we later returned (see, for instance, Lincoln, 1995, 1998a, 1998b). It was a point to which our critics strongly objected before we were sufficiently self-aware to realize the implications of what we had proposed (see, for instance, Sechrest, 1993).

Catalytic and tactical authenticities refer to the ability of a given inquiry to prompt, first, action on the part of research participants and, second, the involvement of the researcher/evaluator in training participants in specific forms of social and political action if participants desire such training. It is here that constructivist inquiry practice begins to resemble forms of critical theorist action, action research, or participative or cooperative inquiry, each of which is predicated on creating the capacity in research participants for positive social change and forms of emancipatory community action. It is also at this specific point that practitioners of positivist and postpositivist social inquiry are the most critical, because any action on the part of the inquirer is thought to destabilize objectivity and introduce subjectivity, resulting in bias. The problem of subjectivity and bias has a long theoretical history, and this chapter is simply too brief for us to enter into the various formulations that either take account of subjectivity or posit it as a positive learning experience, practical, embodied, gendered, and emotive. For purposes of this discussion, it is enough to say that we are persuaded that objectivity is a chimera: a mythological creature that never existed, save in the imaginations of those who believe that knowing can be separated from the knower.

Validity as Resistance, Validity as Poststructural Transgression

Laurel Richardson (1994, 1997) has proposed another form of validity, a deliberately "transgressive" form, the *crystalline*. In writing experimental (i.e., nonauthoritative, nonpositivist) texts, particularly poems and plays, Richardson (1997) has sought to "problematize reliability, validity and truth" (p. 165) in an effort to create new relationships: to her research participants, to her work, to other women, to herself. She says that transgressive forms permit a social scientist to "conjure a different kind of social science . . . [which] means changing one's relationship to one's work, *how* one knows and tells about the sociological" (p. 166). In order to see "how transgression looks and how it feels," it is necessary to "find and deploy methods that allow us to uncover the hidden assumptions and life-denying repressions of sociology; resee/refeel sociology. Reseeing and retelling are inseparable" (p. 167).

The way to achieve such validity is by examining the properties of a crystal in a metaphoric sense. Here we present an extended quotation to give some flavor of how such validity might be described and deployed:

> I propose that the central imaginary for "validity" for postmodernist texts is not the triangle—a rigid, fixed, two-dimensional object. Rather the central imaginary is the crystal, which combines symmetry and substance with an infinite variety of shapes, substances, transmutations, multidimensionalities, and angles of approach. Crystals grow, change, alter, but are not amorphous. Crystals are prisms that reflect externalities *and* refract within themselves, creating different colors, patterns, arrays, casting off in different directions. What we see depends upon our angle of repose. Not triangulation, crystallization. In postmodernist mixed-genre texts, we have moved from plane geometry to light theory, where light can be *both* waves *and* particles. Crystallization, without losing structure, deconstructs the traditional idea of "validity" (we feel how there is no single truth, we see how texts validate themselves); and crystallization provides us with a deepened, complex, thoroughly partial understanding of the topic. Paradoxically, we know more and doubt what we know. (Richardson, 1997, p. 92)

The metaphoric "solid object" (crystal/text), which can be turned many ways, which reflects and refracts light (light/multiple layers of meaning), through which we can see both "wave" (light wave/human currents) and "particle" (light as "chunks" of energy/elements of truth, feeling, connection, processes of the research that "flow" together) is an attractive metaphor for validity. The properties of the crystal-as-metaphor help writers and readers alike see the interweaving of processes in the research: discovery, seeing, telling, storying, re-presentation.

Other "Transgressive" Validities

Laurel Richardson is not alone in calling for forms of validity that are "transgressive" and disruptive of the status quo. Patti Lather (1993) seeks "an incitement to discourse," the purpose of which is "to rupture validity as a regime of truth, to displace its historical inscription . . . via a dispersion, circulation and proliferation of counter-practices of authority that take the crisis of representation into account" (p. 674). In addition to catalytic validity (Lather, 1986), Lather (1993) poses *validity as simulacra/ironic validity; Lyotardian paralogy/neopragmatic validity,* a form of validity that "foster[s] heterogeneity, refusing disclosure" (p. 679); *Derridean rigor/rhizomatic validity,* a form of behaving "via relay, circuit, multiple openings" (p. 680); and *voluptuous/situated validity,* which "embodies a situated, partial tentativeness" and "brings ethics and epistemology together . . . via practices of engagement and self-reflexivity" (p. 686). Together, these form a way of interrupting, disrupting, and transforming "pure" presence into a disturbing, fluid, partial, and problematic presence—a poststructural and decidedly postmodern form of discourse theory, hence textual revelation.

Validity as an Ethical Relationship

As Lather (1993) points out, poststructural forms for validities "bring ethics and epistemology together" (p. 686); indeed, as Parker Palmer (1987) also notes, "every way of knowing contains its own moral trajectory" (p. 24). Peshkin reflects on Noddings's (1984) observation that "the search for justification often carries us farther and farther from the heart of morality" (p. 105; quoted in Peshkin, 1993, p. 24). The *way* in which we know is most assuredly tied up with both *what* we know and our *relationships with our research participants.* Accordingly, one of us worked on trying to understand the ways in which the ethical intersects both the interpersonal and the epistemological (as a form of authentic or valid knowing; Lincoln, 1995). The result was the first set of understandings about emerging criteria for quality that were also rooted in the epistemology/ethics nexus. Seven new standards were derived from that search: positionality, or standpoint, judgments; specific discourse communities and research sites as arbiters of quality; voice, or the extent to which a text has the quality of polyvocality; critical subjectivity (or what might be termed intense self-reflexivity); reciprocity, or the extent to which the research relationship becomes reciprocal rather than hierarchical; sacredness, or the profound regard for how science can (and does) contribute to human flourishing; and sharing the prerequisites of privilege that accrue to our positions as academics with university positions. Each of these standards was extracted from a body of research, often from disciplines as disparate as management, philosophy, and women's studies (Lincoln, 1995).

Voice, Reflexivity, and Postmodern Textual Representation

Texts have to do a lot more work these days than they used to. Even as they are charged by poststructuralists and postmodernists to reflect upon their representational practices, representational practices themselves become more problematic. Three of the most engaging, but painful, issues are the problem of voice, the status of reflexivity, and the problematics of postmodern/poststructural textual representation, especially as those problematics are displayed in the shift toward narrative and literary forms that directly and openly deal with human emotion.

Voice

Voice is a multilayered problem, simply because it has come to mean many things to different researchers. In former eras, the only appropriate "voice" was the "voice from nowhere"—the "pure presence" of representation, as Lather terms it. As researchers became more conscious of the abstracted realities their texts created, they became simultaneously more conscious of having readers "hear" their informants—permitting readers to hear the exact words (and, occasionally, the paralinguistic cues, the lapses, pauses, stops, starts, reformulations) of the informants. Today voice can mean, especially in more participatory forms of research, not only having a real researcher—and a researcher's voice—in the text, but also letting research participants speak for themselves, either in text form or through plays, forums, "town meetings," or other oral and performance-oriented media or communication forms designed by research participants themselves. Performance texts, in particular, give an emotional immediacy to the voices of researchers and research participants far beyond their own sites and locales (see McCall, 2000). Rosanna Hertz (1997) describes voice as

> a struggle to figure out how to present the author's self while simultaneously writing the respondents' accounts and representing their selves. Voice has multiple dimensions: First, there is the voice of the author. Second, there is the presentation of the voices of one's respondents within the text. A third dimension appears when the self is the subject of the inquiry. . . . Voice is how authors express themselves within an ethnography. (pp. xi–xii)

But knowing how to express ourselves goes far beyond the commonsense understanding of "expressing ourselves." Generations of ethnographers trained in the "cooled-out, stripped-down rhetoric" of positivist inquiry (Firestone, 1987) find it difficult, if not nearly impossible, to "locate" themselves deliberately and squarely within their texts (even though, as Geertz [1988] has demonstrated finally and without doubt, the authorial voice is rarely genuinely absent, or even hidden).[3] Specific textual experimentation can help; that is, composing ethnographic work into various literary forms—the poetry and plays of Laurel Richardson are good examples—can help a researcher to overcome the tendency to write in the distanced and abstracted voice of the disembodied "I." But such writing exercises are hard work. This is also work that is embedded in the practices of reflexivity and narrativity, without which achieving a voice of (partial) truth is impossible.

Reflexivity

Reflexivity is the process of reflecting critically on the self as researcher, the "human as instrument" (Guba & Lincoln, 1981). It is, we would assert, the critical subjectivity discussed early on in Reason and Rowan's edited volume *Human Inquiry* (1981). It is a conscious experiencing of the self as both inquirer and respondent, as teacher and learner, as the one coming to know the self within the processes of research itself.

Reflexivity forces us to come to terms not only with our choice of research problem and with those with whom we engage in the research process, but with our selves and with the multiple identities that represent the fluid self in the research setting (Alcoff & Potter, 1993). Shulamit Reinharz (1997), for example, argues that we not only "*bring* the self to the field . . . [we also] *create* the self in the field" (p. 3). She suggests that although we all have many selves we bring with us, those selves fall into three categories: research-based selves, brought selves (the selves that historically, socially, and personally create our standpoints), and situationally created selves (p. 5). Each of those selves comes into play in the research setting and consequently has a distinctive voice. Reflexivity—as well as the poststructural and postmodern sensibilities concerning quality in qualitative research—demands that we interrogate each of our selves regarding the ways in which research efforts are shaped and staged around the binaries, contradictions, and paradoxes that form our own lives. We must question our selves, too, regarding how those binaries and paradoxes shape not only the identities called forth in the field and later in the discovery processes of writing, but also our interactions with respondents, in who we become to them in the process of *becoming* to ourselves. Someone once characterized qualitative research as the twin processes of "writing up" (field notes) and "writing down" (the narrative). But Clandinin and Connelly (1994) have made clear that this bitextual reading of the processes of qualitative research is far too simplistic. In fact, many texts are created in the process of engaging in fieldwork. As Richardson (1994, 1997, 2000; see also Richardson & St. Pierre, Volume 3, Chapter 15) makes clear, writing is not merely the transcribing of some reality. Rather, writing—of all the texts, notes, presentations, and possibilities—is also a process of discovery: discovery of the subject (and sometimes of the problem itself) and discovery of the self.

There is good news and bad news with the most contemporary of formulations. The good news is that the multiple selves—ourselves and our respondents—of postmodern inquiries may give rise to more dynamic, problematic, open-ended, and complex forms of writing and representation. The bad news is that the multiple selves we create and encounter give rise to more dynamic, problematic, open-ended, and complex forms of writing and representation.

Postmodern Textual Representations

There are two dangers inherent in the conventional texts of scientific method: that they may lead us to believe the world is rather simpler than it is, and that they may reinscribe enduring forms of historical oppression. Put another way, we are confronted with a crisis of authority (which tells us the world is "this way" when perhaps it is some other way, or many other ways) and a crisis of representation (which serves to silence those whose lives we appropriate for our social sciences, and which may also serve subtly to re-create *this* world, rather than some other, perhaps more complex, but just one). Catherine Stimpson (1988) has observed:

> Like every great word, "representation/s" is a stew. A scrambled menu, it serves up several meanings at once. For a representation can be an image—visual, verbal, or aural. . . . A representation can also be a narrative, a sequence of images and ideas. . . . Or, a representation can be the product of ideology, that vast scheme for showing forth the world and justifying its dealings. (p. 223)

One way to confront the dangerous illusions (and their underlying ideologies) that texts may foster is through the creation of new texts that break boundaries; that move from the center to the margins to comment on and decenter the center; that forgo closed, bounded worlds for those more open-ended and less conveniently encompassed; that transgress the boundaries of conventional social science; and that seek to create a social science about human life rather than *on* subjects.

Experiments with how to do this have produced "messy texts" (Marcus & Fischer, 1986). Messy texts are not typographic nightmares (although they may be typographically nonlinear); rather, they are texts that seek to break the binary between science and literature, to portray the contradiction and truth of human experience, to break the rules in the service of showing, even partially, how real human beings cope with both the eternal verities of human existence and the daily irritations and tragedies of living that existence. Postmodern representations search out and experiment with narratives that expand the range of understanding, voice, and storied variations in human experience. As much as they are social scientists, inquirers also become storytellers, poets, and playwrights, experimenting with personal narratives, first-person accounts, reflexive interrogations, and deconstruction of the forms of tyranny embedded in representational practices (see Richardson, 2000; Tierney & Lincoln, 1997).

Representation may be arguably the most open-ended of the controversies surrounding phenomenological research today, for no other reasons than that the ideas of what constitutes legitimate inquiry are expanding and, at the same time, the forms of narrative, dramatic, and rhetorical structure are far from being either explored or exploited fully. Because, too, each inquiry, each inquirer, brings a unique perspective to our understanding, the possibilities for variation and exploration are limited only by the number of those engaged in inquiry and the realms of social and intrapersonal life that become interesting to researchers. The only thing that can be said for certain about postmodern representational practices is that they will proliferate as forms and they will seek, and demand much of, audiences, many of whom may be outside the scholarly and academic world. In fact, some forms of inquiry may never show up in the academic world, because their purpose will be use in the immediate context, for the consumption, reflection, and use of indigenous audiences. Those that are produced for scholarly audiences will, however, continue to be untidy, experimental, and driven by the need to communicate social worlds that have remained private and "nonscientific" until now.

▣ A Glimpse of the Future

The issues raised in this chapter are by no means the only ones under discussion for the near and far future. But they are some of the critical ones, and discussion, dialogue, and even controversies are bound to continue as practitioners of the various new and emergent paradigms continue either to look for common ground or to find ways in which to distinguish their forms of inquiry from others.

Some time ago, we expressed our hope that practitioners of both positivist and new-paradigm forms of inquiry might find some way of resolving their differences, such that all social scientists could work within a common discourse—and perhaps even several traditions—once again. In retrospect, such a resolution appears highly unlikely and would probably even be less than useful. This is not, however, because neither positivists nor phenomenologists will budge an inch (although that, too, is unlikely). Rather, it is because, in the postmodern moment, and in the wake of poststructuralism, the assumption that there is no single "truth"—that all truths are but partial truths; that the slippage between signifier and signified in linguistic and textual terms creates re-presentations that are only and always shadows of the actual people, events, and places; that identities are fluid rather than fixed—leads us ineluctably toward the insight that there will be no single "conventional" paradigm to which all social scientists might ascribe in some common terms and with mutual understanding. Rather, we stand at the threshold of a history marked by multivocality, contested meanings, paradigmatic controversies, and new textual forms. At some distance down this conjectural path, when its history is written, we will find that this has been the era of emancipation: emancipation from what Hannah Arendt calls "the coerciveness of Truth," emancipation from hearing only the voices of Western Europe, emancipation from generations of silence, and emancipation from seeing the world in one color.

We may also be entering an age of greater spirituality within research efforts. The emphasis on inquiry that reflects ecological values, on inquiry that respects communal forms of living that are not Western, on inquiry involving intense reflexivity regarding how our inquiries are shaped by our own historical and gendered locations, and on inquiry into "human flourishing," as Heron and Reason (1997) call it, may yet reintegrate the sacred with the secular in ways that promote freedom and self-determination. Egon Brunswik, the organizational theorist, wrote of "tied" and "untied" variables—variables that are linked, or clearly not linked, with other variables—when studying human forms of organization. We may be in a period of exploring the ways in which our inquiries are both tied and untied, as a means of finding where our interests cross and where we can both be and promote others' being, as whole human beings.

Notes

1. There are several versions of critical theory, including classical critical theory, which is most closely related to neo-Marxist theory; postpositivist formulations, which divorce themselves from Marxist theory but are positivist in their insistence on conventional rigor criteria; and postmodernist, poststructuralist, or constructivist-oriented varieties. See, for instance, Fay (1987), Carr and Kemmis (1986), and Lather (1991). See also Kemmis and McTaggart (2000) and Kincheloe and McLaren (2000).

2. For a clearer understanding of how methods came to stand in for paradigms, or how our initial (and, we thought, quite clear) positions came to be misconstrued, see Lancy (1993) or, even more currently, Weiss (1998, esp. p. 268).

3. For example, compare this chapter with, say, the work of Richardson (2000) and Ellis and Bochner (2000), where the authorial voices are clear, personal, vocal, and interior, interacting subjectivities. Although some colleagues have surprised us by correctly identifying which chapters each of us has written in given books, nevertheless, the style of this chapter more closely approximates the more distanced forms of "realist" writing than it does the intimate, personal "feeling tone" (to borrow a phrase from Studs Terkel) of other chapters. Voices also arise as a function of the material being covered. The material we chose as most important for this chapter seemed to demand a less personal tone, probably because there appears to be much more "contention" than calm dialogue concerning these issues. The "cool" tone likely stems from our psychological response to trying to create a quieter space for discussion around controversial issues. What can we say?

References

Addelson, K. P. (1993). Knowers/doers and their moral problems. In L. Alcoff & E. Potter (Eds.), *Feminist epistemologies* (pp. 265–294). New York: Routledge.

Alcoff, L., & Potter, E. (Eds.). (1993). *Feminist epistemologies.* New York: Routledge.

Alpern, S., Antler, J., Perry, E. I., & Scobie, I. W. (Eds.). (1992). *The challenge of feminist biography: Writing the lives of modern American women.* Urbana: University of Illinois Press.

Babbitt, S. (1993). Feminism and objective interests: The role of transformation experiences in rational deliberation. In L. Alcoff & E. Potter (Eds.), *Feminist epistemologies* (pp. 245–264). New York: Routledge.

Bernstein, R. J. (1983). *Beyond objectivism and relativism: Science, hermeneutics, and praxis.* Oxford: Blackwell.

Best, S., & Kellner, D. (1997). *The postmodern turn.* New York: Guilford.

Bloland, H. (1989). Higher education and high anxiety: Objectivism, relativism, and irony. *Journal of Higher Education, 60,* 519–543.

Bloland, H. (1995). Postmodernism and higher education. *Journal of Higher Education, 66,* 521–559.

Bradley, J., & Schaefer, K. (1998). *The uses and misuses of data and models.* Thousand Oaks, CA: Sage.

Carr, W. L., & Kemmis, S. (1986). *Becoming critical: Education, knowledge and action research.* London: Falmer.

Carspecken, P. F. (1996). *Critical ethnography in educational research: A theoretical and practical guide.* New York: Routledge.

Christians, C. G. (2000). Ethics and politics in qualitative research. In N. K. Denzin & Y. S. Lincoln (Eds.), *Handbook of qualitative research* (2nd ed., pp. 133–155). Thousand Oaks, CA: Sage.

Clandinin, D. J., & Connelly, F. M. (1994). Personal experience methods. In N. K. Denzin & Y. S. Lincoln (Eds.), *Handbook of qualitative research* (pp. 413–427). Thousand Oaks, CA: Sage.

Denzin, N. K., & Lincoln, Y. S. (Eds.). (1994). *Handbook of qualitative research.* Thousand Oaks, CA: Sage.

Ellis, C., & Bochner, A. P. (Eds.). (1996). *Composing ethnography: Alternative forms of qualitative writing.* Walnut Creek, CA: AltaMira.

Ellis, C., & Bochner, A. P. (2000). Autoethnography, personal narrative, reflexivity: Researcher as subject. In N. K. Denzin & Y. S. Lincoln (Eds.), *Handbook of qualitative research* (2nd ed., pp. 733–768). Thousand Oaks, CA: Sage.

Enerstvedt, R. (1989). The problem of validity in social science. In S. Kvale (Ed.), *Issues of validity in qualitative research* (pp. 135–173). Lund, Sweden: Studentlitteratur.

Fay, B. (1987). *Critical social science.* Ithaca, NY: Cornell University Press.

Fine, M., Weis, L., Weseen, S., & Wong, L. (2000). For whom? Qualitative research, representations, and social responsibilities. In N. K. Denzin & Y. S. Lincoln (Eds.), *Handbook of qualitative research* (2nd ed., pp. 107–131). Thousand Oaks, CA: Sage.

Firestone, W. (1987). Meaning in method: The rhetoric of quantitative and qualitative research. *Educational Researcher, 16*(7), 16–21.

Foucault, M. (1971). *The order of things: An archaeology of the human sciences.* New York: Pantheon.

Gamson, J. (2000). Sexualities, queer theory, and qualitative research. In N. K. Denzin & Y. S. Lincoln (Eds.), *Handbook of qualitative research* (2nd ed., pp. 347–365). Thousand Oaks, CA: Sage.

Geertz, C. (1988). *Works and lives: The anthropologist as author.* Cambridge: Polity.

Geertz, C. (1993). *Local knowledge: Further essays in interpretive anthropology.* London: Fontana.

Greenwood, D. J., & Levin, M. (2000). Reconstructing the relationships between universities and society through action research. In N. K. Denzin & Y. S. Lincoln (Eds.), *Handbook of qualitative research* (2nd ed., pp. 85–106). Thousand Oaks, CA: Sage.

Guba, E. G., & Lincoln, Y. S. (1981). *Effective evaluation: Improving the usefulness of evaluation results through responsive and naturalistic approaches.* San Francisco: Jossey-Bass.

Guba, E. G., & Lincoln, Y. S. (1982). Epistemological and methodological bases for naturalistic inquiry. *Educational Communications and Technology Journal, 31,* 233–252.

Guba, E. G., & Lincoln, Y. S. (1989). *Fourth generation evaluation.* Newbury Park, CA: Sage.

Guba, E. G., & Lincoln, Y. S. (1994). Competing paradigms in qualitative research. In N. K. Denzin & Y. S. Lincoln (Eds.), *Handbook of qualitative research* (pp. 105–117). Thousand Oaks, CA: Sage.

Harding, S. (1993). Rethinking standpoint epistemology: What is "strong objectivity"? In L. Alcoff & E. Potter (Eds.), *Feminist epistemologies* (pp. 49–82). New York: Routledge.

Heron, J. (1996). *Cooperative inquiry: Research into the human condition.* London: Sage.

Heron, J., & Reason, P. (1997). A participatory inquiry paradigm. *Qualitative Inquiry, 3,* 274–294.

Hertz, R. (1997). Introduction: Reflexivity and voice. In R. Hertz (Ed.), *Reflexivity and voice.* Thousand Oaks, CA: Sage.

Howe, K., & Eisenhart, M. (1990). Standards for qualitative (and quantitative) research: A prolegomenon. *Educational Researcher, 19*(4), 2–9.

Hutcheon, L. (1989). *The politics of postmodernism.* New York: Routledge.

Kemmis, S., & McTaggart, R. (2000). Participatory action research. In N. K. Denzin & Y. S. Lincoln (Eds.), *Handbook of qualitative research* (2nd ed., pp. 567–605). Thousand Oaks, CA: Sage.

Kincheloe, J. L. (1991). *Teachers as researchers: Qualitative inquiry as a path to empowerment.* London: Falmer.

Kincheloe, J. L., & McLaren, P. (2000). Rethinking critical theory and qualitative research. In N. K. Denzin & Y. S. Lincoln (Eds.), *Handbook of qualitative research* (2nd ed., pp. 279–313). Thousand Oaks, CA: Sage.

Kondo, D. K. (1990). *Crafting selves: Power, gender, and discourses of identity in a Japanese workplace.* Chicago: University of Chicago Press.

Kondo, D. K. (1997). *About face: Performing race in fashion and theater.* New York: Routledge.

Kvale, S. (Ed.). (1989). *Issues of validity in qualitative research.* Lund, Sweden: Studentlitteratur.

Kvale, S. (1994, April). *Validation as communication and action.* Paper presented at the annual meeting of the American Educational Research Association, New Orleans.

Lancy, D. F. (1993). *Qualitative research in education: An introduction to the major traditions.* New York: Longman.

Lather, P. (1986). Issues of validity in openly ideological research: Between a rock and a soft place. *Interchange, 17*(4), 63–84.

Lather, P. (1991). *Getting smart: Feminist research and pedagogy with/in the postmodern.* New York: Routledge.

Lather, P. (1993). Fertile obsession: Validity after poststructuralism. *Sociological Quarterly, 34,* 673–693.

Leitch, V. B. (1996). *Postmodern: Local effects, global flows.* Albany: State University of New York Press.

Lincoln, Y. S. (1995). Emerging criteria for quality in qualitative and interpretive research. *Qualitative Inquiry, 1,* 275–289.

Lincoln, Y. S. (1997). What constitutes quality in interpretive research? In C. K. Kinzer, K. A. Hinchman, & D. J. Leu (Eds.), *Inquiries in literacy: Theory and practice* (pp. 54–68). Chicago: National Reading Conference.

Lincoln, Y. S. (1998a). The ethics of teaching qualitative research. *Qualitative Inquiry, 4,* 305–317.

Lincoln, Y. S. (1998b). From understanding to action: New imperatives, new criteria, new methods for interpretive researchers. *Theory and Research in Social Education, 26*(1), 12–29.

Lincoln, Y. S., & Denzin, N. K. (1994). The fifth moment. In N. K. Denzin & Y. S. Lincoln (Eds.), *Handbook of qualitative research* (pp. 575–586). Thousand Oaks, CA: Sage.

Lincoln, Y. S., & Guba, E. G. (1985). *Naturalistic inquiry.* Beverly Hills, CA: Sage.

Marcus, G. E., & Fischer, M. M. J. (1986). *Anthropology as cultural critique: An experimental moment in the human sciences.* Chicago: University of Chicago Press.

McCall, M. M. (2000). Performance ethnography: A brief history and some advice. In N. K. Denzin & Y. S. Lincoln (Eds.), *Handbook of qualitative research* (2nd ed., pp. 421–433). Thousand Oaks, CA: Sage.

Mertens, D. (1998). *Research methods in education and psychology: Integrating diversity with quantitative and qualitative methods.* Thousand Oaks, CA: Sage.

Michael, M. C. (1996). *Feminism and the postmodern impulse: Post–World War II fiction.* Albany: State University of New York Press.

Noddings, N. (1984). *Caring: A feminine approach to ethics and moral education.* Berkeley: University of California Press.

Olesen, V. L. (2000). Feminisms and qualitative research at and into the millennium. In N. K. Denzin & Y. S. Lincoln (Eds.), *Handbook of qualitative research* (2nd ed., pp. 215–255). Thousand Oaks, CA: Sage.

Palmer, P. J. (1987, September-October). Community, conflict, and ways of knowing. *Change, 19,* 20–25.

Peshkin, A. (1993). The goodness of qualitative research. *Educational Researcher, 22*(2), 24–30.

Polkinghorne, D. E. (1989). Changing conversations about human science. In S. Kvale (Ed.), *Issues of validity in qualitative research* (pp. 13–46). Lund, Sweden: Studentlitteratur.

Reason, P. (1993). Sacred experience and sacred science. *Journal of Management Inquiry, 2,* 10–27.

Reason, P., & Rowan, J. (Eds.). (1981). *Human inquiry.* London: John Wiley.

Reinharz, S. (1997). Who am I? The need for a variety of selves in the field. In R. Hertz (Ed.), *Reflexivity and voice* (pp. 3–20). Thousand Oaks, CA: Sage.

Richardson, L. (1994). Writing: A method of inquiry. In N. K. Denzin & Y. S. Lincoln (Eds.), *Handbook of qualitative research* (pp. 516–529). Thousand Oaks, CA: Sage.

Richardson, L. (1997). *Fields of play: Constructing an academic life.* New Brunswick, NJ: Rutgers University Press.

Richardson, L. (2000). Writing: A method of inquiry. In N. K. Denzin & Y. S. Lincoln (Eds.), *Handbook of qualitative research* (2nd ed., pp. 923–948). Thousand Oaks, CA: Sage.

Rorty, R. (1979). *Philosophy and the mirror of nature.* Princeton, NJ: Princeton University Press.

Ryan, K. E., Greene, J. C., Lincoln, Y. S., Mathison, S., & Mertens, D. (1998). Advantages and challenges of using inclusive evaluation approaches in evaluation practice. *American Journal of Evaluation, 19,* 101–122.

Salner, M. (1989). Validity in human science research. In S. Kvale (Ed.), *Issues of validity in qualitative research* (pp. 47–72). Lund, Sweden: Studentlitteratur.

Scheurich, J. J. (1994). Policy archaeology. *Journal of Educational Policy, 9,* 297–316.

Scheurich, J. J. (1996). Validity. *International Journal of Qualitative Studies in Education, 9,* 49–60.

Scheurich, J. J. (1997). *Research method in the postmodern.* London: Falmer.

Schratz, M., & Walker, R. (1995). *Research as social change: New opportunities for qualitative research.* New York: Routledge.

Schwandt, T. A. (1989). Recapturing moral discourse in evaluation. *Educational Researcher, 18*(8), 11–16, 34.

Schwandt, T. A. (1996). Farewell to criteriology. *Qualitative Inquiry, 2,* 58–72.

Schwandt, T. A. (2000). Three epistemological stances for qualitative inquiry: Interpretivism, hermeneutics, and social constructionism. In N. K. Denzin & Y. S. Lincoln (Eds.), *Handbook of qualitative research* (2nd ed., pp. 189–213). Thousand Oaks, CA: Sage.

Sechrest, L. (1993). *Program evaluation: A pluralistic enterprise.* San Francisco: Jossey-Bass.

Smith, J. K. (1993). *After the demise of empiricism: The problem of judging social and educational inquiry.* Norwood, NJ: Ablex.

Smith, J. K., & Deemer, D. K. (2000). The problem of criteria in the age of relativism. In N. K. Denzin & Y. S. Lincoln (Eds.), *Handbook of qualitative research* (2nd ed., pp. 877–896). Thousand Oaks, CA: Sage.

Stimpson, C. R. (1988). Nancy Reagan wears a hat: Feminism and its cultural consensus. *Critical Inquiry, 14,* 223–243.

Tierney, W. G. (2000). Undaunted courage: Life history and the postmodern challenge. In N. K. Denzin & Y. S. Lincoln (Eds.), *Handbook of qualitative research* (2nd ed., pp. 537–553). Thousand Oaks, CA: Sage.

Tierney, W. G., & Lincoln, Y. S. (Eds.). (1997). *Representation and the text: Re-framing the narrative voice.* Albany: State University of New York Press.

Trinh, T. M. (1991). *When the moon waxes red: Representation, gender and cultural politics.* New York: Routledge.

Tschudi, F. (1989). Do qualitative and quantitative methods require different approaches to validity? In S. Kvale (Ed.), *Issues of validity in qualitative research* (pp. 109–134). Lund, Sweden: Studentlitteratur.

Weiss, C. H. (1998). *Evaluation* (2nd ed.). Upper Saddle River, NJ: Prentice Hall.

9

CRITICAL ETHNOGRAPHY

The Politics of Collaboration

Douglas Foley and Angela Valenzuela

Introduction

The purpose of this chapter is to highlight differences between "critical ethnographers" who do academic cultural critiques, who write applied policy studies, and who involve themselves directly in political movements. As we shall see, not all critical ethnographers are politically active. Nor do all produce knowledge that is both universalistic/theoretical and local/practical. Nor do all use reflexive, collaborative research methods. The rubric of critical ethnography glosses over many important differences between practitioners. After characterizing recent trends in contemporary critical ethnography, we portray our own ethnographic practice, which in some ways represents a continuum. On one end, Foley does academic "cultural critiques" and struggles to be more collaborative and politically involved. On the other end, Valenzuela does academic cultural critiques but is much more directly involved in public policy processes. We hope our reflections will encourage others to explore and publish more about their collaborative methodological and political practices.

Some Recent Trends in Critical Ethnography

In the 1960s, "critical ethnography" (Carspecken, 1996) often was based on classic Marxism or neo-Marxist critical theory. As new race, gender, sexual identity, and postcolonial social movements emerged, the philosophical basis for critical ethnography expanded greatly (Foley, Levinson, & Hurtig, 2001; Levinson & Holland, 1996; Villenas & Foley, 2002). These literature reviews underscore the growing disenchantment with the positivist notion of an objective social science that produces value-free ethnographies. Post-1960s critical ethnographers began advocating "cultural critiques" of modern society and its institutions (Marcus, 1998; Marcus & Fischer, 1986). Critical ethnographers not only rejected positivism but also worked the divide between the powerful and the powerless. Most ethnographic cultural critiques studied ruling groups and ruling ideologies and/or the sentiments and struggles of various oppressed peoples. Most were deeply committed to research that promotes an egalitarian society. Most hoped to produce both universalistic theoretical knowledge and local practical knowledge.

As the editors of the *Handbook* have pointed out, qualitative research has become *the* site of philosophical and methodological revolt against positivism. This academic revolt is "political" in the sense that it seeks to transform the knowledge production of the academy. We have both participated in this revolt, which educational philosopher Thomas Schwandt (2000) aptly characterizes as having interpretive, hermeneutic, and constructivist alternatives. Were Schwandt to classify our ethnographic practice, he would note that we have greater affinities with hermeneutic and neo-Marxist critical theorists than with postmodern constructivists. In an earlier article, Foley (2002) advocated utilizing the following complementary reflexive practices: confessional, theoretical, intertextual, and deconstructive. Explicating these types of reflexivity is beyond this chapter, but it is important to note that he situated reflexive practices in a feminist perspective of science.

Donna Haraway (1988) and Sandra Harding (1998) share similar concepts of science that allow politically progressive critical ethnographers to make strong knowledge claims. Harding's discussion of "standpoint theory" and Haraway's notion of "situated knowledge" are so well known that there is little need to elaborate here. Suffice it to say that many critical ethnographers have replaced the grand positivist vision of speaking from a universalistic, objective standpoint with a more modest notion of speaking from a historically and culturally situated standpoint. Speaking from a historically specific standpoint acknowledges the impossibility of what Haraway aptly calls the "god trick" of speaking from an omnipotent standpoint. Critical ethnographers are mere culture-bound mortals speaking from very particular race, class, gender, and sexual identity locations. Because all standpoints represent particular interests and positions in a hierarchical society, they are "ideological" in the sense that they are partial.

Once an ethnographer abandons the positivist fallacy that research techniques can produce a detached, objective standpoint, it makes little sense to ignore more intuitive or subjective ways of knowing. Hence, contemporary critical ethnographers are beginning to use multiple epistemologies. They often value introspection, memory work, autobiography, and even dreams as important ways of knowing. The new, more reflexive critical ethnographer explores the intense self–other interaction that usually marks fieldwork and mediates the production of ethnographic narratives. In the current experimental moment (Denzin & Lincoln, 2000), the road to greater objectivity goes through the ethnographer's critical reflections on her subjectivity and intersubjective relationships. For most critical ethnographers, in a class society marked by class, racial, and sexual conflict, no producers of knowledge are innocent or politically neutral.

One of the early, forceful exponents of this perspective was existentialist sociologist Jack Douglas (1976). He urged social science researchers to abandon the ideal of grand theorizing and universalistic knowledge production. He preferred an "investigative" posture that aggressively studied social and political problems. Tapping into muckraking "new journalism" (T. Wolfe, 1974), Douglas also advocated operating covertly to expose corrupt bureaucrats or hate group leaders. He argued that in a politically corrupt, conflict-filled society, any means used to "get the story" was justifiable if it exposed harmful public practices.

Meanwhile, other anthropologists in the post-1960s era called for "reinventing" the field (Hymes, 1972), "studying up" (Nader, 1996), and studying "people without history" (E. Wolfe, 1982). For the first time, anthropologists began seriously studying imperialism, class and racial oppression, and social movements. They began to occupy the same methodological and ideological terrain occupied by the earlier community sociologists who studied social class inequality. Vidich and Lyman (2000) note that urban sociologists such as the Lynds (Lynd, 1956) and native Americanist anthropologists of the 1920s and 1930s were writing positive portraits of marginalized and stigmatized social, cultural, and occupational groups. Through the post–World War II years, C. Wright Mills (1959) led the way with a series of incisive studies of the national power elites. These early sociological studies of class inequalities and elites were even more critical than the Chicago school of urban sociology. Most of the pre–World War II "critical ethnographers" broke decisively with the positivist idea of value-free ethnographies.

One anthropologist who is often forgotten in histories of critical ethnography is Sol Tax. After doing a classic ethnography of Guatemalan markets (Tax, 1963), he became disenchanted with the academic, structural-functionalist ethnography of the 1940s and 1950s. In the late 1940s, he created a field school on the Mesquaki settlement in my hometown of Tama, Iowa (Foley, 1999). It was to be the testing ground for a new kind of anthropology. Tax advocated that "action anthropologists" be much more collaborative and produce research that the research subjects felt would resolve community problems. Bennett (1996) characterized Tax's orientation as rooted in American pragmatism's liberal, practical notion of science. Consequently, Tax distinguished his approach from academic anthropology and "applied anthropology" in several important ways.

First, action anthropologists were to operate without the sponsorship of government bureaucracies or private nongovernmental organizations (NGO's). They were to find independent funding and work more directly with and for the people they were studying. Second, Tax argued that because action anthropologists became accepted insiders, they were positioned to collect better data on social change and acculturation than were detached scientific ethnographers. Consequently, action anthropologists would help the community while they wrote trustworthy ethnographies. In effect, Tax envisioned a social science that created knowledge that was as practical and useful as it was theoretical and universal. For him, academic social scientists had produced a false notion of science and knowledge that privileged the theoretical over applied, practical knowledge.

Regrettably, Tax's action anthropology project on the Mesquaki settlement promised more than it delivered (Foley, 1999). It produced few lasting changes in the community and even less high-quality ethnography. Moreover, the field of academic anthropology never really embraced Tax's action anthropology. Nevertheless, a former student (Rubinstein, 1986) argues that Tax anticipated much of post-1960s anthropology. He contends that Tax's notion of "action anthropology" has become widely practiced in contemporary anthropology. After reviewing many contemporary studies of American culture, Foley and Moss (2001) would beg to differ. The continental philosophies of post-Marxism, postmodernism, and feminism have had a much greater impact on American anthropology than has philosophical pragmatism. Space does not permit a recapitulation of that review, but the work of Berkeley sociologist Michael Burawoy (1991, 2000) illustrates nicely the "new" critical ethnography, or what Marcus and Fischer (1986) call "the anthropology of cultural critiques." Burawoy and his students try to make the public aware of social inequalities and injustices as they revise the conventional wisdom of reigning academic theories. Because Burawoy explicitly advocates revising and generating social theory, his cultural critiques retain the basic goal of producing universal, scientific knowledge. That makes his studies publishable in the journals of various academic disciplines. The same holds true for many other neo-Marxist and Marxist feminist critical ethnographers (e.g., Brodkin, 2001; Fine & Weis, 1998; Susser, 2001; Zavella, 1987).

Most of these cultural critics break decisively with the positivist notion of value-free, scientific studies. On the other hand, most retain a strong notion of the author as expert and thus still operate in the field much like earlier scientific ethnographers. Their ethnographic practices are not particularly representative of the new postmodern experimental moment in ethnography (Denzin, 1997). The new critical ethnographers usually set the research agenda, collect the data, and write the account with relatively little input from subjects. They are not always inclined to work the self–other hyphen reflexively and to invite their research subjects to co-construct their ethnographic accounts. Characterizing the methodological and political practices of contemporary critical ethnographers is, however, risky business. For whatever reason, many do not report extensively on the extent of their political and methodological collaborations. Fine and Weis's (1998) study of the urban poor is, however, somewhat of an exception. Their formal ethnography and subsequent reflections on field methods (Fine & Weis, 2000; Fine, Weis, Weseen, & Wong, 2000) try to give some idea how collaborative they were politically and methodologically.

The current crop of critical ethnographers seems to be focusing more on dramatic public issues, and they are finding ways to reach wider audiences. Peggy Sanday (1976) was an early advocate of anthropological research that truly served the public interest. Her recent work (1990, 1996) on campus date rape, as well as her involvement and coverage of rape trials, is a case in point. Nancy Scheper-Hughes's (1992; Scheper-Hughes & Sargent,1998) study of child welfare issues and Third World organ harvesting also is exemplary. Finally, our colleague at Rice University, Linda McNeil (2000), has forcefully critiqued many of the political right's educational accountability schemes in Texas. She also has worked tirelessly with local teachers and community educational leaders to reform these educational practices and has appeared on national TV shows such as *60 Minutes.* Increasingly, anthropologists interested in policy studies are advocating a more politicized type of policy studies (Kane & Mason, 2001; Levinson & Sutton, 2001; Okongwu & Mencher, 2000). These surveys of the field and a recent School of American Research conference on critical ethnography (Marcus, 1999) describe a host of new politically relevant cultural critiques in such areas as corporate agriculture, environmental pollution, pharmaceutical dumping, transnational labor migration, the publishing industry, cyberspace hackers, the AIDS crises, media and legal system demonization, and criminalization of urban street life and informal economies based on drugs, sex, and cultural rebellion.

Space does not permit an extensive review of the new, more political policy–oriented ethnographies, but the old labels of "critical ethnography" and "cultural critiques" may no longer capture the new diversity. The number of social scientists who are critiquing questionable legal, medical, educational, media, and corporate practices seems to be exploding. More important, these new critical ethnographers are beginning to write more accessible, less jargon-filled accounts. A few have also "crossed over" into the public sphere and have appeared as "experts" on talk and news shows. They have found new ways to bring their investigations to the public through opinion makers such as Oprah Winfrey, Larry King, and Ted Koppel. Meanwhile, they have quietly provided reporters with expert testimony for their journalistic exposés. Others have become policy advisers to politicians, and they directly influence legislation.

The final type of critical ethnographer is a distinct minority of activists who are deeply involved in progressive social movements and community-based reforms. In the field of educational research, Kemmis and McTaggart (2000) label such activities "participatory action research (PAR)." PAR researchers often base their approach on the philosophy of Latin American social activists Paulo Friere and Fals-Borda. PAR researchers have strong affinities with the more activist-oriented applied anthropologists

(Eddy & Partridge, 1987). They often play the role of democratic facilitator and consciousness-raiser, or "cultural broker" between powerful institutions and the disenfranchised citizens. Anthropology has produced a few activists who are even more collaborative methodologically and politically than are most PAR action researchers. For example, in the early 1970s, anthropologist Carol Talbert, who joined the American Indian Movement (AIM) activists at Wounded Knee, gave an American Anthropological Association presentation about her role as a "pen for hire for AIM." In this particular case, she sought to document the FBI's dubious actions to prop up an anti-AIM faction and indict various AIM members for crimes they may not have committed. Talbert exemplifies a much more direct form of political collaboration. She joined the social movement and gave up much of her academic autonomy and authority to be an independent cultural critic. She researched and wrote what the movement needed.

Another anthropologist, Charles Valentine (1968), joined African American community action groups that conducted studies of landlords and police brutality, and that initiated rent strikes. At an American Anthropological Association meeting in the early 1970s, Valentine and several African American community members dramatized the difference between themselves and academic anthropologists. They flatly refused to present their findings to fellow anthropologists. Their intent was to convey contempt for the politically ineffectual nature of much academic anthropological research. In response, the discussant, Margaret Mead, expressed her anger that a fellow anthropologist would distrust a field that had labored to help the downtrodden. Her rather patronizing commentary set off a lively debate about the political utility/futility of anthropological research.

Although Valentine (1968) produced a classic published critique of the culture of poverty construct, we suspect that many "activist anthropologists" who became deeply involved in local political struggles have stopped writing academic books and articles. Contrary to right-wing propaganda that these "radicals" are taking over academia, our more politically active colleagues often either fail to get tenure or simply leave the academy altogether. For whatever reason, they apparently have been unable to find a way to combine their academic and political work. Unfortunately, we know precious little about where these "pushed out" activists go. To our knowledge, no one has bothered to tell their stories. Are they teaching in community colleges? Are they writing articles for local newspapers? Or have they succumbed to political disillusionment?

Despite such losses, as previously noted, the number of politically active anthropologists and sociologists appears to be growing. The Department of Anthropology at the University of Texas is an excellent case in point. The department now prides itself in ideological, cultural, and gender diversity, as well as a strong "activist anthropology" orientation. Several of our colleagues seem to have found the formula for balancing academic and political activities. For example, Charlie Hale has worked extensively in the land rights struggles of Nicaraguan indigenous groups. He recruits and trains indigenous Mayan anthropologists who actively work for these social movements and write highly critical accounts of Mayan ethnology. He and his students have done very specific research that aids their clients in legal cases, where he has been called upon to testify as an expert witness.

Another UT colleague, Ted Gordon, is a longtime activist among the African Creole populations of Nicaragua. Like Hale, Gordon works directly with ethnic political movements, and his highly successful African Diaspora program has trained many African American and Afro-Caribbean anthropologists. Yet other UT colleagues, Martha Menchaca, director of the borderlands program, and Richard Flores, director of the folklore program, have trained a number of activist Latina/o students. Menchaca has participated directly in legal research on racism and voter redistricting legislation as well. Flores (2002) has written a strong critique of Texas's most sacred cultural icon, the Alamo. Our politically active UT colleagues have all published scholarly, academic cultural critiques (Gordon, 1997; Hale, 1994; Menchaca, 2002). Nevertheless, Hale (n.d.) distances his own ethnographic practice from the Marcus and Fischer (1986) notion of cultural critiques. He contends that too many of the new cultural critics place greater emphasis on creating a "safe academic space" and publishing than on community service and political activism. In contrast, a genuinely "activist anthropologist" is more involved in local political struggles, and, like Sol Tax, Hale claims that such involvement produces better ethnographies.

It would seem that progressive social scientists have gained a foothold in the academy and have created a space for themselves. The browning, queering, and gendering of the academy and the social sciences surely is at work here. People of color, women, gays, and working-class academics are slowly replacing upper-middle-class, white, male gentleman scholars. Furthermore, the emergence of the interdisciplinary field of critical cultural studies has created many new journals and special series in university presses. A market for more critical, investigative ethnographies that expose relations of power and exploitation clearly has evolved. But these developments have their limits.

From a professional survival point of view, the idea of a safe space from which to publish makes considerable sense. It is no secret that Division I research institutions are "publish or perish" meat grinders. You either publish articles in the refereed journals of your field—and books if your department is a "book department"—or you get fired. The rub for many critical ethnographers is that their scholarship must be political in an academically acceptable manner. Consequently, many progressive academics spend most of their time writing and publishing cultural critiques that satisfy the demands of the academy and their peers. This observation is not intended to diminish the exceptional quality of many cultural critiques (Foley & Moss, 2001). Rather, it is meant to highlight the institutional pressures that many activist academics face. Unfortunately, there are few accounts of how the 21st-century knowledge production industry is changing. Most critical ethnographers, our UT colleagues included, rarely chronicle the psychological and monetary price that they pay for their political activism. As we shall see in the following case studies, we have both experienced enough pressures of political correctness to warn fledgling "critical ethnographers" what they too may face.

Case Study 1: A Cultural Critic in Search of Collaborative Methods

Being someone who has written several cultural critiques (Foley, 1990, 1995), I generally agree with Hale's assessment that such studies often are not particularly collaborative or directly political. When I left the anti–Vietnam War movement for academia, I found it a hostile environment for activist social scientists. I have written about my troubled adaptation to academia elsewhere (Foley, 2000). Put simply, in 1970 the University of Texas was a pretty conservative place. George I. Sanchez, a noted Chicano scholar, was the only colleague who encouraged me to do activist research. Like many young scholars with progressive political views, I had to make a number of agonizing compromises. It was the Vietnam War years, which made publishing my dissertation on American neocolonialism in the Philippines difficult. Consequently, I followed Sanchez's advice and began studying colonialism and racism in nearby South Texas. There I was, a former Student for Democratic Society (SDS) activist, wondering whether I was a sold-out academic. Political correctness pressures came from both sides of the American racial divide. Many white faculty saw little point to political activism, and many Chicana/o faculty distrusted *gringo* social scientists who wanted to join the *movimento.* Moreover, being the first ethnographer in a college of education filled with unrepentant positivists, it was difficult to garner high merit evaluations. It seemed as though I would have to produce twice as much as my apolitical colleagues to survive professionally. I felt compelled to cut down on time-consuming political activities so I could produce more publications, and that pattern of adaptation has dogged me throughout my career.

But old political habits die hard, and being a critical ethnographer involves much more than simply writing good cultural critiques. It also involves fighting for institutional reforms, for example, recruiting faculty and mentoring students who have experienced class, race, and gender discrimination. During that era, battling positivism was also a form of political struggle. More important, however, we found a few ways to be directly involved in the Chicano civil rights movement that we were studying (Foley, 1990; Foley with Mota, Post, & Lozano, 1989). Our research team, which included Brazilian Clarice Mota and local Chicano Ignacio Lozano, lived in the barrio, and we frequently voiced our opinions to local Raza Unida Party leaders regarding their political strategies and tactics (Foley, 1999). We also encouraged many local Chicano/a youth to go beyond their high school education. Finally, when La Raza Unida's director of the health care study quit, I went to work for the party and wrote up its research findings.

Nevertheless, our research team also tried to maintain a degree of detachment and neutrality. We wanted to produce a balanced ethnography that spanned the racial divide and included Anglo perspectives as well. We used all the classic methods of good ethnography, including participant observation, interviews, and informant work, in order to write a complex, rich portrait of race relations and the Chicano movement inside and outside schools. In the end, writing a critical ethnography that valorized the Chicano movement's efforts became more important than any direct local political work. As the project evolved, I rationalized my relative lack of political action with a cultural critique argument. We were giving voice to the voiceless Chicana and Chicano masses, thus raising the consciousness of the nation regarding inequality in South Texas. If what I wrote made a few Chicano/as be proud of their movement, or made a few Anglos question their racial attitudes, then my cultural critique was having—to use Patti Lather's (1991) apt phrase—a "catalytic [i.e., political] effect." In addition, the historical ethnography I wrote would have the "professional effect" of getting tenure for me and keeping bread on the family table.

Because we approached the research task in a rather traditional manner, there was very little effort to involve local people in the research process itself. We set the research agenda and wrote the ethnography that we deemed important. Being the lead author, I theorized the data and told the story I wanted to tell. Nevertheless, it is important to underscore some key ways that we tried to make our cultural critique more collaborative than are most "scientific" and/or critical ethnographies. First, like most good ethnographers, we developed a set of intimate, trusting relationships with several highly knowledgeable key community residents. These relationships helped us develop an "insider's" perspective on local life. At times, these relationships evolved into friendships, and some local residents became our "anthropological confidants" or "collaborators." They helped us focus and correct our understanding of local events and relationships. We often shared our interpretations with these locals, and as the relationships developed, we shared more of our mutual biographies. The point here is that good cultural critiques usually are based on a number of intimate, "collaborative" relations with research subjects.

Second, we used a conversational or dialogic style of interviewing, which encouraged the subjects to participate more. We interviewed in a very informal manner, and at times we shared more personal information about ourselves than do conventional interviewers. When these free-flowing conversations were transcribed, they often were shared with the respondents. That provided key informants with the opportunity to see how their own speech objectified and represented them. If they did not like their self-representations, they were free to edit their comments. This, of course, led some informants to censor their negative remarks, but sharing the interviews clearly enhanced local confidence in our intentions to be fair. In short, a more open-ended, conversational interviewing style generated more engaged personal narratives and more candid opinions. It also tended to humanize the interviewer and diminish her power and control of the interview process.

Third, we had a number of community members review our ethnographic manuscript before publication. Very few anthropologists were doing this sort of collaboration with their research subjects in the mid-1970s. I have elaborated elsewhere (Foley, with Mota et al., 1989) just how valuable and ethical this methodological procedure is. It allows us to correct a number of interpretations and representations.

Later, I used the same community review technique in a study of my hometown (Foley, 1995), and it added an important collaborative dimension to our cultural critique. Although this sort of collaboration does not relinquish authorial authority, it does add a great deal of reflexivity to the data collection and representational process. When local actors criticized our representations as slanted or partial, we made a serious effort to better corroborate our interpretations. We also changed the tone and tried to nuance the portrayals of several events and individuals. We took seriously what our local readers criticized, but we did not give them complete control over what we wrote. We created a dialogic, negotiated process that gave them some input into what we wrote, but in the end I wrote what I deemed important. In retrospect, we definitely amended the classic notion of the detached, all-knowing ethnographic scientist, but not entirely.

Finally, I sought to write our ethnography in a much more accessible, engaging ethnographic narrative style. Very early in my career, I came to see the cultural and linguistic gap between the anthropological observer and his subject as elitist and politically unprogressive. Over the years, it became clear that many of my undergraduates could not understand fully the ethnographies we assigned them to read. For political reasons, I came to embrace the ideal that ordinary people must be able to read and understand my ethnography. How can academics possibly serve the people they write about if their subjects cannot understand what they write?

It now seems obvious that academics have to liberate themselves from the pedantic, technical discourse of their disciplines if they hope to write useful stories. Methodologically, writing better is absolutely crucial for creating a kind of linguistic reciprocity between the research subjects and the researcher. This is an important, often unacknowledged form of "collaboration" that leads to more politically useful critical ethnographies.

Unfortunately, no young scholar who has been thoroughly socialized in an academic PhD program can accomplish this easily. At every turn, dissertation committee members, journal editors, and fellow students/colleagues will press a young scholar to retain a pedantic, technical, academic, storytelling style. One's personal identity and professional success seem to depend upon mastering this peculiar form of self-expression. Recent experimentation with mixed genres like autoethnographies has opened up some space in the academy, but the technical, theory-driven academic ethnography remains the standard toward which young scholars must aspire. The senior scholars who control the machinery of academic production and promotion maintain a tight grip on the conventions of social scientific writing. This surely will be the last bastion to fall, if ever it does. In the meantime, the social sciences remain a rather elitist, "high culture" form of social commentary.

To sum up, we opened up the process of producing ethnographies through the following means: a dialogic style of interviewing; intimate, highly personal informant relations; a community review of the manuscript; and writing in ordinary language. These practices, and many more being invented as we speak, make fieldwork—and telling stories about one's fieldwork—more open, more collaborative, and less hierarchical in character. We tried to break significantly with the attitudes and practices of positivistic scientific ethnography and scientific realism (Marcus & Cushman, 1982). Nevertheless, we fell far short of the ethical and political standard that Mâori scholar Linda Tuhiwai Smith (1999) advocates. She urges non-Mâori scholars to collaborate with the tribal elders, who help scholars define what they research and review what they write. In the Mesquaki study (Foley, 1995), I worked with tribal leaders and the tribal council, but the tribal elders neither set my research agenda nor monitored my fieldwork. I also acknowledged their way of knowing through dreams and vision quests, but I made no attempts to utilize those epistemologies. I retained more authorial authority than I would have under the Mâori community review process. Ultimately, I wrote the story I wanted to write—with, however, a good deal of input from key informants and from the community review. As we shall see, I was not as directly involved in community political processes as my coauthor has been.

The most politically active form of action anthropology emphasizes direct involvement in political movements, court cases, and aggressive organizing activities such as rent strikes. Other policy-oriented social scientists "work within the system" and write prizewinning cultural critiques as well as actively shape the public policy process. Accordingly, what follows is Angela Valenzuela's account of how she blends academic research and political commitment in a unique way.

Case Study 2: An "Activist Sociologist" and Her Legislative Involvement

I write to impart my craft—at least with respect to a certain kind of research in which I am currently involved. That is, I conduct "regular" ethnographic research—mostly in schools—using standard qualitative techniques in an attempt to generate better theoretical frameworks through which to both understand social problems and promote the development of just policies and practices in schools. The account that follows, however, reveals how my general interest in politics has evolved into a research approach that may be termed either "the ethnography of public policy" or the "public ethnography of policy."[1]

I am a third-generation Mexican American from West Texas reared in a community where the race and class lines between Anglos and Mexican Americans were sharply drawn for the greater part of the last century. I am also a product of the Texas public school system. I thus have a firsthand sense of its strengths and limitations with respect to the U.S.-Mexican community. I write primarily from my current vantage point as a member of the faculty at the University of Texas at Austin who is involved in the affairs of the Latino community at various levels. As an academic,

I currently hold a tenured, joint appointment in two colleges, Education and Liberal Arts, at the University of Texas. In the College of Education, my appointment is in the Department of Curriculum and Instruction (C & I), and in Liberal Arts, it is in the Center for Mexican American Studies (CMAS). I see myself as situated within a tradition of activist-scholarship previously undertaken by Chicano faculty at the University of Texas at Austin that includes the work of Américo Paredes, George I. Sanchez, and Carlos Castañeda.

Like my colleague Doug Foley, I, too, have endured a prolonged and painful struggle to find my voice and write in a broadly accessible style. However, unlike my colleague, I have long felt a special sense of responsibility that comes precisely from my social and political location as a member of a community lacking in voice, status, and representation at all levels. Acquiring my voice thus has been inseparable from my community's broader agenda to also be heard, and in so doing, to acquire power and political representation. Moreover, my profound desire to write to, and for, my community is what has encouraged me to persist.

I sometimes contemplate how, unlike my Anglo academic colleagues, I have probably been "more liberated" to pursue other rhetorical avenues in both writing and speech. More pointedly, as a minority female scholar, I always suspected that no matter what or how I wrote, I would never quite reap the same privileges and status within the academic hierarchy. The experiences of other minority academics taught me that both acquiring tenure and the goal of institutional validation and legitimacy, generally, are risky pursuits that frequently are characterized by uncertainty and struggle regardless of one's chosen research approach. Consequently, and despite the risks involved, soon after graduating from a positivistic, quantitative Sociology Department at Stanford University, I decided to follow my heart and develop a more humanistic, qualitative research approach. I did so within the context of my first job, a tenure-track position in the Department of Sociology at Rice University in Houston, Texas. It is relevant to note that to date, I am the only Mexican American female professor ever to have been hired for a tenure-track faculty position at Rice.

To best explain my craft, I must first situate myself within my academic/scholarly community and within the broader Latina/o activist community in Texas. What my personal account reveals is the importance of my insider status within the Latino community, coupled with my desire to use research to address the inequities of political and policymaking processes. Although I am less reflexive than some experimental ethnographers (Denzin, 1997), I am collaborative in the first sense that we outline. That is, I have always developed intimate, trusting relationships with collaborators. With respect to the second sense of collaboration, wherein community members review my manuscripts before publication, this has proven somewhat problematic. The process of "studying up" and exposing how elites wield power in my community makes this kind of collaboration either impossible or limited (especially see Valenzuela, 2004a, 2004b). Although I do share my legislative work with select Latina/o leadership, legislators, and State Board of Education members, I nevertheless preserve a great deal of authorial authority. To best explain my current status and position in the legislature, my research background in Houston, Texas, must first be taken into account.

While working at Rice University, I conducted a case study of a local high school that culminated in my book *Subtractive Schooling: U.S.-Mexican Youth and the Politics of Caring* (Valenzuela, 1999). Spanning a 3-year time period, I generated a ground-level ethnography that examined the assimilation experiences of high school youth and how these, in turn, related to achievement and school orientations. Because I wanted the study to appeal directly to the Latino community in Houston, I incorporated an historical perspective and wrote in a language that made it accessible to them. I should add, however, that my desire to be tenured led me to invest a great deal in becoming a "real scholar" within the academy. Combined with my Stanford-based "programming" to develop theory, my academic past had proven to be a constraint of sorts. For example, my deductive-nomological interest in assimilation kept me from seeing, for an extended amount of time, how caring theory could fit into an argument about assimilation (see Valenzuela, 1999, Appendix). It also kept me from seeing—at least to the degree that I now see it—how the testing system itself subtracts resources from students (see Valenzuela, 2000).

My fieldwork on *Subtractive Schooling* nevertheless provided me with an in-depth perspective on local and district policies and politics. I attended various churches, frequented parks, purchased goods and services, exercised, and attended numerous functions in the community surrounding the school that I studied. This experience further provided me with firsthand experiences concerning the frequently challenging conditions of urban life for working-class, Mexican-origin people living in Houston at that time. In short, through my research, I became a trusted member of Houston's inner-city Latino community.

While in Houston, I also was a founding member and chair of the Latino Education Policy Committee (LEPC). The LEPC was composed of researchers, parents, clergy, and community activists. When the former U.S. Secretary of Education, Rodney Paige, was superintendent, the LEPC fought district battles pertaining to the representation of minorities in the district's magnet school programs, as well as another regarding certain Houston Independent School District (HISD) board members' decisions to curtail the bilingual education program in the district. These activities brought me into contact with a rather large array of individuals including League of United Latin American Citizens (LULAC) leadership and council members, city council members, school board members, and state senators and representatives, including State Representative Dora Olivo (D-Rosenberg), with whom I later worked.

Through my work as an associate with the Rice University Center for Education, my network also included large numbers of Houston-area researchers, teachers, administrators, school personnel, and board members. I myself was a board member of the following organizations: Annenberg Foundation, Teach for America, and the Inter-Ethnic Forum. Because of my personal relationship with Lee Brown, I even participated on his transition team when he became Houston's first African American mayor. Despite my multiple political commitments in Houston—which always were part of my larger goal of getting to know the city from multiple perspectives—my professional life continued, primarily through my involvement in professional associations like the American Sociological Association, the American Educational Research Association, and the National Association for Chicana and Chicano Studies.

My family situation also is an important part of my current role as a "participatory action researcher" in the Texas state legislature. My husband, Emilio Zamora, is a Texas historian, award-winning author, and community activist. With my return to Texas from California, I inherited his Houston and Texas network, permitting a smooth and quick transition into the Houston Latino community. Marriage to an academic in a related field also has meant a continuous flow of intellectual and political ideas. We have two children, ages 8 and 11, and in 1998, our family won "Family of the Year" for Houston's 16 of September celebration (marking Mexico's acquisition of independence from Spain in 1810). City officials held a banquet in our honor, and our story appeared as an insert in the city's only major newspaper, the *Houston Chronicle.* Our picture was posted on all of the Metro buses throughout the week of festivities. It is not an overstatement to suggest that at least for a time, the Zamora-Valenzuela family became a virtual household name in the Houston Latino community.

From my standpoint as an activist sociologist, this kind of activity and notoriety had both an upside and a downside. Unfortunately, matters soured for me at Rice University, and I ended up filing a claim against my employer with the Equal Employment Opportunity Commission, alleging gender and national origins discrimination. After a protracted struggle with my employer, we arrived at a mutually agreed upon and amicable settlement. Notwithstanding this moment of personal and familial strife, my research approach surely facilitated my deeper involvement in community political processes. The payoff for me was the community's generous support throughout my tenure review in the form of letters, meetings with university officials, and public recognition of our contributions to Houston's Latino community. In the end, these relationships with key political players helped me both to produce my critical ethnography and to expose the harmful aspects of current educational policies.

During my final year in Houston in 1999, Al Kauffman, lead counsel of the Mexican American Legal Defense and Educational Fund (MALDEF), called on me to testify in a federal suit against the Texas Education Agency and the State Board of Education. The plaintiff's case argued that the state's testing system discriminated against them. All were either Latino/a or African American. They all had obtained the necessary credits for graduation but were denied diplomas because of their inability to pass the high-stakes standardized test. Of all students who fail the state exam statewide, 87% are either Latina/o or African American. During the trial, I was able to bring my own data on immigrant achievement to bear on the questions at hand (see Valenzuela, 1999, 2000).

Unfortunately, MALDEF won the argument that minorities are disproportionately affected by the state's testing system but lost the case because the judge decided that the harm against the plaintiffs did not reach a "constitutional level" (*GI Forum et al. v. Texas Educational Agency et al.*, 2000). That is, due process allegedly was followed in the development of the test and also by allowing students multiple opportunities to take it (see Valenzuela, 2004b). The MALDEF case was transformative because it situated me in the center of crucial state- and national-level policy debates and political activities. I was handed the file for the state, which acquainted me with the policies, evidence, and justifications for the state's testing system. This information helped me to see new ways that the state reproduced educational inequalities while cleverly obscuring them (especially see McNeil & Valenzuela, 2001). My earlier research presented a bottom-up perspective, but participation in the trial helped me develop a more comprehensive, policy-based, top-down analysis as well (Valenzuela, 2002, 2004a, 2004b).

After a year of commuting from Houston to Austin in 1999, during which Emilio secured employment in the School of Information at UT, my family eventually relocated to Austin in the summer of 2000. My work in the legislature began almost immediately upon my arrival when State Representative Dora Olivo asked me to testify on the state's testing system. My Houston network thus followed me, providing me with relatively easy entrée into the Austin lawmaking community.

My interest in policy was further abetted by the CMAS position for which I was hired. That is, my duties included teaching lower- and upper-division courses in public policy, which many CMAS students must take in order to major in Mexican American Studies (the rest pursue a cultural studies concentration). This position forced me to retool and learn more about Texas government, statutes, history, and the policymaking process. Upon completing their policy studies courses, many of our CMAS students pursue internships at the state capitol for which they simultaneously earn college credit. My Mexican American Studies students, in turn, have taught me a great deal and provided me with information that I fold into my writings on educational policy.

At the graduate level, I also offer a course on policy titled Latino Education Policy in Texas. The course is cross-listed with the Lyndon B. Johnson (LBJ) School of Public Affairs. I offer it during every other year when the legislature is in session, and my students, some of whom are former CMAS undergraduates, typically are policy studies majors from either the LBJ school or the College of Education.

Today, I hold the following community-based posts: Education Committee Chair for the Texas League of United Latin American Citizens (LULAC), the nation's oldest Latino civil rights organization; member of an Austin LULAC council called Legislative LULAC; member of the Legislative Committee for the Texas Association for Bilingual Education (TABE); and member of the newly revived La Raza Unida working education group. All of these activities reflect my current position as an advocate for Latina/o youth in the legislature. My legislative activities include advising representatives and senators on different kinds of legislation in the areas of assessment, limited English proficient youth, bilingual education, school vouchers, and school finance. My most intense work has been with State Representative Olivo, with whom I have worked for two biennial legislative sessions to craft and promote legislation in the area of assessment (for a review of this work, see Valenzuela, 2004b, 2000).

Prior to Austin, my research and policy work—particularly through the Latino Education Policy Committee—were somewhat separate tasks. That is, my role was one of bringing my expertise to bear on certain issues. In time, my professional role has evolved from being an ethnographer in the classic sense to being a direct advocate for change. This redefinition of my role as a researcher grew primarily out of a process that began with a deeply felt identification with the political associations—such as LULAC, MALDEF, TABE, and the Intercultural Development Research Association (IDRA)—that advocate on behalf of the U.S.-Mexican community.

Whenever I testified in committee hearings at the state capitol, I found myself generating field notes from all of my experiences. Then I discovered a virtual gold mine of audio archives of committee hearings (at the legislature's Web site, www.capitol.state.tx.us), "data" that are used more by attorneys and legislative staff than researchers. These discoveries dovetailed neatly with my more general interest in informing my community of the politics and process of policy making.

My preference always was (and is) to be the person who merely chronicled and analyzed the unfolding of legislation. My experiences at the capitol, however, have taught me that a number of policy areas, such as assessment and accountability, are woefully under-researched. Upon losing the federal MALDEF trial, the Chicano caucus members anticipated that an appeal would not likely fare well in the conservative Fifth Circuit Court. Consequently, the struggle for a more just assessment system would shift back to the state legislature, where most educational policies originate.

In Fall, 2000, upon moving to Austin, I had hoped to chronicle just such an effort, but I soon realized that both majority and minority advocates were operationally defining equity as *equal access to mandated testing*. That is, the legislative concerns that predominated centered around which students were getting which tests rather than whether a numbers-based, single-number accountability system is a flawed design (McNeil & Valenzuela, 2001; Valenzuela, 2004b). This impoverished definition of equity meant that no one was initiating progressive legislation on the uses of assessment.

In light of this vacuum in leadership, I downloaded the accountability law and revised it from a single-indicator system based on test scores to a multiple-indicator system based on test scores, grades, and teacher recommendations. In this revised version, multiple indicators were to figure into all retention, promotion, and graduation decisions. Much like the admissions processes in most Texas colleges and universities, multiple indicators help compensate for poor test scores. Moreover, because assessment drives curriculum, use of multiple indicators would minimize the teaching to the test, the narrowing of curricula, and the further marginalizing of students that Linda McNeil and I observed to be the case in Houston's inner-city schools (for a more elaborate discussion, see McNeil & Valenzuela, 2001; Valenzuela, 2002).

In November, 2000, I shared the new language of my "multiple indicators" idea with MALDEF attorneys Al Kauffman and Joe Sanchez, who then converted it into legalese. They walked the halls of the capitol searching for a bill sponsor. None of the Anglo representatives on the Committee on Public Education in the House wanted to carry the legislation. Only Representative Dora Olivo, a former teacher who was knowledgeable about the abuses of the testing system, was willing to sponsor it.

I still remember the sense of relief I felt on the day that we found our bill's sponsor. Al Kauffman, lead MALDEF attorney and honorary Mexican, e-mailed me with these words: "On the real difficult issues, *solamente la gente trabaja con nosotros y para nosotros* [only our people work with and for us]."[2] His sincere expression of solidarity and struggle still touches me deeply today.

With his use of Spanish and his reference to "our people," Al Kauffman gave voice to both our struggle for power and also how policy making is racialized independently of the merits of the legislation that we, as minorities, bring to the table. Although our proposal for just assessment practices promised to benefit all children regardless of race, what seemed to matter more in the eyes of the reluctant legislators was *who* was bringing it to their attention rather than *what* the proposal contained. I suspect that if our team both had been Anglo and had not been associated with either civil rights or the MALDEF court case, our proposal would have been received differently. However much they inform policy work, it is impossible to regret such circumstances. They refer to obstacles over which we have no control.

Our strategy has thus been to mobilize our constituents, continue working with our white allies—many of them scholars such as Professors Linda McNeil at Rice University and Walt Haney at Boston University—and educate legislators, newspaper columnists, and the lay public to begin considering how the state's approach to accountability marginalizes either students, the curriculum, or both. With the recent, high-profile exposés of fraudulent accounting of dropouts in the Houston Independent School District by the *New York Times,* coupled with arguments of how such practices are encouraged by design (Schemo 2003a, 2003b; Winerip, 2003), we already have achieved a modicum of success.

Looking back, it was my familiarity with discourse and rhetorical analysis that helped me decipher how state legislators used the slippery term "accountability." My understanding of their rhetoric and logic led me to craft arguments for new accountability practices that were incremental. The idea was to subtly alter, not dismantle, the existing accountability structure. To this end, we contended that because accountability is a large and complex system, it requires a more complex form of assessment. For evaluating students for high-stakes decisions (promotion, retention, and graduation), the state needs an assessment system premised on multiple measures rather than a single, narrow measure based on students' test scores. From a rhetorical standpoint, we framed our proposed legislation in language and justification that was both logical and less threatening to the larger political edifice of accountability (see Valenzuela, 2004b).

Initially, I thought my authority to advocate such an approach before legislative caucus members came from prior research in schools, from my status as a university professor, from my state- and national-level connections, and from being a citizen and having children in the public school system. Yet none of these factors would have been sufficient to convince legislators to rethink the concept of accountability and, in so doing, to consider our proposal seriously. In retrospect, it mattered that I am closely identified with the Mexican community *and* that I am directly involved in the recurrent struggles of Chicana/o legislators to either craft helpful legislation or weigh in on legislation that is not helpful. Moreover, I showed how deeply I was moved by the tragedy of unfairness in the assessment of children of color, as well as for all children generally. Additionally, my demonstrated interest and involvement in issues extending beyond assessment (e.g., legislative issues pertaining to English language learners) manifested my commitment to the Latina/o community, generally, while shielding me from the criticism often heaped upon university academics that their involvement is typically limited and self-serving in nature.

Without these crucial ingredients of identification, direct action, and a principled commitment to the community, my plea for a more humane multiple assessment approach would have lacked moral and ethical force. At first, I resented the circumstances that placed me in this position. I simply wanted to study the reform and not to be the person who was pivotal in achieving it. In time, however, I came to see how my knowledge and expertise could be used for meaningful change and also to appreciate the value of firsthand experience and skills associated with the legislative process. This by now long-term collaboration with Chicana/o political leaders is what pushed me to conduct a deeper, critical analysis of the state's school system. Immersed in the legislative process, I came to see how the Texas Education Agency's official rhetoric and the sanitized test results provided to the media obscured both the material conditions of schooling and the state's purported mission to educate all students equitably and thereby close the achievement gap.

The other side of my collaboration with state legislators is an equally intense collaboration with my graduate students. To date, all of the doctoral students with whom I work directly are engaged in education policy research. Our collective efforts push me to theorize, explain, and represent our observations of the legislature and legislators in new ways.

The dual role that I now play as both researcher and advocate constitutes a major break with my original training as a social scientist. I have found a way of doing social science that goes beyond the insipid, apolitical positivism that I learned in graduate school. At this point, it gives me enormous personal satisfaction to continue using my privileged status as a scholar to support and promote a social justice agenda. Moreover, being a *Tejana* and Mexican American female scholar imbues this calling with a special sense of urgency and purpose.

Conclusion

We have tried to raise some issues and make some distinctions that will move self-proclaimed "critical ethnographers" to interrogate their current ethnographic practice. By contrasting our own ethnographic and political practices, we discovered an interesting difference that helps clarify the notion of collaboration. On one hand, Foley has spent his career writing cultural critiques of American capitalism and its schools, but he has spent considerably less time in direct political involvement. In lieu of joining various progressive political struggles, he joined the ideological struggle against positivism and scientism. Like many progressive academics, this allowed him to survive professionally but left him longing for more direct political involvement as a "citizen anthropologist."

In this regard, he admires the passionate and direct political involvement of his colleague, Angela Valenzuela. She feels a deep moral bond to her ethnic group, and she works tirelessly for its betterment as an expert witness, researcher, and adviser to various Chicana/o legislators. She also mentors many of her students along this path. When Valenzuela responded somewhat apologetically about being less "reflexive" than I am, that mirrored for me how my notion of "collaboration" has shifted over the years. In some ways, I have become "the effect" of the powerful postmodern experimentalist discourse in anthropology. This made it harder for me to see that the following notions of collaboration—decentering the author, deconstructing theory, polyphonic texts, dialogic interviewing, and even community review of the texts—are no more fundamental than Valenzuela's notion of "collaboration."

On the surface, she and her award-winning ethnography do not seem to meet the postmodern ideals of reflexivity and a coproduced narrative. She does not deploy the experimental ethnography discourse rhetorically to make her text more authoritative. Moreover, this chapter is her first attempt at portraying the ethical-political ground of her ethnographic practice. Earlier, she recounted how she is linked to the Chicano political movement and its efforts to change society. Privately, she talks about having a "spiritual" connection with her research subjects—many of whom are political allies. They share a common historical memory of being a racialized, stigmatized people. When she participates in the struggle, she feels affirmed and empowered, and she experiences a shared sense of fate. These feelings compel her to write caring and thoughtful portraits of her people.

In effect, Valenzuela identifies and collaborates with her subjects in a deep psychological and political way. There is a sense of being *carnales* (brothers/sisters) and *camaradas* (comrades). In return, they expect her to be what Antonio Gramsci (1971) would call one of their "organic intellectuals." She has made it through a racist economic and educational system. She now has the academic credentials and the writing skills to be among a select community of experts, authors, and persons who, to use Gayatri Spivak's (1988) apt phrase, "strategically essentialize" their struggle. In the end, they may refuse many of the collaborative methodological practices advocated in experimental, postmodern ethnography. This is not to argue that one notion of collaboration is superior to the other, but it is clear that "native" or insider ethnographers may have to march to the beat of a different drummer. Ethical commitments to their subjects/political allies may compel them to be collaborative in more spiritual and less procedural, methodological ways. Our differences suggest that there are a number of ways of being collaborative. Each ethnographer ultimately develops his or her own notions of collaboration, positionality, and authorship.

Valenzuela's account of how her direct involvement in the legislative process led her to a greater understanding is a ringing endorsement for Hale's notion of activist anthropology. Researchers who are involved directly in the political process are in a better position to understand and theorize about social change. This being true, the academy must find many more ways to reward "citizen-scholars" who are both assisting local communities and producing more deeply grounded research studies. Unfortunately, the academy still mainly rewards scholars who produce universalistic "theoretical knowledge." The ruling academic elite of most disciplines still devalues the production of local, politically useful, "applied knowledge." As a result, many progressive scholars may minimize or even hide their attempts to produce the kind of practical knowledge needed to transform local communities and institutional policies.

At different points in history, the academy has punished progressive scholars for being too active politically. There are signs that the country is presently moving toward a new era of McCarthyism under the banner of fighting terrorism. Notwithstanding the presence of Mexican American Studies centers and other safe spaces that offer protection through a connection to community, the so-called safe space created by post-1960s cultural critics in the academy could disappear rather quickly if political lines harden. Consequently, it is with some urgency that we exhort our academic peers to valorize and share more openly the political dimensions of their fieldwork. There are undoubtedly political risks, but what other choice is there for so-called public intellectuals who live in an empire with enough bombs to destroy the world?

Perhaps future scholars who live in a more humane society and world will look back on this little post-1960s opening of "critical ethnography" with a bit of wonder. What our generation is doing may seem a little like the medical science of leeches or chemotherapy—a modest beginning at best. On a substantive level, we see many promising new varieties of critical ethnography. We have suggested many ways to question our notions of purpose, positionality, collaboration, and writing styles. Transforming the academic knowledge production industry obviously requires much more than challenging the ideology of positivism and scientism. We also need to change the way academic publishing is organized and controlled, and the way promotion and tenure for publication and public service is awarded. We also must continue to open up the academy to underrepresented groups so that they, too, may contribute to scholarship. Critical ethnography that embraces the public interest truly will flower when we can transform academia.

Notes

1. Angela Valenzuela wishes to thank her colleague, Bill Black, for his suggestion of the latter term.
2. Personal communication in 2001 to Angela Valenzuela during the first weeks of the legislative session.

References

Bennett, J. W. (1996). Applied and action anthropology: Ideological and conceptual aspects. *Current Anthropology, 36,* 23–53.

Brodkin, K. (2001). Diversity in anthropological theory. In I. Susser & T. Patterson (Eds.), *Cultural diversity in the United States* (pp. 368–387). Oxford, UK: Blackwell.

Burawoy, M. (1991). *Ethnography unbound.* Berkeley: University of California Press.

Burawoy, M. (2000). *Global ethnography: Forces, connections, and imaginations in a postmodern world.* Berkeley: University of California Press.

Carspecken, P. (1996). *Critical ethnography in educational research: A theoretical and practical guide.* London: Routledge.

Denzin, N. K. (1997). *Interpretive ethnography: Ethnographic practices for the 21st century.* Newbury Park, CA: Sage.

Denzin, N. K., & Lincoln, Y. S. (Eds.). (2000). *Handbook of qualitative research* (2nd ed.). Thousand Oaks, CA: Sage.

Douglas, J. (1976). *Investigative social research.* Beverly Hills, CA: Sage.

Eddy, E., & Partridge, W. (Eds.). (1987). *Applied anthropology in America* (2nd ed.). New York: Columbia University Press.

Fine, M., & Weis, L. (1998). *The unknown city: Lives of poor and working class young adults.* Boston: Beacon.

Fine, M., & Weis, L. (2000). *Speed bumps: A student-friendly guide to qualitative research.* New York: Teachers College Press.

Fine, M., Weis, L., Weseen, S., & Wong, L. (2000). For whom: Qualitative research, representations, and social responsibilities. In N. K. Denzin & Y. S. Lincoln (Eds.), *Handbook of qualitative research* (2nd ed., pp. 107–133). Thousand Oaks, CA: Sage.

Flores, R. (2002). *Remembering the Alamo: Memory, modernity and the master symbol.* Austin: University of Texas Press.

Foley, D. (1990). *Learning capitalist culture: Deep in the heart of Tejas.* Philadelphia: University of Pennsylvania Press.

Foley, D. (1995). *The heartland chronicles.* Philadelphia: University of Pennsylvania Press.

Foley, D. (1999). The Fox project: A reappraisal. *Current Anthropology, 40*(2), 171–191.

Foley, D. (2000, Spring). Studying the politics of Raza Unida politics: Reflections of a white anthropologist. *Reflexiones: New Directions in Mexican American Studies,* 51–81.

Foley, D. (2002). Critical ethnography: The reflexive turn. *International Journal of Qualitative Studies in Education, 15*(4), 469–491.

Foley, D., Levinson, B., & Hurtig, J. (2001). Anthropology goes inside: The new educational ethnography of ethnicity and gender. In W. Secada (Ed.), *Review of research in education* (pp. 37–99). Washington, DC: American Educational Research Association Publications.

Foley, D., & Moss, K. (2001). Studying American cultural diversity: Some non-essentializing perspectives. In I. Susser & T. Patterson (Eds.), *Teaching cultural diversity* (pp. 130–152). London: Blackwell.

Foley, D., with Mota, C., Post, D., & Lozano, I. (1989). *From peones to politicos: Class and ethnicity in a South Texas town, 1900–1987.* Austin: University of Texas Press.

GI Forum et al. v. Texas Educational Agency et al., 87 F. Supp. 667 (W.D. Tex. 2000).

Gordon, E. T. (1997). *Disparate diasporas: Identity and politics in an African-Nicaraguan community.* Austin: University of Texas Press.

Gramsci, A. (1971). *Selections from the prison notebooks.* New York: International Publishers.

Hale, C. R. (1994). *Resistance and contradiction: Miskitu Indians and the Nicaraguan state, 1894–1987.* Stanford, CA: Stanford University Press.

Hale, C. R. (n.d.). *Activist research versus cultural critiques: Contradictions at every turn.* Unpublished paper, Department of Anthropology, University of Texas, Austin.

Haraway, D. (1988). Situated knowledges: The science question in feminism as a site of discourse on the privilege of partial perspective. *Feminist Studies, 14,* 575–599.

Harding, S. (1998). *Is science multicultural? Postcolonialisms, feminisms, and epistemology.* Bloomington: Indiana University Press.

Hymes, D. (Ed.). (1972). *Reinventing anthropology.* New York: Vintage.

Kane, S., & Mason, T. (2001). AIDS and criminal justice. *Annual Review of Anthropology, 30,* 457–479.

Kemmis, S., & McTaggart, R. (2000). Participatory action research. In N. K. Denzin & Y. S. Lincoln (Eds.), *Handbook of qualitative research* (2nd ed., pp. 567–606). Thousand Oaks, CA: Sage.

Lather, P. (1991). *Getting smart: Feminist research and pedagogy within the post-modern.* New York: Routledge.

Levinson, B., & Holland, D. (1996). The cultural production of the educated person: An introduction. In B. Levinson, D. Foley, & D. Hollands (Eds.), *The cultural production of the educated person: Critical ethnographies of schooling and local practice* (pp. 1–54). Albany: State University of New York Press.

Levinson, B., & Sutton, M. (Eds.). (2001). *Policy as practice: Towards a comparative sociological analysis of educational policy.* Westport, CT: Ablex.

Lynd, R. (1956). *Middletown: A study of American culture* (2nd ed.). New York: Harcourt Brace.

Marcus, G. (1998). *Ethnography through thick and thin.* Princeton, NJ: Princeton University Press.

Marcus, G. (Ed.). (1999). *Critical anthropology now: Unexpected contexts, shifting constituencies, changing agendas.* Santa Fe, NM: School of American Research Press.

Marcus, G., & Cushman, D. (1982). Ethnographies as texts. *Annual Review of Anthropology, 11,* 25–69.

Marcus, G., & Fischer, M. (1986). *Anthropology as cultural critique: An experimental moment in the human sciences.* Chicago: University of Chicago Press.

McNeil, L. (2000). *Contradictions of school reform: Educational costs of standardized testing.* New York: Routledge.

McNeil, L., & Valenzuela, A. (2001). The harmful impact of the TAAS system of testing in Texas: Beneath the accountability rhetoric. In M. Kornhaber & G. Orfield (Eds.), *Raising standards or raising barriers? Inequality and high stakes testing in public education* (pp. 127–150). New York: Century Foundation.

Menchaca, M. (2002). *Recovering history, constructing race: The Indian, black and white roots of Mexican Americans.* Austin: University of Texas Press.

Mills, C. W. (1959). *The sociological imagination.* New York: Oxford University Press.

Nader, L. (1996). *Naked science: Anthropological inquiry into boundaries, power, and knowledge.* New York: Routledge.

Okongwu, F., & Mencher, J. P. (2000). The anthropology of public policy: Shifting terrains. *Annual Review of Anthropology, 29,* 107–124.

Rubinstein, R. (1986). Reflections on action anthropology: Some developmental dynamics of an anthropological tradition. *Human Organization, 5,* 270–282.

Sanday, P. R. (1976). *Anthropology and the public interest: Fieldwork and theory.* New York: Academic Press.

Sanday, P. R. (1990). *Fraternity gang rape: Sex, brotherhood and privilege on campus.* New York: New York University Press.

Sanday, P. R. (1996). *A woman scorned: Acquaintance rape on trial.* New York: Doubleday.

Schemo, D. J. (2003a, August 28). For Houston schools, college claims exceed reality. *New York Times.* Retrieved August 28, 2003, from www.nytimes.com

Schemo, D. J. (2003b, July 11). Questions on data cloud luster of Houston schools. *New York Times.* Retrieved July 11, 2003, from www.nytimes.com

Scheper-Hughes, N. (1992). *Death without weeping: The violence of everyday life in Brazil.* Berkeley: University of California Press.

Scheper-Hughes, N., & Sargent, C. (Eds.). (1998). *Small wars: The cultural politics of childhood.* Berkeley: University of California Press.

Schwandt, T. A. (2000). Three epistemological stances for qualitative inquiry: Interpretivism, hermeneutics, and social constructionism. In N. K. Denzin & Y. S. Lincoln (Eds.), *Handbook of qualitative research* (2nd ed., pp. 37–84). Thousand Oaks, CA: Sage.

Smith, L. T. (1999). *Decolonizing methodologies: Research and indigenous peoples.* London: Zed Books.

Spivak, G. (1988). *Other worlds: Essays in cultural politics.* New York: Methuen.

Susser, I. (2001). Poverty and homelessness in US cities. In I. Susser & T. Patterson (Eds.), *Cultural diversity in the United States* (pp. 229–249). Oxford, UK: Blackwell.

Tax, S. (1963). *Penny capitalism: A Guatemalan Indian history.* Chicago: University of Chicago Press.

Valentine, C. (1968). *Culture and poverty: A critique and counter-proposals.* Chicago: University of Chicago Press.

Valenzuela, A. (1999). *Subtractive schooling: U.S.-Mexican youth and the politics of caring.* Albany: State University of New York Press.

Valenzuela, A. (2000). The significance of the TAAS test for Mexican immigrant and Mexican American adolescents: A case study. *Hispanic Journal of the Behavioral Sciences, 22*(4), 524–539.

Valenzuela, A. (2002). High-stakes testing and U.S.-Mexican youth in Texas: The case for multiple compensatory criteria in assessment. *Harvard Journal of Hispanic Policy, 14,* 97–116.

Valenzuela, A. (2004a). Accountability and the privatization agenda. In A. Valenzuela (Ed.), *Leaving children behind: Why Texas-style accountability fails Latino youth* (pp. 263–297). Albany: State University of New York Press.

Valenzuela, A. (2004b). The accountability debate in Texas: Continuing the conversation. In A. Valenzuela (Ed.), *Leaving children behind: Why Texas-style accountability fails Latino youth* (pp. 1–32). Albany: State University of New York Press.

Vidich, A. J., & Lyman, S. (2000). Qualitative methods: Their history in sociology and anthropology. In N. K. Denzin & Y. S. Lincoln (Eds.), *Handbook of qualitative research* (2nd ed., pp. 37–84). Thousand Oaks, CA: Sage.

Villenas, S., & Foley, D. (2002). Chicano/Latino critical ethnography of education: Borderlands cultural productions from La Frontera. In R. R. Valencia (Ed.), *Chicano school failure and success: Past, present, and future* (2nd ed., pp. 195–226). London: Routledge Falmer.

Winerip, M. (2003, August 13). The "zero dropout" miracle: Alas! Alack! A Texas tall tale. *New York Times.* Retrieved August 13, 2003, from www.nytimes .com

Wolfe, E. (1982). *Europe and people without history.* Berkeley: University of California Press.

Wolfe, T. (1974). *The new journalism.* New York: Harper and Row.

Zavella, P. (1987). *Women, work, and family in the Chicano community.* Ithaca, NY: Cornell University Press.

10

EARLY MILLENNIAL FEMINIST QUALITATIVE RESEARCH

Challenges and Contours

Virginia L. Olesen

The only constant in today's world is change.

—Braidotti (2000, p. 1062)

A short time into the "new millennium" (to use a limited, Westernized term), changing themes suffuse feminist qualitative research. These themes challenge feminist work wherever done, bearing on the very articulation of gender, its enactment, and the problems which inhere thereto: economic stagnation that slows growth in Westernized societies and impedes progress in developing countries;

Author's Note. Incisive criticisms from Norman Denzin, Yvonna Lincoln, Patricia Clough, Michelle Fine, Meaghan Morris, and Yen Le Espiritu enhanced the quality of this chapter. I'm grateful to them all as well as to Judith Lorber for generous sharing of feminist research on the Sociologists for Women in Society e-mail list; to Elizabeth Allen for her roster of feminist, critical, and poststructural policy analyses; and to Adele Clarke for continuing, stimulating feminist dialogue.

the potential for war and terrorism of whatever scope; altering relationships among major nation-states, with consequences for isolation and new coalitions; and the unceasingly rapid development of electronic communication which melts borders, transfers resources, and alters identities. Within some societies, both Eastern and Western, conservativism grows or resurges, with substantial potential to shape women's and men's lives. As Evelyn Nakano Glenn has noted, "If one accepts gender as a variable, then one must acknowledge that it is never fixed, but continually constituted and reconstituted" (2002, p. 8).

Feminism and feminist qualitative research remain highly diversified, enormously dynamic, and thoroughly challenging. Contending models of thought jostle, divergent methodological and analytical approaches compete, once clear theoretical differences (see Fee, 1983) blur, and divisions deepen, even as rapprochement occurs. Experimental work with new complexities engages numerous investigators at the same time that many others remain oriented to views of gendered universals and more traditional approaches. Moreover, even within the same wings of feminist research (experimental or traditional), there are disagreements on many issues, such as the most efficacious theoretical stance, treatment of voices, and research for policy use.

What follows here is rooted in an early feminist declaration I wrote for a 1975 conference on women's health in which I argued that "Rage is not enough" (1977, pp. 1–2) and called for incisive scholarship to frame, direct, and harness passion in the interests of redressing grievous problems in many areas of women's health. As a symbolic interactionist working primarily within the interactionist–social constructionist tradition (Denzin, 1992, pp. 1–21), I sympathize with sectors of deconstructive currents in interactionism and feminism that encourage provocative and productive unpacking of taken-for-granted ideas about women in specific material, historical, and cultural contexts to avoid a "fatal unclutteredness" (Mukherjee, 1994, p. 6). Research *for* women should extend and amplify research merely *about* women, to ensure that even the most revealing descriptions of unknown or recognized aspects of women's situations do not remain merely descriptions. It must be remembered, however, as Yen Le Espiritu has commented (personal communication, September 15, 2003), "Women of color have insisted that a social justice agenda address the needs of both men and women of color since they are linked to race and class." Failure to attend closely to how race, class, and gender are relationally constructed leaves feminists of color distanced from feminist agendas.

Research for women that incorporates these critical points is possible in theoretical essays and through a variety of qualitative modes using combinations of both experimental and text-oriented styles, but it is not without difficulties, as will be discussed at the end of this chapter. Feminist work sets the stage for other research, other actions, and policy that transcends and transforms (Olesen, 1993). Feminist inquiry is dialectical, with different views fusing to produce new syntheses that in turn become the grounds for further research, praxis, and policy (Lupton, 1995; Nielsen, 1990, p. 29; Westkott, 1979, p. 430).

I will locate this exploration in changing currents of feminist thought (Benhabib, Butler, Cornell, & Fraser, 1995; Ebert, 1996; entire issue of *Signs*, Vol. 25, No. 4, 2000) and altering, sometimes controversial themes within qualitative research (Denzin, 1997; Gubrium & Holstein, 1997; Gupta & Ferguson, 1997; G. Miller & Dingwall, 1997; Scheurich, 1997). Feminist qualitative research is *not* a passive recipient of transitory intellectual themes and controversies. On the contrary, it influences and alters aspects of qualitative research (Charmaz & Olesen, 1997; DeVault, 1996; D. Smith, 1990a, 1990b; J. Stacey & Thorne, 1985; V. Taylor, 1998), stimulating some and irritating others. Feminisms draw from different theoretical and pragmatic orientations that reflect national contexts where feminist agendas differ widely (Evans, 2002; Morawski, 1997; *Signs*, Vol. 25, No. 4, 2000). Nevertheless, without in anyway positing a global, homogeneous, unified feminism, qualitative feminist research in its many variants, whether or not self-consciously defined as feminist, problematizes women's diverse situations as well as the gendered institutions and material and historical structures that frame those. It refers the examination of that problematic to theoretical, policy, or action frameworks to realize social justice for women (and men) in specific contexts (Eichler, 1986, p. 68; 1997, pp. 12–13). It generates new ideas to produce knowledges about oppressive situations for women, for action or further research (Olesen & Clarke, 1999).[1] Critical race and legal studies have also foregrounded issues to be reviewed here, for instance Patricia Williams's (1991) application of literary theory to analysis of legal discourse to reveal the intersubjectivity of legal constructions or Mari Matsuda's (1996) interrogation of race, gender, and the law.

As background, I will briefly outline the scope of feminist qualitative research, recognizing that this is only a partial glimpse of a substantial literature in many disciplines. This will ground a discussion of emergent complexities in feminist qualitative work and issues that feminist scholars continue to debate. These include the obdurate worries about bias and believability, objectivity and subjectivity for those who continue to rely on these criteria, and for others the demands posed by new experimental approaches in the realm of representation, voice, text, and ethical issues. The accomplishments of, shortfalls in, and future of feminist qualitative research close the chapter.

▣ Scope and Topics of Feminist Qualitative Research

Feminist work goes well beyond views that qualitative research is most useful for inquiries into subjective issues and interpersonal relations or the erroneous assumption that qualitative research cannot handle large scale issues. For reasons found in intellectual themes to be discussed shortly and the multiple use of methods (see Reinharz, 1992), feminists range from assessments of women's lives and experiences that foreground the subjective and production of subjectivities to analyses of relationships through investigation of social movements (Klawiter, 1999; Kuumba, 2002; V. Taylor, 1998; see also two special issues of *Gender and Society*—Vol. 12, No. 6, 1998, and Vol. 13, No. 1, 1999) and research reports in the feminist globalization literature (see the entire issue of *Signs*, Vol. 26, No. 4, 2001 and *International Sociology*, Vol. 18, No. 3, 2003). This includes policy and organizational studies.

It is impossible to cite even a small part of this research here, but two fields, education and health, merit mention. Within the educational realm, the range is indicated by studies such as Sandra Acker's acute observations of classroom experiences (1994), Deborah Britzman's poststructuralist analysis of the "socialization" of student teachers (1991), Diane Reay's research on social class in mothers' involvement in their children's schooling (1998), Susan Chase's narrative analysis of women school superintendents struggling with inhibiting structures (1995), and a study of how women "become gentlemen" in law school (Guinier, Fine, & Balin, 1997). Additionally, educational researchers writing about policy issues in a feminist, critical, and poststructural vein have widened policy analysis (Ball, 1994; Blackmore, 1995; de Castell & Bryson, 1997; Marshall, 1999).

In the field of health and healing, Jennifer Fishman's multimethod study of Viagra demonstrated the emergence of a new disease category, female sexual arousal, which will be the basis for prescribing Viagra-related drugs to women (2001).[2] Jennifer Fosket (1999) showed how women construct breast cancer knowledge, and Janet Shim (2000) revealed gender and other elements in biomedical knowledge formation. Nurse researchers' feminist qualitative inquiries have produced critiques of Asian women's menopausal experiences (Im, Meleis, & Park, 1999) and probed working women's lives (Hattar-Pollara, Meleis, & Nagib, 2000).

Although policy analysis is still largely quantitative and male dominated, some feminist researchers carry out Janet Finch's (1986) early argument that qualitative research can contribute significantly to understanding and framing policy. Some have focused on the substance, construction, and emergence of specific policy issues: Kaufert and McKinlay (1985) documented divergent scientific, clinical, and feminist constructions in the emergence of estrogen replacement therapy; Rosalind Petchesky revealed how women's health was framed in the abortion debate (1985) and the complexities of transnationalizing women's health movements (2003); and Nancy Naples (1997a, 1997b) deployed discourse analysis to demonstrate the state's part in restructuring families and women's roles therein. Others have dealt with processes through which policy is accomplished:[3] Theresa Montini's (1997) triangulated study showed how physicians deflected activists in the movement to provide information to women with breast cancer, away from activists' goals. Accomplishing policy raises issues of control of women: Nancy Fraser's (1989) discourse analysis of women's needs and the state questioned whether definitions are emancipatory or controlling. Wendy Brown (1992) argued that Barbara Ehrenreich and Frances Fox Piven's (1983) positive view of the state for women did not recognize issues of control.[4]

Continuing and Emergent Complexities

Complexity and controversy characterize the qualitative feminist research enterprise: the nature of research, the definition of and relationship with those with whom research is done, the characteristics and location of the researcher, and the creation and presentation of knowledges. If there is a dominant theme, it is the question of knowledges. Whose knowledges? Where and how obtained, and by whom; from whom and for what purposes? As Liz Stanley and Sue Wise (1990) reflected, "Succinctly, feminist theorists have moved away from 'the reactive' stance of the feminist critiques of social science and into the realms of exploring what 'feminist knowledge' could look like" (p. 37). This undergirds influential feminist writing such as Lorraine Code's question, "who can know?" (1991, p. ix), Donna Haraway's conceptualization of situated knowledges (1991), Dorothy Smith's articulation of the everyday world as problematic (1987), and a multitude of texts on feminist qualitative methods and methodology (Behar, 1996; Behar & Gordon, 1995; O. Butler, 1986; Clarke, 2004; DeVault, 1993, 1999; Fine, 1992a; Fonow & Cook, 1991; Hekman, 1990; Holland & Blair with Sheldon, 1995; Lather, 1991; Lewin & Leap, 1996; Maynard & Purvis, 1994; Morawski, 1994; Naples, 2003; Nielsen, 1990; Ramazanoglu with Holland, 2002; Ribbens & Edwards, 1998; Roberts, 1981; Skeggs, 1995a; D. Smith, 1999, in press; Stanley & Wise, 1983; Tom, 1989; Viswesweran, 1994; D. Wolf, 1996a; M. Wolf, 1992, 1996; L. Stanley, 1990).

That there are multiple knowledges was set forth forcefully by Patricia Hill Collins (1990) in her explication of black feminist thought, an influential work that—along with writings of Angela Davis (1981), Bonnie Thornton Dill (1979), Effie Chow (1987), bell hooks (1990), Rayna Green (1990), and Gloria Anzaldúa (1987, 1990)—began to dissolve an unremitting whiteness in feminist research. This continues with exploration of the black female experience (Reynolds, 2002), black women in authority (Forbes, 2001), and the diversities among American Indian women (Mihesuah, 1998, 2000).

This growing emphasis departed from important themes in the early years of feminist research. First, Catherine MacKinnon's assertion that "consciousness raising" is the basis of feminist methodology (1982, p. 535; 1983) gave way as theorists and researchers recognized that women are located structurally in changing organizational and personal contexts that intertwine with subjective assessment to produce knowledge, as Sheryl Ruzek (1978) had earlier demonstrated in her analysis of the women's health movement. Second, observations about women being missing from and invisible in certain arenas of social life, such as Judith Lorber's (1975) research on women in medicine and Cynthia Epstein's (1981) work on women in law, led to complex analyses such as Darlene Clark Hine's (1989) exploration of the structural, interactional, and knowledge-producing elements in the exclusion of and treatment of African American women in American nursing.

Parallel research revealed women as ubiquitous and invisible workers in the domestic sphere (Abel & Nelson, 1990; Finch & Groves, 1983; Graham, 1984, 1985;

Table 10.1 Complexities in Feminist Qualitative Research and Representative Texts

I. Strands in Continuing Complexities

Work by and About Specific Groups of Women

Writing by Women of Color
Dill (1979), A. Y. Davis (1981), Zinn (1982), Collins (1986), Zavella (1987), Garcia (1989), Hurtado (1989), Anzaldúa (1990), Green (1990), hooks (1990), Espiritu (1997), Mihesuah (1998), Reynolds (2002)

Lesbian Research and Queer Theory
Krieger (1983), Anzaldúa (1990), Hall & Stevens (1991), Terry (1991), Weston (1991), J. Butler (1990, 1993), Kennedy & Davis (1993), Lewin (1993), Alexander (1997)

Disabled Women
Asch & Fine (1992), Morris (1995), Lubelska & Mathews (1997)

II. Approaches

Postcolonial Feminist Thought

Mohanty (1988, 2003), Spivak (1988), Trinh (1989, 1992), Heng (1997)

Globalization

Marchand & Runyan (2000), Misra (2000), Naples (2002), Runyon & Marchand (2000), Bergeron (2001), Fernandez-Kelly & Wolf (2001), Freeman (2001), Kelly et al. (2001), Kofman et al. (2001), Young (2001), Barndt (2002)

Standpoint Theory
Hartsock (1983, 1997b), Harding (1987,1990), D. Smith (1987, 1997), Collins (1990, 1998), Haraway (1991), Weeks (1998), Ramazanoglu with Holland (2002), Naples (2003)

Postmodern and Deconstructive Theory
Flax (1987), Hekman (1990), Nicholson (1990), Haraway (1991), Clough (1998), Haraway (1997), Collins (1998b), Lacsamana (1999)

III. Consequences of Complexity

Problematizing Researcher and Participant

Behar (1993), Frankenberg & Mani (1993), Lincoln (1993, 1997), Ellis (1995), Reay (1996a), Lather & Smithies (1997)

Problematizing Unremitting Whiteness

Frankenberg (1994), Hurtado & Stewart (1997)

Destabilizing Insider-Outsider

Kondo (1990), Lewin (1993), Ong (1995), Zavella (1996), Naples (1996, 2003), Weston (1996), B. Williams (1996), Narayan (1997)

Deconstructing Traditional Concepts

Experience
Scott (1991), O'Leary (1997)

Difference
hooks (1990), Felski (1997)

Gender
West & Zimmerman (1987), J. Butler (1990, 1993), Lorber (1994), Poster (2002)

IV. Enduring Issues

"Bias" and Objectivity

Fine (1992), Scheper-Hughes (1992), Holland & Ramazanoglu (1994), Phoenix (1994), Harding (1991, 1996, 1998), Haraway (1997), Diaz (2002)

"Validity" and Trustworthiness

Lather (1993), Richardson (1993), K. Manning (1997)

Participants' Voices

Maschia-Lees et al. (1989), Fine (1992a), Opie (1992), Lincoln (1993, 1997), Reay (1996b), Kincheloe (1997), Ribbens & Edwards (1998)

Presenting the Account

Behar & Gordon (1995), Ellis (1995), Kondo (1995), Lather & Smithies (1997), McWilliam (1997), Richardson (1997), Gray & Sinding (2002)

Research Ethics

Finch (1984), Stacey (1988), Lincoln (1995), Fine & Weis (1996), Reay (1996b), D. Wolf (1996), M. Wolf (1996), Ribbens & Edwards (1998), Edwards & Mauthner (2002), Mauthner et al. (2002)

Transcending, Transforming the Academy

Stacey & Thorne (1985), Abu-Lughod (1990), Fine & Gordon (1992), Behar (1993), Morawski (1994), Cancian (1996), D. Smith (1999), Gergen (2001), Messer-Davidow (2002), Anglin (2003)

Making Feminist Work Count

Laslett & Brenner (2001), Stacey (2003)

M. K. Nelson, 1990). Evelyn Nakano Glenn's (1990) work on Japanese domestic workers, Judith Rollins's (1985) participant observation study of doing housecleaning, Mary Romero's (1992) interview study of Latina domestic workers, and Pierrette Hondagneu-Sotelo's (2001) interview study of employers, Latina workers, and heads of employment agencies laid bare the race, class, and gender issues in domestic service and household work and concomitant contexts of knowledge, seemingly banal, but ultimately critical to everyday life. This work problematized further the concept of care and spurred a surge of later conceptual and research projects (Cancian, Kurz, London, Reviere, & Tuominen, 2000). Margery DeVault's (1991) research on domestic food preparation, Anne Murcott's (1993) analysis of conceptions of food, and Arlie Hochschild and Anne Machung's findings (1989) that household labor is imbedded in the political economy of household emotions further demonstrated the dynamics of knowledge production and control within gendered relationships in the domestic sphere.

Thus, emergent complexities moved feminist research from justly deserved criticisms of academic disciplines (J. Stacey & Thorne, 1985, 1996), social institutions, and the lack of or flawed attention to women's lives and experiences to debate and discussion of critical epistemological issues.[5] Researchers became more sensitive to differences among women, even in the same group, and to concerns about the researcher's own characteristics. As the concept of a universalized "woman" or "women" faded, understanding grew that multiple identities and subjectivities are constructed in particular historical and social contexts (Ferguson, 1993).

Strands Contributing to and Sustaining Complexities

Major strands that continue to sustain complexities in feminist research include work by and about specific groups of women (women of color, gay and lesbian/queer women, and disabled women) and approaches to the study of women (postcolonial, globalization, standpoint theory, postmodern theory, and deconstructive theory). These are not always discrete, as, for instance, researchers who are women of color may utilize standpoint theory, as is noted elsewhere.

Writing by Women of Color. Beyond the eye-opening analyses cited earlier, other work by women of color significantly shaped new understandings that displaced taken-for-granted views of women of color and revealed the extent to which whiteness can be a factor in creating "otherness," for example, Asianness in Britain (Puar, 1996). Aside from the critical task of differentiation, greater recognition of the interplay of race, class, and gender in shaping women's oppression and white women's advantage is displayed in writing by Maxine Baca Zinn (1982), Patricia Hill Collins (1986), Aida Hurtado (1989), A. M. Garda (1989), and research by Patricia Zavella on Mexican American cannery workers (1987) and by Elaine Bell Kaplan on black teenage mothers (1997). As Yen Le Espiritu has noted, "Racism affects not only people of color, but organizes and shapes experiences of all women" (personal communication, September 15, 2003). At the same time, Gloria Anzaldúa's experimental writing and work (1987) foregrounded the conceptualization of borders, crossing borders and fluidities in women's lives—familial, national, sexual, and international—adding further dimensions and complexities. Recognition of the importance of borders and fluidities, albeit in a very different form, emerged from feminist researchers working on women and immigration (Espin, 1995; Hondagneu-Sotelo, 2001). Yet feminist scholars Vanessa Bing and P. T. Reid (1996) warned against misapplication of white feminist knowledge, a caveat echoed by legal scholar Kimberly Crenshaw (1992) in her discussion of white feminists' appropriation of the 1991 Clarence Thomas hearings.

Parallel to these developments have been critical investigations that problematize not only the construction of women of color in relationship to whiteness, but also whiteness itself. Ruth Frankenberg's (1994) interview study shifts whiteness from privileged, unnamed taken-for-grantedness to a critical issue that must be raised about all research participants. Noting that "whiteness" is the "natural" state of affairs, Aida Hurtado and Abigail J. Stewart (1997, pp. 309–310) call for studies of whiteness from the standpoint of people of color to find what they call a critical, counterhegemonic presence in the research. Dealing with untangling whiteness and the existence of a global color line, Chandra Talpade Mohanty (2003) urged feminists to consider questions of power, equality, and justice in ways that address context and recognition of questions of history and experience.

Postcolonial Feminist Thought. If the criticisms of an unremitting whiteness in feminist research in Western, industrialized societies began to unsettle feminist research frames, powerful and sophisticated research and feminist thought from postcolonial theorists further shifted the grounds of feminist research with regard to "woman" and "women," the very definitions of feminism itself, and constructions of color (Mohanty, 2003). Feminism, these theorists argued, takes many different forms depending on the context of contemporary nationalism (Heng, 1997). Concerned about the invidious effects of "othering" (invidious, oppressive defining of the persons with whom research is done), they argued that Western feminist models were inappropriate for thinking of research with women in postcolonial sites (Kirby, 1991, p. 398). Postcolonial feminists raised incisive questions such as Gayatri Chakravorti Spivak's (1988) query as to whether subordinates can speak or are forever silenced by virtue of representation within elite thought. (See also Mohanty, 1988.) They also asked about whether Third World women or indeed all women could be conceptualized as unified subjectivities easily located in the category of "woman." Drawing on her expertise as a filmmaker, Trinh T. Minh-ha (1989, 1992) articulated a fluid framing of woman (as other and not other) and undermined the very doing of ethnographic research by undercutting the concept of woman, the assumptions of subjectivity and objectivity, and the utility of the interview. This literature also pointed to issues in globalization.

Globalization. Feminist theorists' and researchers' explorations of the international march of capital, shifting labor markets, and recruitment thereto have foregrounded the implications of these vast political and economic processes for women in highly divergent contexts (Barndt, 2002; R. M. Kelly, Bayes, Hawkesworth, & Young, 2001; Kofman, Phizacklea, Raghuran, & Sales, 2001; Marchand & Runyan, 2000; see also the entire issue of *Signs,* Vol. 26, No. 4, 2001) and expanded the scope of feminist qualitative research. Feminists complicate homogeneous views of globalization, which is not "unified and noncontradictory, an inevitable accumulation on a world wide basis or solely determined by powerful economic institutions" (Bergeron, 2001, p. 996), but rife with contradictions (Naples, 2002) and the potential to produce multiple subjectivities (see also Fernandez-Kelly & Wolf, 2001; C. Freeman, 2001; Runyan & Marchand, 2000; Young, 2001). This complicating maneuver has produced research that reflects divergent views on two critical issues: (a) the interplay of the dominance of the state and these economic forces in women's lives and women's enactment of or potential resistance and (b) the production of new opportunities and/or the continuation of old oppressions. Rhacel Parrenas's (2001) research on Filipina domestic workers finds acts of resistance in everyday life, but these did not intervene against structural processes. Millie Thayer's (2001) analysis of rural Brazilian women shows that the women's local movement drew on their own resources to exert power, defend the movement's autonomy, and negotiate access to resources. These studies and others (Constable, 1997; Guevarra, 2003) stretch feminist qualitative researchers, as they require multiple methods (ethnography, interviews, documentary analysis). They also invoke contentious issues found elsewhere in feminist qualitative work: the efficacy of postmodern thinking (Lacsamana, 1999); the risk of reproducing Eurocentric concepts of feminism (Grewal & Caplen, 1994; Kempadoo, 2001; Rudy, 2000; Shohat, 2001); theoretical tensions between local particulars and the political economy of labor (Lacsamana, 1999); and, particularly in sex traffic research, questions of female agency (Doezema, 2000; Ho, 2000; Hanochi, 2001) and working conditions (Gulcur & Ilkkaracan, 2002; Poudel & Carryer, 2000; Pyle, 2001).

Lesbian Research. In research that quickly laid to rest Stanley and Wise's (1990, pp. 29–34) criticism that little attention had been paid to lesbians, feminist scholars upended theoretical and research frames saturated with stigma that essentially had rendered lesbians invisible and, where visible, despicable. Here, as Yen Le Espiritu has pointed out, it is useful to differentiate studies that focus on sexuality as an object of study from those that make sexuality a central concept (personal communication, September 15, 2003). The former type of research dissolved a homogeneous view of lesbians: Susan Krieger's (1983) ethnography of a lesbian community; Patricia Stevens and Joanne Hall's (1991) analysis of how medicine has invidiously defined lesbianism; Kath Weston's (1991) study of lesbian familial relationships; Ellen Lewin's (1993) research on lesbian mothers, which shows the surpassing importance of the maternal rather than sexual identity; and Jennifer Terry

(1994) on theorizing "deviant" historiography. Other work (Anzaldúa, 1987, 1990; Kennedy & Davis, 1993; Lewin,1996) further differentiated these views by revealing race and class issues within lesbian circles and the multiple bases of lesbian identity. Jacqui Alexander's (see Alexander & Mohanty, 1997) work is of the second category, as she conceptualizes sexuality as fundamental to gender inequality and as a salient marker of otherness that has been central to racist and colonial ideologies.

The very meaning of gender also came in for incisive critical review by Judith Butler (1990, 1993), whose philosophical analysis for some feminists evoked themes contained in an earlier sociological statement by Candace West and Don Zimmerman (1987). In both cases, but for different theoretical reasons, these scholars pointed to sexual identity as performative rather than given or socially ascribed and thus undercut a dualistic conception of gender that had informed feminist thought for decades.

The term "queer" has been used as a synonym for homosexual identity and also to question norms around heterosexual marriage. The emergence of the term "queer theory," referring to those gay men and women who refuse assimilation into either gay culture or oppressive heterosexual culture, also has been loosely used as a cover term for gay and lesbian studies. In addition, it refers to a more precise political stance (Lewin, 1996, pp. 6–9). Ellen Lewin's (1998) research on gay and lesbian marriages shows how those ceremonies simultaneously reflect accommodation and subversion. This stance of resistance carries conceptual implications that bear directly on feminist research and that require recognition of the complex contributions of race and class (J. Butler, 1994) to diverse expressions of identity(ies), always in formation and always labile. The stability of the very categories of "man" and "woman" is questioned, as Leila Rupp and Verta Taylor show in their study of drag queens (2003).

Disabled Women. Recognition of differences among women also emerged with the disability rights movement and publication by feminist women who were themselves disabled. "Socially devalued, excluded from the playing field as women and invisible" (Gill, 1997, p. 96), disabled women were essentially depersonalized and degendered, sometimes even, regrettably, within feminist circles (Lubelska & Mathews, 1997, p. 135). A. Asch and Michelle Fine, reviewing the emergence of disabled women as a problematic issue for feminists, pointed out that even sympathetic research on women with disabilities tended to overlook women's multiple statuses and view women solely in terms of their disability (1992, p. 142; see also J. Morris, 1995).

Standpoint Research. Building on a loosely related set of theoretical positions by feminist scholars from several disciplines, standpoint research (much of that noted earlier can be thusly categorized) took up the feminist criticism of the absence of women from or marginalized women in research accounts and foregrounded women's knowledge as emergent from women's situated experiences (Harding, 1987, p. 184). Aptly summarized by Donna Haraway, whose influential work in the history of science undergirded standpoint thinking, "standpoints are cognitive-emotional-political achievements, crafted out of located social-historical-bodily experience—itself always constituted through fraught, noninnocent, discursive, material, collective practices" (1997, p. 304, n. 32).[6] Research and writing by sociologist Dorothy Smith, sociologist Patricia Hill Collins, political scientist Nancy Hartsock, and philosopher Sandra Harding dissolved the concept of essentialized, universalized woman, which was to be replaced by the ideas of a situated woman with experiences and knowledge specific to her place in the material division of labor and the racial stratification systems.

This implies that knowledge claims are socially located and that some social locations, especially those at the bottom of social and economic hierarchies, are better than others as starting points for seeking knowledge not only about those particular women but others as well. (This does *not* assume that the researcher's own life or group is the best starting point, nor does it assert the relativist position that all social locations are equally valuable for knowledge projects.) Although they have been grouped under the rubric of "standpoint," standpoint theorists are by no means identical, and in their differing versions they offer divergent approaches for qualitative researchers (Harding, 1997, p. 389). It is worthwhile to review these theorists while recognizing the inevitable violence done to subtle thought in such a brief review. (See Naples, 2003, pp. 37–88; Ramazanoglu with Holland, 2002, pp. 60–69; and Weeks, 1998, pp. 3–11 for useful summaries of standpoint theorists, their critics, and misinterpretations.)

Dorothy Smith focuses on women's standpoints and conceptualizes the everyday world as a problematic—that is, continually created, shaped, and known by women within it—and its organization, which is shaped by external material factors or textually mediated relations (1987, p. 91). Thus, the "everyday, everynight activities" of women's lives are at the center. To understand that world, the researcher must not objectify the woman, as traditionally would be done in sociology, which divides subject and object, researcher and participant. The researcher must be able to "work very differently than she is able to do with established sociological strategies of thinking and inquiry" (D. Smith, 1992, p. 96) that are not outside the relations of ruling. This requires a high degree of reflexivity from the researcher and a recognition of how feminist sociologists "participate as subjects in the relations of ruling" (p. 96). Smith's work with Alison Griffith (see D. Smith, 1987) discloses how she and her colleague found in their own discussions the effects of the North American discourse on mothering of the 1920s and 1930s (D. Smith, 1992, p. 97). Smith (in press) herself has fully explicated institutional ethnography, as this approach is called, as a method of inquiry. A growing cadre of researchers is utilizing and developing her ideas of institutional ethnography (M. Campbell, 1998, 2002; M. Campbell & Gregor, 2002; M. Campbell & Manicom, 1995). They attempt to discover how textually mediated relationships occur and are sustained in institutional settings, thus knitting an important link between the classic problem of micro and macro issues (D. Smith, 1997).

Patricia Hill Collins (1990) grounds her articulation of black women's standpoint in black women's material circumstances and political situation. Methodologically, this requires "an alternative epistemology whose 'criteria for substantiated knowledge' and 'methodological adequacy' will be compatible with the experiences and consciousness of Black women" (O'Leary, 1997, p. 62). Collins's writings and those of bell hooks (1984, 1990) moved feminist thinking and research in the direction of more particularized knowledge and away from any sense of the universal. Collins refuses to abandon situated standpoints and links the standpoint of black women with intersectionality, "the ability of social phenomena, race, class, and gender to mutually construct one another" (1998a, p. 205), but *always* within keen consideration for power and structural relations (1998a, pp. 201–228). This substantially amplifies standpoint theory. Thinking through this complexity is, as she recognizes, a "daunting task" (1998a, p. 225), and doing qualitative research within such a frame is equally daunting. Nevertheless, embracing new understandings of social complexity—and the locales of power relationships—is vital to the task of developing black feminist thought as critical social theory and new forms of visionary pragmatism (1998a, p. 228).

Sandra Harding, a philosopher, early recognized three types of feminist inquiry, which she termed "transitional epistemologies" (1987, p. 186). Harding's concerns about modernity and science in general, and science questions in feminism, led her to rest these types on how those modes of inquiry relate to traditional science and the problem of objectivity. (a) *Feminist empiricism* is of two types: first, "spontaneous feminist empiricism" (rigorous adherence to existing research norms and standards), and second, following Helen Longino (1990), "contextual empiricism" (recognition of the influence of social values and interests in science) (Harding, 1993, p. 53). (b) *Standpoint theory* "claims that all knowledge attempts are socially situated and that some of these objective social locations are better than others for knowledge projects" (Harding, 1993, p. 56). (c) *Postmodern theories* void the possibility of a feminist science in favor of the many and multiple stories women tell about the knowledge they have (Harding, 1987, p. 188). These are still useful ways to look at different styles of feminist qualitative work, but many projects display elements of several or all three as feminist researchers creatively borrow from multiple styles in their search "to escape damaging limitations of the dominant social relations and their schemes" (Harding, 1990, p. 101).

At issue here is the very form of science and whether "all possible science and epistemology . . . must be containable within modern, androcentric, Western, bourgeois forms" (Harding, 1990, p. 99). Harding argues that other forms of science are quite possible and likely. Her concerns with feminist research as a scientific activity and the attempt to generate "less false stories" prompted her to reject reliance on processes strictly governed by methodological rules and to argue that researchers critically examine their own personal and historical commitments with which they construct their work (1993, pp. 70–71). She points to the critical difference between sociological, cultural, and historical relativism (listening carefully to others' views) and judgmental relativism (abandoning any claims for adjudicating between different systems of beliefs and their social origins). Her solution is a posture of "strong objectivity" (1991).[7] Strong objectivity contrasts sharply with value-free objectivity and posits the interplay of the researcher and participant. Her contribution on "strong objectivity" is discussed in greater detail later in this chapter, under issues of validity.

Key to Nancy Hartsock's Marxist formulation of standpoint theory is her view that women's circumstances in the material order provide them with experiences that generate particular and privileged knowledge that reflects oppression and women's resistance (1983, 1985). Like the proletariat in Marxist theory, their knowledges provide a basis for criticism of domination and for political action (Hartsock, 1997b, p. 98). This does not assume that such knowledge is innately essential or that all women have the same experiences or, indeed, the same knowledge. Rather, Hartsock articulates the possibility of a "concrete multiplicity" of perspectives (1990, p. 171). Each of these constitutes a different world, and each represents a differential influence of power, a consideration that distinguishes standpoint theory from feminist empiricism (Hundleby, 1997, p. 41). Such knowledge is not merely individual but derives from "interaction of people and groups with each other" and is always transitional (Hundleby, 1997, p. 36). As Hartsock has observed, "the subjects who matter are not individual subjects, but collective subjects, or groups" (1997a, p. 371).

Standpoint theories and their implications for feminist qualitative research have not gone uncriticized. Some fretted that standpoint theories contained risks of relativism (Harding, 1987, p. 187), were overly simplistic (Hawkesworth, 1989), and raised issues around validity (Ramazanoglu, 1989). Criticisms arose about the potential for essentialism (Lemert, 1992, p. 69), neglect of traditions of knowledge among women of color (Collins, 1992), problems of evaluating accounts from different perspectives (Hekman, 1997b, p. 355; Longino, 1993, p. 104; Maynard, 1994b; Welton, 1997, p. 21), questions about understanding fragmented identities (Lemert, 1992, p. 68), and the potentially untenable basis of experience as a starting point for investigation if it is continually mediated and constructed from unconscious desire (Clough, 1993a). Others have argued that queer theory, with its destabilizing elements, undercut the possibility for standpoint thinking, which, in this view, presumed the replication of heterosexual categories (Clough, 1994, p. 144).

For their part, standpoint theorists have not been silent. Dorothy Smith's robust exchange with Patricia Clough highlighted the centrality of experience, the place of desire, and the primacy of text (Clough, 1993a, p. 169; Clough, 1993b; Smith, 1993). Clough argued that Smith had not gone far enough in deconstructing sociology as a dominant discourse of experience, a point Smith rejected, claiming that Clough's view is overly oriented to text and neglects experience. Susan Hekman's critical review of standpoint theory (1997a, 1997b) addressed questions of whether women's knowledge is privileged and how truth claims can be settled. Responses from Dorothy Smith (1997), Patricia Hill Collins (1997), Nancy Hartsock (1997a), and Sandra Harding (1997) show clearly that standpoint theories have been and are continually revised (Harding, 1997, p. 389). Feminist qualitative researchers thinking of using standpoint theories in their work must read these theorists carefully and in their latest version if they are to avoid misinterpretation and if they are to explore new connections between standpoint theories and postmodernism (Hirschman, 1997). Indeed, Sandra Harding has observed that "poststructural approaches have been especially helpful in enabling standpoint theories systematically to examine critically pluralities of power relations, of the sort indicated in the earlier discussion of gender as shaped by class, race and other historical cultural forces and how these are disseminated through 'discourses' that are both structural and symbolic" (1996, p. 451). Patricia Hill Collins, while warning about the corrosive effects of postmodern and deconstructive thought for black women's group authority and hence social action (1998b, p. 143), also points to postmodernism's powerful analytic tools as useful in challenging dominant discourses and the very rules of the game (1998b, p. 154).[8] Nancy Naples argues for a multidimensional approach to standpoint research that recognizes both the embodied aspects of standpoint theory and the multiplicity of perspectives that researchers and participants achieve in dynamic social and political environments (2003, pp. 197–198).

These controversies show no sign of abating (see the exchange between Walby, 2001a, 2001b Sprague, 2001, and Harding, 2001). At the same time, research using standpoint theory is abundant and wide ranging: ethnographic research in a Latino community (Eichenberger, 2002), sexual harassment (Dougherty, 2001), gendered relations in organizations (P. Y. Martin, 2001), African American women managers (Forbes, 2001), mothers with HIV (Tanenberg, 2000), backlash politics (Hawkesworth, 1999), and women's political practice (Naples, 1999; Naples & Sachs, 2000).

Postmodern and Deconstructive Thought. Complexities probably would have arisen in feminist qualitative research thanks to any of the themes discussed here, but multiple seductive intellectual aspects of postmodern and deconstructive thought honed complexities.[9] Indeed, in varying degrees postmodernism and deconstructionism are present in many of the foregoing themes, sometimes constituting the central stance (as in Judith Butler or Trinh T. Minh-ha's analyses), occasionally anticipating future problematics (as in Frankenberg's deconstruction of whiteness), and frequently reflecting trends and themes firmly set out by feminists not oriented to these modes of thought (as in Collins's analysis of black feminist thought or Lewin's research on lesbian cultures).

Concerned that it is difficult, if not impossible, to produce more than a partial story of women's lives in oppressive contexts, postmodern feminists regard "truth" as a destructive illusion. They see the world as a series of stories or texts that sustain the integration of power and oppression and actually "constitute us as subjects in a determinant order" (Hawkesworth, 1989, p. 549). Feminist researchers in anthropology, sociology, history, political science, cultural studies, and social studies of science as well as in the experimental wings in educational and nursing research (see the Australian journal *Nursing Inquiry*) have drawn on these ideas.

Carrying the imprint of feminist forebears from deconstruction and postmodernism (French feminists such as Irigaray and Cixous, and Foucault, Deleuze, Lyotard, and Baudrillard), feminist research in cultural studies stresses representation and text. This area is particularly complex for feminist researchers because some scholars also utilize Marxist theory from Althusser, French feminist theory, literary criticism (Abel, Christian, & Moglen, 1997), historical analysis, and psychoanalytic views (Lacan—not all feminists agree on Lacan's utility for feminist research; see Ferguson, 1993, p. 212, n. 3). In contrast to classical Marxist feminist studies of women, work, and social class such as Karen Sacks's investigation of hospital workers (1988) and Nona Glazer's analysis of race and class issues in the profession of nursing (1991), materialist feminist research in an Althusserian mode looks at ideology and its place in the shaping of subjectivity, desire, and authority (Clough, 1994, p. 75). Here enters the elusive and difficult issue of how desire is expressed in or inferred from cultural products ranging from ethnographic accounts through films. This confronts the feminist qualitative researcher with questions that go far beyond the easy recognition of intersubjectivity and invokes deeper cultural forms and questions.[10] (For a feminist materialist analysis of narrative, see Roman, 1992.)

These inquiries typically take the form of the analysis of cultural objects (film, etc.) and their meanings (Balsamo, 1993; Clough, 2000; de Lauretis, 1987; Denzin, 1992, p. 80; M. Morris, 1998). Included are textual analysis of these objects and the discourses surrounding them (Denzin, 1992, p. 81) and the "study of lived cultures and experiences which are shaped by the cultural meanings that circulate in everyday life" (Denzin, 1992, p. 81). This anticipates Valerie Walkerdine's (1995) important call for the analysis of understanding the media as the site of production of subjectivity.

Here will be found the voluminous and sophisticated feminist work in gender and science, wherein science, the sacred cow of the Enlightenment, modernity, and the contemporary moment, is dismembered as a culture to reveal its practices, discourses, and implications for control of women's lives (Haraway, 1991, 1997; E. Martin, 1987, 1999), including their health (Clarke & Olesen, 1999), and to provide avenues for resistance and/or intervention. Research about women's reproductive status, an issue central to feminist qualitative research from the very start and long productive of influential work (Ginzburg, 1998; Gordon, 1976; Joffe, 1995; Luker, 1984, 1996), has moved into the gender and science area (Balsamo, 1993, 1998; Casper, 1998; Hartouni, 1997; Mamo, 2002; Rapp, 1999). Because this work utilizes interdisciplinary borrowing, it is not easily classified. Studies often appear as hybrids and radical in terms of form, substance, and content, as, for instance, in Donna Haraway's deft interweaving of fiction, biology, history, humor, religion, and visual imagery in her feminist unpacking of technosciences (1997). These productions can be uncomfortable, threatening, and subversive, not only for male-dominated institutions such as science, but also for feminism itself.

These styles of thought continue to sharpen and enhance the emerging complexities: the sites (gender, race, and class) of where and how "women" are controlled, and how the multiple, shifting identities and selves that supplant earlier notions of a stable identity (self) are produced (Clough, 1998; Ferguson, 1993; Flax, 1990; Fraser, 1997, p. 381). They shift from binary frameworks to fluid conceptualizations of women's experiences, places, and spaces (Anzaldúa, 1987; Trinh, 1989, 1992). This move emphasized discourse, narrative and text, and experimental writing of standard research account presentations. Postmodernism and deconstructionism also called into question, as had standpoint theorists, feminist qualitative researchers' unexamined embrace of and adherence to traditional positivist qualitative approaches. Known as feminist empiricism, these were thought to forward the feminist agenda, but rather, the critics averred, merely repeated structures of oppression. The postmodern position produced an uneasy and anxious concern that the shifting sands of meaning, text, locale, and the continual proliferation of identities left no grounds for reform-oriented research, reinforced the status quo, erased structural power, and failed to address problems or to represent a cultural system (Benhabib, 1995; Collins, 1998b; Ebert, 1996; Hawkesworth, 1989; Johannsen, 1992; Maschia-Lees, Sharpe, & Cohen, 1989; Maynard, 1994a; Ramazanoglu, 1989). This impact raised questions that will be discussed more fully in the section on issues in feminist qualitative research.

Consequences of Growing Complexities

Writing from women of color, gay/lesbian/ queer theorists, postcolonial and globalization researchers, disabled women, standpoint theorists, and analysts persuaded to a postmodern stance opened and upended taken-for-granted conceptualizations of feminist research as well as critical key concepts such as experience, difference, and gender. Nowhere has this been more and more incisively pursued than in rethinking the topic of woman as research participant, a point discussed above, and in the destabilization of the conception of the feminist researcher as an all-knowing, unified, distanced, and context-free seeker of objectified knowledge whose very gender guarantees access to women's lives and knowledges.

The dissolution of this assumption took two directions. A first direction came with recognition that the researcher, too, has attributes; characteristics; a history; and gender, class, race, and social attributes that enter the research interaction. Yvonna Lincoln captured this in her comment that, "We are not single persons, but a multitude of possibilities any one of which might reveal itself in a specific field situation" (1997, p. 42). However, these possibilities are not static elements; they are, rather, reflections of the intersections of structures and practices. In this vein, borrowing from cultural studies, Ruth Frankenberg and Lata Mani articulated a conjecturalist approach that "firmly centers the analysis of subject formation and cultural practice within matrices of domination and subordination" and that "asserts that there is an effective but not determining relationship between subjects and their histories, a relationship that is complex, shifting and not 'free'" (1993, p. 306). Although they wrote in a postcolonial, deconstructionist vein, their conceptualization of a conjecturalist approach still has applicability to the dynamics of feminist research wherever found because it recognizes that both researcher and participant are positioned and are being positioned by virtue of history and context.

A number of feminist researchers have described the dynamics of conjecturalism in their work: Foregrounding her own trajectory from the working class to middle-class researcher, Diane Reay (1996a) reflected on class in her analysis of mothers' involvement in their children's primary schooling; Ann Phoenix's (1994) work on young people's social identities demonstrated that the taken-for-granted assumption that matching race and gender of interviewers is too simplistic; and Catherine Kohler Riessman (1987) pointed out how ethnic and class differences override gender in achieving understandings in interviews. Several researchers examined problems with their feminist views in their research: D. Millen (1997) examined potential problems when feminist researchers work with women not sympathetic to feminism, and Denise Cuthbert's (2000) study of non-Aboriginal women who adopted Aboriginal children necessitated a departure from feminist methodology. (In a related vein, see also Andrews, 2002; Gaskell & Eichler, 2001.)

A second direction recognized the impact of research on the feminist researcher in light of the multiple positions, selves, and identities at play in the research process. The subjectivity of the researcher, as much as that of the researched, became foregrounded, an indication of the blurring phenomenological and epistemological boundaries between the researcher and the researched. This did not go unmarked among more traditional researchers, who worried that the emphasis on subjectivity comes "too close . . . to a total elimination of intersubjective validation of description and explanation" (Komarovsky, 1988, p. 592; 1991). This issue led directly into questions about objectivity, "validity and reliability," and nature of the text and the voices in it, to be discussed shortly. In spite of these misgivings, feminists began to publish provocative and even influential work that reflected the blurring of these boundaries: Ruth Behar's (1993) analysis of her Mexican respondent's life and her own crosses multiple national, disciplinary, and personal borders, as do Carolyn Ellis's (1995) poignant account of a terminal illness and Patti Lather's (Lather & Smithies, 1997) work with HIV-positive women.

These views of the researcher's part in the research also bred a host of influential reflections that rethought the important issue of whether being an "insider" gave feminist researchers access to inside knowledge, a view that partook of Patricia Hill Collins's important conceptualization of "insider/outsider"(1986): Patricia Zavella's (1996) discovery that her Mexican background did not suffice in studying Mexican women doing factory work; Ellen Lewin's (1993) analysis of lesbian mothers showed the surpassing importance of motherhood over sexual orientation; Kirin Narayan (1997) asked how native is a "native" anthropologist?; Dorinne Kondo (1990) reported unexpected and sometimes unsettling experiences doing fieldwork in Japan around her Japanese identity; and Brackette Williams (1996) found that kinship as well as racial identity affected her research with elderly African Americans. These papers and others, such as Aihwa Ong's (1995) account of work with immigrant Chinese women and Nancy Naples's (1996) research with women in Iowa, problematized the idea that a feminist researcher who shared some attributes of a cultural background would, by virtue of that background, have full access to women's knowledge in that culture. They also troubled the hidden assumption that insider knowledge is unified, stable, and unchanging and the view that insider/outsider positions are fixed and unchanging (Naples, 2003, p. 40). Kath Weston's report of her struggles with these issues summarizes the problems: "A single body can not bridge that mythical divide between insider and outsider, researcher and researched. I am neither, in any simple way, and yet I am both" (1996, p. 275).

If the play of increasing complexities destabilized once-secure views of the researcher and those with whom research is done, it also generated critical examination of once-taken-for-granted concepts. Although feminist qualitative researchers working in the empiricist and standpoint frames still foreground women's reports of experience as key, there is growing recognition that merely focusing on those reports does not account for how that "experience" emerged (Morawski, 1990; Scott, 1991) and the characteristics of the material, historical, and social circumstances. One of the problems with taking experience in an unproblematic way is that the research, even standpoint research, though less prone to this problem, replicates rather than criticizes oppressive systems and carries a note of essentialism. Personal experience is not a self-authenticating claim to knowledge (O'Leary, 1997, p. 47), a point postmodernists raise in pointing to the risk of essentialism in unthinking reliance on experience. Historian Joan Scott comments, "Experience is at once already an interpretation and in need of interpretation" (1991, p. 779).

Feminist research in sociology and anthropology analyzes both women's representations of experience and the material, social, economic, or gendered conditions that articulate the experience: Arlie Hochschild's (1983) research on how flight attendants manage emotions (1983), Nona Glazer's (1997) examination of racism and classism in professional nursing, Nancy Scheper-Hughes's (1992) exploration of motherhood and poverty in northeastern Brazil, and Jennifer Pierce's (1995) ethnographic study of how legal assistants play a part in the production of their oppression in law firms. Historian Linda Kerber's (1998) analysis of women's legal obligations as well as their rights also falls into this category.

The recognition of difference, a conceptual move that pulled feminist thinkers and researchers away from the view of a shared gynocentric identity, surfaced in the dynamics of trends just discussed but very quickly gave way to concerns about the almost unassailable nature of the concept and whether its use led to an androcentric or imperialistic "othering" (Felski, 1997; hooks, 1990). Arguing for the use of such concepts as hybridity, creolization, and metissage, Rita Felski (1997) claims that these metaphors "not only recognize differences within the subject, fracturing and complicating holistic notions of identity, but also address connections between subjects by recognizing affiliations, cross-pollinations, echoes, and repetitions, thereby unseating difference from a position of absolute privilege" (p. 12).

Theorist Nancy Tuana enunciated a balance of possible common interests and observable differences in a way that would allow feminist qualitative researchers to grapple with these issues in their work:

> It is more realistic to expect pluralities of experiences that are related through various intersections or resemblances of some of the experiences of various women to some of the experiences of others. In other words, we are less likely to find a common core of shared experiences that are immune to economic conditions, cultural imperatives, etc., than a family of resemblances with a continuum of similarities, which allows for significant differences between the experience of, for example, an upper-class white American woman and an Indian woman from the lowest caste. (1993, p. 283)

While echoing much of this thinking, bell hooks (1990) and Patricia Hill Collins (1990) nevertheless reminded feminist researchers that identity cannot be dropped entirely. Rather, they see differences as autonomous, not fragmented, producing knowledge that accepts "the existence of, and possible solidarity with, knowledges from other standpoints" (O'Leary, 1997, p. 63). These views reflect Gadamer's little-recognized concept of the "fusion of horizons" "which carries double or dual vision and dialectical notions a step further than do standpoint epistemologies because it indicates a transcendent third and new view or synthesis" (Nielsen, 1990, p. 29).

Gender, the workhorse concept of feminist theory and research, also has undergone changes that make contemporary use of this concept much more complex and differentiated than at the outset of the "second wave." Theoretical insights going as far back as Suzanne Kessler and Wendy McKenna's classic ethnomethodological framing of gender (1978), including Judith Butler's philosophical outline of gender as performative (1990) and Judith Lorber's argument that gender is wholly constructed (1994, p. 5), shifted research possibilities. Whereas in an earlier time, work on gender differences looked for explanations or characteristics of autonomous individuals (Gilligan, 1982), now production and realization of gender in a complex matrix of material, racial, and historical circumstances become the research foci. Differences among women as well as similarities between men and women are acknowledged (Brabeck, 1996; Lykes, 1994). (Gender as causal explanation and as analytic category and the implications for research are examined in the exchange between Hawkesworth, 1997a, and McKenna and Kessler, 1997; Scott, 1997; S. G. Smith, 1997; and Connell, 1997; and the reply from Hawkesworth, 1997b.) Global ethnography also has stimulated reconsideration of gender (Poster, 2002).

Issues and Tensions

The shifting currents depicted earlier emphasize and alter tensions to produce new issues about the conduct of the research, including new worries about ethics. Whereas in an earlier era, concerns about the research enterprise tended to reflect traditional worries about the qualitative research enterprise (how to manage "bias," what about validity, etc.), the newer worries display uneasiness about voice, the text, and ethical conduct. Feminist empiricists and those working within one of the standpoint frameworks are apt to share all these concerns, whereas those who pursue a deconstructionist path are less likely to worry about bias and validity and more about voice and text, and about key issues in representation, although there are important exceptions here (Lather & Smithies, 1997). There is a good deal of borrowing across these lines; hence, many grapple simultaneously with these issues because much remains to be articulated, particularly in work that experiments with writing, narrative, voice, and form.

Dissolving the distance between the researcher and those with whom the research is done and the recognition that both are labile, nonunitary subjects (Britzman, 1998, p. ix) steps beyond traditional criticisms about researcher bias (Denzin, 1992, pp. 49–52; Huber, 1973) and leads to strong arguments for "strongly reflexive" accounts about the researcher's part (Fine, 1992a; Holland & Ramazanoglu, 1994; Phoenix, 1994; Warren, 1988) and reflections from the participants (Appleby, 1997), but Susan Speer (2002) argues that many feminist researchers do not yet have the skills to do reflexivity well.

What Nancy Scheper-Hughes called "the cultural self" that all researchers take into their work (1992) is not a troublesome element to be eradicated or controlled, but a set of resources. Indeed, Susan Krieger (1991) early argued that utilization of the self was fundamental to qualitative work. If the researcher is sufficiently reflexive about her project, she can evoke these resources to guide gathering, creating, and interpreting her own behavior (Casper, 1997; Daniels, 1983; J. Stacey, 1998). Leslie Rebecca Bloom (1998, p. 41) goes further to urge that researchers and their participants work out how they will communicate and that this be part of research account. Nevertheless, researcher reflexivity needs to be tempered with acute awareness as to the contributions of hidden or unrecognized elements in the researchers' background. Sherry Gorelick identifies potential problems when inductivist feminist researchers who espouse a Marxist framework "fail to take account of the hidden structure of oppression (the research participant is not omniscient) and the hidden relations of oppression (the participant may be ignorant of her relative privilege over and difference from other women)" (1991, p. 461). Nancy Scheper-Hughes (1983) also warned about feminists unwittingly replicating androcentric perspectives in their work. Thus, there is recognition that both researcher and participant produce interpretations that are "the data" (Diaz, 2002).

Forgoing traditional and rigid ideas about objectivity, feminist researchers have opened new spaces to consider the enduring question of bias (Cannon, Higginbotham, & Leung, 1991). Arguing that observers' experiences can be useful, Sandra Harding suggests a strategy of "strong objectivity" that takes researchers as well as those researched as the focus of critical, causal, scientific explanations (1993, p. 71) and calls for critical examination of the researcher's social location (1996, 1998). She notes, "Strong objectivity requires that we investigate the relation between subject and object rather than deny the existence of, or seek unilateral control over, this relation" (1991, p. 152). She asks that the participants in the inquiry be seen by the feminist researcher as "gazing back" and that the researcher take their view in looking at her own socially situated project.[11] This goes beyond mere reflection on the conduct of the research and demands a steady, uncomfortable assessment of the interpersonal and interstitial knowledge-producing dynamics of qualitative research. As Janet Holland and Caroline Ramazanoglu illustrate in their research on young women's sexuality, there is no way to neutralize the social nature of interpretation. They argue:

> Feminist researchers can only try to explain the grounds on which selective interpretations has been made by making explicit the processes of decision making which produce the interpretation and the logic of the method on which these decisions are based. This entails acknowledging complexity and contradiction which may be beyond the researchers' experience, and recognizing the possibility of silences and absences in their data. (Holland & Ramazanoglu, 1994, p. 133)[12]

Donna Haraway urges going beyond even strong objectivity to the exercise of diffracting, which turns the lenses with which researchers view phenomena to show multiple fresh combinations and possibilities (1997, p. 16).

Rescuing feminist objectivity from being in thrall to classical positivist definitions and from being lost in an inchoate relativism (all views are equal), Donna Haraway (1988) recognizes the merging of researcher and participant to foreground a position of situated knowledge, accountability (the necessity to avoid reproducing oppressive views of women), and partial truths. In Haraway's apt and oft-quoted phrase, "the view from nowhere" becomes "the view from somewhere," that of connected embodied, situated participants. (For an example of Haraway's conceptualization of objectivity in use, see Kum-Kum Bhavani's [1994] research on young, working-class people in Britain.)

Related to the question of objectivity is the old question of the degree to which the account reflects or depicts that which the researcher and her participants have mutually constructed, a question which goes to the heart of whether feminist qualitative research will be deemed credible, a potent question if the research addresses key issues in women's lives. Feminist qualitative researchers address or worry about validity (Holland & Ramazanoglu, 1995), also known in more recent incarnations as "trustworthiness" in different ways, depending on how researchers frame their approaches (Denzin, 1997, pp. 1–14). For those who work in a traditional vein reflecting the positivist origins of social science (there is a reality to be discovered), the search for validity will turn to well-established techniques. Those who disdain the positivistic origins, but nevertheless believe that ways of achieving validity that reflect the nature of qualitative work are possible, seek out ways to establish credibility by such strategies as audit trails and member "validation," techniques that reflect their postpositivist views but that do not hold out hard and fast criteria for according "authenticity" (Lincoln & Guba, 1985; K. Manning, 1997). Feminist qualitative researchers who worry about whether their research will respect or appreciate those with whom they work, and, indeed, may transform those others into another version of themselves, reach for something new, as in Laurel Richardson's manifesto (1993, p. 695):

> I challenge different kinds of validity and call for different kinds of science practices. The science practice I model is a feminist-postmodernist one. It blurs genres, probes lived experiences, enacts science, creates a female imagery, breaks down dualisms, inscribes female labor and emotional response as valid, deconstructs the myth of an emotion-free social science, and makes a space for partiality, self-reflexivity, tension and difference.

Among new ways of imagining validity (Denzin, 1997, pp. 9–14; Scheurich, 1997, pp. 88–92), Patti Lather's transgressive validity is the most completely worked out feminist model, one that calls for a subversive move ("retaining the term to circulate and break with the signs that code it," 1993, p. 674) in a feminist deconstructionist mode. To ensure capturing differences but within a transformative space that can lead to a critical political agenda, she rests transgressive validity on four subtypes, here highly condensed: (a) ironic validity, which attends to the problems in representation; (b) paralogical validity, which seeks out differences, oppositions, and uncertainties; (c) rhizomatic validity, which counters authority with multiple sites; and (b) voluptuous validity, which deliberately seeks excess and authority via self-engagement and reflexivity (1993, pp. 685–686). Whether even in these bold steps Lather has gone far enough to overcome what some see as the almost obdurate problem in legitimation (the inevitable replication of researcher within the analyzed views of the researched) (Scheurich, 1997, p. 90), this formulation nevertheless retains a feminist emancipatory stance while providing leads for feminist qualitative researchers to work out and work on the inherent problems in validity. Lather's research with Chris Smithies on women with AIDS illustrates these strategies of validity and challenges feminist qualitative researchers (1997).

Problems of Voice, Reflexivity, and Text

Irrespective of the approach they take, feminist qualitative researchers continue to worry about the question of voice and the nature of the account, which, as William Tierney and Yvonna Lincoln argue in *Representation and the Text*, now "comes under renewed scrutiny" (1997, p. viii), a position echoed in Rosanna Hertz's *Reflexivity and Voice* (1997). This concern goes back to the earliest beginnings of feminist research and the attempts, noted earlier in this chapter, to find and express women's voices. When women of color and postcolonial critics raised concerns about how participants' voices are to be heard, with what authority and in what form, they sharpened and extended this issue. Within these questions lie anxiety-provoking matters of whether the account will only replicate hierarchical conditions found in parent disciplines, such as sociology (D. Smith, 1989, p. 43) and the difficult problems of translating private matters from women's lives into the potentially oppressive and distorting frames of social science (Ribbens & Edwards, 1998). To address this, some feminist researchers have articulated strategies involving voice-centered relational methods (Mauthner & Doucet, 1998), reconstructing research narratives (Birch, 1998), and writing the voices of the less powerful (Standing, 1998).

How to make women's voices heard without exploiting or distorting those voices is also a vexatious question. When literary devices are borrowed to express voice, hidden problems of control may occur (Maschia-Lees et al., 1989, p. 30). Even though researchers and participants both shape the flow of silences and comments, the researcher, who writes up the account and has responsibility for the text, remains in the more powerful position (Lincoln, 1997; Phoenix, 1994; J. Stacey, 1998). Merely letting the tape recorder run to present the respondent's voice does not overcome the problem of representation, because the respondent's comments are already mediated when they are made in the interview (Lewin, 1991). Even taking the account back for comment or as simple courtesy, or shaping the account with respondents, may not work, as J. Acker, Barry, and Esseveld (1991) found in their participatory project. Women wanted them to do the interpreting. Moreover, the choice of audience shapes how voice is found and fashioned (Kincheloe, 1997; Lincoln, 1993, 1997).[13] Michelle Fine raises serious questions about voices (use of pieces of narrative, taking individual voices to reflect group ideas, assuming that voices are free of power relations, failing to make clear the researcher's own position in relationship to the voices or becoming a "ventriloquist"). She forcefully urges feminist researchers to "articulate how, how not, and within what limits voices are framed and used (1992b, pp. 217–219).[14] She also (personal communication) points to the tension between treating voices as if they were untouched by ideology, hegemony, or interpretation and critically analyzing the contexts in which they arise and the hegemonic pressures out of which they are squeezed. The issue of voice leads into the form, nature, and content of the account. Experimental writing, based on research or on highly reflexive and insightful interpretations, is growing. Some manipulate or work within the printed text, while others opt for performances of the account.

Experimentation blooms.[15] Marjorie Wolf presents three versions of voices from her anthropological fieldwork in Taiwan: a piece of fiction, her anthropological field notes, and a social science article (1992). Ruth Behar (1993) explodes the traditional anthropological form of life history to intertwine her own voice with that of her cocreator in an extended double voiced text. Patti Lather and Chris Smithies (1997) use a split-page textual format to present their research, their respondents' views, and their own reflections on themselves and their research. Laurel Richardson (1997) continues to pioneer writing and presenting sociological poetry and tales. (See also Richardson & St. Pierre, Volume 2, Chapter 15.) Carolyn Ellis's accounts (1995), both presented and written, deal with emotionally difficult topics such as an abortion, death in the family, an experience with black-white relations, and the death of her partner; this work has given research in the sociology of emotions a decidedly experimental and feminist tone. "Auto-ethnography," Ellis's term for this form, locates the researcher's deeply personal and emotional experiences as topics in a context related to larger social issues. Here, the personal, biographical, political, and social are interwoven with the autoethnography, which in turn illuminates them (Denzin, 1997, p. 200) as in Laura Ellingson's reflexive account of communications within a medical setting (1998). These stances link the personal and political, and they undercut criticisms that personal reflections are merely solipsistic (Patai, 1994). As autoethnography has matured (Ellis & Bochner, 1996) researchers have developed careful reflections with which to evaluate this new style of ethnographic work (see *Qualitative Inquiry*, Vol. 6, No. 2, 2000, and R. H. Brown, 1998).

At the same time, some feminists, borrowing from avant-garde art (Wheeler, 2003), create performance pieces, dramatic readings, or plays performed at academic conferences. This is related to feminist analysis of performance theory, where the key question is "How can the consideration of the engendered live body in performance provide a site for possible feminist subversions, making performance a vital paradigm for any study of social relations?" (Case & Abbitt, 2004, p. 937). The work of the early 1990s (Michal McCall and Howard Becker on the art world, 1990; the late Marianne Paget's poignant play, based on her own research, about a woman with an incorrect cancer diagnosis, 1990; Jackie Orr's performance of a panic diary, 1993) continues. Anthropologist Dorinne Kondo's play *Dis(Graceful) Conduct*, about sexual and racial harassment in the academy, embraces a paradigm that shifts "away from the purely textual to the performative, the evanescent, the nondiscursive, the collaborative" and attempts to intervene in another register in what she calls "powerfully engaging modes quite different from conventional academic prose" (1995, p. 51). Canadian social scientists (Gray & Sinding, 2002) who performed their research about women diagnosed with metastatic breast cancer with the women themselves also videotaped the performance, which allows showing it in many venues. They also discuss production of performance pieces. Performance pieces vary with regard to preparation and audience involvement (Denzin, 1997, pp. 90–125). Creating a performance piece of whatever type is not easy (Olesen, 1997). High literary skills and sensitivities are necessary if the piece is not to founder or be deemed sophomoric by audiences accustomed to the polished presentations in contemporary visual media. Because performance pieces are still developing, deploying them to reach new audiences or to display feminist research has yet to be fully explored, though Judith Stacey's candid insights into taking feminist research public suggest that performance pieces might be useful (2003, p. 28). In the meantime, thoughtful practitioners of performance and dramatic work have begun to examine how to evaluate such work (McWilliam, 1997; see also *Qualitative Inquiry*, Vol. 9, No. 2, 2003).

Ethics in Feminist Qualitative Research

Feminist qualitative researchers recognize and discuss ethical issues, such as privacy, consent, confidentiality, deceit, and deception, that also trouble the larger field.

They try to avoid harm of whatever sort (undue stress, unwanted publicity, loss of reputation, invasion of privacy) throughout the research, negotiating access, gathering and analyzing, and writing text (Ribbens & Edwards, 1998; D. Wolf, 1996). However, feminist writing on research ethics has moved beyond universalist positions in moral philosophy (duty ethics of principles, utilitarian ethics of consequences) to become more complex, emphasizing specificity and context and drawing on feminist ethics of care (Mauthner, Birch, Jessop, & Miller, 2002). Rosalind Edwards and Melanie Mauthner's (2002) helpful review of ethical models (deontological—based on unbreakable principles; consequential utilitarianism—based on consequences; virtue ethics of skills—based on situated negotiations; communitarian—based on ethics of care) shows the strengths and shortcomings of each and tensions among them. They suggest close attention to specifics of particular research contexts (pp. 20–28) as an ethical approach. This echoes Yvonna Lincoln's insight that standards for quality are now intertwined with ethical ones, for example, the demand that the researcher conduct and make explicit open and honest negotiations around gathering materials, analysis, and presentation (1995, p. 287). These are closely tied to issues of how and where knowledge is created, as are the enduring questions of privacy, confidentiality, disclosure, informed consent, and researcher "power."

Regarding privacy and confidentiality, few face having their empirical materials subpoenaed (Scarce, 2002), but regulations offering anyone access to such materials gathered in federally funded studies occasion renewed worries about assurance of privacy and confidentiality. Those who work on women's reproductive health, especially abortion; sexual activity, and orientation; experience with stigmatized illness or health conditions; and homeless women are particularly sensitive to these issues, though all feminist qualitative researchers face them.

The worries exist uneasily with concerns about deceit and about fully informing participants of research goals, strategies, and styles. The older qualitative or feminist literature treated informed consent as unproblematic, stable, and durable. However, some have questioned the very meaning of informed consent (who is consenting to what?) and pointed to the fact that consent may fade or alter, so that participants express curiosity, skepticism about, or resistance to the research at a later stage (Casper, 1997; Corrigan, 2003, pp. 784–786; Fine & Weis, 1996; May, 1980; T. Miller & Bell, 2002; see also Fine, Weis, Weseen, & Wong, 2000).

Although feminists rarely conduct covert research, there remain gray areas where the researcher may deliberately withhold or blur personal information (D. Wolf, 1996, pp. 11–12), or views on sex, religion, politics, money, social class, or race are lost in the complexities of interactions characterized by both participants' and researchers' mobile subjectivities and multiple realities. The former is a research strategy; the latter is characteristic of everyday social life. In both cases, the lack of information may influence the mutual construction of stories and representations.

Relationships with participants lie at the heart of feminist ethical concerns. Earlier, some believed that friendly relationships could occur (Oakley, 1981), but this quickly gave way to more distanced views. Feminist qualitative researchers became sensitive to ethical issues arising from concern for and even involvement with participating individuals. Janet Finch's (1984) early observation about researchers' unwitting manipulation of participants hungry for social contact anticipated Judith Stacey's widely cited paper (1988) and Lila Abu-Lughod's (1990) analysis of contradictions in feminist qualitative methodology. Stacey raised the uncomfortable question of getting information from respondents as a means to an end, along with the difficult compromises that may be involved in promising respondents control over the report. These issues characterize qualitative work, which can never resolve all ethical dilemmas that arise (Wheatley, 1994).

Other ethical dilemmas abound, among them the hazard of "stealing women's words" (Opie, 1992; Reay, 1996b), negotiating meanings with participants (Jones, 1997), "validating" or challenging women's taken-for-granted views when they do not accord with feminist perspectives (Kitzinger & Wilkinson, 1997), research where professional and research roles may conflict (Bell & Nutt, 2002; Field, 1991), blurred boundaries between research and counseling (Birch & Miller, 2000), how to represent findings in respondents' own words (S. A. Freeman & Lips, 2002; Skeggs, 1995b).

The view, long held in feminist research, that the researcher occupies a more powerful position continues to be worrisome. However, closer examination of research relations has recognized that the researcher's "power" is often only partial (Ong, 1995), illusory (D. Wolf, 1996; Viswesweran, 1994), tenuous (J. Stacey, 1998; D. Wolf, 1996, p. 36), and confused with researcher responsibility (Bloom, 1998, p. 35), even though the researcher may be more powerfully positioned when out of the field, because she usually will write the account (Luff, 1999).

These ethical issues and those of voice and account emerge even more vividly in activist studies, where researchers and participants collaborate on topics of concern in their lives and worlds. Participatory research (fully discussed in McKemmis & Taggart, Volume 2, Chapter 10) confronts both researchers and participants-who-are-also-researchers with challenges about women's knowledge, representations of women, modes of gathering empirical materials, analysis, interpretation and writing the account, and relationships between and among the collaborating parties. Although it is not as widely done as might be hoped, nevertheless there is a growing body of research projects and thoughtful discussion of such issues as othering and dissemination (Lykes, 1997). Linda Light and Nancy Kleiber's (1981) early study of a Vancouver women's health collective describes their conversion from traditional field workers to coresearchers with the members of the women's health collective and the difficulties of closing the distance between researchers and participants both fully engaged in the research. Questions of the ownership of the research materials also arise (Renzetti, 1997). Issues of power remain, as collaborative research does not dissolve competing interests (Lykes, 1989, p. 179). Alice McIntyre and M. Brinton Lykes (1998) urge feminist participatory action researchers to exercise reflexivity to interrogate power, privilege, and multiple hierarchies.

In a certain sense, participants are always "doing" research, for they, along with researchers, construct the meanings that are interpreted and turned into "findings." Whereas in customary research, the researcher frames interpretations, in participatory action research researchers and participants undertake this together (Cancian, 1996; Craddock & Reid, 1993). This raises issues of evaluation (Lykes, 1997) and management of distortion. Based on her collaborative work, Maria Mies's conceptualization of "conscious partiality," achieved through partial identification with research participants, creates a critical conceptual distance between the researcher and participants dialectically to facilitate correction of distortions on both sides (Mies, 1993, p. 68; Skeggs, 1994).

Feminist Research on Ethics. Feminist research on ethics has been done on (a) questions referential to larger issues of moral beingness and (b) practices and situations in health care. Research on moral beingness has a long history reaching back to Carol Gilligan's well-known and controversial study of young girls' moral development (Gilligan, 1982; see also Benhabib, 1987; Brabeck, 1996; Koehn, 1998; Larrabee, 1993). This history overlaps complex arguments around the question of care (Larrabee, 1993; R. C. Manning, 1992; Tronto, 1993) and the substantial conceptual and empirical feminist literature on caregiving (Cancian et al., 2000; Noddings, 2002). Ideas from that literature have filtered into discussions of research ethics.

Theorists and researchers have shifted away from the view that ethical or moral behavior is inherent in gender (the essentialist view that women are "natural" carers) to the social construction of gender, which recognizes that a trait such as caring emerges from an interaction between the individual and the milieu (Seigfried, 1996, p. 205). These newer positions on an ethic of care go beyond a focus on personal relationships in the private sphere to concerns with the just community (Seigfried, 1996, p. 210) and the potential for transforming society in the public sphere (Tronto, 1993, pp. 96–97). (See also Walker, 1998; DesAutels & Wright, 2001; Fiore & Nelson, 2003.)

Feminist researchers' long-standing concerns about and work on ethical (or nonethical) treatment of women in health care systems have carried into inquiries on aspects of new technologies, such as assisted reproduction and genetic screening, and into the regrettably enduring problems of equitable care for elderly, poor women of all ethnic groups (Holmes & Purdy, 1992; Sherwin, 1992; Tong, 1997).

Unrealized Agendas

In the early millennial moment, feminist qualitative research remains a complex, diverse, and highly energized enterprise. There is no single approach, nor can any approach claim dominance or a privileged position. Given the substantive range, theoretical complexity, and empirical difficulties, the multiplicity of voices is apt. None of these approaches is beyond criticism, which could and should sharpen and improve them. Feminists should celebrate, not condemn, the diversity and multiplicity of these approaches. The strained binary that posed rigid adherence to traditional methods against the view that all competing knowledge claims are valid should be abandoned. More profitable and realistic are attempts, as theorist Joan Alway (1995) has argued, "to try to produce less false, less partial and less perverse representations without making any claims about what is absolutely and always true" (p. 225). This posture rests on the important assumption that women in specific contexts are best suited to help develop presentations of their lives, contexts that are located in specific structures and historical-material moments. This point is particularly critical as feminists work to understand—through text, discourses, and encounters with women—how their lives are contextualized and framed.

Unrealized agendas remain. Foremost among these is deeper exploration of how race, class, and gender emerge, interlock, and achieve their various effects. Patricia Hill Collins's analysis of "real mothers" (1999); Yen Le Espiritu's (1997) research on gender-based immigration, labor policies, and labor conditions in 19th- and 20th-century America; and Sheila Allen's (1994) discussion of race, ethnicity, and nationality accomplish this critical task. Complicating this agenda is the still-unfinished job of problematizing whiteness and its links to privilege, discussed earlier, and the realization of different agendas, contexts, and dynamics for women of color and varying social status. A promising start is Dorothy Smith's (1997) proposal to utilize the metaphor of the map to discover the ongoing ways by which people coordinate their activities, particularly "those forms of social organization and relations that connect up multiple and various sites of experience" (p. 175). Olivia Espin's (1995) analysis of racism and sexuality in immigrant women's narratives does this.

Much remains to be done to open traditional approaches of data gathering, analysis, and representation to experimental moves, though some feminist researchers are appreciative of the new moves.[16] However, this poses two issues for all feminist qualitative researchers. First is the obdurate necessity to attend to representation, voice, and text in ways that avoid replication of the researcher and instead display participants' representations. Simply presenting research materials or findings in new or shocking ways will not resolve this difficulty. It speaks to the ethical and analytic difficulties inherent as researcher and participant engage in the mutual creation of interpretations that the researcher usually brings to the fore. Researchers cannot avoid responsibility for the account, the text, and the voices.

Patricia Clough (1993a) further complicates this point: "The textuality never refers to a text, but to the processes of desire elicited and repressed, projected and interjected in the activity of reading and writing" (p. 175). Apt though this is, it presents an even much more elusive question than choosing and positioning voices and texts, and it merits much more thoughtful attention.

A second and parallel task is how to address overarching issues of credibility or, put another way, how to indicate that the claims produced are less false, less perverse, and less partial, without falling back into positivist standards that measure acceptability of knowledge in terms of some ideal, unchanging body of knowledge. One way forward, proposed by authors reviewed here, is scrupulous and open interrogation of the feminist researcher's own postures, views, and practices, turning back on herself the very lenses with which she is scrutinizing the lives of the women with which she works, always looking for tensions, contradictions, and complicity (Humphries, 1997, p. 7). Uncomfortable though this may be, it is a strategy both for feminist qualitative researchers who reach for new and experimental approaches and for those who take more familiar paths. Such unremitting reflexivity is not without difficulties: Rachel Wasserfall (1997) reveals deep and tension-laden differences between herself and her participants; Rebecca Lawthom (1997) discloses problems in her work as a feminist researcher in nonfeminist research; and Kathy Davis and Ine Gremmen (1998) found that feminist ideals sometimes can stand in the way of doing feminist research.

The Influence of Contexts on Agendas

It is important to note some contexts that shape and are shaped by feminist qualitative research agendas.

Academic Life. The traditional structure of academic life—at least in the United States—has influenced feminist qualitative research, and not always in the direction of transformations. Ellen Messer-Davidow's (2002) extended and critical account of feminist scholarship within the academy argues that the very structures it sought to reform shaped it. Her incisive historical inquiry addresses Dorothy Smith's earlier question, "What is it about the academy that undermines and reworks the project of claiming it for women in general?" (1999, p. 228). Carolyn Dever's (2004) skeptical exploration of "the boundaries with which academic feminists have constructed their work" (p. xvi) raises fundamental issues about exclusivity and about canonization of feminist theory and knowledge that undergird research.

Whereas much of the early impetus for reform and transformation emerged outside the academy, one finds major feminist research energies of recent decades in such traditional departments as anthropology, sociology, psychology, political science, philosophy, history, interdisciplinary women's studies, and cultural studies and in such professional programs as education, nursing, and social work, where it is not surprising to read thoughtful research and essays on issues discussed in this chapter such as quality of the work and the utility of standpoint theory. Dispersal of feminist qualitative research as well as the feminisms that support it results in highly variegated approaches and levels of maturity. It also means differential reception of qualitative feminist work, ranging from dismissal or hostility to admiration if well, truly, and brilliantly done (depending on evaluators' predilection for traditional or experimental approaches). How these responses translate into job recruitment, tenure review, and acceptance of publications and research funding is a crucial question. Francesca Cancian's (1996, pp. 198–204) academic colleagues doing activist participatory research revealed conflicts and tensions with other colleagues that necessitated working out strategies to enable them to continue such work while trying to succeed academically. Still, as Margaret Randall (2004) observed, "Academics capable of rigorous scholarship and motivated to test that scholarship in activist politics are in a privileged position with regard to exercising the social change so necessary to the survival of humankind"(p. 23).

A different but intriguing issue arises when other scholars borrow feminist research strategies in qualitative feminist research, some taken from traditional qualitative approaches and then modified, others newly created, thus creating a problem of differentiating feminist work from these other projects. Some feminist qualitative researchers would argue that criteria for feminist work (see footnote 1) would differentiate methodologically similar qualitative projects from feminist research. The question of whether feminist qualitative research can transform traditional disciplines is lodged in the complexities of feminist research and the structural nature of the site. Sectors of sociology and psychology tenaciously hold positivistic outlooks along with diverse theoretical views that blunt or facilitate feminist transformation (J. Stacey & Thorne, 1985). Whether such transformative research stances as Dorothy Smith's radical critique of sociology (1974, 1989, 1990a, 1990b; Collins, 1992) or Patricia Hill Collins's concerns about the impact of dualistic thought and the tendency to perpetuate racism (1986, 1990) will reshape sociology remains to be seen. Or will changes come from more deconstructive approaches of abandoning ethnography and focusing on "re-readings of representations in every form of information processsing," which Patricia Clough (1998, p. 137) urges, or Ann Game's embrace of discourses rather than the focus on "the social" (1991, p. 47)?

Within anthropology, Ruth Behar (1993) and Lila Abu-Lughod (1990) argue that influential themes discussed earlier (dissolution of self/other, subject/object boundaries) that are fundamental to traditional ethnographic approaches may liberate the discipline from its colonial and colonizing past (Behar, 1993, p. 302). In psychology, Michelle Fine and Susan Merle Gordon (1992, p. 23) urge that feminist psychologists work in the space between the personal and the political to reconstitute psychology. They urge activist research,[17] while Mary Gergen (2001) formulates a constructionist, postmodern agenda for revisioning psychology. Noting that feminists in psychology have made local and partial alterations to established methods rather than creating a programmatic metatheory, Jill Morawski (1994) foresees the basis for radically new forms of psychological inquiry even though feminist psychology remains in transition.

It is too early to detect the transformative potential of feminist cultural studies and the vital multidisciplined social studies of science. Here, as in other disciplinary sites, the plight of the fiscally strained academic department will shape feminist qualitative research. Downsized departments or programs relying on part-time faculty are not fertile arenas for experimental or even traditional transformative work. In all these contexts, the balance of demands from home, family, and career is an obdurate "every day, every night issue" (to use Dorothy Smith's felicitous phrase) that confronts feminist qualitative researchers who are serious about research for women and its transformative potentials. Counterbalancing these issues is the strong presence of established feminist researchers who take mentoring seriously and who connect politically to other scholars, feminist or not, and to other feminists, academic or not.

Parochialism and Publishing Practices. For at least the last two decades and with no apparent end in sight, publishers have brought out thousands of feminist titles—theoretical, empirical, experimental, and methodological (Messer-Davidow, 2002). This abundance has nourished the emergence and growing complexity of qualitative feminist research. As positive as this is, given the relatively limited number of offerings three decades ago, it nevertheless is worrisome because much of this often very sophisticated literature, which includes work by feminists from countries other than the United States and the United Kingdom, is published in English. Translation difficulties and marketing pressures make English language publication necessary (Maynard, 1996; Meaghan Morris, personal communication; Schiffrin, 1998).[18] It is not surprising that there are undifferentiated views and limited or nonexistent understandings of feminist research done outside Westernized, bureaucratized societies.

Fortunately, different perspectives—such as those of postcolonial, Marxist feminists—come through these publications to undercut Westernizing and homogenizing assumptions about "women" anywhere and everywhere. The leading English-language feminist journals increasingly publish essays from researchers in Asia, Africa, Latin America, the Arab Middle East, and Eastern Europe. Special issues featuring international researchers are common. Leading university and trade presses that publish feminist books frequently have non-U.S. feminists on their lists.[19] However, even when published in English, a feminist research-oriented monograph such as Cynthia Nelson and Soraya Altorki's Arab Regional Women's Studies Workshop (1997) may not easily reach interested Western feminists if it is published outside the United States or Great Britain.

Some, but not enough, of that work is heard at international conferences such as the International Congresses on Women's Health Issues, which meet biannually in such countries as New Zealand, Denmark, Botswana, Thailand, Egypt, and South Korea and draw substantial numbers of international participants. In sum, greater access to international researchers' work balances English-language publications and the dominance of English-language feminism, particularly around international feminist concerns about the problems and complexities of globalization. Given the increasing complexity in feminist qualitative research, some of which derives from postcolonial feminist thinking, new approaches and tactics from international scholars will attract attention not only among open-minded English language feminist researchers but also among publishers with an eye to profitable publication in an era when the economics of publishing are highly problematic.

Qualitative researchers who wish to go beyond research in the Anglophone world increasingly find valuable feminist talk lists and Web sites that offer information about international feminist work, conferences, and publications. Many originate outside the United States or Great Britain. Limited space here prohibits listing even a small proportion of this abundance, but a powerful search engine will produce a cornucopia of worthwhile addresses and sites. Particularly notable among these burgeoning resources that redress Westernized parochialism in feminist research is the Sociologists for Women in Society talk list, where Judith Lorber, herself a leading feminist qualitative researcher, regularly shares such information. Regrettably, computer and Internet resources may not be readily available to all feminist qualitative researchers, particularly those in disadvantaged countries.

Conclusion

If anything, feminist qualitative research is stronger than in the past because theorists and researchers both critically examine its foundations, even as they try new research approaches, both experimental and traditional. Above all, they are much more self-conscious, aware of and sensitive to issues in the formulation and conduct of research. More sophisticated approaches and more incisive understandings enable feminists to grapple with the innumerable problems in women's lives, contexts, and situations in the hope of achieving, if not emancipation, at least some modest intervention and transformation. Yet there is more to do, as many of the authors cited in this chapter make clear. Given the diversity and complexity of feminist qualitative research, it is not likely that any orthodoxy—experimental or traditional—will prevail; nor, in my opinion, should it.

Feminist researchers have articulated thoughtful and incisive directions on feminist research and the potential for change or transformation. Judith Stacey outlined the difficulties of taking feminist work public: "We must take our work public with extraordinary levels of reflexivity, caution and semiotic and rhetorical sophistication" (2003, p. 28). Barbara Laslett and Johanna Brenner (2001) urged feminist researchers to recognize the way higher education institutions work (p. 1233) while noting that "we will need new strategies that correspond to new opportunities as well as the difficulties of these times" (p. 1234). Mary Anglin (2003, p. 3), chair of the Association for Feminist Anthropology of the American Anthropological Association (2003–2005), renewed the call for feminists to reconsider how to bridge academic theories/research with gender equity and social justice.

I conclude with a statement Adele Clarke and I published in 1999:

> It is important to recognize that knowledge production is continually dynamic—new frames open which give way to others which in turn open again and again. Moreover, knowledges are only partial. Some may find these views discomfiting and see in them a slippery slope of ceaseless constructions with no sure footing for action of whatever sort. It is not that there is no platform for action, reform, transformation or emancipation, but that

> the platforms are transitory. If one's work is overturned or altered by another researcher with a different, more effective approach, then one should rejoice and move on. . . . What is important for concerned feminists is that new topics, issues of concerns and matters for feminist inquiry are continually produced and demand attention to yield a more nuanced understanding of action on critical issues. (Olesen & Clarke, 1999, p. 356)[20]

Early millennial feminist qualitative research, outlined far too sketchily here because of space limitations, offers strategies to lay foundations for action on critical projects, large and small, to realize social justice in different feminist versions, a challenge that thoughtful feminists must accept and carry forward. The range of problems is too great and the issues are too urgent to do otherwise. As poet and activist Margaret Randall declared in her realistic plenary talk to the Winter, 2004, Sociologists for Women in Society meeting, "our mission . . . must be nothing short of rethinking and reworking our future" (Randall, 2004, p. 23).

Accepting this, what can feminist qualitative researchers expect? Ruth Chance, a feminist and legendary director of the Rosenberg Foundation (1958–1974), wisely and realistically observed:

> I think the more modest you are about what you are doing, the better off you'll be. You can count on it that time is going to upset your solutions, and that a period of great ferment and experimentation will be followed by one of examination to see what should be absorbed or modified or rejected . . . but that shouldn't discourage us from acting on the issues as we see them at a given time. The swing of the pendulum will come and maybe you'll start all over again, but it does seem to inch us forward in understanding how complex and remote solutions are. (Chance, quoted in Gorfinkel, 2003, p. 27)

NOTES

1. Even though feminist qualitative research may not directly relieve women's suffering in certain contexts, the research nevertheless can contribute to legislation, policy, or agencies' actions (Maynard, 1994a). Beyond the relevance of the findings, the very conduct of the research provides grounds for evaluating the degree to which it is feminist: Does it depict the researched as abnormal, powerless, or without agency? Does it include details of the micropolitics of the research? How is difference handled in the study? Does it avoid replicating oppression? (Bhavnani, 1994, p. 30). Francesca Cancian enunciates a similar list of criteria for regarding research as feminist (1992).

2. Feminist research on health and illness ranges very widely. Lora Bex Lempert (1994) linked accounts of battered women's experiences to constructions of the battering and structural issues. Her subjective approach contrasted with Dorothy Broom's (1991) analysis of how the emergence of state-sponsored women's health clinics in Australia created contradictions with feminist principles that feminists had to handle as they worked within the health care system. Linda Hunt, Brigitte Jordan, S. Irwin, and Carole Browner's (1989) interview study found that women did not comply with medical regimes for reasons that made sense in their

own lives and were not "cranks," a finding similar to Anne Kasper's (1994) in her study of women with breast cancer. At a different level, Sue Fisher's (1995) analysis showed that nurse practitioners provide more attentive care than do physicians but still exert considerable control over patients. Addressing large-scale issues, Susan Yadlon's (1997) analysis of discourses around causes for breast cancer revealed that women were blamed for being poor mothers or too skinny, but the discourses overlooked environmental and other extracorporal causes (1997). Sarah Nettleton's (1991) deconstructive analysis of discursive practices in dentistry showed how ideal mothers are created, while Kathy Davis's (1995) research on cosmetic surgery highlighted women's dilemmas.

3. Policy research raises the issue of "studying up." It also invokes the oft-noted comment that feminist researchers, like many other qualitative (and quantitative) investigators, find it easier to access respondents in social groups open to them rather than high-status lawmakers or elected officials, an important exception being Margaret Stacey's (1992) analysis of the British Medical Council. Furthermore, feminist concerns focus on elite policy sites, overlooking the fact that significant policy is made at local levels (institutions, city government, school boards, community groups). The work developing Dorothy Smith's theories of institutional ethnography (M. Campbell & Manicom, 1995) and particularly Marie Campbell's (1998) analysis of how texts are enacted as policy in a Canadian nursing home offers new and promising leads in the area of feminist policy analysis. Carroll Estes and Beverly Edmonds's (1981) symbolic interactionist model of how emergent policy issues become framed remains a valuable approach for feminists interested in policy analysis. Additionally a growing number of explicitly feminist examinations of policy construction (Bacchi, 1999), policy and social justice (N. D. Campbell, 2000), critical policy analysis (Marshall, 1997), and policy and politics (Staudt, 1998) provide foundations for policy-oriented qualitative feminist researchers, as does the new area of feminist comparative policy (Mazur, 2002). However, as Ronnie Steinberg's (1996) account of her considerable experience as a feminist advocacy policy researcher shows, there are substantial "challenges, frustrations, and unresolvable double-bind associated with conducting (feminist) research in a political context for social change" (p. 254). Another difficulty, documented in a Canadian report about feminist policy analysis (Burt, 1995), lies in the tensions between traditional approaches that often overlook women and feminist policy challenges.

4. In Adele Clarke's phrase, these are "meso analyses" that refer to how societal and institutional forces mesh with human activity. Clarke's own feminist sociohistorical analysis shows how these processes play out around such issues as production of contraceptives (1990, 1998a, 1998b). These studies elevate research for women to an important critique of historically male-dominated science and policy making and control, not just of women but also of the policy processes, for example, Linda Gordon's (1994) sociohistorical analysis of welfare mothers, which showed how outmoded ideas about women's place are carried into new eras and misplaced policies.

5. This shift has evoked worried comments that feminist researchers have moved away from the political agendas of an earlier time, concerned with understanding and alleviating women's oppression, to descriptions of women's lives or arcane epistemological questions (Glucksman, 1994, p. 150; L. Kelly, Burton, & Regan, 1994, p. 28). Clearly, widespread interest in epistemological issues flourishes among those seeking to understand, improve, or destabilize feminist approaches, but there is abundant work oriented to intervention and change on

numerous fronts. Patti Lather and Chris Smithies's (1997) participatory study with HIV-positive women combines poststructural approaches with a clear reform agenda, Rachel Pfeffer's (1997) ethnographic inquiry into lives of young homeless women points to programmatic possibilities, and Diana Taylor and Katherine Dower's (1995) policy-oriented focus group research with community women in San Francisco details women's concerns. Olesen, Taylor, Ruzek, & Clarke (1997) extensively review feminist research oriented to ameliorating women's health, and qualitative feminist researchers discuss difficult issues in researching sexual violence against women—for example, sexual harassment of the researcher (Huff, 1997), cross-race research (Huisman, 1997), and managing one's own and others' emotions (Mattley, 1997). Adele Clarke and I argue that "discursive constructions and signifying practices can be handled as constitutive rather than determinative" (1999a, p. 13). Sally Kenney and Helen Kinsella (1997) detail the political and reform implications of standpoint theory. Moreover, a number of journals (*Qualitative Research in Health Care*, *Qualitative Studies in Education*, *Feminism and Psychology*, *Western Journal of Nursing Research*, *Journal of Social Issues*, *Sociology of Health and Illness*, *Qualitative Inquiry*, *Qualitative Sociology*, *Journal of Contemporary Ethnography*, *Feminist Studies*, *Feminist Review*, *Gender & Society*, and *Social Problems*) publish feminist qualitative reform–oriented research. However, here, as elsewhere, space limits on length of essays (25 pages double-spaced) make constructing both an argument and a reform stance difficult, given the necessity for detail in qualitative reporting.

6. Work by feminist legal scholars (Ashe, 1988; Bartlett, 1990; Fry, 1992; MacKinnon, 1983; Matsuda, 1992, 1996; P. J. Williams, 1991) also falls within this genre.

7. Yvonna Lincoln, in a personal communication, has reminded me that relativism "spreads over a continuum" ranging from radical relativists who believe that "anything goes" to those who disavow absolute standards for evaluating accounts but who hold that standards should be developed in specific contexts, and these standards should incorporate participants' ideas of which account represents useful knowledge. This latter view does not jettison any notion of quality but rather serves as a way to avoid utilizing "scientific standards" in contexts where "they act in oppressing, disabling or power-freighted ways."

8. Beyond the original texts of standpoint theorists cited here, useful interpretive reviews can be found in Denzin (1997), Clough (1998), and Kenney and Kinsella (1997). Harding's summary of standpoint theories' chronology also is instructive (1997, p. 387).

9. The extensive and occasionally difficult literature on deconstructionism, postmodernism, and feminism is not always as accessible as it should be for those who are starting to explore or wish to deepen their understanding. Some useful works are the Spring, 1988, issue of *Feminist Studies*, Nicholson (1990, 1997), Hekman (1990), Flax (1987, 1990), Rosenau (1992), Lemert (1997), Charmaz's (1995) insightful and evenly balanced analysis of positivism and postmodernism in qualitative research, and Collins's (1998b, pp. 114–154) incisive discussion of what postmodernism means for black feminists.

10. Feminist researchers who look to deconstruction or psychoanalytic feminist semiotics disavow attention to experience (Clough, 1993a, p. 179). They argue that irrespective of how close the researcher, experience is always created in discourse and textuality. Text is central to incisive analysis as a fundamental mode of social criticism. In this work, the emphasis on desire seems to refer to (a) passion, (b) the mysterious and mischievous contributions of the unconscious, (c) libidinal resources not squeezed out of us by childhood and adult socialization, and (d) the sexuality and politics of cultural life and its representations.

11. Kamela Visweswaran (1994) makes a useful differentiation between reflexive ethnography, which questions its own authority, confronts the researcher's processes of interpretation, and emphasizes how the researcher thinks she knows, and deconstructive ethnography, which abandons authority, confronts power in the interpretive processes, and emphasizes how we think we know what we know is not innocent.

12. Other feminist accounts that have explicated how decisions are made include Janet Finch and Jennifer Mason's detailed report on how they sought "negative cases" (1990) and Catherine Kohler Riessman's worries about her analysis of divorced persons' reports and the sociologist's interpretive voice (1990). Jennifer Ring, following Hegel, avers that dialectical thought prevents stabilizing the border between objectivity and subjectivity (1987, p. 771).

13. Considerations of voice and preparation of text or alternative presentation raise the question of type of publication. Presenting research materials in popular magazines may reach audiences who would be unlikely to have access to or see more traditional or even experimental accounts in academic sources. At present, few of the academic review processes leading to tenure, promotion, or even merit increases acknowledge these lay publications as important. Patti Lather and Chris Smithies (1997), in their research with HIV-positive women in which they consulted with women throughout, initially took their manuscript directly into a publication for the mass audience reachable through such outlets as supermarkets.

14. Earlier feminist accounts developed innovative ways to reflect and present voice, though not all would be free of the problems Fine discusses. (For an extensive list of such accounts, see Maschia-Lees et al., 1989, pp. 7–8, n. 1.) Two contrasting examples: Marjorie Shostak (1981) gave a verbatim dialogic account of her voice and that of her K!ung respondent, Nissa, and Susan Krieger (1983) used the device of a polyphonic chorus to represent voices of women in a Midwest lesbian community. Krieger's voice is absent, though she clearly selected the materials for the account.

15. Under the editorship of Barbara and Dennis Tedlock, the flagship journal *The American Anthropologist* adopted a policy of publishing experimental texts, as have several sociological journals long sympathetic to the new modes (*Qualitative Inquiry*, *Journal of Contemporary Ethnography*, *The Midwest Sociological Quarterly*, and *Qualitative Sociology*).

16. In a review essay by five women at the University of Michigan's Institute for Research on Women and Gender, discussing Laurel Richardson's *Fields of Play* (1997), Lora Bex Lempert argues that scholars who have moved into the experimental spaces have created intellectual and representation spaces for others in the work of social transformation, an agenda shared with the traditionalists (Dutton, J., Groat, L., Hassinger, J., Lempert, L., Riehl, C., 1998).

17. Activist-oriented research agendas in women's health are outlined by Narrigan, Zones, Worcester, and Grad (1997) and by Ruzek, Olesen, and Clarke (1997).

18. I am indebted here to a lively exchange on these issues with Meaghan Morris, Norman Denzin, Patricia Clough, and Yvonna Lincoln. In a helpful critical reading of this section of the chapter, Annie George of the University of California, San Francisco Department of Social and Behavioral Sciences Graduate Program in Sociology pointed out that many English-language publications in non-Western countries are not listed or cited in major databases such as SocAbstracts and ERIC.

19. Notable recent issues of English-language feminist journals with international feminist research include *Feminist Review* (Summer, 1998), "Rethinking Caribbean Difference"; and *Signs* (Winter, 1998), "Gender, Politics and Islam." Research by Chinese and Japanese feminists

on women office workers (Ogasawara, 1998) and on women factory workers in Hong Kong and South China (Lee, 1998) exemplifies international work published by university and trade presses, as do writings by international scholars on their relationship to feminism and scholarship in their home and adopted societies (John, 1996; U. Narayan, 1997).

20. As Deborah Lupton (1995) has noted, "The point is not to seek a certain 'truth,' but to uncover varieties of truth that operate, to highlight the nature of truth as transitory and political and the position of subjects as fragmentary and contradictory" (pp. 160–161).

References

Abel, E., Christian, B., & Moglen, H. (Eds.). (1997). *Female subjects in black and white: Race, psychoanalysis, criticism.* Berkeley: University of California Press.

Abel, E. K., & Nelson, M. K. (Eds.). (1990). *Circles of care: Work and identity in women's lives.* Albany: State University of New York Press.

Abu-Lughod, L. (1990). Can there be a feminist ethnography? *Women and Performance, 5,* 7–27.

Acker, J., Barry, K., & Esseveld, J. (1991). Objectivity and truth: Problems in doing feminist research. In M. M. Fonow & J. A. Cook (Eds.), *Beyond methodology: Feminist scholarship as lived research* (pp. 133–153). Bloomington: University of Indiana Press.

Acker, S. (1994). *Gendered education: Sociological reflections on women, teaching and feminism.* Buckingham, UK: Open University Press.

Alexander, M. J., & Mohanty, C. T. (1997). *Feminist genealogies, colonial legacies, democratic futures.* New York: Routledge.

Allen, S. (1994). Race, ethnicity and nationality: Some questions of identity. In H. Afshar & M. Maynard (Eds.), *The dynamics of "race" and gender: Some feminist interventions* (pp. 85–105). London: Taylor and Francis.

Alway, J. (1995). The trouble with gender: Tales of the still missing feminist revolution in sociological theory. *Sociological Theory, 13,* 209–228.

Andrews, M. (2002). Feminist research with non- feminist and anti-feminist women: Meeting the challenge. *Feminism and Psychology, 12,* 55–77.

Anglin, M. (2003). Feminism in practice. *Voices: A Publication of the Association for Feminist Anthropology, 6,* 3.

Anzaldúa, G. (1987). *Borderlands/La frontera.* San Francisco: Auntie Lute.

Anzaldúa, G. (1990). *Making sou: Haciendo caras.* San Francisco: Auntie Lute.

Appleby, Y. (1997). How was it for you? Intimate exchanges in feminist research. In M. Ang-Lyngate, C. Corrin, & H. S. Millson (Eds.), *Desperately seeking sisterhood: Still challenging and building* (pp. 127–147). London: Taylor and Francis.

Asch, A., & Fine, M. (1992). Beyond the pedestals: Revisiting the lives of women with disabilities. In M. Fine (Ed.), *Disruptive voices: The possibilities of feminist research* (pp. 139–174). Ann Arbor: University of Michigan Press.

Ashe, M. (1988). Law-language of maternity: Discourse holding nature in contempt. *New England Law Review, 521,* 44–70.

Bacchi, C. (1999). *Women, policy and politics.* Thousand Oaks, CA: Sage.

Ball, S. J. (1994). *Education reform: A critical and post-structural approach.* Buckingham, UK: Open University Press.

Balsamo, A. (1993). On the cutting edge: Cosmetic surgery and the technological production of the gendered body. *Camera Obscura, 28,* 207–237.

Balsamo, A. (1999). Technologies of surveillance: Constructing cases of maternal neglect. In A. E. Clarke & V. L. Olesen (Eds.), *Revisioning women, health and healing: Feminist cultural and technoscience perspectives* (pp. 231–253). New York: Routledge.

Barndt, D. (2002). *Tangled routes: Women, work and globalization on the tomato trail.* New York: Rowman & Littlefield.

Bartlett, K. (1990). Feminist legal methods. *Harvard Law Review, 103,* 45–50.

Behar, R. (1993). *Translated woman: Crossing the border with Esperanza's story.* Boston: Beacon.

Behar, R. (1996). *The vulnerable observer.* Boston: Beacon.

Behar, R., & Gordon, D. (Eds.). (1995). *Women writing culture.* Berkeley: University of California Press.

Bell, L., & Nutt, L. (2002). Divided loyalties, divided expectations: Research ethics, professional and occupational responsibilities. In M. Mauthner, M. Birch, J. Jessop, & T. Miller (Eds.), *Ethics in qualitative research* (pp. 70–90). Thousand Oaks, CA: Sage.

Benhabib, S. (1987). The generalized and the concrete other: The Kohlberg-Gilligan controversy and feminist theory. In S. Benhabib & D. Cornell (Eds.), *Feminism as critique* (pp. 77–95). Minneapolis: University of Minnesota Press.

Benhabib. S. (1995). Feminism and postmodernism: An uneasy alliance. In S. Benhabib, J. Butler, D. Cornell, & N. Fraser (Eds.), *Feminist contentions: A philosophical exchange* (pp. 17–34). New York: Routledge.

Benhabib, S., Butler, J., Cornell, D., & Fraser, N. (Eds.). (1995). *Feminist contentions: A philosophical exchange.* New York: Routledge.

Bergeron, S. (2001). Political economy discourses of globalization and feminist politics. *Signs, 26,* 984–1006.

Bhavnani, K.-K. (1994). Tracing the contours: Feminist research and feminist objectivity. In H. Afshar & M. Maynard (Eds.), *The dynamics of "race" and gender: Some feminist interventions* (pp. 26–40). London: Taylor and Francis.

Bing, V. M., & Reid, P. T. (1996). Unknown women and unknowing research: Consequences of color and class in feminist psychology. In N. R. Goldberger, J.M.M. Tarule, B. McVicker, & M. Field (Eds.), *Knowledge, difference and power: Essays inspired by women's ways of knowing* (pp. 175–205). New York: Basic Books.

Birch, M. (1998). Reconstructing research narratives: Self and sociological identity in alternative settings. In J. Ribbens & R. Edwards (Eds.), *Feminist dilemmas in qualitative research: Public knowledge and private lives* (pp. 171–185). Thousand Oaks, CA: Sage.

Birch, M., & Miller, T. (2000). Inviting intimacy: The interview as therapeutic opportunity. *International Review of Social Research Methodology, 3,* 189–202.

Blackmore, J. (1995). Policy as dialogue: Feminist administrators working for educational change. *Gender and Education, 7,* 293–313.

Bloom, L. R. (1998). *Under the sign of hope: Feminist methodology and narrative interpretation.* Albany: State University of New York Press.

Brabeck, M. M. (1996). The moral self, values and circles of belonging. In K. F. Wyche & F. J. Crosby (Eds.), *Women's ethnicities: Journeys through psychology* (pp. 145–165). Boulder, CO: Westview.

Braidotti, R. (2000). Once upon a time in Europe. *Signs, 25,* 1061–1064.

Britzman, D. P. (1991). *Practice makes practice: A critical study of learning to teach.* Albany: State University of New York Press.

Britzman, D. P. (1998). Foreword. In L. R. Bloom, *Under the sign of hope: Feminist methodology and narrative interpretation* (pp. ix–xi). Albany: State University of New York Press.

Broom, D. (1991). *Damned if we do: Contradictions in women's health care.* Sydney: Allen and Unwin.

Brown, R. H. (1998). Review of *Fields of Play: Constructing an Academic Life* by Laurel Richardson. *Contemporary Sociology, 27,* 380–383.

Brown, W. (1992). Finding the man in the state. *Feminist Studies, 18,* 7–34.

Burt, S. (1995). Gender and public policy: Making some difference in Ottawa. In F.-P. Gingras (Ed.), *Gender and politics in contemporary Canada* (pp. 86–105). Toronto: Oxford University Press.

Butler, J. (1990). *Gender trouble: Feminism and the subversion of identity.* London: Routledge.

Butler, J. (1993). *Bodies that matter: On the discursive limits of "sex."* London: Routledge.

Butler, J. (1994). Against proper objects. *Differences, 6,* 1–16.

Butler, O. (1986). *Feminist experiences in feminist research.* Manchester, UK: University of Manchester Press.

Campbell, M. (1998). Institutional ethnography and experience as data. *Qualitative Sociology, 21,* 55–74.

Campbell, M. (2002). Textual accounts, ruling action: The intersection of knowledge and power in the routine conduct of nursing work. *Studies in Cultures, Organizations and Societies, 7,* 231–250.

Campbell, M., & Gregor, F. (2002). *Mapping social relations: A primer in doing institutional ethnography.* Toronto: Garamond.

Campbell, M., & Manicom, A. (Eds.). (1995). *Knowledge, experience and ruling relations.* Toronto: University of Toronto Press.

Campbell, N. D. (2000). *Using women: Gender, drug policy, and social justice.* New York: Routledge.

Cancian, F. M. (1992). Feminist science: Methodologies that challenge inequality. *Gender and Society, 6,* 623–642.

Cancian, F. M. (1996). Participatory research and alternative strategies for activist sociology. In H. Gottfried (Ed.), *Feminism and social change* (pp. 187–205). Urbana: University of Illinois Press.

Cancian, F. M., Kurz, D., London, A. S., Reviere, R., & Tuominen, M. C. (Eds.). (2000). *Child care and inequality: Re-thinking care work for children and youth.* New York: Routledge.

Cannon, L. W., Higginbotham, E., & Leung, M.L.A. (1991). Race and class bias in qualitative research on women. In M. M. Fonow & J. A. Cook (Eds.), *Beyond methodology: Feminist scholarship as lived research on women* (pp. 107–118). Bloomington: Indiana University Press.

Case, S.-E., & Abbitt, E. W. (2004). Disidentifications, diaspora and desire. Questions on the future of the feminist critique of performance. *Signs, 29,* 925–938.

Casper, M. J. (1997). Feminist politics and fetal surgery: Adventures of a research cowgirl on the reproductive frontier. *Feminist Studies, 23,* 233–262.

Casper, M. J. (1998). *The making of the unborn patient: Medical work and the politics of reproduction in experimental fetal surgery.* New Brunswick, NJ: Rutgers University Press.

Charmaz, K. (1995). Between positivism and postmodernism: Implications for methods. In N. K. Denzin (Ed.), *Studies in symbolic interaction* (Vol. 17, pp. 43–72). Greenwich, CT: JAI.

Charmaz, K., & Olesen, V. L. (1997). Ethnographic research in medical sociology: Its foci and distinctive contributions. *Sociological Methods and Research, 25,* 452–494.

Chase, S. E. (1995). *Ambiguous empowerment: The work narratives of women school superintendents.* Amherst: University of Massachusetts Press.

Chow, E. N. (1987). The development of feminist consciousness among Asian American women. *Gender and Society, 1,* 284–299.

Clarke, A. (1990). A social worlds research adventure: The case of reproductive science. In S. E. Cozzens & T. F. Gieryn (Eds.), *Theories of science in society* (pp. 15–43). Bloomington: Indiana University Press.

Clarke, A. (1998a). *Disciplining reproduction: Modernity, American life sciences, and the problems of "sex."* Berkeley: University of California Press.

Clarke, A., & Olesen, V. L. (Eds.). (1999). *Revisioning women, health and healing: Feminist, cultural and technoscience perspectives.* New York: Routledge.

Clarke, A., & Olesen, V. (1999a). Revising, diffracting, acting. In A. E. Clarke & V. L. Olesen (Eds.), *Revisioning women, health and healing: Feminist, cultural and technoscience perspectives* (pp. 3–38). New York: Routledge.

Clarke, A. (2005). *Situational analysis: Grounded theory after the postmodern turn.* Thousand Oaks, CA: Sage.

Clough, P. T. (1993a). On the brink of deconstructing sociology: Critical reading of Dorothy Smith's standpoint epistemology. *The Sociological Quarterly, 34,* 169–182.

Clough, P. T. (1993b). Response to Smith's response. *The Sociological Quarterly, 34,* 193–194.

Clough, P. T. (1994). *Feminist thought: Desire, power and academic discourse.* London: Basil Blackwell.

Clough, P. T. (1998). *The end(s) of ethnography* (Rev. ed.). Newbury Park, CA: Sage.

Clough, P. T. (2000). *Autoaffection: The unconscious in the age of teletechnology.* Minneapolis: University of Minnesota Press.

Code, L. (1991). *What can she know? Feminist theory and the construction of knowledge.* Ithaca, NY: Cornell University Press.

Collins, P. H. (1986). Learning from the outsider within: The sociological significance of Black feminist thought. *Social Problems, 33,* 14–32.

Collins, P. H. (1990). *Black feminist thought: Knowledge, consciousness and the politics of empowerment.* Boston: Unwin Hyman.

Collins, P. H. (1992). Transforming the inner circle: Dorothy Smith's challenge to sociological theory. *Sociological Theory, 10,* 73–80.

Collins, P. H. (1997). Comment on Hekman's "Truth and method: Feminist standpoint theory revisited." *Signs, 22,* 375–381.

Collins, P. H. (1998a). *Fighting words: Black women and the search for justice.* Minneapolis: University of Minnesota Press.

Collins, P. H. (1998b). What's going on? Black feminist thought and the politics of postmodernism. In P. H. Collins, *Fighting words: Black women and the search for justice* (pp. 124–154). Minneapolis: University of Minnesota Press.

Collins, P. H. (1999). Will the "real" mother please stand up? The logic of eugenics and American national family planning. In A. E. Clarke & V. L. Olesen (Eds.), *Revisioning women, health and healing: Feminist, cultural and technoscience perspectives* (pp. 266–282). New York: Routledge.

Connell, R. W. (1997). Comment on Hawkesworth's "Confounding gender." *Signs, 22,* 702–706.

Constable, N. (1997). *Maid to order in Hong Kong: Stories of Filipina workers.* Ithaca, NY: Cornell University Press.

Corrigan, O. (2003). Empty ethics: The problem with informed consent. *Sociology of Health and Illness, 25,* 768–792.

Craddock, E., & Reid, M. (1993). Structure and struggle: Implementing a social model of a well woman clinic in Glasgow. *Social Science and Medicine, 19,* 35–45.

Crenshaw, K. (1992). Whose story is it, anyway? Feminist and antiracist appropriations of Anita Hill. In T. Morrison (Ed.), *Race-ing justice, engendering power* (pp. 402–436). New York: Pantheon.

Cuthbert, D. (2000). "The doctor from the university is at the door . . .": Methodological reflections on research with non-Aboriginal adoptive and foster mothers of Aboriginal children. *Resources for Feminist Research/Documentation sur la Recherche Feminists, 28,* 209–228.

Daniels, A. K. (1983). Self-deception and self-discovery in field work. *Qualitative Sociology, 6,* 195–214.

Davis, A. Y. (1981). *Women, race and class.* London: The Women's Press.

Davis, K. (1995). *Reshaping the female body: The dilemma of cosmetic surgery.* New York: Routledge.

Davis, K., & Gremmen, I. (1998). In search of heroines: Some reflections on normativity in feminist research. *Feminism and Psychology, 8,* 133–153.

de Castell, S., & Bryson, M. (1997). En/gendering equity: Paradoxical consequences of institutionalized equity policies. In S. de Castell & M. Bryson (Eds.), *Radical In(ter)ventions: Identity politics and difference/s in educational praxis* (pp. 85–103). Albany: State University of New York Press.

de Lauretis, T. (1987). *Technologies of gender: Essays on theory, film, and fiction.* Bloomington: Indiana University Press.

Denzin, N. K. (1992). *Symbolic interactionism and cultural studies.* Oxford, UK: Basil Blackwell.

Denzin, N. K. (1997). *Interpretive ethnography: Ethnographic practices for the 21st century.* Thousand Oaks, CA: Sage.

DesAutels, P., & Wright, J. (2001). *Feminists doing ethics.* Boulder, CO: Rowman and Littlefield.

DeVault, M. (1991). *Feeding the family: The social organization of caring as gendered work.* Chicago: University of Chicago Press.

DeVault, M. (1993). Different Voices: Feminists' methods of social research. *Qualitative Sociology, 16,* 77–83.

DeVault, M. (1996). Talking back to sociology: Distinctive contributions of feminist methodology. *Annual Review of Sociology, 22,* 29–50.

DeVault, M. (1999). *Liberating method: Feminism and social research.* Philadelphia: Temple University Press.

Dever, C. (2004). *Skeptical feminism, activist theory, activist practice.* Minneapolis: University of Minnesota Press.

Diaz, C. (2002). Conversational heuristic as a reflexive method for feminist research. *International Review of Sociology, 12*(2), 249–255.

Dill, B. T. (1979). The dialectics of Black womanhood. *Signs, 4,* 543–555.

Doezema, J. (2000). Loose women or lost women? The emergence of the myth of white slavery in contemporary discourses on trafficking in women. *Gender Issues, 18,* 23–50.

Dougherty, D. S. (2001). Sexual harassment as [dys]functional process: A feminist standpoint analysis. *Journal of Applied Communication Research, 29,* 372–402.

Dutton, J., Groat, L., Hassinger, J., Lempert, L., Riehl, C. (1998). Academic lives. *Qualitative Sociology, 21,* 195–203.

Ebert, T. (1996). *Ludic feminism and after: Postmodernism, desire, and labor in late capitalism.* Ann Arbor: University of Michigan Press.

Edwards, R., & Mauthner, M. (2002). Ethics and feminist research: Theory and practice. In M. Mauthner, M. Birch, J. Jessop, & T. Miller (Eds.), *Ethics in qualitative research* (pp. 14–31). Thousand Oaks, CA: Sage.

Ehrenreich, B., & Fox Piven, F. (1983). Women and the welfare state. In I. Howe (Ed.), *Alternatives: Proposals for America from the democratic left* (pp. 30–45). New York: Pantheon.

Eichenberger, S. E. (2002). *Perceived identity: Researching a Latino/a Catholic community.* Paper presented at the meeting of the Southern Sociological Society.

Eichler, M. (1986). The relationship between sexist, non-sexist, woman-centered and feminist research. *Studies in Communication, 3,* 37–74.

Eichler, M. (1997). Feminist methodology. *Current Sociology, 45,* 9–36.

Ellingson, L. L. (1998). "Then you know how I feel": Empathy, identity and reflexivity in fieldwork. *Qualitative Inquiry, 4,* 492–514.

Ellis, C. (1995). *Final negotiations: A story of love, loss and chronic illness.* Philadelphia: Temple University Press.

Ellis, C., & Bochner, A. P. (1996). *Composing ethnography: Alternative forms of writing.* Walnut Creek, CA: AltaMira.

Epstein, C. F. (1981). *Women in law.* New York: Basic Books.

Espin, O. M. (1995). "Race," racism and sexuality in the life narratives of immigrant women. *Feminism and Psychology, 5,* 223–228.

Espiritu, Y. L. (1997). *Asian American women and men: Labor, laws and love.* Thousand Oaks, CA: Sage.

Estes, C. L., & Edmonds, B. C. (1981). Symbolic interaction and social policy analysis. *Symbolic Interaction, 4,* 75–86.

Evans, S. M. (2002). Re-viewing the second wave. *Feminist Studies, 28,* 259–267.

Fee, E. (1983). Women and health care: A comparison of theories. In E. Fee (Ed.), *Women and health: The politics of sex in medicine* (pp. 10–25). Englewood Cliffs, NJ: Baywood.

Felski, R. (1997). The doxa of difference. *Signs, 23,* 1–22.

Ferguson, K. (1993). *The man question: Visions of subjectivity in feminist theory.* Berkeley: University of California Press.

Fernandez-Kelly, P., & Wolf, D. (2001). A dialogue on globalization. *Signs, 26,* 1243–1249.

Field, P. A. (1991). Doing fieldwork in your own culture. In J. M. Morse (Ed.), *Qualitative nursing research: A contemporary dialogue* (pp. 91–104). Newbury Park, CA: Sage.

Finch, J. (1984). It's great to have someone to talk to. In C. Bell & H. Roberts (Eds.), *Social researching: Politics, problems, practice* (pp. 70–87). London: Routledge and Kegan Paul.

Finch, J. (1986). *Research and policy: The uses of qualitative research in social and educational research.* London: Falmer.

Finch, J., & Groves, D. (1983). *A labour of love: Women, work and caring.* London: Routledge and Kegan Paul.

Finch, J., & Mason, J. (1990). Decision taking in the fieldwork process: Theoretical sampling and collaborative working. In R. G. Burgess (Ed.), *Studies in qualitative methodology: Vol. 2. Reflections on field experience* (pp. 25–50). Greenwich, CT: JAI.

Fine, M. (Ed.). (1992a). *Disruptive voices.* Ann Arbor: University of Michigan Press.

Fine, M. (1992b). Passions, politics and power: Feminist research possibilities. In M. Fine (Ed.), *Disruptive voices* (pp. 205–232). Ann Arbor: University of Michigan Press.

Fine, M., & Gordon, S. M. (1992). Feminist transformations of/despite psychology. In M. Fine (Ed.), *Disruptive voices* (pp. 1–25). Ann Arbor: University of Michigan Press.

Fine, M., & Weis, L. (1996). Writing the "wrongs" of fieldwork: Confronting our own research/ writing dilemma in urban ethnographies. *Qualitative Inquiry, 2,* 251–274.

Fine, M., Weis, L., Weseen, S., & Wong, L. M. (2000). For whom? Qualitative research, representations and social responsibilities. In N. K. Denzin & Y. S. Lincoln (Eds.), *Handbook of qualitative research* (2nd ed., pp. 107–132). Thousand Oaks, CA: Sage.

Fiore, R. N., & Nelson, H. L. (2003). *Recognition, responsibility and rights: Feminist ethics and social theory.* Boulder, CO: Rowan and Littlefield.

Fisher, S. (1995). *Nursing wounds: Nurse practitioners, doctors, women patients, and the negotiation of meaning.* New Brunswick, NJ: Rutgers University Press.

Fishman, J. (2001). Drugs and sex: Clinical research. *Molecular Interventions, 2,* 12–16.

Flax, J. (1987). Postmodernism and gender relations in feminist theory. *Signs, 14,* 621–643.

Flax, J. (1990). *Thinking fragments: Psychoanalysis, feminism and postmodernism in the contemporary West.* Berkeley: University of California Press.

Fonow, M. M., & Cook, J. A. (1991). *Beyond methodology: Feminist scholarship as lived research.* Bloomington: University of Indiana Press.

Forbes, D. A. (2001). Black women in authority: An oxymoron? A black feminist analysis of the organizational experiences of selected African-descended women managers in the United States and Jamaica. *Dissertation Abstracts International-* 61/08, February, p. 3367.

Fosket, J. R. (1999). Problematizing biomedicine: Women's constructions of breast cancer knowledge. In L. Potts (Ed.), *Ideologies of breast cancer: Feminist perspectives* (pp. 15–36). London: Macmillan.

Frankenberg, R. (1994). *White women, race matters: The social construction of whiteness.* Minneapolis: University of Minnesota Press.

Frankenberg, R., & Mani, L. (1993). Cross currents, cross talk: Race, postcoloniality and the politics of location. *Cultural Studies, 7,* 292–310.

Fraser, N. (1989). Struggle over needs: Outline of a socialist-feminist critical theory of late capitalist political culture. In N. Fraser, *Unruly practices: Power, discourse and gender in contemporary social theory* (pp. 161–187). Minneapolis: University of Minnesota Press.

Fraser, N. (1997). *Justice interruptus: Critical reflections on the post-socialist condition.* New York: Routledge.

Freeman, C. (2001). Is local:global as feminine: masculine? Rethinking the gender of globalization. *Signs, 26,* 1007–1038.

Freeman, S. A., & Lips, H. M. (2002). Harsh judgements and sharp impressions: Audience responses to participants in a study of heterosexual feminist identities. *Feminism and Psychology, 12,* 275–281.

Fry, M. J. (1992). *Postmodern legal feminism.* London: Routledge.

Game, A. (1991). *Undoing the social: Towards a deconstructive sociology.* Milton Keynes, UK: Open University Press.

Garcia, A. M. (1989). The development of Chicana discourse. *Gender & Society,* 3, 217–238.

Gaskell, J., & Eichler, M. (2001). White women as burden: On playing the role of feminist "experts" in China. *Women's Studies International Forum, 24,* 637–651.

Gergen, M. (2001). *Feminist reconstructions in psychology: Narrative, gender, and performance.* Newbury Park, CA: Sage.

Gill, C. J. (1997). The last sisters: Health issues of women with disabilities. In S. B. Ruzek, V. L. Olesen, & A. E. Clarke (Eds.), *Women's health: Complexities and differences* (pp. 96–112). Columbus: The Ohio State University Press.

Gilligan, C. (1982). *In a different voice: Psychological theory and women's development.* Cambridge, MA: Harvard University Press.

Ginzburg, F. (1998). *Contested lives: The abortion debate in an American community* (new ed.). Berkeley: University of California Press.

Glazer, N. Y. (1991). "Between a rock and a hard place": Women's professional organizations in nursing and class, racial and ethnic inequalities. *Gender and Society, 5,* 351–372.

Glenn, E. N. (1990). The dialectics of wage work: Japanese-American women and domestic service, 1905–1940. In E. C. DuBois & V. Ruiz (Eds.), *Unequal sisters: A multi-cultural reader in U.S. women's history* (pp. 345–372). London: Routledge.

Glenn, E. N. (2002). *Unequal freedom: How race and gender shaped American citizenship and labor.* Cambridge, MA: Harvard University Press.

Glucksman, M. (1994). The work of knowledge and the knowledge of women's work. In M. Maynard & J. Purvis (Eds.), *Researching women's lives from a feminist perspective* (pp. 149–165). London: Taylor and Francis.

Gordon, L. *Women's body, women's right.* New York: Grossman.

Gordon, L. (1994). *Pitied but not entitled: Single mothers and the history of welfare.* New York: Free Press.

Gorelick, S. (1991). Contradictions of feminist methodology. *Gender and Society, 5,* 459–477.

Gorfinkel, C. (2003). *Much remains to be done: Ruth Chance and California's 20th century movements for social justice.* Pasadena, CA: International Productions.

Graham, H. (1984). *Women, health and the family.* Brighton, UK: Wheatsheaf Harvester.

Graham, H. (1985). Providers, negotiators and mediators: Women as the hidden carers. In E. Lewin & V. L. Olesen (Eds.), *Women, health and healing: Toward a new perspective* (pp. 25–52). London: Tavistock.

Gray, R., & Sinding, C. (2002). *Standing ovation: Performing social science research about cancer.* Boulder, CO: Rowman & Littlefield.

Green, R. (1990). The Pocahontas perplex: The image of Indian women in American culture. In E. C. DuBois & V. L. Ruiz (Eds.), *Unequal sisters: A multi-cultural reader in U.S. women's history* (pp. 15–21). London: Routledge.

Grewal, I., & Caplen, K. (1994). *Scattered hegemonies: Postmodernity and trans-national practices.* Minneapolis: University of Minnesota Press.

Gubrium, J. B., & Holstein, J. A. (1997). *The new language of qualitative method.* New York: Oxford University Press.

Guevarra, A. (2003). *Manufacturing bodies for sale: The biopolitics of labor export in the Philippines.* Unpublished doctoral dissertation, Department of Social and Behavioral Sciences, University of California, San Francisco.

Guinier, L., Fine, M., & Balin, J. (1997). *Becoming gentlemen: Women, law school and institutional change.* Boston: Beacon.

Gulcur, L., & Ilkkaracan, P. (2002). The "Natasha" experience: Migrant sex workers from the former Soviet Union and Eastern Europe in Turkey. *Women's Studies International Forum, 25,* 411–421.

Gupta, A., & Ferguson, J. (1997). *Anthropological locations: Boundaries and grounds of a field science.* Berkeley: University of California Press.

Hamochi, S. (2001). Japan and the global sex industry. In R. M. Kelly, J. H. Hayes, M. H. Hawkesworth, & B. Young (Eds.), *Gender, globalization, and democratization* (pp. 137–146). Lanham, MD: Roman & Littlefield.

Haraway, D. J. (1988). Situated knowledges: The science question in feminism and the privilege of partial perspectives. *Feminist Studies, 14,* 575–599.

Haraway, D. J. (1991). *Simians, cyborgs and women: The reinvention of nature.* London: Routledge.

Haraway, D. J. (1997). *Modest-Witness@Second-Millennium.FemaleMan-Meets-OncoMouse.* New York: Routledge.

Harding, S. (1987). Conclusion: Epistemological questions. In S. Harding (Ed.), *Feminism and methodology* (pp. 181–190). Bloomington: Indiana University Press.

Harding, S. (1990). Feminism, science and the anti-enlightenment critiques. In L. J. Nicholson (Ed.), *Feminism/postmodernism* (pp. 83–105). New York: Routledge.

Harding, S. (1991). "Strong objectivity" and socially situated knowledge. In S. Harding, *Whose science, whose knowledge?* (pp. 138–163). Ithaca, NY: Cornell University Press.

Harding, S. (1993). Rethinking standpoint epistemology: What is "strong objectivity?" In L. Alcoff & E. Potter (Eds.), *Feminist epistemologies* (pp. 49–82). New York: Routledge.

Harding, S. (1996). Gendered ways of knowing and the "epistemological crisis" of the West. In N. R. Goldberger, J. M. Tarule, B. M. Clinchy, & M. F. Belenky (Eds.), *Knowledge, difference and power: Essays inspired by women's ways of knowing* (pp. 431–454). New York: Basic Books.

Harding, S. (1997). Comment on Hekman's "Truth and method: Feminist standpoint theory revisited." *Signs, 22,* 382–391.

Harding, S. (1998). *Is science multicultural? Postcolonialisms, feminisms and epistemologies.* Bloomington: Indiana University Press.

Harding, S. (2001). Comment on Walby's "Against epistemological chasms: The science question in Feminism Revisited": Can democratic values and interests ever play a rationally justifiable role in the evaluation of scientific worth? *Signs, 26,* 511–576.

Hartouni, V. (1997). *Cultural conceptions: On reproductive technologies and the remaking of life.* Minneapolis: University of Minnesota Press.

Hartsock, N. (1983). The feminist standpoint: Developing the ground for a specifically feminist historical materialism. In S. Harding & M. B. Hintikka (Eds.), *Discovering reality* (pp. 283–310). Amsterdam: D. Reidel.

Hartsock, N. (1985). *Money, sex, and power: Towards a feminist historical materialism.* Boston: Northeastern University Press.

Hartsock, N. (1990). Foucault on power: A theory for women? In L. J. Nicholson (Ed.), *Feminism and postmodernism* (pp. 157–175). New York: Routledge.

Hartsock, N. (1997a). Comment on Hekman's "Truth and method: Feminist standpoint theory revisited": Truth or justice? *Signs, 22,* 367–374.

Hartsock, N. (1997b). Standpoint theories for the next century. In S. J. Kenney & H. Kinsella (Eds.), *Politics and feminist standpoint theory* (pp. 93–101). New York: Haworth.

Hattar-Pollara, M., Meleis, A. I., & Nagib, H. (2000). A study of the spousal role of Egyptian women in clerical jobs. *Health Care for Women International, 21,* 305–317.

Hawkesworth, M. E. (1989). Knowers, knowing, known: Feminist theory and claims of truth. *Signs, 14,* 533–557.

Hawkesworth, M. E. (1997a). Confounding gender. *Signs, 22,* 649–686.

Hawkesworth, M. E. (1997b). Reply to McKenna and Kessler, Smith, Scott and Connell: Interrogating gender. *Signs, 22,* 707–713.

Hawkesworth, M. (1999). Analyzing backlash: Feminist standpoint theory as analytical tool. *Women's Studies International Forum, 22,* 135–155.

Hekman, S. (1990b). *Gender and knowledge: Elements of a post-modern feminism.* Boston: Northeastern University Press.

Hekman, S. (1997a). Reply to Hartsock, Collins, Harding and Smith. *Signs, 22,* 399–402.

Hekman, S. (1997b). Truth and method: Feminist standpoint theory revisited. *Signs, 22,* 341–365.

Heng, G. (1994). "A great way to fly": Nationalism, the state and varieties of Third World feminism. In M. J. Alexander & C. T. Mohanty (Eds.), *Feminist genealogies, colonial legacies, democratic futures* (pp. 30–45). New York: Routledge.

Hertz, R. (Ed.). (1997). *Reflexivity and voice.* Thousand Oaks, CA: Sage.

Hine, D. C. (1989). *Black women in white: Racial conflict and cooperation in the nursing profession, 1890–1950.* Bloomington: University of Indiana Press.

Hirschman, N. J. (1997). Feminist standpoint as postmodern strategy. In S. J. Kenney & H. Kinsella (Eds.), *Politics and feminist standpoint theories* (pp. 73–92). New York: Haworth.

Ho, J. C. (2000). Self–empowerment and "professionalism": Conversations with Taiwanese sex workers. *Inter-Asian Cultural Studies, 1,* 283–299.

Hochschild, A. R. (1983). *The managed heart: Commercialization of human feeling.* Berkeley: University of California Press.

Hochschild, A. R. (with Machung, A.). (1989). *The second shift.* New York: Avon.

Holland, J., & Blair, M., with Sheldon, S. (Eds.). (1995). *Debates and issues in feminist research and pedagogy.* Clevedon, UK: Open University Press.

Holland, J., & Ramazanoglu, C. (1994). Coming to conclusions: Power and interpretation in researching young women's sexuality. In M. Maynard & J. Purvis (Eds.), *Researching women's lives from a feminist perspective* (pp. 125–148). London: Taylor and Francis.

Holland, J., & Ramazanoglu, C. (1995). Accounting for sexuality, living sexual politics: Can feminist research be valid? In J. Holland & M. Blair (with S. Sheldon) (Eds.), *Debates and issues in feminist research and pedagogy.* Clevedon, UK: The Open University Press.

Holmes, H. B., & Purdy, L. M. (Eds.). (1992). *Feminist perspectives in medical ethics.* Bloomington: University of Indiana Press.

Hondagneu-Sotelo, P. (2001). *Domestica: Immigrant workers cleaning and caring in the shadows of affluence.* Berkeley: University of California Press.

Hondagneu-Sotelo, P. (Ed.). (2003). *Gender in U.S. immigration: Continuing trends.* Berkeley: University of California Press.

hooks, b. (1984). *Feminist theory from margin to center.* Boston: South End Press.

hooks, b. (1990). Culture to culture: Ethnography and cultural studies as critical intervention. In b. hooks, *Yearning: Race, gender and cultural politics* (pp. 123–133). Boston: South End.

Huber, J. (1973). Symbolic interaction as a pragmatic perspective: The bias of emergent theory. *American Sociological Review, 38,* 274–284.

Huff, J. K. (1997). The sexual harassment of researchers by research subjects: Lessons from the field. In M. D. Schwartz (Ed.), *Researching sexual violence against women: Methodological and personal perspectives* (pp. 115–128).Thousand Oaks, CA: Sage.

Huisman, K. A. (1997). Studying violence against women of color: Problems faced by white women. In M. D. Schwartz (Ed.), *Researching sexual violence against women: Methodological and personal perspectives* (pp. 179–192). Thousand Oaks, CA: Sage.

Humphries, B. (1997). From critical thought to emancipatory action: Contradictory research goals. *Sociological Research Online, 2*(1), 1–9.

Hundleby, C. (1997). Where standpoint stands now. In S. J. Kenney & H. Kinsella (Eds.), *Politics and feminist standpoint theories* (pp. 25–44). New York: Haworth.

Hunt, L. M., Jordan, B., Irwin, S., & Browner, C. H. (1989). Compliance and the patient's perspective: Controlling symptoms in everyday life. *Culture, Medicine and Psychiatry, 13,* 315–334.

Hurtado, A. (1989). Relating to privilege: Seduction and rejection in the subordination of white women and women of color. *Signs, 14,* 833–855.

Hurtado, A., & Stewart, A. J. (1997). Through the looking glass: Implications of studying whiteness for feminist methods. In M. Fine, L. Weis, L. C. Powell, & L. M. Wong (Eds.), *Off white: Readings on race, power and society* (pp. 297–311). New York: Routledge.

Im, E. O., Meleis, A. I., & Park, Y. S. (1999). A feminist critique of menopausal experience of Korean women. *Research in Nursing and Health, 22,* 410–420.

Joffe, C. (1995). *Doctors of conscience: The struggle to provide abortion before and after* Roe v. Wade. Boston: Beacon.

Johannsen, A. M. (1992). Applied anthropology and post-modernist ethnography. *Human Organization, 51,* 71–81.

John, M. E. (1996). *Discrepant dislocations: Feminism, theory and postcolonial histories.* Berkeley: University of California Press.

Jones, S. J. (1997). Reflexivity and feminist practice: Ethical dilemmas in negotiating meaning. *Feminism and Psychology, 7,* 348–353.

Kaplan, E. B. (1997). *Not our kind of girl: Unraveling the myths of black teenage motherhood.* Berkeley: University of California Press.

Kasper, A. (1994). A feminist qualitative methodology: A study of women with breast cancer. *Qualitative Sociology, 17,* 263–281.

Kaufert, P. A., & McKinlay, S. M. (1985). Estrogen-replacement therapy: The production of medical knowledge and the emergence of policy. In E. Lewin & V. L. Olesen (Eds.), *Women, health and healing: Toward a new perspective* (pp. 113–138). London: Tavistock.

Kelly, L., Burton, S., & Regan, L. (1994). Researching women's lives or studying women's oppression? Reflections on what constitutes feminist research. In M. Maynard & J. Purvis (Eds.),

Researching women's lives from a feminist perspective (pp. 27–48). London: Taylor and Francis.

Kelly, R. M., Bayes, J. M., Hawkesworth, M. E., & Young, B. (2001). *Gender, globalization and democratization.* Lanham, MD: Rowman & Littlefield.

Kempadoo, K. (2001). Women of color and the global sex trade: Transnational feminist perspectives. *Meridians, Feminism, Race, Transnationalism, 1,* 28–51.

Kennedy, E. L., & Davis, M. (1993). *Boots of leather, slippers of gold: The history of a lesbian community.* New York: Routledge.

Kenney, S. J., & Kinsella, H. (Eds.). (1997). *Politics and feminist standpoint theories.* Binghamton, NY: Haworth.

Kerber, L. (1998). *No constitutional right to be ladies: Women and the obligation of citizenship.* New York: Hill and Wang.

Kessler, S., & McKenna, W. (1978). *Gender: An ethnomethodological approach.* New York: Wiley.

Kincheloe, J. (1997). Fiction formulas: Critical constructivism and the representation of reality. In W. G. Tierney & Y. S. Lincoln (Eds.), *Representation and the text: Reframing the narrative voice* (pp. 57–80). Albany: State University of New York Press.

Kirby, V. (1991). Comment on Maschia-Lees, Sharpe, and Cohen's "The postmodernist turn in anthropology: Cautions from a feminist perspective." *Signs, 16,* 394–400.

Kitzinger, C., & Wilkinson, S. (1997). Validating women's experiences? Dilemmas in feminist research. *Feminism and Psychology, 7,* 566–574.

Klawiter, M. (1999). Racing for the cure, walking, women and toxic touring: Mapping cultures of action within the Bay Area terrain of breast cancer. *Social Problems, 46,* 104–126.

Koehn, D. (1998). *Rethinking feminist ethics: Care, trust and empathy.* New York: Routledge.

Kofman, E., Phizacklea, A., Raghuran, P., & Sales, R. (2001). *Gender and internal migration in Europe: Employment, welfare, politics.* New York: Routledge.

Komarovsky, M. (1988). The new feminist scholarship: Some precursors and polemics. *Journal of Marriage and the Family, 50,* 585–593.

Komarovsky, M. (1991). Some reflections on the feminist scholarship in sociology. *Annual Review of Sociology, 17,* 1–25.

Kondo, D. K. (1990). *Crafting selves: Power, gender, and discourses of identity in a Japanese workplace.* Chicago: University of Chicago Press.

Kondo, D. K. (1995). Bad girls: Theater, women of color, and the politics of representation. In R. Behar & D. Gordon (Eds.), *Women writing culture* (pp. 49–64). Berkeley: University of California Press.

Krieger, S. (1983). *The mirror dance: Identity in a women's community.* Philadelphia: Temple University Press.

Krieger, S. (1991). *Social science and the self: Personal essays as an art form.* New Brunswick, NJ: Rutgers University Press.

Kuumba, M. B. (2002). "You've struck a rock": Comparing gender, social movements, and transformation in the United States and South Africa. *Gender and Society, 4,* 504–523.

Lacsamana, A. E. (1999). Colonizing the South: Postmodernism, desire and agency. *Socialist Review, 27,* 95–106.

Larrabee, M. J. (Ed.). (1993). *An ethic of care: Feminist and interdisciplinary perspectives.* New York: Routledge.

Laslett, B., & Brenner, J. (2001). Twenty-first century academic feminism in the United States: Utopian visions and practical actions. *Signs, 25,* 1231–1236.

Lather, P. (1991). *Getting smart: Feminist research and pedagogy within the postmodern.* New York: Routledge.

Lather, P. (1993). Fertile obsession: Validity after post-structuralism. *The Sociological Quarterly, 34,* 673–694.

Lather, P. (1995). Feminist perspectives on empowering research methodologies. In J. Holland & M. Blair with S. Sheldon (Eds.), *Debates and issues in feminist research and pedagogy* (pp. 292–307). Clevedon, UK: Open University Press.

Lather, P., & Smithies, C. (1997). *Troubling the angels: Women living with AIDS.* Boulder, CO: Westview.

Lawthom, R. (1997). What can I do? A feminist researcher in non-feminist research. *Feminism and Psychology, 7,* 533–538.

Lee, C. K. (1998). *Gender and the south China miracle: Two worlds of factory women.* Berkeley: University of California Press.

Lemert, C. (1992). Subjectivity's limit: The unsolved riddle of the standpoint. *Sociological Theory, 10,* 63–72.

Lemert, C. (1997). *Postmodernism is not what you think.* Malden, MA: Blackwell.

Lempert, L. B. (1994). Narrative analysis of abuse: Connecting the personal, the rhetorical and the structural. *Journal of Contemporary Ethnography, 22,* 411–441.

Lewin, E. (1991). Writing gay and lesbian culture: What the natives have to say for themselves. *American Ethnologist, 18,* 786–792.

Lewin, E. (1993). *Lesbian mothers.* Ithaca, NY: Cornell University Press.

Lewin, E. (Ed.). (1996). *Inventing lesbian cultures in America.* Boston: Beacon.

Lewin, E. (1998). *Recognizing ourselves: Ceremonies of lesbian and gay commitment.* New York: Columbia University Press.

Lewin, E., & Leap, W. L. (Eds.). (1996). *Out in the field: Reflections of gay and lesbian anthropologists.* Chicago: University of Illinois Press.

Light, L., & Kleiber, N. (1981). Interactive research in a feminist setting. In D. A. Messerschmidt (Ed.), *Anthropologists at home in North America: Methods and issues in the study of one's own society* (pp. 167–184). Cambridge, UK: Cambridge University Press.

Lincoln, Y. S. (1993). I and thou: Method, voice, and roles in research with the silenced. In D. McLaughlin & W. G. Tierney (Eds.), *Naming silenced lives: Personal narratives and processes of educational change* (pp. 20–27). New York: Routledge.

Lincoln, Y. S. (1995). Emerging criteria for quality in qualitative and interpretive research. *Qualitative Inquiry, 1,* 275–289.

Lincoln, Y. S. (1997). Self, subject, audience, text: Living at the edge, writing in the margins. In W. G. Tierney & Y. S. Lincoln (Eds.), *Representation and the text* (pp. 37–55). Albany: State University of New York Press.

Lincoln, Y. S., & Guba, E. G. (1985). *Naturalistic inquiry.* Beverly Hills, CA: Sage.

Longino, H. (1990). *Science as social knowledge.* Princeton, NJ: Princeton University Press.

Longino, H. (1993). Subjects, power and knowledge: Description and prescription in feminist philosophies of science. In L. Alcott & E. Potter (Eds.), *Feminist epistemologies* (pp. 101–120). New York: Routledge.

Lorber, J. (1975). Women and medical sociology: Invisible professionals and ubiquitous patients. In M. M. Millman & R. M. Kanter (Eds.), *Another voice: Feminist perspectives on social life and social science* (pp. 75–105). Garden City, NY: Anchor Books.

Lorber, J. (1994). *Paradoxes of gender.* New Haven, CT: Yale University Press.

Lubelska, C., & Mathews, J. (1997). Disability issues in the politics and processes of feminist studies. In M. Ang-Lygate, C. Corrin, & M. S. Henry (Eds.), *Desperately seeking sisterhood: Still challenging and building* (pp. 117–137). London: Taylor and Francis.

Luker, K. (1984). *The politics of motherhood.* Berkeley: University of California Press.

Luker, K. (1996). *Dubious conceptions: Politics of teen-age pregnancy.* Cambridge, MA: Harvard University Press.

Luff, D. (1999). Dialogue across the divides: "Moments of rapport" and power in research with anti-feminist women. *Sociology, 33,* 689–703.

Lupton, D. (1995). *The imperative of health: Public health and the regulated body.* Thousand Oaks, CA: Sage.

Lykes, M. B. (1989). Dialogue with Guatemalan Indian women: Critical perspectives on constructing collaborative research. In R. Unger (Ed.), *Representations: Social constructions of gender* (pp. 167–184). Amityville, NY: Baywood.

Lykes, M. B. (1994). Whose meeting at which crossroads? A response to Brown and Gilligan. *Feminism and Psychology, 4,* 345–349.

Lykes, M. B. (1997). Activist participatory research among the Maya of Guatemala: Constructing meanings from situated knowledge. *Journal of Social Issues, 53,* 725–746.

MacKinnon, C. (1982). Feminism, Marxism, method and the state: An agenda for theory. *Signs, 7,* 515–544.

MacKinnon, C. (1983). Feminism, Marxism and the state: Toward feminist jurisprudence. *Signs, 8,* 635–658.

Mamo, L. (2002). Sexuality, reproduction, and biomedical negotiations: An analysis of achieving pregnancy in the absence of heterosexuality. *Dissertation Abstracts.* International-A63/04, October, p. 1565.

Manning, K. (1997). Authenticity in constructivist inquiry: Methodological considerations without prescription. *Qualitative Inquiry, 3,* 93–116.

Manning, R. C. (1992). *Speaking from the heart: A feminist perspective on ethics.* Lanham, MD: Rowman & Littlefield.

Marchand, M. H., & Runyan, A. S. (Eds.). (2000a). *Gender and global restructuring: Sightings, sites and resistances.* London: Routledge.

Marchand, M. H., & Runyan, A. S. (2000). Introduction: Feminist sightings of global restructuring, conceptualizations and reconceptualizations. In M. H. Marchand & S. Runyan (Eds.), *Gender and global restructuring: Sightings, sites and resistances* (pp. 1–22). London: Routledge.

Marshall, C. (1997). *Feminist critical policy analysis.* Washington, DC: Falmer.

Marshall, C. (1999). Researching the margins: Feminist critical policy analysis. *Educational Policy, 13,* 59–76.

Martin, E. (1987). *The woman in the body: A cultural analysis of reproduction.* Boston: Beacon.

Martin, E. (1999). The woman in the flexible body. In A. E. Clarke & V. L. Olesen (Eds.), *Revisioning women, health and healing: Feminist, cultural and technoscience perspectives* (pp. 97–118). New York: Routledge.

Martin, P. Y. (2001). "Mobilizing masculinities": Women's experiences of men at work. *Organization, 8,* 587–618.

Maschia-Lees, F. E., Sharpe, P., & Cohen, C. B. (1989). The postmodern turn in anthropology: Cautions from a feminist perspective. *Signs, 15,* 7–33.

Matsuda, M. (1992). *Called from within: Early women lawyers of Hawaii.* Honolulu: University of Hawaii Press.

Matsuda, M. (1996). *Where is your body?: And other essays on race, gender and the law.* Boston: Beacon.

Mattley, C. (1997). Field research with phone sex workers: Managing the researcher's emotions. In M. D. Schwartz (Ed.), *Researching sexual violence against women: Methodological and personal perspectives* (pp. 101–114). Thousand Oaks, CA: Sage.

Mauthner, M., Birch, M., Jessop, J., & Miller, T. (Eds.). (2002). *Ethics in qualitative research.* Thousand Oaks, CA: Sage.

Mauthner, N., & Doucet, A. (1998). Reflections on a voice-centered relational method: Analyzing maternal and domestic voices. In J. Ribbens & R. Edwards (Eds.), *Feminist dilemmas in qualitative research: Public knowledge and private lives* (pp. 119–146). Thousand Oaks, CA: Sage.

May, K. A. (1980). Informed consent and role conflict. In A. J. Davis & J. C. Krueger (Eds.), *Patients, nurses, ethics* (pp. 109–118). New York: American Journal of Nursing.

Maynard, M. (1994a). Methods, practice and epistemology: The debate about feminism and research. In M. Maynard & J. Purvis (Eds.), *Researching women's lives from a feminist perspective* (pp. 10–26). London: Taylor and Francis.

Maynard, M. (1994b). Race, gender and the concept of "difference" in feminist thought. In H. Afshar & M. Maynard (Eds.), *The dynamics of "race" and gender: Some feminist interventions* (pp. 9–25). London: Taylor and Francis.

Maynard, M. (1996). Challenging the boundaries: Towards an anti-racist women's studies. In M. Maynard & J. Purvis (Eds.), *New frontiers in women's studies: Knowledge, identity and nationalism* (pp. 11–29). London: Taylor and Francis.

Maynard, M., & Purvis, J. (Eds.). (1994). *Researching women's lives from a feminist perspective.* London: Taylor and Francis.

Mazur, A. G. (2002). *Theorizing feminist policy.* Oxford, UK: Oxford University Press.

McCall, M., & Becker, H. (1990). Performance science. *Social Problems, 37,* 117–132.

McIntyre, A., & Lykes, M. B. (1998). Who's the boss? Confronting whiteness and power differences within a feminist mentoring relationship in participatory action research. *Feminism and Psychology, 8,* 427–444.

McKenna, W., & Kessler, S. (1997). Comment on Hawkesworth's "Confounding gender": Who needs gender theory? *Signs, 22,* 687–691.

McWilliam, E. (1997). Performing between the posts: Authority, posture and contemporary feminist scholarship. In W. G. Tierney & Y. S. Lincoln (Eds.), *Representation and the text: Reframing the narrative voice* (pp. 219–232). Albany: State University of New York Press.

Messer-Davidow, E. (2002). *Disciplining feminism: From social activism to academic discourse.* Durham, NC: Duke University Press.

Mies, M. (1993). Towards a methodology for feminist research. In M. Hammersley (Ed.), *Social research: Philosophy, politics and practice* (pp. 64–82). Newbury Park, CA: Sage.

Mihesuah, D. A. (1998). Commonality of difference: American Indian women and history. In D. A. Mihesuah (Ed.), *Natives and academics: Researching and writing about American Indians* (pp. 37–54). Lincoln: University of Nebraska Press.

Mihesuah, D. A. (2000). A few cautions at the millennium on the merging of feminist studies with American Indian Women's Studies. *Signs, 25,* 1246–1251.

Millen, D. (1997). Some methodological and epistemological issues raised by doing feminist research on non-feminist women. *Sociological Research Online, 2* (3), 2–18.

Miller, G., & Dingwall, R. (1997). *Context and method in qualitative research.* Thousand Oaks, CA: Sage.

Miller, T., & Bell, L. (2002). Consenting to what? Issues of access, gate-keeping and "informed" consent." In M. Mauthner, M. Birch, J. Jessop, & T. Miller (Eds.), *Ethics in qualitative research* (pp. 37–54). New York: Routledge.

Misra, J. (2000). Gender and the world-system: Engaging the feminist literature on development. In T. D. Hall (Ed.), *A world-systems reader: New perspectives on gender, urbanism, cultures, indigenous peoples, and ecology* (pp. 105–130). Lanham, MD: Rowman & Littlefield.

Mohanty, C. (1988). Under Western eyes: Feminist scholarship and colonial discourses. *Feminist Review, 30,* 60–88.

Mohanty, C. (2003). *Feminism without borders: Decolonizing theory, practicing solidarity.* Durham, NC: Duke University Press.

Montini, T. (1997). Resist and redirect: Physicians respond to breast cancer informed consent legislation. *Women and Health, 12,* 85–105.

Morawski, J. (1990). Toward the unimagined: Feminism and epistemology in psychology. In R. Hare-Mustin & J. Marecek (Eds.), *Making a difference: Psychology and the construction of gender* (pp. 159–183). New Haven, CT: Yale University Press.

Morawski, J. (1994). *Practicing feminisms, reconstructing psychology: Notes on a liminal science.* Ann Arbor: University of Michigan Press.

Morawski, J. (1997). The science behind feminist research methods. *Journal of Social Issues, 53,* 667–681.

Morris, J. (1995). Personal and political: A feminist perspective on researching physical disability. In J. Holland & M. Blair with S. Sheldon (Eds.), *Debates and issues in feminist research and pedagogy* (pp. 262–272). Clevedon, UK: Open University Press.

Morris, M. (1998). *Too soon, too late: History in popular culture.* Bloomington: University of Indiana Press.

Mukherjee, B. (1994). *The holder of the world.* London: Virago.

Murcott, A. (1993). On conceptions of good food, or anthropology between the laity and professionals. *Anthropology in Action, 14,* 11–13.

Naples, N. A. (1996). A feminist revisiting of the insider/outsider debate: The "outsider phenomenon" in rural Iowa. *Qualitative Sociology, 19,* 83–106.

Naples, N. A. (1997a). Contested needs: Shifting the standpoint in rural economic development. *Feminist Economics, 3,* 63–98.

Naples, N. A. (1997b). The "new consensus on the gendered social contract": The 1997–1998 U.S. Congressional hearings on welfare reform. *Signs, 22,* 907–945.

Naples, N. A. (1999). Towards comparative analyses of women's political praxis: Explicating multiple dimensions of standpoint epistemology for feminist methodology. *Women & Politics, 20*(1), 29–57.

Naples, N. (2002). The challenges and possibilities of transnational feminist praxis. In N. A. Naples & M. Desai (Eds.), *Women's activism and globalization: Linking local struggles and global politics* (pp. 267–282). New York: Routledge.

Naples, N. A. (2003). *Feminism and method, ethnography, discourse analysis and activist research.* New York: Routledge.

Naples, N., & Sachs, G. (2000). Standpoint epistemology and the uses of self-reflection in feminist enthnography. *Rural Sociology, 65,* 194–214.

Narayan, K. (1997). How native is a "native" anthropologist? In L. Lamphere, H. Ragone, & P. Zavella (Eds.), *Situated lives, gender and culture in everyday life* (pp. 23–41). New York: Routledge.

Narayan, U. (1997). *Dislocating cultures: Identities and Third World feminism.* New York: Routledge.

Narrigan, D., Zones, J. S., Worcester, N., & Grad, M. J. (1997). Research to improve women's health: An agenda for equity. In S. B. Ruzek, V. L. Olesen, & A. E. Clarke (Eds.), *Women's health: Complexities and differences* (pp. 551–579). Columbus: The Ohio State University Press.

Nelson, C., & Altorki, S. (Eds.). (1997). *Arab Regional Studies Workshop: Cairo Papers in Social Science* (Vol. 20, No. 3). Cairo, IL: The American University in Cairo Press.

Nelson, M. K. (1990). *Negotiated care: The experience of family day care givers.* Philadelphia: Temple University Press.

Nettleton, S. (1991). Wisdom, diligence and teeth: Discursive practices and the creation of mothers. *Sociology of Health and Illness, 13,* 98–111.

Nicholson, L. (Ed.). (1990). *Feminism/postmodernism.* London: Routledge.

Nicholson, L. (Ed.). (1997). *The second wave.* New York: Routledge.

Nielsen, J. M. (Ed.). (1990). *Feminist research methods: Exemplary readings in the social sciences.* Boulder, CO: Westview.

Noddings, N. (2002). *Starting at home: Caring and social policy.* Berkeley: University of California Press.

Oakley, A. (1981). Interviewing women: A contradiction in terms? In H. Roberts (Ed.), *Doing feminist research* (pp. 30–61). London: Routledge & Kegan Paul.

Ogasawara, Y. (1998). *Office ladies and salaried men: Power, gender and work in Japanese companies.* Berkeley: University of California Press.

O'Leary, C. M. (1997). Counteridentification or counterhegemony? Transforming feminist standpoint theory. In S. J. Kenney & H. Kinsella (Eds.), *Politics and feminist standpoint theories* (pp. 45–72). New York: Haworth.

Olesen, V. L. (1977). Rage is not enough: Scholarly feminism and research in women's health. In V. L. Olesen (Ed.), *Women and their health: Research implications for a new era* (DHEW Publication No. HRA-3138) (pp. 1–2). Rockville, MD: Health Resources Administration, National Center for Health Services Research.

Olesen, V. L. (1993). Unfinished business: The problematics of women, health and healing. *The Science of Caring, 5,* 27–32.

Olesen, V. L. (1997). "Do whatever you want": Audiences created, creating, recreated. *Qualitative Inquiry, 3,* 511–515.

Olesen, V. L., & Clarke, A. E. (1999). Resisting closure, embracing uncertainties, creating agendas. In A. E. Clarke & V. L. Olesen (Eds.), *Revisioning women, health and healing: Feminist cultural studies and technoscience perspectives* (pp. 355–357). New York: Routledge.

Olesen, V. L., Taylor, D., Ruzek, S. B., & Clarke, A. E. (1997). Strengths and strongholds in women's health research. In S. B. Ruzek, V. L. Olesen, & A. E. Clarke (Eds.), *Women's health: Complexities and differences* (pp. 580–606). Columbus: The Ohio State University Press.

Ong, A. (1995). Women out of China: Traveling tales and traveling theories in postcolonial feminism. In R. Behar & D. Gordon (Eds.), *Women writing culture* (pp. 350–372). Berkeley: University of California Press.

Opie, A. (1992). Qualitative research, appropriation of the "other" and empowerment. *Feminist Review, 40,* 52–69.

Orr, J. (1993). Panic diary: (Re)constructing a partial politics and poetics of disease. In J. Holstein & G. Miller (Eds.), *Reconsidering social constructionism: Debates in social problems theory* (pp. 441–482). New York: Aldine de Gruyter.

Paget, M. (1990). Performing the text. *Journal of Contemporary Ethnography, 19,* 136–155.

Parrenas, R. S. (2001). Transgressing the nation state: The partial citizenship and imagined (global) community of migrant Filipina domestic workers. *Signs, 26,* 1129–1135.

Patai, D. (1994, February 23). Sick and tired of nouveau solipsism. *The Chronicle of Higher Education,* p. A52.

Petchesky, R. P. (1985). Abortion in the 1980's: Feminist morality and women's health. In E. Lewin & V. Olesen (Eds.), *Women, health and healing: Toward a new perspective* (pp. 139–173). London: Tavistock.

Petchesky, R. P. (2003). *Global prescriptions: Gendering health and human rights.* New York: Zed Books.

Pfeffer, R. (1997). *Children of poverty: Studies on the effect of single parenthood, the feminization of poverty and homelessness.* New York: Garland.

Phoenix, A. (1994). Practicing feminist research: The intersection of gender and "race" in the research process. In M. Maynard & J. Purvis (Eds.), *Researching women's lives from a feminist perspective* (pp. 35–45). London: Taylor and Francis.

Pierce, J. L. (1995). *Gender trials: Emotional lives in contemporary law firms.* Berkeley: University of California Press.

Poster, W. R. (2002). Racialism, sexuality, and masculinity: Gendering "global ethnography" of the workplace. *Social Politics, 9,* 126–158.

Poudel, P., & Carryer, J. (2000). Girl-trafficking, HIV/AIDS and the position of women in Nepal. *Gender and Development, 8,* 74–79.

Puar, J. K. (1996). Resituating discourses of "whiteness" and "Asianness" in northern England: Second-generation Sikh women and constructions of identity. In M. Maynard & J. Purvis (Eds.), *New frontiers in women's studies* (pp. 125–150). London: Taylor and Francis.

Pyle, J. L. (2001). Sex, maids and export processing: Risks and reasons for gendered global production networks. *International Journal of Politics, Culture and Society, 15,* 55–76.

Ramazanoglu, C. (1989). Improving on sociology: The problems of taking a feminist standpoint. *Sociology, 23,* 427–442.

Ramazanoglu, C., with Holland, J. (2002). *Feminist methodology: Challenges and choices.* London: Sage.

Randall, M. (2004). Know your place: The activist scholar in today's political culture. *SWS Network News, 21,* 20–23.

Rapp, R. (1999). *Testing women, testing the foetus: The social impact of amniocentesis in America.* New York: Routledge.

Reay, D. (1996a). Dealing with difficult differences. *Feminism and Psychology, 6,* 443–456.

Reay, D. (1996b). Insider perspectives or stealing the words out of women's mouths: Interpretation in the research process. *Feminist Review, 53,* 57–73.

Reay, D. (1998). Classifying feminist research: Exploring the psychological impact of social class on mothers' involvement in children's schooling. *Feminism & Psychology, 8,* 155–171.

Reinharz, S. (1992). *Feminist methods in social research.* Oxford, UK: Oxford University Press.

Renzetti, C. M. (1997). Confessions of a reformed positivist: Feminist participatory research as good social science. In M. D. Schwartz (Ed.), *Researching sexual violence against women: Methodological and personal perspectives* (pp. 131–143). Thousand Oaks, CA: Sage.

Reynolds, T. (2002). Rethinking a black feminist standpoint. *Ethnic and Racial Studies, 25,* 591–606.

Ribbens, J., & Edwards, R. (1998). *Feminist dilemmas in qualitative research: Public knowledge and private lives.* Thousand Oaks, CA: Sage.

Richardson, L. (1993). Poetics, dramatics and transgressive validity: The case of the skipped line. *The Sociological Quarterly, 34,* 695–710.

Richardson, L. (1997). *Fields of play: Constructing an academic life.* New Brunswick, NJ: Rutgers University Press.

Riessman, C. K. (1987). When gender is not enough: Women interviewing women. *Gender and Society, 2,* 172–207.

Riessman, C. K. (1990). *Divorce talk: Women and men make sense of personal relationships.* New Brunswick, NJ: Rutgers University Press.

Ring, J. (1987). Toward a feminist epistemology. *American Journal of Political Science, 31,* 753–772.

Roberts, H. (1981). *Doing feminist research.* London: Routledge.

Rollins, J. (1985). *Between women: Domestics and their employers.* Philadelphia: Temple University Press.

Roman, L. (1992). The political significance of other ways of narrating ethnography: A feminist materialist analysis. In M. D. LeCompte, W. L. Millroy, & J. Preissle (Eds.), *The handbook of qualitative research in education* (pp. 555–594). San Diego: Academic Press.

Romero, M. (1992). *Maid in the U.S.A.* London: Routledge.

Rosenau, P. M. (1992). *Post-modernism and the social sciences: Insights, inroads and intrusions.* Princeton, NJ: Princeton University Press.

Rudy, K. (2000). Difference and indifference: A US feminist response to global politics. *Signs, 25,* 1051–1053.

Runyan, A. S., & Marchand, M. H. (2000). Conclusion: Feminist approaches to global restructuring. In M. H. Marchand & A. S. Runyan (Eds.), *Gender and global restructuring* (pp. 225–230). London: Routledge.

Rupp, L. J., & Taylor, V. (2003). *Drag queens at the 801 Cabaret.* Chicago: University of Chicago Press.

Ruzek, S. B. (1978). *The women's health movement: Feminist alternatives to medical care.* New York: Praeger.

Ruzek, S. B., Olesen, V. L., & Clarke, A. E. (Eds.). (1997). *Women's health: Complexities and differences.* Columbus: The Ohio State University Press.

Sacks, K. B. (1988). *Caring by the hour: Women, work and organizing at Duke Medical Center.* Urbana: University of Illinois Press.

Scarce, R. (2002). Doing time as an act of survival. *Symbolic Interaction, 25,* 303–321.

Scheper-Hughes, N. (1983). Introduction: The problem of bias in androcentric and feminist anthropology. *Women's Studies, 19,* 109–116.

Scheper-Hughes, N. (1992). *Death without weeping: The violence of everyday life in Brazil.* Berkeley: University of California Press.
Scheurich, J. J. (1997). The masks of validity: A deconstructive investigation. In J. J. Scheurich, *Research method in the postmodern* (pp. 80–93). London: Falmer.
Schiffrin, A. (1998, November 20). Transactional publishing in microcosm: The Frankfurt book fair. *The Chronicle of Higher Education,* pp. B6–B7.
Scott, J. (1991). The evidence of experience. *Critical Inquiry, 17,* 773–779.
Scott, J. (1997). Comment on Hawkesworth's "Confounding gender." *Signs, 22,* 697–702.
Seigfried, C. H. (1996). *Pragmatism and feminism: Reweaving the social fabric.* Chicago: University of Chicago Press.
Sherwin, S. (1992). *No longer patient: Feminist ethics and health care.* Philadelphia: Temple University Press.
Shim, J. K. (2000). Bio-power and racial, class and gender formation in biomedical knowledge production. In J. J. Kronenfield (Ed.), *Research in the sociology of health care* (pp. 173–195). Stamford, CT: JAI.
Shohat, E. (2001). Area studies, transnationalism and the feminist production of knowledge. *Signs, 26,* 1269–1272.
Shostak, M. (1981). *Nisa: The life and words of a !Kung woman.* Cambridge, MA: Harvard University Press.
Skeggs, B. (1994). Situating the production of feminist ethnography. In M. Maynard & J. Purvis (Eds.), *Researching women's lives from a feminist perspective* (pp. 72–92). London: Taylor and Francis.
Skeggs, B. (Ed.). (1995a). *Feminist cultural theory: Process and production.* New York: Manchester University Press.
Skeggs, B. (1995b). Theorizing ethics and representation in feminist ethnography. In B. Skeggs (Ed.), *Feminist cultural theory: Process and production* (pp. 190–206). New York: Manchester University Press.
Smith, D. (1974). Women's perspective as a radical critique of sociology. *Sociological Inquiry, 4,* 1–13.
Smith, D. (1987). *The everyday world as problematic.* Boston: Northeastern University Press.
Smith, D. (1989). Sociological theory: Methods of writing patriarchy. In R. A. Wallace (Ed.), *Feminism and sociological theory* (pp. 34–64). Newbury Park, CA: Sage.
Smith, D. (1990a). *The conceptual practices of power: A feminist sociology of knowledge.* Boston: Northeastern University Press.
Smith, D. (1990b). *Texts, facts and femininity: Exploring the relations of ruling.* London: Routledge.
Smith, D. (1992). Sociology from women's experience: A reaffirmation. *Sociological Theory, 10,* 88–98.
Smith, D. (1993). High noon in textland: A critique of Clough. *Sociological Quarterly, 30,* 183–192.
Smith, D. (1997). Telling the truth after postmodernism. *Symbolic Interaction, 19,* 171–202.
Smith, D. (1999). *Writing the social.* Toronto: University of Toronto Press.
Smith, D. (in press). *Institutional ethnography: A sociology from people's standpoint.* Walnut Creek, CA: AltaMira Press.
Smith, S. G. (1997). Comment on Hawkesworth's "Confounding gender." *Signs, 22,* 691–697.

Speer, S. A. (2002). What can conversational analysis contribute to feminist methodology? Putting reflexivity into practice. *Discourse and Society, 13,* 783–803.

Spivak, G. C. (1988). Subaltern studies: Deconstructing historiography. In G. C. Spivak, *In other worlds: Essays in cultural politics* (pp. 197–221). London: Routledge.

Sprague, J. (2001). Comment on Walby's "Against epistemological chasms: The science question in feminism revisited": Structured knowledge and strategic methodology. *Signs, 26,* 527–536.

Stacey, J. (1988). Can there be a feminist ethnography? *Women's Studies International Forum, 11,* 21–27.

Stacey, J. (1998). *Brave new families: Stories of domestic upheaval in late twentieth century America.* Berkeley: University of California Press.

Stacey, J. (2003). Taking feminist sociology public can prove less progressive than you wish. *SWS Network News, 20,* 27–28.

Stacey, J., & Thorne, B. (1985). The missing feminist revolution in sociology. *Social Problems, 32,* 301–316.

Stacey, J., & Thorne, B. (1996). Is sociology still missing its feminist revolution? *Perspectives: The ASA Theory Section Newsletter, 18,* 1–3.

Stacey, M. (1992). *Regulating British medicine: The General Medical Council.* New York: Wiley.

Standing, K. (1998). Writing the voices of the less powerful. In J. Ribbens & R. Edwards (Eds.), *Feminist dilemmas in qualitative research: Public knowledge and private lives* (pp. 186–202). Thousand Oaks, CA: Sage.

Stanley, L. (Ed.). (1990). *Feminist praxis: Research, theory, and epistemology in feminist sociology.* London: Routledge.

Stanley, L., & Wise, S. (1983). *Breaking out: Feminist consciousness and feminist research.* London: Routledge and Kegan Paul.

Stanley, L., & Wise, S. (1990). Method, methodology and epistemology in feminist research processes. In L. Stanley (Ed.), *Feminist praxis: Research, theory and epistemology in feminist sociology* (pp. 20–60). London: Routledge.

Staudt, K. (1998). *Policy, politics and gender: Women gaining ground.* West Hartford, CT: Kumarian Press.

Steinberg, R. J. (1996). Advocacy research for feminist policy objectives: Experiences with comparable worth. In H. Gottfried (Ed.), *Feminism and social change: Bridging theory and practice* (pp. 250–255). Urbana: University of Illinois Press.

Stevens, P. E., & Hall, J. H. (1991). A critical historical analysis of the medical construction of lesbianism. *International Journal of Health Services, 21,* 271–307.

Tanenberg, K. (2000). Marginalized epistemologies: A feminist approach to understanding the experiences of mothers with HIV. *Affilia, 15,* 31–48.

Taylor, D., & Dower, K. (1995). Toward a women-centered health care system: Women's experiences, women's voices, women's needs. *Health Care for Women International, 18,* 407–422.

Taylor, V. (1998). Feminist methodology in social movements research. *Qualitative Sociology, 21,* 357–379.

Terry, J. (1994). Theorizing deviant historiography. In A.-L. Shapiro (Ed.), *Feminists revision history* (pp. 20–30). New Brunswick, NJ: Rutgers University Press.

Thayer, M. (2001). Transnational feminism: Reading Joan Scott in the Brazilian sertão. *Ethnography, 2,* 243–271.

Tierney, W. G., & Lincoln, Y. S. (1997). *Representation and the text: Reframing the narrative voice.* Albany: State University of New York Press.

Tom, W. (1989). *Effects of feminist research on research methods.* Toronto: Wilfred Laurier Press.

Tong, R. (1997). *Feminist approaches to bioethics: Theoretical reflections and practical applications.* Boulder, CO: Westview.

Trinh, T. M-ha. (1989). *Woman, native, other: Writing post-coloniality and feminism.* Bloomington: University of Indiana Press.

Trinh, T. M-ha. (1992). *Framer framed.* New York: Routledge.

Tronto, J. C. (1993). *Moral boundaries: A political argument for an ethic of care.* New York: Routledge.

Tuana, N. (1993). With many voices: Feminism and theoretical pluralism. In P. England (Ed.), *Theory on gender: Feminism on theory* (pp. 281–289). New York: Aldine de Gruyter.

Visweswaran, K. (1994). *Fictions of feminist ethnography.* Minneapolis: University of Minnesota Press.

Walby, S. (2001a). Against epistemological chasms: The science question in feminism revisited. *Signs, 26,* 485–510.

Walby, S. (2001b). Reply to Harding and Sprague. *Signs, 26,* 537–540.

Walker, M. V. (1998). *Moral understandings: A feminist study in ethics.* New York: Routledge.

Walkerdine, V. (1995). Postmodernity, subjectivity and the media. In T. Ibanez & L. Iniguez (Eds.), *Critical social psychology* (pp. 169–177). London: Sage.

Warren, C.A.B. (1988). *Gender issues in field research.* Newbury Park, CA: Sage.

Wasserfall, R. R. (1997). Reflexivity, feminism and difference. In R. Hertz (Ed.), *Reflexivity and voice* (pp. 150–168). Thousand Oaks, CA: Sage.

Weeks, K. C. (1998). *Constituting feminist subjects.* Ithaca, NY: Cornell University Press.

Welton, K. (1997). Nancy Hartsock's standpoint theory: From content to "concrete multiplicity." In S. J. Kenney & H. Kinsella (Eds.), *Politics and feminist standpoint theories* (pp. 7–24). New York: Haworth.

West, C., & Zimmerman, D. (1987). Doing gender. *Gender and Society, 1,* 125–151.

Westkott, M. (1979). Feminist criticism of the social sciences. *Harvard Educational Review, 4,* 422–430.

Weston, K. (1991). *Families we choose: Lesbians, gays, kinship.* New York: Columbia University Press.

Weston, K. (1996). Requiem for a street fighter. In E. L. Lewin & W. L. Leap (Eds.), *Out in the field: Reflections of lesbian and gay anthropologists* (pp. 274–286). Urbana: University of Illinois Press.

Wheatley, E. (1994). How can we engender ethnography with a feminist imagination: A rejoinder to Judith Stacey. *Women's Studies International Forum, 17,* 403–416.

Wheeler, B. (2003). The institutionalization of an American avant-garde: Performance art as democratic culture, 1970–2000. *Sociological Perspectives, 46,* 491–512.

Williams, B. (1996). Skinfolk, not kinfolk: Comparative reflections on the identity of participant-observation in two field situations. In D. Wolf (Ed.), *Feminist dilemmas in fieldwork* (pp. 72–95). Boulder, CO: Westview.

Williams, P. J. (1991). *The alchemy of race and rights.* Cambridge, MA: Harvard University Press.

Wolf, D. (Ed.). (1996). *Feminist dilemmas in fieldwork.* Boulder, CO: Westview.

Wolf, M. (1992). *A thrice told tale: Feminism, postmodernism and ethnographic responsibility.* Stanford, CA: Stanford University Press.

Wolf, M. (1996). Afterword: Musings from an old gray wolf. In D. Wolf (Ed.), *Feminist dilemmas in fieldwork* (pp. 214–222). Boulder, CO: Westview.

Yadlon, S. (1997). Skinny women and good mothers: The rhetoric of risk, control and culpability in the production of knowledge about breast cancer. *Feminist Studies, 23,* 645–677.

Young, B. (2001). Globalization and gender: A European perspective. In R. M. Kelly, J. H. Bayes, M. E. Hawkesworth, & B. Young (Eds.), *Gender, globalization, and democratization* (pp. 27–48). New York: Rowman & Littlefield.

Zavella, P. (1987). *Women's work and Chicano families: Cannery workers of the Santa Clara Valley.* Ithaca, NY: Cornell University Press.

Zavella, P. (1996). Feminist insider dilemmas: Constructing ethnic identity with Chicana informants. In D. Wolf (Ed.), *Feminist dilemmas in fieldwork* (pp. 138–159). Boulder, CO: Westview.

Zinn, M. B. (1982). Mexican-American women in the social sciences. *Signs, 8,* 251–272.

11

THE MORAL ACTIVIST ROLE OF CRITICAL RACE THEORY SCHOLARSHIP

Gloria Ladson-Billings and Jamel Donnor

It doesn't matter who you are, or how high you rise. One day you will get your call. The question is how will you respond?

—African American University Senior Administrator

The epigraph that opens this chapter comes from a colleague and friend who serves as a top administrator at a major university. His use of the term "your call" is his reference to what in African American vernacular would be known as being called the "N-word." Rather than focus on the controversy over the term and its appropriateness (see Kennedy, 2002), this chapter looks more specifically at the meaning of the "call" and the ways it should mobilize scholars of color[1] and others who share commitments to equity, social justice, and human liberation. This friend was referring to the way African Americans almost never are permitted to break out of the prism (and prison) of race that has been imposed by a racially coded and constraining society. Clearly, this same hierarchy and power dynamic operates for all people of color, women, the poor, and other "marginals."[2] The call is that moment at which, regardless of one's stature and/or accomplishments, race (and other categories of otherness) is recruited to remind one that he or she still remains locked in the racial construction. Below, we provide examples from popular culture, and each of the authors demonstrates how the "call" is mobilized to maintain the power dynamic and hierarchical racial structures of society.

The first example comes from the 1995 murder trial of Orenthal James Simpson, more commonly known as O. J. Simpson. Simpson was an American hero. He was revered for his exploits on the football field at the University of Southern California, and with the professional football franchises in Buffalo and San Francisco, coupled with his good looks and "articulateness."[3] The latter two qualities allowed Simpson to turn his postcompetition years into a successful sports broadcasting career and a mediocre but profitable acting career. Simpson moved comfortably in the world of money and power—the white world. He was said to be someone who "transcended race" (Roediger, 2002), which is a code expression for those people of color that whites claim they no longer think of as people of color. Michael Jordan and Colin Powell also are considered in this vein. They are, according to Dyson (1993), "symbolic figures who embodied social possibilities of success denied to other people of color" (p. 67).

Some might argue that Simpson did not get a "call," that he was a murderer who got the notoriety and degradation he deserved, while also getting away with a heinous crime. Our point is not to argue Simpson's guilt or innocence (and from where we stand, he indeed looks guilty), but rather to describe his devolution from white to black in the midst of the legal spectacle. Simpson learned quickly that the honorary white status accorded to him by the larger society was tentative and ephemeral. Some might argue that anyone charged with murder would receive the same treatment, but consider that Ray Carruth, a National Football League player who was convicted of a murder-for-hire of his pregnant girlfriend, was regarded as "just another black hoodlum." His actions barely caused a collective raised eyebrow in the larger society. We argue that Simpson's crimes are not only the murder of Nicole Brown and Ron Goodman but also the perceived "betrayal" of white trust.

Simpson went from conceptually white to conceptually black (King, 1995)—from a "Fresh Prince of Brentwood" to the "Pariah of Portrero Hill" (the San Francisco community in which he grew up). One of the weekly newsmagazines admitted to "colorizing" Simpson's police mug shot on its cover, resulting in a more sinister look. We perceive that editorial decision as a symbol of Simpson's "return to black." He no longer transcended race. He was just another N-word who was dangerous, sinister, and unworthy of honorary white status. O. J. Simpson received his call.

Of course, the bizarre and circus-like circumstances of the Simpson trial make it an outlier example of receiving a call. Therefore, we use more personal examples that better situate this argument in our everyday life experiences. Ladson-Billings (1998b) describes her experience of being invited to a major university to be a speaker in the distinguished scholars lecture series. After the speech, she returned to her hotel and decided to unwind in the hotel's concierge floor lounge. Dressed in business attire and reading the newspaper, she noticed a white man who popped his head in the door. "What time are y'all serving?" he asked. Because she was the only person in the lounge, it was clear that he was addressing Ladson-Billings. She politely but firmly replied, "I don't know what time *they* are serving. I'm here as a guest." Red-faced and clearly embarrassed, the man quietly left. One might argue that he made a simple mistake. Perhaps he would have asked the same question of anyone who was sitting in the lounge. Nevertheless, the moment reminded Ladson-Billings that no matter what her scholarly reputation, at any time she could be snapped back into the constraining racial paradigm, complete with all the limitations such designations carry.

Donnor asserts that one of his many calls came when he served as an instructor for a "diversity" class that enrolled only white, middle-class teachers. Because this was a graduate course, Donnor expected the students to adhere to the rigors of a master's-level class. After assigning homework following the first class meeting, Donnor was challenged by one of the few male students about the amount of homework. When Donnor told the student that he expected students to complete the assignment, the inquirer responded, "It ain't going to happen." At the next class meeting, the program's site coordinator, a white woman, arrived at the class, ostensibly to share some program information with the students. However, as she addressed the students, she began to talk to them about modifications in assignments and contacting her if they had issues and concerns regarding the course.

The issue with the student's complaint about the volume of work is a common one in a society that regularly rejects intellectual pursuits. However, graduate students typically exercise some level of courtesy and skill in negotiating the amount of work they are willing (or able) to do. The blatant remark that "it ain't going to happen" may reflect the certainty with which the student approached the racial power dynamic. As a white male approaching an African American male, this student understood that he could challenge Donnor's credentials and abilities. More pointedly, the experience with the site coordinator underscored the fact that although Donnor was hired to teach the course, authority flowed to the white woman. Students could essentially discount Donnor whenever he did anything they disagreed with. Both incidents serve as powerful reminders for Donnor that despite his academic credentials and experience, his racial identity always serves as a mitigating factor in determining his authority and legitimacy.

Receiving a call is a regular reminder of the liminal space of alterity (Wynter, 1992) that racialized others occupy. But it is important not to regard the liminal space solely as a place of degradation and disadvantage. Wynter (1992) assures us that this place of alterity offers a perspective advantage whereby those excluded from the center (of social, cultural, political, and economic activity) experience "wide-angle" vision. This perspective advantage is not due to an inherent racial/cultural difference but instead is the result of the dialectical nature of constructed otherness that prescribes the liminal status of people of color as beyond the normative boundary of the conception of Self/Other (King, 1995).

In the previous iteration of this chapter, Ladson-Billings (2000)[4] cited King (1995), who argued that the epistemic project that scholars of color and their allies must undertake is more than simply adding multiple perspectives or "pivoting" the center. Such scholars occupy a liminal position whose perspective is one of alterity. This liminal position or point of alterity that we inhabit attempts to transcend an "either/or" epistemology. Alterity is not a dualistic position such that there are multiple or equally partial standpoints that are either valid or inexorably ranked hierarchically. Recognizing the alterity perspective does not essentialize other perspectives such as blackness, Indian-ness, Asian-ness, or Latino-ness as homogenizing reverse epistemics (West, 1990).

Ethiopian anthropologist Asmaron Legesse (1973) asserts that the liminal group is that which is forcibly constrained to play the role of alter ego to the ideal self prescribed by the dominant cultural model. This dominant model sets up prescriptive rules and canons for regulating thought and action in the society. Thus, the "issue is about the 'nature of human knowing' of the social reality, in a model of which the knower is already a socialized subject" (Wynter, 1992, p. 26).

> The system-conserving mainstream perspectives of each order (or well-established scholarship) therefore clash with the challenges made from the perspectives of alterity. . . . For, it is the task of established scholarship to rigorously maintain those prescriptions which are critical to the order's existence. (Wynter, 1992, p. 27)

This focus on the ways of the dominant order is important in helping us explore the ways such an order distorts the realities of the Other in an effort to maintain power relations that continue to disadvantage those who are excluded from that order. As Wynter (1992) so eloquently argues, this liminal perspective is the condition of the dominant order's self-definition that "can empower us to free ourselves from the 'categories and prescriptions' of our specific order and from its 'generalized horizon of understanding'" (p. 27).

In this iteration of the handbook, we move away from solely describing the epistemological terrain (both dominant and liminal) to advocating the kinds of moral and ethical responsibilities various epistemologies embody. We do this in hopes of mobilizing scholarship that will take a stance on behalf of human liberation. The subsequent sections of this chapter examine the position of intellectuals as constructors of ethical epistemologies, the discursive and material limits of liberal ideology, new templates for ethical action, moving from research to activism, reconstructing the intellect, and the search for a revolutionary habitus.

We admit at the outset that this is an ambitious project and that we are likely to fall short of our stated goals. However, because a task is hard does not imply that we should not undertake it. Similarly, Derrick Bell (1992) argued that even though racism was a permanent fixture of American life, we must still struggle against it. Our success will not necessarily come in the form of a tightly constructed scholarly treatise but rather in the form of scores of other community, student, and scholar activists who continue or take up this cause rather than merely waiting for "the call."

Intellectual Marginals as Constructors of Ethical Epistemologies

> *The special function of the Negro intellectual is a cultural one. He [sic] should . . . assail the stultifying blight of the commercially depraved white middle-class who has poisoned the structural roots of the American ethos and transformed the American people into a nation of intellectual dolts.*
>
> —Harold Cruse (1967/1984, p. 455)

We would be remiss if we did not acknowledge the incredible volume of work that scholars of color have produced that we regard as ethical epistemologies. Clearly, in a chapter of this length, it is impossible to do justice to all (or even most) of this work. Thus, we will attempt to make this "review of the literature" more a grand tour (Spradley, 1979) to outline the contours of the foundation on which we are building. We start our foundational work with a look at W.E.B. DuBois's (1903/1953) construct of "double consciousness," with which he argues that the African American "ever feels his two-ness . . . two souls, two thoughts, two unreconciled strivings" (p. 5). David Levering Lewis (1993, p. 281) addressed the importance of DuBois's conception stating:

> It was a revolutionary concept. It was not just revolutionary; the concept of the divided self was profoundly mystical, for DuBois invested this double consciousness with a capacity to see incomparably farther and deeper. The African American . . . possessed the gift of "second sight in this American world," an intuitive faculty enabling him/her to see and say things about American society that possessed heightened moral validity.

Ladson-Billings (2000) argued that DuBois's work had an important synchronic aspect in that he raised the issues of double consciousness prior to the formation of the Frankfurt School, out of which critical theories emerged. Coincidentally, DuBois had studied at the University of Berlin in the late 1800s, yet his name is never mentioned in the same context as those of Max Horkheimer, Theodor Adorno, and Herbert Marcuse. DuBois remains a "Negro" intellectual concerned with the "Negro" problem, but it was in Germany that DuBois recognized the race problems in the Americas, Africa, and Asia, as well as the political development of Europe, as being one problem that was part of a shared ideology. This was the period of his life that united his studies of history, economics, and politics into a scientific approach of social research.

DuBois's notion of double consciousness applies not only to African Americans but to all people who are constructed outside the dominant paradigm. Although DuBois refers to a double consciousness, we know that our sense of identity may evoke multiple consciousness, and it is important to read our discussion of multiple consciousness as a description of complex phenomena that impose essentialized concepts of "blackness," "Latina/o-ness," "Asian American-ness," or "Native American-ness" on specific individuals or groups.[5]

In addition to DuBois's conception of double consciousness, we rely on Anzaldúa's (1987) perspective that identities are fractured not only by gender, class, race, religion, and sexuality, but also by geographic realities such as living along the U.S.-Mexico border, in urban spaces, or on government-created Indian reservations. Anzaldúa's work continues a long intellectual history of Chicanas/os (see Acuna, 1972; Almaguer, 1974; Balderrama, 1982; Gomez-Quinones, 1977; Mirande & Enriquez, 1979; Padilla, 1987; Paz, 1961) and extends what Delgado Bernal (1998) calls a Chicana feminist epistemology. This work includes writers such as Alarcon (1990), Castillo (1995), and de la Torre and Pesquera (1993) to illustrate the intersections of race, class, and gender.

Our reliance on these scholars is not to assume a unified Latino/a (or even Chicano/a) subject. Oboler (1995) challenges the amalgamation of Spanish speakers in the Western Hemisphere under the rubric "Hispanic." The Hispanic label belies the problem inherent in attempts to create a unitary consciousness from one that is much more complex and multiple than imagined or constructed. According to Oboler:

> Insofar as the ethnic label Hispanic homogenizes the varied social and political experiences of 23 million people of different races, classes, languages, and national origins, genders, and religions, it is perhaps not so surprising that the meanings and uses of the term have become the subject of debate in the social sciences, government agencies, and much of society at large. (1995, p. 3)

Oboler's (1995) argument is enacted in a scene in Rebecca Gilman's (2000) play *Spinning into Butter.* In one scene, a college student is told that he is eligible for a "minority" fellowship. When the student objects to the term "minority," the dean informs him that he can designate himself as "Hispanic." He becomes more offended at that term, and when the dean asks him how he would like to identify himself, he says, "Newyorican." The dean then suggests that he list "Puerto Rican," but the student explains to her that he is not Puerto Rican. "I have never been to Puerto Rico and I would be as lost as any American tourist there." They continue to argue over what label or category is appropriate. The dean cannot understand that a key feature of self-determination lies in the ability to name oneself. The failure of the dean to recognize Newyorican as an identity does not de-legitimate it, except in her mainstream world, which not insignificantly controls the resources that the student needs to be successful at the college.

American Indians grapple with similar questions of what it means to be Indian. Despite movements toward "Pan-Indianism" (Hertzberg, 1971), the cultures of American Indians are both broad and diverse. Although we warn against essentializing American Indians, we do not want to minimize the way the federal government's attempt to "civilize" and de-tribalize Indian children through boarding schools helped various groups of Indians realize that they shared a number of common problems and experiences (Snipp, 1995). Lomawaima (1995) stated that "since the federal government turned its attention to the 'problem' of civilizing Indians, its overt goal has been to educate Indians to be non-Indians" (p. 332).

Much of the double consciousness that Indians face revolves around issues of tribal sovereignty. A loss of sovereignty is amplified by four methods of disenfranchisement experienced by many American Indians (Lomawaima, 1995). Those four methods included relocation by colonial authorities (e.g., to missions or reservations), systematic eradication of the native language, religious conversion (to Christianity), and restructuring of economies toward sedentary agriculture, small-scale craft industry, and gendered labor.

Warrior (1995) asks whether or not an investigation of early American Indian writers can have a significant impact on the way contemporary Native intellectuals develop critical studies. He urges caution in understanding the scholarship of Fourth World formulations such as those of Ward Churchill and M. Annette Jaimes because it tends to be essentializing in its call for understanding American Indian culture as a part of a global consciousness shared by all indigenous people in all periods of history. Warrior's work is a call for "intellectual sovereignty" (p. 87)—a position free from the tyranny and oppression of the dominant discourse.

Despite the attempts to eradicate an Indian identity, the mainstream continues to embrace a "romantic" notion of the Indian. In Eyre's (1998) adaptation of Sherman Alexie's (1993) *The Lone Ranger and Tonto Fistfight in Heaven*, which became the film *Smoke Signals*, we see an excellent example of this. The character Victor tells his traveling companion Thomas that he is not Indian enough. Playing on the prevailing stereotypes that whites have about Indians, Victor instructs Thomas to be "more stoic," to allow his hair to flow freely, and to get rid of his buttoned-down look. We see the humor in this scene because we recognize the ways we want Indians to appear to satisfy our preconceived notions of "Indian-ness."

Among Asian Pacific Islanders, there are notions of multiple consciousness. Lowe (1996) expresses this in terms of "heterogeneity, hybridity, and multiplicity" (p. 60). She points out that

> The articulation of an "Asian American identity" as an organizing tool has provided unity that enables diverse Asian groups to understand unequal circumstances and histories as being related. The building of "Asian American culture" is crucial to this effort, for it articulates and empowers the diverse Asian-origin community vis-à-vis the institutions and apparatuses that exclude and marginalize it. Yet to the extent that Asian American culture

> fixes Asian American identity and suppresses differences—of national origin, generation, gender, sexuality, class—it risks particular dangers: not only does it underestimate the differences and hybridities among Asians, but it may inadvertently support the racist discourse that constructs Asians as a homogenous group . . . (pp. 70–71)

Espiritu (1992) also reminds us that "Asian American" as an identity category came into being within the past 30 years. Prior to that time, most members of the Asian-descent immigrant population "considered themselves culturally and politically distinct" (p. 19). Indeed, the historical enmity that existed between and among various Asian groups made it difficult for groups to transcend their national allegiances to see themselves as one unified group. In addition, the growing anti-Asian sentiments with which the various Asian immigrant groups were faced in the United States caused specific groups to "disassociate themselves from the targeted group so as not to be mistaken for members of it and suffer any possible negative consequences" (p. 20).

Trinh Minh-ha (1989) and Mohanty (1991) offer postmodern analyses of Asian American-ness that challenge any unitary definitions of "Asian American." Rather than construct a mythical solidarity, their work examines the ways that Asian-ness is represented in the dominant imagination. One of the most vivid examples of the distorted, imagined Asian shows up in the work of David Henry Hwang, whose play *M. Butterfly* demonstrated how a constellation of characteristics—size, temperament, submissiveness—allowed a French armed services officer to intimately mistake a man for a woman.

Lowe (1996) reminds us that "the grouping 'Asian American' is not a natural or static category; it is a socially constructed unity, a situationally specific position assumed for political reasons" (p. 82). But it coexists with a "dynamic fluctuation and heterogeneity of Asian American culture . . ." (p. 68).

What each of these groups (i.e., African Americans, Native Americans, Latinos, and Asian Americans) has in common is the experience of a racialized identity. Each group is composed of myriad other national and ancestral origins, but the dominant ideology of the Euro-American epistemology has forced them into an essentialized and totalized unit that is perceived to have little or no internal variation. However, at the same moment, members of these groups have used these unitary racialized labels for political and cultural purposes. Identification with the racialized labels means an acknowledgment of some of the common experiences that group members have had as outsiders and others.

Along with this notion of double-consciousness that we argue pervades the experience of racialized identities, we believe it is imperative to include another theoretical axis—that of postcolonialism. Whereas double consciousness speaks to the struggle for identities, postcolonialism speaks to the collective project of the modern world that was in no way prepared for the decolonized to talk back and "act up." As West (1990) asserts, decolonization took on both "impetuous ferocity and moral outrage" (p. 25). Frantz Fanon (1968) best describes this movement:

> Decolonization, which sets out to change the order of the world, is obviously a program of complete disorder. . . . Decolonization is the meeting of two forces, opposed to each other by their very nature, which in fact owe their originality to that sort of substantification which results from and is nourished by the situation in the colonies. In decolonization, there is therefore the need of a complete calling in question of the colonial situation. (p. 35)

Fanon (1994) helped us understand the dynamics of colonialism and why decolonization had to be the major project of the oppressed:

> Colonial domination, because it is total and tends to over-simplify, very soon manages to disrupt in spectacular fashion the cultural life of a conquered people. This cultural obliteration is made possible by the negation of national reality, by new legal relations introduced by the occupying power, by the banishment of the natives and their customs to outlying districts by colonial society, by expropriation, and by the systematic enslaving of men and women. (p. 45)

Postcolonial theory serves as a corrective to our penchant for casting these issues into a strictly U.S. context. It helps us see the worldwide oppression against the "other" and the ability of dominant groups to define the terms of being and non-being, of civilized and uncivilized, of developed and undeveloped, of human and non-human. But even as we attempt to incorporate the term "postcolonial" into our understanding of critical race theory, we are reminded of the limits of such terminology to fully explain conditions of hierarchy, hegemony, racism, sexism, and unequal power relations. As McClintock (1994) asserts, "'post-colonialism' (like postmodernism) is unevenly developed globally. . . . Can most of the world's countries be said, in any meaningful or theoretically rigorous sense, to share a single 'common past,' or single common 'condition,' called 'the post-colonial condition,' or 'post- coloniality'" (p. 294)? Indeed, McClintock (1994) reminds us that "the term 'post-colonialism' is, in many cases, prematurely celebratory. Ireland may, at a pinch, be 'post-colonial,' but for the inhabitants of British-occupied Northern Ireland, not to mention the Palestinian inhabitants of the Israeli Occupied Territories and the West Bank, there may be nothing 'post' about colonialism at all"(p. 294). As Linda Tuhiwai Smith (1998) queries, "Post . . . have they left yet?"

"Is-ness" Versus "Us-ness": The Discursive and Material Limits of Liberal Ideology

> *To the extent that we interpret our experience from within the master narrative, we reinforce our own subordination. Whether [people of color] can counter racism may depend, finally, on our ability to claim identities outside the master narrative.*
>
> —Lisa Ikemoto (1995, pp. 312–313)

In the previous section, we addressed axes of moral and ethical epistemology on which much of the work of scholars of color rests (i.e., double consciousness, sovereignty, hybridity, heterogeneity, postcolonialism). In this section, we point toward the problems of dichotomy provoked by current political and social rhetoric.

After the September 11, 2001, terrorist attacks on the World Trade Center, the Pentagon, and a plane that crashed in Pennsylvania, George W. Bush addressed the nation (and ostensibly the world), letting the audience know that there were but two choices—to be with "us" or with the "terrorists." Those dichotomous choices were not nearly as simple as Bush suggested. For one thing, who is the "us"? Is the "us" the United States, regardless of the situation and circumstance? Is the "us" the United States even when it oppresses you? Is the "us" the supporters of the U.S. Patriot Acts I and II? Second, who are the terrorists? Clearly, we are not confused about al-Qaeda or the Taliban, but does objecting to U.S. foreign policy place us in league with them? If we stand in solidarity with the Palestinian people, are "with the terrorists"? If we acknowledge the legitimacy of the claims of the Northern Ireland Catholics, have we lost our claim on being a part of "us"? In the face of this sharp dividing line, many liberals chose George W. Bush's "us."

Choosing this unified "us" is not unlike Lipsitz's (1998) argument that the United States has been constructed as a nation of white people whose public policy, politics, and culture are designed to serve the interests of whites. Such a construction serves to maintain white privilege and justify the subordination of anyone outside this racial designation. Thus, even in the reporting of war casualties, we list the number of Americans (read: white, even if this is not the actual case) killed while ignoring the number of "the enemy" who are killed. What is important here is that whiteness is not attached to phenotype but to rather a social construction of who is worthy of inclusion in the circle of whiteness. The enemy is never white. His identity is subsumed in a nationality or ideology that can be defined as antithetical to whiteness (e.g., Nazis, fascists, communists, Muslims).

In one of her classes, Ladson-Billings used to show students a videotape of the Rodney King beating and, following the viewing, distributed copies of blind editorials about the beating. She then asked the students to determine the political perspective of the writers. Without benefit of newspaper mastheads or authors' names, many of the students struggled to locate the writers' ideological views. Predictably, the students divided the editorials into "liberal" and "conservative." No students identified moderate, radical, or reactionary perspectives. Their failure to see a broader ideological continuum is indicative of the polarization and dichotomization of our discourses.

We make a specific assumption about where the discursive battles must be fought. We do not engage the conservative ideology because we take for granted its antagonism toward the issues we raise. We understand that conservative rhetoric has no space for discussions of ethical epistemologies, double consciousness, hybridity, or postcolonialism. Our battle is with liberals who presume the moral high ground and who have situated themselves as "saviors" of the oppressed while simultaneously maintaining their white skin privilege (McIntosh, 1988).

A wonderful literary example of the moral vacuum in current liberal discourse appears in a novel by Bebe Moore Campbell (1995), *Your Blues Ain't Like Mine.* The novel is a fictionalized account of the horrible Emmett Till murder of the 1950s. Instead of focusing solely on the victim's family and perspective, the author provides multiple perspectives, including that of the perpetrators, the various families, and the townspeople. One character, Clayton, is a classic white liberal. He is from a privileged family and is afraid to truly relinquish his access to that privilege. Therefore, although Clayton tries to "help" various black characters, at the end of the novel, when he discovers that he is related to one of the black characters, he adamantly refuses to share his inheritance with her. Clayton's behavior is a metaphor for white liberalism. It is prepared to go only so far.

A real-life example of this moral vacuum was exemplified in the Clinton presidency. We are not referring to his personal transgressions and sexual exploits but rather his retreat from the political left by packaging himself as a "New Democrat," which can only be described as an "Old Moderate Republican"—think Nelson Rockefeller, George Romney, or Lowell Weicker. The actual Clinton presidency record indicates, according to columnist Steve Perry (1996), that [he] . . . co-opted the great middle while leaving liberals with no place to go" (p. 2). Randall Kennedy (2001) suggests:

> For all Clinton's much-expressed concern about social justice in general and racial justice in particular, his programs, policies, and gestures have done painfully little to help those whom Professor William Julius Wilson calls "the truly disadvantaged"—impoverished people, disproportionately colored, who are locked away in pestilent and crime-ridden inner cities or forgotten rural or small-town wastelands, people who are bereft of money, training, skills, or education needed to escape their plight. True, Clinton had to contend with a reactionary, Republican-led Congress for much of his presidency. But, even before the Gingrichian deluge of 1994 he had made it plain that his sympathies lay predominantly with "the middle class." For those below it, he offered chastising lectures that legitimated the essentially conservative notions that the predicament of the poor results primarily from their conduct and not from the deformative deprivations imposed on them by a grievously unfair social order that is in large part a class hierarchy and in smaller part a pigmentocracy.

Progressive columnist Malik Miah (1999) argues that Clinton's ease and fellow feeling with African Americans should not be interpreted as solidarity with the cause of African American or other people suffering oppression:

> While it is true Clinton plays the sax and is right at home visiting a Black church, his real policies have done more damage to the Black community than any president since the victory of civil rights movement in the 1960s. . . .
>
> On the issue of families and welfare he's ended programs that, while inadequate, provided some relief for the poorest sections of the population. Ironically, Nixon, Reagan and Bush—who all promised to end welfare—couldn't get it done. Clinton not only did it but claimed it as a great accomplishment of his first term in office. . . .

> He pushed through Congress a crime bill that restricts civil liberties and makes it easier to impose the death penalty. . . .
>
> The strong support [of African Americans] for Clinton is thus seen as "using common sense" and doing what's best for the future of our children, much more than having big illusions in Clinton and the "new" Democrats. The new middle-class layers in these communities also provide new potential voters and supporters for the two main parties of the rich.

Like Campbell's (1995) fictional character, Clayton, Bill Clinton was prepared to go only so far in his support of people of color. His liberal credentials relied on superficial and symbolic acts (e.g., associating with blacks, attending black churches, playing the saxophone); thus, in those areas where people of color were most hurting (e.g., health, education, welfare), he was unwilling to spend political capital. Such a retreat from liberal ideals represented a more severe moral failing than afternoon trysts with a White House intern.

With the George W. Bush administration, people of color and poor people are faced with a more pressing concern—the legitimacy of their being. Rather than argue over whether or not they are "with us" or "with the terrorists," we must constantly assert that we *are* rather than reflect a solidarity with an overarching "us" that actively oppresses. At this writing, we are watching a movement in California to prohibit the state from collecting data that identify people by racial categories (California Proposition 54). Passage of this proposition would mean that the state would not be able to report about the disparities that exist between whites and people of color in school achievement, incarceration, income levels, health concerns, and other social and civic concerns. Thus, this so-called color-blind measure effectively erases the races while maintaining the social, political, economic, and cultural status quo. The significance of this proposition is lost in the media circus of the California gubernatorial recall and cast of characters seeking to be governor of the most populous (and one of the most diverse) states in the nation.

At the same moment that the society seeks to erase and ignore the Other, it maintains a curious desire to consume and co-opt it. The appropriation of cultural forms from communities of color is not really flattery; it is a twisted embrace that simultaneously repels the Other. The complexity of this relationship allows white people, as performance artist Roger Guenveur Smith (Tate, 2003, p. 5) suggests, to love black music and hate black people. The mainstream community despises rap music for its violence, misogyny, and racial epithets but spends millions of dollars to produce and consume it. The mainstream decries illegal immigration from Mexico and Central America while refusing to acknowledge its own complicity in maintaining immigrants' presence through its demand for artificially price-depressed produce, domestic service, and the myriad jobs that "Americans" refuse to do. The mainstream fights what it sees as the "overrepresentation" of Asian-descent people in certain industries or high-status universities but cultivates fetishes over "Oriental" artifacts—martial arts, feng shui, sushi, and "docile," "petite" women. The mainstream remained silence while the indigenous population was massacred and displaced onto reservations but now runs eagerly to participate in sweat lodges and powwows. Such fascination does nothing to liberate and enrich the Other. Instead, they remain on the margins and are conveniently exploited for the political, economic, social, and cultural benefit of the dominant group. We are not a part of the "us" or "the terrorists." We are the struggling to exist—to just "be."

New Templates for Ethical Action

> *The past history of biology has shown that progress is equally inhibited by an anti-intellectual holism and a purely atomistic reductionism.*
>
> —Ernst Mayr (1976)

In his book *Ethical Ambition*, legal scholar Derrick Bell (2002) addresses a question that plagues many scholars of color: "How can I succeed without selling my soul?" He argues that the qualities of passion, risk, courage, inspiration, faith, humility, and love are the keys to success that maintain one's integrity and dignity. He contends that scholars must consider these as standards of behavior in both scholarship and relationships. Clearly, this is a different set of standards than those the academy typically applies to research and scholarship. But how well have the usual standards served communities of color?

> From 1932 to 1972, 399 poor black sharecroppers in Macon County, Alabama were denied treatment for syphilis and deceived by physicians of the United States Public Health Service. As part of the Tuskegee Syphilis Study, designed to document the natural history of the disease, these men were told that they were being treated for "bad blood." In fact, government officials went to extreme lengths to insure that they received no therapy from any source. As reported by the *New York Times* on 26 July 1972, the Tuskegee Syphilis Study was revealed as "the longest nontherapeutic experiment on human beings in medical history." (Tuskegee Syphilis Study Legacy Committee, 1996)

The Health News Network (2000; www.healthnewsnet.com) details a long list of unethical and egregious acts performed in the name of science. For example, in 1940, 400 prisoners in Chicago were infected with malaria to study the effects of new and experimental drugs to combat the disease. In 1945, Project Paperclip was initiated by the U.S. State Department, Army intelligence, and the CIA to recruit Nazi scientists and offer them immunity and secret identities in exchange for work on top secret government projects in the United States. In 1947, the CIA began a study of LSD as a potential weapon for use by U.S. intelligence. In this study, human subjects (both civilian and military) were used with and without their knowledge. In 1950, the U.S. Navy sprayed a cloud of bacteria over San Francisco to determine how susceptible a U.S. city would be to biological attack. In 1955, the CIA released a bacteria over Tampa Bay, Florida, that had been withdrawn from the Army's biological warfare arsenal to determine its ability to infect human populations with biological agents. In 1958, the Army Chemical Welfare Laboratories tested LSD on 95 volunteers to determine its effect on intelligence. In 1965, prisoners at the Holmesburg State Prison in Philadelphia were subjected to dioxin, the highly toxic chemical compound of Agent Orange used in Vietnam. In 1990, more than 1,500 6-month-old black and Latino babies in Los Angeles were given an "experimental" measles vaccine that had never been licensed for use in the United States. The Centers for Disease Control later admitted that the parents were never informed that their babies were receiving an experimental vaccine.

Although these examples in the life sciences are extreme, it is important to recognize that social sciences have almost always tried to mimic the so-called hard sciences. We have accepted their paradigms and elevated their ways of knowing even when "hard scientists" themselves challenge them (Kuhn, 1962). The standards that require research to be "objective," precise, accurate, generalizable, and replicable do not simultaneously produce moral and ethical research and scholarship. The current calls for "scientifically based" and "evidence-based" research in education from the United States Department of Education have provoked an interesting response from the education research community (Shavelson & Towne, 2003).

The National Research Council Report *Scientific Research in Education* (Shavelson & Towne, 2003) outlines what it terms a "set of fundamental principles" for "a healthy community of researchers" (p. 2). These principles include:

1. Pose significant questions that can be investigated empirically.
2. Link research to relevant theory.
3. Use methods that permit direct investigation of the question.
4. Provide a coherent and explicit chain of reasoning.
5. Replicate and generalize across studies.
6. Disclose research to encourage professional scrutiny and critique. (pp. 3–5)

On their face, these seem to be "reasonable" principles around which the "scientific" community can coalesce. Although it is beyond the scope of this chapter to do a thorough review of the NRC report, we do want to point out some of the problems such thinking provokes, particularly in the realm of ethics and moral activism. The first principle suggests that we "pose significant questions that can be investigated empirically." We cannot recall the last time a researcher asserted that he or she was investigating something "insignificant." Scholars research that which interests them, and no one would suggest that they are interested in insignificant things. More important, this principle assumes the supremacy of empirical work. Without taking our discussion too far into the philosophical, we assert that what constitutes "the empirical" is culturally coded. For example, many years ago, a researcher from a prestigious university was collecting data in an urban classroom. The researcher reported on the apparent chaos and disorder of the classroom and described her observation of some students openly snorting drugs in the back of the classroom. Later, a graduate student who knew the school and the community talked with some of the students and learned that the students knew that the researchers expected them to be "dangerous," "uncontrollable," and "frightening." Determined to meet the researcher's expectations, the students gathered up the chalk dust from the blackboard ledge and began treating it like a powdered drug. What the researcher actually saw were students who decided to fool a researcher. This may have been empirical work, but clearly it was wrong.

In a less extreme example, an anthropology of education professor regularly displayed a set of photographic slides to his class and required students to describe the contents of each slide. In one slide, a photo of a farmhouse in a small German village, there is a huge pile of manure (at least one full story high) in front of the house. Not one student out of a lecture section of about 100 noted the manure pile. Even if one might argue that it was difficult to determine what it was in the slide, not one student noted that there was a "pile of something" sitting in front of the farmhouse. Our point here is that our ability to access the empirical is culturally determined and always shaped by moral and political concerns.

Popkewitz (2003) argues that the NRC report rests on a number of assumptions that expose the writers' misunderstanding of scientific inquiry. These assumptions include:

> (1) There is a unity of foundational assumptions that cross all the natural and social sciences. This unity involves: (2) the importance of rigorous methods and design models; (3) the cumulative, sequential development of knowledge; (4) science is based on inferential reasoning; (5) the empirical testing and development of knowledge. Finally, the assumptions provide the expertise of what government needs—showing what works. This last point is important as the Report has a dual function. It is to outline a science of education and to propose how government can intervene in the development of a science that serves policy reforms. (pp. 2–3)

Popkewitz (2003) is elegant in his rebuttal of the NRC report, and we are limited in our ability to expend space to offer additional critique. However, our task is to point out that with all the emphasis on "scientific principles," the NRC report fails to include the moral and ethical action in which scholars must engage. Is it enough to follow protocols for human subjects? That sets a very minimalist standard that is likely to continue the same moral and ethical abuses. For example, in a recent National Public Radio broadcast of *All Things Considered* (Mann, 2003) titled "New York Weighs Lead-Paint Laws," the reporter indicated that researchers were testing children for the levels of lead in their blood. Although there was consensus that many of the children had elevated levels of lead, the researchers rejected the recommendation that the levels of lead in the building be tested. This second, more efficient method would allow for class action on the part of the building residents, but the researchers chose to persist in examining individuals. Rather than raise the moral bar by insisting that it is unsafe to live in buildings with lead-based paint and to test the buildings for that paint, individuals (many who are poor and disenfranchised) are responsible for coming forth to be tested. One might argue that the researchers are abiding by the standards of scientific inquiry; however, these standards are not inclusive of the moral and ethical action that must be taken.

In addition to Bell's (2002) call for ethical behavior in the academy, Guinier and Torres (2002) have argued that it is important to move past the current racial discourses because such discourses invariably keep us locked in race-power hierarchies that depend on a winner-take-all conclusion. Instead, Guinier and Torres (2002) give birth to a new construct—"political race"—that relies on building cross-racial coalitions and alliances that involve grassroots workers who strive to remake the terms of participation and invigorate democracy. Their work points to the coalition of African Americans and Latinos who devised the 10% decision to address inequity in Texas higher education. This decision means that all students in the state of Texas who graduate in the top 10% of their class are eligible for admission at the two flagship Texas universities—University of Texas at Austin and Texas A&M. We would also point to the work of the modern civil rights movement of the 1960s and the anti-apartheid work in South Africa. In both instances, we saw broad coalitions of people working for human liberation and justice. The aim of such work is not merely to remedy past racial injustice but rather to enlarge the democratic project to include many more participants. In the case of the United States, the civil rights movement became a template for addressing a number of undemocratic practices against women, immigrants, gays and lesbians, the disabled, and linguistic minorities. The point of moral and ethical activism is not to secure privileges for one's own group; it is to make democracy a reality for increasing numbers of groups and individuals. Such work permits us to look at multiple axes of difference and take these intersections seriously.

In *Miner's Canary*, Guinier and Torres (2002) point out that our typical response to inequity is to feel sorry for the individuals but ignore the structure that produces such inequity. We would prefer to prepare the dispossessed and disenfranchised to better fit in a corrupt system rather than rethink the whole system. Instead of ignoring racial differences, as the color-blind approach suggests, political race urges us to understand the ways that race and power intertwine at every level of the society and to further understand that only through cross-racial coalitions can we expose the embedded hierarchies of privilege and destroy them (www.minerscanary.org/about.shtml, retrieved December 1, 2003). Guinier and Torres (2002) call this notion of enlisting race to resist power "political race." It requires diagnosing systemic injustice and organizing to resist it.

Political race challenges the social and economic consequences of race in a "third way" (www.minerscanary.org/about.shtml) that proposes a multitextured political strategy rather than the traditional legal solutions to the issues of racial justice. The authors argue that "political race dramatically transforms the use of race from a signifier of individual culpability and prejudice to an early warning sign of larger injustices" (Ibid.) When they speak of political, they are not referring to conventional electoral politics. Rather, their notion of political race challenges social activists and critical scholars to rethink what winning means and if winning in a corrupt system can ever be good enough. Instead, their focus is on the power of change through collective action and how such action can change (and challenge) us all to work in new ways.

We seek a methodology and a theory that, as Gayatri Spivak (1990) argues, seeks not merely reversal of roles in a hierarchy, but rather displacement of taken-for-granted norms around unequal binaries (e.g., male-female, public-private, white-non-white, able-disabled, native-foreign). We see such possibility in Critical Race Theory (CRT), and we point out that CRT is not limited to the old notions of race. Rather, CRT is a new analytic rubric for considering difference and inequity using multiple methodologies—story, voice, metaphor, analogy, critical social science, feminism, and postmodernism. So visceral is our reaction to the word "race" that many scholars and consumers of scholarly literature cannot see beyond the word to appreciate the value of CRT for making sense of our current social condition. We would argue that scholars such as Trinh Minh-ha, Robert Allen Warrior, Gloria Anzaldúa, Ian Haney Lopez, Richard Delgado, Lisa Lowe, David Palumbo-Liu, Gayatri Spivak, Chandra Mohanty, and Patricia Hill Collins all produce a kind of CRT. They are not bogged down with labels or dogmatic constraints; rather, they are creatively and passionately engaging new visions of scholarship to do work that ultimately will serve people and lead to human liberation.

Thus, we argue that the work of critical scholars (from any variety of perspectives) is not merely to try to replicate the work of previous scholars in a cookie-cutter fashion but rather to break new epistemological, methodological, social activist, and moral ground. We do not need Derrick Bell, Lani Guinier, or Gerald Torres clones. We need scholars to take up their causes (along with causes they identify for themselves) and creatively engage them. We look to them because of their departure from the scholarly mainstream, not to make them idols.

Moving From Research to Activism—Street-Level Research in Ivory Towers

Conflict—the real world kind, I mean—can be bloody, misguided, and wholly tragic. It behooves us always to try to understand how and why bloodshed breaks out as it does. But the very narratives and stories we tell ourselves and each other afterwards, in an effort to explain, understand, excuse, and assign responsibility for conflict, may also be, in a sense, the source of the very violence we abhor.

—Lisa Ikemoto (1995, p. 313)

Earlier in this chapter, we referenced Harold Cruse and *The Crisis of the Negro Intellectual* (1967/1984), and indeed we recognize that the crisis Cruse identifies is a crisis for all intellectuals of color. Cruse's point that "While Negro intellectuals are busy trying to interpret the nature of the black world and its aspirations to the whites, they should, in fact, be defining their own roles as intellectuals within both worlds" (p. 455) is applicable to all scholars of color. Novelists such as Toni Morrison (1987), Shawn Wong (1995), Ana Castillo (1994), Sherman Alexie (1993), and Jhumpa Lahiri (1999) deftly accomplish what Cruse asks. They sit comfortably within the walls of the academy and on the street corners, barrios, and reservations of the people. They are "cultural brokers" who understand the need to be "in" the academy (or mainstream) but not "of" the academy.

In the foreword to Cruse's book, Allen and Wilson (1984) summarize the central tasks that this book outlines for "would-be intellectuals" (p. v):

1. To familiarize themselves with their own intellectual antecedents and with previous political and cultural movements;

2. To analyze critically the bases for the pendulum swings between the two poles of integration and [black] nationalism, and try to synthesize them into a single and consistent analysis;

3. To identify clearly the political, economic, and cultural requisites for black advancement in order to meld them into a single politics of progressive black culture. This process requires greater attention both to Afro-American popular culture and to the macroeconomic, structural context of modern capitalism in which group culture either flourishes or atrophies;

4. To recognize the uniqueness of American conditions and to insist that one incorporate this uniqueness when studying numbers 1 through 3 above.

Despite Cruse's (1967/1984) focus on African Americans and their experiences in the United States, it is clear to us that such work is important for any marginalized group. All scholars of color must know the intellectual antecedents of their cultural, ethnic, or racial group. This is important for combating the persistent ideology of white supremacy that denigrates the intellectual contributions of others. All scholars of color must look to the epistemological underpinnings and legitimacy of their cultures and cultural ways of knowing. They must face the tensions that emerge in their communities between assimilation into the U.S. mainstream and the creation of separate and distinct cultural locations. For example, the construction of Asian

Americans as articulated previously by Lowe (1996) and Espiritu (1992) are powerful examples of the synthesis Cruse speaks of. All scholars of color need to acknowledge the salience of popular culture in shaping our research and scholarly agendas, for it is in the popular that our theories and methodologies become living, breathing entities.

Martin Luther King, Jr. had a theory about "nonviolence" that came from his study of Gandhi and Dietrich Bonhoeffer, but the theory was actualized in the hearts and minds of ordinary people—Fannie Lou Hamer, Esau Jenkins, Septima Clark, and many others. So great is the desire for survival and liberation that it transcends geopolitical boundaries, languages, and cultures. The modern civil rights movement in the United States was replayed in China's Tiananmen Square, in the cities and townships of South Africa, and in liberation struggles the world over. In each instance, the power of the popular brings music, art, and energy to the struggle. Ordinary people become the "street-level bureaucrats" (Lipsky, 1983) who translate theory into practice. However, we want to be clear that we are not suggesting that such "street-level bureaucrats" begin to behave as functionaries of the state and thereby become the new power brokers. Rather, we are suggesting a new vision of Lipsky's (1983) concept in which people from the community represent a new form of leadership that is unafraid of shared power and real democracy.

But scholars who take on the challenge of moral and ethical activist work cannot rely solely on others to make sense of their work and translate it into usable form. Patricia Hill Collins (1998) speaks of a "visionary pragmatism" (p. 188) that may be helpful in the development of more politically and socially engaged scholarship. She uses this term to characterize the perspective of the working-class women of her childhood:

> The Black women on my block possessed a "visionary pragmatism" that emphasized the necessity of linking caring, theoretical vision with informed, practical struggle. A creative tension links visionary thinking and practical action. Any social theory that becomes too out of touch with everyday people and their lives, especially oppressed people, is of little use to them. The functionality and not just the logical consistency of visionary thinking determines its worth. At the same time, being too practical, looking only to the here and now—especially if present conditions seemingly offer little hope—can be debilitating. (p. 188)

Scholars must also engage new forms of scholarship that make translations of their work more seamless. Guinier and Torres (2002) speak to us of "political race" as a new conception we can embrace. Castillo (1994) offers magical realism as a rubric for Chicano coalescence. Lowe (1996) has taken up notions of hybridity, heterogeneity, and multiplicity to name the material contradictions that characterize immigrant groups—particularly Asian-descent immigrants—who are routinely lumped together and homogenized into a unitary and bounded category. Espiritu (2003) helps us link the study of race and ethnicity to the study of imperialism so that we can better understand transnational and diasporic lives. Similarly, Ong (1999) warns of the growing threat of global capital that destabilizes notions of cultural unity and/or allegiance.

Instead, the overwhelming power of multinational corporations creates economic cleavages that force people, regardless of their racial, cultural, and ethnic locations, to chase jobs and compete against each other to subsist.

Promising scholarship that may disrupt the fixed categories that whiteness has instantiated appears in work by Prashad (2002), who examines the cross-racial and interracial connections that reflect the reality of our histories and current conditions. Prashad argues that instead of the polarized notions of either "color-blindness" or a primordial "multiculturalism," what we seek is a "polyculturalism," a term he borrows from Robin D. G. Kelley (1999), who argues that "so-called 'mixed-race' children are not the only ones with a claim to multiple heritages. All of us, and I mean ALL of us, are the inheritors of European, African, Native-American, and even Asian pasts, even if we can't exactly trace our bloodlines to all of these continents" (p. 6). Kelley (1999) further argues that our various cultures "have never been easily identifiable, secure in their boundaries, or clear to all people who live in or outside our skin. We were multi-ethnic and polycultural from the get-go" (p. 6). This challenge to notions of ethnic purity moves us away from the futile chase for "authenticity" and troubles the reification of ethnic and racial categories. We begin to understand, as political activist Rev. Al Sharpton has said, that "all my skin folks, ain't my kin folks." Just because people look like us by no means implies that they have our best interests at heart.

At the street level, we must acknowledge the power of hip-hop culture. It is important that we distinguish our acknowledgment from the negatives that corporate interests promulgate—violence, racism, misogyny, and crass consumerism—from hip-hop as a vehicle for cross-racial, cross-cultural, and international coalitions. Organizations such as El Puente Academy for Peace and Justice in the Williamsburg section of Brooklyn, New York, and the Urban Think Tank Institute (www.Urban ThinkTank .org) provide a more democratic and politically progressive discourse. The Urban Think Tank Institute argues that the hip-hop generation "has become more politically sophisticated . . . [and needs] a space whereby grassroots thinkers, activists, and artists can come together, discuss relevant issues, devise strategies, and then articulate their analysis to the public and to policy makers" (see Yvonne Bynoe on the Urban Think Tank Web site). Such organizations have corollaries in the earlier work of Myles Horton (1990; Horton & Freire, 1990), Paulo Freire (1970), Septima Clark (with Brown, 1990), Marcus Garvey's Universal Negro Improvement Association (Prashad, 2002), and the Boggs Center (Boggs, 1971). It also resembles the worldwide liberation movements we have seen in India, South Africa, China, Brazil, Zimbabwe, and most everywhere in the world where people have organized to resist oppression and domination.

The hip-hop movement reminds us of the stirrings of the youth and young adults in the modern civil rights movement. When it became clear that the older, more conservative leadership was unwilling to make a space for young people in the movement, we began to see a new form of liberation work. Instead of attempting to assimilate and assert our rights as Americans, young people began to assert their rights to a distinct identity in which being an American may have been constitutive of this identity but it was not the all-encompassing identity. Hip-hop's wide appeal, across geopolitical and ethnic boundaries (we found hip-hop Web sites in Latvia, Russia, Italy, and Japan) makes it a potent force for mobilizing young people worldwide. Unfortunately, most scholars (and, for that matter, most adults) have narrow views of hip hop.[6] They see it merely as rap music and "gangsta" culture. However, the power of hip hop is in its diffuseness. It encompasses art, music, dance, and self-presentation. Although much of the media attention has focused on notorious personalities such as Biggie Smalls, Snoop Dogg, P. Diddy, 50-Cent, Nelly, and others, there is a core group of hip-hop artists whose major purpose was to provide social commentary and awaken a somnambulant generation of young people from their drug, alcohol, and materialistic addictions. Some of these artists sought to contextualize the present conditions of the African American and other marginalized communities of color and call for action by making historical links to ideas (e.g., Black Power), social movements (e.g., cultural nationalism), and political figures (e.g., Malcolm X, Che Guevara). The need for this kind of work is not unlike the call of Ngugi wa Thiongo (1991), who argued, in speaking of the emerging independent African nations, that we needed a radically democratic proposal for the production of art, literature, and culture based on our political praxis. Looking at the U.S. scene, Dyson (1993) argues:

> Besides being the most powerful form of Black musical expression today, rap music projects a style of self into the world that generates forms of cultural resistance and transforms the ugly terrain of ghetto existence into a searing portrait of life as it must be lived by millions of voiceless people. For that reason alone, rap deserves attention and should be taken seriously. (p. 15)

Counted among these visionary hip-hop leaders[7] are Grandmaster Flash, Public Enemy, Run-DMC, The Fugees, Lauryn Hill, KRS-1, Diggable Planets, Arrested Development, the Roots, Mos Def, Common, Erykah Badu, the whole host of Nuyorican poets, and the organic intellectuals that produce *YO Magazine* in the San Francisco Bay area. These are the people who have the ears (and hearts and minds) of young people. It is among this group that new forms of scholarship that take up moral and ethical positions will be forged. Scholars who choose to ignore the trenchant pleas of the hip-hop generation will find themselves increasingly out of touch and irrelevant to the everyday lives of people engaged in the cause of social justice.

A number of scholars have made connections with the hip-hop generation: Miguel Algarin, with his ties to both the academy and the Nuyorican Poet's Café; Cornel West and Michael Eric Dyson, with their face-to-face conversations with the hip-hop generation; and bell hooks, with her revolutionary black feminism. The late poet June Jordan, Toni Morrison, Pablo Neruda, Carlos Bulosan, John Okada, Diego Rivera, Leslie

Marmon Silko, Sherman Alexie, and others have deployed their art to speak across the generations.

Social scientists must similarly situate themselves to play a more active and progressive role in the fight for equity and social justice. Their work must transcend narrow disciplinary boundaries if it is to have any impact on people who reside in subaltern sites or even on policy makers. Unfortunately, far too many academics spend their time talking to each other in the netherworld of the academy. We write in obscure journals and publish books in languages that do not translate to the lives and experiences of real people. We argue not for the seeming "simplicity" of the political right, but for the relevancy and the power of the popular.

Reconstruction of the Work of the Intellect

Don't push me, cause I'm close to the edge I'm trying not to lose my head. It's like a jungle sometimes, it makes me wonder How I keep from going under.

—From *The Message*, by Grandmaster Flash

It is typical for institutional recommendations to call for a "transformation" of some kind. In this case, were we to suggest that the academy needed to be transformed, we imagine that many would agree. However, transformation implies a change that emanates from an existing base. Clark Kent transformed himself into Superman, but underneath the blue tights, he was still Clark Kent. Britt Reid transformed himself into the Green Hornet, but underneath the mask he was still Britt Reid. Captain John Reid's brother Dan transformed himself into the Lone Ranger, but under that powder blue, skintight outfit and mask he was still Dan Reid. What we are urging is the equivalent of having Jimmy Olsen, Kato, and Tonto assume the leadership and implement the plan.

Reconstruction comes after the destruction of what was. The Union Army did not attempt to massage the South into a new economy after the U.S. Civil War. The Cuban Revolution was not Fidel Castro's attempt to adapt the Battista regime. The new South Africa is not trying to organize a new form of apartheid with black dominance. Rather, these are instances where we see the entire destruction of the old in an attempt to make something new. So it may have to be with the academy in order for it to be responsive to the needs of everyday people.

The student movement at San Francisco State College (Prashad, 2002) revolutionized not only that local campus but also campuses across the country. It formed the basis for the development of what Wynter (1992) called "new studies" in black, Latino, Asian, and Native American studies. It provided a template for women's studies, gay and lesbian studies, and disability studies. It reconfigured knowledge from static, fixed disciplines with the perception of cumulative information, to a realization of the dynamic and overlapping nature of knowledge and a more fluid sense of epistemology and methodology. But even with the strides made by these new studies, they still represent a very small crack in the solid, almost frozen traditions of the university. Indeed, the more careerist interests have made a more indelible imprint on colleges and universities in the United States. Instead of seeing colleges and universities as the site of liberal education and free thinking, increasing numbers of young people (and their parents) see the university as a job training facility. Courses and programs of study in hotel and restaurant management, criminal justice, and sports management,[8] while representing legitimate job and career choices, are less likely to promote overall university goals of educating people to engage with knowledge and critical thinking across a wide variety of disciplines and traditions.

A reconstructed university would displace much of the credentialing function of the current system and organize itself around principles of intellectual enrichment, social justice, social betterment, and equity. Students would see the university as a vehicle for public service, not merely personal advancement. Students would study various courses and programs of study in an attempt to improve both their minds and the condition of life in the community, society, and the world. Such a program has little or no chance of success in our current sociopolitical atmosphere. Although colleges and universities are legitimately categorized as nonprofit entities, they do have fiscal responsibilities. Currently, those fiscal responsibilities are directed to continued employment of elites, supplying a well-prepared labor force, and increasing endowments. In a reconstructed university, the fiscal responsibility would be directed toward community development and improving the socioeconomic infrastructure.

A reconstructed university would have a different kind of reward system in which teaching and service were true equals to research and scholarship. Perhaps these components would be more seamlessly wedded and more tightly related. Excellence would be judged by quality efforts in all areas. Admission to such a university would involve more complex standards being applied in evaluating potential students. Instead of examining strict grade point averages, class rankings, standardized test scores, and inflated résumés,[9] colleges and universities could begin to select students for their ability to contribute to the body politic that will be formed on a particular campus.

Democracy is a complicated system of government, and it requires an educated citizenry to participate actively in it. By educated, we are referring not merely to holding degrees and credentials, but to knowing enough to, as Freire (1970) insists, "read the word and the world." We recognize the need for "organic intellectuals"[10] to help us as credentialed intellectuals do the reconstructive work. We find it interesting (and paradoxical) that education at the two ends of the continuum (precollegiate and adult education) seem to be more progressive and proactive (at least from the point of view of the literature they produce and respond to). Colleges and universities seem to function as incubators for the soon-to-be (or wannabe) guardians of the status quo. Too many of our college and university students want to assume a place in the current society without using their collegiate years as an opportunity to consider how the society could be different and how it could be more just.

Among precollegiate educators, Grace Boggs (1971) has developed a "new system of education" that makes a radical break from the current system that is designed to "prepare the great majority [of citizens] for labor and to advance a few out of their ranks to join the elite in governing" (p. 32). Boggs's (1971) vision is for a "new system of education that will have as its means and its ends the development of the great masses of people *to govern over themselves and to administer over things*" (p. 32). Boggs's system of education calls for an education that must do the following:

- Be based on a philosophy of history—in order to realize his or her highest potential as a human being, every young person must be given a profound and continuing sense (a) of his or her own life as an integral part of the continuing evolution of the human species; and (b) of the unique capacity of human beings to shape and create reality in accordance with conscious purposes and plans;
- Include productive activity—productive activity, in which individuals choose a task and participate in its execution from beginning to end, remains the most effective and rapid means to internalize the relationship between cause and effect, between effort and result, between purposes (ends) and programs (means), an internalization which is necessary to rational behavior, creative thinking, and responsible activity;
- Include living struggles—every young person must be given expanding opportunities to solve the problems of his [*sic*] physical and social environment, thereby developing the political and technical skills which are urgently needed to transform the social institutions as well as the physical environments of our communities and cities;
- Include a wide variety of resources and environments—in our complex world, education must be consciously organized to take place not only in schools and not only using teachers and technology, but also a multiplicity of physical and social environments (e.g., the countryside, the city, the sea, factories, offices, other countries, other cultures);
- Include development in bodily self-knowledge and well-being—increased scientific and technological knowledge necessitates more active participation by lay people and a greater focus on preventive medicine. Students must learn how to live healthy lives and work to reverse the devastating health conditions in poor and working-class communities;
- Include clearly defined goals—education must move away from achieving more material goods and/or fitting people into the existing unequal structure. Education's primary purpose must be governing. (pp. 33–36)

Early scholars in adult education (Freire, 1970; M. Horton, 1990; M. Horton & Freire, 1990) understood the need to develop education imbued with social purpose and grounded in grassroots, popular organizing movements. Although there are a number of such examples, because of space limitations we will focus on the Highlander Folk School. Aimee Horton (1989) documents the school's history and points out that its relationship with social movements is the key to understanding both the strength and the limitations of its adult education program. The two—social movement and adult education—form a symbiotic relationship. As Myles Horton (1990) himself suggests:

> It is only in a movement that an idea is often made simple enough and direct enough that is can spread rapidly. . . . We cannot create movements, so if we want to be a part of a movement when it comes, we have to get ourselves into a position—by working with organizations that deal with structural change—to be on the inside of that movement when it comes, instead of on the outside trying to get accepted. (p. 114)

Highlander always saw itself as part of the larger goals of social movements while simultaneously "maintaining a critical and challenging voice within" (Heaney,1995, p. 57). Highlander based its work on two major components—an education grounded in the "real and realizable struggles of people for democratic control over their lives" (Heaney, 1995, p. 57) and the need to challenge people to consider the present and the future simultaneously as they move toward social change.

The Citizenship Schools (which functioned between 1953 and 1961), one of Highlander's programs, were designed to help African American citizens of the deep South to become literate *and* protest for their rights. According to Horton (1990), "you can't read and write yourself into freedom. You [have] to fight for that and you [have] to do it as part of a group, not as an individual" (p. 104). The Citizenship Schools are a far cry from current adult literacy and vocational programs that have no political commitment and encourage individual and simple solutions to major social problems (Heaney, 1995).

We are skeptical of the academy's ability to reconstruct itself because of the complicity of its intellectuals with the current social order. Thus, we agree with Foucault (1977), who insists:

> Intellectuals are no longer needed by the masses to gain knowledge: the masses know perfectly well, without illusion; they know far better than the intellectual and they are certainly capable of expressing themselves. But there exists a system of power which blocks, prohibits, and invalidates this discourse and this knowledge, a power not only found in manifest authority of censorship, but one that profoundly and subtly penetrates an entire societal network. Intellectuals are themselves agents of this system of power—the idea of their responsibility for "consciousness" and discourse forms part of the system. (p. 207)

Concluding Thoughts: In Search of Revolutionary Habitus

> *As soon as possible he [the white man] will tell me that it is not enough to try to be white, but that a white totality must be achieved.*
>
> —Frantz Fanon (1986)

Our previous section suggests an almost nihilistic despair about the role of the intellectual in leading us toward more just and equitable societies. Actually, we point to the limits of the academy and suggest that committed intellectuals must move into spaces beyond the academy to participate in real change. Indeed, such a move may mean that academics take on less prominent roles in order to listen and learn from people actively engaged in social change. Thus, we speak to an audience who is willing to search for a revolutionary habitus.

Bourdieu (1990) brought us the concept of habitus, which he vaguely defines as a system of

> durable, transposable dispositions, structured structures predisposed to function as structuring structures, that is, as principles which generate and organize practices and representations that can be objectively adapted to their outcomes without presupposing a conscious aiming at ends or an express mastery of the operations necessary in order to attain them. Objectively "regulated" and "regular" without being in any way the product of obedience to the rules, they can be collectively orchestrated without being the product of the organizing action of a conductor. (p. 53)

Thus, according to Palumbo-Liu (1993), "individuals are inclined to act in certain ways given their implicit understanding of, their 'feel for,' the field" (p. 6). The habitus "expresses first the result of an organizing action with a meaning close to that of words such as structure: it also designates a way of being, a habitual state (especially of the body) and, in particular, a disposition, a tendency, propensity, or inclination" (Bourdieu, 1977, p. 214). This work provides us with both "the flexibility of what might otherwise be thought of as a strictly determinative structure (the field) and the ambiguity of a predisposed but not mandated agency (habitus) [and] signal Bourdieu's desire to go beyond the usual binary categories of external/internal, conscious/unconscious, determinism/free agency" (Palumbo-Liu, 1993, p. 7).

Our call for a revolutionary habitus recognizes that the "field" (Bourdieu, 1990) in which academics currently function constrains the social (and intellectual) agency that might move us toward social justice and human liberation. As Palumbo-Liu (1993) points out, a field is

> a particular grid of relations that governs specific areas of social life (economics, culture, education, politics, etc.): individuals do not act freely to achieve their goals and the creation of dispositions must be understood within historically specific formations of fields; each field had its own rules and protocols that open specific social positions for different agents. Yet this is not a static model: the field in turn is modified according to the manner in which those positions are occupied and mobilized. (p. 6)

Thus, despite notions of academic freedom and tenure, professors work within a field that may delimit and confine political activity and views unpopular with university administrators, state and national legislators, and policy makers. Subtle and not so subtle sanctions have the power to shape how individuals' habituses conform to the field. We must imagine new fields and new habituses that constitute a new vision of what it means to do academic work. According to Palumbo-Liu (1993), "The habitus we might imagine for social agents has not yet become habituated to postmodern globalized culture that continues to be reshaped as we speak. The field of culture must now be understood to accommodate both dominant and emergent social groups who differently and significantly inflect the consumption and production of an increasingly global and hybrid culture" (p. 8).

Perhaps our notion of a revolutionary habitus might better be realized through Espiritu's (2003) powerful conceptualization of "home," in which there is a keen awareness of the way racialized immigrants "from previously colonized nations are not exclusively formed as racial minorities within the United States but also as colonized nationals while in their 'homeland'—one that is deeply affected by U.S. influences and modes of social organization" (p. 1). Espiritu points out that the notion of home is not merely a physical place but is also "a concept and desire—a place that immigrants visit through the imagination" (p. 10). We assert that even those long-term racialized residents of the United States (e.g., African Americans, American Indians, Latinos) have experienced (and continue to experience) colonial oppression (Ladson-Billings, 1998a).

What Espiritu (2003) offers is a way to think about the permeable nature of concepts like race, culture, ethnicity, gender, and ability. Rather than become fixated on who is included and who is excluded, we need to consider the way that we are all border dwellers who negotiate and renegotiate multiple places and spaces. According to Mahmud (cited in Espiritu, 2003), "immigrants call into question implicit assumptions about 'fixed identities, unproblematic nationhood, invisible sovereignty, ethnic homogeneity, and exclusive citizenship'" (p. 209).

Thus, the challenge of those of us in the academy is not how to make those outside the academy more like us, but rather to recognize the "outside the academy" identities that we must recruit for ourselves in order to be more effective researchers on behalf of people who can make use of our skills and abilities. We must learn to be "at home" on the street corners and in the barrios, churches, mosques, kitchens, porches, and stoops of people and communities, so that our work more accurately reflects their concerns and interests. Our challenge is to renounce our paternalistic tendencies and sympathetic leanings to move toward an empathic, ethical, and moral scholarship that propels us to a place where we are prepared to forcefully and courageously answer "the call."

Notes

1. We are using the term "of color" to refer to all people who are raced and outside the construction of whiteness (Haney Lopez, 1998).

2. Paulo Freire (1970) insists that "that the oppressed are not 'marginals,' are not men living 'outside' society. They have always been 'inside'—inside the structure that made them 'beings' for others" (p. 71).

3. "Articulate" is a term seemingly reserved for African Americans and is seen by African Americans as a way to suggest that one speaks better than would be expected of "your kind."

4. We are restating at length portions of Ladson-Billings's (2000) discussion on alterity and liminality that appeared in the second edition of the *Handbook.*

5. We remind the reader that we are aware of the dilemma of using racialized categories and that the boundaries between and among various racial, ethnic, and cultural groups are more permeable and more complex than the categories imply.

6. MacArthur Fellow and civil rights leader Bernice Johnson Reagon asserts that no one has the right to tell the next generation what their freedom songs should be (Moyers, 1991).

7. We are aware that we are not acknowledging all of the artists in this tradition.

8. We want to be clear that we do not disparage these career choices; however, we question whether they represent what is meant by "liberal arts."

9. Increasingly, students seeking admission to selective colleges and universities participate in extracurricular activities (e.g., sports, clubs, the arts) and volunteer efforts not because of interests and commitments but rather because such participation may give them an advantage over other applicants.

10. We use this term to describe those grassroots people whose intellectual power convicts and persuades the masses of people to investigate and explore new ideas for human liberation. The late John Henrik Clark (New York), Clarence Kailin, (Madison, WI), and the late James Boggs and his wife Grace Lee Boggs (Detroit) are examples of organic intellectuals.

▣ References

Acuna, R. (1972). *Occupied America: The Chicano struggle toward liberation.* New York: Canfield Press.

Alarcon, N. (1990). Chicana feminism: In the tracks of "the" native woman. *Cultural Studies, 4,* 248–256.

Alexie, S. (1993). *The Lone Ranger and Tonto fistfight in heaven.* New York: Atlantic Monthly Press.

Allen, B., & Wilson, E. J. (1984). Foreword. In H. Cruse, *The crisis of the Negro intellectual* (pp. i–vi). New York: Quill.

Almaguer, T. (1974). Historical notes on Chicano oppression: The dialectics of racial and class domination in North America. *Aztlan, 5*(1–2), 27–56.

Anzaldúa, G. (1987). *Borderlands/la frontera: The new mestiza.* San Francisco: Ante Lute Press.

Balderrama, F. E. (1982). *In defense of La Raza: The Los Angeles Mexican consulate and the Mexican community, 1929–1936.* Tucson: University of Arizona Press.

Bell, D. (1992). *Faces at the bottom of the well: The permanence of racism.* New York: Basic Books.

Bell, D. (2002). *Ethical ambition.* New York: Bloomsbury.

Boggs, G. L. (1971). *Education to govern* [Pamphlet]. Detroit: All-African People's Union.

Bourdieu, P. (1977). *Outline of a theory of practice.* Cambridge: Cambridge University Press.

Bourdieu, P. (1990). *The logic of practice* [R. Nice, Trans.]. Stanford, CA: Stanford University Press.

Campbell, B. M. (1995). *Your blues ain't like mine.* New York: Ballantine.

Castillo, A. (1994). *So far from God.* New York: Plume.

Castillo, A. (1995). *Massacre of the dreamers: Essays on Xicanisima.* New York: Plume.

Clark, S. (with Brown, C. S., ed.). (1990). *Ready from within: A first person narrative.* Trenton, NJ: Africa World Press.

Collins, P. H. (1998). *Fighting words: Black women and the search for justice.* Minneapolis: University of Minnesota Press.

Cruse, H. (1984). *The crisis of the Negro intellectual.* New York: Quill. (Original work published 1967)

de la Torre, A., & Pesquera, B. (Eds.). (1993). *Building with our hands: New directions in Chicano studies.* Berkeley: University of California Press.

Delgado Bernal, D. (1998). Using a Chicana feminist epistemology in educational research. *Harvard Educational Review, 68,* 555–582.

DuBois, W.E.B. (1953). *The souls of black folks.* New York: Fawcett. (Original work published 1903)

Dyson, M. E. (1993). *Reflecting Black: African American cultural criticism.* Minneapolis: University of Minnesota Press.

Espiritu, Y. L. (1992). *Asian American panethnicity: Bridging institutions and identities.* Philadelphia: Temple University Press.

Espiritu, Y. L. (2003). *Home bound: Filipino American lives across cultures, communities, and countries.* Berkeley: University of California Press.

Eyre, C. (Director). (1998). *Smoke signals* [Motion picture]. Los Angeles: Miramax.

Fanon, F. (1968). *The wretched of the earth.* New York: Grove.

Fanon, F. (1986). *Black skin, white masks.* London: Pluto Press.

Fanon, F. (1994). On national culture. In P. Williams & L. Chrisman (Eds.), *Colonial discourse and post-colonial theory* (pp. 36–52). New York: Columbia University Press.

Foucault, M. (1977). *Language, counter-memory, practice.* Ithaca, NY: Cornell University Press.

Freire, P. (1970). *Pedagogy of the oppressed.* New York: Continuum.

Gilman, R. (2000). *Spinning into butter.* Woodstock, IL: Dramatic Publishing.

Gomez-Quinones, J. (1977). On culture. *Revista Chicano-Riquena, 5*(2), 35–53.

Guinier, L., & Torres, G. (2002). *Miner's canary: Enlisting race, resisting power, transforming democracy.* Cambridge, MA: Harvard University Press.

Haney Lopez, I. (1998). *White by law: The legal construction of race.* New York: New York University Press.

Health News Network. (2000). *A history of secret human experimentation.* Retrieved December 28, 2004, from www.skyhighway.com/~chemtrails 911/docs/human_experiments.html

Heaney, T. (1995). When adult education stood for democracy. *Adult Education Quarterly,* 43(1), 51–59.

Hertzberg, H. W. (1971). *The search for an American Indian identity.* Syracuse, NY: Syracuse University Press.

Horton, A. (1989). *The Highlander Folk School: A history of its major programs, 1932–1961.* Brooklyn, NY: Carlson.

Horton, M., with Kohl, H., & Kohl, J. (1990). *The long haul: An autobiography.* New York: Doubleday.

Horton, M., & Freire, P. (1990). *We make the road by walking: Conversations on education and social change.* Philadelphia: Temple University Press.

Ikemoto, L. (1995). Traces of the master narrative in the story of African American/Korean American conflict: How we constructed "Los Angeles." In R. Delgado (Ed.), *Critical race theory: The cutting edge* (pp. 305–315). Philadelphia: Temple University Press.

Kelley, R.D.G. (1999). People in me. *Colorlines, 1*(3), 5–7.

Kennedy, R. (2001, February). The triumph of robust tokenism. *The Atlantic online*. Retrieved from http://www.theatlantic.com/issues/2001/02/kennedy.htm

Kennedy, R. (2002). *Nigger: The strange career of a troublesome word.* New York: Pantheon.

King, J. E. (1995). Culture centered knowledge: Black studies, curriculum transformation, and social action. In J. A. Banks & C. M. Banks (Eds.), *Handbook of research on multicultural education* (pp. 265–290). New York: Macmillan.

Kuhn, T. (1962). *The structure of scientific revolutions.* Chicago: University of Chicago Press.

Ladson-Billings, G. (1998a). From Soweto to the South Bronx: African Americans and colonial education in the United States. In C. A. Torres & T. Mitchell (Eds.), *Sociology of education: Emerging perspectives* (pp. 247–264). Albany: SUNY Press.

Ladson-Billings, G. (1998b). Just what is critical race theory and what is it doing in a "nice" field like education? *International Journal of Qualitative Studies in Education, 11,* 7–24.

Ladson-Billings, G. (2000). Racialized discourses and ethnic epistemologies. In N. Denzin & Y. Lincoln (Eds.), *Handbook of qualitative research* (2nd ed., pp. 257–277). Thousand Oaks, CA: Sage.

Lahiri, J. (1999). *Interpreter of maladies.* Boston: Houghton Mifflin.

Legesse, A. (1973). *Gada: Three approaches to the study of an African society.* New York: Free Press.

Lewis, D. L. (1993). *W.E.B. DuBois: Biography of a race (1868-1919).* New York: Henry Holt.

Lipsitz, G. (1998). *The possessive investment in whiteness: How white people profit from identity politics.* Philadelphia: Temple University Press.

Lipsky, M. (1983). *Street-level bureaucrats.* New York: Russell Sage Foundation.

Lomawaima, K. T. (1995). Educating Native Americans. In J. A. Banks & C. M. Banks (Eds.), *Handbook of research on multicultural education* (pp. 331–347). New York: Macmillan.

Lowe, L. (1996). *Immigrant acts: On Asian-American cultural politics.* Durham, NC: Duke University Press.

Mann, B. (2003, October 6). New York weighs lead-paint laws [Radio broadcast]. *All Things Considered.* Washington, DC: National Public Radio.

Mayr, E. (1976). *Evolution and the diversity of life.* Cambridge, MA: Belknap Press.

McClintock, A. (1994). The angel of progress: Pitfalls of the term "post-colonialism." In P. Williams & L. Chrisman (Eds.), *Colonial discourse and post-colonial theory* (pp. 291–304). New York: Columbia University Press.

McIntosh, P. (1988). *White privilege and male privilege: A personal account of coming to see correspondences through work in women's studies* (Working Paper 189). Wellesley, MA: Wellesley College Center for Research on Women.

Miah, M. (1999). Race and politics: Black voters and "brother" Clinton. *Against the Current.* Retrieved from http://solidarity.igc.org/atc/78Miah.html

Minh-ha, T. (1989). *Woman, narrative, other: Writing postcoloniality and feminism.* Bloomington: Indiana University Press.

Mirande, A., & Enriquez, E. (1979). *La Chicana: The Mexican American woman.* Chicago: University of Chicago Press.

Mohanty, C. T. (1991). Under western eyes: Feminist scholarship and colonial discourses. In C. T. Mohanty, A. Russo, & L. Torres (Eds.), *Third World women and the politics of feminism* (pp. 50–80). Bloomington: Indiana University Press.

Morrison, T. (1987). *Beloved.* New York: Vintage Books.

Moyers, B. (Producer), & Pellett, G. (Director). (1991, February). *The songs are free: Interview with Bernice Johnson Reagon* [Video recording]. Princeton, NJ: Films for the Humanities & Sciences.

Oboler, S. (1995). *Ethnic lives, ethnic labels.* Minneapolis: University of Minnesota Press.

Ong, A. (1999). *Flexible citizenship: The cultural logics of transnationality.* Raleigh, NC: Duke University Press.

Padilla, F. (1987). *Latino ethnic consciousness.* Notre Dame, IN: Notre Dame University Press.

Palumbo-Liu, D. (1993). Introduction: Unhabituated habituses. In D. Palumbo-Liu & H. U. Gumbrecht (Eds.), *Streams of cultural capital: Transnational cultural studies* (pp. 1–21). Stanford, CA: Stanford University Press.

Paz, O. (1961). *The labyrinth of solitude: Life and thought in Mexico.* New York: Random House.

Perry, S. (1996, May 29). *Bill Clinton's politics of meaning.* Retrieved from ww.citypages.com/databank/17/808/article2724.asp

Popkewitz, T. (2003). Is the National Research Council Committee's report on scientific research in education scientific? On trusting the manifesto. *Qualitative Inquiry, 10*(1), 62–78.

Prashad, V. (2002). *Everybody was Kung Fu fighting: Afro-Asian connections and the myth of cultural purity.* New York: Beacon.

Roediger, D. (2002). *Colored White: Transcending the racial past.* Berkeley: University of California Press.

Shavelson, R., & Towne, L. (Eds.). (2003). *Scientific research in education.* Washington, DC: National Academies Press.

Smith, L. T. (1998). *Decolonising methodologies: Research and indigenous peoples.* London: Zed Books.

Snipp, C. M. (1995). American Indian studies. In J. A. Banks & C. M. Banks (Eds.), *Handbook of research on multicultural education* (pp. 245– 258). New York: Macmillan.

Spivak, G. C. (1990). Explanation and culture: Marginalia. In R. Ferguson, M. Gever, & T. T. Minh-ha (Eds.), *Out there: Marginalization and contemporary cultures* (pp. 377–393). Cambridge: MIT Press.

Spradley, J. (1979). *The ethnographic interview.* New York: Holt, Rinehart & Winston.

Tate, G. (2003). Introduction: Nigs R Us, or how Blackfolks became fetish objects. In G. Tate (Ed.), *Everything but the burden: What white people are taking from Black culture* (pp. 1–14). New York: Broadway Books.

Tuskegee Syphilis Study Legacy Committee. (1996, May 26). *Final report.* Washington, DC: Author.

wa Thiongo, N. (1991). *Decolonising the mind.* Nairobi: Heinemann Kenya.

Warrior, R. A. (1995). *Tribal secrets: Recovering American Indian intellectual traditions.* Minneapolis: University of Minnesota Press.

West, C. (1990). The new cultural politics of difference. In R. Ferguson, M. Gever, & T. T. Minh-ha (Eds.), *Out there: Marginalization and contemporary cultures* (pp. 19–36). Cambridge: MIT Press.

Wong, S. (1995). *American knees.* New York: Simon & Schuster.

Wynter, S. (1992). *Do not call us "negros": How "multicultural" textbooks perpetuate racism.* San Francisco: Aspire Books.

12

RETHINKING CRITICAL THEORY AND QUALITATIVE RESEARCH

Joe L. Kincheloe and Peter McLaren

Our Idiosyncratic Interpretation of Critical Theory and Critical Research

Over the past 25 years of our involvement in critical theory and critical research, we have been asked by hundreds of people to explain more precisely what critical theory is. We find that question difficult to answer because (a) there are many critical theories, not just one; (b) the critical tradition is always changing and evolving; and (c) critical theory attempts to avoid too much specificity, as there is room for disagreement among critical theorists. To lay out a set of fixed characteristics of the position is contrary to the desire of such theorists to avoid the production of blueprints of sociopolitical and epistemological beliefs. Given these disclaimers, we will now attempt to provide one idiosyncratic "take" on the nature of critical theory and critical research in the first decade of the 21st century. Please note that this is merely our subjective analysis and that there are many brilliant critical theorists who will find many problems with our pronouncements. In this spirit, we tender a description of an ever-evolving criticality, a reconceptualized critical theory that was critiqued and overhauled by the "post-discourses" of the last quarter of the 20th century and has been further extended in the first years of the 21st century (Bauman, 1995; Carlson & Apple, 1998; Collins, 1995; Giroux, 1997; Kellner, 1995; Peters, Lankshear, & Olssen, 2003; Roman & Eyre, 1997; Steinberg & Kincheloe, 1998; Weil & Kincheloe, 2003).

In this context, a reconceptualized critical theory questions the assumption that societies such as the United States, Canada, Australia, New Zealand, and the nations in the European Union, for example, are unproblematically democratic and free. Over the 20th century, especially after the early 1960s, individuals in these societies were acculturated to feel comfortable in relations of domination and subordination rather than equality and independence. Given the social and technological changes of the last half of the century that led to new forms of information production and access, critical theorists argued that questions of self-direction and democratic egalitarianism should be reassessed. In this context, critical researchers informed by the "post-discourses" (e.g., postmodern, critical feminism, poststructuralism) came to understand that individuals' view of themselves and the world were even more influenced by social and historical forces than previously believed. Given the changing social and informational conditions of late 20th-century and early 21st-century media-saturated Western culture, critical theorists have needed new ways of researching and analyzing the construction of individuals (Agger, 1992; Flossner & Otto, 1998; Hinchey, 1998; Leistyna, Woodrum, & Sherblom, 1996; Quail, Razzano, & Skalli, 2004; Skalli, 2004; R. Smith & Wexler, 1995; Sünker, 1998; Wesson & Weaver, 2001).

Partisan Research in a "Neutral" Academic Culture

In the space available here, it is impossible to do justice to all of the critical traditions that have drawn inspiration from Marx, Kant, Hegel, Weber, the Frankfurt School theorists; Continental social theorists such as Foucault, Habermas, and Derrida; Latin American thinkers such as Paulo Freire; French feminists such as Irigaray, Kristeva, and Cixous; or Russian sociolinguists such as Bakhtin and Vygotsky—most of whom regularly find their way into the reference lists of contemporary critical researchers. Today there are criticalist schools in many fields, and even a superficial discussion of the most prominent of these schools would demand much more space than we have available.

The fact that numerous books have been written about the often-virulent disagreements among members of the Frankfurt School only heightens our concern with the "packaging" of the different criticalist schools. Critical theory should not be treated as a universal grammar of revolutionary thought objectified and reduced to discrete formulaic pronouncements or strategies. Obviously, in presenting our idiosyncratic version of a reconceptualized critical theory or an evolving criticality, we have defined the critical tradition very broadly for the purpose of generating understanding; as we asserted earlier, this will trouble many critical researchers. In this move, we decided to focus on the underlying commonality among critical schools of thought, at the cost of focusing on differences. This, of course, is always risky business in terms of suggesting a false unity or consensus where none exists, but such concerns are unavoidable in a survey chapter such as this.

We are defining a criticalist as a researcher or theorist who attempts to use her or his work as a form of social or cultural criticism and who accepts certain basic assumptions:

that all thought is fundamentally mediated by power relations that are social and historically constituted; that facts can never be isolated from the domain of values or removed from some form of ideological inscription; that the relationship between concept and object and between signifier and signified is never stable or fixed and is often mediated by the social relations of capitalist production and consumption; that language is central to the formation of subjectivity (conscious and unconscious awareness); that certain groups in any society and particular societies are privileged over others and, although the reasons for this privileging may vary widely, the oppression that characterizes contemporary societies is most forcefully reproduced when subordinates accept their social status as natural, necessary, or inevitable; that oppression has many faces and that focusing on only one at the expense of others (e.g., class oppression versus racism) often elides the interconnections among them; and, finally, that mainstream research practices are generally, although most often unwittingly, implicated in the reproduction of systems of class, race, and gender oppression (Kincheloe & Steinberg, 1997).

In today's climate of blurred disciplinary genres, it is not uncommon to find literary theorists doing anthropology and anthropologists writing about literary theory, political scientists trying their hand at ethnomethodological analysis, or philosophers doing Lacanian film criticism. All these inter-/cross-disciplinary moves are examples of what Norman Denzin and Yvonna Lincoln (2000) have referred to as bricolage—a key innovation, we argue, in an evolving criticality. We will explore this dynamic in relation to critical research later in this chapter. We offer this observation about blurred genres not as an excuse to be wantonly eclectic in our treatment of the critical tradition but to make the point that any attempts to delineate critical theory as discrete schools of analysis will fail to capture the evolving hybridity endemic to contemporary critical analysis (Kincheloe, 2001a; Kincheloe & Berry, 2004).

Readers familiar with the criticalist traditions will recognize essentially four different "emergent" schools of social inquiry in this chapter: the neo-Marxist tradition of critical theory associated most closely with the work of Horkheimer, Adorno, and Marcuse; the genealogical writings of Michel Foucault; the practices of poststructuralist deconstruction associated with Derrida; and postmodernist currents associated with Derrida, Foucault, Lyotard, Ebert, and others. In our view, critical ethnography has been influenced by all these perspectives in different ways and to different degrees. From critical theory, researchers inherit a forceful criticism of the positivist conception of science and instrumental rationality, especially in Adorno's idea of negative dialectics, which posits an unstable relationship of contradiction between concepts and objects; from Derrida, researchers are given a means for deconstructing objective truth, or what is referred to as "the metaphysics of presence."

For Derrida, the meaning of a word is constantly deferred because the word can have meaning only in relation to its difference from other words within a given system of language. Foucault invites researchers to explore the ways in which discourses are implicated in relations of power and how power and knowledge serve as dialectically reinitiating practices that regulate what is considered reasonable and true. We have characterized much of the work influenced by these writers as the "ludic" and "resistance" postmodernist theoretical perspectives. Critical research can be understood best in the context of the empowerment of individuals. Inquiry that aspires to the name "critical" must be connected to an attempt to confront the injustice of a particular society or public sphere within the society. Research thus becomes a transformative endeavor unembarrassed by the label "political" and unafraid to consummate a relationship with emancipatory consciousness. Whereas traditional researchers cling to the guardrail of neutrality, critical researchers frequently announce their partisanship in the struggle for a better world (Grinberg, 2003; Horn, 2000; Kincheloe, 2001b).

The work of Brazilian educator Paulo Freire is instructive in relation to constructing research that contributes to the struggle for a better world. The research of both authors of this chapter has been influenced profoundly by the work of Freire (1970, 1972, 1978, 1985). Always concerned with human suffering and the pedagogical and knowledge work that helped expose the genesis of it, Freire modeled critical research throughout his career. In his writings about research, Freire maintained that there are no traditionally defined objects of his research—he insisted on involving, as partners in the research process, the people he studied as subjects. He immersed himself in their ways of thinking and modes of perception, encouraging them all along to begin thinking about their own thinking. Everyone involved in Freire's critical research, not just the researcher, joined in the process of investigation, examination, criticism, and reinvestigation—everyone learned to see more critically, think at a more critical level, and to recognize the forces that subtly shape their lives.

Whereas traditional researchers see their task as the description, interpretation, or reanimation of a slice of reality, critical researchers often regard their work as a first step toward forms of political action that can redress the injustices found in the field site or constructed in the very act of research itself. Horkheimer (1972) puts it succinctly when he argues that critical theory and research are never satisfied with merely increasing knowledge (see also Agger, 1998; Andersen, 1989; Britzman, 1991; Giroux, 1983, 1988, 1997; Kincheloe, 1991, 2003c; Kincheloe & Steinberg, 1993; Quantz, 1992; Shor, 1996; Villaverde & Kincheloe, 1998). Research in the critical tradition takes the form of self-conscious criticism—self-conscious in the sense that researchers try to become aware of the ideological imperatives and epistemological presuppositions that inform their research as well as their own subjective, intersubjective, and normative reference claims. Thus, critical researchers enter into an investigation with their assumptions on the table, so no one is confused concerning the epistemological and political baggage they bring with them to the research site.

Upon detailed analysis, critical researchers may change these assumptions. Stimulus for change may come from the critical researchers' recognition that such assumptions are not leading to emancipatory actions. The source of this emancipatory action involves the researchers' ability to expose the contradictions of the world of appearances accepted by the dominant culture as natural and inviolable (Giroux, 1983,

1988, 1997; McLaren, 1992, 1997; San Juan, 1992; Zizek, 1990). Such appearances may, critical researchers contend, conceal social relationships of inequality, injustice, and exploitation. For instance, if we view the violence we find in classrooms not as random or isolated incidents created by aberrant individuals willfully stepping out of line in accordance with a particular form of social pathology, but as possible narratives of transgression and resistance, then this could indicate that the "political unconscious" lurking beneath the surface of everyday classroom life is not unrelated to practices of race, class, and gender oppression but rather intimately connected to them.

An Evolving Criticality

In this context, it is important to note that we understand a social theory as a map or a guide to the social sphere. In a research context, it does not determine how we see the world but helps us devise questions and strategies for exploring it. A critical social theory is concerned in particular with issues of power and justice and the ways that the economy; matters of race, class, and gender; ideologies; discourses; education; religion and other social institutions; and cultural dynamics interact to construct a social system (Beck-Gernsheim, Butler, & Puigvert, 2003; Flecha, Gomez, & Puigvert, 2003). Thus, in this context we seek to provide a view of an evolving criticality or a reconceptualized critical theory. Critical theory is never static; it is always evolving, changing in light of both new theoretical insights and new problems and social circumstances.

The list of concepts elucidating our articulation of critical theory indicates a criticality informed by a variety of discourses emerging after the work of the Frankfurt School. Indeed, some of the theoretical discourses, while referring to themselves as critical, directly call into question some of the work of Horkheimer, Adorno, and Marcuse. Thus, diverse theoretical traditions have informed our understanding of criticality and have demanded understanding of diverse forms of oppression including class, race, gender, sexual, cultural, religious, colonial, and ability-related concerns. The evolving notion of criticality we present is informed by, while critiquing, the post-discourses—for example, postmodernism, poststructuralism, and postcolonialism. In this context, critical theorists become detectives of new theoretical insights, perpetually searching for new and interconnected ways of understanding power and oppression and the ways they shape everyday life and human experience.

In this context, criticality and the research it supports are always evolving, always encountering new ways to irritate dominant forms of power, to provide more evocative and compelling insights. Operating in this way, an evolving criticality is always vulnerable to exclusion from the domain of approved modes of research. The forms of social change it supports always position it in some places as an outsider, an awkward detective always interested in uncovering social structures, discourses, ideologies, and epistemologies that prop up both the status quo and a variety of forms of privilege. In the epistemological domain, white, male, class elitist, heterosexist, imperial, and colonial privilege often operates by asserting the power to claim objectivity and neutrality. Indeed, the owners of such privilege often own the "franchise" on reason and rationality. Proponents of an evolving criticality possess a variety of tools to expose such oppressive power politics. Such proponents assert that critical theory is well-served by drawing upon numerous liberatory discourses and including diverse groups of marginalized peoples and their allies in the nonhierarchical aggregation of critical analysts (Bello, 2003; Clark, 2002; Humphries, 1997).

In the present era, emerging forms of neocolonialism and neo-imperialism in the United States move critical theorists to examine the ways American power operates under the cover of establishing democracies all over the world. Advocates of an evolving criticality argue—as we do in more detail later in this chapter—that such neocolonial power must be exposed so it can be opposed in the United States and around the world. The American Empire's justification in the name of freedom for undermining democratically elected governments from Iran (Kincheloe, 2004), Chile, Nicaragua, and Venezuela to Liberia (when its real purpose is to acquire geopolitical advantage for future military assaults, economic leverage in international markets, and access to natural resources) must be exposed by criticalists for what it is—a rank imperialist sham (McLaren, 2003a, 2003b; McLaren & Jaramillo, 2002; McLaren & Martin, 2003). Critical researchers need to view their work in the context of living and working in a nation-state with the most powerful military-industrial complex in history that is shamefully using the terrorist attacks of September 11 to advance a ruthless imperialist agenda fueled by capitalist accumulation by means of the rule of force (McLaren & Farahmandpur, 2003).

Chomsky (2003), for instance, has accused the U.S. government of the "supreme crime" of preventive war (in the case of its invasion of Iraq, the use of military force to destroy an invented or imagined threat) of the type that was condemned at Nuremburg. Others, like historian Arthur Schlesinger (cited in Chomsky, 2003), have likened the invasion of Iraq to Japan's "day of infamy," that is, to the policy that imperial Japan employed at the time of Pearl Harbor. David G. Smith (2003) argues that such imperial dynamics are supported by particular epistemological forms. The United States is an epistemological empire based on a notion of truth that undermines the knowledges produced by those outside the good graces and benevolent authority of the empire. Thus, in the 21st century, critical theorists must develop sophisticated ways to address not only the brute material relations of class rule linked to the mode and relations of capitalist production and imperialist conquest (whether through direct military intervention or indirectly through the creation of client states) but also the epistemological violence that helps discipline the world. Smith refers to this violence as a form of "information warfare" that spreads deliberate falsehoods about countries such as Iraq and Iran. U.S. corporate and governmental agents become more sophisticated in the use of such episto-weaponry with every day that passes.

Obviously, an evolving criticality does not promiscuously choose theoretical discourses to add to the bricolage of critical theories. It is highly suspicious—as we detail later—of theories that fail to understand the malevolent workings of power, that fail to critique the blinders of Eurocentrism, that cultivate an elitism of insiders and outsiders, and that fail to discern a global system of inequity supported by diverse forms of ideology and violence. It is uninterested in any theory—no matter how fashionable—that does not directly address the needs of victims of oppression and the suffering they must endure. The following is an elastic, ever-evolving set of concepts included in our evolving notion of criticality. With theoretical innovations and shifting zeitgeists, they evolve. The points that are deemed most important in one time period pale in relation to different points in a new era.

Critical Enlightenment. In this context, critical theory analyzes competing power interests between groups and individuals within a society—identifying who gains and who loses in specific situations. Privileged groups, criticalists argue, often have an interest in supporting the status quo to protect their advantages; the dynamics of such efforts often become a central focus of critical research. Such studies of privilege often revolve around issues of race, class, gender, and sexuality (Allison, 1998; V. Carter, 1998; Howell, 1998; Kincheloe & Steinberg, 1997; Kincheloe, Steinberg, Rodriguez, & Chennault, 1998; McLaren, 1997; Rodriguez & Villaverde, 2000; Sleeter & McLaren, 1995). In this context, to seek critical enlightenment is to uncover the winners and losers in particular social arrangements and the processes by which such power plays operate (Cary, 1996; Dei, Karumanchery, & Karumanchery-Luik, 2004; Fehr, 1993; King, 1996; Pruyn, 1994; Wexler, 1996a).

Critical Emancipation. Those who seek emancipation attempt to gain the power to control their own lives in solidarity with a justice-oriented community. Here, critical research attempts to expose the forces that prevent individuals and groups from shaping the decisions that crucially affect their lives. In this way, greater degrees of autonomy and human agency can be achieved. In the first decade of the 21st century, we are cautious in our use of the term "emancipation" because, as many critics have pointed out, no one is ever completely emancipated from the sociopolitical context that has produced him or her. Concurrently, many have used the term "emancipation" to signal the freedom an abstract individual gains by gaining access to Western reason—that is, becoming reasonable. Our use of "emancipation" in an evolving criticality rejects any use of the term in this context. In addition, many have rightly questioned the arrogance that may accompany efforts to emancipate "others." These are important caveats and must be carefully taken into account by critical researchers. Thus, as critical inquirers who search for those forces that insidiously shape who we are, we respect those who reach different conclusions in their personal journeys (Butler, 1998; Cannella, 1997; Kellogg, 1998; Knobel, 1999; Steinberg & Kincheloe, 1998; Weil, 1998).

The Rejection of Economic Determinism. A caveat of a reconceptualized critical theory involves the insistence that the tradition does not accept the orthodox Marxist notion that "base" determines "superstructure"—meaning that economic factors dictate the nature of all other aspects of human existence. Critical theorists understand in the 21st century that there are multiple forms of power, including the aforementioned racial, gender, and sexual axes of domination. In issuing this caveat, however, a reconceptualized critical theory in no way attempts to argue that economic factors are unimportant in the shaping of everyday life. Economic factors can never be separated from other axes of oppression (Aronowitz & DiFazio, 1994; Carlson, 1997; Gabbard, 1995; Gee, Hull, & Lankshear, 1996; Gibson, 1986; Kincheloe, 1995, 1999; Kincheloe & Steinberg, 1999; Martin & Schuman, 1996). Mechanistic formulations of economic determinism are often misreadings of the work of Marx. McLaren's work, for instance, does not reject the base/superstructure model *tout court*, but only undialectical formulations of it (see McLaren & Farahmandpur, 2001).

The Critique of Instrumental or Technical Rationality. A reconceptualized critical theory sees instrumental/technical rationality as one of the most oppressive features of contemporary society. Such a form of "hyper-reason" involves an obsession with means in preference to ends. Critical theorists claim that instrumental/technical rationality is more interested in method and efficiency than in purpose. It delimits its topics to "how to" instead of "why should." In a research context, critical theorists claim that many rationalistic scholars become so obsessed with issues of technique, procedure, and correct method that they forget the humanistic purpose of the research act. Instrumental/technical rationality often separates fact from value in its obsession with "proper" method, losing in the process an understanding of the value choices always involved in the production of so-called facts (Alfino, Caputo, & Wynyard, 1998; Giroux, 1997; Hinchey, 1998; Kincheloe, 1993; McLaren, 1998; Ritzer, 1993; Stallabrass, 1996; M. Weinstein, 1998).

The Concept of Immanence. Critical theory is always concerned with what could be, what is immanent in various ways of thinking and perceiving. Thus, critical theory should always move beyond the contemplative realm to concrete social reform. In the spirit of Paulo Freire, our notion of an evolving critical theory possesses immanence as it imagines new ways to ease human suffering and produce psychological health (A.M.A. Freire, 2001; Slater, Fain, & Rossatto, 2002). Critical immanence helps us get beyond egocentrism and ethnocentrism and work to build new forms of relationship with diverse peoples. Leila Villaverde (2003) extends this point about immanence when she maintains that critical theory helps us "retain a vision of the not yet." In the work of the Frankfurt School critical theory and the hermeneutics of Hans-Georg Gadamer (1989) we find this concern with immanence. Gadamer argues that we must be more cautious in our efforts to determine "what is" because it holds such dramatic consequences for how we engage "what ought to be." In Gadamer's view, the process of understanding involves interpreting meaning and applying the concepts gained to the historical moment that faces us. Thus, immanence in the context of qualitative research involves the use of human wisdom in the process of bringing about a better and more just world, less suffering, and more individual fulfillment. With this notion in mind, critical theorists critique researchers whose scholarly work operates to adapt individuals to the world as it is. In the context of immanence, critical researchers are profoundly concerned with who we are, how we got this way, and where we might go from here (Weil & Kincheloe, 2003).

A Reconceptualized Critical Theory of Power: Hegemony. Our conception of a reconceptualized critical theory is intensely concerned with the need to understand the various and complex ways that power operates to dominate and shape consciousness. Power, critical theorists have learned, is an extremely ambiguous topic that demands detailed study and analysis. A consensus seems to be emerging among criticalists that power is a basic constituent of human existence that works to shape the oppressive and productive nature of the human tradition. Indeed, we are all empowered and we are all unempowered, in that we all possess abilities and we are all limited in the attempt to use our abilities. Because of limited space, we will focus here on critical theory's traditional concern with the oppressive aspects of power, although we understand that an important aspect of critical research focuses on the productive aspects of power—its ability to empower, to establish a critical democracy, to engage marginalized people in the rethinking of their sociopolitical role (Apple, 1996; Fiske, 1993; A.M.A. Freire, 2000; Giroux, 1997; Macedo, 1994; Nicholson & Seidman, 1995). In the context of oppressive power and its ability to produce inequalities and human suffering, Antonio Gramsci's notion of hegemony is central to critical research. Gramsci understood that dominant power in the 20th century was not always exercised simply by physical force but also was expressed through social psychological attempts to win people's consent to domination through cultural institutions such as the media, the schools, the family, and the church. Gramscian hegemony recognizes that the winning of popular consent is a very complex process and must be researched carefully on a case-by-case basis. Students and researchers of power, educators, sociologists, all of us are hegemonized as our field of knowledge and understanding is structured by a limited exposure to competing definitions of the sociopolitical world. The hegemonic field, with its bounded sociopsychological horizons, garners consent to an inequitable power matrix—a set of social relations that are legitimated by their depiction as natural and inevitable. In this context, critical researchers note that hegemonic consent is never completely established, as it is always contested by various groups with different agendas (Grossberg, 1997; Lull, 1995; McLaren, 1995a, 1995b; McLaren, Hammer, Reilly, & Sholle, 1995; West, 1993). We note here that Gramsci famously understood Marx's concept of laws of tendency as implying a new immanence and a new conception of necessity and freedom that cannot be grasped within a mechanistic model of determination (Bensaid, 2002).

A Reconceptualized Critical Theory of Power: Ideology. Critical theorists understand that the formation of hegemony cannot be separated from the production of ideology. If hegemony is the larger effort of the powerful to win the consent of their "subordinates," then ideological hegemony involves the cultural forms, the meanings, the rituals, and the representations that produce consent to the status quo and individuals' particular places within it. Ideology vis-à-vis hegemony moves critical inquirers beyond explanations of domination that have used terms such as "propaganda" to describe the ways media, political, educational, and other sociocultural productions coercively manipulate citizens to adopt oppressive meanings. A reconceptualized critical research endorses a much more subtle, ambiguous, and situationally specific form of domination that refuses the propaganda model's assumption that people are passive, easily manipulated victims. Researchers operating with an awareness of this hegemonic ideology understand that dominant ideological practices and discourses shape our vision of reality (Lemke, 1995, 1998). Thus, our notion of hegemonic ideology is a critical form of epistemological constructivism buoyed by a nuanced understanding of power's complicity in the constructions people make of the world and their role in it (Kincheloe, 1998). Such an awareness corrects earlier delineations of ideology as a monolithic, unidirectional entity that was imposed on individuals by a secret cohort of ruling-class czars. Understanding domination in the context of concurrent struggles among different classes, racial and gender groups, and sectors of capital, critical researchers of ideology explore the ways such competition engages different visions, interests, and agendas in a variety of social locales—venues previously thought to be outside the domain of ideological struggle (Brosio, 1994; Steinberg, 2001).

A Reconceptualized Critical Theory of Power: Linguistic/Discursive Power. Critical researchers have come to understand that language is not a mirror of society. It is an unstable social practice whose meaning shifts, depending upon the context in which it is used. Contrary to previous understandings, critical researchers appreciate the fact that language is not a neutral and objective conduit of description of the "real world." Rather, from a critical perspective, linguistic descriptions are not simply about the world but serve to construct it. With these linguistic notions in mind, criticalists begin to study the way language in the form of discourses serves as a form of regulation and domination. Discursive practices are defined as a set of tacit rules that regulate what can and cannot be said, who can speak with the blessings of authority and who must listen, whose social constructions are valid and whose are erroneous and unimportant. In an educational context, for example, legitimated discourses of power insidiously tell educators what books may be read by students, what instructional methods may be utilized, and what belief systems and views of success may be taught. In all forms of research, discursive power validates particular research strategies, narrative formats, and modes of representation. In this context, power discourses undermine the multiple meanings of language, establishing one correct reading that implants a particular hegemonic/ideological message into the consciousness of the reader. This is a process often referred to as the attempt to impose discursive closure. Critical researchers interested in the construction of consciousness are very attentive to these power dynamics. Engaging and questioning the use value of particular theories of power is central to our notion of an evolving criticality (Blades, 1997; Gee, 1996; Lemke, 1993; McWilliam & Taylor, 1996; Morgan, 1996; Steinberg, 2001).

Focusing on the Relationships Among Culture, Power, and Domination. In the last decades of the 20th century, culture took on a new importance in the critical effort to understand power and domination. Critical researchers have argued that culture has to be viewed as a domain of struggle where the production and transmission of knowledge is always a contested process (Giroux, 1997; Kincheloe & Steinberg, 1997; McLaren, 1997; Steinberg & Kincheloe, 1997). Dominant and subordinate cultures deploy differing systems of meaning based on the forms of knowledge produced in their cultural domain. Popular culture, with its TV, movies, video games, computers, music, dance, and other productions, plays an increasingly important role in critical research on power and domination. Cultural studies, of course, occupies an ever-expanding role in this context, as it examines not only popular culture but also the tacit rules that guide cultural production. Arguing that the development of mass media has changed the way the culture operates, cultural studies researchers maintain that cultural epistemologies in the first decade of the 21st century are different from those of only a few decades ago. New forms of culture and cultural domination are produced as the distinction between the real and the simulated is blurred. This blurring effect of hyperreality constructs a social vertigo characterized by a loss of touch with traditional notions of time, community, self, and history. New structures of cultural space and time generated by bombarding electronic images from local, national, and international spaces shake our personal sense of place. This proliferation of signs and images functions as a mechanism of control in contemporary Western societies. The key to successful counterhegemonic cultural research involves (a) the ability to link the production of representations, images, and signs of hyperreality to power in the political economy and (b) the capacity, once this linkage is exposed and described, to delineate the highly complex effects of the reception of these images and signs on individuals located at various race, class, gender, and sexual coordinates in the web of reality (R. Carter, 2003; Cary, 2003; Ferguson & Golding, 1997; Garnham, 1997; Grossberg, 1995; Jackson & Russo, 2002; Joyrich, 1996; O'Riley, 2003; Rose & Kincheloe, 2003; Sanders-Bustle, 2003; Steinberg, 1997a, 1997b; Thomas, 1997; Wexler, 2000).

The Centrality of Interpretation: Critical Hermeneutics. One of the most important aspects of a critical theory–informed qualitative research involves the often-neglected domain of the interpretation of information. The critical hermeneutic tradition (Grondin, 1994; Gross & Keith,1997; Rosen, 1987; Vattimo, 1994) holds that in qualitative research, there is only interpretation, no matter how vociferously many researchers may argue that the facts speak for themselves. The hermeneutic act of interpretation involves, in its most elemental articulation, making sense of what has been observed in a way that communicates understanding. Not only is all research merely an act of interpretation, but, hermeneutics contends, perception itself is an act of interpretation. Thus, the quest for understanding is a fundamental feature of human existence, as encounter with the unfamiliar always demands the attempt to make meaning, to make sense. The same, however, is also the case with the familiar. Indeed, as in the study of commonly known texts, we come to find that sometimes the familiar may be seen as the most strange. Thus, it should not be surprising that even the so-called objective writings of qualitative research are interpretations, not value-free descriptions (Denzin, 1994; Gallagher, 1992; Jardine, 1998; Mayers, 2001; D. G. Smith, 1999). Learning from the hermeneutic tradition and the postmodern critique, critical researchers have begun to reexamine textual claims to authority. No pristine interpretation exists—indeed, no methodology, social or educational theory, or discursive form can claim a privileged position that enables the production of authoritative knowledge. Researchers must always speak/write about the world in terms of something else in the world, "in relation to . . ." As creatures of the world, we are oriented to it in a way that prevents us from grounding our theories and perspectives outside it. The critical hermeneutics that grounds critical qualitative research moves more in the direction of a normative hermeneutics in that it raises questions about the purposes and procedures of interpretation. In its critical theory–driven context, the purpose of hermeneutical analysis is to develop a form of cultural criticism revealing power dynamics within social and cultural texts. Qualitative researchers familiar with critical hermeneutics build bridges between reader and text, text and its producer, historical context and present, and one particular social circumstance and another. Accomplishing such interpretive tasks is difficult, and researchers situated in normative hermeneutics push ethnographers, historians, semioticians, literary critics, and content analysts to trace the bridge-building processes employed by successful interpretations of knowledge production and culture (Gallagher, 1992; Kellner, 1995; Kogler, 1996; Rapko, 1998). Grounded by this hermeneutical bridge building, critical researchers in a hermeneutical circle (a process of analysis in which interpreters seek the historical and social dynamics that shape textual interpretation) engage in the back-and-forth of studying parts in relation to the whole and the whole in relation to parts. Deploying such a methodology, critical researchers can produce profound insights that lead to transformative action (Berger, 1995; Cary, 1996; Clough, 1998; Coben,1998; Gadamer, 1989; Goodson, 1997; Kincheloe & Berry, 2004; Miller & Hodge, 1998; Mullen, 1999; Peters & Lankshear, 1994).

The Role of Cultural Pedagogy in Critical Theory. Cultural production often can be thought of as a form of education, as it generates knowledge, shapes values, and constructs identity. From our perspective, such a framing can help critical researchers make sense of the world of domination and oppression as they work to bring about a more just, democratic, and egalitarian society. In recent years, this educational dynamic has been referred to as cultural pedagogy (Berry, 1998; Giroux, 1997; Kincheloe, 1995; McLaren, 1997; Pailliotet, 1998; Semali, 1998; Soto, 1998). "Pedagogy" is a useful term that traditionally has been used to refer only to teaching and schooling. By using the term "cultural pedagogy," we are specifically referring to the ways particular cultural agents produce particular hegemonic ways of seeing. In our critical interpretive context, our notion of cultural pedagogy asserts that the new "educators" in the electronically wired contemporary era are those who possess the financial resources to use mass media. This corporate-dominated pedagogical process has worked so well that few complain about it in the first decade of the 21st century—such informational politics doesn't make the evening news. Can we imagine another institution in contemporary society gaining the pedagogical power that corporations now assert over information and signification systems? What if the Church of Christ was sufficiently powerful to run pedagogical "commercials" every few minutes on TV and radio touting the necessity for everyone to accept that denomination's faith? Replayed scenes of Jews, Muslims, Hindus, Catholics, and Methodists being condemned to hell if they rejected the official pedagogy (the true doctrine) would greet North Americans and their children 7 days a week. There is little doubt that many people would be outraged and would organize for political action. Western societies have to some degree capitulated to this corporate pedagogical threat to democracy, passively watching an elite gain greater control over the political system and political consciousness via a sophisticated cultural pedagogy. Critical researchers are intent on exposing the specifics of this process (Deetz, 1993; Drummond, 1996; Kincheloe, 2002; Molnar, 1996; Pfeil, 1995; Rose & Kincheloe, 2003; Steinberg & Kincheloe, 1997).

Critical Research and Cultural Studies

Cultural studies is an interdisciplinary, transdisciplinary, and sometimes counterdisciplinary field that functions within the dynamics of competing definitions of culture. Unlike traditional humanistic studies, cultural studies questions the equation of culture with high culture; instead, cultural studies asserts that myriad expressions of cultural production should be analyzed in relation to other cultural dynamics and social and historical structures. Such a position commits cultural studies to a potpourri of artistic, religious, political, economic, and communicative activities. In this context, it is important to note that although cultural studies is associated with the study of popular culture, it is not primarily about popular culture. The interests of cultural studies are much broader and generally tend to involve the production and nature of the rules of inclusivity and exclusivity that guide academic evaluation—in particular, the way these rules shape and are shaped by relations of power. The rules that guide academic evaluation are inseparable from the rules of knowledge production and research. Thus, cultural studies provides a disciplinary critique that holds many implications (Abercrombie, 1994; Ferguson & Golding, 1997; Grossberg, 1995; Hall & du Gay, 1996; Kincheloe, 2002; McLaren, 1995a; Oberhardt, 2001; Woodward, 1997).

One of the most important sites of theoretical production in the history of critical research has been the Centre for Contemporary Cultural Studies (CCCS) at the University of Birmingham. Attempting to connect critical theory with the particularity of everyday experience, the CCCS researchers have argued that all experience is vulnerable to ideological inscription. At the same time, they have maintained that theorizing outside everyday experience results in formal and deterministic theory. An excellent representative of the CCCS's perspectives is Paul Willis, whose *Learning to Labour: How Working Class Kids Get Working Class Jobs* was published in 1977, 7 years after Colin Lacey's *Hightown Grammar* (1970). Redefining the nature of ethnographic research in a critical manner, *Learning to Labour* inspired a spate of critical studies: David Robins and Philip Cohen's *Knuckle Sandwich: Growing Up in the Working-Class City* in 1978, Paul Corrigan's *Schooling the Smash Street Kids* in 1979, and Dick Hebdige's *Subculture: The Meaning of Style* in 1979. Also following Willis's work were critical feminist studies, including an anthology titled *Women Take Issue* (Women's Studies Group, 1978). In 1985, Christine Griffin published *Typical Girls?*, the first extended feminist study produced by the CCCS. Conceived as a response to Willis's *Learning to Labour*, *Typical Girls?* analyzes adolescent female consciousness as it is constructed in a world of patriarchy. Through their recognition of patriarchy as a major disciplinary technology in the production of subjectivity, Griffin and the members of the CCCS gender study group moved critical research in a multicultural direction.

In addition to the examination of class, gender and racial analyses are beginning to gain in importance (Quantz, 1992). Poststructuralism frames power not simply as one aspect of a society but as the basis of society. Thus, patriarchy is not simply one isolated force among many with which women must contend; patriarchy informs all aspects of the social and effectively shapes women's lives (see also Douglas, 1994; Finders, 1997; Fine, Powell, Weis, & Wong, 1997; Frankenberg, 1993; Franz & Stewart, 1994; Shohat & Stam, 1994). Cornel West (1993) pushes critical research even further into the multicultural domain as he focuses critical attention on women, the Third World, and race. Adopting theoretical advances in neo-Marxist postcolonialist criticism and cultural studies, he is able to shed greater light on the workings of power in everyday life.

In this context, Ladislaus Semali and Joe Kincheloe, in *What Is Indigenous Knowledge? Voices from the Academy* (1999), explore the power of indigenous knowledge as a resource for critical attempts to bring about social change. Critical researchers, they argue, should analyze such knowledges in order to understand emotions, sensitivities, and epistemologies that move in ways unimagined by many Western knowledge producers. In this postcolonially informed context, Semali and Kincheloe employ concerns raised by indigenous knowledge to challenge the academy, its "normal science," and its accepted notions of certified information. Moving the conversation about critical research in new directions, these authors understand the conceptual inseparability of valuing indigenous knowledge, developing postcolonial forms of resistance, academic reform, the reconceptualization of research and interpretation, and the struggle for social justice.

In *Schooling as a Ritual Performance,* Peter McLaren (1999) integrates poststructuralist, postcolonialist, and Marxist theory with the projects of cultural studies, critical pedagogy, and critical ethnography. He grounds his theoretical analysis in the poststructuralist claim that the connection of signifier and signified is arbitrary yet shaped by historical, cultural, and economic forces. The primary cultural narrative that defines school life is the resistance by students to the school's attempts to marginalize their street culture and street knowledge. McLaren analyzes the school as a cultural site where symbolic capital is struggled over in the form of ritual dramas. *Schooling as a Ritual Performance* adopts the position that researchers are unable to grasp themselves or others introspectively without social mediation through their positionalities with respect to race, class, gender, and other configurations. The visceral, bodily forms of knowledge, and the rhythms and gestures of the street culture of the students, are distinguished from the formal abstract knowledge of classroom instruction. The teachers regard knowledge as it is constructed informally outside the culture of school instruction as threatening to the universalist and decidedly Eurocentric ideal of high culture that forms the basis of the school curriculum.

As critical researchers pursue the reconceptualization of critical theory pushed by its synergistic relationship with cultural studies, postmodernism, and poststructuralism, they are confronted with the post-discourses' redefinition of critical notions of democracy in terms of multiplicity and difference. Traditional notions of community often privilege unity over diversity in the name of Enlightenment values. Poststructuralists in general and poststructuralist feminists in particular see this communitarian dream as politically disabling because of the suppression of race, class, and gender differences and the exclusion of subaltern voices and marginalized groups whom community members are loath to engage. What begins to emerge in this instance is the movement of feminist theoretical concerns to the center of critical theory. Indeed, after the feminist critique, critical theory can never return to a paradigm of inquiry in which the concept of social class is antiseptically privileged and exalted as the master concept in the Holy Trinity of race, class, and gender.

A critical theory reconceptualized by poststructuralism and feminism promotes a politics of difference that refuses to pathologize or exoticize the Other. In this context, communities are more prone to revitalization and revivification (Wexler, 1996b, 1997); peripheralized groups in the thrall of a condescending Eurocentric gaze are able to edge closer to the borders of respect, and "classified" objects of research potentially acquire the characteristics of subjecthood. Kathleen Weiler's *Women Teaching for Change: Gender, Class, and Power* (1988) serves as a good example of critical research framed by feminist theory. Weiler shows not only how feminist theory can extend critical research but also how the concept of emancipation can be reconceptualized in light of a feminist epistemology. In this context, we clearly observe the way our notion of an evolving criticality operates. Criticalists inform poststructuralists and feminists, who in turn critique and extend the subject matter and the approach of more traditional forms of critical research. Though not always without contention, such a process is in the long-term interests of a vibrant critical theory that continues to matter in the world (Aronowitz & Giroux, 1991; Behar & Gordon, 1995; Bersani, 1995; Brents & Monson, 1998; Britzman, 1995; Christian-Smith & Keelor, 1999; Clatterbaugh, 1997; Clough, 1994; Cooper, 1994; Hedley, 1994; Johnson, 1996; Kelly, 1996; King & Mitchell, 1995; Lugones, 1987; Maher & Tetreault, 1994; Morrow, 1991; Rand, 1995; Scott, 1992; Sedgwick, 1995; Steinberg, 1997b; I. Young, 1990).

In the last few years, Norman Denzin (2003) has initiated a major turn in cultural studies with his notion of a performative ethnography. As a critical and emancipatory discourse, a performative cultural studies connects Giroux's, McLaren's, and Kincheloe's articulations of critical pedagogy with new ways of writing and performing cultural politics. Denzin carefully argues that performance-based human disciplines can catalyze democratic social change. Moving like the coyote trickster, Denzin proposes a cultural studies of action that decenters subjectivity as it questions the status quo. Defining performance as an "act of intervention, a method of resistance, a form of criticism, a way of revealing agency" (p. 9), Denzin shapes his notion of performativity in the spirit of Henry Giroux's (2003) work in cultural studies and critical pedagogy. Performance in cultural studies becomes public pedagogy when it employs the aesthetic and performative in the effort to portray the interactions connecting politics, institutions, and experience. Thus, performance for Denzin becomes a form of human agency that brings individuals together with culture in an enacted manner.

Denzin's important ideas intersect with Peter Reason and William Torbert's (2001) concept of the action turn. In the action turn, Reason and Torbert reconceptualize the nature and purpose of social science. Because human beings, they tell us,

> are all participating actors in the world, the purpose of inquiry is not simply or even primarily to contribute to the fund of knowledge in a field, to deconstruct taken-for-granted realities, or even to develop emancipatory theory, but rather to forge a more direct link between intellectual knowledge and moment-to-moment personal and social action, so that inquiry contributes directly to the flourishing of human persons, their communities, and the ecosystems of which they are part. (p. 2)

In this context, we find an intersection between Denzin's performativity and the shift to action from social science's emphasis on abstract knowledge. In both articulations, the focus of social research is critical, as it focuses on the improvement of the human condition, community development, and the strengthening of the ecosystems in which people and communities operate. In this spirit, Denzin, in *Performative Ethnography* (2003), uses racism as an example of a problem that can be addressed by a critical performative social science. Connecting his work to the research of W.E.B. DuBois and bell hooks, Denzin seeks to write and perform cultural dynamics around race in innovative ways. In this context, he positions political acts as pedagogical and performative. In this way, the researcher opens fresh venues for democratic citizenship and transformative dialogue. In light of the racial violence of the contemporary era, Denzin applies his performative ethnography to help us imagine alternative social realities, new modes of discourse, and fresh experiences in schools, workplaces, wilderness areas, and other public spaces.

Thus, Denzin pushes cultural studies and its attendant criticality that moves from textual ethnography to a performative autoethnography, while connecting it to critical pedagogy's concept of making the political more pedagogical and the pedagogical more political. Critical in the way it confronts mainstream ways of knowing and representing the world, Denzin's performativity is better tailored to engage postcolonial and subaltern cultural practices. In addition to connecting to the action turn in research documented by Reason and Torbert, Denzin's performativity also connects to Humberto Mautaurana and Francisco Varela's Santiago school of Enactivism in cognitive theory. If performance ethnography and cultural studies highlight immediacy and involvement, then Enactivism's concern with the importance of *enacting* cognition in the complexity and complications of lived experience can possibly synergize our insights into the realm of performance. With the help of the social, pedagogical, political, and cognitive theories, critical researchers begin to understand that the social world may be more complex than we have been taught. Denzin's performativity helps us get closer to this complexity.

This interaction connecting performance ethnography, the action turn, and Enactivism moves critical researchers to explore their work in relation to recent inquiry about our evolving view of the human mind. Looking at the concept of mind from biological, psychological, and social perspectives, Enactivists begin the reparation process necessitated by the Western rationalistic abstraction, reduction, and fragmentation of the world. When Enactivism is added to our notion of an evolving criticality, we emerge with a powerful grounding for a reconceptualization of the research act. Kincheloe and Steinberg (1993, 1996, 1999) and numerous other cognitive theorists have argued, in the spirit of Lev Vygotsky, over the last two decades, that cognition and the knowledge it produces are socially situated activities that take place in concrete historical situations (Kincheloe, 2003b). Varela adds to this description, arguing that it is in the particular historical circumstance that we realize who we are and what we can become. Indeed, we realize our cognitive capabilities in the specific concrete circumstance while concurrently gaining the power to imagine what capabilities we can develop.

As criticalists engage Denzin's performativity, the action turn, and Enactivist principles of systemic self-organization (autopoiesis), critical research moves into a new zone of emergent complexity. In this context, when advocates of a critical form of inquiry use the term "transformative action," they gain a deeper sense of what this might mean using the enactivist concept of readiness-for-action. Knowledge must be enacted—understood at the level of human beings' affect and intellect. In a critical context, the knowledge we produce must be enacted in light of our individual and collective struggles. Without this dimension, the research act becomes a rather abstract enterprise. Nothing new *emerges*, as knowledges and concepts are merely produced rather than related to one another and enacted (performed) in the world. In this enacted context, Denzin argues, cultural studies develops a new way of encountering the cosmos. Epistemological notions of performance and performativity enter into a dynamic tension between doing and the done, the saying and the said. In this productive tension, distance and detachment are overcome in the act of performing. Improvisation, a key dynamic in all these intersecting discourses of inquiry, constructs the moment where resistance emerges, where the doing and the done merge.

In this performative, action-oriented moment, criticalists escape the confines of the stale debate between positivist empiricism and postmodern interpretivism. A new dawn breaks for our evolving criticality and research in cultural studies, as researchers study themselves in relation to others in the effort to produce a practical form of knowledge represented in an action-oriented, performative manner. A new performative, action-oriented, and Enactivist-informed paradigm helps critical researchers develop new ways of inquiring in action-based everyday interactions and lived processes. These interactions and processes are always "sensuous and contingent," Denzin notes. In order for an ethnographer or cultural studies researcher to represent such dynamics, new modes of research are necessary. By definition, the performative ethnography that Denzin offers shatters the textual conventions that traditionally have operated to represent lived experiences. Critical ethnography and cultural studies will never be the same after performativity and the participatory epistemology on which it is based explode the boundaries of acceptable research practice.

◼ Critical Research Encounters the Bricolage

Using the concept of bricolage, as articulated by the editors of this handbook, Norman Denzin and Yvonna Lincoln, Joe Kincheloe develops the notion as an extension of the concept of evolving criticality developed in this chapter. Lincoln and Denzin use the term in the spirit of Claude Levi-Strauss (1966) and his lengthy discussion of it in *The Savage Mind.* The French word *bricoleur* describes a handyman or handywoman who makes use of the tools available to complete a task (Harper, 1987). Some connotations of the term involve trickery and cunning and remind me of the chicanery of

Hermes, in particular his ambiguity concerning the messages of the gods. If hermeneutics came to connote the ambiguity and slipperiness of textual meaning, then bricolage can also imply the fictive and imaginative elements of the presentation of all formal research. Indeed, as cultural studies of science have indicated, all scientific inquiry is jerry-rigged to a degree; science, as we all know by now, is not nearly as clean, simple, and procedural as scientists would have us believe. Maybe this is an admission that many in our field would wish to keep in the closet.

In the first decade of the 21st century, bricolage typically is understood to involve the process of employing these methodological strategies as they are needed in the unfolding context of the research situation. While this interdisciplinary feature is central to any notion of the bricolage, critical qualitative researchers must go beyond this dynamic. Pushing to a new conceptual terrain, such an eclectic process raises numerous issues that researchers must deal with in order to maintain theoretical coherence and epistemological innovation. Such multidisciplinarity demands a new level of research self-consciousness and awareness of the numerous contexts in which any researcher is operating. As one labors to expose the various structures that covertly shape our own and other scholars' research narratives, the bricolage highlights the relationship between a researcher's ways of seeing and the social location of his or her personal history. Appreciating research as a power-driven act, the critical researcher-as-bricoleur abandons the quest for some naïve concept of realism, focusing instead on the clarification of his or her position in the web of reality and the social locations of other researchers and the ways they shape the production and interpretation of knowledge.

In this context, bricoleurs move into the domain of complexity. The bricolage exists out of respect for the complexity of the lived world and the complications of power. Indeed, it is grounded on an epistemology of complexity. One dimension of this complexity can be illustrated by the relationship between research and the domain of social theory. All observations of the world are shaped either consciously or unconsciously by social theory—such theory provides the framework that highlights or erases what might be observed. Theory in a modernist empiricist mode is a way of understanding that operates without variation in every context. Because theory is a cultural and linguistic artifact, its interpretation of the object of its observation is inseparable from the historical dynamics that have shaped it. The task of the bricoleur is to attack this complexity, uncovering the invisible artifacts of power and culture, and documenting the nature of their influence on not only their own works but on scholarship in general. In this process, bricoleurs act upon the concept that theory is not an explanation of nature—it is more an explanation of our relation to nature.

In its hard labors in the domain of complexity, the bricolage views research methods actively rather than passively, meaning that we actively construct our research methods from the tools at hand rather than passively receiving the "correct," universally applicable methodologies. Avoiding modes of reasoning that come from certified processes of logical analysis, bricoleurs also steer clear of preexisting guidelines and checklists developed outside the specific demands of the inquiry at hand. In its embrace of complexity, the bricolage constructs a far more active role for humans both in shaping reality and in creating the research processes and narratives that represent it. Such an active agency rejects deterministic views of social reality that assume the effects of particular social, political, economic, and educational processes. At the same time and in the same conceptual context, this belief in active human agency refuses standardized modes of knowledge production (Bresler & Ardichvili, 2002; Dahlbom, 1998; Mathie & Greene, 2002; McLeod, 2000; Selfe & Selfe, 1994; T. Young & Yarbrough, 1993).

Some of the best work in the study of social complexity is now taking place in the qualitative inquiry of numerous fields including sociology, cultural studies, anthropology, literary studies, marketing, geography, media studies, informatics, library studies, women's studies, various ethnic studies, education, and nursing. Denzin and Lincoln (2000) are acutely aware of these dynamics and refer to them in the context of their delineation of the bricolage. Yvonna Lincoln (2001), in her response to Kincheloe's development of the bricolage, maintains that the most important border work between disciplines is taking place in feminism and race-ethnic studies.

In many ways, there is a form of instrumental reason, of rational irrationality, in the use of passive, external, monological research methods. In the active bricolage, we bring our understanding of the research context together with our previous experience with research methods. Using these knowledges, we *tinker* in the Levi-Straussian sense with our research methods in field-based and interpretive contexts. This tinkering is a high-level cognitive process involving construction and reconstruction, contextual diagnosis, negotiation, and readjustment. Researchers' interactions with the objects of their inquiries, bricoleurs understand, are always complicated, mercurial, unpredictable, and, of course, complex. Such conditions negate the practice of planning research strategies in advance. In lieu of such rationalization of the process, bricoleurs enter into the research act as methodological negotiators. Always respecting the demands of the task at hand, the bricolage, as conceptualized here, resists its placement in concrete as it promotes its elasticity. Critical researchers are better informed as to the power of the bricolage in light of Yvonna Lincoln's (2001) delineation of two types of bricoleurs: those who (a) are committed to research eclecticism, allowing circumstance to shape methods employed, and (b) want to engage in the genealogy/archeology of the disciplines with some grander purpose in mind. My purpose entails both of Lincoln's articulations of the role of the bricoleur.

Research method in the bricolage is a concept that receives more respect than in more rationalistic articulations of the term. The rationalistic articulation of method subverts the deconstruction of wide varieties of unanalyzed assumptions embedded in passive methods. Bricoleurs, in their appreciation of the complexity of the research process, view research method as involving far more than procedure. In this mode of analysis, bricoleurs come to understand research method as also a technology of justification, meaning a way of defending what we assert we know and the process by which we know it. Thus, the education of critical researchers demands that everyone take a step back from the process of learning research methods. Such a step back allows us a conceptual distance that produces a critical consciousness. Such a consciousness refuses the passive acceptance of externally imposed research methods that tacitly certify modes justifying knowledges that are decontextualized, reductionistic, and inscribed by dominant modes of power (Denzin & Lincoln, 2000; Fenwick, 2000; Foster, 1997; McLeod, 2000).

In its critical concern for just social change, the bricolage seeks insight from the margins of Western societies and the knowledge and ways of knowing of non-Western peoples. Such insight helps bricoleurs reshape and sophisticate social theory, research methods, and interpretive strategies, as they discern new topics to be researched. This confrontation with difference so basic to the concept of the bricolage enables researchers to produce new forms of knowledge that inform policy decisions and political action in general. In gaining this insight from the margins, bricoleurs display once again the blurred boundary between the hermeneutical search for understanding and the critical concern with social change for social justice. Kincheloe has taken seriously Peter McLaren's (2001) important concern—offered in his response to Kincheloe's (2001a) first delineation of his conception of the bricolage—that merely focusing on the production of meanings may not lead to "resisting and transforming the existing conditions of exploitation" (McLaren, 2001, p. 702). In response, Kincheloe maintained that in the critical hermeneutical dimension of the bricolage, the act of understanding power and its effects is merely one part—albeit an inseparable part—of counterhegemonic *action.* Not only are the two orientations not in conflict, they are synergistic (DeVault, 1996; Lutz, Kendall, & Jones, 1997; Soto, 2000; Steinberg, 2001).

To contribute to social transformation, bricoleurs seek to better understand both the forces of domination that affect the lives of individuals from race, class, gender, sexual, ethnic, and religious backgrounds outside of dominant culture(s) and the worldviews of such diverse peoples. In this context, bricoleurs attempt to remove knowledge production and its benefits from the control of elite groups. Such control consistently operates to reinforce elite privilege while pushing marginalized groups farther away from the center of dominant power. Rejecting this normalized state of affairs, bricoleurs commit their knowledge work to helping address the ideological and informational needs of marginalized groups and individuals. As detectives of subjugated insight, bricoleurs eagerly learn from labor struggles, women's marginalization, the "double consciousness" of the racially oppressed, and insurrections against colonialism (Kincheloe & Steinberg, 1993; Kincheloe, Steinberg, & Hinchey, 1999; T. Young & Yarbrough, 1993). In this way, the bricolage hopes to contribute to an evolving criticality.

Thus, the bricolage is dedicated to a form of rigor that is conversant with numerous modes of meaning-making and knowledge production—modes that originate in diverse social locations. These alternative modes of reasoning and researching always consider the relationships, the resonances, and the disjunctions between formal and rationalistic modes of Western epistemology and ontology and different cultural, philosophical, paradigmatic, and subjugated expressions. In these latter expressions, bricoleurs often uncover ways of accessing a concept without resorting to a conventional validated set of prespecified procedures that provide the distance of objectivity (Thayer-Bacon, 2003). This notion of distance fails to take into account the rigor of the hermeneutical understanding of the way meaning is preinscribed in the act of being in the world, the research process, and objects of research. This absence of hermeneutical awareness undermines the researcher's quest for a thick description and contributes to the production of reduced understandings of the complexity of social life (Paulson, 1995; Selfe & Selfe, 1994).

The multiple perspectives delivered by the concept of difference provide bricoleurs with many benefits. Confrontation with difference helps us to see anew, to move toward the light of epiphany. A basic dimension of an evolving criticality involves a comfort with the existence of alternative ways of analyzing and producing knowledge. This is why it's so important for a historian, for example, to develop an understanding of phenomenology and hermeneutics. It is why it is so important for a social researcher from New York City to understand forms of indigenous African knowledge production. The incongruities between such cultural modes of inquiry are quite valuable, for within the tensions of difference rest insights into multiple dimensions of the research act. Such insights move us to new levels of understanding of the subjects, purposes, and nature of inquiry (Burbules & Beck, 1999; Mayers, 2001; Semali & Kincheloe, 1999; Willinsky, 2001).

Difference in the bricolage pushes us into the hermeneutic circle as we are induced to deal with parts in their diversity in relation to the whole. Difference may involve culture, class, language, discipline, epistemology, cosmology, ad infinitum. Bricoleurs use one dimension of these multiple diversities to explore others, to generate questions previously unimagined. As we examine these multiple perspectives, we attend to which ones are validated and which ones have been dismissed. Studying such differences, we begin to understand how dominant power operates to exclude and certify particular forms of knowledge production and why. In the criticality of the bricolage, this focus on power and difference always leads us to an awareness of the multiple dimensions of the social. Paulo Freire (1970) referred to this as the need for perceiving social structures and social systems that undermine equal access to resources and power. As bricoleurs answer such questions, we gain new appreciations of the way power tacitly shapes what we know and how we come to know it.

The Bricolage, a Complex Ontology, and Critical

A central dimension of the bricolage that holds profound implications for critical research is the notion of a critical ontology (Kincheloe, 2003a). As bricoleurs prepare to explore that which is not readily apparent to the ethnographic eye, that realm of complexity in knowledge production that insists on initiating a conversation about what it is that qualitative researchers are observing and interpreting in the world, this clarification of a complex ontology is needed. This conversation is especially important because it hasn't generally taken place. Bricoleurs maintain that this object of inquiry is ontologically complex in that it can't be described as an encapsulated entity. In this more open view, the object of inquiry is always a part of many contexts and processes; it is culturally inscribed and historically situated. The complex view of the object of inquiry accounts for the historical efforts to interpret its meaning in the world and how such efforts continue to define its social, cultural, political, psychological, and educational effects.

In the domain of the qualitative research process, for example, this ontological complexity undermines traditional notions of triangulation. Because of its in-process (processual) nature, inter-researcher reliability becomes far more difficult to achieve. Process-sensitive scholars watch the world flow by like a river in which the exact contents of the water are never the same. Because all observers view an object of inquiry from their own vantage points in the web of reality, no portrait of a social phenomenon is ever exactly the same as another. Because all physical, social, cultural, psychological, and educational dynamics are connected in a larger fabric, researchers will produce different descriptions of an object of inquiry depending on what part of the fabric they have focused on—what part of the river they have seen. The more unaware observers are of this type of complexity, the more reductionistic the knowledge they produce about it. Bricoleurs attempt to understand this fabric and the processes that shape it in as thick a way as possible (Blommaert, 1997).

The design and methods used to analyze this social fabric cannot be separated from the way reality is construed. Thus, ontology and epistemology are linked inextricably in ways that shape the task of the researcher. The bricoleur must understand these features in the pursuit of rigor. A deep interdisciplinarity is justified by an understanding of the complexity of the object of inquiry and the demands such complications place on the research act. As parts of complex systems and intricate processes, objects of inquiry are far too mercurial to be viewed by a single way of seeing or as a snapshot of a particular phenomenon at a specific moment in time.

A deep interdisciplinarity seeks to modify the disciplines and the view of research brought to the negotiating table constructed by the bricolage. Everyone leaves the table informed by the dialogue in a way that idiosyncratically influences the research methods they subsequently employ. The point of the interaction is not standardized agreement as to some reductionistic notion of "the proper interdisciplinary research method" but awareness of the diverse tools in the researcher's toolbox. The form such deep interdisciplinarity may take is shaped by the object of inquiry in question. Thus, in the bricolage the context in which research takes place always affects the nature of the deep interdisciplinarity employed. In the spirit of the dialectic of disciplinarity, the ways these context-driven articulations of interdisciplinarity are constructed must be examined in light of the power literacy previously mentioned (Blommaert, 1997; Friedman, 1998; Pryse, 1998; Quintero & Rummel, 2003; T. Young & Yarbrough, 1993).

In social research, the relationship between individuals and their contexts is a central dynamic to be investigated. This relationship is a key ontological and epistemological concern of the bricolage; it is a connection that shapes the identities of human beings and the nature of the complex social fabric. Thus, bricoleurs use multiple methods to analyze the multidimensionality of this type of connection. The ways bricoleurs engage in this process of putting together the pieces of the relationship may provide a different interpretation of its meaning and effects. Recognizing the complex ontological importance of relationships alters the basic foundations of the research act and knowledge production process. Thin reductionistic descriptions of isolated things-in-themselves are no longer sufficient in critical research (Foster, 1997; Zammito, 1996).

What the bricolage is dealing with in this context is a double ontology of complexity: first, the complexity of objects of inquiry and their being-in-the-world; second, the nature of the social construction of human subjectivity, the production of human "being." Such understandings open a new era of social research where the process of becoming human agents is appreciated with a new level of sophistication. The complex feedback loop between an unstable social structure and the individual can be charted in a way that grants human beings insight into the means by which power operates and the democratic process is subverted. In this complex ontological view, bricoleurs understand that social structures do not *determine* individual subjectivity but *constrain* it in remarkably intricate ways. The bricolage is acutely interested in developing and employing a variety of strategies to help specify these ways subjectivity is shaped.

The recognitions that emerge from such a multiperspectival process get analysts beyond the determinism of reductionistic notions of macrosocial structures. The intent of a usable social or educational research is subverted in this reductionistic context, as human agency is erased by the "laws" of society. Structures do not simply "exist" as objective entities whose influence can be predicted or "not exist" with no influence over the cosmos of human affairs. Here fractals enter the stage with their loosely structured characteristics of irregular shape—fractal structures. While not *determining* human behavior, for example, fractal structures possess sufficient order to affect other systems and entities within their environment. Such structures are never stable or universally present in some uniform manifestation (Varenne, 1996; T. Young & Yarbrough, 1993). The more we study such dynamics, the more diversity of expression we find. Taking this ontological and epistemological diversity into account, bricoleurs understand there are numerous dimensions to the bricolage (Denzin & Lincoln, 2000). As with all aspects of the bricolage, no description is fixed and final, and all features of the bricolage come with an elastic clause.

▣ Critical Research in a Globalized, Privatized World

A critical postmodern research requires researchers to construct their perception of the world anew, not just in random ways but in a manner that undermines what appears natural, that opens to question what appears obvious (Slaughter, 1989). Oppositional and insurgent researchers as maieutic agents must not confuse their research efforts with the textual suavities of an avant-garde academic posturing in which they are awarded the sinecure of representation for the oppressed without actually having to return to those working-class communities where their studies took place. Rather, they need to locate their work in a transformative praxis that leads to the alleviation of suffering and the overcoming of oppression.

Rejecting the arrogant reading of metropolitan critics and their imperial mandates governing research, insurgent researchers ask questions about how what is has come to be, whose interests are served by particular institutional arrangements, and where our own frames of reference come from. Facts are no longer simply "what is"; the truth of beliefs is not simply testable by their correspondence to these facts. To engage in research grounded on an evolving criticality is to take part in a process of critical world-making, guided by the shadowed outline of a dream of a world less conditioned by misery, suffering, and the politics of deceit. It is, in short, a pragmatics of hope in an age of cynical reason. The obstacles that critical research has yet to overcome in terms of a frontal assault against the ravages of global capitalism, the new American Empire and its devastation of the global working class, has led McLaren to a more sustained and sympathetic engagement with Marx and the Marxist tradition.

One significant area of concern that has been addressed in the recent Marxist work of McLaren and Scatamburlo-D'Annibale (2004) and Antonia Darder and Rodolfo Torres (2004) is that of critical pedagogy and its intersection with critical multiculturalism, especially with respect to the influence that critical race theory has had on recent work in these interconnected domains. Darder and Torres (2004) point to the fact that much of the work within critical race theory is grounded in the popular intersectionality argument of the post-structuralist and post-modernist era that stipulates that race, class, gender, and sexual orientation should all receive equal attention in understanding the social order and the institutions and ideologies that constitute it. That is, various oppressions are to be engaged with equal weight as one ascribes pluralized sensibilities to any political project that theorizes about social inequalities (2004).

This reduces capitalist exploitation and relations of capitalist production to one set of relations, among others, that systematically denies the totality of capitalism that is constitutive of the process of racialized class relations. This is not to argue that the pernicious ideology of racism is not integral to the process of capitalist accumulation but, as Darder and Torres argue, it is to antiseptically separate politics and economics as distinct spheres of power or ensembles of social relations. Rather than focus on race, or raced identity (i.e., shared phenotypical traits or cultural attributes), Darder and Torres make the case for concentrating upon the ideology of racism and racialized class relations within a larger materialist understanding of the world, thereby bringing the analysis of political economy to the center of the debate.

In a similar fashion, McLaren and Scatamburlo-D'Annibale (2004) argue that the separation of the economic and the political within current contributions of multiculturalism premised on identity politics has had the effect of replacing a *historical materialist class analysis* with a *cultural analysis of class*. As a result, many critical race theorists as well as post-Marxists writing in the realm of cultural studies have also stripped the idea of class of precisely that element which, for Marx, made it radical—namely its status as a universal form of exploitation whose abolition required (and was also central to) the abolition of all manifestations of oppression (Marx, 1978, p. 60). With regard to this issue, Kovel (2002) is particularly insightful, for he explicitly addresses an issue that continues to vex the Left—namely the priority given to different categories of what he calls "dominative splitting"—those categories of gender, class, race, ethnic and national exclusion, and so on.

Kovel argues that we need to ask the question of *priority* with respect to what? He notes that if we mean priority with respect to time, then the category of gender would have priority because there are traces of gender oppression in all other forms of oppression. If we were to prioritize in terms of existential significance, Kovel suggests that we would have to depend on the immediate historical forces that bear down on distinct groups of people—he offers examples of Jews in 1930s Germany who suffered from brutal forms of anti-Semitism and Palestinians today who experience anti-Arab racism under Israeli domination. The question of what has political priority, however, would depend on which transformation of relations of oppression are practically more urgent, and while this would certainly depend upon the preceding categories, it would also depend on the fashion in which all the forces acting in a concrete situation are deployed.

As to the question of which split sets into motion all the others, the priority would have to be given to *class* because class relations

> entail the state as an instrument of enforcement and control, and it is the state that shapes and organizes the splits that appear in human ecosystems. Thus, class is both logically and historically distinct from other forms of exclusion (hence, we should not talk of "classism" to go along with "sexism" and "racism," and "species-ism"). This is, first of all, because class is an essentially human-made category, without root in even a mystified biology. We cannot imagine a human world without gender distinctions—although we can imagine a world without domination by gender. But a world without class is eminently imaginable—indeed, such was the human world for the great majority of our species's time on earth, during all of which considerable fuss was made over gender. Historically, the difference arises because "class" signifies one side of a larger figure that includes a state apparatus whose conquests and regulations create races and shape gender relations. Thus, there will be no true resolution of racism so long as class society stands, inasmuch as a racially oppressed society implies the activities of a class-defending state. Nor can gender inequality be enacted away so long as class society, with its state, demands the super-exploitation of women's labor. (Kovel, 2002, pp. 123–124)

Rethinking Class and Class Consciousness

Recently, McLaren and Scatamburlo-D'Annibale (2004) have reexamined some of the ethnographic and conceptual work of Paul Willis (1977, 1978, 2000; Willis, Jones, Cannan, & Hurd, 1990) in an attempt to rethink a research agenda involving the participation of working-class subjects and constituencies. We believe that ethnographic models of research such as those developed by Willis would best serve the interests of the working class if they could be accompanied by a larger strategy for socialist transformation, one that proceeds from an assessment of the objective factors and capabilities latent in the current conditions of class struggle. McLaren and Scatamburlo-D'Annibale maintain that the worldwide social movement against anticorporate globalization, as well as the anti-imperialist/antiwar movements preceding and following the U.S. invasion of Iraq, have provided new contexts (mostly through left-wing independent publications and resources on the Internet) for enabling various publics (and non-publics beyond the institutions that serve majority groups) to become more critically literate about the relationship between current world events, global capitalism, and imperialism. For many researchers and educators on the left, this will require a socialist "education" of working-class consciousness. This, in turn, means challenging the mediated social forms in which we live and learn to labor.

One way of scrutinizing the production of everyday meanings so that they are less likely to provide ballast to capitalist social relations is to study working-class consciousness. Bertell Ollman (1971, 1993, 2003) has developed a systematic approach to dialectics that can be brought to bear on the study of working-class consciousness. Such an approach is in need of serious consideration by progressive researchers, especially because most current studies of working-class consciousness have been derived from non-Marxist approaches. Ollman (1993) advises that class consciousness is much more than individual consciousness writ large. The subject of class consciousness is, after all, class. Viewing class consciousness from the perspective of the labor theory of value and the materialist conception of history, as undertaken in Ollman's account, stipulates that we view class in the context of the overall integrated functions of capital and wage labor.

Although people can certainly be seen from the functionalist perspective as embodiments of social-economic functions, we need to expand this view and understand the subjective dimensions of class and class consciousness. Ollman follows Marx's advice in recommending that in defining "class" or any other important notion, we begin from the whole and proceed to the part (see also Ilyenkov, 1977, 1982a, 1982b). According to McLaren and Scatamburlo-D'Annibale (2004), class must be conceived as a complex social relation in the context of Marx's dialectical approach to social life. (This discussion is based on McLaren and Scatamburlo-D'Annibale [2004]). It is important in this regard to see class as a function (from the perspective of the place of a function within the system), as a group (qualities that are attributed to people such as race and gender), and as a complex relation (that is, as the abstracted common element in the social relationship of alienated individuals). A class involves, therefore, the alienated quality of the social life of individuals who function in a certain way within the system. The salient features of class—alienated social relation, place/function, and group—are all mutually dependent.

Class as function relates to the objective interests of workers; class as group relates to their subjective interests. Subjective interests refer to what workers actually believe to be in their own best interests. Those practices that serve the workers in their function as wage laborers refer to their objective interests. Ollman summarizes class consciousness as

> one's identity and interests (subjective and objective) as members of a class, something of the dynamics of capitalism uncovered by Marx (at least enough to grasp objective interests), the broad outlines of the class struggle and where one fits into it, feelings of solidarity toward one's own class and of rational hostility toward opposition classes (in contrast to the feelings of mutual indifference and inner-class competition that accompany alienation), and the vision of a more democratic and egalitarian society that is not only possible but that one can help bring about. (1993, p. 155)

Ollman underscores importantly the notion that explaining class consciousness stipulates seeking what is not present in the thinking of workers as well as what is present. It is an understanding that is "appropriate to the objective character of a class and its objective interests" (1993, p. 155). But in addition to the objective aspect of class consciousness, we must include the subjective aspect of class consciousness, which Ollman describes as "the consciousness of the group of people in a class in so far as their understanding of who they are and what must be done develops from its economistic beginnings toward the consciousness that is appropriate to their class situation" (1993, p. 155). But what is different between this subjective consciousness and the actual consciousness of each individual in the group? Ollman writes that subjective consciousness is different from the actual consciousness of the individual in the group in the following three ways:

> (1) It is a group consciousness, a way of thinking and a thought content, that develops through the individuals in the group interacting with each other and with opposing groups in situations that are peculiar to the class; (2) it is a consciousness that has its main point of reference in the situation and objective interests of a class, viewed functionally, and not in the declared subjective interests of class members (the imputed class consciousness referred to above has been given a role here in the thinking of real people); and (3) it is in its essence a process, a movement from wherever a group begins in its consciousness of itself to the consciousness appropriate to its situation. In other words, the process of becoming class conscious is not external to what it is but rather at the center of what it is all about. (1993, p. 155)

Class consciousness is therefore something that Ollman describes as "a kind of 'group think,' a collective, interactive approach to recognizing, labeling, coming to understand, and acting upon the particular world class members have in common" (1993, p. 156). Class consciousness is different from individual consciousness in the sense of "having its main point of reference in the situation of the class and not in the already recognized interests of individuals" (1993, p. 157). Class consciousness is something that exists "in potential" in the sense that it represents "the appropriate consciousness of people in that position, the consciousness that maximizes their chances of realizing class interests, including structural change where such change is required to secure other interests" (1993, p. 157). Ollman stresses that class consciousness "exists in potential," that is, "class consciousness is a consciousness waiting to happen" (1993, p. 187). It is important here not to mistake class consciousness as some kind of "abstract potential" because it is "rooted in a situation unfolding before our very eyes, long before understanding of real people catches up with it" (1993, p. 157). Class consciousness, then, is not something that is fixed or permanent but is always in motion. The very situatedness of the class establishes its goal—it is always in the process of becoming itself, if we understand the notion of process dialectically. Consequently, we need to examine class from the perspective of Marx's philosophy of internal relations, as that "which treats the relations in which anything stands as essential parts of what it is, so that a significant change in any of these relations registers as a qualitative change in the system of which it is a part" (Ollman, 2003, p. 85).

Focusing on Critical Ethnography

As critical researchers attempt to get behind the curtain, to move beyond assimilated experience, to expose the way ideology constrains the desire for self-direction, and to confront the way power reproduces itself in the construction of human consciousness, they employ a plethora of research methodologies. In this context, Patti Lather (1991, 1993) extends our position with her notion of catalytic validity. Catalytic validity points to the degree to which research moves those it studies to understand the world and the way it is shaped in order for them to transform it. Noncritical researchers who operate within an empiricist framework will perhaps find catalytic validity to be a strange concept. Research that possesses catalytic validity will not only display the reality-altering impact of the inquiry process; it will also direct this impact so that those under study will gain self-understanding and self-direction.

Theory that falls under the rubric of *postcolonialism* (see McLaren, 1999; Semali & Kincheloe, 1999) involves important debates over the knowing subject and object of analysis. Such works have initiated important new modes of analysis, especially in relation to questions of imperialism, colonialism, and neocolonialism. Recent attempts by critical researchers to move beyond the objectifying and imperialist gaze associated with the Western anthropological tradition (which fixes the image of the so-called informant from the colonizing perspective of the knowing subject), although laudatory and well-intentioned, are not without their shortcomings

(Bourdieu & Wacquaat, 1992). As Fuchs (1993) has so presciently observed, serious limitations plague recent efforts to develop a more reflective approach to ethnographic writing. The challenge here can be summarized in the following questions: How does the knowing subject come to know the Other? How can researchers respect the perspective of the Other and invite the Other to speak (Abdullah & Stringer, 1999; Ashcroft, Griffiths, & Tiffin, 1995; Brock-Utne, 1996; Goldie, 1995; Macedo, 1994; Myrsiades & Myrsiades, 1998; Pieterse & Parekh, 1995; Prakash & Esteva, 1998; Rains, 1998; Scheurich & Young, 1997; Semali & Kincheloe, 1999; Viergever, 1999)?

Although recent confessional modes of ethnographic writing attempt to treat so-called informants as "participants" in an attempt to avoid the objectification of the Other (usually referring to the relationship between Western anthropologists and non-Western culture), there is a risk that uncovering colonial and postcolonial structures of domination may, in fact, unintentionally validate and consolidate such structures as well as reassert liberal values through a type of covert ethnocentrism. Fuchs (1993) warns that the attempt to subject researchers to the same approach to which other societies are subjected could lead to an " 'othering' of one's own world" (p. 108). Such an attempt often fails to question existing ethnographic methodologies and therefore unwittingly extends their validity and applicability while further objectifying the world of the researcher. Michel Foucault's approach to this dilemma is to "detach" social theory from the epistemology of his own culture by criticizing the traditional philosophy of reflection. However, Foucault falls into the trap of ontologizing his own methodological argumentation and erasing the notion of prior understanding that is linked to the idea of an "inside" view (Fuchs, 1993). Louis Dumont fares somewhat better by arguing that cultural texts need to be viewed simultaneously from the inside and from the outside.

However, in trying to affirm a "reciprocal interpretation of various societies among themselves" (Fuchs, 1993, p. 113) through identifying both transindividual structures of consciousness and transsubjective social structures, Dumont aspires to a universal framework for the comparative analysis of societies. Whereas Foucault and Dumont attempt to "transcend the categorical foundations of their own world" (Fuchs, 1993, p. 118) by refusing to include themselves in the process of objectification, Pierre Bourdieu integrates himself as a social actor into the social field under analysis. Bourdieu achieves such integration by "epistemologizing the ethnological content of his own presuppositions" (Fuchs, 1993, p. 121). But the self-objectification of the observer (anthropologist) is not unproblematic. Fuchs (1993) notes, after Bourdieu, that the chief difficulty is "forgetting the difference between the theoretical and the practical relationship with the world and of imposing on the object the theoretical relationship one maintains with it" (p. 120). Bourdieu's approach to re-search does not fully escape becoming, to a certain extent, a "confirmation of objectivism," but at least there is an earnest attempt by the researcher to reflect on the preconditions of his or her own self-understanding—an attempt to engage in an "ethnography of ethnographers" (p. 122).

Postmodern ethnography often intersects—to varying degrees—with the concerns of postcolonialist researchers, but the degree to which it fully addresses issues of exploitation and the social relations of capitalist exploitation remains questionable. Postmodern ethnography—and we are thinking here of works such as Paul Rabinow's *Reflections on Fieldwork in Morocco* (1977), James Boon's *Other Tribes, Other Scribes* (1982), and Michael Taussig's *Shamanism, Colonialism, and the Wild Man* (1987)—shares the conviction articulated by Marc Manganaro (1990) that "no anthropology is apolitical, removed from ideology and hence from the capacity to be affected by or, as crucially, to effect social formations. The question ought not to be if an anthropological text is political, but rather, what kind of sociopolitical affiliations are tied to particular anthropological texts" (p. 35).

Judith Newton and Judith Stacey (1992–1993) note that the current postmodern textual experimentation of ethnography credits the "post-colonial predicament of culture as the opportunity for anthropology to reinvent itself" (p. 56). Modernist ethnography, according to these authors, "constructed authoritative cultural accounts that served, however inadvertently, not only to establish the authority of the Western ethnographer over native others but also to sustain Western authority over colonial cultures" (p. 56). They argue (following James Clifford) that ethnographers can and should try to escape the recurrent allegorical genre of colonial ethnography—the pastoral, a nostalgic, redemptive text that preserves a primitive culture on the brink of extinction for the historical record of its Western conquerors. The narrative structure of this "salvage text" portrays the native culture as a coherent, authentic, and lamentably "evading past," whereas its complex, inauthentic, Western successors represent the future (p. 56).

Postmodern ethnographic writing faces the challenge of moving beyond simply the reanimation of local experience, an uncritical celebration of cultural difference (including figural differentiations within the ethnographer's own culture), and the employment of a framework that espouses universal values and a global role for interpretivist anthropology (Silverman, 1990). What we have described as resistance postmodernism can help qualitative researchers challenge dominant Western research practices that are underwritten by a foundational epistemology and a claim to universally valid knowledge at the expense of local, subjugated knowledges (Peters, 1993). The choice is not one between modernism and postmodernism, but one of whether or not to challenge the presuppositions that inform the normalizing judgments one makes as a researcher.

Vincent Crapanzano (1990) warns that "the anthropologist can assume neither the Orphic lyre nor the crown of thorns, although I confess to hear salvationist echoes" in his desire to protect his people (p. 301).

Connor (1992) describes the work of James Clifford, which shares an affinity with ethnographic work associated with Georges Bataille, Michel Lerris, and the College de Sociologie, as not simply the "writing of culture" but rather "the interior disruption of categories of art and culture correspond[ing] to a radically dialogic form of ethnographic writing, which takes place across and between cultures" (p. 251). Clifford (1992) describes his own work as an attempt "to multiply the hands and discourses involved in 'writing culture' . . . not to assert a naïve democracy of plural authorship, but to loosen at least somewhat the monological control of the executive writer/anthropologist and to open for discussion ethnography's hierarchy and negotiation of discourses in power-charged, unequal situations" (p. 100). Citing the work of Marcus and Fischer (1986), Clifford warns against modernist ethnographic practices of "representational essentializing" and "metonymic freezing" in which one aspect of a group's life is taken to represent the group as a whole; instead, Clifford urges forms of multilocale ethnography to reflect the "transnational political, economic and cultural forces that traverse and constitute local or regional worlds" (p. 102). Rather than culture being fixed into reified textual portraits, it needs to be better understood as displacement, transplantation, disruption, positionality, and difference.

Although critical ethnography allows, in a way conventional ethnography does not, for the relationship of liberation and history, and although its hermeneutical task is to call into question the social and cultural conditioning of human activity and the prevailing sociopolitical structures, we do not claim that this is enough to restructure the social system. But it is certainly, in our view, a necessary beginning. We follow Patricia Ticineto Clough (1992) in arguing that "realist narrativity has allowed empirical social science to be the platform and horizon of social criticism" (p. 135). Ethnography needs to be analyzed critically not only in terms of its field methods but also as reading and writing practices. Data collection must give way to "rereadings of representations in every form" (p. 137). In the narrative construction of its authority as empirical science, ethnography needs to face the unconscious processes upon which it justifies its canonical formulations, processes that often involve the disavowal of oedipal or authorial desire and the reduction of differences to binary oppositions. Within these processes of binary reduction, the male ethnographer is most often privileged as the guardian of "the factual representation of empirical positivities" (Clough, 1992, p. 9).

▣ New Questions Concerning Validity in Critical Ethnography

Critical research traditions have arrived at the point where they recognize that claims to truth are always discursively situated and implicated in relations of power. Yet, unlike some claims made within "ludic" strands of postmodernist research, we do not suggest that because we cannot know truth absolutely, truth can simply be equated with an effect of power. We say this because truth involves regulative rules that must be met for some statements to be more meaningful than others. Otherwise, truth becomes meaningless and, if that is the case, liberatory praxis has no purpose other than to win for the sake of winning. As Phil Carspecken (1993, 1999) remarks, every time we act, in every instance of our behavior, we presuppose some normative or universal relation to truth. Truth is internally related to meaning in a pragmatic way through normative referenced claims, intersubjective referenced claims, subjective referenced claims, and the way we deictically ground or anchor meaning in our daily lives. Carspecken explains that researchers are able to articulate the normative evaluative claims of others when they begin to see them in the same way as their participants by living inside the cultural and discursive positionalities that inform such claims.

Claims to universality must be recognized in each particular normative claim, and questions must be raised about whether such norms represent the entire group. When the limited claim of universality is seen to be contradictory to the practices under observation, power relations become visible. What is crucial here, according to Carspecken, is that researchers recognize where they are located ideologically in the normative and identity claims of others and at the same time be honest about their own subjective referenced claims and not let normative evaluative claims interfere with what they observe. Critical research continues to problematize normative and universal claims in a way that does not permit them to be analyzed outside a politics of representation, divorced from the material conditions in which they are produced, or outside a concern with the constitution of the subject in the very acts of reading and writing.

In his book *Critical Ethnography in Educational Research* (1996), Carspecken addresses the issue of critical epistemology, an understanding of the relationship between power and thought, and power and truth claims. In a short exposition of what is "critical" to critical epistemology, he debunks facile forms of social constructivism and offers a deft criticism of mainstream epistemologies by way of Continental phenomenology, poststructuralism, and postmodernist social theory, mainly the work of Edmund Husserl and Jacques Derrida. Carspecken makes short work of facile forms of constructivist thought, purporting that what we see is strongly influenced by what we already value and that criticalist research simply indulges itself in the "correct" political values. For instance, some constructivists argue that all that criticalists need to do is to "bias" their work in the direction of social justice.

This form of constructivist thought is not viable, according to Carspecken, because it is plainly ocular-centric; that is, it depends upon visual perception to form the basis of its theory. Rather than rely on perceptual metaphors found in mainstream ethnographic accounts, critical ethnography, in contrast, should emphasize communicative experiences and structures as well as cultural typifications. Carspecken argues that critical ethnography needs to differentiate among ontological categories (i.e., subjective, objective, normative-evaluative) rather than adopt the position of "multiple realities" defended by many constructivists. He adopts a principled position that research value orientations should not determine research findings, as much as this is possible. Rather, critical ethnographers should employ a critical epistemology; that is, they should uphold epistemological principles that apply to all researchers. In fecundating this claim, Carspecken rehabilitates critical ethnography from many of the misperceptions of its critics who believe that it ignores questions of validity.

To construct a socially critical epistemology, critical ethnographers need to understand holistic modes of human experience and their relationship to communicative structures. Preliminary stages of this process that Carspecken articulates include examining researcher bias and discovering researcher value orientations. Following stages include compiling the primary record through the collection of monological data, preliminary reconstructive analysis, dialogical data generation, discovering social systems relations, and using systems relations to explain findings. Anthony Giddens's work forms the basis of Carspecken's approach to systems analysis. Accompanying discussions of each of the complex stages Carspecken develops are brilliantly articulated approaches to horizontal and vertical validity reconstructions and pragmatic horizons of analysis. In order to help link theory to practice, Carspecken uses data from his study of an inner-city Houston elementary school program that is charged with helping students learn conflict management skills.

Another impressive feature is Carspecken's exposition and analysis of communicative acts, especially his discussion of meaning as embodiment and understanding as intersubjective, not objective or subjective. Carspecken works from a view of intersubjectivity that combines Hegel, Mead, Habermas, and Taylor. He recommends that critical ethnographers record body language carefully because the meaning of an action is not in the language, it is rather in the action and the actor's bodily states. In Carspecken's view, subjectivity is derivative from intersubjectivity (as is objectivity), and intersubjectivity involves the dialogical constitution of the "feeling body." Finally, Carspecken stresses the importance of macro-level social theories, environmental conditions, socially structured ways of meeting needs and desires, effects of cultural commodities on students, economic exploitation, and political and cultural conditions of action. Much of Carspecken's inspiration for his approach to validity claims is taken from Habermas's theory of communicative action. Carspecken reads Habermas as grasping the prelinguistic foundations of language and intersubjectivity, making language secondary to the concept of intersubjectivity.

Yet Carspecken departs from a strict Habermasian view of action by bringing in an expressive/praxis model roughly consistent with Charles Taylor's work. Although Habermas and Taylor frequently argue against each other's positions, Carspecken puts them together in a convincing manner. Taylor's emphasis on holistic modes of understanding and the act constitution that Carspecken employs make it possible to link the theory of communicative rationality to work on embodied meaning and the metaphoric basis of meaningful action. It also provides a means for synthesizing Giddens's ideas on part/whole relations, virtual structure, and act constitution with communicative rationality. This is another way in which Carspecken's work differs from Habermas and yet remains consistent with his theory and the internal link between meaning and validity.

Recent Innovations in Critical Ethnography

In addition to Carspecken's brilliant insights into critically grounded ethnography, the late 1990s witnessed a proliferation of deconstructive approaches as well as reflexive approaches (this discussion is based on Trueba and McLaren [2000]). In her important book *Fictions of Feminist Ethnography* (1994), Kamala Visweswaran maintains that reflexive ethnography, like normative ethnography, rests on the "declarative mode" of imparting knowledge to a reader whose identity is anchored in a shared discourse.

Deconstructive ethnography, in contrast, enacts the "interrogative mode" through a constant deferral or a refusal to explain or interpret. Within deconstructive ethnography, the identity of the reader with a unified subject of enunciation is discouraged. Whereas reflexive ethnography maintains that the ethnographer is not separate from the object of investigation, the ethnographer is still viewed as a unified subject of knowledge that can make hermeneutic efforts to establish identification between the observer and the observed (as in modernist interpretive traditions). Deconstructive ethnography, in contrast, often disrupts such identification in favor of articulating a fractured, destabilized, multiply positioned subjectivity (as in postmodernist interpretive traditions). Whereas reflexive ethnography questions its own authority, deconstructive ethnography forfeits its authority.

Both approaches to critical ethnography can be used to uncover the clinging Eurocentric authority employed by ethnographers in the study of Latino/a populations. The goal of both these approaches is criticalist in nature: that is, to free the object of analysis from the tyranny of fixed, unassailable categories and to rethink subjectivity itself as a permanently unclosed, always partial, narrative engagement with text and context. Such an approach can help the ethnographer to caution against the damaging depictions propagated by Anglo observers about Mexican immigrants. As Ruth Behar (1993) notes, in classical sociological and ethnographic accounts of the Mexican and Mexican American family, stereotypes similar to those surrounding the black family perpetuated images of the authoritarian, oversexed, and macho husband and the meek and submissive wife surrounded by children who adore their good and suffering mother. These stereotypes have come under strong critique in the last few years, particularly by Chicana critics, who have sought to go beyond the various "deficiency theories" that continue to mark the discussion of African American and Latino/a family life (p. 276).

The conception of culture advanced by critical ethnographers generally unpacks culture as a complex circuit of production that includes myriad dialectically reinitiating and mutually informing sets of activities such as routines, rituals, action conditions, systems of intelligibility and meaning-making, conventions of interpretation, systems relations, and conditions both external and internal to the social actor (Carspecken, 1996). In her ethnographic study *A Space on the Side of the Road* (1996), Kathleen Stewart cogently illustrates the ambivalent character of culture, as well as its fluidity and ungraspable multilayeredness, when she remarks:

> Culture, as it is seen through its productive forms and means of mediation, is not, then, reducible to a fixed body of social value and belief or a direct precipitant of lived experience in the world but grows into a space on the side of the road where stories weighted with sociality take on a life of their own. We "see" it . . . only by building up multilayered narratives of the poetic in the everyday life of things. We represent it only by roaming from one texted genre to another—romantic, realist, historical, fantastic, sociological, surreal. There is no final textual solution, no way of resolving the dialogic of the interpreter/interpreted or subject/object through efforts to "place" ourselves in the text, or to represent "the fieldwork experience," or to gather up the voices of the other as if they could speak for themselves. (p. 210)

According to E. San Juan (1996), a renewed understanding of culture—as both discursive and material—becomes the linchpin for any emancipatory politics. San Juan writes that the idea of culture as social processes and practices that are thoroughly grounded in material social relations—in the systems of maintenance (economics), decision (politics), learning and communication (culture), and generation and nurture (the domain of social reproduction)—must be the grounding principle, or paradigm if you like, of any progressive and emancipatory approach (p. 177; Gresson, 1995). Rejecting the characterization of anthropologists as either "adaptationalists" (e.g., Marvin Harris) or "ideationalists" (e.g., cognitivists, Lévi-Straussian structuralists, Schneiderian symbolists, Geertzian interpretivists), E. Valentine Daniel remarks in his recent ethnography *Charred Lullabies: Chapters in an Anthropology of Violence* (1996) that culture is "no longer something out there to be discovered, described, and explained, but rather something into which the ethnographer, as interpreter, enter[s]" (p. 198). Culture, in other words, is cocreated by the anthropologist and informant through conversation. Yet even this semeiosic conceptualization of culture is not without its problems. As Daniel himself notes, even if one considers oneself to be a "culture-comaking processualist," in contrast to a "culture-finding essentialist," one still has to recognize that one is working within a logocentric tradition that, to a greater or lesser extent, privileges words over actions.

Critical ethnography has benefited from this new understanding of culture and from the new hybridic possibilities for cultural critique that have been opened up by the current blurring and mixing of disciplinary genres—those that emphasize experience, subjectivity, reflexivity, and dialogical understanding. The advantage that follows such perspectives is that social life is not viewed as preontologically available for the researcher to study. It also follows that there is no perspective unspoiled by ideology from which to study social life in an antiseptically objective way. What is important to note here is the stress placed on the ideological situatedness of any descriptive or socioanalytic account of social life. Critical ethnographers such as John and Jean Comaroff (1992) have made significant contributions to our understanding of the ways in which power is entailed in culture, leading to practices of domination and exploitation that have become naturalized in everyday social life. According to Comaroff and Comaroff, hegemony refers to "that order of signs and practices, relations and distinctions, images and epistemologies—drawn from a historically situated cultural field—that come to be taken-for-granted as the natural and received shape of the world and everything that inhabits it" (p. 23). These axiomatic and yet ineffable discourses and practices that are presumptively shared become "ideological" precisely when their internal contradictions are revealed, uncovered, and viewed as arbitrary and negotiable. Ideology, then, refers to a highly articulated worldview, master narrative, discursive regime, or organizing scheme for collective symbolic production. The dominant ideology is the expression of the dominant social group.

Following this line of argument, hegemony "is nonnegotiable and therefore beyond direct argument," whereas ideology "is more susceptible to being perceived as a matter of inimical opinion and interest and therefore is open to contestation" (Comaroff & Comaroff, 1992, p. 24). Ideologies become the expressions of specific groups, whereas hegemony refers to conventions and constructs that are shared and naturalized throughout a political community. Hegemony works both through silences and through repetition in naturalizing the dominant worldview. There also may exist oppositional ideologies among subordinate or subaltern groups—whether well formed or loosely articulated—that break free of hegemony. In this way, hegemony is never total or complete; it is always porous.

▣ Critical Research, 9/11, and the Effort to Make Sense of the American Empire in the 21st Century

The dominant power of these economic dynamics has been reinforced by post-9/11 military moves by the United States. Critical researchers cannot escape the profound implications of these geopolitical, economic, social, cultural, and epistemological issues for the future of knowledge production and distribution. An evolving criticality is keenly aware of these power dynamics and the way they embed themselves in all dimensions of the issues examined here. In this context, it is essential that critical researchers work to expose these disturbing dynamics to both academic and general audiences. In many ways, 9/11 was a profound shock to millions of Americans who obtain their news and worldviews from the mainstream, corporately owned media and their understanding of American international relations from what is taught in most secondary schools and in many colleges and universities. Such individuals are heard frequently on call-in talk radio and TV shows expressing the belief that America is loved internationally because it is richer, more moral, and more magnanimous than other nations. In this mind-set, those who resist the United States hate its freedom for reasons never quite specified. These Americans, the primary victims of a right-wing corporate-government produced miseducation (Kincheloe & Steinberg, 2004), have not been informed by their news sources of the societies that have been undermined by covert U.S. military operations and U.S. economic policies (Parenti, 2002). Many do not believe, for example, the description of the human effects of American sanctions on Iraq between the first and second Gulf Wars. Indeed, the hurtful activities of the American Empire are invisible to many of the empire's subjects in the United States itself.

The complexity of the relationship between the West (the United States in particular) and the Islamic world demands that we be very careful in laying out the argument we are making about this cultural pedagogy, this miseducation. The activities of the American Empire have not been the only forces at work creating an Islamist extremism that violently defies the sacred teaching of the religion. But American misdeeds have played an important role in the process. A new critical orientation toward knowledge production and research based on an appreciation of difference can help the United States redress some of its past and present policies toward the diverse Islamic world. Although these policies have been invisible to many Americans, they are visible to the rest of the world—the Islamic world in particular. Ignoring the *history* of the empire, Kenneth Weinstein (2002) writes in the Thomas B. Fordham Foundation's (2002) *September 11: What Our Children Need to Know* that the Left "admits" that differences exist between cultures but paradoxically downplays their violent basis through relativism and multiculturalism. It views cultural diversity and national differences as matters of taste, arguing that the greatest crime of all is judgmentalism. Weinstein concludes this paragraph by arguing that Americans are just too nice and, as such, are naïve to the threats posed by many groups around the world.

The Fordham Foundation's *September 11: What Our Children Need to Know* (2002) is right-wing educator Chester Finn's epistle to the nation about the incompetence of U.S. educators. The report's list of contributors is a virtual who's who of the theorists of the 21st-century American Empire, including the wife of Vice President Dick Cheney, Lynne Cheney, as well as William Bennett. Critical researchers should be aware of the politics of knowledge operating in this well-financed discreditation of thoughtful educators. As Finn puts it, he had to act because so much "nonsense" was being put out by the educational establishment. What Finn describes as nonsense can be read as scholarship attempting to provide perspective on the long history of Western-Islamic relations. Finn's use of "so much" in relation to this "nonsense" is crass exaggeration. Most materials published about 9/11 for educators were rather innocuous pleas for helping children deal with the anxiety produced by the attacks. Little elementary or secondary school material devoted to historicizing or contextualizing the Islamic world and its relation with the West appeared in the first 2 years after the tragic events of 9/11.

Kenneth Weinstein and many other Fordham authors set up a classic straw man argument in this context. The Left that is portrayed by them equates difference with a moral relativism that is unable to condemn the inhumane activities of particular groups. Implicit throughout *September 11: What Our Children Need to Know* is the notion that this fictional American Left does not condemn al-Qaeda and its crimes against humanity. It is the type of distortion that equated opposition to the second Gulf War with support for Saddam Hussein's Iraqi regime. How can these malcontents oppose America, the Fordham authors ask. Their America is a new empire that constantly denies its imperial dimensions. The new empire is not like empires in previous historical eras that overtly boasted of conquest and the taking of colonies. The 21st century is the era of the postmodern empire that speaks of its moral duty to unselfishly liberate nations and return power to the people. Empire leaders speak of free markets, the rights of the people, and the domino theory of democracy. The new American Empire employs public relations people to portray it as the purveyor of freedom around the world. When its acts of liberation and restoration of democracy elicit protest and retaliation, its leaders express shock and disbelief that such benevolent actions could arouse such "irrational" responses.

In Joe Kincheloe's chapter on Iran in *The Miseducation of the West: Constructing Islam* (2004), he explores the inability of American leaders to understand the impact of empire building in the Persian Gulf on the psyches of those personally affected by such activities. Indeed, the American public was ignorant of covert U.S. operations that overthrew the democratically elected government of Iran so a totalitarian regime more sympathetic to the crass needs of the American Empire could be installed. The citizens of Iran and other peoples around the Muslim world, however, were acutely aware of this imperial action and the contempt for Muslims it implied. When this was combined with a plethora of other U.S. political, military, and economic initiatives in the region, their view of America was less than positive. In the case of Iraq in the second Gulf War, American leaders simply disregarded the views of nations around the world, the Muslim world in particular, as they expressed their opposition to the American invasion. History was erased as Saddam Hussein was viewed in a psychological context as a madman. References to times when the United States supported the madman were deleted from memory. The empire, thus, could do whatever it wanted, regardless of its impact on the Iraqi people or the perceptions of others (irrational others) around the world. An epistemological naïveté—the belief that dominant American ways of seeing both itself and the world are rational and objective and that differing perspectives are irrational—permeate the official information of the empire (Abukhattala, 2004; Kellner, 2004; Progler, 2004; Steinberg, 2004). As John Agresto (2002) writes in the Fordham report:

> It is not very helpful to understand other cultures and outlooks and not understand our own country and what it has tried to achieve. What is it that has brought tens of millions of immigrants to America, not to bomb it, but to better its future and their own? What is it about the promise of liberty and equal treatment, of labor that benefits you and your neighbor, of an open field for your enterprise, ambition, determination and pluck? *Try not to look at America through the lens of your own ideology or political preference but see it as it really is.* Try, perhaps, to see the America most American see. That can be a fine antidote to smugness and academic self-righteousness. (emphasis ours)

Studying the Fordham Foundation's ways of looking at and teaching about America with its erasures of history deployed in the very name of a call to teach history, we are disturbed. When this is combined with an analysis of media representations of the nation's war against terrorism and the second Gulf War in Iraq, we gain some sobering insights into America's future. The inability or refusal of many Americans, especially those in power, to see the problematic activities of the "invisible" empire does not portend peace in the world in the coming years. The way knowledge is produced and transmitted in the United States by a corporatized media and an increasingly corporatized/privatized educational system is one of the central political issues of our time. Yet, in the mainstream political and educational conversations it is not even on the radar. A central task of critical researchers must involve putting these politics of knowledge on the public agenda. The power literacies and the concern with social change delineated in our discussion of critical theoretical research have never been more important to the world.

References

Abdullah, J., & Stringer, E. (1999). Indigenous knowledge, indigenous learning, indigenous research. In L. Semali & J. L. Kincheloe (Eds.), *What is indigenous knowledge? Voices from the academy.* Bristol, PA: Falmer.

Abercrombie, N. (1994). Authority and consumer society. In R. Keat, N. Whiteley, & N. Abercrombie (Eds.), *The authority of the consumer.* New York: Routledge.

Abukhattala, I. (2004). The new bogeyman under the bed: Image formation of Islam in the Western school curriculum and media. In J. L. Kincheloe & S. R. Steinberg (Eds.), *The miseducation of the West: Constructing Islam.* New York: Greenwood.

Agger, B. (1992). *The discourse of domination: From the Frankfurt school to postmodernism.* Evanston, IL: Northwestern University Press.

Agger, B. (1998). *Critical social theories: An introduction.* Boulder, CO: Westview.

Agresto, J. (2002). Lessons of the Preamble. In Thomas B. Fordham Foundation, *September 11: What our children need to know.* Retrieved from www.edexcellence.net/institute/publication/publication.cfm?id=65#743

Alfino, M., Caputo, J., & Wynyard, R. (Eds.). (1998). *McDonaldization revisited: Critical essays on consumer and culture.* Westport, CT: Praeger.

Allison, C. (1998). Okie narratives: Agency and whiteness. In J. L. Kincheloe, S. R. Steinberg, N. M. Rodriguez, & R. E. Chennault (Eds.), *White reign: Deploying whiteness in America.* New York: St. Martin's.

Andersen, G. (1989). Critical ethnography in education: Origins, current status, and new directions. *Review of Educational Research, 59,* 249–270.

Apple, M. (1996). *Cultural politics and education.* New York: Teachers College Press.

Aronowitz, S., & DiFazio, W. (1994). *The jobless future.* Minneapolis: University of Minnesota Press.

Aronowitz, S., & Giroux, H. (1991). *Postmodern education: Politics, culture, and social criticism.* Minneapolis: University of Minnesota Press.

Ashcroft, B., Griffiths, G., & Tiffin, H. (Eds.). (1995). *The post-colonial studies reader.* New York: Routledge.

Bauman, Z. (1995). *Life in fragments: Essays in postmodern morality.* Cambridge, MA: Blackwell.

Beck-Gernsheim, E., Butler, J., & Puigvert, L. (2003). *Women and social transformation.* New York: Peter Lang.

Behar, R. (1993). *Translated woman: Crossing the border with Esperanza's story.* Boston: Beacon.

Behar, R., & Gordon, D. A. (Eds.). (1995). *Women writing culture.* Berkeley: University of California Press.

Bello, W. (2003). The crisis of the globalist project and the new economics of George W. Bush. *New Labor Forum.* Retrieved from www.globalpolicy.org/globaliz/econ/2003/0710 bello.htm

Bensaid, D. (2002). *Marx for our times: Adventures and misadventures of a critique* (G. Elliot, Trans.). London: Verso.

Berger, A. A. (1995). *Cultural criticism: A primer of key concepts.* Thousand Oaks, CA: Sage.

Berry, K. (1998). Nurturing the imagination of resistance: Young adults as creators of knowledge. In J. L. Kincheloe & S. R. Steinberg (Eds.), *Unauthorized methods: Strategies for critical teaching.* New York: Routledge.

Bersani, L. (1995). Loving men. In M. Berger, B. Wallis, & S. Watson (Eds.), *Constructing masculinity.* New York: Routledge.

Blades, D. (1997). *Procedures of power and curriculum change: Foucault and the quest for possibilities in science education.* New York: Peter Lang.

Blommaert, J. (1997). *Workshopping: Notes on professional vision in discourse.* Retrieved from http:// africana_rug.ac.be/texts/research-publications/publications_on-line/workshop ping.htm

Boon, J. A. (1982). *Other tribes, other scribes: Symbolic anthropology in the comparative study of cultures, histories, religions, and texts.* Cambridge, UK: Cambridge University Press.

Bourdieu, P., &Wacquaat, L. (1992). *An invitation to reflexive sociology.* Chicago: University of Chicago Press.

Brents, B., & Monson, M. (1998). Whitewashing the strip: The construction of whiteness in Las Vegas. In J. L. Kincheloe, S. R. Steinberg, N. M. Rodriguez, & R. E. Chennault (Eds.), *White reign: Deploying whiteness in America.* New York: St. Martin's.

Bresler, L., & Ardichvili, A. (Eds.). (2002). *Research in international education: Experience, theory, and practice.* New York: Peter Lang.

Britzman, D. (1991). *Practice makes practice: A critical study of learning to teach.* Albany: State University of New York Press.

Britzman, D. (1995). What is this thing called love? *Taboo: The Journal of Culture and Education, 1,* 65–93.

Brock-Utne, B. (1996). Reliability and validity in qualitative research within Africa. *International Review of Education, 42,* 605–621.

Brosio, R. (1994). *The radical democratic critique of capitalist education.* New York: Peter Lang.

Burbules, N., & Beck, R. (1999). Critical thinking and critical pedagogy: Relations, differences, and limits. In T. Popkewitz & L. Fendler (Eds.), *Critical theories in education.* New York: Routledge.

Butler, M. (1998). Negotiating place: The importance of children's realities. In S. R. Steinberg & J. L. Kincheloe (Eds.), *Students as researchers: Creating classrooms that matter.* London: Taylor & Francis.

Cannella, G. (1997). *Deconstructing early childhood education: Social justice and revolution.* New York: Peter Lang.

Carlson, D. (1997). *Teachers in crisis.* New York: Routledge.

Carlson, D., & Apple, M. (Eds.). (1998). *Power/ knowledge/ pedagogy: The meaning of democratic education in unsettling times.* Boulder, CO: Westview.

Carspecken, P. F. (1993). *Power, truth, and method: Outline for a critical methodology.* Unpublished manuscript, Indiana University.

Carspecken, P. F. (1996). *Critical ethnography in educational research: A theoretical and practical guide.* New York: Routledge.

Carspecken, P. F. (1999). *Four scenes for posing the question of meaning and other essays in critical philosophy and critical methodology.* New York: Peter Lang.

Carter, R. (2003). Visual literacy: Critical thinking with the visual image. In D. Weil & J. Kincheloe (Eds.), *Critical thinking and learning: An encyclopedia for parents and teachers.* Westport, CT: Greenwood.

Carter, V. (1998). Computer-assisted racism: Toward an understanding of cyber-whiteness. In J. L. Kincheloe, S. R. Steinberg, N. M. Rodriguez, & R. E. Chennault (Eds.), *White reign: Deploying whiteness in America.* New York: St. Martin's.

Cary, R. (1996). I.Q. as commodity: The "new" economics of intelligence. In J. L. Kincheloe, S. R. Steinberg, & A. D. Gresson III (Eds.), *Measured lies: The bell curve examined.* New York: St. Martin's.

Cary, R. (2003). Art and aesthetics. In D. Weil & J. Kincheloe (Eds.), *Critical thinking and learning: An encyclopedia for parents and teachers.* Westport, CT: Greenwood.

Chomsky, N. (2003, August 11). Preventive war "the supreme crime." *Znet.* Retrieved from www.zmag.org/content/showarticle.cfm?SectionID=40&ItemID=4030

Christian-Smith, L., & Keelor, K. S. (1999). *Everyday knowledge and women of the academy: Uncommon truths.* Boulder, CO: Westview.

Clark, L. (2002). *Critical theory and constructivism. Theory and methods for the teens and the new media @ home project.* Retrieved from www.colorado.edu/journalism/mcm/qmr crit-theory.htm

Clatterbaugh, K. (1997). *Contemporary perspectives on masculinity: Men, women, and politics in modern society.* Boulder, CO: Westview.

Clifford, J. (1992). Traveling cultures. In L. Grossberg, C. Nelson, & P. A. Treichler (Eds.), *Cultural studies.* New York: Routledge.

Clough, P. T. (1992). *The end(s) of ethnography: From realism to social criticism.* Newbury Park, CA: Sage.

Clough, P. T. (1994). *Feminist thought: Desire, power and academic discourse.* Cambridge, MA: Blackwell.

Clough, P. T. (1998). *The end(s) of ethnography: From realism to social criticism* (2nd ed.). New York: Peter Lang.

Coben, D. (1998). *Radical heroes: Gramsci, Freire and the politics of adult education.* New York: Garland.

Collins, J. (1995). *Architectures of excess: Cultural life in the information age.* New York: Routledge.

Comaroff, J., & Comaroff, J. (1992). *Ethnography and the historical imagination.* Boulder, CO: Westview.

Connor, S. (1992). *Theory and cultural value.* Cambridge, MA: Blackwell.

Cooper, D. (1994). Productive, relational, and everywhere? Conceptualizing power and resistance within Foucauldian feminism. *Sociology, 28,* 435–454.

Corrigan, P. (1979). *Schooling the Smash Street Kids.* London: Macmillan.

Crapanzano, V. (1990). Afterword. In M. Manganaro (Ed.), *Modernist anthropology: From fieldwork to text.* Princeton, NJ: Princeton University Press.

Dahlbom, B. (1998). *Going to the future.* Retrieved from http://www.viktoria.infomatik.gu.se/~max/bo/papers.html

Daniel, E. V. (1996). *Charred lullabies: Chapters in an anthropology of violence.* Princeton, NJ: Princeton University Press.

Darder, A., & Torres, R. (2004). *After race: Racism after multiculturalism.* New York: New York University Press.

DeLissovoy, N., & McLaren, P. (2003). Educational "accountability" and the violence of capital: A Marxian reading. *Journal of Education Policy, 18,* 131–143.

Deetz, S. A. (1993, May). *Corporations, the media, industry, and society: Ethical imperatives and responsibilities.* Paper presented at the annual meeting of the International Communication Association, Washington, DC.

Dei, G., Karumanchery, L., & Karumanchery-Luik, N. (2004). *Playing the race card: Exposing white power and privilege.* New York: Peter Lang.

Denzin, N. K. (1994). The art and politics of interpretation. In N. K. Denzin & Y. S. Lincoln (Eds.), *Handbook of qualitative research.* Thousand Oaks, CA: Sage.

Denzin, N. K. (2003). *Performative ethnography: Critical pedagogy and the politics of culture.* Thousand Oaks, CA: Sage.

Denzin, N. K., & Lincoln, Y. S. (2000). Introduction: The discipline and practice of qualitative research. In N. K. Denzin & Y. S. Lincoln (Eds.), *Handbook of qualitative research* (2nd ed.). Thousand Oaks, CA: Sage.

DeVault, M. (1996). Talking back to sociology: Distinctive contributions of feminist methodology. *Annual Review of Sociology, 22,* 29–50.

Douglas, S. (1994). *Where the girls are: Growing up female in the mass media.* New York: Times Books.

Drummond, L. (1996). *American dreamtime: A cultural analysis of popular movies and their implications for a science of humanity.* Lanham, MD: Littlefield Adams.

Fehr, D. (1993). *Dogs playing cards: Powerbrokers of prejudice in education, art, and culture.* New York: Peter Lang.

Fenwick, T. (2000). *Experiential learning in adult education: A comparative framework.* Retrieved from www.ualberta.ca/~tfenwick/ext/aeq.htm

Ferguson, M., & Golding, P. (Eds.). (1997). *Cultural studies in question.* London: Sage.

Finders, M. (1997). *Just girls: Hidden literacies and life in junior high.* New York: Teachers College Press.

Fine, M., Powell, L. C., Weis, L., & Wong, L. M. (Eds.). (1997). *Off white: Readings on race, power and society.* New York: Routledge.

Fiske, J. (1993). *Power works, power plays.* New York: Verso.

Flecha, R., Gomez, J., & Puigvert, L. (Eds.). (2003). *Contemporary sociological theory.* New York: Peter Lang.

Flossner, G., & Otto, H. (Eds.). (1998). *Towards more democracy in social services: Models of culture and welfare.* New York: de Gruyter.

Fordham Foundation. (2002). *September 11: What our children need to know.* Retrieved www.edexcellence.net/institute/publication/publication.cfm?id=65

Foster, R. (1997). Addressing epistemologic and practical issues in multimethod research: A procedure for conceptual triangulation. *Advances in Nursing Education, 20*(2), 1–12.

Frankenberg, R. (1993). *White women, race matters: The social construction of whiteness.* Minneapolis: University of Minnesota Press.

Franz, C., & Stewart, A. (Eds.). (1994). *Women creating lives.* Boulder, CO: Westview.

Freire, A. M. A. (2000). Foreword. In P. McLaren, *Che Guevara, Paulo Freire, and the pedagogy of revolution.* Boulder, CO: Rowman and Littlefield.

Freire, A. M. A. (2001). *Chronicles of love: My life with Paulo Freire.* New York: Peter Lang.

Freire, P. (1970). *Pedagogy of the oppressed.* New York: Herder and Herder.

Freire, P. (1972). *Research methods.* Paper presented to a seminar in Studies in Adult Education, Dar-es-Salaam, Tanzania.

Freire, P. (1978). *Education for critical consciousness.* New York: Seabury.

Freire, P. (1985). *The politics of education: Culture, power, and liberation.* South Hadley, MA: Bergin & Garvey.

Friedman, S. (1998). (Inter)disciplinarity and the question of the women's studies Ph.D. *Feminist Studies, 24*(2), 301–326.

Fuchs, M. (1993). The reversal of the ethnological perspective: Attempts at objectifying one's own cultural horizon. Dumont, Foucault, Bourdieu? *Thesis Eleven, 34,* 104–125.

Gabbard, D. (1995). NAFTA, GATT, and Goals 2000: Reading the political culture of post-industrial America. *Taboo: The Journal of Culture and Education, 2,* 184–199.

Gadamer, H.-G. (1989). *Truth and method* (2nd rev. ed.) (J. Weinsheimer & D. G. Marshall, Eds. & Trans.). New York: Crossroad.

Gallagher, S. (1992). *Hermeneutics and education.* Albany: State University of New York Press.

Garnham, N. (1997). Political economy and the practice of cultural studies. In M. Ferguson & P. Golding (Eds.), *Cultural studies in question.* London: Sage.

Gee, J. (1996). *Social linguistics and literacies: Ideology in discourses* (2nd ed.). London: Taylor & Francis.

Gee, J., Hull, G., & Lankshear, C. (1996). *The new work order: Behind the language of the new capitalism.* Boulder, CO: Westview.

Gibson, R. (1986). *Critical theory and education.* London: Hodder & Stoughton.

Giroux, H. (1983). *Theory and resistance in education: A pedagogy for the opposition.* South Hadley, MA: Bergin & Garvey.

Giroux, H. (1988). Critical theory and the politics of culture and voice: Rethinking the discourse of educational research. In R. Sherman & R. Webb (Eds.), *Qualitative research in education: Focus and methods.* New York: Falmer.

Giroux, H. (1992). *Border crossings: Cultural workers and the politics of education.* New York: Routledge.

Giroux, H. (1997). *Pedagogy and the politics of hope: Theory, culture, and schooling.* Boulder, CO: Westview.

Giroux, H. (2003). *The abandoned generation: Democracy beyond the culture of fear.* New York: Palgrave.

Goldie, T. (1995). The representation of the indigene. In B. Ashcroft, G. Griffiths, & H. Tiffin (Eds.), *The post-colonial studies reader.* New York: Routledge.

Goodson, I. (1997). *The changing curriculum: Studies in social construction.* New York: Peter Lang.

Gresson, A. (1995). *The recovery of race in America.* Minneapolis: University of Minnesota Press.

Griffin, C. (1985). *Typical girls? Young women from school to the job market.* London: Routledge & Kegan Paul.

Grinberg, J. (2003). Only the facts? In D. Weil & J. L. Kincheloe (Eds.), *Critical thinking and learning: An encyclopedia for parents and teachers.* Westport, CT: Greenwood.

Grondin, J. (1994). *Introduction to philosophical hermeneutics* (J. Weinsheimer, Trans.). New Haven, CT: Yale University Press.

Gross, A., & Keith, W. (Eds.). (1997). *Rhetorical hermeneutics: Invention and interpretation in the age of science.* Albany: State University of New York Press.

Grossberg, L. (1995). What's in a name (one more time)? *Taboo: The Journal of Culture and Education, 1,* 1–37.

Grossberg, L. (1997). *Bringing it all back home: Essays on cultural studies.* Durham, NC: Duke University Press.

Hall, S., & du Gay, P. (Eds.). (1996). *Questions of cultural identity.* London: Sage.

Harper, D. (1987). *Working knowledge: Skill and community in a small shop.* Chicago: University of Chicago Press.

Hebdige, D. (1979). *Subculture: The meaning of style.* London: Methuen.

Hedley, M. (1994). The presentation of gendered conflict in popular movies: Affective stereotypes, cultural sentiments, and men's motivation. *Sex Roles, 31,* 721–740.

Hinchey, P. (1998). *Finding freedom in the classroom: A practical introduction to critical theory.* New York: Peter Lang.

Horkheimer, M. (1972). *Critical theory.* New York: Seabury.

Horn, R. (2000). *Teacher talk: A post-formal inquiry into educational change.* New York: Peter Lang.

Howell, S. (1998). The learning organization: Reproduction of whiteness. In J. L. Kincheloe, S. R. Steinberg, N. M. Rodriguez, & R. E. Chennault (Eds.), *White reign: Deploying whiteness in America.* New York: St. Martin's.

Humphries, B. (1997). From critical thought to emancipatory action: Contradictory research goals? *Sociological Research Online, 2*(1). Retrieved from www.socresonline.org.uk/socresonline/2/1/3.html

Ilyenkov, E. V. (1977). *Dialectical logic: Essays on its history and theory.* Moscow: Progress.

Ilyenkov. E. V. (1982a). *The dialectics of the abstract and the concrete in Marx's Capital* (S. Syrovatkin, Trans.). Moscow: Progress.

Ilyenkov. E. V. (1982b). *Leninist dialectics and the metaphysics of positivism.* London: New Park Publications.

Jackson, S., & Russo, A. (2002). *Talking back and acting out: Women negotiating the media across cultures.* New York: Peter Lang.

Jardine, D. (1998). *To dwell with a boundless heart: Essays in curriculum theory, hermeneutics, and the ecological imagination.* New York: Peter Lang.

Johnson, C. (1996). Does capitalism really need patriarchy? Some old issues reconsidered. *Women's Studies International Forum, 19,* 193–202.

Joyrich, L. (1996). *Reviewing reception: Television, gender, and postmodern culture.* Bloomington: Indiana University Press.

Kellner, D. (1995). *Media culture: Cultural studies, identity, and politics between the modern and the postmodern.* New York: Routledge.

Kellner, D. (2004). September 11, terror war, and blowback. In J. L. Kincheloe & S. R. Steinberg (Eds.), *The miseducation of the West: Constructing Islam.* New York: Greenwood.

Kellogg, D. (1998). Exploring critical distance in science education: Students researching the implications of technological embeddedness. In S. R. Steinberg & J. L. Kincheloe (Eds.), *Students as researchers: Creating classrooms that matter.* London: Falmer.

Kelly, L. (1996). When does the speaking profit us? Reflection on the challenges of developing feminist perspectives on abuse and violence by women. In M. Hester, L. Kelly, & J. Radford (Eds.), *Women, violence, and male power.* Bristol, PA: Open University Press.

Kincheloe, J. L. (1991). *Teachers as researchers: Qualitative paths to empowerment.* London: Falmer.

Kincheloe, J. L. (1993). *Toward a critical politics of teacher thinking: Mapping the postmodern.* Granby, MA: Bergin & Garvey.

Kincheloe, J. L. (1995). *Toil and trouble: Good work, smart workers, and the integration of academic and vocational education.* New York: Peter Lang.

Kincheloe, J. L. (1998). Critical research in science education. In B. Fraser & K. Tobin (Eds.), *International handbook of science education* (Pt. 2). Boston: Kluwer.

Kincheloe, J. L. (1999). *How do we tell the workers? The socioeconomic foundations of work and vocational education.* Boulder, CO: Westview.

Kincheloe, J. L. (2001a). Describing the bricolage: Conceptualizing a new rigor in qualitative research. *Qualitative Inquiry, 7*(6), 679–692.

Kincheloe, J. L. (2001b). *Getting beyond the facts: Teaching social studies/social sciences in the twenty-first century* (2nd ed.). New York: Peter Lang.

Kincheloe, J. L. (2002). *The sign of the burger: McDonald's and the culture of power.* Philadelphia: Temple University Press.

Kincheloe, J. L. (2003a). Critical ontology: Visions of selfhood and curriculum. *JCT: Journal of Curriculum Theorizing, 19*(1), 47–64.

Kincheloe, J. L. (2003b). Into the great wide open: Introducing critical thinking. In D. Weil & J. L. Kincheloe (Eds.), *Critical thinking and learning: An encyclopedia for parents and teachers.* Westport, CT: Greenwood.

Kincheloe, J. L. (2003c). *Teachers as researchers: Qualitative paths to empowerment* (2nd ed.). London: Falmer.

Kincheloe, J. L. (2004). Iran and American miseducation: Coverups, distortions, and omissions. In J. L. Kincheloe & S. Steinberg (Eds.), *The miseducation of the West: Constructing Islam.* New York: Greenwood.

Kincheloe, J. L., & Berry, K. (2004). *Rigour and complexity in educational research: Conceptualizing the bricolage.* London: Open University Press.

Kincheloe, J. L., & Steinberg, S. R. (1993). A tentative description of post-formal thinking: The critical confrontation with cognitive theory. *Harvard Educational Review, 63,* 296–320.

Kincheloe, J. L., & Steinberg, S. R. (1996). Who said it can't happen here? In J. L. Kincheloe, S. Steinberg, & A. D. Gresson III (Eds.), *Measured lies: The bell curve examined.* New York: St. Martin's.

Kincheloe, J. L., & Steinberg, S. R. (1997). *Changing multiculturalism: New times, new curriculum.* London: Open University Press.

Kincheloe, J. L., & Steinberg, S. R. (1999). Politics, intelligence, and the classroom: Postformal teaching. In J. Kincheloe, S. Steinberg, & L. Villaverde (Eds.), *Rethinking intelligence: Confronting psychological assumptions about teaching and learning.* New York: Routledge.

Kincheloe, J. L., & Steinberg, S. R. (Eds.). (2004). *The miseducation of the West: Constructing Islam.* New York: Greenwood.

Kincheloe, J. L., Steinberg, S. R., & Hinchey, P. (Eds.). (1999). *The post-formal reader: Cognition and education.* New York: Falmer.

Kincheloe, J. L., Steinberg, S. R., Rodriguez, N. M., & Chennault, R. E. (Eds.). (1998). *White reign: Deploying whiteness in America.* New York: St. Martin's.

King, J. (1996). Bad luck, bad blood, bad faith: Ideological hegemony and the oppressive language of hoodoo social science. In J. L. Kincheloe, S. R. Steinberg, & A. D. Gresson III (Eds.), *Measured lies: The bell curve examined.* New York: St. Martin's.

King, J., & Mitchell, C. (1995). *Black mothers to sons.* New York: Peter Lang.

Knobel, M. (1999). *Everyday literacies: Students, discourse, and social practice.* New York: Peter Lang.

Kogler, H. (1996). *The power of dialogue: Critical hermeneutics after Gadamer and Foucault.* Cambridge: MIT Press.

Kovel, J. (2002). *The enemy of nature: The end of capitalism or the end of the world?* London: Zed Books.

Lacey, C. (1970). *Hightown Grammar: The school as a social system.* London: Routledge & Kegan Paul.

Lather, P. (1991). *Getting smart: Feminist research and pedagogy with/in the postmodern.* New York: Routledge.

Lather, P. (1993). Fertile obsession: Validity after poststructuralism. *Sociological Quarterly, 34,* 673–693.

Leistyna, P., Woodrum, A., & Sherblom, S. (1996). *Breaking free: The transformative power of critical pedagogy.* Cambridge, MA: Harvard Educational Review.

Lemke, J. (1993). Discourse, dynamics, and social change. *Cultural Dynamics, 6,* 243–275.

Lemke, J. (1995). *Textual politics: Discourse and social dynamics.* London: Taylor & Francis.

Lemke, J. (1998). Analyzing verbal data: Principles, methods, and problems. In B. Fraser & K. Tobin (Eds.), *International handbook of science education* (Pt. 2). Boston: Kluwer.

Levi-Strauss, C. (1966). *The savage mind.* Chicago: University of Chicago Press.

Lincoln, Y. (2001). An emerging new bricoleur: Promises and possibilities—a reaction to Joe Kincheloe's "Describing the bricoleur." *Qualitative Inquiry, 7*(6), 693–696.

Lugones, M. (1987). Playfulness, "world"-traveling, and loving perception. *Hypatia, 2*(2), 3–19.

Lull, J. (1995). *Media, communication, culture: A global approach.* New York: Columbia University Press.

Lutz, K., Kendall, J., & Jones, K. (1997). Expanding the praxis debate: Contributions to clinical inquiry. *Advances in Nursing Science, 20*(2), 23–31.

Macedo, D. (1994). *Literacies of power: What Americans are not allowed to know.* Boulder, CO: Westview.

Maher, F., & Tetreault, M. (1994). *The feminist classroom: An inside look at how professors and students are transforming higher education for a diverse society.* New York: Basic Books.

Manganaro, M. (1990). Textual play, power, and cultural critique: An orientation to modernist anthropology. In M. Manganaro (Ed.), *Modernist anthropology: From fieldwork to text.* Princeton, NJ: Princeton University Press.

Marcus, G. E., & Fischer, M.M.J. (1986). *Anthropology as cultural critique: An experimental moment in the human sciences.* Chicago: University of Chicago Press.

Martin, H., & Schuman, H. (1996). *The global trap: Globalization and the assault on democracy and prosperity.* New York: Zed Books.

Marx, K. (1978). Economic and philosophical manuscripts of 1844. In *The Marx-Engels reader* (2nd ed., R. C. Tucker, Ed.). New York: W. W. Norton.

Mathie, A., & Greene, J. (2002). Honoring difference and dialogue in international education and development: Mixed-method frameworks for research. In L. Bresler & A. Ardichvili (Eds.), *Research in international education: Experience, theory, and practice.* New York: Peter Lang.

Mayers, M. (2001). *Street kids and streetscapes: Panhandling, politics, and prophecies.* New York: Peter Lang.

McLaren, P. (1992). Collisions with otherness: "Traveling" theory, post-colonial criticism, and the politics of ethnographic practice—the mission of the wounded ethnographer. *International Journal of Qualitative Studies in Education, 5,* 77–92.

McLaren, P. (1995a). *Critical pedagogy and predatory culture: Oppositional politics in a postmodern era.* New York: Routledge.

McLaren, P. (1995b). *Life in schools* (3rd ed.). New York: Longman.

McLaren, P. (1997). *Revolutionary multiculturalism: Pedagogies of dissent for the new millennium.* New York: Routledge.

McLaren, P. (1998). Revolutionary pedagogy in post-revolutionary times: Rethinking the political economy of critical education. *Educational Theory, 48,* 431–462.

McLaren, P. (1999). *Schooling as a ritual performance: Toward a political economy of educational symbols and gestures* (3rd ed.). Boulder, CO: Rowman & Littlefield.

McLaren, P. (2001). Bricklayers and bricoleurs: A Marxist addendum. *Qualitative Inquiry, 7*(6), 700–705.

McLaren, P. (2002). Marxist revolutionary praxis: A curriculum of transgression. *Journal of Curriculum Inquiry Into Curriculum and Instruction, 3*(3), 36–41.

McLaren, P. (2003a). Critical pedagogy in the age of neoliberal globalization: Notes from history's underside. *Democracy and Nature, 9*(1), 65–90.

McLaren, P. (2003b). The dialectics of terrorism: A Marxist response to September 11 (Part Two: Unveiling the Past, Evading the Present). *Cultural Studies/Critical Methodologies 3*(1), 103–132.

McLaren, P., & Farahmandpur, R. (2001). The globalization of capitalism and the new imperialism: Notes towards a revolutionary critical pedagogy. *The Review of Education, Pedagogy & Cultural Studies, 23*(3), 271–315.

McLaren, P., & Farahmandpur, R. (2003). Critical pedagogy at ground zero: Renewing the educational left after 9–11. In D. Gabbard & K. Saltman (Eds.), *Education as enforcement: The militarization and corporatization of schools.* New York: Routledge.

McLaren, P., Hammer, R., Reilly, S., & Sholle, D. (1995). *Rethinking media literacy: A critical pedagogy of representation.* New York: Peter Lang.

McLaren, P., & Jaramillo, N. (2002). Critical pedagogy as organizational praxis: Challenging the demise of civil society in a time of permanent war. *Educational Foundations, 16*(4), 5–32.

McLaren, P., & Martin, G. (2003, Summer). The "big lie" machine devouring America. *Socialist Future Review,* pp. 18–27.

McLaren, P., & Scatamburlo-D'Annibale, V. (2004). Paul Willis, class consciousness, and critical pedagogy: Toward a socialist future. In N. Dolby & G. Dimitriadis with P. Willis (Eds.), *Learning to labor in new times.* New York: RoutledgeFalmer.

McLeod, J. (2000, June). *Qualitative research as bricolage.* Paper presented at the annual conference of the Society for Psychotherapy Research, Chicago.

McWilliam, E., & Taylor, P. (Eds.). (1996). *Pedagogy, technology, and the body.* New York: Peter Lang.

Miller, S., & Hodge, J. (1998). *Phenomenology, hermeneutics, and narrative analysis: Some unfinished methodological business.* Unpublished manuscript, Loyola University, Chicago.

Molnar, A. (1996). *Giving kids the business: The commercialization of America's schools.* Boulder, CO: Westview.

Morgan, W. (1996). Personal training: Discourses of (self) fashioning. In E. McWilliam & P. Taylor (Eds.), *Pedagogy, technology, and the body.* New York: Peter Lang.

Morrow, R. (1991). Critical theory, Gramsci and cultural studies: From structuralism to post-structuralism. In P. Wexler (Ed.), *Critical theory now.* New York: Falmer.

Mullen, C. (1999). Whiteness, cracks and ink-stains: Making cultural identity with Euroamerican preservice teachers. In P. Diamond & C. Mullen (Eds.), *The postmodern educator: Arts-based inquiries and teacher development.* New York: Peter Lang.

Myrsiades, K., & Myrsiades, L. (Eds.). (1998). *Race-ing representation: Voice, history, and sexuality.* Lanham, MD: Rowman & Littlefield.

Newton, J., & Stacey, J. (1992–1993). Learning not to curse, or, feminist predicaments in cultural criticism by men: Our movie date with James Clifford and Stephen Greenblatt. *Cultural Critique, 23,* 51–82.

Nicholson, L. J., & Seidman, S. (Eds.). (1995). *Social postmodernism: Beyond identity politics.* New York: Cambridge University Press.

Oberhardt, S. (2001). *Frames within frames: The art museum as cultural artifact.* New York: Peter Lang.

Ollman, B. (1971). *Alienation: Marx's conception of man in capitalist society.* New York: Cambridge University Press.

Ollman, B. (1993). *Dialectical investigations.* New York: Routledge.

Ollman, B. (2003). Marxism, this tale of two cities. *Science & Society, 67*(1), 80–86.

O'Riley, P. (2003). *Technology, culture, and socioeconomics: A rhizoanalysis of educational discourses.* New York: Peter Lang.

Pailliotet, A. (1998). Deep viewing: A critical look at visual texts. In J. L. Kincheloe & S. R. Steinberg (Eds.), *Unauthorized methods: Strategies for critical teaching.* New York: Routledge.

Parenti, M. (2002). *The terrorism trap: September 11 and beyond.* San Francisco: City Lights Books.

Paulson, R. (1995). Mapping knowledge perspectives in studies of educational change. In P. W. Cookson, Jr., & B. Schneider (Eds.), *Transforming schools.* New York: Garland.

Peters, M. (1993). *Against Finkielkraut's la defaite de la pensee: Culture, postmodernism and education.* Unpublished manuscript, University of Glasgow.

Peters, M., & Lankshear, C. (1994). Education and hermeneutics: A Freirean interpretation. In P. McLaren & C. Lankshear (Eds.), *Politics of liberation: Paths from Freire.* New York: Routledge.

Peters, M., Lankshear, C., & Olssen, M. (Eds.). (2003). *Critical theory and the human condition.* New York: Peter Lang.

Pfeil, F. (1995). *White guys: Studies in postmodern domination and difference.* New York: Verso.

Pieterse, J., & Parekh, B. (1995). Shifting imaginaries: Decolonization, internal decolonization, postcoloniality. In J. Pieterse & B. Parekh (Eds.), *The decolonization of imagination: Culture, knowledge, and power.* Atlantic Highlands, NJ: Zed.

Prakash, M., & Esteva, G. (1998). *Escaping education: Living as learning within grassroots cultures.* New York: Peter Lang.

Progler, Y. (2004). Schooled to order: Education and the making of modern Egypt. In J. Kincheloe & S. Steinberg (Eds.), *The miseducation of the West: Constructing Islam.* New York: Greenwood.

Pruyn, M. (1994). Becoming subjects through critical practice: How students in an elementary classroom critically read and wrote their world. *International Journal of Educational Reform, 3*(1), 37–50.

Pryse, M. (1998). Critical interdisciplinarity, women's studies, and cross-cultural insight. *NWSA Journal, 10*(1), 1–11.

Quail, C. B., Razzano, K. A., & Skalli, L. H. (2004). *Tell me more: Rethinking daytime talk shows.* New York: Peter Lang.

Quantz, R. A. (1992). On critical ethnography (with some postmodern considerations). In M. D. LeCompte, W. L. Millroy, & J. Preissle (Eds.), *The handbook of qualitative research in education.* New York: Academic Press.

Quintero, E., & Rummel, M. K. (2003). *Becoming a teacher in the new society: Bringing communities and classrooms together.* New York: Peter Lang.

Rabinow, P. (1977). *Reflections on fieldwork in Morocco.* Berkeley: University of California Press.

Rains, F. (1998). Is the benign really harmless? Deconstructing some "benign" manifestations of operationalized white privilege. In J. L. Kincheloe, S. R. Steinberg, N. M. Rodriguez, & R. E. Chennault (Eds.), *White reign: Deploying whiteness in America.* New York: St. Martin's.

Rand, E. (1995). *Barbie's queer accessories.* Durham, NC: Duke University Press.

Rapko, J. (1998). Review of *The power of dialogue: Critical hermeneutics after Gadamer and Foucault. Criticism, 40*(1), 133–138.

Reason, P., & Torbert, W. R. (2001). Toward a transformational science: A further look at the scientific merits of action research. *Concepts and Transformations, 6*(1), 1–37.

Ritzer, G. (1993). *The McDonaldization of society.* Thousand Oaks, CA: Pine Forge.

Robins, D., & Cohen, P. (1978). *Knuckle sandwich: Growing up in the working-class city.* Harmondsworth, UK: Penguin.

Rodriguez, N. M., & Villaverde, L. (2000). *Dismantling white privilege.* New York: Peter Lang.

Roman, L., & Eyre, L. (Eds.). (1997). *Dangerous territories: Struggles for difference and equality in education.* New York: Routledge.

Rose, K., & Kincheloe, J. (2003). *Art, culture, and education: Artful teaching in a fractured landscape.* New York: Peter Lang.

Rosen, S. (1987). *Hermeneutics as politics.* New York: Oxford University Press.

San Juan, E., Jr. (1992). *Articulations of power in ethnic and racial studies in the United States.* Atlantic Highlands, NJ: Humanities Press.

San Juan, E., Jr. (1996). *Mediations: From a Filipino perspective.* Pasig City, Philippines: Anvil.

Sanders-Bustle, L. (2003). *Image, inquiry, and transformative practice: Engaging learners in creative and critical inquiry through visual representation.* New York: Peter Lang.

Scheurich, J. J., & Young, M. (1997). Coloring epistemologies: Are our research epistemologies racially biased? *Educational Researcher, 26*(4), 4–16.

Scott, J. W. (1992). Experience. In J. Butler & J. W. Scott (Eds.), *Feminists theorize the political.* New York: Routledge.

Sedgwick, E. (1995). Gosh, Boy George, you must be awfully secure in your masculinity! In M. Berger, B. Wallis, & S. Watson (Eds.), *Constructing masculinity.* New York: Routledge.

Selfe, C. L., & Selfe, R. J., Jr. (1994). *The politics of the interface: Power and its exercise in electronic contact zones.* Retrieved from www.hu.mtu.edu/~cyselfe/texts/politics.html

Semali, L. (1998). Still crazy after all of these years: Teaching critical media literacy. In J. L. Kincheloe & S. R. Steinberg (Eds.), *Unauthorized methods: Strategies for critical teaching.* New York: Routledge.

Semali, L., & Kincheloe, J. L. (1999). *What is indigenous knowledge? Voices from the academy.* New York: Falmer.

Shohat, E., & Stam, R. (1994). *Unthinking Eurocentrism: Multiculturalism and the media.* New York: Routledge.

Shor, I. (1996). *When students have power: Negotiating authority in a critical pedagogy.* Chicago: University of Chicago Press.

Silverman, E. K. (1990). Clifford Geertz: Towards a more "thick" understanding? In C. Tilley (Ed.), *Reading material culture.* Cambridge, MA: Blackwell.

Skalli, L. (2004). Loving Muslim women with a vengeance: The West, women, and fundamentalism. In J. L. Kincheloe & S. R. Steinberg (Eds.), *The miseducation of the West: Constructing Islam.* New York: Greenwood.

Slater, J., Fain, S., & Rossatto, C. (2002). *The Freirean legacy: Educating for social justice.* New York: Peter Lang.

Slaughter, R. (1989). Cultural reconstruction in the post-modern world. *Journal of Curriculum Studies, 3,* 255–270.

Sleeter, C., & McLaren, P. (Eds.). (1995). *Multicultural education, critical pedagogy, and the politics of difference.* Albany: State University of New York Press.

Smith, D. G. (1999). *Pedagon: Interdisciplinary Essays in the Human Sciences, Pedagogy, and Culture.* New York: Peter Lang.

Smith, D. G. (2003). On enfraudening the public sphere, the futility of empire and the future of knowledge after "America." *Policy Futures in Education, 1*(3), 488–503.

Smith, R., & Wexler, P. (Eds.). (1995). *After post- modernism: Education, politics, and identity.* London: Falmer.

Soto, L. (1998). Bilingual education in America: In search of equity and social justice. In J. L. Kincheloe & S. R. Steinberg (Eds.), *Unauthorized methods: Strategies for critical teaching.* New York: Routledge.

Soto, L. (Ed.). (2000). *The politics of early childhood education.* New York: Peter Lang.

Stallabrass, J. (1996). *Gargantua: Manufactured mass culture.* London: Verso.

Steinberg, S. R. (1997a). The bitch who has everything. In S. R. Steinberg & J. L. Kincheloe (Eds.), *Kinderculture: The corporate construction of childhood.* Boulder, CO: Westview.

Steinberg, S. (1997b). Kinderculture: The cultural studies of childhood. In N. Denzin (Ed.), *Cultural studies: A research volume.* Greenwich, CT: JAI.

Steinberg, S. (Ed.). (2001). *Multi/intercultural conversations.* New York: Peter Lang.

Steinberg, S. R. (2004). Desert minstrels: Hollywood's curriculum of Arabs and Muslims. In J. L. Kincheloe & S. R. Steinberg (Eds.), *The miseducation of the West: Constructing Islam.* New York: Greenwood.

Steinberg, S. R., & Kincheloe, J. L. (Eds.). (1997). *Kinderculture: Corporate constructions of childhood.* Boulder, CO: Westview.

Steinberg, S. R., & Kincheloe, J. L. (Eds.). (1998). *Students as researchers: Creating classrooms that matter.* London: Taylor & Francis.

Stewart, K. (1996). *A space on the side of the road: Cultural poetics in an "other" America.* Princeton, NJ: Princeton University Press.

Sünker, H. (1998). Welfare, democracy, and social work. In G. Flosser & H. Otto (Eds.), *Towards more democracy in social services: Models of culture and welfare.* New York: de Gruyter.

Taussig, M. (1987). *Shamanism, colonialism, and the wild man: A study in terror and healing.* Chicago: University of Chicago Press.

Thayer-Bacon, B. (2003). *Relational "(e)pistemologies."* New York: Peter Lang.

Thomas, S. (1997). Dominance and ideology in cultural studies. In M. Ferguson & P. Golding (Eds.), *Cultural studies in question.* London: Sage.

Trueba, E. T., & McLaren, P. (2000). Critical ethnography for the study of immigrants. In E. T. Trueba & L. I. Bartolomé (Eds.), *Immigrant voices: In search of educational equity.* Boulder, CO: Rowman & Littlefield.

Varenne, H. (1996). The social facting of education: Durkheim's legacy. *Journal of Curriculum Studies, 27,* 373–389.

Vattimo, G. (1994). *Beyond interpretation: The meaning of hermeneutics for philosophy.* Stanford, CA: Stanford University Press.

Viergever, M. (1999). Indigenous knowledge: An interpretation of views from indigenous peoples. In L. Semali & J. L. Kincheloe (Eds.), *What is indigenous knowledge? Voices from the academy.* Bristol, PA: Falmer.

Villaverde, L. (2003). Developing curriculum and critical pedagogy. In J. Kincheloe & D. Weil (Eds.), *Critical thinking and learning: An encyclopedia.* Westport, CT: Greenwood.

Villaverde, L., & Kincheloe, J. L. (1998). Engaging students as researchers: Researching and teaching Thanksgiving in the elementary classroom. In S. R. Steinberg & J. L. Kincheloe (Eds.), *Students as researchers: Creating classrooms that matter.* London: Falmer.

Visweswaran, K. (1994). *Fictions of feminist ethnography.* Minneapolis: University of Minnesota Press.

Weil, D. (1998). *Towards a critical multicultural literacy: Theory and practice for education for liberation.* New York: Peter Lang.

Weil, D., & Kincheloe, J. (Eds.). (2003). *Critical thinking and learning: An encyclopedia for parents and teachers.* Westport, CT: Greenwood.

Weiler, K. (1988). *Women teaching for change: Gender, class, and power.* South Hadley, MA: Bergin & Garvey.

Weinstein, K. (2002). Fighting complacency. In Thomas B. Fordham Foundation, *September 11: What our children need to know.* Retrieved from www.edexcellence.net/institute/publication/publication.cfm?id=65#764

Weinstein, M. (1998). *Robot world: Education, popular culture, and science.* New York: Peter Lang.

Wesson, L., & Weaver, J. (2001). Administration– Educational standards: Using the lens of post-modern thinking to examine the role of the school administrator. In J. Kincheloe & D. Weil (Eds.), *Standards and schooling in the United States: An encyclopedia* (3 vols.). Santa Barbara, CA: ABC-CLIO.

West, C. (1993). *Race matters.* Boston: Beacon.

Wexler, P. (1996a). *Critical social psychology.* New York: Peter Lang.

Wexler, P. (1996b). *Holy sparks: Social theory, education, and religion.* New York: St. Martin's.

Wexler, P. (1997, October). *Social research in education: Ethnography of being.* Paper presented at the International Conference on the Culture of Schooling, Halle, Germany.
Wexler, P. (2000). *The mystical society: Revitalization in culture, theory, and education.* Boulder, CO: Westview.
Willinsky, J. (2001). Raising the standards for democratic education: Research and evaluation as public knowledge. In J. Kincheloe & D. Weil (Eds.), *Standards and schooling in the United States: An encyclopedia* (3 vols.). Santa Barbara, CA: ABC-CLIO.
Willis, P. E. (1977). *Learning to labour: How working class kids get working class jobs.* Farnborough, UK: Saxon House.
Willis, P. (1978). *Profane culture.* London: Routledge & Kegan Paul.
Willis, P., Jones, S., Cannan, J., & Hurd, G. (1990). *Common culture.* Milton Keynes, UK: Open University Press.
Willis, P. (2000). *The ethnographic imagination.* Cambridge, UK: Polity.
Women's Studies Group, Centre for Contemporary Cultural Studies. (1978). *Women take issue: Aspects of women's subordination.* London: Hutchinson, with Centre for Contemporary Cultural Studies, University of Birmingham.
Woodward, K. (Ed.). (1997). *Identity and difference.* London: Sage.
Young, I. (1990). The ideal of community and the politics of difference. In L. J. Nicholson (Ed.), *Feminism/postmodernism.* New York: Routledge.
Young, T., & Yarbrough, J. (1993). *Reinventing sociology: Missions and methods for postmodern sociology* (Transforming Sociology Series, 154). Red Feather Institute. Retrieved from www.etext.org/Politics/Progressive.Sociologists/authors/Young.TR/reinventing-sociology
Zammito, J. (1996). *Historicism, metahistory, and historical practice: The historicization of the historical subject.* Retrieved from http://cohesion.rice.edu/humanities/csc/conferences .cfm?doc_id=378
Zizek, S. (1990). *The sublime object of ideology.* London: Verso.

13

METHODOLOGIES FOR CULTURAL STUDIES

An Integrative Approach

Paula Saukko

In this chapter, I discuss the characteristic methodological approaches of cultural studies and how recent intellectual and historical developments have modified them. I also propose an integrative methodological framework that interlaces the different philosophical and methodological commitments of the paradigm. By doing this, I hope to point beyond debates that have underpinned cultural studies since its inception over whether the focus of research should be culture, people, or the real—or texts, audiences, or production in communication studies (e.g., Ferguson & Golding, 1997; Grossberg, 1998; McGuigan, 1997; McRobbie, 1997).

The distinctive feature of cultural studies is the way in which it combines a hermeneutic focus on lived realities, a (post)structuralist critical analysis of discourses that mediate our experiences and realities, and a contextualist/realist investigation of historical, social, and political structures of power. This creative combining of different approaches has accounted for the productivity and popularity of cultural studies since the golden years of the Birmingham Centre for Contemporary Cultural Studies in the 1970s. However, it also has resulted in philosophical and political tensions. The hermeneutic interest in lived realities runs into a contradiction with the poststructuralist interest in

Author's Note. The support of the Economic and Social Science Research Council (ESRC) is gratefully acknowledged. This work forms part of the research program on Genomics in Society (Egenis). The author would also like to thank Pertti Alasuutari and Norman Denzin for comments.

Table 13.1. The Three Validities or Methodological Programs in Cultural Studies in an Integrated Framework

	Contextual Validity	*Dialogic Validity*	*Self-Reflexive Validity*
Contextual dimension	**Social reality**	Local realities in social context	Research shapes "real" social processes
Dialogic dimension	Local repercussions of social processes	**Local realities**	Local awareness of social shaping of reality
Self-reflexive dimension	Research shapes social processes or reality	Local realities are socially shaped	**Social shaping of reality**

critical analysis of discourses, posing the question: How can one be true to lived experiences and, at the same time, criticize discourses that form the very stuff out of which our lived realities are made? Furthermore, hermeneutics and poststructuralism explore the lived and political dimensions of realities in the plural. On the contrary, contextualism is always wedded to an implicit or explicit realism or the idea that social structures of power constitute the bottom line or the reality against which the meaning and effectiveness of discourses and experiences should be evaluated. These frictions between different methodological approaches structured the chapters on cultural studies in the previous editions of the *Handbook of Qualitative Research*, addressing the long-standing juxtaposition of research on production and consumption in media studies (Fiske, 1994) and discussing multiperspectival research (Frow & Morris, 2000).

In the spirit of contributing to a handbook on methodology, and following in the footsteps of pioneers such as Lincoln and Guba (1985, 1994) and Lather (1993), I intend that this chapter will start to make sense of the three methodological currents in cultural studies by translating them into three "validities." In traditional social research–speak, validity refers to various measures that aim to guarantee the "truthfulness" of research or that attempt to ensure that research accurately and objectively describes reality. The three modes of inquiry in cultural studies, however, open distinctive perspectives on reality or define truth differently. The hermeneutic impulse in cultural studies evaluates the value of research in terms of how sensitive it is to the lived realities of its informants (Lincoln & Guba, 1985, 1994). The poststructuralist bent in the paradigm assesses research in terms of how efficiently it exposes the politics embedded in the discourses through which we construct and perceive realities (Lather, 1993). The contextual and realist commitment of cultural studies most closely mirrors the traditional criteria for validity in that it evaluates how accurately or truthfully research makes sense of the historical and social reality.

In this chapter, I propose an integrative and multidimensional framework for combining the hermeneutic or dialogic, poststructuralist or self-reflexive, and contextual validities that form the methodological basis of cultural studies. I do not argue that these different validities are united by a common reference to truth. However, nor do I argue that they refer to different truths. Instead, I explore how the three validities interlace one another, so that each validity or research program is rendered multidimensional by the other two (see Table 13.1). For example, contextualist analysis of social structures and processes may focus on what these structures "are." Such analysis will be enriched, however, by paying attention to the way in which these social processes may be experienced very differently in particular local contexts (dialogism). It also will benefit from thinking through how the research itself, for its small or big part, influences the processes it is studying (self-reflexivity).

The proposed methodological framework builds on the long-term tradition of doing empirical research in cultural studies, while also pushing it in new directions. The days are gone when social research could speak from the top-down or ivory-tower position of autonomy and objectivism. Gone also are the days when cultural studies could speak from the bottom-up, romantic/populist position of "the margin." Current theories, such as actor-network theory (Latour, 1993, also Haraway, 1997), as well as institutional pressures to attain external funding and produce more and more monetary, social, and intellectual "outcomes," view scholarship in less vertical and more horizontal terms. Research is viewed as being not above or below but in the middle, as one among many actors that forges connections between different institutions, people, and things, creating, fomenting, and halting social processes. The integrated but multidimensional methodological framework hopes to offer both a survival kit and a critical toolbox in this brave new world, helping to make sense of what it is, how it affects different peoples, and what our role is in it.

Methodological Histories

Before discussing the three validities and their dimensions in more detail, I will revisit the history of cultural studies as a means of grounding the current approaches. As Stuart Hall (1982) analyzed in a classic article, cultural studies as a paradigm carved itself a space in the early 1970s, between and beyond right-wing positivist functionalism and left-wing Marxist political economy. It did this by innovatively combining hermeneutics, structuralism, and New Leftism (Hall, 1980), and these three philosophical/political currents shaped and continue to shape empirical inquiry in the paradigm (on the early works, see Gurevitch, Woollacott, Bennett, & Curran, 1982; Hall, Hobson, Lowe, & Willis, 1980).

Two early landmark studies in cultural studies, Paul Willis's *Learning to Labour* (1977) and Janice Radway's *Reading the Romance* (1984), highlight the both fruitful and problematic nature of this multimethodological approach. Both Willis and Radway empathetically studied the everyday life of a subordinated group. Willis investigated the misbehavior of working-class schoolboys, and Radway analyzed fantasies of middle-class women involving a relationship with a nurturing man that drive these women to read romances. On the surface, these popular activities may appear to be of little importance or even silly. However, Willis and Radway argue that they address important, "real" structural inequalities, namely working-class children's alienation within the middle-class school-culture and women's dissatisfaction with intimate relationships structured by patriarchy. The authors, however, conclude that despite their creative and resistant nature, these activities do not transform the structures of power they address. Instead, they end up consolidating the structures, as underperformance at school leads working-class boys to blue-collar jobs and the seductive powers of romance novelettes hold women under the spell of an imaginary nurturing or true love.

The methodological innovativeness of these early works lies in their ability to take seriously a popular, often ignored, practice, such as disobedience at school or reading of romance literature, trying to understand its significance from the point of view of the people involved as well as against the backdrop of the wider social context. However, this strength also constitutes the Achilles' heel of the methodology. Willis and Radway argue that the misbehaving working-class boys and romance-reading women resist real structures of power (alienating education, patriarchy), yet they posit that this resistance is "imaginary," in that it gives people a sense of power or pleasure but does little to transform class or gender structures. These underlying distinctions, however, raise the question of how to separate wheat from chaff or real from imaginary resistance.[1]

As critical commentators (Ang, 1996; Marcus, 1986) have noted, what counts as the "real," against which the per se interesting popular acts are to be evaluated, reflects the authors' preferred theoretical frameworks, namely Marxist labor theory and feminism. This highlights a constitutive tension between a hermeneutic interest in subordinated experiences/realities and the New Leftist project of evaluating their relevance against the social context or "system." Three decades after his classic study, Willis (2000) defends his reading of the schoolboys' culture through theory, stating that field material needs to be brought to "forcible contact with outside concepts" in order to locate it as part of a wider whole (p. xi). The question, however, remains how to forge the micro and the macro in a way that does not reduce the local experiences to props for social theories.

When these canonical pieces are examined from a contemporary perspective, they come across as lodged in a decidedly modern and vertical imaginary of "foundations"—structuring theories, such as the Marxist base/superstructure model, the Freudian theory of the unconscious, and the idea of genes as the blueprint of life. All these theories refer to a deep or hidden layer of reality that is excavated or brought to light by science in order to provide the final explanation (structures of labor, the unconscious, DNA) of societies, people, or life.

What is interesting about Willis's and Radway's works is that they compare and contrast experiences in different sites. These innovative contrasts, however, are interpreted in vertical or hierarchical terms, so that one (the factory, intimate relations) is more "real," whereas the other one (the school, romance reading) is less so. However, one also can juxtapose multiple sites and social processes in a more horizontal manner that does not necessarily privilege one process over another but highlights how they interact and interrupt each other (see Marcus, 1998). Maybe having to do with her spatial field of geography, Doreen Massey (1994) has, like Willis, examined the marginalization of working-class men while drawing attention to the contradictions of the process. Exploring the aftermath of the British Miners' Strike, she notes that the benefits of government regeneration programs went to the wives of the former miners. After a long history of domestic servitude, these women offered the perfect labor pool for the new industries that wanted a "flexible" and non-unionized labor force that was willing to take up temporary and part-time jobs for low pay. Looking at the formation of these new labor markets from several perspectives (how it marginalized men yet allowed women to gain a level of economic independence, even if within a controversial economic configuration) highlights the multidimensionality of the process instead of interpreting it as simply a loss or a victory. Exploring several perspectives in an open fashion may enrich systemic analyses by focusing attention on developments that do not fit the initial framework, such as Marxist labor theory, and perhaps also pave the way for more inclusive and multidimensional political responses.

Contextual Validity

Willis's and Radway's studies are examples of cultural studies research that emphasize the social context, providing a convenient bridge to start a discussion on the contextual validity in cultural studies. The contextual dimension of research refers to an analysis of social and historical processes, and the worth or validity of the project depends on how thoroughly and defensibly or correctly this has been done. Few cultural studies projects embark on a major analysis of social, political, or economic processes. Such analyses usually involve an examination of large sets of statistical data and documents. Many cultural studies projects, however, make reference to social structures and processes, such as labor structures or, more recently, globalization or neoliberalism (e.g., Rose, 1999; Tomlinson, 1999). Therefore, relating to and assessing contextual developments may be seen as a prerequisite for doing high-quality cultural studies. I also argue in this section that not only does cultural studies benefit from contextualization but contextual analysis also benefits from being aware, in the dialogic spirit, of local realities that may challenge general analyses as well as being self-reflexively conscious of the political nature of its analysis.

To discuss the contextual approach, I have chosen to focus on a body of work that does not fall within cultural studies but is a prime example of an ambitious, realist analysis of contemporary global reality widely used by scholars in the field: Manuel Castells's highly acclaimed trilogy on the information society (Castells, 1996, 1997, 1998). Castells's oeuvre is based on a formidable amount of statistical and other data on social, technological, and economic developments in different parts of the world. Drawing on the data, he states that the world increasingly has been split into the sphere of The Net and the sphere of The Self. The Net emerges from flows, such as Internet communication and financial transactions as well as the globally mobile managerial elite, that operate beyond or above particular places. Castells argues that this space of flows begins to live a life of its own, as happens in places like New York or Mexico City, where the local elite is connected to global financial and other networks and disconnected from local marginalized people (Castells, 1996, p. 404). Most people, however, do not inhabit the ungrounded Net but are caught in places. In this sphere of The Self, Castells argues, people construct new identities and social movements that could challenge the elusive and elitist tendencies of the global Net. Castells distinguishes three kinds of identities and movements. A "legitimizing" identity validates dominant institutions, an example being trade unionists who bargain with the welfare state. A "resistant" identity reacts to globalization by isolating into a community of believers, ranging from Islamic fundamentalists and American patriots to Mexican Zapatistas on the Yucatán peninsula. A "project" identity, such as a feminist or environmentalist identity, on the contrary, reaches outward to connect with other people and issues and, therefore, according to Castells, has the potential to provide a counterforce to the global Net (Castells, 1997).

Castells's description of resistant identity appears prophetic against the backdrop of the September 11, 2001, attacks on the World Trade Center and the Pentagon. Those attacks seem to epitomize the resentful and futile violence of a "resistant" social movement that, instead of paving the way for social transformation, sparked a massive military retaliation against an entire region. This prophetic or critical insight of Castells's analysis is, however, troubled by his relentless dichotomizing categories, such as The Net/The Self, resistant/project, reactive/proactive, history/future, inward-looking/outward-looking, disconnected/connected (also Friedmann, 2000; Watermann, 1999). Despite Castells's understanding or analytical attitude toward the resistant movements, his polarizing logic underlines the prevailing idea that these groups are simply misguided, dangerous, and wrong, thereby fueling the kind of social division and mistrust that in other ways he is trying to address critically. This highlights the methodological blind spot of the realism that Castells represents. In its belief that through an analysis of, for example, statistics, it can describe how the world "really is," it is not able to reflect critically on the political nature of the categories it creates to excavate the "truth" out of these data.

The political nature and implications of Castells's conceptual framework become particularly clear when contrasting them to Ien Ang's (2001) analysis of another "resistant" movement, namely Pauline Hanson's right-wing populism and Patomäki's

(2003) critical comment on Castells's eulogization of the Finnish model of combining a free-market information society and social equality (Castells & Himanen, 2002).

Drawing on Castells's analysis, Ang locates the roots of Hansonism in the white working class's loss of cultural and economic privilege amid the processes of a globalizing economy and transnational migration. She also notes the xenophobia embedded in the movement's rallying against being "swamped by Asians" and the futility of its strategy as it further disinvests its supporters from the contemporary economic and symbolic hard currency of multicultural ease and flexibility. However, halfway through the essay, Ang shifts gears and begins to reflect critically on her own position as a female intellectual of Asian origin who migrated to Australia in the 1990s when the New Labour, neoliberal government of Paul Keating was rebranding the continent as a "multicultural Australia in Asia." Ang interrogates how her enthusiasm with the inclusive reinterpretation of Australian nationality implicitly supports the harsh discourse on economic restructuring and competition for the Asian market that wants to transform Australia into "a future-oriented nation which is not just capable of change but actively desires change, turning necessity into opportunity in times of altered economic and geopolitical circumstances" (2001, p. 155). Castells invites radical cultural studies intellectuals to feel that in their outward-directedness they are "in the right," in relation to both global forces of capitalism and the self-enclosed fundamentalists. On the contrary, Ang suggests that intellectuals should critically reflect on their cultural and political frames of reference that may be complicit with the new global "survival of the fittest," in which Hansonites are the losers.

Patomäki (2003) challenges Castells's analytical framework from a rather different perspective. He refers to Castells's (Castells & Himanen, 2002) work that frames my own country of origin, Finland, as an exemplar of the successful combining of a free-market information economy—epitomized by Nokia mobile-phones and Linux open-source software—and social equality. Patomäki argues that Castells's interpretation of the mutual compatibility of Finland's aggressive liberalization and transformation into information economy during the 1990s, on one hand, and social equality, on the other, is an "optical illusion." Noting that Castells uses old statistics on income equality to make his point, Patomäki states that his analysis is misguiding, as it neglects the rapid steepening of social disparities in Finland during the 1990s, precisely when the country took the leap toward liberalization and information society. Thus, Patomäki's comment illustrates the danger that a strong commitment to a particular theory may carry the analyst away, to see what he or she wants to see in the data (that a liberal information economy is the only solution but that it can be harnessed to social equality).

To draw a preliminary conclusion, Castells's work is a brilliant example of meticulous and extraordinarily broad analysis of a social and global transformation, identifying it from an enormous material of pivotal tendencies. As such, it is a great exemplar of contextual validity and how to do a remarkable job in making sense of social reality. However, the works by Ang and Patomäki highlight that contextual analysis would benefit from the dialogic principle of being sensitive to local realities. As illustrated by the Australian Hansonites and the Finnish version of an information economy, paying close attention to these local cases might complicate the conceptual framework, drawing attention to complexities and incongruencies that do not fit the model. Furthermore, Ang and Patomäki also draw attention to the need to be self-reflexively aware of the political commitments embedded in the concepts and categories that drive one's work. Castells is deeply committed to the distinction between the Net and the Self and that the way forward is to give the Net a humane face (in the shape of the environmentalist and feminist movements or the Finnish model economy). This commitment makes him blind to the way in which his pronouncements may breed the kind of intolerance and hostility (against various peoples branded "fundamentalists") he laments and to the possibility that his socioeconomic analysis may legitimate the negative underpinnings of the new economy he criticizes.

▣ Dialogic Validity

Taking local realities seriously is the starting point for the second, dialogic, validity or research program in cultural studies. Dialogic validity has its roots in the classical ethnographic and hermeneutic project of capturing "the native's point of view" or, to quote Bronislaw Malinowski, "to realize *his* vision of *his* world" (Malinowski, 1922/1961, p. 25; see also Alasuutari, 1998, pp. 61–66). Classic ethnography, however, believed that it was possible for research to comprehend the internal universe of informants objectively, or through the rigorous use of a method, such as participant observation. More recent interpretations of the hermeneutic principle of understanding local realities view research in more interactive terms, as happening in the dialogic space between the Self of the researcher and the Other world of the person being researched (e.g., Buber, 1970; Maso, 2001). On the dialogic end of the hermeneutic continuum, research participants are involved in the project of capturing or constructing their reality as coworkers, involved in designing, executing, and reporting on the study, in some cases even sharing authorship (Lincoln, 1995). The dialogic interest in Other worlds also lays significant emphasis on emotional and embodied forms of knowledge and understanding, understood to be neglected by rationalistic "facts"-focused scientific research (e.g., Denzin, 1997).

An outstanding example of dialogic work that aims to understand a decidedly different or hard-to-comprehend world is Faye Ginsburg's (1989/1998) ethnography on prolife and prochoice women. After her fieldwork, Ginsburg's aim became to communicate the "counterintuitive" fact that prolife women, perceived as foes of feminism, saw themselves as defending female values of care, nurturance, and selflessness against violent masculine competitiveness and materialism (Ginsburg, 1997). One of her informants, Karen, explained that abortion has become accepted because materialist and individualist society does not value caring, and that "housewives don't mean much because we do the caring and mothering kinds of things which are not important" (Ginsburg, 1989/1998, p. 185). Thus, rather than fit Karen and her likes into an overarching social theory, Ginsburg aimed to comprehend how prolife women define the world and their place in it, and she allowed that view to trouble presuppositions about these women. Still, Ginsburg also provided another angle on abortion and described how the prochoice women saw their reward coming when women who have come to the clinic thank them for making a difference in their life and being "so warm, and so caring and so non-judgemental" (p. 155).

The extraordinary feature of Ginsburg's work on these two ways of experiencing female caring is that it enables the reader to relate to the contrasting realities of both of these groups of women and to comprehend them, even if not necessarily accepting them. Furthermore, Ginsburg also reaches outward from these intimate feelings, stating that they reflect the way in which the women's lives are shaped by the distinction between private care and public freedom that still structured the American society in the late 20th century. In making the two nearly incomprehensibly different worldviews comprehensible, as well as pointing out how they both address same-gendered structures of inequality, Ginsburg gestures toward political dialogues that would acknowledge both differences and points of common interest between the two groups. In her attempt to imagine ways to bridge different worlds, Ginsburg comes close to Ang's visions of forging tentative dialogues with the Hanson supporters.

Ginsburg's ethnographic work is exemplary in its intimate depth, social breadth, and balanced nuance. However, just as in research on social context, research on lived experiences is sometimes oblivious of other dimensions of life and reality. The literature in my current area of research, genetic testing, is rife with descriptions of intense intimate experiences that are strangely lacking in terms of critical social analysis. For example, Smith, Michie, Stephenson, and Quarrel (2002) have used interpretative phenomenological analysis to make sense of the way in which people who have relatives with Huntington's disease perceive their risk and make decisions about taking a predictive test. Huntington's disease is a genetic neurodegenerative disorder that will lead to deterioration of the person's mental and physical capacities and premature death in mid-life. It is a dominantly inherited condition: A person with one parent with Huntington's has a 50% chance of being afflicted. Smith et al. set out to get a "holistic" understanding of the "knife edge predicament" facing people who are deciding whether to take the test. They recount how one of their informants, Linda, psyched herself up for bad news and rationalized that, even if her result were negative, it would affect one of her children: "Even if you say for 100 percent it's gonna miss me, it's gonna cop for one of mine or both of mine. I says so how do you think that makes me feel?" (Smith et al., 2002, p. 135). Smith et al. succinctly capture the feel of such tough decisions—you can almost hear Linda speaking in her rolling and thick working-class British accent. However, even if the description stays true to the texture of the experience, it ends up fixated on perceptions (and misunderstanding) of clinical, probabilistic risk estimates.

Smith et al. set out to resuscitate a warm, flesh-and-blood, and emotional lived experience that has been ignored by mainstream medicine. However, when doing it, they reaffirmed the scientist's distinction between real, probabilistic risk estimates and perceptions of them, ending up exploring how these "facts feel" (Wynne, 2001). This fixation on clinical risk underlines the necessity to underpin the dialogic aim to capture the experience of the Other with a self-reflexive awareness that both our understanding of other people as well as their understanding of themselves is mediated by social discourses. Without this self-reflexive understanding, research may end up moving in a circle, where the starting point of research is a common social discourse (clinical risk) and the study then lends emotional or existential support to this common sense, dwelling in its intensity (Atkinson & Silverman, 1997). There are no "cracks" in this story that would allow for a moment of critical reflection on these new identities and discourses formed around "risk." Furthermore, the analysis seems as if it floats in a timeless and placeless emotional intensity, where not only the mediated nature but also the social context or contextual dimension of the experience fall out of the picture. In the analysis of predictive testing for Huntington's disease, the social ramifications of genetic testing—such as how it interacts with other social regimes, including the contemporary, contradictory social and political discourse emphasizing taking "responsibility" of, or enhancing, one's self, health, and life (see Novas & Rose, 2000)—are entirely absent in the picture. Dialogic research sees itself seeking to give voice to experiences that have been neglected by mainstream society. If the methodological framework does not leave space for the experiences to address the discourses and social contexts that shape them, the experiences cannot speak about or back to the social structures that neglected them in the first place.

▣ Self-Reflexive Validity

Critical reflection on how social discourses and processes shape or mediate how we experience our selves and our environment is, perhaps, the most prominent feature of cultural studies. Analyses of popular media texts—such as the romances studied by Radway—and how they shape the way we understand our selves are the trademark of cultural studies research. Self-reflexive awareness of mediation, thus, is the most characteristic criterion for good or valid research in the paradigm.

Most critically reflexive research in cultural studies, including Radway's work, is "objectivist," or marked by the scholar's detached scrutiny of a body of texts or talk in terms of the social discourses that underpin them. The trouble with objectivist analyses is that they may end up forgetful of the discourses that guide the analysis itself, as happens in Radway's study, which pronounces women as falling short of becoming fully fledged feminists.

When I initiated my research on women who, like myself, had been anorexic, I was aggravated or insulted by objectivist analyses—both psychiatric (e.g., Bruch, 1978) and feminist (e.g., Bordo, 1993)—that examined the way in which women who starved were influenced by social discourses, such as beauty ideals. I felt that these diagnostic analyses oversimplified anorexia and fueled the notion that anorexic women are dis-ordered, or incapable of reliably assessing their thoughts or actions. Thus, when I interviewed women who had had anorexia, I asked them to tell about their experience with the condition, which inevitably led to a discussion of beauty and gender norms, as well as to tell me what they thought of the diagnostic notions of anorexia. By doing this, I wanted to avoid diagnosing the women, from the outside, in terms of identifying discourses that informed their self-understanding. I rather wanted to invite them to "do" poststructuralism with me, from the inside, on both the discourses that informed their starving and the discourses that informed their diagnosis.

The response that I got was varied. An American woman, Jeanne, stated that her starving was informed by the "Reagan years, when women were supposed to have it all, be extremely successful in all realms and be extremely thin and good-looking." The attempt to live up to this ideal led her to exercise to the extreme, work in popular campus bars, and use the money she earned to buy clothing to "show off" her thin body. She also was an excellent student who would spend her nights in the undergraduate lounge, where she would "smoke, and smoke, and smoke and drink diet sodas and just study into the night." In a similar fashion, a Finnish woman, Taru, associates her starving with having danced ballet. For 15 years, since the age of 5, she did everything she could to become a professional dancer: strong, light, and flawless. To achieve this, she put herself through an excruciating regime of exercises, long stays abroad, crossing half of Finland to attend lessons, and assuaging her hunger by nibbling on rice and Tabasco sauce, which "made her stomach feel warm."

Despite the similarities of their experience of anorexia, Jeanne and Taru assessed the diagnostic discourses on the condition rather differently. Reflecting on her years of starving and the diagnostic notions of eating disorders, Jeanne noted that she was a relatively typical middle-class anorexic. She concluded that she is "not proud" for having had anorexia, which with hindsight seemed "just so self-indulgent." Rather differently, Taru was sharply critical of notions of anorexia, noting that they were similar to stories she encountered when dancing ballet and reading fitness and sports magazines, which frame women as always "weaker" than men. She concluded that she did not want to analyze the causes of her anorexia too much, as she was afraid it just "reveals more weaknesses and abnormalities."

Both of the women's stories bear witness to the way in which their starving was informed by the competitive individualist ideal of strength and success. Looking back to it, Jeanne defined her quest for strength as both self-destructive and self-indulgent. Somewhat differently, Taru criticized the diagnostic discourses of anorexia that define women's pursuit of strength as merely pathological, noting that it simply added to the discourses that define women as too weak in mind and body, which informs the anorexic's fierce starving to overcome her shortcomings in the first place. Making sense of these similarities and differences, I resorted to an e-mail that I received from a third woman, Eleanora, who commented on an article that I had written (Saukko, 2000), based partly on her interview. She wrote that she did not recognize herself in the description of a lonely and pained child, noting that it fueled the notion of anorexic women as mere victims and did not acknowledge that they can also be strong. In the same e-mail, she added that the pursuit of strength also can be limiting and that her decision to follow her lover to a foreign country had sidetracked her adamant career orientation but also made her more happy, even if also insecure. What the stories of Jeanne, Taru, and Eleanora tell about is the merciless judgment that the cultural, highly gendered discourse on strength passes on these women. This normative discourse leaves little space for the kind of ambivalence communicated by Eleanora's personal story, which contemplates on how self-determination may enable women, or people in general, to get ahead in their lives but that it may also limit their lives, even if alternative paths are not without their problems.

Methodologically speaking, paying attention to social discourses, such as the individualist discourse on strength, allows us to illuminate deep-seated belief systems that guide our thoughts and actions and shape our societies. However, if done in an objectivist manner, these analyses may end up passing on problematic cultural diagnoses based on uninterrogated cultural assumptions. This happens, for example, when anorexic women are diagnosed as being subjugated by cultural ideals of strength and self-control and, in the same breath, defined as weak and out of control, affirming the same norms of strength and control. Opening this critical reflexive bite to other views benefits from being complemented with a dialogic dimension or sensitivity to local critiques of discourses. The rarely stated but usually assumed presumption in poststructuralism is that "lay" people are blind to social discourses that guide them and that critical analysis of mediation can be executed only by an expert. However, the idea that only experts can analyze expert discourses may render the analysis moving in a circle, as there is no way for critical outside insight to break into the cycle. This is particularly true when analyzing people like anorexics, whose critical comments on their diagnosis or treatment have been all too easily dismissed as defiance or symptomatic of their dis-order.

A more concrete or contextual dimension of self-reflexivity calls attention to the "real" implications our research has for the reality we are studying. This refers back to Foucault's argument with Derrida, in which Foucault (1979) noted that the discourse on madness did not simply symbolically affirm the Enlightenment notion of rationality (that stood in opposition to the definition of irrationality or madmen) but also very concretely locked the mad in institutions, ripping from them any basic human rights. When initiating my research on anorexia, I deliberately did not want to study anorexic women in a treatment context, as I wanted to critically analyze diagnostic practices. However, looking back to it, I have had second thoughts about this decision. Even though my work has been adopted by scholars and teachers working in psychology, I feel it would have had more of an impact on the treatment of anorexia if I had directly engaged with the therapeutic institution.

This question of whether research should be "in" or "out" of the institutional context it is addressing has been discussed at length in cultural studies, particularly in the so-called policy debates in the 1990s. Tony Bennett (1998) started these debates by suggesting that cultural studies as a paradigm should get engaged in policy making and advice, arguing that it would make the discipline more politically effective as well as acknowledge the fact that, despite claims of autonomy, research always legitimates political arrangements, such as the liberal humanism of the liberal state. Bennett's suggestion was met with criticism in some circles. The criticism drew parallels between his approach and so-called administrative communication research in postwar America that was funded by government and industry and concentrated on polling and marketing research and against which cultural and critical communication studies defined itself (Hardt, 1992). Tomaselli (1996) noted that the usefulness of the policy approach depended on the context, and that working for the South African government during apartheid may have been counterproductive, whereas collaboration with the new state was a different case.

The British Minister of Education, Charles Clarke, recently refueled the policy debate by stating that he does not "mind there being some medievalists around for ornamental purposes, but there is no reason for the state to pay for them." He later clarified that he wanted to underline the task of British universities to deal with challenges posed by "global change" to the national economy and society ("Devil's Advocate Ignites Row," 2003, p. 2). What this means can be exemplified by the fact that during Clarke's reign in office, the legendary Department of Cultural Studies at the Birmingham University was "restructured" out of existence in the summer of 2002. In this situation, there does not seem to exist a choice to be outside the system or do research that is not externally funded and socially or economically "relevant." This, however, does not mean that critical inquiry has had its day, but it does force scholars in the field to rethink self-reflexivity. The introspective interrogating of the discourses that impinge on other people's or on one's own self-understanding no longer is sufficient. What is called for is an outward-directed exploration of what kinds of concrete realities our research, for its big or small part, helps to create (Haraway, 1997). This returns this chapter back full circle to contextual validity, or the need to assess research in terms of how well it is able to make sense of gritty social and historical processes and the role it plays in those processes.

Conclusion

Perhaps, in a way that was symptomatic of the newest of new times (Hall & Jacques, 1989) in cultural studies, about a year ago I decided to change gears in my academic career. I left communication studies and moved into social scientific research on genomics. I thought genomics as an area was intellectually interesting, socially relevant, and timely, and, in a utilitarian fashion, probably a better bet to get funding than reading media texts.

The first surprise in my new job came when I had to wait for 6 months to get a go-ahead from the local ethics board for my study. In the aftermath of several scandals, including the so-called Bristol case—where tissue samples from children, who had died in cardiac surgery, were kept and used for research without permission over a long period of time—the governance of ethics in medical research in the United Kingdom has become part of a long-winded, multistage bureaucratic procedure. While waiting to study "real" people, I began following a virtual discussion group. The group that I was reading was for people with a relatively low "polygenic" susceptibility to developing deep vein thrombosis (as opposed to more familiar monogenic or deterministic genetic diseases, such as Huntington's). When I contacted the moderator and the hematologist working with the group about the study I was contemplating, they told me they were in the process of establishing an organization for patients, in collaboration with the Centers for Disease Control in Atlanta. They stated that my research on the group might serve the patient information project they were planning. One of the first priorities of the newly formed group was to negotiate a reduced price from La Roche for a machine that would allow home testing of blood-coagulation levels (to save people numerous trips to clinics). On the list, people also expressed hopes that the new organization would lobby for the House to pass the bill, approved by the Senate, that would ban insurance companies and employers from discriminating against people based on genetic information.

Rabinow (1996) has made sense of these new social sensibilities and modes of action with his term "biosociality" (as opposed to the old sociobiology), which refers to the ways in which people with shared genetic characteristics form identities and projects around them. They may form patient organizations that use virtual and real modes of communication and organization to forge connections between themselves, regulatory bodies, medical practitioners and scientists, pharmaceutical companies, and cultural studies scholars to produce often-contradictory political projects (also Heath, Koch, Ley, & Montova, 1999).

This current situation is significantly different from that of the early part of the 20th century, when geneticists James V. Neel and Victor McKusick based their research on the indigenous people in Amazonia and the old order Amish. They would go to these communities and harvest indigenous knowledge, plant and human DNA, family trees, family photographs, and life stories (Lindee, 2003; Santos, 2003). As Lindee has aptly noted, the material that McKusick collected consisted of very different kinds of knowledges, being like a "patchwork quilt, pulled together from multiple fabrics" (Lindee, 2003, p. 50). Yet the heterogeneity of these knowledges was rendered invisible in the final product of genetic knowledge that gives the appearance of pure, objective science. Those days of free harvesting, however, are gone. Nowadays, indigenous people and people with genetic conditions or susceptibilities do not necessarily simply lend themselves to be investigated but want to negotiate the collaboration.

As a consequence, research can no longer retreat to the space of apparent autonomy and objectivity and make statements about the social system, people, or nature. But neither can research render people with genetic conditions targets of their own romantic projections about the "margin." Instead, the researcher, like the people with their newly found biosociality, is caught in a messier and more horizontal network, forging and negotiating links between social and cultural research, medical research and practice, policy, patients, companies, and funding bodies, and possibly being funded by government research councils, health care providers, companies, or the patient organizations.

In this scenario, the old distinction between the system and the people blurs. This refers to the intersections between contextual and dialogic validities in Table 13.1. Thus, systems are comprehensible only through their local implications or manifestations, such as the mundane need for reasonably priced home testing machines, which may complicate or confound grand systemic pronouncements about the goodness or badness of our "genomic future" (on opposite views, see Department of Health, 2003; GeneWatch/UK, 2002). Yet, similarly, the local needs are intelligible only within the system. These might include the emerging use of genomic knowledge to prevent common illnesses, which has costs and benefits for the people using preventive tests and drugs, the health care and insurance system, and the companies producing the test machines.

The other side of the equation, the relationship between the people and the system, seems equally indistinguishable. This refers to the intersection between dialogic and self-reflexive validities in Table 13.1. The local people or realities or biosociality that we study do not exist—anymore than "genes" do—in "nature" or in a socially untouched state of authenticity, but are instead formed by the genomic configuration or system. Furthermore, local people cannot be presumed to be "dupes" or unaware of their relationship with the wider system. On the contrary, they actively engage with it, forming alliances, inserting pressure on, and bargaining with other social organizations, including cultural studies research projects, to advance their interests, such as better and affordable care.

Furthermore, we can observe a collapse of the distinctions that have formed the cornerstones of many of the methodological debates in cultural studies between the researcher and the research object/subject and virtual and real. This refers to the intersection of the self-reflexive and contextual validities in Table 13.1. Research on, for example, social implications of genomics cannot assume to be neutral, as it forms part of the busy network of actors who shape policy, regulations, treatment practices, scientific and funding priorities, and everyday lives. The influences exerted by the different constituencies within this network—cultural studies and genomic research, people with the genetic susceptibilities, policy makers, companies, and so on—are also both symbolic and real or "material/semiotic," to quote Haraway

(1997). They not only represent people, genes, risk, cures, prevention, costs, and benefits but also forge them in concrete terms, giving rise to particular everyday routines of care, health care priorities, policies, and so on.

In the end, the task of the integrative methodological approach is to facilitate empirical inquiry into social reality in a way that takes into account that the reality is shot through with a mosaic of different realities and that our research is part of the processes forming this social mosaic or a "patchwork quilt" (Deleuze & Guattari, 1987; Lindee, 2003; Saukko, 2000). This integrative quilting approach aims to address some novel historical and intellectual factors, but it is close to exploring the nexuses between the local and global, the cultural and the real, and the personal and the political, which have fascinated and infatuated cultural studies throughout its history. I make no claim in this chapter to point "beyond" these positions or debates; I simply hope to contribute to the ongoing project of making the incompatible compatible in an analytically sophisticated, methodologically practical, and politically productive way that has fueled the paradigm for over three decades.

Note

1. This distinction reflects Antonio Gramsci's separation between "good sense" and "common sense" (Gramsci, 1971, p. 333) as well as the later concept of "double articulation" (Grossberg, 1997, p. 217).

References

Alasuutari, P. (1998). *An invitation to social research.* London: Sage.

Ang, I. (1996). *Living room wars: Rethinking media audiences for a postmodern world.* London: Routledge.

Ang, I. (2001). *On not speaking Chinese: Living between Asia and the West.* London: Routledge.

Atkinson, P., & Silverman, D. (1997). Kundera's *Immortality*: The interview society and the invention of the self. *Qualitative Inquiry, 3,* 304–325.

Bennett, T. (1998). *Culture: A reformer's science.* London: Sage.

Bordo, S. (1993). *The unbearable weight: Feminism, Western culture, and the body.* Berkeley: University of California Press.

Bruch, H. (1978). *The golden cage: The enigma of anorexia nervosa.* Cambridge, MA: Harvard University Press.

Buber, M. (1970). *I and thou.* New York: Charles Scribner's Sons.

Castells, M. (1996). *The rise of the network society.* London: Blackwell.

Castells, M. (1997). *The power of identity.* London: Blackwell.

Castells, M. (1998). *End of millennium.* London: Blackwell.

Castells, M., & Himanen, P. (2002). *The information society and the welfare state: The Finnish model.* Oxford, UK: Oxford University Press.

Deleuze, G., & Guattari, F. (1987). *A thousand plateaus: On capitalism and schizophrenia.* Minneapolis: University of Minnesota Press.

Denzin, N. (1997). *Interpretive ethnography: Ethnographic practices for the 21st century.* Thousand Oaks, CA: Sage.

Department of Health. (2003). *Our inheritance, our future: Realising the potential of genetics in the NHS.* London: The Stationery Office. Available at www.dh.gov.uk/PolicyAndGuidance/HealthAndSocialCareTopics/Genetics/GeneticsGeneralInformation/GeneticsGeneralArticle/fs/en?CONTENTID=4016430&chk=RnGBgL

Devil's advocate ignites row . . . (2003, May 16). *Times Higher Education Supplement,* pp. 1–3.

Ferguson, M., & Golding, P. (Eds.). (1997). *Cultural studies in question.* London: Sage.

Fiske, J. (1994). Audiencing: Cultural practice and cultural studies. In N. K.Denzin & Y. S. Lincoln (Eds.), *Handbook of qualitative research* (pp. 189–198). Thousand Oaks, CA: Sage.

Foucault, M. (1979). My body, this paper, this fire. *Oxford Literary Review, 4,* 9–28.

Friedmann, J. (2000). Reading Castells: *Zeitdiagnose* and social theory. *Environment and Planning D: Society and Space, 18,* 111–120.

Frow, J., & Morris, M. (2000). Cultural studies. In N. K. Denzin & Y. S. Lincoln (Eds.), *Handbook of qualitative research* (2nd ed., pp. 315–346). Thousand Oaks, CA: Sage.

GeneWatch/UK. (May, 2002). *Genetics and "predictive medicine": Selling pills, ignoring causes* (Briefing Number 18). Available at www.genewatch.org/HumanGen/publications/briefings.htm#Brief18

Ginsburg, F. (1997). The case of mistaken identity: Problems in representing women on the Right. In R. Hertz (Ed.), *Reflexivity and voice* (pp. 283–299). London: Sage.

Ginsburg, F. (1998). *Contested lives: The abortion debate in an American community.* Berkeley: University of California Press. (Original work published 1989)

Gramsci, A. (1971). *Selections from the prison notebooks of Antonio Gramsci* (Q. Hoare & J. Nowell Smith, Ed. and Trans.). London: Lawrence & Wishart.

Grossberg, L. (1997). *Bringing it all back home: Essays on cultural studies.* Durham, NC: Duke University Press.

Grossberg, L. (1998). The victory of culture. Part I. Against the logic of mediation. *Angelaki, 3*(3), 3–29.

Gurevitch, M., Woollacott, J., Bennett, T., & Curran, J. (Eds.). (1982). *Culture, society and the media.* London: Methuen.

Hall, S. (1980). Cultural studies: Two paradigms. *Media, Culture and Society, 2*(1), 59–72.

Hall, S. (1982). The rediscovery of ideology: Return of the repressed in media studies. In M. Gurevitch, J. Woollacott, T. Bennett, & J. Curran (Eds.), *Culture, society and the media* (pp. 56–90). London: Methuen.

Hall, S., Hobson, D., Lowe, A., & Willis, P. (Eds.). (1980). *Culture, media, language: Working papers in cultural studies, 1972–79.* London: Hutchinson.

Hall, S., & Jacques, M. (Eds.). (1989). *New times: The changing face of politics in the 1990s.* London: Lawrence and Wishart.

Haraway, D. (1997). *Modest-Witness@Second-Millennium. FemaleMan-Meets-OncoMouse: Feminism and technoscience.* London: Routledge.

Hardt, H. (1992). *Critical communication studies: Essays on communication, history and theory in America.* London: Routledge.

Heath, D., Koch, E., Ley, B., & Montova, M. (1999). Nodes and queries: Linking locations in networked fields of inquiry. *American Behavioral Scientist, 43*(3), 450–463.

Lather, P. (1993). Fertile obsessions. Validity after poststructuralism. *The Sociological Quarterly, 34*(4), 673–693.

Latour, B. (1993). *We have never been modern.* Cambridge, MA: Harvard University Press.

Lincoln, Y., & Guba, E. (1985). *Naturalistic inquiry.* London: Sage.

Lincoln, Y., & Guba, E. (1994). Competing paradigms in qualitative research. In N. K. Denzin & Y. S. Lincoln (Eds.), *Handbook of qualitative research* (pp. 105–117). Thousand Oaks, CA: Sage.

Lindee, M. S. (2003). Provenance and pedigree: Victor McKusick's fieldwork with the old order Amish. In A. Goodman, D. Heath, & M. S. Lindee (Eds.), *Genetic nature/culture: Anthropology and science beyond the two-culture divide* (pp. 41–76). Berkeley: University of California Press.

Malinowski, B. (1961). *Argonauts of the Western Pacific.* New York: E. P. Dutton. (Original work published 1922)

Marcus, G. (1986). Contemporary problems of ethnography in the modern world system. In J. Clifford & G. Marcus (Eds.), *Writing culture: The politics and poetics of ethnography* (pp. 165–193). Berkeley: University of California Press.

Marcus, G. (1998). *Ethnography through thick and thin.* Princeton, NJ: Princeton University Press.

Maso, I. (2001). Phenomenology and ethnography. In P. Atkinson, A. J. Coffey, S. Delamont, J. Lofland, & L. H. Lofland (Eds.), *Handbook of ethnography* (pp. 136–144). London: Sage.

Massey, D. (1994). *Space, place and gender.* London: Polity.

McGuigan, J. (Ed.). (1997). *Cultural methodologies.* London: Sage.

McRobbie, A. (Ed.). (1997). *Back to reality? Social experience and cultural studies.* Manchester, UK: Manchester University Press.

Novas, C., & Rose, N. (2000). Genetic risks and the birth of the somatic individual. *Economy and Society, 29*(4), 485–513.

Patomäki, H. (2003). An optical illusion: The Finnish model for the information age. *Theory, Culture, and Society, 20*(3), 136–145.

Radway, J. (1984). *Reading the romance: Women, patriarchy, and popular literature.* Chapel Hill: University of North Carolina Press.

Rose, N. (1999). *Powers of freedom: Reframing political thought.* Cambridge, UK: Cambridge University Press.

Santos, R. V. (2003). Indigenous peoples, changing social and political landscapes, and human genetics in Amazonia. In A. Goodman, D. Heath, & M. S. Lindee (Eds.), *Genetic nature/culture: Anthropology and science beyond the two-culture divide* (pp. 23–40). Berkeley: University of California Press.

Saukko, P. (2000). Between voice and discourse: Quilting interviews on anorexia. *Qualitative Inquiry, 6*(3), 299–317.

Smith, J., Michie, S., Stephenson, M., & Quarrel, O. (2002). Risk perception and decision-making in candidates for genetic testing for Huntington's disease: An interpretative phenomenological analysis. *Journal of Health Psychology, 7*(2), 131–144.

Tomaselli, K. (1996, December). *Cultural policy & politics: South Africa and the Australian cultural policy "moment."* Paper delivered at the Cultural Studies Association of Australia

Conference "In Search of the Public." Retrieved from www.nu.ac.za/ccms/anthropology/culturalpolicy.asp?ID=1

Tomlinson, J. (1999). *Globalization and culture.* London: Polity.

Watermann, P. (1999). The brave new world of Manuel Castells: What on earth (or in the ether) is going on? *Development and Change, 20,* 357–380.

Willis, P. (1977). *Learning to labour: How working-class kids get working-class jobs.* Westmead: Saxon House.

Willis, P. (2000). *The ethnographic imagination.* Cambridge, UK: Polity.

Wynne, B. (2001). Creating public alienation: Expert cultures of risk and ethics on GMOs. *Science as Culture, 10*(4), 445–481.

14

CRITICAL HUMANISM AND QUEER THEORY

Living With the Tensions

Ken Plummer

Failure to examine the conceptual structures and frames of reference which are unconsciously implicated in even the seemingly most innocent factual inquires is the single greatest defect that can be found in any field of inquiry.

—John Dewey (1938, p. 505)

Most people in and outside of the academy are still puzzled about what queerness means, exactly, so the concept still has the potential to disturb or complicate ways of seeing gender and sexuality, as well as the related areas of race, ethnicity and class.

—Alexander Doty (2000, p. 7)

Research—like life—is a contradictory, messy affair. Only on the pages of "how-to-do-it" research methods texts or in the classrooms of research methods courses can it be sorted out into linear stages, clear protocols, and firm principles.

My concern in this chapter lies with some of the multiple, often contradictory assumptions of inquiries. Taking my interest in sexualities/gay/queer research as a starting point and as a tension, I see "queer theory" and "critical humanism" as one of my own tensions. I have tried to depict each and to suggest some overlaps, but my aim has not been to reconcile the two. That is not possible and probably is not even desirable. We have to live with the tensions, and awareness of them is important background for the self-reflexive social researcher.

Social Change and Zombie Research

This discussion should be seen against a background of rapid social change. Although for many, research methods remain the same over time (they just get a bit more refined with each generation), for others of us, changes in society are seen to bring parallel changes in research practices. To put it bluntly, many claim we are moving into a postmodern, late modern, globalizing, risk, liquid society. A new global order is in the making that is much more provisional and less authoritative than that of the past; it is a society of increasing self-reflexivity and individuation, a network society of flows and mobilities, a society of consumption and waste (Bauman, 2000, 2004; Beck, 2003; Giddens,1991; Urry, 2000).

As we tentatively move into these new worlds, our tools for theory and research need radical overhaul. German sociologist Ulrich Beck, for example, speaks of "zombie categories"; we move among the living dead! Zombie categories are categories from the past that we continue to use even though they have long outlived their usefulness and even though they mask a different reality. We probably go on using them because at present we have no better words to put in their place. Yet dead they are.

Beck cites the example of the concept of "the family" as an instance of a zombie category, a term that once had life and meaning but for many now means very little. I suggest that we could also cite most of our massive research methodology apparatus as partially zombified. I am not a major fan of television, but when I choose to watch a documentary, I often am impressed by how much more I get from it than from the standard sociological research tract. Yet the skills of a good documentary maker are rarely the topics of research methods courses, even though these skills—from scriptwriting and directing to camera movements and ethics—are the very stuff of good 21st-century research. And yes, some research seems to have entered the world of cyberspace, but much of it simply replicates the methods of quantitative research, making qualitative research disciplined, quantitative, and antihumanistic. Real innovation is lacking. Much research at the end of the 20th century—to borrow Beck's term again—truly was zombie research (Beck, 2003).

Table 14.1 suggests some links between social change and social research styles. The background is the authoritative scientific account with standard research protocols. As the social world changes, so we may start to sense new approaches to making inquiries. My concern in this chapter is largely with the arrival of queer theory.

A Reflexive Introduction

How research is done takes us into various language games—some rational, some more contradictory, some qualitative, some quantitative. The languages we use bring with them all manner of tensions. Although they sometimes help us chart the ways we do research, they often bring their own contradictions and problems. My goal here is to address some of the incoherencies I have found in my own research languages and inquiries and to suggest ways of living with them. Although I will draw widely from a range of sources and hope to provide some paradigmatic instances, the chapter inevitably will be personal. Let me pose the key contradiction of my inquiries. (We all have our own.)

The bulk of my inquiries have focused on sexualities, especially lesbian and gay concerns, with an ultimate eye on some notion of sexual justice. In the early days, I used a relatively straightforward symbolic interactionism to guide me in relatively straightforward fieldwork and interviewing in and around London's gay scene of the late 1960s. At the same time, I engaged politically, initially with the Homosexual Law Reform Society and then with the Gay Liberation Front in its early years. I read my Becker, Blumer, Strauss, and Denzin! At the same time, I was coming out as a young gay man and finding my way in the very social world I was studying. More recently, such straightforwardness has come to be seen as increasingly problematic. Indeed, there was always a tension there: I just did not always see it (Plummer, 1995).

On one hand, I have found myself using a language that I increasingly call that of critical humanism, one allied to symbolic interactionism, pragmatism, democratic thinking, storytelling, moral progress, redistribution, justice, and good citizenship (Plummer, 2003). Inspirations range from Dewey to Rorty, Blumer to Becker. All of these are quite old and traditional ideas, and although I have sensed their postmodernized affinities (as have others), they still bring more orthodox claims around experience, truths, identities, belonging to groups, and a language of moral responsibilities that can be shared through dialogues (Plummer, 2003).

By contrast, I also have found myself at times using a much more radicalized language that nowadays circulates under the name of queer theory. The latter must usually be seen as at odds with the former: Queer theory puts everything out of joint, out of order. "Queer," for me, is the postmodernization of sexual and gender studies. "Queer" brings with it a radical deconstruction of all conventional categories of sexuality and gender. It questions all the orthodox texts and tellings of the work of gender and sexuality in the modern world (and all worlds). It is a messy, anarchic affair—not

Table 14.1. Shifting Research Styles Under Conditions of Late Modernity

Current Social Changes	*Possible Changes in Research Style*
Toward a late modern world	Toward a late modern research practice
Postmodern/fragmentation/pluralization	The 'polyphonic' turn
Mediazation	The new forms of media as both technique and data
Stories and the death of the grand narrative	The storytelling/narrative turn
Individualization/choices/unsettled identities	The self-reflexive turn
Globalization-glocalization hybridization/ diaspora	The hybridic turn: decolonizing methods (L. T. Smith, 1999)
High tech/mediated/cyborg /post-human	The high-tech turn
Knowledge as contested	The epistemological turn
Postmodern politics and ethics	The political/ethical turn
The network society	Researching flows, mobilities, and contingencies
Sexualities as problematic	The queer turn

much different from intellectual anarchists or political International Situationists. "Queer" would seem to be antihumanist, to view the world of normalization and normality as its enemy, and to refuse to be sucked into conventions and orthodoxy. If it is at all sociological (and it usually is not), it is gothic and romantic, not classical and canonical (Gouldner, 1973). It transgresses and subverts.

On one hand, then, I am quite happy about using the "new language of qualitative method" (Gubrium & Holstein, 1997); on the other, I am quite aware of a queer language that finds problems everywhere with orthodox social science methods (Kong, Mahoney, & Plummer, 2002). Again, these tensions are very much products of their time (queer theory did not exist before the late 1980s). Yet, retrospectively, it would seem that I have always walked tightropes between an academic interactionism, a political liberalism, a gay experience, and a radical critique.

But of course, as usual, there are more ironies here. Since the late 1980s, I have more or less considered myself "post-gay." So who was that young man from the past who studied the gay world? Likewise, those wild queer theorists have started to build their textbooks, their readers, and their courses, and they have proliferated their own esoteric cultlike worlds that often seem more academic than the most philosophical works of Dewey. Far from breaking boundaries, queer theorists often have erected them, for while they may not wish for closure, they nevertheless find it. Queer theories have their gurus, their followers, and their canonical texts. But likewise, humanists and new qualitative researchers—finding themselves under siege from postmodernists, queer theorists, some feminists, and multiculturalists and the like—have also fought back, rewriting their own histories and suggesting that many of the critiques laid at their door are simply false. Some, like Richard Rorty—the heir apparent to the modern pragmatism of Dewey and James—fall into curious traps: Himself labeled a postmodernist by others, he condemns postmodernists as "posties" (Rorty, 1999). Methodological positions often lead in directions different from those originally claimed.[1]

So here am I, like many others, a bit of a humanist, a bit post-gay, a sort of a feminist, a little queer, a kind of a liberal, and seeing that much that is queer has the potential for an important radical change. In the classic words of interactionism, Who am I? How can I live with these tensions?

This chapter is not meant to be an essay of overly indulgent self-analysis, but rather one in which, starting to reflect on such a worry, I am simply showing tensions that many must confront these days. Not only am I not alone in such worries, but I also am fairly sure that all reflective qualitative inquiries will face their own versions of them, just as most people face them in their daily lives. Ambivalence is the name of the game.

In this chapter, I plan to deal with three interconnected issues raised by qualitative research—all focused on just how far we can "push" the boundaries of qualitative research into new fields, strategies, and political/moral awareness—and how this has been happening continuously in my own work. New languages of qualitative method benefit from new ideas that at least initially may be seen as opposition. This is how they grow and how the whole field of qualitative research becomes more refined. In what follows, I will explore:

- What is critical humanism and how to do a critical humanist method
- What is queer and how to do a queer method
- How the contradictions can be lived through

The Critical Humanist Project

> *How different things would be . . . if the social sciences at the time of their systematic formation in the nineteenth century had taken the arts in the same degree they took the physical science as models.*
>
> —Robert Nisbet (1976, p. 16)

> *There is an illusive center to this contradictory, tension-ridden enterprise that seems to be moving further and further away from grand narratives and single, overarching ontological, epistemological, and methodological paradigms. This center lies in the humanistic commitment of the qualitative researcher to study the world always from the perspective of the interacting individual. From this*

> *simple commitment flow the liberal and radical politics of qualitative research. Action, feminist, clinical, constructivist, ethnic, critical, and cultural studies researchers all unite on this point. They all share the belief that a politics of liberation must always begin with the perspectives, desires, and dreams of those individuals and groups who have been oppressed by the larger ideological, economic, and political forces of a society or a historical moment.*
>
> —Denzin & Lincoln (1994, p. 575)

I use the term "critical humanism" these days to suggest orientations to inquiry that focus on human experience—that is, with the structure of experience and its daily lived nature—and that acknowledge the political and social role of all inquiry. It goes by many names—symbolic interactionism,[2] ethnography, qualitative inquiry, reflexivity, cultural anthropology, and life story research, among others—but they all have several concerns at heart. All these research orientations have a focus on human subjectivity, experience, and creativity: They start with people living their daily lives. They look at their talk, their feelings, their actions, and their bodies as they move around in social worlds and experience the constraints of history and a material world of inequalities and exclusions. They make methodological claims for a naturalistic "intimate familiarity" with these lives, recognizing their own part in such study. They make no claims for grand abstractions or universalism—assuming an inherent ambivalence and ambiguity in human life with no "final solutions," only damage limitations—while simultaneously sensing both their subjects' ethical and political concerns and their own in conducting such inquiries. They have pragmatic pedigrees, espousing an epistemology of radical, pragmatic empiricism that takes seriously the idea that knowing—always limited and partial—should be grounded in experience (Jackson, 1989). It is never neutral, value-free work, because the core of the inquiry must be human values. As John Dewey remarked long ago, "Any inquiry into what is deeply and inclusively (i.e., significantly) human enters perforce into the specific area of morals" (1920, p. xxvi). Impartiality may be suspect; but a rigorous sense of the ethical and political sphere is a necessity. Just why would one even bother to do research were it not for some wider concern or value?

What are these values? In the most general terms, critical humanism champions those values that give dignity to the person,[3] reduce human sufferings, and enhance human well-being. There are many such value systems, but at a minimum they probably must include the following:

1. A commitment to a whole cluster of *democratizing values* (as opposed to totalitarian ones) that aim to *reduce/remove human sufferings.* They take as a baseline *the value of the human being* and often provide a number of suggested *human rights*—freedom of movement, freedom of speech, freedom of association, freedom against arbitrary arrest, and so on. They nearly always include the *right to equality.* This commitment is strongly antisuffering and provides a major thrust toward both equality and freedom for all groups, including those with "differences" of all kinds (Felice, 1996).

2. An ethics of *care* and *compassion.* Significantly developed by feminists, this is a value whereby looking after the other takes on a prime role and whereby *sympathy*, *love*, and even *fidelity* become prime concerns (Tronto, 1993).

3. A politics of *recognition* and *respect.* Following the work of Axel Honneth (1995) and significantly shaped earlier by George Herbert Mead, this is a value whereby others are always acknowledged and a certain level of empathy is undertaken.

4. The importance of *trust.* This value recognizes that no social relationships (or society, for that matter) can function unless humans have at least some modicum of trust in each other (O'Neill, 2002).

Of course, many of these values bring their own tensions: We must work through them and live with them. A glaring potential contradiction, for example, may be to talk of humanistic values under capitalism, for many of the values of humanism must be seen as stressing nonmarket values. They are values that are not necessarily given a high ranking in a capitalist economy. Cornel West has put this well:

> In our own time it is becoming extremely difficult for non-market values to gain a foothold. Parenting is a non-market activity; so much sacrifice and service go into it without any assurance that the providers will get anything back. Mercy, justice: they are non market. Care, service: non market. Solidarity, fidelity: non market. Sweetness and kindness and gentleness. All non market. Tragically, non-market values are relatively scarce. . . . (West, 1999, p. 11)

The Methodologies of Humanism

These values strongly underpin critical humanism. In his classic book *The Human Perspective in Sociology*, T. S. Bruyn (1966) locates this humanistic perspective as strongly allied to the methods of participant observation. Elsewhere, I have suggested an array of life story strategies for getting at human experience. The task is a "fairly complete narrating of one's entire experience of life as a whole, highlighting the most important aspects" (R. Atkinson, 1998, p. 8). These may be long, short, reflexive, collective, genealogical, ethnographic, photographic, even auto/ethnographic (Plummer, 2000). Life stories are prime humanistic tools, but it is quite wrong to suggest that this means that the stories only have a concern with subjectivity and personal experience.[4]

Throughout all of this, there is a pronounced concern not only with the humanistic understanding of experience but also with ways of telling the stories of the research. Usually, the researcher is present in many ways in the text: The text rarely is neutral, with a passive observer. Chris Carrington's (1999) study of gay families, for example, makes it very clear from the outset his own location within a single-parent family: "I grew up in a working-poor, female-headed, single parent family. Throughout much of my childhood, in order to make ends meet, my mother worked nights as bar tender. There were periods where she could not get enough hours and our family had to turn to food stamps and welfare" (p. 7). Likewise, Peter Nardi's (1999) study of gay men's friendships is driven by his own passion for friends: "What follows is partly an attempt to make sense of my own experiences with friends" (p. 2). Humanistic inquiries usually reveal humanistic researchers.

Most commonly, as in Josh Gamson's *Freaks Talk Back* (1998) and Leila Rupp and Verta Taylor's *Drag Queens at the 801 Cabaret* (2003), the method employed will entail triangulation—a combination of cultural analysis tools.[5] Here, multiple sources of data pertaining to texts, production, and reception are collected and the intersections among them analyzed. In Rupp and Taylor's study of drag queens, they observed, tape recorded, and transcribed 50 drag performances, along with the dialogue, music, and audience interactions, including photographs and dressing up themselves. They collected data on the performances through weekly meetings of the drag artists and semi-structured life histories, and they conducted focus groups on people who attended the performances. In addition, they looked at weekly newspapers (such as the gay paper *Celebrate*) and others to partially construct the history of the groups. Their research has a political aim, humanistic and sociological, and yet queer too, showing that combinations are possible. Enormous amounts of research have been written on all of this (e.g., Clifford & Marcus, 1986; Coffey, 1999; Coles, 1989; Ellis & Flaherty, 1992; Hertz, 1992; Reed-Danahay, 1997; Ronai, 1992).

A further recent example of such work is Harry Wolcott's (2002) account of Brad, the Sneaky Kid. Wolcott, an educational anthropologist, is well known for his methodological writings and books, especially in the field of education. This book started life in the early 1980s as a short journal article on the life story of Brad, a troubled 19-year-old. The story is aimed at getting at the human experience of educational failure, in particular, the lack of support for those who are not well served by our educational systems.

This would have been an interesting life story but an unexceptional one had it not been for all the developments that subsequently emerged around it. What are not told in the original story are the details of how Wolcott met Brad, how he had gay sex with him, and how he got him to tell his life story. Much follows after the original story, which later takes curious turns: Brad develops schizophrenia and returns one night to Wolcott's house to burn it down in an enraged attempt to kill him. This leads to the complete destruction of Wolcott's home and all his belongings (and those of his schoolteacher partner). A serious court case ensues in which Brad is tried and sent to prison. Despite Brad's guilt, Wolcott is himself scrutinized regarding his relationship, his homosexuality, and even his role as an anthropologist. Brad's family is especially unhappy about the relationship with Wolcott, but so are many academics. Ultimately, Brad is institutionalized. Eventually, the story is turned into an intriguing ethnographic play. I have only read the text of the play and not seen it performed. Judging by the text presented here, it comes across as a collage of 1980s pop music, sloganized slides, and a drama in two layers—one about Brad's relationship with Wolcott and another about Wolcott's ruminations, as a professor, on the plights of ethnography.

I mention this study because although it started out as a life story gloss—a simple relaying of Brad's story—because of the curious circumstances that it led to, a much richer and complex story was revealed that generated a host of questions and debates about the ethical, personal, and practical issues surrounding fieldwork. Sexuality and gender were pretty much at the core. It is a gripping tale of the kinds of issues highlighted by all humanistic research. Indeed, within the book a second major narrative starts to appear—that of Harry Wolcott himself. He was always present, of course, but his story takes over as he reveals how he had regular sex with the young man, his partner's disapproval of Brad, and how one night he returns to his house to find a strong smell of oil and Brad screaming "You fucker. I'm going to kill you. I'm going to kill you. I'm going to tie you up and leave you in the house and set the house on fire" (p. 74). Luckily, Harry escapes, but unluckily, his house does not. It goes up entirely in flames, with all of his and his partner's belongings. This may be one of the core dramatic moments in life story telling—certainly an "epiphany"! After that, a major chapter follows that tells of the working of the court and how Wolcott himself is almost on trial.

When the story of Sneaky Kid was first published in 1983, it was a 30-page essay; it has grown into a book of more than 200 pages (Wolcott, 2002). The original article does not tell much about the relationship from which it grew or much of the other background; the book tells much more, but it raises sharply the issue of just how much remains left out. The book serves as a sharp reminder that all social science, including life stories, consists of only partial selections of realities. There is always much going on behind the scenes that is not told. Here we have the inevitable bias, the partiality, the limits, the selectivity of all stories told—but I will not take these issues further here.

▣ The Troubles With Humanism

Although I think humanism has a lot to offer qualitative inquiry, it is an unfashionable view these days: Many social scientists seem to want to turn only to discourse and language. But this discourse is not incompatible with doing this, as it evokes the humanities (much more so than other traditions), widens communities of understanding by dialoguing with the voices of others, and takes a strong democratic impulse as the force behind its thinking and investigating. As a form of imagery to think about social life, this is all to the good. It brings with it the possibility for such inquiry to engage in poetry and poetics, drama and performance, philosophy and photography, video and film, narrative and stories.

Nevertheless, these days humanism remains a thoroughly controversial and contested term—and not least among queer theorists themselves. We know, of course, the long-standing attacks on humanism from theologies, from behavioral psychologies, and from certain kinds of philosophers: There is a notorious debate between the humanist Sartre's *Existentialism and Humanism* and Heidegger's *Letter on Humanism*. More recent attacks have denounced "humanism" as a form of white, male, Western, elite domination and colonization that is being imposed throughout the world and that brings with it too strong a sense of the unique individual. It is seen as contra postmodernism. In one telling statement, Foucault proclaims, "The modern individual—objectified, analyzed, fixed—is a historical achievement. There is no universal person on whom power has performed its operations and knowledge, its enquiries" (1979, pp. 159–160). The "Human Subject" becomes a Western invention. It is not a progress or a liberation, merely a trapping on the forces of power.

This loose but important cluster of positions critical of humanism—usually identified with a postmodern sensibility—would include queer theorists, multicultural theorists, postcolonialists, many feminists, and antiracists, as well as poststructural theorists. Although I have much sympathy with these projects and the critical methodologies they usually espouse (e.g., L. T. Smith, 1999), I also believe in the value of the pragmatic and humanist traditions. How can I live with this seeming contradiction?

Let me look briefly at what the critics say. They claim that Humanists propose some kind of common and hence universal "human being" or self: a common humanity that blinds us to wider differences and positions in the world. Often this is seen as a powerful, actualizing, and autonomous force in the world: The individual agent is at the center of the action and of the universe. This is said to result in overt individualism strongly connected to the Enlightenment project (Western, patriarchal, racist, colonialist, etc.) which turns itself into a series of moral and political claims about progress through a liberal and democratic society. Humanism is linked to a universal, unencumbered "self" and to the "modern" Western liberal project. Such ideas of the human subject are distinctly "Western" and bring with them a whole series of ideological assumptions about the centrality of the white, Western, male, middle-class/ bourgeois position; hence, they become the enemies of feminism (human has equaled male), ethnic movements (human has equaled white superiority), gays (human has equaled heterosexual), and all cultures outside the Western Enlightenment project (human here has equaled the middle-class West).

A More Complex Humanism?

Such claims made against "humanism" demean a complex, differentiated term into something far too simple. Humanism can, it is true, come to mean all of the above, but the term does not have to. Alfred McLung Lee (1978, pp. 44–45) and others have charted both a long history of humanism and many forms of it. Attacks usually are waged at a high level of generality, and specifics of what constitutes "the human" often are seriously overlooked. But, as I have suggested elsewhere, for me this "human being" is never a passive, helpless atom. Humans must be located in time and space: They are always stuffed full of their culture and history, and they must "nest" in a universe of contexts. Human beings are both embodied, feeling animals and creatures with great symbolic potential. They engage in symbolic communication and are dialogic and intersubjective: There is no such thing as the solitary individual. Human lives are shaped by chance, fateful moments, epiphanies, and contingencies. There is also a continuous tension between the specificities and varieties of humanities at any time and place, and the universal potentials that are to be found in all humans. And there is a continuous engagement with moral, ethical, and political issues.

Curiously, it is also clear that many of the seeming opponents of humanism can be found wanting to hold onto some version of humanism after all. Indeed, it is odd that some of the strongest opponents lapse into a kind of humanism at different points in their argument. For instance, Edward Said—a leading postcolonial critic of Western-style humanism—actually urges another kind of humanism, "shorn of all its 'unpleasantly triumphalist weight,'" and in recent work he actually claims to be a humanist (Said, 1992, p. 230; 2003).

Indeed, at the start of the 21st century, there have been many signs that the critique of humanism that pervaded the previous century has started to be reinvigorated as a goal of inquiry. More and more contemporary commentators, well aware of the attacks above, go on to make some kinds of humanist claims. It would not be hard to find signs of humanism (even if the authors disclaimed them!) in major studies such as Nancy Scheper-Hughes's *Death Without Weeping* (1994), Stanley Cohen's *States of Denial* (1999), and Martha Nussbaum's *Sex and Social Justice* (1999). For me, they are clearly inspired by a version of humanism with the human being at the heart of the analysis, with care and justice as core values, and with the use of any methods at hand that will bring out the story.[6] So whatever the critiques, it does appear that a critical humanism still has its place in social science and qualitative inquiry. But before going too far, we should see what queer theory has to say on all this.

A Queer Project

> *Queer articulates a radical questioning of social and cultural norms, notions of gender, reproductive sexuality and the family.*
>
> —Cherry Smith (2002, p. 28)

> *Queer is by definition whatever is at odds with the normal, the legitimate, the dominant. There is nothing in particular to which it necessarily refers.*
>
> —David Halperin (1995, p. 62)

Queer theory emerged around the mid- to late 1980s in North America, largely as a humanities/multicultural-based response to a more limited "lesbian and gay studies." While the ideas of Michel Foucault loom large (with his talks of "regimes of truth" and "discursive explosions"), the roots of queer theory (if not the term) usually are seen to lie in the work of Teresa de Lauretis (Halperin, 2003, p. 339) and Eve Kosofsky Sedgwick, who argued that

> many of the major nodes of thought and knowledge in twentieth century Western culture as a whole are structured—indeed fractured—by a chronic, now endemic crisis of homo/heterosexual definition, indicatively male, dating from the end of the nineteenth century. . . . an understanding of any aspect of modern Western culture must be, not merely incomplete, but damaged in its central substance to the degree that it does not incorporate a critical analysis of modern Homo/heterosexual definition. (1990, p. 1)

Judith Butler's work has been less concerned with the deconstruction of the homo/heterosexual binary divide and more interested in deconstructing the sex/gender divide. For her, there can be no kind of claim to any essential gender: It is all "performative," slippery, unfixed. If there is a heart to queer theory, then, it must be seen as a radical stance around sexuality and gender that denies any fixed categories and seeks to subvert any tendencies toward normality within its study (Sullivan, 2003).

Despite these opening suggestions, the term "queer theory" is very hard to pin down (some see this as a necessary virtue for a theory that refuses fixed identity). It has come to mean many things: Alexander Doty can suggest at least six different meanings, as follow. Sometimes it is used simply as a synonym for lesbian, gay, bisexual, transgender (LGBT). Sometimes it is an "umbrella term" that puts together a range of so-called "non-straight positions." Sometimes it simply describes any non-normative expression of gender (which could include straight). Sometimes it is used to describe "non-straight things" not clearly signposted as lesbian, gay, bisexual, or transgender but that bring with them a possibility for such a reading, even if incoherently. Sometimes it locates the "non-straight work, positions, pleasures, and readings of people who don't share the same sexual orientation as the text they are producing or responding to." Taking it even further, Doty suggests that "queer" may be a particular form of cultural readership and textual coding that creates spaces not contained within conventional categories such as gay, straight, and transgendered. Interestingly, what all his meanings have in common is that they are in some way descriptive of texts and they are in some way linked to (usually transgressing) categories of gender and sexuality (Doty, 2000, p. 6).

In general, "queer" may be seen as partially deconstructing our own discourses and creating a greater openness in the way we think through our categories. Queer theory must explicitly challenge any kind of closure or settlement, so any attempts at definition or codification must be nonstarters. Queer theory is, to quote Michael Warner, a stark attack on "normal business in the academy" (1992, p. 25). It poses the paradox of being inside the academy while wanting to be outside it. It suggests that a "sexual order overlaps with a wide range of institutions and social ideologies, to challenge the sexual order is sooner or later to encounter these institutions as a problem" (Warner, 1993, p. 5). Queer theory is really poststructuralism (and postmodernism) applied to sexualities and genders.

To a limited extent, queer theory may be seen as another specific version of what Nancy Harstock and Sandra Harding refer to as standpoint theory (though I have never seen it discussed in this way). Initially developed as a way to analyze a position of women's subordination and domination, it suggests that an "opposition consciousness" can emerge that transcends the more taken-for-granted knowledge. It is interesting that hardly any men have taken this position up, but other women—women of race and disability, for example—have done so. Men seem to ignore the stance, and so too do queer theorists, yet what we may well have in queer theory is really something akin to a "queer standpoint."

Certain key themes are worth highlighting. Queer theory is a stance in which

- both the heterosexual/homosexual binary and the sex/gender split are challenged.
- there is a de-centering of identity.
- all sexual categories are open, fluid, and nonfixed (which means that modern lesbian, gay, bisexual, and transgender identities are fractured, along with all heterosexual ones).
- it offers a critique of mainstream or "corporate" homosexuality.
- it sees power as being embodied discursively. Liberation and rights give way to transgression and carnival as a goal of political action, what has been called a "politics of provocation."
- all normalizing strategies are shunned.
- academic work may become ironic, is often comic and paradoxical, and is sometimes carnivalesque: "What a difference a gay makes," "On a queer day you can see forever" (cf. Gever, Greyson, & Parmar, 1993).
- versions of homosexual subject positions are inscribed everywhere, even in heterosexualities.
- the deviance paradigm is fully abandoned, and the interest lies in a logic of insiders/outsiders and transgression.
- its most common objects of study are textual—films, videos, novels, poetry, visual images.
- its most frequent interests include a variety of sexual fetishes, drag kings and drag queens, gender and sexual playfulness, cybersexualities, polyamoury, sadomasochism, and all the social worlds of the so-called radical sexual fringe.

A Queer Methodology?

What are the implications of queer theory for method (a word it rarely uses)? In its most general form, queer theory is a refusal of all orthodox methods—a certain disloyalty to conventional disciplinary methods (Halberstam,1998, pp. 9–13). What, then, does queer method actually do? What does it look like? In summary, let me give a few examples of what a queer methodology can be seen to offer.

The Textual Turn: Rereadings of Cultural Artifacts. Queer methods overwhelmingly employ an interest in and analysis of texts—films, literature, television, opera, musicals. This is perhaps the most commonly preferred strategy of queer theory. Indeed, Michael

Warner has remarked that "almost everything that would be called queer theory is about ways in which texts—either literature or mass culture of language—shape sexuality." More extremely, he continues, "you can't eliminate queerness . . . or screen it out. It's everywhere. There's no place to hide, hetero scum!" (Warner, 1992, p. 19). The locus classicus of this way of thinking usually is seen to be Sedgwick's *Between Men* (1985), in which she looked at a number of key literary works (from Dickens to Tennyson) and reread these texts as driven by homosexuality, homosociality, and homophobia. Whereas patriarchy might condemn the former, it positively valorizes the latter (Sedgwick, 1985). In her wake have come hosts of rereadings around such themes. In later works, she gives readings to work as diverse as Diderot's *The Nun*, Wilde's *The Importance of Being Earnest*, and authors such as James and Austen (Sedgwick, 1990, 1994). In her wake, Alexander Doty gives queer readings to mass culture products such as "the sitcom"—from lesbian readings of the sitcoms *I Love Lucy* or *The Golden Girls*, to the role of "feminine straight men" such as Jack Benny, to the bisexual meanings in *Gentlemen Prefer Blondes* (Doty, 1993, 2000). Indeed, almost no text can escape the eyes of the queer theorist.

Subversive Ethnographies: Fieldwork Revisited. These are often relatively straightforward ethnographies of specific sexual worlds that challenge assumptions. Sasho Lambevski (1999), for instance, attempted to write "an insider, critical and experiential ethnography of the multitude of social locations (class, gender, ethnicity, religion) from which 'gays' in Macedonia are positioned, governed, controlled and silenced as subaltern people" (p. 301). As a "gay" Macedonian (are the terms a problem in this context?) who had spent time studying HIV in Australia, he looks at the sexual conflicts generated between the gay Macedonians and gay Albanians (never mind the Australian connection). Lambevski looks at the old cruising scenes in Skopje, known to him from before, that now take on multiple and different meanings bound up with sexualities, ethnicities, gender playing, and clashing cultures. Cruising for sex here is no straightforward matter. He describes how, in approaching and recognizing a potential sex partner as an Albanian (in an old cruising haunt), he feels paralyzed. Both bodies are flooded with ethnic meaning, not simple sexual ones, and ethnicities reek of power. He writes: "I obeyed by putting the (discursive) mask of my Macedonicity over my body" (p. 398). In another time and place, he may have reacted very differently.

Lambevski is overtly critical of much ethnography and wishes to write a queer experiential ethnography, not a confessional one (1999, p. 298). He refuses to commit himself to what he calls "a textual lie," which "continues to persist in much of what is considered a real ethnographic text." Here bodies, feelings, sexualities, ethnicities, and religions all can be left out easily. Nor, he claims, can ethnography simply depend on site observation or one-off interviewing. There is a great chain of connection: "The gay scene is inextricably linked to the Macedonian school system, the structuring of Macedonian and Albanian families and kinship relations, the Macedonian state and its political history, the Macedonian medical system with its power to mark and segregate 'abnormality' (homosexuality)" (1999, p. 400). There is a chain of social sites, and at the same time his own life is an integral part of this (Macedonian queer, Australian, gay). Few researchers have been so honest regarding the tensions that infuse their lives and the wider chains of connectedness that shape their work.

I find it hard to believe that this is not true for all research, but it is usually silenced. Laud Humphreys's classic *Tearoom Trade* (1970), for example—admittedly, written some 30 years earlier—cannot speak of Humphreys's own gayness, his own bodily presence (though there is a small footnote on the taste of semen!), his emotional worlds, his white middle-classness, or his role as a white married minister. To the contrary, although he does remind the reader of his religious background and his wife, this serves more as a distraction. As important as it was in its day, this is a very different kind of ethnography. The same is true of a host that followed it. They were less aware of the problematic nature of categories and the links to material worlds. They were, in a very real fashion, "naïve ethnographies"—somehow thinking "the story could be directly told as it was." We live in less innocent times, and queer theory is a marker for this.

Scavenger Methodologies: The Raiding of Multiple Texts to Assemble New Ones. A fine example of queer "method" is Judith Halberstam's work on "female masculinity" (1998). Suggesting that we have failed to develop ways of seeing that can grasp the different kinds of masculinities that women have revealed both in the past and the present, she wrote a study that documents the sheer range of such phenomena. In her own work, she "raids" literary textual methods, film theory, ethnographic field research, historical survey, archival records, and taxonomy to produce her original account of emerging forms of "female masculinity" (Halberstam, 1998, pp. 9–13). Here we have aristocratic European cross-dressing women of the 1920s, butch lesbians, dykes, drag kings, tomboys, black "butch in the hood" rappers, trans-butches, the tribade (a woman who practices "unnatural vices" with other women), the gender invert, the stone butch, the female-to-male transsexual (FTM), and the raging bull dyke! She also detects—through films as diverse as *Alien* and *The Killing of Sister George*—at least six prototypes of the female masculine: tomboys, Predators, Fantasy Butches, Transvestites, Barely Butches, and Postmodern Butches (1998, chap. 6).

In introducing this motley collection, she uses a "scavenger methodology . . . [of] different methods to collect and produce information on subjects who have been deliberately or accidentally excluded from traditional studies of human behavior" (1998, p. 13). She borrows from Eve Kosofsky Sedgwick's "nonce taxonomy": "The making and unmaking and remaking and redissolution of hundreds of old and new categorical meanings concerning all the kinds it takes to make up a world" (Sedgwick, 1990, p. 23). This is the mode of "deconstruction," and in this world the very idea that types of people called homosexuals or gays or lesbians (or, more to the point, "men" and "women") can be simply called up for study becomes a key problem in itself. Instead, the researcher should become more and more open to start sensing new worlds of possibilities.

Many of these social worlds are not immediately transparent, whereas others are amorphously nascent and forming. All this research brings to the surface social worlds only dimly articulated hitherto—with, of course, the suggestion that there are more, many more, even more deeply hidden. In one sense, Halberstam captures rich fluidity and diversity—all this going on just beneath the surface structures of society. But in another sense, her very act of naming, innovating terms, and categorizing tends itself to create and assemble new differences.

Performing Gender and Ethnographic Performance. Often drawing upon the work of Judith Butler, who sees gender as never essential, always unfixed, not innate, never natural, but always constructed through performativity—as a "stylized repetition of acts" (1990, p. 141)—much of the work in queer theory has been playing around with gender. Initially fascinated by drag, transgender, and transsexualism, and with Divas, Drag Kings, and key cross-genderists such as Del LaGrace Volcano and Kate Bornstein (1995), some of it has functioned almost as a kind of subversive terrorist drag. It arouses curious, unknown queered desires emancipating people from the constraints of the gendered tyranny of the presumed "normal body" (Volcano & Halberstam, 1999). Others have moved out to consider a wide array of playing with genders—from "faeries" and "bears," to leather scenes and the Mardi Gras, and on to the more commercialized/normalized drag for mass consumption: RuPaul, Lily Savage, and Graham Norton.

Sometimes performance may be seen as even more direct. It appears in the work of alternative documentaries, in "video terrorism" and "street theater," across cable talk shows, experimental artworks, and activist tapes. By the late 1980s, there was a significant expansion of lesbian and gay video (as well as film and film festivals), and in the academy, posts were created to deal with this—along with creation of more informal groupings. (See, for example, Jennie Livingston's film *Paris Is Burning* [1990], which looks at the "ball circuit" of poor gay men and transgenderists, usually black, in the late 1980s in New York City, or Ang Lee's *Wedding Banquet* [1993], which reconfigured the dominant "rice queen" image).[7]

Exploring New/Queered Case Studies. Queer theory also examines new case studies. Michael Warner, for example, looks at a range of case studies of emergent publics. One stands out to me: It is the details of a queer cabaret (a counter-public?) that involves "erotic vomiting." Suggesting a kind of "national heterosexuality" that, along with "family values," saturates much public talk, he argues that multiple queer cultures work to subvert these. He investigates the queer counter public of a "garden variety leather bar" where the routines are "spanking, flagellation, shaving, branding, laceration, bondage, humiliation, wrestling—as they say, you know, the usual" (Warner, 2002, pp. 206–210). But suddenly this garden-variety S&M bar is subverted by the less than usual: a cabaret of what is called erotic vomiting.

The Reading of the Self. Most of the researches within queer theory play with the author's self: It is rarely absent. D. A. Miller's (1998) account, for example, of the Broadway musical and the role its plays in queer life is an intensely personal account of the musical, including snapshots of the author as child, with the albums played.

What's New?

As interesting as many of these methods, theories, and studies most certainly are, I suggest that there is really very little that could be called truly new or striking here. Often, queer methodology means little more than literary theory rather belatedly coming to social science tools such as ethnography and reflexivity (although sometimes it is also a radical critique of orthodox social science—especially quantitative—methods). Sometimes it borrows some of the oldest of metaphors, such as drama. Queer theory does not seem to me to constitute any fundamental advance over recent ideas in qualitative inquiry—it borrows, refashions, and retells. What is more radical is its persistent concern with categories and gender/sexuality—although, in truth, this has long been questioned, too (cf. Plummer, 2002; Weston, 1998). What seems to be at stake, then, in any queering of qualitative research is not so much a methodological style as a political and substantive concern with gender, heteronormativity, and sexualities. Its challenge is to bring stabilized gender and sexuality to the forefront of analyses in ways they are not usually advanced and that put under threat any ordered world of gender and sexuality. This is just what is, indeed, often missing from much ethnographic or life story research.

The Troubles With Queer

Responses to queer theory have been mixed. It would not be too unfair to say that outside the world of queer theorists—the world of "straight academia"—queer theory has been more or less ignored and has had minimal impact. This has had the unfortunate consequence of largely ghettoizing the whole approach. Ironically, those who may most need to understand the working of the heterosexual-homosexual binary divide in their work can hence ignore it (and they usually do), whereas those who least need to understand it actively work to deconstruct terms that really describe themselves. Thus, it is comparatively rare in mainstream literary analysis or sociological theory for queer to be taken seriously (indeed, it has taken three editions of the *Handbook* to include something on it, and the so-called seventh moment of inquiry [see Lincoln & Denzin, Epilogue, this volume] has so far paid only lip service to it!).

More than this, many gays, lesbians, and feminists themselves see no advance at all in a queer theory that, after all, would simply "deconstruct" them, along with all their political gains, out of existence. Queer theorists often write somewhat arrogantly, as if they have a monopoly on political validity, negating both the political and theoretical gains of the past. Let me reflect on some of the standard objections to queer theory.

First, for many, the term itself is provocative: a pejorative and stigmatizing phrase from the past is reclaimed by that very same stigmatized grouping and had its meaning renegotiated; as such, it has a distinct generational overtone. Younger academics love it; older ones hate it. It serves to write off the past worlds of research and create new divisions.

Second, it brings a category problem, what Josh Gamson (1995) has described as a Queer Dilemma. He claims that there is simultaneously a need for a public collective identity (around which activism can galvanize) and a need to take apart and blur boundaries. As he says, fixed identity categories are the basis for both oppression and political power. Although it is important to stress the "inessential, fluid and multiple sited" forms of identity emerging within the queer movement, he also can see that there are very many from within the lesbian, gay, bisexual, and transgender movement (LGBT, as it is currently clumsily called) who also reject its tendency to deconstruct the very idea of gay and lesbian identity—hence abolishing a field of study and politics when it has only just gotten going.

There are also many radical lesbians who view it with even more suspicion, as it tends to work to make the lesbian invisible and to reinscribe tacitly all kinds of male power (in disguise), bringing back well-worn arguments about S&M, porn, and transgender politics as anti-women. Radical lesbian feminist Sheila Jeffreys (2003) is particularly scathing, seeing the whole queer movement as a serious threat to the gains of radical lesbians in the late 20th century. With the loss of the categories of woman-identified-woman and radical lesbian in a fog of (largely masculinist) queer deconstruction, it becomes impossible to see the roots of women's subordination to men. She also accuses it of a major elitism: The languages of most of its proponents ape the language of male academic elites, and lose all the gains that were made by the earlier, more accessible writings of feminists who wrote for and spoke to women in the communities, not just other academics. Lilian Faderman claims it is "resolutely elitist" and puts this well:

> The language queer scholars deploy sometimes seems transparently aimed at what lesbian feminists once called the "big boys" at the academy. Lesbian-feminist writing, in contrast, had as primary values clarity and accessibility, since its purpose was to speak directly to the community and in so doing reflect change. (1997, pp. 225–226).[8]

There are many other critics. Tim Edwards (1998) worries about a politics that often collapses into some kind of fan worship, celebration of cult films, and weak cultural politics. Stephen O. Murray hates the word "queer" itself because it perpetuates binary divisions and cannot avoid being a tool of domination, and he worries about excessive preoccupation with linguistics and with textual representation (2002, pp. 245–247). Even some of queer theory's founders now worry if the whole radical impulse has gotten lost and queer theory has become normalized, institutionalized, even "lucrative" within the academy (Halperin, 2003).

From many sides, then, doubts are being expressed that all is not well in the house of queer. There are problems that come with the whole project, and in some ways I still find the language of the humanists more conducive to social inquiry.

Queer Theory Meets Critical Humanism: The Conflictual Worlds of Research

Conflict is the gadfly of thought . . . a sine qua non of reflection and ingenuity.

— John Dewey (*Human Nature and Conduct*, p. 300)

And so we have two traditions seemingly at serious odds with each other. There is nothing unusual about this—all research positions are open to conflict from both within and without. Whereas humanism generally looks to experience, meaning, and human subjectivity, queer theory rejects this in favor of representations. Whereas humanism generally asks the researcher to get close to the worlds he or she is studying, queer theory almost pleads for distance—a world of texts, defamiliarization, and deconstruction. Whereas humanism brings a liberal democratic project with "justice for all," queer theory aims to prioritize the oppressions of sexuality and gender and urges a more radical change. Humanism usually favors a calmer conversation and dialogue, whereas queer is carnivalesque, parodic, rebellious, and playful. Humanism champions the voice of the public intellectual; queer theory is to be found mainly in the universities and its own self-generated social movement of aspiring academics.

Yet there are some commonalities. Both, for instance, would ask researchers to adopt a critically self-aware stance. Both would seek out a political and ethical background (even though, in a quite major way, they may differ on this—queer theory has a prime focus on radical gender change, and humanism is broader). And both assume the contradictory messiness of social life, such that no category system can ever do it justice.

On a closer look, several of the above differences overlap. Many critical humanisms can focus on representations (though fewer queer theorists are willing to focus on experience). Critical humanists often are seen as social constructionists, and this hardly can be seen as far removed from deconstructionists. There is no reason why critical humanism cannot take the value and political stances of queer theorists (I have and I do), but the moral baselines of humanism are wider and less specifically tied to gender. Indeed, contemporary humanistic method enters the social worlds of different "others" to work a catharsis of comprehension. It juxtaposes differences and complexities with similarities and harmonies. It recognizes the multiple possible worlds of social research—not necessarily the standard interviews or ethnographies, but the roles of photography, art, video, film, poetics, drama, narrative, autoethnography, music, introspection, fiction, audience participation, and street theater. It also finds multiple ways of presenting the "data," and it acknowledges that a social science of any consequences must be located in the political and moral dramas of its time. One of those political and moral dramas is "queer."

But there again, the histories, canons, and gurus of critical humanism and queer theory are indeed different, even though, in the end, they are not nearly as at odds with each other as one could be led to believe. Yes, they are not the same; and it is right that they should maintain some of their key differences. But no, they are not so very different either. It is no wonder, then, that I find that I can live with both. Contradiction, ambivalence, and tension reside in all critical inquiries.

▣ Notes

1. As Dmitri Shalin noted more than a decade ago, "The issues that symbolic interactionism has highlighted since its inception and that assured its maverick status in American sociology bear some uncanny resemblance to the themes championed by postmodernist thinkers" (1993, p. 303). It investigates "the marginal, local, everyday, heterogeneous and indeterminate" alongside the "socially constructed, emergent and plural" (p. 304). Likewise, David Maines (2001) has continued to sustain an earlier argument that symbolic interactionism, by virtue of its interpretive center, finds an easy affinity with much of postmodernism, but because of that same center, has no need for it (pp. 229–233). He finds valuable the resurgence of interest in interpretive work, the importance now given to writing "as intrinsic to method," the concern over multiple forms of presentation, and the reclaiming of value positions and "critical work" (Maines, 2001, p. 325). In addition, as is well known, Norman K. Denzin has been at the forefront in defending postmodernism within sociology/cultural studies and symbolic interactionism, in numerous books and papers (e.g., Denzin, 1989,1997, 2003).

2. For some, "interactionism" has become almost synonymous with sociology; see Maines (2001) and P. Atkinson and Housley (2003).

3. The liberal, humanist feminist philosopher Martha Nussbaum (1999, p. 41) suggests a long list of "human capabilities" that need cultivating for a person to function as a human being. These include concerns such as "bodily health and integrity" senses, imagination, and thought; emotions; practical reason; affiliation; concern for other species; play; control over one's environment; and life itself. To this I might add the crucial self-reflexive process, a process of communication that is central to the way we function.

4. In Bob Connell's rich study of *Masculinities* (1995)—a study that is far from being either avowedly "humanist" or "queer"—he takes life stories as emblematic/symptomatic of "crisis tendencies in power relations (that) threaten hegemonic masculinity directly" (p. 89). He looks at four groups of men under crisis—radical environmentalists, gay and bisexual networks, young working-class men, and men of the new class. Connell implies that I do not take this seriously (1995, p. 89). However, even in the first edition of my book *Documents of Life* (Plummer, 1983), I make it quite clear that among the contributions of the life story, it can be seen as a "tool for history," as a perspective on totality, and as a key focus on social change! (pp. 68–69).

5. Or, as Rupp and Taylor call it, "the tripartite model of cultural investigation" (2003, p. 223).

6. Likewise, I can sense a humanism at work in the writings of Cornel West, Jeffrey Weeks, Seyla Benhabib, Anthony Giddens, Zygmunt Bauman, Agnes Heller, Jürgen Habermas, Michel Bakhtin, and many others. Never mind the naming game, in which they have to come out as humanists (though some clearly do); what matters are the goals that they see will produce adequate understanding and social change for the better. In this respect, a lot of them read like humanists manqué.

7. See, for example, *Jump Cut*, *Screen*, *The Celluloid Closet*, *Now You See It?*, *The Bad Object Choices* collective, and the work of Tom Waugh and Pratibha Parmar.

8. See also Simon Watney's critiques to be found in *Imagine Hope* (2000). Watney is far from sympathetic to radical lesbianism, but his account has distinct echoes. Queer theory has often let down AIDS activism.

▣ References

Atkinson, P., & Housley, W. (2003). *Interactionism.* London: Sage.

Atkinson, R. (1998). *The life story interview.* Thousand Oaks, CA: Sage.

Bauman, Z. (1991). *Modernity and ambivalence.* Cambridge, UK: Polity.

Bauman, Z. (2000). *Liquid society.* Cambridge, UK: Polity.

Bauman, Z. (2004). *Wasted lives: Modernity and its outcasts.* Cambridge, UK: Polity.

Beck, U. (2003). *Individualization.* London: Sage.

Bornstein, K. (1995). *Gender outlaw.* New York: Vintage.

Bruyn, T. S. (1966). *The human perspective in sociology.* Englewood Cliffs, NJ: Prentice Hall.

Butler, J. (1990). *Gender trouble.* London: Routledge.

Carrington, C. (1999). *No place like home: Relationships and family life among lesbians and gay men.* Chicago: University of Chicago Press.

Clifford, J., & Marcus, G. E. (Eds.). (1986). *Writing culture.* Berkeley: University of California Press.

Coffey, A. (1999). *The ethnographic self: Fieldwork and the representation of identity.* London: Sage.

Cohen, S. (1999). *States of denial.* Cambridge, UK: Polity.

Coles, R. (1989). *The call of stories: Teaching and the moral imagination.* Boston: Houghton Mifflin.

Connell, R. W. (1995). *Masculinities.* Cambridge, UK: Polity.

Denzin, N. K. (1989). *Interpretive biography.* London: Sage.

Denzin, N. K. (1997). *Interpretive ethnography: Ethnographic practices for the 21st century.* London: Sage.

Denzin, N. K. (2003). *Performance ethnography.* London: Sage.

Denzin, N., & Lincoln, Y. (Eds.). (1994). *Handbook of qualitative research.* London: Sage.

Dewey, J. (1920). *Reconstruction of philosophy.* New York: Henry Holt.

Dewey, J. (1938). *Logic of inquiry.* New York: Henry Holt.

Dewey, J. (19XX). *Human nature and conduct.* New York: Henry Holt.

Doty, A. (1993). *Making things perfectly queer: Interpreting mass culture.* Minneapolis: University of Minnesota Press.

Doty, A. (2000). *Flaming classics: Queering the film canon.* London: Routledge.

Edwards, T. (1998). Queer fears: Against the cultural turn. *Sexualities, 1*(4), 471–484.

Ellis, C., & Flaherty, M. G. (Eds.). (1992). *Investigating subjectivity: Research on lived experience.* London: Sage.

Faderman, L. (1997). Afterword. In D. Heller (Ed.), *Cross purposes: Lesbians, feminists and the limits of alliance.* Bloomington: Indiana University Press.

Felice, W. F. (1996). *Taking suffering seriously.* Albany: State University of New York Press.

Foucault, M. (1979). *The history of sexuality.* Middlesex, UK: Harmondsworth.

Gamson, J. (1995). Must identity movements self-destruct?: A queer dilemma. *Social Problems, 42*(3), 390–407.

Gamson, J. (1998). *Freaks talk back: Tabloid talk shows and sexual nonconformity.* Chicago: University of Chicago Press.

Gever, M., Greyson, J., & Parmar, P. (Eds.). (1993). *Queer looks: Perspectives on lesbian and gay film and video.* New York: Routledge.

Giddens, A. (1991). *Modernity and self-identity.* Cambridge, UK: Polity.

Gouldner, A. (1973). *For sociology: Renewal and critique in sociology today.* London: Allen Lane.

Gubrium, J., & Holstein, J. (1997). *The new language of qualitative research.* Oxford, UK: Oxford University Press.

Halberstam, J. (1998). *Female masculinity.* Durham, NC: Duke University Press.

Halperin, D. (1995). *Saint Foucault: Towards a gay hagiography.* New York: Oxford University Press.

Halperin, D. (2003). The normalization of queer theory. *Journal of Homosexuality, 45*(2–4), 339–343.

Hertz, R. (Ed.). (1997). *Reflexivity and voice.* Thousand Oaks, CA: Sage.

Honneth, A. (1995). *The struggle for recognition: The moral grammar of social conflicts.* Cambridge, UK: Polity.

Humphreys, L. (1970). *Tearoom trade.* Chicago: Aldine.

Jackson, M. (1989). *Paths toward a clearing: Radical empiricism and ethnographic inquiry.* Bloomington: Indiana University Press.

Jeffreys, S. (2003). *Unpacking queer politics.* Oxford, UK: Polity.

Kong, T., Mahoney, D., & Plummer, K. (2002). Queering the interview. In J. F. Gubrium & J. A. Holstein (Eds.), *The handbook of interview research* (pp. 239–257). Thousand Oaks, CA: Sage.

Lambevski, S. A. (1999). Suck my nation: Masculinity, ethnicity and the politics of (homo)sex. *Sexualities, 2*(3), 397–420.

Lee, A. (Director). (1993). *The wedding banquet* [Motion picture]. Central Motion Pictures Corporation.

Lee, A. M. (1978). *Sociology for whom?* Oxford: Oxford University Press.

Lincoln, Y. S., & Denzin, N. K. (1994). The fifth moment. In N. K. Denzin & Y. S. Lincoln (Eds.), *Handbook of qualitative research* (pp. 575–586). Thousand Oaks, CA: Sage.

Livingston, J. (Director), & Livingston, J., & Swimar, B. (Producers). (1990). *Paris Is Burning* [Motion picture]. Off White Productions.

Maines, D. (2001). *The fault lines of consciousness: A view of interactionism in sociology.* New York: Aldine de Gruyter.

Miller, D. A. (1998). *Place for us: Essay on the Broadway musical.* Cambridge, MA: Harvard University Press.

Murray, S. O. (2002). Five reasons I don't take queer theory seriously. In K. Plummer (Ed.), *Sexualities: Critical concepts in sociology* (Vol. 3, pp. 245–247). London: Routledge.

Nardi, P. (1999). *Gay men's friendships: Invincible communities.* Chicago: University of Chicago Press.
Nisbet, R. (1976). *Sociology as an art form.* London: Heinemann.
Nussbaum, M. C. (1999). *Sex and social justice.* New York: Oxford University Press.
O'Neill, O. (2002). *A question of trust: The BBC Reith Lectures 2002.* Cambridge, UK: Cambridge University Press.
Plummer, K. (1983). *Documents of life.* London: Allen and Unwin.
Plummer, K. (1995). *Telling sexual stories.* London: Routledge.
Plummer, K. (2001). *Documents of life 2: An invitation to a critical humanism.* London: Sage.
Plummer, K. (Ed.). (2002). *Sexualities: Critical concepts in sociology* (4 vols.). London: Routledge.
Plummer, K. (2003). *Intimate citizenship.* Seattle: University of Washington Press.
Reed-Danahay, D. E. (Ed.). (1997). *Auto/ethnography: Rewriting the self and the social.* Oxford, UK: Berg.
Ronai, C. R. (1992). A reflexive self through narrative: A night in the life of an erotic dancer/researcher. In C. Ellis & M. G. Flaherty (Eds.), *Investigating subjectivity: Research on lived experience* (pp. 102–124). Newbury Park, CA: Sage.
Rorty, R. (1999). *Philosophy and social hope.* Middlesex, UK: Penguin.
Rupp, L., & Taylor, V. (2003). *Drag queens at the 801 Cabaret.* Chicago: University of Chicago Press.
Said, E. (2003). *Orientalism* (2nd ed.). New York: Cambridge.
Scheper-Hughes, N. (1994). *Death without weeping.* Berkeley: University of California Press.
Sedgwick, E. K. (1985). *Between men: English literature and male homosexual desire.* New York: Columbia University Press.
Sedgwick, E. K. (1990). *Epistemology of the closet.* Berkeley: University of California Press.
Sedgwick, E. K. (1994). *Tendencies.* London: Routledge.
Shalin, D. N. (1993). Modernity, postmodernism and pragmatic inquiry. *Symbolic Interaction, 16*(4), 303–332.
Smith, L. T. (1999). *Decolonizing methodologies: Research and indigenous peoples.* London: Zed Books.
Smyth, C. (1992). Lesbians talk queer notions. London: Scarlet Press.
Sullivan, N. (2003). *A critical introduction to queer theory.* Edinburgh: University of Edinburgh Press.
Tronto, J. (1993). *Moral boundaries: A political argument for an ethic of care.* London: Routledge.
Urry, J. (2000). *Sociology beyond societies: Mobilities for the twenty-first century.* London: Routledge.
Volcano, D. L., & Halberstam, J. (1999). *The drag king book.* London: Serpent's Tail.
Warner, M. (1991). *Fear of a queer planet: Queer politics and social theory.* Minneapolis: University of Minnesota.
Warner, M. (1992, June). From queer to eternity: An army of theorists cannot fail. *Voice Literary Supplement, 106,* pp. 18–26.
Warner, M. (1999). *The trouble with normal: Sex, politics, and the ethics of queer life.* Cambridge, MA: Harvard University Press.
Warner, M. (2002). *Public and counterpublics.* New York: Zone Books.
Watney, S. (2000). *Imagine hope: AIDS and gay identity.* London: Routledge.
West, C. (1999). The moral obligations of living in a democratic society. In D. B. Batstone & E. Mendieta (Eds.), *The good citizen* (pp. 5–12). London: Routledge.
Weston, K. (1998). *longslowburn: Sexuality and social science.* London: Routledge.
Wolcott, H. F. (2002). *Sneaky kid and its aftermath.* Walnut Creek, CA: AltaMira.

Part III

THE FUTURE OF QUALITATIVE RESEARCH

And so we come to the end, which is only the starting point for a new beginning. Several observations have structured our arguments to this point. The field of qualitative research continues to transform itself. The changes that took shape during the early 1990s are gaining momentum, even as they confront multiple forms of resistance during the first decade of this century. The gendered narrative turn has been taken. Foundational epistemologies, what Schwandt (1997, p. 40) calls epistemologies with the big *E*, have been replaced by constructivist, hermeneutic, feminist, poststructural, pragmatist, critical race, and queer theory approaches to social inquiry. Epistemology with a small *e* has become normative, displaced by discourses on ethics and values, conversations on and about the good, and conversations about the just and moral society.

We have argued throughout that qualitative inquiry is under assault from three sides. First, on the *political right* are the methodological conservatives who are connected to neoconservative governmental regimes. These critics support evidence-based, experimental methodologies or mixed methods. This stance consigns qualitative research to the methodological margins. Second, on the *epistemological right* are neotraditionalist methodologists who look with nostalgia at the Golden Age of qualitative inquiry. These critics find in the past all that is needed for inquiry in the present. Third, on the *ethical right* are mainstream biomedical scientists and traditional social science researchers who invoke a single ethical model for human subject research. The ethical right refuses to engage the arguments of those researchers who engage in collaborative, consciousness-raising, empowering inquiry.

Qualitative researchers in the seventh and eighth moments must navigate among these three oppositional forces, each of which threatens to deny the advances in qualitative research over the past three decades. These critics do not recognize the influences of indigenous, feminist, race, queer, and ethnic border studies. We need to protect ourselves from these criticisms. We also need to create spaces for dialogue and public scholarly engagement of these issues.

The chapters in this volume speak collectively to the great need for a compassionate, critical, interpretive civic social science. This is an interpretive social science that blurs both boundaries and genres. Its participants are committed to politically informed action research, inquiry directed to praxis and social change. Hence, as the reformist movement called qualitative research gains momentum, its places in the discourses of a free democratic society become ever more clear. With the action researchers, we seek a set of disciplined interpretive practices that will produce radical democratizing transformations in the public and private spheres of the global postcapitalist world. Qualitative research is the means to these ends. It is the bridge that joins multiple interpretive communities. It stretches across many different landscapes and horizons, moving back and forth between the public and the private, the sacred and the secular.

Paradigm shifts and dialogues have become a constant presence within and across the theoretical frameworks that organize both qualitative inquiry and the social and human sciences. The move to standpoint epistemologies has accelerated. No one still believes in the concept of a unified sexual subject or, indeed, of any unified subject. Epistemology has come out of the closet. The desire for critical, multivoiced, postcolonial ethnographies increases as capitalism extends its global reach.

We now understand that the civic-minded qualitative researcher uses a set of material practices that bring the world into play. These practices are not neutral tools. This researcher thinks historically and interactionally, always mindful of the structural processes that make race, gender, and class potentially repressive presences in daily life. The material practices of qualitative inquiry turn the researcher into a methodological (and epistemological) *bricoleur.* This person is an artist, a quilt maker, a skilled craftsperson, a maker of montages and collages. The interpretive bricoleur can interview, observe, study material culture, think within and beyond visual methods, write poetry or fiction, write autoethnography, construct narratives that tell explanatory stories, use qualitative computer software, do text-based inquiries, construct *testimonios* using focus group interviews, and even engage in applied ethnography and policy formulation.

It is apparent that the constantly changing field of qualitative research is defined by a series of tensions and contradictions as well as emergent understandings. These tensions and understandings have been felt in every chapter in this volume. Here, as in the first and second editions of the *Handbook,* we list many of them for purposes of summary only. They take the form of questions and assertions:

1. Will the performance turn in qualitative inquiry lead to performances that decolonize theory and help to deconstruct that global postcolonial world?
2. Will critical, indigenous interpretive paradigms, epistemologies, and pedagogies flourish in the eighth moment?

3. Will critical, indigenous interpretive paradigms, epistemologies, and pedagogies lead to the development and use of new inquiry practices, including counternarratives, autoethnographies, cultural poetics, and arts-based methodologies?

4. Can indigenous and nonindigenous qualitative researchers take the lead in decolonizing the academy?

5. Will the emphasis on multiple standpoint epistemologies and moral philosophies crystallize around a set of shared understandings concerning the contributions of qualitative inquiry to civil society, civic discourse, and critical race theory?

6. Will the criticisms from the methodological, political, and ethical conservatives stifle this field?

7. Will the performance turn in ethnography produce a shift away from attempts to represent the stream of consciousness, and the world of internal meanings, of the conscious subject?

8. How will feminist, communitarian, and indigenous ethical codes change institutional review boards (IRBs)? Will the two- and three-track IRB models become normative?

9. Will a new interpretive paradigm, with new methods and strategies of inquiry, emerge out of the interactions that exist between and among the many paradigms and perspectives we have presented in this volume?

10. How will indigenous, ethnic, queer, postcolonial, and feminist paradigms be fitted to this new synthesis if it comes?

11. Will the postmodern, antifoundational sensibility begin to form its own foundational criteria for evaluating the written and performed text?

12. When all universals, including the postmodern worldview, are gone in favor of local interpretations, how can we continue to talk and learn from one another?

There is no definitive answer to any of these questions. Here we can only suggest, in the barest of detail, our responses to them. In our concluding chapter (Epilogue), we elaborate these responses, grouping them around several basic themes or issues: text and voice, the existential sacred text, reflexivity and being in the text, working the hyphen, ethics and critical moral consciousness, and the textual subject, including our presence in the text. Examined from another angle, the 12 questions just listed focus on the social text, history, politics, ethics, the other, and interpretive paradigms more broadly.

Into the Future

Zygmunt Bauman (Chapter 15) reflexively moves qualitative inquiry (and sociology) into the new century, telling us that the work of the poet and the sociologist—and of history—is to uncover, in ever new situations, "human possibilities previously hidden." Writing and inquiry are not innocent practices. In its representational and political practices, qualitative inquiry, like sociology, makes visible the possibility of "living together differently with less misery or no misery. . . . Disclosure is the beginning—not the end—of the war against human misery." We have no choice; we are always already political, always already engaged. A neutral noncommitted form of inquiry is an impossibility. In a truly democratic society, Bauman observes (quoting Cornelius Castorladis), everyone is free to question "everything that is pre-given. . . . In such a society, all individuals are free to create for their lives the meanings they will." In such a society, qualitative inquiry becomes a vehicle for questioning all that is pre-given. Thus does Bauman lead us into the future.

▣ ▣ ▣

Douglas Holmes and George Marcus (Chapter 16) extend this argument, calling for a "refunctioning of ethnography," a regrounding of ethnography in the contemporary moment. They are quite explicit, observing that "a new set of regulative norms of fieldwork are needed to release ethnographers-in-the-making from the . . . imaginary" of classic ethnography. Contemporary ethnography could profitably be oriented to para-ethnography; that is, to the ecologies of knowledge, existing discourses, and local practices that are in place in field settings. The ethnographer finds the "literal field" by working through complex scenes, levels, and multiple sites that connect the local to the global.

Holmes and Marcus observe that recognizing the multisited nature of fieldwork produces a "rethinking of a whole set of issues in fieldwork—complicity instead of rapport, . . . the necessity of collaborations and their personal politics, the uneven distribution or depth of knowing, . . . the changing nature of the object of study, the grounding of abstract relations . . . in forms of human action and knowing." Thus do they offer terms of a refunctioned ethnography where subjects, now called para-ethnographers, are treated as experts, as collaborators and partners in research. They ground their interpretation of the para-ethnographer in the analysis of a famous political actor, the French nationalist Jean-Marie Le Pen.

Para-ethnography goes beyond merely identifying a new ethnographic subject. Rather, it opens the door for deeper questions of how "culture operates within a continuously unfolding contemporary." More deeply, and more radically, Holmes and Marcus believe that "spontaneously generated para-ethnographies are built into the structure of the contemporary and give form and content to a continuously unfolding skein of experience."

▣ ▣ ▣

The collapse of foundational epistemologies has led to emerging innovations in methodology. These innovations reframe what is meant by validity. They have shaped the call for increased textual reflexivity, greater textual self-exposure, multiple voicing, stylized forms of literary representation, and performance texts. These innovations shade into the next issues surrounding representation.

Representational issues involve how the other will be presented in the text. Representational strategies converge with a concern over the place of politics in the text. We can no longer separate ideology and politics from methodology. Methods always acquire their meaning within broader systems of meaning, from epistemology to ontology. These systems are themselves embedded in ethical and ideological frameworks as well as in particular interpretive communities. Our methods are always grafted into our politics.

Scientific practice does not stand outside ideology. As argued in the first and second editions of the *Handbook,* a poststructural social science project seeks its external grounding not in science but rather in a commitment to post-Marxism and an emancipatory feminism. A good text is one that invokes these commitments. A good text exposes how race, class, and gender work their ways into the concrete lives of interacting individuals.

We foresee a future where research becomes more relational, where working the hyphen becomes both easier and more difficult, for researchers are always on both sides of the hyphen. We also see a massive spawning of populist technology. This technology will serve to undermine qualitative inquiry as we know it, including disrupting what we mean by a stable subject (where is the cyberself located?). The new information technologies also increase the possibilities of dialogue and communication across time and space. We may be participating in the reconstruction of the social sciences. If so, qualitative inquiry is taking the lead in this reconstruction.

Finally, we predict that there will be no dominant form of qualitative textuality in the seventh and eighth moments; rather, several different hybrid textual forms will circulate alongside one another. The first form will be the classic, realist ethnographic text, redefined in poststructural terms. We will hear more from the first-person voice in these texts. The second hybrid textual form will blend and combine poetic, fictional, and performance texts into critical interventionist presentations. The third textual form will include testimonios and first-person (autoethnographic) texts. The fourth form will be narrative evaluation texts, which work back and forth between first-person voices and the testimonios. These forms will be evaluated in terms of an increasingly sophisticated set of local, indigenous, antifoundational, moral, and ethical criteria.

Variations on these textual forms will rest on a critical rethinking of the notion of the reflexive, self-aware subject. Lived experience cannot be studied directly. We study representations of experience—stories, narratives, performances, dramas. We have no direct access to the inner psychology and inner world of meanings of the reflexive subject. The subject in performance ethnographies becomes a performer. We study performers and performances, persons making meaning together, the how of culture as it connects persons in moments of cocreation and coperformance.

History, Paradigms, Politics, Ethics, and the Other

Many things are changing as we write our way out of writing culture and move into the eighth moment of qualitative research. Multiple histories and theoretical frameworks now circulate in this field, whereas before there were just a few. Today foundationalism and postpositivism are challenged and supplemented by a host of competing paradigms and perspectives. Many different applied action and participatory research agendas inform program evaluation and analysis.

We now understand that we study the other to learn about ourselves, and many of the lessons we have learned have not been pleasant. We seek a new body of ethical directives fitted to postmodernism. The old ethical codes failed to examine research as a morally engaged project. They never seriously located the researcher within the ruling apparatuses of society. A feminist, communitarian ethical system will continue to evolve, informed at every step by critical race, postcolonial, and queer theory sensibilities. Blatant voyeurism in the name of science or the state will continue to be challenged.

Performance-based cultural studies and critical theory perspectives, with their emphases on moral criticism, will alter the traditional empiricist foundations of qualitative research. The dividing line between science and morality will continue to be erased. A postmodern, feminist, poststructural communitarian science will move closer to a sacred science of the moral universe.

As we edge our way into the 21st century, looking back and borrowing Max Weber's metaphor, we see more clearly how we were trapped by the 20th century and its iron cage of reason and rationality. Like a bird in a cage, for too long we were unable to see the pattern in which we were caught. Coparticipants in a secular science of the social world, we became part of the problem. Entangled in the ruling apparatuses that we wished to undo, we perpetuated systems of knowledge and power that we found, underneath, to be all too oppressive. It is not too late to get out of the cage. Today we leave that cage behind.

And so do we enter, or leave, the eighth moment. In our concluding chapter (Epilogue), we elaborate our thoughts about the next generation of qualitative research.

Reference

Schwandt, T. A. (1997). *Qualitative inquiry.* Thousand Oaks, CA: Sage.

15

AFTERTHOUGHT

On Writing; on Writing Sociology

Zygmunt Bauman

The need in thinking is what makes us think.

—Theodor W. Adorno

Quoting the Czech poet Jan Skacel's opinion on the plight of the poet (who, in Skacel's words, only discovers the verses that "were always, deep down, there"), Milan Kundera comments (in *l'Art du roman,* [1986]): "To write, means for the poet to crush the wall behind which something that 'was always there' hides." In this respect, the task of the poet is not different from the work of history, which also discovers rather than "invents"; history, like poets, uncovers—in ever new situations—human possibilities previously hidden.

What history does matter-of-factly is a challenge, a task, and a mission for the poet. To rise to this mission, the poet must refuse to serve up truths known beforehand and well worn, truths already "obvious" because they have been brought to the surface and left floating there. It does not matter whether such truths "assumed in advance" are classified as revolutionary or dissident, Christian or atheist—or how right and proper, noble and just, they are or have been proclaimed to be. Whatever their denomination, those "truths" are not this "something hidden" that the poet is called to uncover; they are,

Author's Note. An earlier version of this essay was first published in *Theory, Culture and Society*, 2000, 1.

rather, parts of the wall that the poet's mission is to crush. Spokespersons for the obvious, self-evident, and "what we all believe, don't we?" are *false poets,* says Kundera. But what, if anything, does the poet's vocation have to do with the sociologist's calling? We sociologists rarely write poems. (Some of us who do take a leave of absence from our professional pursuits for the time of writing.) And yet if we do not wish to share the fate of "false poets" and resent being "false sociologists," we ought to come as close as the true poets do to the yet hidden human possibilities. For that reason, we need to pierce the walls of the obvious and self-evident, of that prevailing ideological fashion of the day whose commonality is taken for the proof of its sense. Demolishing such walls is as much the sociologist's calling as the poet's calling—and for the same reason; the walling up of possibilities belies human potential while obstructing the disclosure of its bluff.

Perhaps the verses that the poet seeks "were always there." One cannot be so sure, though, about the human potential discovered by history. Do humans—the makers and the made, the heroes and the victims of history—indeed carry forever the same volume of possibilities waiting for the right time to be disclosed? Or is it rather that, as human history goes, the opposition between discovery and creation is null and void and makes no sense? Because history is the endless process of human creation, is not history for the same reason (and by the same token) the unending process of human self-discovery? Is not the propensity to disclose/create ever new possibilities, to expand the inventory of possibilities already discovered and made real, the sole human potential that always has been, and always is, "already there"? The question of whether the new possibility has been created or "merely" uncovered by history is no doubt welcome nourishment to many a scholastic mind. As for history itself, it does not wait for an answer and can do quite well without one.

Niklas Luhmann's most seminal and precious legacy to fellow sociologists has been the notion of *autopoiesis–self-creation* (from Greek: do, create, give form, be effective; the opposite of suffering, being an object—not the source—of the act), meant to grasp and encapsulate the gist of the human condition. The choice of the term was itself a creation or discovery of the link (inherited kinship rather than chosen affinity) between history and poetry. Poetry and history are two parallel currents ("parallel" in the sense of the non-Euclidean universe ruled by Bolyai and Lobachevski's geometry) of that autopoiesis of human potentialities, in which creation is the sole form that discovery can take, whereas self-discovery is the principal act of creation.

Sociology, one is tempted to say, is a third current running in parallel with those two. Or at least this is what it should be if it is to stay inside that human condition that it tries to grasp and make intelligible. This is what it has tried to become since its inception, although it has been repeatedly diverted from trying by mistaking the seemingly impenetrable and not-yet-decomposed walls for the ultimate limits of human potential and going out of its way to reassure the garrison commanders and the troops they command that the lines they have drawn to set aside the off-limits areas will never be transgressed.

Alfred de Musset suggested nearly two centuries ago that "great artists have no country." Two centuries ago, these were militant words, a war cry of sorts. They were written down amid deafening fanfares of youthful and credulous, and for that reason arrogant and pugnacious, patriotism. Numerous politicians were discovering their vocation in building nation-states of one law, one language, one worldview, one history, and one future. Many poets and painters were discovering their mission in nourishing the tender sprouts of national spirit, resurrecting long-dead national traditions or conceiving of brand-new ones that never lived before, and offering the nation as not-yet-fully-enough-aware-of-being-a-nation the stories, the tunes, the likenesses, and the names of heroic ancestors—something to share, love, and cherish in common and so to lift the mere living together to the rank of belonging together, opening the eyes of the living to the beauty and sweetness of belonging by prompting them to remember and venerate their dead and to rejoice in guarding their legacy. Against that background, de Musset's blunt verdict bore all the marks of a rebellion and a call to arms; it summoned his fellow writers to refuse cooperation with the enterprise of the politicians, the prophets, and the preachers of closely guarded borders and gun-bristling trenches. I do not know whether de Musset intuited the fratricidal capacities of the kind of fraternities that nationalist politicians and ideologists laureate were determined to build or whether his words were but an expression of the intellectual's disgust with and resentment of narrow horizons, backwaters, and parochial mentality. Whatever the case then, when read now with the benefit of hindsight through a magnifying glass stained with the dark blots of ethnic cleansings, genocides, and mass graves, de Musset's words seem to have lost nothing of their topicality, challenge, and urgency, nor have they lost any of their original controversiality. Now, as then, they aim at the heart of the writers' mission and challenge their consciences with the question decisive for any writer's *raison d'être.*

A century and a half later, Juan Goytisolo, probably the greatest among living Spanish writers, took up the issue once more. In a recent interview ("Les batailles de Juan Goytisolo" in *Le Monde,* February 12, 1999), he points out that once Spain had accepted, in the name of Catholic piety and under the influence of the Inquisition, a highly restrictive notion of national identity, the country became, toward the end of the 16th century, a "cultural desert." Let us note that Goytisolo writes in Spanish but for many years lived in Paris and in the United States before finally settling in Morocco. And let us note that no other Spanish writer has had so many of his works translated into Arabic. Why? Goytisolo has no doubt about the reason. He explains, "Intimacy and distance create a privileged situation. Both are necessary." Although each for a different reason, both these qualities make their presence felt in Goytisolo's relations to his native Spanish and acquired Arabic, French, and English—the languages of the countries that, in succession, became his chosen substitute homes.

Because Goytisolo spent a large part of his life away from Spain, the Spanish language ceased for him to be the all-too-familiar tool of daily, mundane, and ordinary communication, always at hand and calling for no reflection. His intimacy with his childhood language was not—and could not be—affected, but now it has been supplemented with distance. The Spanish language became the authentic homeland in his exile, a territory that was known and felt and lived through from the inside and yet, because it also became remote and was full of surprises and exciting discoveries. That intimate/distant territory lends itself to the cool and detached scrutiny *sine ira et studio*, laying bare the pitfalls and the yet untested possibilities invisible in vernacular uses, showing previously unsuspected plasticity, admitting and inviting creative intervention. It is the combination of intimacy and distance that allowed Goytisolo to realize that the unreflexive immersion in a language—just the kind of immersion that exile makes all but impossible—is fraught with dangers: "If one lives only in the present, one risks disappearing together with the present." It was the "outside" detached look at his native language that allowed Goytisolo to step beyond the constantly vanishing present and so to enrich his Spanish in a way that otherwise was unlikely, perhaps altogether inconceivable. He brought back into his prose and poetry ancient terms, long fallen into disuse, and by doing so blew away the storeroom dust that had covered them, wiped out the patina of time, and offered the words' new and previously unsuspected (or long forgotten) vitality.

In *La Contre Allée*, a book published recently in cooperation with Catherine Malabou, Jacques Derrida invites his readers to think in *travel*—or, more exactly, to "think travel." That means to think that unique activity of departing, going away from *chez soi*, going far toward the unknown, taking all of the risks, pleasures, and dangers that the "unknown" has in store (even the risk of not returning).

Derrida is obsessed with "being away." There is some reason to surmise that the obsession was born when, in 1942, the 12-year-old Derrida was sent down from the school that, by the decree of the Vichy administration of North Africa, was ordered to purify itself of Jewish pupils. This is how Derrida's "perpetual exile" started. Since then, Derrida has divided his life between France and the United States. In the United States, he was a Frenchman. In France, however hard he tried to avoid it, time and time again the Algerian accent of his childhood kept breaking through his exquisite French *parole*, betraying a *pied noir* hidden under the thin skin of the Sorbonne professor. (This is, some people think, why Derrida came to extol the superiority of writing and composed the axiological myth of priority to support the axiological assertion.) Culturally, Derrida was to remain "stateless." This did not mean, though, having no cultural homeland. Quite the contrary; being "culturally stateless" meant having more than one homeland, building a home of one's own on the crossroads between cultures. Derrida became and remained a *métèque*—a cultural hybrid. His "home on the crossroads" was built of language.

Building a home on cultural crossroads proved to be the best conceivable occasion to put language to tests it seldom passes elsewhere, to see through its otherwise unnoticed qualities, to find out what language is capable of and what promises it makes but can never deliver. From that home on the crossroads came the exciting and eye-opening news about the inherent plurality and undecidability of sense (in *l'Ecriture et la différence*), about the endemic impurity of origins (in *De la grammatologie*), and about the perpetual unfulfillment of communication (in *La Carte postale*), as Christian Delacampagne notes in *Le Monde* (March 12, 1999).

Goytisolo's and Derrida's messages are different from that of de Musset. It is not true, the novelist and the philosopher suggest in unison, that great art has no homeland; on the contrary, art, like the artists, may have many homelands and most certainly has more than one. Rather than homelessness, the trick is to be at home in many homes but to be in each inside and outside at the same time, to combine intimacy with the critical look of an outsider, involvement, with detachment—a trick that sedentary people are unlikely to learn. Learning the trick is the chance of the exile— *technically* one that is *in* but not *of* the place. The unconfinedness that results from this condition (that *is* this condition) reveals the homely truths to be manmade and unmade and reveals the mother tongue to be an endless stream of communication between generations and a treasury of messages always richer than any of their readings and forever waiting to be unpacked anew.

George Steiner has named Samuel Beckett, Jorge Luis Borges, and Vladimir Nabokov as among the greatest contemporary writers. What unites them and what made them all great, he says, is that each of the three moved with equal ease—was equally "at home" in several linguistic universes, not one. (A reminder is in order here. "Linguistic universe" is a pleonastic phrase; the universe in which each one of us lives is, and cannot be anything but, "linguistic"—made of words. Words light the islands of visible forms in the dark sea of the invisible and mark the scattered spots of relevance in the formless mass of the insignificant. It is words that slice the world into the classes of nameable objects and bring out their kinship or enmity, closeness or distance, affinity or mutual estrangement. And so long as they stay alone in the field, they raise all such artifacts to the rank of reality—the only reality there is.) One needs to live, to visit, to know intimately more than one such universe to spy out human invention behind any universe's imposing and apparently indomitable structure and to discover just how much human cultural effort is needed to divine the idea of nature with its laws and necessities—all that is required to muster, in the end, the audacity and the determination to join in that cultural effort *knowingly*, aware of its risks and pitfalls but also of the boundlessness of its horizons.

To create (and so also to discover) always means breaking a rule; following a rule is mere routine, more of the same—not an act of creation. For the exile, breaking rules is not a matter of free choice but rather an eventuality that cannot be avoided. Exiles do not know enough of the rules reigning in their country of arrival, nor do they treat these rules unctuously enough for their efforts to observe them and conform to be perceived as genuine and approved. As for their country of origin, going into exile has been recorded there as their original sin, in the light of which all that the sinners later may do may be taken down and used against them as evidence of their rule breaking. By commission or by omission, rule breaking becomes a trademark of the exiles. This is unlikely to endear them to the natives of any of the countries between which their life itineraries are plotted. But paradoxically, it also allows them to bring to all of the countries involved gifts that they need badly without even knowing it—gifts that they could hardly expect to receive from any other source.

Let me clarify. The "exile" under discussion here is not necessarily a case of physical bodily mobility. It may involve leaving one country for another, but it need not. As Christine Brook-Rose puts it (in her essay "Exsul"), the distinguishing mark of all exile, and particularly the writer's exile (i.e., the exile articulated in words and thus made into a communicable *experience*) is the refusal to be integrated—the determination to stand out from the physical space, to conjure up a place of one's own, different from the place in which those around are settled, a place unlike the places left behind and unlike the place of arrival. The exile is defined not in relation to any particular physical space, or to the oppositions among a number of physical spaces, but rather through the autonomous stand taken toward space as such. Ultimately, asks Brooke-Rose, is not every poet or "poetic" (exploring, rigorous) novelist an exile of sorts, looking in from outside into a bright desirable image in the mind's eye, of the little world created, for the space of the writing effort and the shorter space of the reading? This kind of writing, often at odds with publishers and the public, is the last solitary, nonsocialized creative art.

The resolute determination to stay "nonsocialized"; the consent to integrate solely with the condition of nonintegration; the resistance—often painful and agonizing, yet ultimately victorious—to the overwhelming pressure of the place, old or new; the rugged defense of the right to pass judgment and choose; the embracing of ambivalence or calling ambivalence into being—these are, we may say, the constitutive features of exile. Note that all of them refer to attitude and life strategy and to spiritual mobility rather than physical mobility.

Michel Maffesoll (in *Du nomadisme: Vagabondages initiatiques,* 1997) writes of the world we *all* inhabit nowadays as a "floating territory" in which "fragile individuals" meet "porous reality." In this territory, only such things or persons may fit as are fluid, ambiguous, in a state of perpetual becoming, and in a constant state of self-transgression. "Rootedness," if any, can be only dynamic; it needs to be restated and reconstituted daily, precisely through the repeated act of "self-distantiation"—that foundational, initiating act of "being in travel," on the road. Having compared all of us—the inhabitants of the present-day world—to nomads, Jacques Attali (in *Chemins de sagesse,* 1996) suggests that, apart from traveling light and being kind, friendly, and hospitable to strangers whom they meet on their way, nomads must be constantly on the watch, remembering that their camps are vulnerable and have no walls or trenches to stop intruders. Above all, nomads, struggling to survive in the world of nomads, need to grow used to the state of continuous disorientation and to traveling along roads of unknown direction and duration, seldom looking beyond the next turn or crossing. They need to concentrate all of their attention on that small stretch of road that they need to negotiate before dusk.

"Fragile individuals," doomed to conduct their lives in a "porous reality," feel like skating on thin ice, and "in skating over thin ice," Ralph Waldo Emerson remarks in his essay "Prudence," "our safety is in our speed." Individuals, whether fragile or not, need safety, crave safety, and seek safety, and so they try, to the best of their ability, to maintain a high speed in whatever they do. When running among fast runners, slowing down means being left behind; when running on thin ice, slowing down also means the real threat of being drowned. Speed, therefore, climbs to the top of the list of survival values.

Speed, however, is not conducive to thinking, not to thinking far ahead, not to long-term thinking at any rate. Thought calls for pause and rest, for "taking one's time," recapitulating the steps already taken, and looking closely at the place reached and the wisdom (or imprudence, as the case may be) of reaching it. Thinking takes one's mind away from the task at hand, which is always the running and keeping speed and whatever else it may be. And in the absence of thought, the skating on thin ice, which is the *fate* of fragile individuals in the porous world, may well be mistaken for their *destiny.*

Taking one's fate for destiny, as Max Scheler insists in his *Ordo amoris,* is a grave mistake: "Destiny of man is not his fate. . . . The assumption that fate and destiny are the same deserves to be called fatalism." Fatalism is an error of judgment because in fact fate has "a natural and basically comprehensible origin." Moreover, although fate is not a matter of free choice, and particularly of individual free choice, it "*grows up* out of the life of a man or a people." To see all that, to note the difference and the gap between fate and destiny, and to escape the trap of fatalism, one needs resources not easily attainable when running on thin ice—"time off" to think and a distance allowing a long view. "The image of our destiny," Scheler warns, "is thrown into relief only in the recurrent traces left when we turn away from it." Fatalism, however, is a self-corroborating attitude; it makes the "turning away," that *conditio sine qua non* of thinking, appear useless and unworthy of trying.

Taking distance and taking time to separate destiny and fate, to emancipate destiny from fate, and to make destiny free to confront fate and challenge it—this is the calling of sociology. And this is what sociologists may do if they consciously, deliberately, and earnestly strive to reforge the calling they have joined—their fate—into their destiny.

"Sociology is the answer. But what was the question?" states—and asks—Ulrich Beck in *Politik in der Risikogesellschaft.* A few pages previously, Beck seems to articulate the question he seeks—the chance of a democracy that goes beyond "expertocracy," a kind of democracy that "begins where debate and decision making are opened about whether we *want* a life under the conditions that are being presented to us."

This chance is under a question mark not because someone has deliberately and malevolently shut the door on such a debate and prohibited an informed decision taking; hardly ever in the past was the freedom to speak out and to come together to discuss matters of common interest as complete and unconditional as it is now. The point is, though, that more than a formal freedom to talk and pass resolutions is needed for the kind of democracy that Beck thinks is our imperative to start in earnest. We also need to know what it is we need to talk about and what the resolutions we pass ought to be concerned with. And all of this needs to be done in our type of society, in which the authority to speak and resolve issues is the reserve of experts who own the exclusive right to pronounce on the difference between reality and fantasy and to set apart the possible from the impossible. (Experts, we may say, are almost by definition people who "get the facts straight," who take the facts as they come and think of the least risky way of living in their company.)

Why this is not easy, and is unlikely to become easier unless something is done, Beck explains in his *Risikogesellscbaft: auf dem Weg andere Moderne:* "What food is for hunger, eliminating risks, *or interpreting them away,* is for the consciousness of risks." In a society haunted primarily by material want, such an option between "eliminating" misery and "interpreting it away" did not exist. In our society, haunted by risk rather than want, it does exist—and is taken daily. Hunger cannot be assuaged by denial; in hunger, subjective suffering and its objective cause are indissolubly linked, and the link is self-evident and cannot be belied. But risks, unlike material want, are not subjectively experienced; at least, they are not "lived" directly unless they are mediated by knowledge. They may never reach the realm of subjective experience. They may be trivialized or downright denied before they arrive there, and the chance that they will indeed be barred from arriving *grows* together with the extent of the risks.

What follows is that *sociology is needed today more than ever before.* The job in which sociologists are the experts—the job of restoring to view the lost link between objective affliction and subjective experience—has become more vital and indispensable than ever, while being less likely than ever to be performed without their professional help, because its performance by the spokesmen and practitioners of other fields of expertise has become utterly improbable. If all experts deal with practical problems and all expert knowledge is focused on their resolution, sociology is one branch of expert knowledge where the practical problem it struggles to resolve is *enlightenment aimed at human understanding.* Sociology is perhaps the sole field of expertise in which (as Pierre Bourdieu pointed out in *La Misère du monde*) Dilthey's famed distinction between *explanation* and *understanding* has been overcome or cancelled.

To understand one's fate means to be aware of its difference from one's destiny. And to understand one's fate is to know the complex network of causes that brought about that fate and its difference from that destiny. To work in the world, as distinct from being "worked out and about" by it, one needs to know how the world works.

The kind of enlightenment that sociology is capable of delivering is addressed to freely choosing individuals and aimed at enhancing and reinforcing their freedom of choice. Its immediate objective is to reopen the allegedly shut case of explanation and so to promote understanding. It is the self-formation and self-assertion of individual men and women, the preliminary condition of their ability to decide whether they want the kind of life that has been presented to them as their fate, that may gain in vigor, effectiveness, and rationality as a result of sociological enlightenment. The cause of the autonomous society may profit together with the cause of the autonomous individual; they can only win or lose together.

To quote from Cornelius Castorladis's *Le Délabrement de l'Occident:*

> An autonomous society, a truly democratic society, is a society which questions everything that is pre-given and by the same token *liberates the creation of new meanings.* In such a society, all individuals are free to create for their lives the meanings they will (and can).

Society is truly autonomous once it "knows, must know, that there are no 'assured' meanings, that it lives on the surface of chaos, that it itself is a chaos seeking a form, but a form that is never fixed once for all." The absence of guaranteed meanings—of absolute truths, of preordained norms of conduct, of predrawn borderlines between right and wrong no longer needing attention, of guaranteed rules of successful action—is the *conditio sine qua non* of, simultaneously, a truly autonomous society and truly free individuals; autonomous society and the freedom of its members depend on each other. Whatever safety democracy and individuality muster depends not on fighting the endemic contingency and uncertainty of human condition but rather on recognizing it and facing its consequences point blank.

If orthodox sociology, born and developed under the aegis of solid modernity, was preoccupied with the conditions of human obedience and conformity, then the prime concern of sociology made to measure of liquid modernity needs to be the promotion of autonomy and freedom; such sociology must, therefore, put individual self-awareness, understanding, and *responsibility* at its focus. For the denizens of modern society in its solid and managed phase, the major opposition was one between conformity and deviance. For the major opposition of modern society in its present-day liquefied and decentered phase, the opposition that needs to be faced up to so as to pave the way to a truly autonomous society is one between taking up responsibility and seeking a shelter where responsibility for one's own actions need not be taken by the actors.

That other side of the opposition, seeking shelter, is a seductive option and a realistic prospect. Alexis de Tocqueville (in the second volume of his *De la démocratie en Amerique*), notes that if selfishness, that bane haunting humankind during all periods of its history, "desiccated the seeds of all virtues," then individualism, a novel and typically modern affliction, dries up only "the source of public virtues"; the individuals affected are busy cutting out small companies for their own use, while leaving the "great society" to its own fate. The temptation to do so has grown considerably since de Tocqueville jotted down his observation.

Living among a multitude of competing values, norms, and lifestyles without a firm and reliable guarantee of being in the right is hazardous and commands a high psychological price. No wonder that the attraction of the second response—of hiding from the requisites of responsible choice—gathers in strength. As Julia Kristeva puts it (in *Nations Without Nationalism*), "It is a rare person who does not invoke a primal shelter to compensate for personal disarray." And we all, to a greater or lesser extent, sometimes more and sometimes less, find ourselves in that state of personal disarray. Time and again, we dream of a "great simplification." Unprompted, we engage in regressive fantasies of which the images of the prenatal womb and the walled-up home are prime inspirations. The search for a primal shelter is "the other" of responsibility, just like deviance and rebellion were the other of conformity. The yearning for a primal shelter these days has come to replace rebellion, which has now ceased to be a sensible option. As Pierre Rosanvallon points out (in a new preface to his classic *Le Capitalisme utopique*), there is no longer a "commanding authority to depose and replace. There seems to be no room left for a revolt, as social fatalism vis-à-vis the phenomenon of unemployment testifies."

Signs of malaise are abundant and salient, yet as Pierre Bourdieu observes repeatedly, they seek in vain a legitimate expression in the world of politics. Short of articulate expression, they need to be read out, obliquely, from the outbursts of xenophobic and racist frenzy—the most common manifestations of the primal shelter nostalgia. The available, and no less popular, alternative to neotribal moods of scapegoating and militant intolerance—the exit from politics and the withdrawal to behind the fortified walls of the private—is no longer prepossessing and, above all, no longer an adequate response to the genuine source of the ailment. And so it is at this point that sociology, with its potential for explanation that promotes understanding, comes into its own more than at any other time in its history.

According to the ancient but never bettered Hippocratic tradition, as Pierre Bourdieu reminds the readers of *La Misère du monde,* genuine medicine begins with the recognition of the invisible disease—"facts of which the sick does not speak or forgets to report." What is needed in the case of sociology is the "revelation of the structural causes which the apparent signs and talks disclose only through distorting them (*ne devoilent qu'en les voilant*). One needs to see through—explain and understand—the sufferings characteristic of the social order that "no doubt pushed back the great misery (though as much as it is often said), while . . . at the same time multiplying the social spaces . . . offering favourable conditions to the unprecedented growth of all sorts of little miseries."

To diagnose a disease does not mean the same as curing it. This general rule applies to sociological diagnoses as much as it does to medical verdicts. But one should note that the illness of society differs from bodily illnesses in one tremendously important respect: In the case of an ailing social order, the absence of an adequate diagnosis (elbowed out or silenced by the tendency to "interpret away" the risks spotted by Ulrich Beck) is a crucial, perhaps decisive, part of the disease. As Cornelius Castorladis famously puts it, society is ill if it stops questioning itself. And it cannot be otherwise considering that—whether it knows it or not—society is autonomous (its institutions are nothing but human-made and so, potentially, human-unmade) and that suspension of self-questioning bars the awareness of autonomy while promoting the illusion of heteronomy with its unavoidably fatalistic consequences. To restart questioning means to take a long step toward the cure. If in the history of human condition discovery equals creation, if in thinking about the human condition explanation and understanding are one, then in the efforts to improve human condition diagnosis and therapy merge.

Pierre Bourdieu expressed this perfectly in the conclusion of *La Misère du monde:* "To become aware of the mechanisms which make life painful, even unlivable, does not mean to neutralize them; to bring to light the contradictions does not mean to resolve them." And yet, skeptical as one can be about the social effectiveness of the sociological message, the effects of allowing those who suffer to discover the possibility of relating their sufferings to social causes cannot be denied, nor can one dismiss the effects of becoming aware of the social origin of unhappiness "in all its forms, including the most intimate and most secret of them."

Nothing is less innocent, Bourdieu reminds us, than laissez-faire. Watching human misery with equanimity while placating the pangs of conscience with the ritual incantation of the TINA ("there is no alternative") creed means complicity. Whoever willingly or by default partakes in the cover-up or, worse still, the denial of the human-made, noninevitable, contingent, and alterable nature of social order, notably the kind of order responsible for unhappiness, is guilty of immorality—of refusing help to a person in danger.

Doing sociology and writing sociology are aimed at disclosing the possibility of living together differently with less misery or no misery— the possibility that is daily withheld, overlooked, or unbelieved. Not seeing, not seeking, and thereby suppressing this possibility is itself part of human misery and a major factor in its perpetuation. Its disclosure does not by itself predetermine its use. Also, when known, possibilities might not be trusted enough to be put to the test of reality. Disclosure is the beginning—not the end—of the war against human misery. But that war cannot be waged in earnest, let alone with a chance of at least partial success, unless the scale of human freedom is revealed and recognized so that freedom can be fully deployed in the fight against the social sources of all, including the most individual and private—unhappiness.

There is no choice between "engaged" and "neutral" ways of doing sociology. A noncommittal sociology is an impossibility. Seeking a morally neutral stance among the many brands of sociology practiced today, brands stretching all the way from the outspokenly libertarian to the staunchly communitarian, would be a vain effort. Sociologists may deny or forget the worldview effects of their work, and the impact of that view on human singular or joint actions, only at the expense of forfeiting that responsibility of choice that every other human faces daily. The job of sociology is to see to it that the choices are genuinely free and that they remain so—increasingly so—for the duration of humanity.

Notes

1. Herbert Marcuse, "Liberation from the Affluent Society," quoted from *Critical Theory and Society: A Reader,* edited by Stephen Eric Bronner and Douglas MacKay Kellner (London: Routledge, 1989), p. 277.

2. David Conway, *Classical Liberalism: The Unvanquished Ideal* (New York: St. Martin's, 1955), p. 48.

3. Charles Murray, *What It Means to Be a Libertarian: A Personal Interpretation* (New York: Broadway Books, 1997), p. 32. See also Jeffrey Friedman's pertinent comments in "What's Wrong with Libertarianism," *Critical Review,* Summer 1997, pp. 407–467.

4. From *Sociologie et philosophie* (1924). Here quoted in *Emile Durkheim: Selected Writings,* translated by Anthony Giddens (Cambridge, UK: Cambridge University Press, 1972), p. 115.

5. Erich Fromm, *Fear of Freedom* (London: Routledge, 1960), pp. 51, 67.

6. Richard Sennett, *The Corrosion of Character: The Personal Consequences of Work in the New Capitalism* (New York: Norton, 1998), p. 44.

7. Giles Deleuze and Felix Guattari, *Anti-Oedipus: Capitalism and Schizophrenia,* translated by Robert Hurley (New York: Viking, 1977), p. 42.

8. Alain Touraine, "Can We Live Together, Equal and Different?" *European Journal of Social Theory,* November 1998, p. 177.

9. (Frankfurt am Main, Germany: Suhrkamp, 1986); Ulrich Beck, *Risk Society: Towards a New Modernity,* translated by Mark Ritter (London: Sage, 1998), p. 138.

10. See Jean-Paul Besset and Pascale Kremer, "Le Nouvel attrait pour les residences 'sécurisées'," *Le Monde,* 15 May 1999, p. 10.

11. Richard Sennett, "The Myth of Purified Community," in *The Uses of Disorder: Personal Identity and City Style* (London: Faber & Faber, 1996), pp. 36, 39.

12. Quoted from *Emile Durkheim: Selected Writings,* edited by Anthony Giddens (Cambridge, UK: Cambridge University Press, 1972), pp. 94, 115.

13. See Jim MacLaughlin, "Nation-Building, Social Closure, and Anti-Traveller Racism in Ireland," *Sociology,* February 1999, pp. 129–151.

14. See Jean Clair, "De Guernica à Belgrade," *Le Monde,* 21 May 1999, p. 16.

15. *Newsweek,* 21 June 1999.

16. See Chris Bird, "Serbs Flee Kosovo Revenge Attacks," *The Guardian,* 17 July 1999.

17. See Daniel Vernet, "Les Balkans face au risque d'une tourmente sans fin," *Le Monde,* 15 May, p. 18

18. Ibid.

19. Eric Hobsbawm, "The Nation and Globalization," *Constellations,* March 1998, pp. 4–5.

20. Rene Girard, *La Violence et le sacre* (Paris: Grasset, 1972). Here quoted from *Violence and the Sacred,* translated by Patrick Gregory (Baltimore, MD: Johns Hopkins University Press, 1979), pp. 8, 12–13.

21. Arne Johan Vetlesen, "Genocide: A Case for the Responsibility of the Bystander," unpublished manuscript, July 1998.

22. Arne Johan Vetlesen, "Yugoslavia, Genocide, and Modernity," unpublished manuscript, January 1999.

16

REFUNCTIONING ETHNOGRAPHY

The Challenge of an Anthropology of the Contemporary

Douglas R. Holmes and George E. Marcus

We begin this chapter with some basic orientations that are driving our work these days. Part of it is sticking with the so-called *Writing Culture* critiques of anthropology (Clifford & Marcus, 1986) and trying to figure out what are their most productive legacies in the present. Part of it has to do with the changing circumstances of producing anthropological research that we experience every day in the supervision of graduate students. And relatedly, part of it has to do with contemplating the systematic changes that are necessary in the practice of ethnography to accommodate the kinds of new social and cultural formations that are emerging within frames of work that are conceived distinctively as contemporary. We see a need to "refunction ethnography" or at least to provide it with an alternative formulation to the classic Malinowskian one so as to address certain problems of research. We are pursuing this as a project by producing a series of small studies and discussion papers (Holmes, 1993; Holmes & Marcus, 2004; Marcus, 1999b, 1999d, 2001, 2002a, 2002b, 2003).

Beyond Malinowski's Staging

Early in the essay in *Argonauts of the Western Pacific*, in which fieldwork is evoked and its practices are inculcated, Malinowski (1928/1961) intones, "Imagine yourself, suddenly set down surrounded by all your gear, alone on a tropical beach close to a native village, while the launch or dinghy which has brought you sails away out of sight" (p. 46). Anthropologists have always thought about each other's fieldwork and about teaching it to initiates not just in terms of stories or tales of the field but also, in more analytic moments, strongly in terms of images and scenarios. Such a dramaturgical regime of method is most effective when the experience of fieldwork actually corresponds at least roughly to the imaginary that anthropologists make out of what they report to each other from distant experiences that are theirs alone. There is a great premium placed on ethnography that is able to set scenes that can be entered through concretely visualized and situated thought experiments.

Another distinctive, if not peculiar, aspect of the professional lore about fieldwork in anthropology is that it is highly specific and richly evoked for the early phases of fieldwork experience with the image (as per Malinowski) of "first contact" and heightened otherness in mind. The initiate's experience of fieldwork is how the imaginary is slanted, even when it expresses the experience of seasoned field-workers. But what about the continuing research of an anthropologist who has been working in a particular site for a decade or even decades? Is there any model of method in anthropology for what fieldwork is like for the virtuoso? Is it even recognizable as fieldwork according to the Malinowskian mise-en-scène? Our point is that the later work of mature ethnographers usually operates free of the tropes of their earlier work. And we would argue that somehow initiatory fieldwork in certain arenas where many younger anthropologists are working today requires something of the more diffuse and open idea of what fieldwork can be that seems to be characteristic of virtuoso fieldwork, if only it were articulated in the traditional imaginary under which ethnographers-in-the-making train. So this is a problem of pedagogy. Students now enter anthropology inspired by complex social and cultural theories from the interdisciplinary ferment of the 1980s and early 1990s, as well as by the examples of mature second and third works of senior anthropologists—themselves deeply influenced by this period of interdisciplinary ferment—that they admire and want to emulate, and then are faced with a still powerful culture of method that insists that they do something less ambitious. We insist that a new set of regulative norms of fieldwork are needed to release ethnographers-in-the-making from the emphatic and vivid "being there-ness" of the classic imaginary of fieldwork.

Now, turning to the actual challenges to the traditional fieldwork imaginary, what in the world (today) has led to fieldwork's entanglements in multiple and heterogeneous sites of investigation and in complicitous forms of collaboration that have changed markedly what anthropologists want from "natives" as subjects and have deeply compromised claims to authoritative knowledge even of the revised sorts reinstantiated by the reflexive critiques of the 1980s? The conventional understanding of these developments has lain in certain presumptions about the nature of postmodernity that circulated widely in the arenas of interdisciplinary work of the past two decades, namely that as cultures and settled populations have fragmented and become mobile and transnational, as well as more cosmopolitan locally (or at least more invaded or intervened on), fieldwork has simply had literally to follow, when it could, these processes in space. Furthermore, the weight of political and ethical critique of the traditional fieldwork relationship that generated ethnographic data, as revealed by the scrupulous reflexive probing of the postmodern gaze, broke the modicum of innocence and naïveté necessary to sustain the distance in the ethnographer's relationship to subjects, so that complicity with subjects—a state of ambiguity and improper seeming alliance—now pervades the scene of fieldwork, signaling a loss of innocence in the wake of postmodern exposures. Herein both the intensity of focus and the integrity of relationship that have shaped the Malinowskian scene of fieldwork have been challenged.

Although we are sympathetic to this conventional understanding of the challenges to the traditional composure of fieldwork, they do not arise simply from the complexities of a postmodern or now globalizing world. After all, many anthropologists can easily continue doing the same thing, and in fact many do; in many situations, it is even valuable to do so. But our take on what generates multisitedness and complicit relations in fieldwork projects today has more to do with the self-esteem of anthropology in the diminution of its distinctive documentary function amid many competing and overlapping forms of representation comparable to its own. In effect, every project of ethnography enters sites of fieldwork through zones of collateral counterpart knowledge that it cannot ignore in finding its way to the preferred scenes of ordinary everyday life with which it is traditionally comfortable. This condition alone makes fieldwork both multisited in nature, and heterogeneously so, as well as complicit with certain subjects (often experts or authorities in the scene of fieldwork, so to speak), who are crucial to bounding fieldwork and giving it orientation. The fundamental problem here is in confronting the politics of knowledge that any project of fieldwork involves and the ethnographer's trying to gain position in relation to this politics by making this terrain itself part of the design of fieldwork investigation.

Thus, since the 1980s, any critical anthropology worthy of the name not only tries to speak truth to power—truth as subaltern and understood within the closely observed everyday lives of ordinary subjects as the traditional milieu of fieldwork, power as conceptualized and theorized but not usually investigated by the strategies of fieldwork—but also tries to understand power and its agencies in the same ethnographically committed terms and in the same boundaries of fieldwork in which the subaltern is included. Ethnographic understanding itself, as a dominated segment of the dominant (in Pierre Bourdieu's terms), suggests an alternative modality relevant to the circumstances of contemporary fieldwork in which incorporating a second-order perspective on often overlapping, kindred official, expert, and academic discourses as counterpart to the ethnographer's own is an essential and complicating formulation of the traditional mise-en-scène of fieldwork. It is what accounts most cogently for making much of contemporary fieldwork multisited and political. It also makes contemporary fieldwork both slightly alienated and slightly paranoid in ways that are both inevitable and productive (Marcus, 1999c).

The keenly reflexive critical anthropology after the 1980s is well suited to this incorporation of cultures of the rational as a strategic part of its sites of fieldwork. Indeed, if there was one great success of these earlier critiques, it was to create an anthropology of current formations of knowledge and their distributions in a way that was thoroughly new and original. In a sense, all anthropology since has been most effectively an intimate critique of diffused Western knowledge practices in the name of specific communities of subjects misrepresented by, excluded from, seduced by, or victimized by such practices. The emerging innovation of fieldwork currently is to treat such power/knowledges as equal subjects of fieldwork in their complex and obscured connections to the scenes of everyday life as the cultivated and favored milieu of classic ethnography. But to be effective, such fieldwork has to do something more with this complex field of engagements than just provide distanced, however reflexive, description and interpretation. At the moment, a pervasive and sometimes cloying discourse and rhetoric of moral redemption holds this vacant place of an alternative, fully imagined and worked out alternative function for ethnography. Eventually, this rhetorical placeholder might be replaced by more active techniques that are styled in the range between ideas of experimentation and ideas of activism.

So contemporary critical ethnography orients itself through the imaginaries of expert others—through what we call para-ethnography—and operates through found zones of powerful official or expert knowledge-making practices so as to find more traditional subjects for itself. But what does it want of the complicit collaborations it makes with counterpart subjects in these domains, and what does it make of the scene of ethnography? This is distinctly not about an ethnography of elite cultures (Marcus, 1983); rather, it is about an access to a construction of an imaginary for fieldwork that can be shaped only by alliances with makers of visionary knowledge who are already in the scene or within the bounds of the field. The imaginaries of knowledge makers who have preceded the ethnographer are what the dreams of contemporary fieldwork are made of. But what are the practices/aesthetics of technique that go along with such complicitous, multisited fieldwork investigations?

Ecologies of Knowledge

As the anthropologist arrives at the gleaming headquarters of a multinational pharmaceutical corporation in New Jersey, the imposing governmental offices of the Bank of Japan, the sprawling alternative arts space in an urban ward of Cape Town, the courtrooms of the War Crimes Tribunal in The Hague, the offices of software engineers in Uttar Pradesh, or the research laboratories of the World Health Organization in Hong Kong, he or she is faced with unsettling questions. What do I do now? How do I start the fieldwork that is at the heart of my profession? How do I engage the human subjects who can enliven my research and can make my theoretical ideas anthropological? These are not just the questions that haunt the graduate student facing his or her first stint of fieldwork. They are the deep preoccupations that arise on a more or less daily basis, and it is with a veritable ethnographic treatment of the politics and ecologies of such knowledge forms that every project of the ethnography of the contemporary begins.[1] This initial ethnographic treatment produces both the context and the scaffolding of fieldwork. We suppose that this sensitivity to the zones of discourses in play as the portal through which every ethnographic project enters, and indeed constitutes the field, comes from the emphases of the 1980s critiques on reflexivity, representation, rhetorics, and especially politics. But rather than viewing these functions as constitutive of the Malinowskian project within its traditional boundaries, we see them as shaping different and methodologically more challenging conceptions of this theme of fieldwork and the practices they elicit. For us, the kind of reflexivity that is most valuable is the one that positions anthropologists within a field of already existing discourses as subjects of ethnography themselves so that they can find their way to the classic subjects of ethnography.

The work of Fortun (2001), Maurer (1995, 1999, 2002a, 2002b), Riles (2000, 2004a, 2004b, in press), and Miyazaki (2000, 2003, 2004), among many others,[2] demonstrates this rethinking of how projects of ethnography can begin deeply and critically within discourses of the rational that evoke ecologies and politics of knowledge that can be examined ethnographically. Moreover, the work of these authors has identified the deeply reflexive and complicit character of this kind of ethnography and the ways in which *theory* becomes implicated in this work. As Miyazaki (2003) notes regarding his work on Japanese securities traders,

> My ultimate goal is to carve out a space for a different kind of anthropological knowledge formation that finds an opportunity, rather than a problem, in social theorists' collective sense of belatedness. I suggest that the explicit construction of temporal incongruity as an opportunity in financial transactions makes financial markets a particularly suitable site for such exploration. (p. 256)

He further notes how the dilemmas of his subjects, securities traders, are analogous to those of the social theorists and how this convergence creates the basis of a distinctive kind of knowledge production:

> I suggested that social theorists' attention to financial markets as a new target of criticism has resulted from, and in turn intensified, their own collective sense of a temporal incongruity between their knowledge and its object of contemplation, the market. My response to this condition has been to point to analogues of such a sense of temporal incongruity in the

> financial markets themselves. I have argued that the traders I knew generated prospective momentum in their work precisely by reorienting the temporality of their work so as to continually re-create various forms of temporal incongruity. These analogies to the problems of social theory would suggest that the task of social theorists must be not so much to find new objects of contemplation on the constantly receding horizon of the new, such as financial markets, as to reflect on the work of temporal incongruity as an engine of knowledge formation, more generally. (p. 262)

In a sense, then, the anthropologist finds the literal field by working through the imaginaries of his or her counterparts who are already there, so to speak. This transforms the well-established scene of fieldwork as the encounter with the "other" into a much more complex scene of multiple levels, sites, and kinds of association in producing ethnographic knowledge.

We have become associated with discussing the predicament that we have been describing in terms of the emergence of multisited ethnographic research (Marcus, 1999b). Anthropology cannot remain local but rather must follow its objects and subjects as they move and circulate. This is true, and there are special problems with this, both practical and otherwise. But multisited fieldwork arises as much from the hypersensitivity of anthropology to the ecologies and politics of knowledge in which it operates that are necessary to constitute any subject today for fieldwork investigation. It cannot bracket these in the name of disciplinary authority but rather must incorporate them within the field of fieldwork, so to speak. This in itself is what generates multisitedness in its most pragmatic and feasible sense because there is no doubt that anthropological studies of the contemporary have most often taken the form of examining the relation of institutions to subjects, of systems to everyday life, and of domination to resistance. It is just that now these leading tropes of the contemporary terrain of fieldwork must be thought through in terms of the specific capacities and limits of ethnography as method and as a matter of design in how these tropes literally emerge in the constitution of fieldwork strategies, serendipity, and opportunities. The self-consciously multisited character of fieldwork comes into being as an epiphenomenon of the need to constitute the field and the object of study by incorporating both communities of often elite discourse and communities of often subaltern subjects. From this comes a rethinking of a whole set of issues of fieldwork—complicity instead of rapport (Marcus, 2001), the necessity of collaborations and their personal politics, the uneven distribution or depth of knowing in ethnography (both thickness and thinness as virtues of ethnographic description are in play), the changing nature of the object of study, the grounding of abstract relations that define cultural systems in forms of human action and knowing.

For us, one of the most important settings for developing this project of refunctioning that we are proposing is a pedagogical one. We want to give a sense of what, during recent years, has made the traditional regulative ideals of fieldwork unstable in the work of anthropology and an object for refunctioning. Part of it has to do with failures in the reigning folkloric, storytelling mode of inculcating ethnography as the distinctive practice in the professional culture of anthropology by which fieldwork has long been regulated, thought about, and idealized. This involves articulating certain dimensions that were always there in the Malinowskian staging or mise-en-scène of fieldwork but are now more important than ever in guiding adequately student ethnographers-in-the-making in the kinds of research they are increasingly undertaking. Yet at the same time, it is not clear—based on old governing tropes—what fieldwork is to be experientially in these student projects and what kinds of data it is supposed to generate. Thus, part of the destabilization has to do with the conditions that are reshaping research projects and demanding both more and different emphases from the old ethos in its vision and imaginings of what fieldwork is. This is hardly worthy of the term "crisis" as in the 1980s "crisis of representation," but like the diffusely articulated reflexively critical tendencies growing before the critique of ethnographic writing, there is now a comparable situation with regard to fieldwork. The Malinowskian mise-en-scène is by no means an empty term or guide, but it only roughly covers the forms and norms it actually takes now when applied to new projects.

In our recent work, we have been making a diverse range of arguments about this changing nature of fieldwork, especially for students in new topical arenas, grouped around the notion of what the multisited terrain of contemporary projects does to the focused Malinowskian mise-en-scène and around the concept of complicity as redefining the core relationship of collaboration in fieldwork on which authoritative ethnographic claims to knowledge have always depended. We have used the term mise-en-scène several times in referring to the imaginary that mediates and regulates the expression of method in anthropology. Fieldwork has been a vividly theatrical object of thought in anthropology from its very inception and ideological consolidation by Malinowski as the key symbol, initiatory rite, and method of anthropology. Much of the rest of this chapter is devoted to elucidating the terms of a refunctioned ethnography.

For Method

In earlier post-1986 writing, we emphasized the problem of passing through zones of representation and somehow incorporating them into the purview of fieldwork. As we noted, *acting* on this problem immediately generates the special problems of multisited fieldwork to which we have been alluding. But our efforts here are also a specific response to the possibilities that we both have encountered in pursuing initially the ethnography of elites, and now the ethnography of expertise, in the potential for these figures to define the reflexive politics of positioning for any anthropological research on the contemporary. Probing the ecologies of discourse that orient fieldwork projects today is indeed what the ethnography of elites, and now experts, has most productively become.

If the opening gambit of the ethnography is an orienting foray into a strategically selected culture of expertise, then that milieu of fieldwork cannot be treated conventionally or traditionally. Experts are to be treated not as collateral colleagues helping to inform fieldwork to occur elsewhere but instead as subjects fully within our own analytical ambit whose cognitive purview and social action range potentially over multiple, if not countless, sites and locales. Nor can they be treated as conventional "natives" or tokens of their cultures to be systematically understood; instead, they must be treated as agents who actively participate in shaping emergent social realms. These subjects must be treated like collaborators or partners in research, a fiction to be sustained more or less strongly around the key concept of para-ethnography.[3]

The para-ethnographic is a self-conscious critical faculty operating in expert domains as a way of dealing with contradictions, exceptions, and facts that are fugitive, suggesting a social realm and social processes not in alignment with conventional representations and reigning modes of analysis. Making ethnography from the found para-ethnographic redefines the status of the subject or informant and asks what different accounts one wants from such key figures in the fieldwork process. We have conceptualized the para-ethnographic as a kind of *social* thought—expressed in genres such as "the anecdotal," "hype," and "intuition"—within institutions dominated by a technocratic ethos, an ethos that, under changed contemporary circumstances, simply does not discipline thought and action as efficiently as it once did.

The para-ethnographer is an expert subject like the genetic engineer who is perplexed by the significance of his or her own cognitive practices and who, in the shadow of his or her formal knowledge work, creates intricate *cultural* narratives that might never be fully voiced but nonetheless mimic the form and the content of an ethnographic engagement with the world. Various fragmentary discourses are continuously spun off from this kind of knowledge work that connects formal scientific inquiry to the existential condition of the scientist cum para-ethnographer, on the one hand, and to a wider social imaginary, on the other. Ethical and moral apprehensions as well as professional and commercial preoccupations, although typically not fully articulated, nonetheless circulate in complex relationship to formal scientific practices, thereby constituting the substance of para-ethnography as well as part of the ecology of discourse that creates the field or ground in which strategies and designs of anthropological research take form. The questions, motives, and purposes that project anthropologists into fieldwork are not simply those raised within the discipline of anthropology or posed by the contextualizing social theories or historical narratives of contiguous academic specializations; rather, they arise from orienting engagements with counterparts and actors already defined within the field of ethnographic inquiry. Through this process, the formal *problematic* of contemporary ethnography is established (Fischer, 1999, 2003; Marcus, 1999a; Rabinow, 2003).

Under the conditions we are stipulating, where meaning is fugitive and social facts are elusive, distinct dilemmas are created for the individual. Cultural innovations continually destabilize social consensus, posing characteristic struggles for the perplexed subject—struggles that gain expression through various manifestations of the para-ethnographic. We are interested in how these para-ethnographic narratives become linked together among different expert subjects, conferring a distinctive *social* character on, for the most part, technical knowledge. What we refer to as internarratives not only link domains of expertise, often in unlikely ways, but also allow expertise to be juxtaposed in ways that render them acutely relevant to a broad range of anthropological questions. Expertise in science, politics, law, business, finance, and art must increasingly confront reciprocal expertise (and subaltern discourses) on human rights, social justice, and environmentalism, to name just a few. These critical and insurgent discourses can emerge from what are very familiar ethnographic concerns—the economic, political, and/or environmental plights of subaltern subjects or indigenous peoples—but they gain articulation in courts and through legal proceedings, in government bureaus and scientific agencies, within universities and museums, in nongovernmental organizations and a diverse range of international forums as well as through our own anthropological practices of representation and advocacy. The interchange between and among various established and alternative domains of expertise can create decisive axes of analysis that can orient a multisited staging of fieldwork. Thus, these bridging discourses can link the ethnography of experts to the lives and struggles of ordinary people. In this way, inquiry into cultures of expertise may well become an aspect of virtually all major projects pursued by anthropologically informed ethnography, even those projects that start from highly localized sets of interests and concerns.[4]

Our delineation of para-ethnography developed out of analysis of the unusual expertise of an infamous political actor, the French nationalist Jean-Marie Le Pen. Observations of Le Pen and his colleagues revealed an eerie convergence between their insurgent forms of political experimentation and those practices that encompass the professional métier of the ethnographer. Insurgent political narratives are, for the most part, designed not merely to circulate among experts but also to shape social thought and action across countless sites and among diverse publics. Le Pen's para-ethnography demonstrates the potential of this kind of narrative to establish a multisited scene providing the intellectual substance and the conceptual links between and among sites. By aligning the work of the anthropologist with that of highly problematic political figures such as Le Pen, we establish the problem of "complicity" as pivotal in defining the ethics and politics of fieldwork—in ways that were disguised in the Malinowskian scene in the off-stage presence of the colonial official.

▣ Schematic Exchange

We turn to a particular case of political expertise that illustrates the shift in the staging of the ethnographic encounter we have been discussing. We draw on an interview that was part of a multisited ethnographic project that moved from the rural districts of northeast Italy, to the political and bureaucratic precincts of the European Parliament in Strasbourg and Brussels, and finally to the impoverished districts of the East End of

London. The subject of the exchange on which we focus here is Le Pen. Holmes conducted the interview at the headquarters of the European Parliament in Strasbourg during the early 1990s. The voice—the "I"—here is superficially that of Douglas Holmes, but it actually represents our combined responses to this unusual conversation.

What made it pivotal for our thinking is that the exchange began with rather conventional premises whereby the subject, Le Pen, served as an informant, as an interlocutor who could provide an "insider account" or the "native point of view," as it were, on a distinctive form of extreme right-wing French nationalism, but in the course of the exchange a series of disruptions introduced by Le Pen (and tacitly accepted by Holmes) revealed the operation of what we are terming the para-ethnographic. In what follows, we show that what initially appeared to be a subtle shift in the staging of the encounter, in which Le Pen's role was recast from "key informant" to "para-ethnographer," incites a wide-ranging reassessment of anthropological ethnography. We present the case as a scenario—as a thought experiment—that focuses on the nature of the encounter and how it operated in the service of anthropological knowledge. The scenario also encompasses the technical language and terminology that we have developed to rebuild and refunction ethnography.

Fieldwork at the European Parliament, the consultative body of the European Union (EU), was as part of a study of European integration that spanned the decade from late 1980s to the late 1990s, focusing on interviews with a very broad range of political figures. The meeting with Le Pen, leader of the National Front, was unplanned and came after discussions with other leaders of the party.[5]

The conversation with Le Pen defied my expectations and understanding of how the ethnographic relationship is staged and how ideas are shaped and exchanged through this kind of relationship. This sense that something about the ethnographic relation was shifting as I was participating in it had been building over the course of my work at the parliament. But only when I encountered Le Pen, with his lurid charms, his extravagance, and his audacity in openly challenging the tenets of the interview process, did I fully grasp the extent to which the ethnographic relationship was being recast. In one important way, this was not a surprise; Le Pen's theatricality is renowned, and his performances are widely acknowledged to be masterful and compelling despite (or because of) their extremist character. He prides himself on the texture, the subtlety, and the range of his emotional message. What others consider to be distasteful about his performance, Le Pen claims as the distinctive means by which he engages the intimate struggles that circumscribe the lives of his public. Linking the theatrical and emotional dimensions of his political practice is a formidable intellectual tradition that intersects with the foundational concepts of humanistic anthropology—the traditions and lineages of what Isaiah Berlin terms the "Counter-Enlightenment." From this intellectual tradition, Le Pen distills what he believes to be the essence of human nature and the character of cultural affinity and difference, ideas that imbue fervent political yearning and foreshadow an exclusionary political economy.

The manner in which Le Pen insinuated this vision into our meeting was decisive in both defining the key *theoretical* issue of Holmes's project—the supranational character of advanced European integration—and fully revealing the possibilities of what we refer to here as the para-ethnographic. Acknowledging the operation of the para-ethnographic also exposed the interleaved affinities—or what we term "complicities"—linking the knowledge work of figures such as Le Pen and our own knowledge work.

My first impression during the meeting was that Le Pen was parodying and baiting me. In retrospect, I think that there is no doubt that was exactly what he was doing. It was, however, by no means merely a rhetorical maneuver on his part; rather, it was a deep substantive challenge. He was asserting that the distinctive domain of his political expertise was "culture." He was claiming a mastery over cultural ideas, cultural practices, and cultural meanings that far exceeded anything I, or any other mere academic, was capable of exercising.

To demonstrate his prowess, he laid out a remarkable vision of Europe, a vision predicated on solving the central conundrum—the core riddle of advanced European integration. He asserted that European integration that presents itself, at least at the time of the interview, as a wide-ranging economic undertaking was in fact a radical social and cultural project aimed at creating a *supranational* multiracial and multicultural Europe. Moreover, the project, as he understood it, was unfolding unmarked, unrecognized, and unnarrated. He had assumed for himself the task of giving voice to this process, giving the project of European integration a language and thereby a new political reality.

He recognized that at the heart of the project is a deep antagonism toward the political economy of the European nation-state, its regulatory regimes, and its cognitive purview. He saw integration as a wide-ranging scheme to usurp the powers of the nation-state, a scheme that ironically was engineered through the nation-state itself. The state, in this view, is by no means irrelevant, particularly as it has come to operate intergovernmentally within the EU; rather, it no longer constitutes the preeminent instrument defining *society* in Europe (Connolly, 1995; Milward, 1999; Moravcsik, 1998).

Framing Le Pen's insights are a number of fundamental analytical challenges. As the dominant position of the European nation-state is usurped through the process of integration, so too are many of the phenomenological, epistemological, and methodological assumptions that underpin the social sciences. Inquiry into the supranational operation of the EU reveals how deeply our extant repertoire of analytical concepts, our historical perspectives, and even our ethical and moral assumptions are predicated on the nation-state as a social fact. Thus, when we seek to examine European integration, we must confront phenomena that aggressively challenge all of our means and methods by which we produce knowledge. But of course, this is precisely what makes the EU—as it continually reinvents itself—such a profoundly important object of study (Holmes, 2003).

Le Pen's ambition during the early 1990s was to define the discourse on the emergence of a multiracial and multicultural society by eviscerating its moral and intellectual foundations. He thereby escaped the tightly sequestered world of right-wing French nationalism and established the premises of a supranational politics of Europe, a politics emphatically opposed to integration. Indeed, during the early 1990s, Le Pen was the first to elaborate what could be construed as a new political articulation of what is at stake in advanced European integration.

Le Pen's political innovations are compelling intellectually and have had a powerful appeal for new *European* constituencies—despite their overt fascist resonance. What Le Pen delineated exceeds what is conventionally understood as "politics"; rather, he conjured a complex sociology and metaphysics that tethers the new political economy of the EU to emerging existential struggles taking shape in the lives of virtually all Europeans. He recognized that integration was paradoxically creating new domains of alienation and estrangement in which radical formation of meaning are being contested (Bauman, 1997, 2001; Holmes, 2000, pp. 59–74).

Le Pen was hardly inclined to submit to the role of mere informant for someone else's project; on the contrary, he sought to both control and disrupt our interchange at every turn. As I became essentially the audience for his performance, I detected something oddly familiar about Le Pen's discourse, particularly the way in which he conceptualized overarching social and cultural struggles that could be read in the sacred and profane experience of situated subjects. The way in which he drew on anecdotal accounts to create intricately woven narratives about contemporary Europe sounded ethnographic to me; indeed, our exchange in some ways sounded like the musings of social anthropologists. His narratives were, of course, hardly disinterested, yet they seemed at least superficially to be ethnographic. In other words, what struck me was that Le Pen needed something akin to an ethnographic purview to pursue his political insurgency. This insight provoked a series of questions with which we continue to grapple. What is the nature of this kind of "ethnographic" purview? How does it operate? How do we draw these knowledge practices of our subjects into a broader anthropological project? How does this kind of collaborative knowledge practice recast our relationship to our subjects? And what are the ethical implications of this kind of collaboration? More broadly, we recognized even with this initial rendering of the para-ethnographic that new strategies and designs for problematizing research had become possible (Rabinow, 2003).

▣ Complicities

As we examined carefully the intersection between ethnography and para-ethnography, we developed the notion of the "illicit discourse" to mark out domains of complicity. Le Pen's discourse was overtly "illicit" insofar as it was predicated on malevolent cultural distinctions, but it was also "illicit" insofar as it challenges our claim as anthropologists to have a unique authority over this form of knowledge practice. More broadly, we have used the concept of illicit discourse to mark a conceptual space for working out the formidable moral and ethical challenges posed by the collaborative imperatives of para-ethnography. The para-ethnographer in this case is not merely involved in a complex "sensemaking" but rather is involved in an aggressive knowledge practice in the service of wide-ranging theoretical and ideological agendas. Le Pen's para-ethnography draws on "theory" and "ideology" that seek to explain cultural and racial affinity and difference in ways that challenge the culture concept as it has come to underwrite humanistic anthropology. On this kind of complex collaborative terrain, our ethical and moral conceits are open to direct challenge from the theoretically and ideologically informed positions of our subjects (Holmes, 2000).

The most powerful illicit discourse that we discerned from the engagement with Le Pen focused on the problem of "society" as key to our reciprocal practices of "ethnography." Le Pen and we sought constructions of European society as a moral framework, an analytical construct, and an empirical fact; we needed to conjure new representations of society to do our respective work. This was the foundation of a deep convergence of our ethnography and Le Pen's para-ethnography. Le Pen used his representation of society to configure deeply rancorous political meaning. We created a representation of society to configure a critical analysis of European politics, most notably of politics like those framed by Le Pen (Holmes, 1993).

Le Pen understands viscerally that as society framed by the bourgeois nation-state is eclipsed, a space is created for a radical politics that draws on latent cultural idioms to align a new conceptualization of collectivity. This view of society espoused by Le Pen could be used, as Holmes demonstrated, to frame an analytic of European integration. But Le Pen's disturbing "theoretical" innovation also depends on a "method"—a para-ethnography—that allowed him to narrate the usurpation of the nation-state and its significance not just for those traditional political constituencies displaced and estranged by this process but also for all Europeans. Inlaid in his narrative was a complex structure of feeling that configured a new emotional landscape for a supranational Europe on which sublime yearnings are crosscut by acute fears and anxieties. Again, he recognized that integration was paradoxically creating new domains of alienation and estrangement in which radical formation of meaning were establishing the terms of struggle over multiracial and multicultural society. Le Pen had, in this way, defined a distinctive tableau not only for his political insurgency but also for our ethnographic experimentation. In other words, European integration became a domain that we could enter analytically via the ecology of discourses that Le Pen had articulated (Marcus, 1999a, 1999b).

▣ Connective Tissue

Political narratives defining European pluralism are obviously designed not merely to circulate within the political precincts of the EU but also to shape social thought and action within countless sites across this burgeoning polity. Thus, Le Pen's para-ethnography is decisive in another crucial way in that he demonstrates the potential of what we term the "internarrative" in the construction of a multisited scene.

Internarratives serve as the connective tissue and the intellectual substance, as it were, of multisited ethnography; they provide the conceptual bridges between and among sites.

Insurgent politicians seek to create narratives that can enter the lifeworlds of a newly constituted public. The initial trajectory of this kind of communicative action is, in the case of Le Pen, from his headquarters in Paris to the homes, bars, workplaces, sports clubs, and so on of French and European citizens, where his narratives circulate in informal conversations, in press accounts, and in the shop talk of local politicians. These political narratives are interpreted and endowed with distinctive configurations of meaning in these diverse local contexts. They are also refracted back to Paris, to Le Pen's headquarters, and to the political offices of all those who seek to oppose him, where they can be recalibrated and recommunicated to align a complex discursive field.

By taking a marginal nationalist discourse and recrafting it as a supranational European discourse, Le Pen set the terms of debate on a multiracial and multicultural Europe and, for our purposes, established an analytical tableau that extends across innumerable sites. Thus, the discourse on pluralism that he crafted can take profoundly different forms depending, for example, on whether it is configured across the borderlands of Ireland or Poland within working-class neighborhoods of Marseille or Vilnius. In these diverse sites, this narrative enlivens distinctive human predicaments, conferring on them a fraught conceptual and emotional substance that can be explored ethnographically. Thus, a multisited ethnography was constructed across this tableau inspired by Le Pen, revealing how contemporary formulations of European pluralism gain expression as intimate cultural practices in rural districts of northeast Italy, as a racialized political economy within the institutions of the EU, and as a violent idiom of alienation and estrangement in the East End of London (Holmes, 2000). In this staging, multiple points of entry, through which one can discover countless interlocutors who endow European integration with diverse human voices, were established.

▣ Creative Possibilities

In our effort to reconcile the troubling affinities between the knowledge work of figures like Le Pen and our own knowledge work, we recognized an unusual creative process—an "intimate artifice"—whereby the ethnographer and para-ethnographer create either a shared framework of analysis or frameworks that operate in some kind of reciprocal relationship through which interleaved formations of knowledge are generated and exchanged dialectically. These collaborative exchanges operate at each stage of the ethnographic project.

The creative challenge posed by the type of fieldwork on which we focus here involves delineating the phenomenon to be studied, establishing an analytic tableau populated with human subjects who define it, endowing it with social form and cultural content. For us, this is a complex collaborative process whereby a discursive space on which a multisited ethnography can be staged is created, a discursive space where the actions of our subjects and our own analytical practices can be observed and where they and we shape a social reality.

In the case that we have discussed, a discursive space was circumscribed—Holmes terms it "integralism"—allowing us to view European integration simultaneously from the standpoints of its diverse theoretical underpinnings, its intellectual lineages, and its technocratic practices as well as allowing us to engage ethnographically the ways in which integrations inspire political insurgencies radically opposed to its abiding ideals. Moreover, the collaborative space encompassed by integralism created a dynamic purview from which we can view integration in terms of its manifold contradictions, revealing not merely its institutional manifestations but also its profoundly human character—the ways in which it has come to align consciousness and mediate intimacy. For us, this is the essence of a multisited mise-en-scène, a staging that can reveal the interplay between metatheoretical issues and the intricacies of human experience.

Inevitably, as we explore the dilemmas of expertise in other domains, we reciprocally expose our own professional limitations and liabilities. Not the least of these is the curious effect of observing how what we claim to be our distinctive practices as ethnographers can be deployed in creative ways by our subjects, conferring on their knowledge work a status that equals, if not exceeds, our own. To do an engaged and critical ethnography of expertise, we not only must build into our projects, as a methodological first principle, an acknowledgment of the uncertain nature of our own intellectual practices as ethnographers but also must actively exploit this unsettling condition as a driving force of our inquiry. By drawing complicity to the heart of our methods and ethics, a circumstantial *activism* becomes plausible (Marcus, 1999b).

We view this kind of collaboration as not merely an elicitation of preexisting social and cultural elements but also the systematic crafting of discursive spaces that capture newly constituted social and cultural phenomena as they take form within a continuously unfolding contemporary. We believe that this kind of activism rekindles the most radical aspirations of the anthropological project. In this collaborative framing—this intimate artifice—an activism that is theoretical, empirical, ethical, political, and existential in its scope and purview can be built into the constitution of the ethnographic relationship (Fortun, 2001).

Thus, para-ethnography is not merely a matter of identifying a new ethnographic subject—an accomplished autodidact; rather, it opens far deeper questions of how culture operates within a continuously unfolding contemporary. What is at stake in our conceptualization of the para-ethnographic are formations of culture that are *not* fully contingent on convention, tradition, and "the past" but rather constitute future-oriented cognitive practices that can generate novel configurations of meaning and action. Indeed, this gives rise to our most radical assertion—that spontaneously generated para-ethnographies are built into the structure of the contemporary and give form and content to a continuously unfolding skein of experience.

Notes

1. Most of the graduate projects that we supervise begin or end with such encounters, even though they may operate for considerable periods of time in the traditional mise-en-scène of anthropological fieldwork of sustained residence among ordinary (accessible?) people—in villages, on shop floors, in neighborhoods, on hospital wards, in classrooms. But these encounters are now given ethnographic import and treatment, and the main puzzle of fieldwork becomes their multileveled relation to these other more conventional and manageable sites of fieldwork. For example, we currently have a student who is researching the implementation of "freedom of information act" laws in Poland as an index of "democratization" there, the initial challenge of which has been to understand, by self-conscious fieldwork strategy, the "local" intellectual and official culture by which these laws have been conceived and formulated. Another student who has worked on concepts of risk among financiers in Korea moved back and forth between and among firms and particular neighborhoods in Seoul, sites that offered her variably "thick" and "thin" ethnography but created the context of relationship in which she found her focused object of study—not what went on in either set of sites but rather the nature of the real and imaginary relationships between and among them. A third student has spent long periods among contemporary Mayan villagers who live on or near ancient ruins, but the project has achieved its cogency only by extending fieldwork into the daily operations of the formidable regional and national bureaucracies of cultural heritage in Mexico. Of work that has been published by former students, that of Bargach (2002), Fortun (2001), and Hernandez (2002) exemplifies this emergence of multisited fieldwork in very different styles, but each study requires the sort of refunctioning of traditional notions of fieldwork that we have described.

2. The ethnographic studies of contemporary politics, of science and technology, of corporate business and markets, and of art worlds are the primary arenas of contemporary life where the refunctioning of ethnography that we describe has been emerging. The primary example that we work through in this essay comes from European politics. The recent study of Australian aboriginal painting by Myers (2002) is probably the most important example of such ethnography on art worlds. The Late Editions volume edited by Marcus (1998) provides sources on the ethnographic study of corporations. See also the work of Maurer (1995, 1999, 2002a, 2002b). However, it is in the burgeoning field of science and technology studies that the most impressive shift in the practice of ethnography can be observed. See Downey and Dumit (1997), Latour and Woolgar (1988), Marcus (1995), Pickering (1995), Rabinow (1999), Reid and Traweek (2000), Strathern (1992), and Traweek (1988).

3. Although we try to give our own specific conception to para-ethnography as an object of fieldwork investigation, it is certainly deeply connected to the long-standing interest in American cultural anthropology of probing "native points of view" through ethnographic investigation. Put simply, anthropology works through the understandings of others and the claim to be able to achieve knowledge of these understandings through fieldwork investigation. The influential discussions in social theory (Beck, Giddens, & Lash, 1994) of the importance of reflexivity itself as a major structural dimension of contemporary life have only enhanced this traditionally rooted interest in the para-ethnographic as an object of ethnography. For an elaborated discussion of this connection between the native point of view and para-ethnography, see Holmes and Marcus (2004).

4. A superb case in point is the recent work by Petryna (2002) on Chernobyl nuclear accident survivors that was named winner of the best first book published by an anthropologist, awarded in 2003 by the American Ethnological Society. Petryna worked closely with a group of survivors, participating in their everyday lives, characteristic of the vantage point of traditional ethnography. But she quickly found that to do justice to her topic, and to her subjects, she had to conduct multiple parallel ethnography: "My decision to abstain from judgment is also supported on empirical grounds. . . . Worlds of science, statistics, bureaucracy, suffering, power, and biological processes coevolve here in particular and unstable ways. How to discern their patterns as locally observable realities that affect people's daily lives and sense of moral and bodily integrity—or put another way, how to do an ethnography of the relationships among biological, political, and social processes as those relationships evolve—is a major creative challenge of this work" (p. 120).

5. The anthropology of contemporary Europe is a particularly cogent setting for the refunctioning of ethnography based in multisited strategies of fieldwork. The emergence of the EU and its institutions has made every locally focused study in Europe—no matter the specific venue or topic—at the same time a study of the overarching EU frame. With everything parallel processed, so to speak, there is no likely topic on contemporary Europe that is not at least multisited in its social space. Thus, this area of anthropology has been especially prescient in the refunctioning of ethnography as we discuss it. To understand the new anthropology of Europe that has emerged around the problematic of advanced European integration, see Abélès (1992, 1995, 1996, 2000), Bellier (1994, 1997), and Shore (2000).

References

Abélès, M. (1992). *La vie Quotidienne au Parlement Européen.* Paris: Hachette.

Abélès, M. (1995). Pour une anthropologie des instituitions. *L'Homme, 135,* 65–85.

Abélès, M. (1996). *En attente d'Europe: Débat avec Jean-Louis Bourlanges.* Paris: Hachette.

Abélès, M. (2000). Virtual Europe. In I. Bellier & T. Wilson (Eds.), *An anthropology of the European Union: Building, imagining, and experiencing the new Europe* (pp. 31–52). Oxford, UK: Berg.

Bargach, J. (2002). *Orphans of Islam: Family, abandonment, and secret adoption in Morocco.* Lanham, MD: Rowman & Littlefield.

Bauman, Z. (1997, January 24). No way back to bliss: How to cope with the restless chaos of modernity. *Times Literary Supplement,* p. 5.

Bauman, Z. (2001). Identities in a globalizing world. *Social Anthropology, 9,* 127.

Beck, U., Giddens, A., & Lash, S. (1994). *Reflexive modernization: Politics, tradition, and aesthetics in the modern social order.* Stanford, CA: Stanford University Press.

Bellier, I. (1994). *La Commission européenne: Hauts fonctionnaries et "culture du management."* Revue française d'administration, Publique 70.

Bellier, I. (1997). The commission as an actor: An anthropologist's view. In H. Wallace & A. R. Young (Eds.), *Participation and policy-making in the European Union* (pp. 91–115). Oxford, UK: Clarendon.

Clifford, J., & Marcus, G. E. (Eds.). (1986). *Writing culture: The poetics and politics of ethnography.* Berkeley: University of California Press.

Connolly, B. (1995). *The rotten heart of Europe: The dirty war for Europe's money.* London: Faber & Faber.

Downey, G. L., & Dumit, J. (Eds.). (1997). *Cyborgs and citadels.* Santa Fe, NM: School of American Research Press.

Fischer, M. M. J. (1999). Emergent forms of life: Anthropologies of late or postmodernities. *Annual Review of Anthropology, 28,* 455–478.

Fischer, M. M. J. (2003). *Emergent forms of life and the anthropology of voice.* Durham, NC: Duke University Press.

Fortun, K. (2001). *Advocacy after Bhopal: Environmentalism, disaster, new global orders.* Chicago: University of Chicago Press.

Hernandez, M. T. (2002). *Delirio: The fantastic, the demonic, and the reel.* Austin: University of Texas Press.

Holmes, D. R. (1993). Illicit discourse. In G. Marcus (Ed.), *Perilous states: Conversations on culture, politics, and nation* (Late Editions, No. 1, pp. 255–281). Chicago: University of Chicago Press.

Holmes, D. R. (2000). *Integral Europe: Fast-capitalism, multiculturalism, neofascism.* Princeton, NJ: Princeton University Press.

Holmes, D. R. (2003). [Review of Cris Shore, 2000, *Building Europe: The Cultural Politics of European Integration*]. *American Anthropologist, 105,* 464–466.

Holmes, D. R., & Marcus, G. E. (2004). Cultures of expertise and the management of globalization: Toward the re-functioning of ethnography. In A. Ong & S. J. Collier (Eds.), *Global assemblages: Technology, politics, and ethics as anthropological problems* (pp. 235–252). London: Blackwell.

Latour, B., & Woolgar, S. (1988). *The pasteurization of France.* Cambridge, MA: Harvard University Press.

Malinowski, B. (1961). *Argonauts of the Western Pacific.* New York: Dutton. (Original work published 1928)

Marcus, G. E. (1983). *Elites: Ethnographic issues.* Albuquerque: University of New Mexico Press.

Marcus, G. E. (Ed.). (1995). *Technoscientific imaginaries: Conversations, profiles, and memoirs* (Late Editions 2). Chicago: University of Chicago Press.

Marcus, G. E. (Ed.). (1998). *Corporate futures: The diffusion of the culturally sensitive corporate form* (Late Editions, No. 5). Chicago: University of Chicago Press.

Marcus, G. E. (1999a). Critical anthropology now: An introduction. In G. E. Marcus (Ed.), *Critical anthropology now: Unexpected contexts, shifting constituencies, changing agendas* (pp. 3–28). Santa Fe, NM: School of American Research Press.

Marcus, G. E. (1999b). *Ethnography through thick and thin.* Princeton, NJ: Princeton University Press.

Marcus, G. E. (Ed.). (1999c). *Paranoia within reason: A casebook on conspiracy as explanation* (Late Editions, No. 6). Chicago: University of Chicago Press.

Marcus, G. E. (1999d). What is at stake—and not—in the idea and practice of multi-sited ethnography. *Canberra Anthropology, 22*(2), 6–14.

Marcus, G. E. (2001). From rapport under erasure to the theater of complicit reflexivities. *Qualitative Inquiry, 7,* 519–528.

Marcus, G. E. (2002a). Beyond Malinowski and after *Writing Culture:* On the future of cultural anthropology and the predicament of ethnography. *Australian Journal of Anthropology, 13,* 191–199.

Marcus, G. E. (2002b). On the problematic contemporary reception of ethnography as the stimulus for innovations in its forms and norms in teaching and research. *Anthropological Journal on European Cultures, 11,* 191–206.

Marcus, G. E. (2003). The unbearable slowness of being an anthropologist now: Notes on a contemporary anxiety in the making of ethnography. *Xcp, 12,* 7–20.

Maurer, B. (1995). Complex subjects: Offshore finance, complexity theory, and the dispersion of the modern. *Socialist Review, 25,* 113–145.

Maurer, B. (1999). Forget Locke? From proprietor to risk-bearer in new logics of finance. *Public Culture, 11,* 47–67.

Maurer, B. (2002a). Anthropological and accounting knowledge in Islamic banking and finance: Rethinking critical accounts. *Journal of the Royal Anthropological Institute, 8,* 645–667.

Maurer, B. (2002b). Repressed futures: Financial derivatives' theological unconscious. *Economy and Society, 31*(1), 15–36.

Milward, A. S. (1999). *The European rescue of the nation-state.* London: Routledge.

Miyazaki, H. (2000). Faith and its fulfillment: Agency, exchange, and the Fijian aesthetics of completion. *American Ethnologist, 27,* 31–51.

Miyazaki, H. (2003). The temporalities of the market. *American Anthropologist, 105,* 255–265.

Miyazaki, H. (2004). *The method of hope.* Stanford, CA: Stanford University Press.

Moravcsik, A. (1998). *The choices for Europe: Social purpose and state power from Messina to Maastricht.* Ithaca, NY: Cornell University Press.

Myers, F. (2002). *Painting culture: The making of an aboriginal high art.* Durham, NC: Duke University Press.

Petryna, A. (2002). *Life exposed: Biological citizens after Chernobyl.* Princeton, NJ: Princeton University Press.

Pickering, A. (1995). *The mangle of practice: Time, agency, and science.* Chicago: University of Chicago Press.

Rabinow, P. (1999). *French modern: Norms and forms of the social environment.* Chicago: University of Chicago Press.

Rabinow, P. (2003). *Anthropos today: Reflections on modern equipment.* Princeton, NJ: Princeton University Press.

Reid, R., & Traweek, S. (Eds.). (2000). *Doing science + culture.* New York: Routledge.

Riles, A. (2000). *The network inside out.* Ann Arbor: University of Michigan Press.

Riles, A. (2004a). Property as legal knowledge: Means and ends. *Journal of the Royal Anthropological Institute, 10,* 773–793.

Riles, A. (2004b). Real time: Unwinding technocratic and anthropological knowledge. *American Ethnologist, 31*(3), 1–14.

Riles, A. (in press). Introduction. In A. Riles (Ed.), *Documents: Artifacts of modern knowledge.* Durham, NC: Duke University Press.

Shore, C. (2000). *Building Europe: The cultural politics of European integration.* London: Routledge.

Strathern, M. (1992). *Reproducing the future: Essays on anthropology, kinship, and the new reproductive technologies.* New York: Routledge.

Traweek, S. (1988). *Beamtimes and lifetimes: The world of high energy physicists.* Cambridge, MA: Harvard University Press.

EPILOGUE

The Eighth and Ninth Moments—Qualitative Research in/and the Fractured Future

Yvonna S. Lincoln and Norman K. Denzin

The end of a work such as this should signal neither a conclusion nor a final word, but rather a punctuation in time that marks a stop merely to take a breath, and, indeed, that is what we intend in this epilogue. The breadth that the contributors to this volume have tried to span marks a multidimensional map of territory traversed, including multiple moments, multiple histories, multiple influences, and multiple paradigms, perspectives, and methods, as well as increasing sensitivity to and awareness of new issues and problems. The contributors have also marked out this territory as terra incognita to be explored. Many have been as provocative as they have been historical, and that is as it should be, for we merely pause now on the border of a new vision for the social sciences. We would characterize this new vision as the realization of the seventh moment (although not its fulfillment) and a course charted toward the eighth and ninth moments in qualitative research.

The realization of the seventh moment lies in two signal achievements. First, we see, with the *Handbook* and the growing body of literature on specific methods, theoretical lenses, and paradigms, that a mature sophistication now characterizes the choices that qualitative researchers, practitioners, and theoreticians deploy in inquiring into social issues. No longer is it possible to categorize practitioners of various perspectives, interpretive practices, or paradigms in a singular or simplistic way. The old categories have fallen away with the rise of conjugated and complex new perspectives. Poststructuralist feminist qualitative researchers are joined by critical indigenous qualitative researchers. Critical poststructural feminist reconstructionists work in tandem with postmodern performance ethnographers. Labels perform double duty, or they are not applied at all. The important thing to note about many practicing interpretivists today is that they have been shaped by and influenced toward postmodern perspectives, the critical turn (as powerful an influence as the interpretive turn and the postmodern turn were in their own times), the narrative or rhetorical turn, and the turn toward a rising tide of *voices.* These are the voices of the formerly disenfranchised, the voices of subalterns everywhere, the voices of indigenous and postcolonial peoples, who are profoundly politically committed to determining their own destiny. We are at the "end of history" (Fukuyama, 1989, 1992), or at least at the end of history as we have known it. We are all "after the fact" (Geertz, 1995).

Although Hammersley (1999) objects to our historicizing, or punctuating, moments in the awakening or creation of qualitative research, we believe that there are genuine ruptures in the fabric of our own histories, precise or fuzzy points at which we are irrevocably changed. A sentence, a luminous argument, a compelling paper, a personal incident—any of these can create a breach between what we practiced previously and what we can no longer practice, what we believed about the world and what we can no longer hold onto, who we will be as field-workers as distinct from who we have been in earlier research. Indeed, we would argue that what we call moments are themselves the appearances of new sensibilities, times when qualitative researchers become aware of issues they had not imagined before. They are the "ah-ha" moments, the epiphanies, much like the "click" moments so deliciously recounted 30 years ago in the pages of *Ms.* magazine by women coming to consciousness. So, believing in our project as one of description and interpretation—the ethnographer's job—we continue to think of even the most contemporary history as a history emphasized and underscored by revelatory moments that shudder through the interpretive communities we inhabit. Those are the moments we try to describe, with the full understanding that, in the poststructural moment, our textual descriptions fall far short of what the lived experiences of individual researchers and inquiry and disciplinary communities look and feel like.

We have called the current moment the *methodologically contested present,* and we have described it as a time of great tension, substantial conflict, methodological retrenchment in some quarters (see Denzin & Lincoln, Chapter 1, this volume), and the disciplining and regulation of inquiry practices to conform with conservative, neoliberal programs and regimes that make claims regarding Truth (Cannella & Lincoln, 2004a, 2004b; Lincoln & Cannella, 2004a, 2004b). It is also a time of great tension *within* the qualitative research community, simply because the methodological, paradigmatic, perspectival, and inquiry contexts are so open and varied that it is easy to believe that researchers are everywhere. What appears to be chaos to outsiders, however, is nothing less than the intense desire of a growing number of people to explore the multiple unexplored places of a global society in transition. But where these people study, what they study, with whom they study, how they study the phenomena of interest with a communitarian sensibility, what they write about what they have studied, who writes about what they have studied—all these are subject to debate and struggle.

Out of this debate, struggle, and contestation will come the next moment. In some ways, it will share characteristics with the present moment; for example, it seems clear that the next moment will also be methodologically contested. The National Research Council's *Scientific Research in Education* (2002) will now stand next to the National Science Foundation's *Workshop on Scientific Foundations of Qualitative Research* (Ragin, Nagel, & White, 2004) as a boundary of the contested ground. It may well be the case that, as Alasuutari (2004) contends, we are undergoing a stunning compression of time, of moments, at this period in our history. Certainly, from our perspective as the editors of this volume, we see that advances in qualitative methods and models of inquiry appear to be developing somewhat more swiftly than in the past, with inventions, improvisations, and other forms of bricolage becoming both more sophisticated and more highly adaptable and adapted. It is also clear that many "moments"—in the form of real practitioners facing real problems in real fields and bringing with them real and material practices—will continue to circulate at the same time. Thus practitioners, scholars, and researchers are spread out, to varying degrees, over nine moments, often moving between moments as they seek—or are found by—new sites for inquiry. We are not discomfited by this; on the contrary, we believe it adds to the strength of qualitative research as a field and discipline, for it signifies that practitioners are willing to live with many forms of practice, many paradigms, without demanding conformity or orthodoxy.

There will also be some differences in the next moment. In the pages that follow, we try to portray some of the shifts, repositionings, and metamorphoses that we see coming and that we have asked this volume's contributors to address.

◘ The Eighth and Ninth Moments

Although methodological contestation will continue within and among the many disciplinary communities of qualitative research—business, marketing, nursing, psychology, communications studies, cultural studies, education, sociology, anthropology, medical clinical practice and epidemiology, and others—methodological sophistication will grow. The days when the teachers of qualitative research courses needed to search hard for good methodology texts are over; multiple enriched, cosmopolitan, transnational, and practice-seasoned literatures—and internal critiques of these same literatures—have been created, resulting in a veritable feast of paradigmatic arguments, interpretive practices, analytic and data management choices, and application issues. The problem for these scholars today is not in finding sound materials, but rather in choosing among and between them so as not to appear extravagant in assigning readings for classes.[1]

The next generation of qualitative researchers will face the same areas of contestation as did their earlier counterparts, but they will also face several new improvisations on old issues. It seems to us that arguments around four major issues will characterize the forthcoming generations, or moments, of the history of qualitative research. These issues are the reconnection of social science to social purpose, the rise of indigenous social science(s) crafted for the local needs of indigenous peoples, the decolonization of the academy, and the return "home" of Western social scientists as they work in their own settings using approaches that are vastly different from those employed by their predecessors. We provide some explanation of each of these major issues in the pages that follow. We then complete our forecast by discussing other issues that we believe will mark the next moment.

The Reconnection of Social Science to Social Purpose

Ruth Bleier (1984, 1986) has argued that the resources available to social science are too short, too scarce, to be used simply to satisfy scientific curiosity. Rather, she proposes, social science research should be driven by an ameliorative purpose; it should seek to solve some problem, to allay some maldistribution of resources, to meet a genuine need. Too often, however, guided by the modernist presupposition of objectivity in science, social scientists have lost sight of the purposive, intentional meanings of their work, circled back to their disciplinary roots, and left to chance and heaven the wending of findings into the policy arena. In contrast, seeking an engaged social science leads to what Conklin (2003) and Wildavsky (1975) have called "speaking truth to power." Addressing the issue of indigenous advocacy, Conklin (2003) suggests that "we can start to sort out these sticky issues," particularly the places where "the priorities of academic and activists diverge," by "locating points where professional ethics and political effectiveness converge" (p. 5). Roth (1990) suggests much the same thing when he observes that "anthropological knowledge [indeed, any putative knowledge] is also to be judged in regard to how it integrates with what else passes as knowledge" (p. 276).

The professional ethics issue that has begun to engage social scientists, particularly interpretivist qualitative researchers, most forcefully is the issue of social justice. The coupling of historically reified structures of oppression—whether educational, medical, ecological, nutritional, economic, social, or cultural—with unjust distribution of social goods and services creates a flood tide of injustice that threatens to engulf developed and developing nations and indigenous peoples alike.

The rise of a new ethic—communitarian, egalitarian, democratic, critical, caring, engaged, performative, social justice oriented—and a new emphasis on ethics that includes the reformulation of ethical issues in response to the new felt ethic signals a new interpretive community (Christians & Traber, 1997; de Laine, 2000; Zeni, 2001; see also Christians, Chapter 6, this volume). This new community is characterized by a sense of "interpersonal responsibility" (Mieth, 1997, p. 93) and moral obligation on the part of qualitative researchers, responsibility and obligation to participants, to respondents, to consumers of research, and to themselves as qualitative field-workers. This includes the quality of "*being with* and *for* the other, not *looking at*" the other (de Laine, 2000, p. 16). The new participatory, feminist, and democratic values of interpretive qualitative research mandate a stance that is democratic, reciprocal, and reciprocating rather than objective and objectifying.

The methods and methodologies game is not for members of the Western or European interpretive community only, however. The rise of multiple voices, some of them previously all but ignored by Eurocentric researchers, heralds a new era in qualitative inquiry. The firmness with which African American, Asian American, Native American, Latina/o, and border voices have begun to assert themselves lends a frisson of excitement, uncertainty, anticipation, and unpredictability to the field. These developments are yet another characteristic of the next wave, the eighth and ninth moments.

The Rise of Indigenous Social Science(s)

The rise of a social science that is indigenously designed and indigenously executed, more or less independent of Western or colonial and postcolonial influences, except where invited, is already a reality (De Soto & Dudwick, 2000; Fahim, 1982; Gugelberger, 1996; Gupta & Ferguson, 1997, 1999; Harrison, 2001; Smith, 1999; see also in this volume Smith, Chapter 4; Bishop, Chapter 5). Indigenism, a label once paradoxically manipulated to distinguish between the so-called civilized and the uncivilized (Ramos, 1998), now provides a framework for both critique of Western deployment of social science methods among native peoples and the creative genesis of new forms of systematic inquiry into community conditions, problems, and concerns devised by members of indigenous communities themselves. As we point out in Chapter 1 of this volume, Linda Tuhiwai Smith (1999) succinctly describes the state of social science research in her own Māori community as well as other indigenous communities: "The term 'research' is inextricably linked to European imperialism and colonialism" because "imperialism frames the indigenous experience. It is part of our story, our version of modernity" (pp. 1, 19).

Why should this generative spirit arise in social science at this particular moment in history? A tremendous number of forces have collided in the political economy of nations to create conditions that are favorable for subaltern and indigenous peoples to speak. Most prominent among these forces are the rising numbers of individuals from indigenous communities who have achieved terminal degrees and taken their places on faculties or in other positions where they can make their voices heard; the forces of globalization, which have enabled individuals all around the world to be connected via media in ways unknown a generation ago; a profound resistance to some forms of this same globalization and its Westernized, late-capitalist formations that result in the importation of Western ideas and corporatist values at the expense of local and indigenous languages, cultures, customs, and traditions; and the deep desire f self-determination among indigenous peoples everywhere. Education (and, more generally, literacy), access to means of mass communication (including the Internet), and powerful urges toward voice, liberty, and self-determination have foregrounded the dreams of oppressed peoples all over the globe. Indigenous voices are not all heard in the same ways, however; rather, the geography of place (Bhabha, 1990; Gupta & Ferguson, 1999) lends a distinctive tang to the expression of indigenous desire, as do indigenous peoples' particular experiences of colonialism and postcolonialism.

Indigenous voices in Latin America. Yúdice (1996) has a slightly different take on the emergence of indigenous assertions to the right to speak:

> More than any other form of writing in Latin America, the *testimonio* has contributed to the demise of the traditional role of the intellectual/artist as spokesperson for the "voiceless." As some major writers . . . increasingly take neoconservative positions and as the subordinated and oppressed feel more enabled to opt to speak for themselves in the wake of the new social movements, Liberation Theology, and other consciousness-raising grassroots movements, there is less of a social and cultural imperative for concerned writers to heroically assume the grievances and demands of the oppressed. . . .
>
> In contrast, the *testimonialista* gives his or her personal testimony "directly," addressing a specific interlocutor. . . . The speaker does not speak for or represent a community but rather performs an act of identity-formation that is simultaneously personal and collective. (p. 42)

Yúdice's implication is that when the intellectual/artist retreated into neoconservative (or neoliberal) political stances, the subordinated found a need to speak for themselves. And they did so, although not through any genre or rhetorical form known in the conventions of Western writing, or from any political stance previously recognized in Western literary traditions. *Testimonio,* a particularly Latin American form, serves the critical historical function of *witnessing* (see Beverley, Volume 2, Chapter 9; Hartnett & Engels, Volume 3, Chapter 18), often in the form of testifying to events unknown or unwitnessed by Western and colonial/postcolonial observers. *Testimonio* serves the political function of supporting solidarity while also serving the psychological purpose of establishing a separate and clear cultural identity for the group whose identity is being witnessed. In some ways, *testimonio* is unique among indigenous writings in that both its form and its political capacity are quite unknown in the Eurocentric and colonial rhetorical panoply.

Native voices in India and the Middle East. The experience of postcolonialism and an [illegible]onal ethnographic method are worked out very differently in India and the [illegible] Mohanty, 1988; O'Hanlon, 1988). Whereas Latin American forms, par- [illegible] (but also other forms of writing around the oppressed), appear to [illegible]ll, on the relationship between the colonized and the colonizer, [illegible]nd Near Eastern, and south Asian indigenous writings are frequently indexed to a sharp awareness of the presence of the colonizer and postcolonizer. The works of Ashis Nandy, Edward Said, Chandra Mohanty, Gayatri Spivak, and Homi Bhabha explore this colonial presence in several ways: by deconstructing how this presence has been responsible for suppressing or destroying portions of national or regional identities and languages, by capturing a mourning for what has been lost, by exploring indigenous means for recovering the lost "self" of national identity, and by providing critiques of the ways in which representations created—indeed, invented—by the West have shaped ongoing relations between the East and West (Said, 1979) in arenas as wide ranging as tourism and foreign policy. Indeed, as all of these authors have argued (albeit in different ways), social scientists' failure to grasp the cultural grounds and boundaries of the colonized has led to recurring missteps, gaffes, and social and political displacements. Much of the indigenous critique that proceeds from the Orient, consequently, revolves around the deconstruction of the culture-erasing effects of colonialism and postcolonialism; it does not seek a specific genre of ancient knowledge in which to ground new forms of social inquiry or auto-critique (Conklin, 2003).

Indigenous inquiry at the antipodes and the United States. Harrison (2001) notes that the voices of the indigenous peoples of Australia, New Zealand, the United States, and Canada are often juxtaposed for the simple reason that

> the First Nations peoples of Canada, Native Americans and Alaska Natives in the United States, Aborigines in Australia, and Māori in New Zealand have established regular means of communicating about the things that they now have in common. . . . Political movements aimed at achieving recognition of sovereignty of indigenous groups have developed among the indigenous peoples in all four countries. (p. 23)

In these four countries, indigenous peoples have established a particular form of relationship with the federal governments that now shapes a distinctive collective dialogue around political movement toward self-determination for indigenous peoples as well as issues of education, health care, and social welfare, broadly conceived. It is from the indigenous peoples in these countries that we have both the clearest critique of modernist social science and the richest proposal for an indigenous knowledge-based education (Ah Nee-Benham & Cooper, 2000) and inquiry model (Smith, 1999).

A variety of indigenous groups have proposed guidelines for social science that take account of signal characteristics deeply embedded in non-Western cosmologies and epistemologies. Three elements of such guidelines are especially sensitive and telling. First, in manifestos and agreements indigenous peoples from these four countries and others have asserted their right to have "all investigations in our territories . . . carried out with our consent and under joint control and guidance" (Charter of the Indigenous Tribal Peoples of the Tropical Forests, as quoted in Smith, 1999, p. 119). This is a clear indication that although social scientists may find that collaboration is possible, or even useful, they can no longer carry on with their usual practice of simply inserting themselves into the context to study what and when they will.

Second, indigenous peoples in many parts of the world, but especially the four nations that frame this discussion, are troubling the entire process of researchers' seeking informed consent and institutional review board approval. One of us (Yvonna) first became aware of this at a conference in Australia when an audience member respectfully informed her that Aboriginal tribal elders consider the use of informed consent forms insulting, and so researchers working with this population in Australia simply do not use such forms. Given that Australian federal law requires a process similar to that required in the United States, in that researchers must secure the informed consent of all human participants in a research project, Yvonna asked the audience member what researchers in Australia do about this requirement; he simply replied, shrugging his shoulders, "We ignore it." We have no idea how a local institutional review board may feel about this course of action, but it is quite clear that Australian Aborigines have made their own decisions regarding the utility of the informed consent process, and, as far as they are concerned, the federal government has no say in the matter. Indeed, Linda Smith (1999) outlines a whole series of objections that indigenous peoples have to this process, including the entirely Western assumption that it is the *individual* who owns knowledge and who can participate or withdraw from a study as she or he pleases. In many indigenous cultures this construction undermines the sense of the collective, the tribal, and the concept of communal and ancestral knowledge. That such knowledge should belong to all the members of a group is not a construct that rests easy in Western epistemologies, based as they are on 18th- and 19th-century philosophical formulations of the autonomous individual (Gergen, 1991).

Third, many indigenous peoples have now established their rights to exclusive ownership of their cultural and intellectual properties, including the right to "protect and control dissemination of that knowledge [about themselves]"; further, they have established that the "first beneficiaries of indigenous knowledge must be direct indigenous descendants of that knowledge" (Smith, 1999, pp. 118–119). Where tribal, cultural, or indigenous treaties, compacts, agreements, and other formal documents exist to support such rights, it is absolutely clear that Western scholars do not have first claim on the knowledge they may help to generate. Rather, they must negotiate for that knowledge and respect the forms in which the "owners" may wish to have it presented or re-presented. Indigenous peoples pursuing self-determination with ferocity and single-mindedness have successfully challenged Western scholars' propensity to believe that they can own whatever they appropriate.

In much the same way, and with the same effects, Canadian First Nations peoples have secured a status for themselves that includes extensive local control over education, Native language and cultural instruction, and health care and other social services. In some broad ways, Canadian First Nations peoples, the Māori in New Zealand, and Australia's Aborigines have stronger and clearer voices in their self-determination than do Native Americans and Native Hawaiians in the United States or South Pacific peoples (e.g., Tongans). Nevertheless, members of all these groups are able to articulate what respect for indigenous cultural customs and epistemologies might look like, and all have assumed increasing control over the form and shape of research conducted in their midst, with some groups retaining the right to determine the research agenda and the use of methods that display maximum cultural sensitivity. This is not true of indigenous peoples in all parts of the world (Reagan, 2005).

The Decolonization of the Academy

Finkelstein, Seal, and Schuster (1998) catalog the myriad changes currently under way in the American professoriate, none of which is more visible or has greater potential to change the face of academe than the "composition of the new entrants into the faculty" (p. xi). The startling gains of women in the past 15 years, of non-native-born faculty members, of faculty of color (the most impressive gains being made by women faculty of color), and of Asians and Pacific Islanders on faculties point to a dramatic demographic shift between new hires and senior faculty (those nearing retirement). Further, the greatest changes have occurred in public, doctoral-granting institutions, with public comprehensive institutions next and private doctoral-granting institutions third.[2]

Because the greatest demographic shift is occurring in institutions that grant doctoral and master's degrees, the most profound impact of this massive diversification in the faculty ranks is being felt, at least immediately, in graduate research (Finkelstein et al., 1998). Beyond the forces impinging on graduate study, this shift is resulting in two additional changes. First, new faculty members are far less wedded to traditional forms of academic reporting than were their predecessors. Particularly in the social sciences, they are more interested in newer theoretical currents that suggest the dividing line between art and science is far more fluid and permeable than the previous academic generation believed it to be. As a consequence, the very shapes and forms of texts—whether books, journal articles, or conference presentations—are likely to be less traditional. Experimental, "messy," layered poetic and performance texts are beginning to appear in journals and on conference podiums. Second, the students of these new faculty tend to be equally comfortable with experimentation, and they are increasingly preparing research papers and dissertations that are, at a minimum, bilingual—writings that address the needs of multiple rather than singular audiences, often across national borders (see, for instance, Gonzaléz y Gonzaléz, 2004). They deploy this kind of strategy deliberately, with a globalized impact in mind. Models of academic research such as Anzaldúa's (1999) bilingual, border-focused work open up possibilities for students, especially as these many-layered and multilingual texts have become textbooks for graduate study. It is no longer unheard of, or even strange, for students to produce doctoral dissertations that include portions that some of the members of their dissertation committees may not be able to translate.

The decolonization of the academy is taking other forms as well. The influx into the American professoriate of vast numbers of individuals who were not born in the United States has brought cultural richness and diversity of experience to academia, but these individuals have also brought with them traditions that are different from those of earlier faculty, including the peculiarly American tradition of shared governance. A consequence of this may be an inadvertent undermining of the extent to which faculty participate in policy making and administrative decision making. In the same vein, just as new European theoretical currents have become deeply embedded in critical research and curricular concerns, the globalizing influence of international faculty may lead to a more pronounced set of sensibilities regarding the cultural, political, and artistic variety that is possible and desirable as a positive outcome of globalization.

International faculty also bring to U.S. colleges and universities both subtle and pronounced differences in modes of graduate training and graduate mentoring. Institutions of higher education in the United States have grappled for some time with the issue of how to mentor graduate students, including how to socialize them into faculty roles of their own. The perspectives of international faculty members, as well as those of the increasing numbers of faculty of color, bring to the fore new considerations regarding what mentoring might mean and how different forms of mentoring might be effective for diverse students (and for diverse new young faculty members, for that matter; see Stanley & Lincoln, 2005) as well as how the academy's range and repertoire of possible collegial relationships may be expanded through mentoring. Each of these changes opens the academy to decolonization by lessening the hegemony of the Western canon and creating a new consciousness of global citizenry.

Most important, the infusion into U.S. institutions of non-Western, indigenous, and "colored" epistemologies has created a vital mix of new paradigmatic perspectives, new methods and strategies for research, contested means for establishing validity in texts, new criteria for judging research and scholarship, and competing cosmologies from which knowledge and understanding might grow. The era of a shared and largely modernist model of inquiry has likely passed away. Some scholarship will still be presented and judged from a positivist paradigm, but other scholarship will be traveling the margins and borders, searching for new and innovative forms through which to express non-Western modes of knowing and being in the world.

The Homecoming of Western Social Science

Perhaps the most striking hallmark of the next moment will be the reconsideration of how the social sciences are practiced in the West as well. The phenomenological, postpositivist, postmodern, emancipatory, qualitative, liberationist sensibility that challenges modernist master narratives holds within it the seeds of a reformulated vision of what the social sciences might accomplish and how ethnographers might reconnoiter what they have already produced for evidence of its contributions to a democratic imaginary on its own soil.

We are now approaching a serious moral confrontation in Western social science. On the one hand, some social scientists (including the two of us and the contributors to this volume) are examining critically the purposes and projects of past and future social science, questioning whether, when, and under what conditions our knowledge has served to enhance democratic ends and extend social justice as well as when and under what conditions it has served to reify historical power and resource distributions. On the other hand, other, equally responsible, inquirers and researchers are seeking to reestablish the supremacy of "one method/one truth," the "gold standard" of research strategies. Political battles that are normally fought in legislative circles, leaving social scientists untouched and unmoved, have shifted directly into the arenas of educational, social, and behavioral sciences. The evolving political struggles between liberal and neoconservative/neoliberal views of the world have become progressively sharper and more distinct in Western life, concomitantly creating more fissures in American life than have existed for a half century. This is reflected in legislation affecting education (e.g., the No Child Left Behind Act of 2001) and in policy documents that represent stances on what research designs are to be considered appropriate and meaningful (e.g., National Research Council, 2002).

This is the first of the serious fractures in the social science community. What had been a sometimes mild-mannered disagreement between research methodologists, leading to a courteous détente between schools of thought (Lincoln, 2004), has become a firefight, with substantial resources, including funding through grants and contracts, and political and policy power hanging in the balance. This methodologically contested moment will not subside anytime soon.

In the meantime, qualitative research practitioners are engaged in earnest and consequential work of their own. Despite accusations of "advocacy" and of "ideology parading as intellectual inquiry" (Mosteller & Boruch, 2002, p. 2), postpositivist inquirers of all perspectives and paradigms have joined in the collective struggle for a socially responsive, democratic, communitarian, moral, and justice-promoting set of inquiry practices and interpretive processes (for a review of some of this literature, see Scheurich, 2002). The search for "culturally sensitive" research approaches—approaches that are attuned to the specific cultural practices of various groups and that "both recognize ethnicity and position culture as central to the research process" (Tillman, 2002)—is already under way (Anzaldúa, 1987; Bernal, 1998; Bishop, 1998; Collins, 2000; Dillard, 2000; Gunaratnam, 2003; Harrison, 2001; Hurtado, 1996; Parker & Lynn, 2002; Sandoval, 2000; Smith, 1999; Wing, 2000). Many of the issues associated with such approaches are captured with comprehensiveness and nuance in this volume. Qualitative researchers' concerns for social justice, moral purpose, and "liberation methodology" will mark this next moment with passion, urgency, purpose, and verve. When we argued in an earlier edition of the *Handbook* that qualitative research had "come of age," we were mistaken. It had merely reached a zesty and robustly athletic late youth. The genuine coming of age in methodology, we see now, will be the maturing of the field into a new set of practices and purposes—a new praxis that is deeply responsive and accountable to those it serves.

▣ The Next Moment, the Fractured Future

We predict that in the ninth moment the world of methods will enter what we term a *fractured future*—a future in which, unless an intervention we cannot currently imagine takes place, methodologists will line up on two opposing sides of a great divide. Randomized field trials, touted as the "gold standard" of scientific educational research, will occupy the time of one group of researchers while the pursuit of a socially and cultural responsive, communitarian, justice-oriented set of studies will consume the meaningful working moments of another. A world in which both sides might be heard, and their results carefully considered as differently produced and differently purposed views on social realities, now seems somewhat far away, mixed-methods advocates notwithstanding.

In a battle where the warriors on the frontlines are fairly evenly matched and not much progress is being made, the skirmishes, conflicts, and engagements are likely to move elsewhere. We predict that the next encounter will be a scrimmage over federal ethics regulations. Extremely useful, but out of date for the purposes of qualitative research and entirely useless for the development of culturally, racially, and ethnically sensitive methods (for a critique of the ways in which federal regulations fail to respond to qualitative research, see Lincoln & Guba, 1989; but see also Lincoln, 2001), the current federal regulations—regarding informed consent, privacy of records, confidentiality, and the role of deception—form one kind of quality floor under research practices. As the American Association of University Professors (2001) has argued well, however, the current regulations and laws are better suited to biomedical research than to social science.

In the absence of a substantive effort to revisit the federal regulations on human subjects protections or any grave reconsideration of the applicability of the regulations either to the social sciences or, more specifically, to qualitative research (writ large, as in the pages of this book), several professional associations have constructed their own statements on professional and field ethics. The American Anthropological Association, the American Sociological Association, the American Historical Association, and the American Educational Research Association have all constructed exemplary statements on professional ethics. The American Anthropological Association in particular has been extremely attentive to concerns about the rights of indigenous peoples, and the association's newsletter, *Anthropology News,* features a continuing dialogue, pursued for more than a decade, on field ethics, indigenous rights, and other ethical dilemmas of an "engaged anthropology."

We know from the applications of technology we see around us that technology frequently sweeps far ahead of both public policy and civic engagement in debates around public policy. The technologies associated with genetic engineering and cloning are good examples. Currently, scientists' ability to clone living organisms is much further advanced than any rational civic debate about whether and under what circumstances cloning should be allowed. We have no idea what Americans' "moral boiling point" is with respect to cloning. In precisely the same way, "McDonaldizing," "corporatizing," and globalizing efforts around the world have ensnared social scientists who wish to understand the effects of late capitalism's expansion and penetration around the globe. Technologies and technoimaginaries of communication, travel, and cyberspace have far outpaced deliberate and considered debate about what is moral, useful, and culturally respectful. The ethics, aesthetics, and teleologies necessary for a globalized world have not yet come into being, although they are being born in this volume and elsewhere. Social scientists, men and women of conscience, are devising their own standards in collaboration with indigenous peoples, people of color, and marginalized groups everywhere, but it would be heartening to see the U.S. federal government take some additional leadership role in this arena.

Qualitative researchers in the next moment will face another struggle, too, around the continuing issue of representation. On the one hand, creating open-ended, problematic, critical, polyphonic texts, given the linearity of written formats and the poststructural problem of the distance between representation and reality(ies), grows more difficult. On the other hand, engaging performative forms of social science can be difficult in many venues. Traditional texts are far more portable, albeit far less emotionally compelling. Performing social justice, examining ways in which our work can serve social justice, may be the teleological framework for a reimagined social science. Attention to the representations we make, to the possibility that messages may further disenfranchise or oppress (Fine, Weis, Weseen, & Wong, 2000; see also Tedlock, Volume 2, Chapter 5) when they begin circulating in the wider world, and respect for the wisdom of people who are not like us, who know all too well the unfortunate images that surround their lives, may be the start of our performance of justice. It is a place to begin.

Notes

1. Ivan Brady (2004) makes this point in a recent journal article titled "In Defense of the Sensual," as do Hartnett and Engels in Chapter 18 of Volume 3: The "unfinalizable" nature of ethnography arises not so much from the problem of unknowables (although they always exist) as it does from the overriding problem of plural "knowabilities" and the frustration that having to choose among them causes. Worse still for the researcher is having someone choose for him or her, some individual or some institution with the power to enforce the choice. See Brady (2004, p. 632).

2. Finkelstein et al. (1998) make the point that public institutions of higher education have diversified more swiftly than have private institutions, likely because of public pressures to do so. This has resulted in the exposure of a broader range of graduate students to diversity, given that public institutions, as a group, typically produce more doctorates than do private institutions in any given period of time.

References

Ah Nee-Benham, M. K. P., & Cooper, J. E. (Eds.). (2000). *Indigenous educational models for contemporary practice: In our mother's voice.* Mahwah, NJ: Lawrence Erlbaum.

Alasuutari, P. (2004). The globalization of qualitative research. In C. Seale, G. Gobo, J. F. Gubrium, & D. Silverman (Eds.), *Qualitative research practice* (pp. 595–608). London: Sage.

American Association of University Professors. (2001). Protecting human beings: Institutional review boards and social science research. *Academe, 87*(3), 55–67.

Anzaldúa, G. (1999). *Borderlands/la frontera: The new mestiza* (2nd ed.). San Francisco: Aunt Lute.

Bernal, D. (1998). Using a Chicana feminist epistemology in educational research. *Harvard Educational Review, 68,* 555–582.

Bhabha, H. K. (Ed.). (1990). *Nation and narration.* New York: Routledge.

Bishop, R. (1998). Freeing ourselves from neo-colonial domination in research: A Māori approach to creating knowledge. *International Journal of Qualitative Studies in Education, 11,* 199–219.

Bleier, R. (1984). *Science and gender: A critique of biology and its theories on women.* Oxford: Pergamon.

Bleier, R. (Ed.). (1986). *Feminist approaches to science.* Oxford: Pergamon.

Brady, I. (2004). In defense of the sensual: Meaning construction in ethnography and poetics. *Qualitative Inquiry, 10,* 622–644.

Cannella, G. S., & Lincoln, Y. S. (2004a). Dangerous discourses II: Comprehending and countering the redeployment of discourses (and resources) in the generation of liberatory inquiry. *Qualitative Inquiry, 10,* 165–174.

Cannella, G. S., & Lincoln, Y. S. (2004b). Epilogue: Claiming a critical public social science—reconceptualizing and redeploying research. *Qualitative Inquiry, 10,* 298–309.

Christians, C. G., & Traber, M. (Eds.). (1997). *Communication ethics and universal values.* Thousand Oaks, CA: Sage.

Collins, P. H. (2000). *Black feminist thought: Knowledge, consciousness, and the politics of empowerment* (2nd ed.). New York: Routledge.

Conklin, B. (2003, October). Speaking truth to power: Mapping an engaged anthropology. *Anthropology News, 44,* 5.

de Laine, M. (2000). *Fieldwork, participation and practice: Ethics and dilemmas in qualitative research.* London: Sage.

De Soto, H. G., & Dudwick, N. (2000). *Fieldwork dilemmas: Anthropologists in postsocialist states.* Madison: University of Wisconsin Press.

Dillard, C. (2000). The substance of things hoped for, the evidence of things not seen: Examining an endarkened feminist epistemology in educational research an leadership. *International Journal of Qualitative Studies in Education, 13,* 661–681.

Fahim, H. (Ed.). (1982). *Indigenous anthropology in non-Western countries.* Durham, NC: Carolina Academic Press.

Fine, M., Weis, L., Weseen, S., & Wong, L. (2000). For whom? Qualitative research, representations, and social responsibilities. In N. K. Denzin & Y. S. Lincoln (Eds.), *Handbook of qualitative research* (2nd ed., pp. 107–131). Thousand Oaks, CA: Sage.

Finkelstein, M. J., Seal, R. K., & Schuster, J. H. (1998). *The new academic generation: A profession in transformation.* Baltimore: Johns Hopkins University Press.

Fukuyama, F. (1989, Summer). The end of history? *National Interest, 16,* 3–18.

Fukuyama, F. (1992). *The end of history and the last man.* New York: Free Press.

Geertz, C. (1995). *After the fact: Two countries, four decades, one anthropologist.* Cambridge, MA: Harvard University Press.

Gergen, K. J. (1991). *The saturated self: Dilemmas of identity in contemporary life.* New York: Basic Books.

Gonzaléz y Gonzaléz, E. M. (2004). *Perceptions of selected senior administrators of higher education institutions in Mexico regarding needed administrative competencies.* Unpublished doctoral dissertation, Texas A&M University.

Gugelberger, G. M. (Ed.). (1996). *The real thing: Testimonial discourse and Latin America.* Durham, NC: Duke University Press.

Gunaratnam, Y. (2003). *Researching "race" and ethnicity: Methods, knowledge and power.* London: Sage.

Gupta, A., & Ferguson, J. (Eds.). (1997). *Anthropological locations: Boundaries and grounds of a field science.* Berkeley: University of California Press.

Gupta, A., & Ferguson, J. (Eds.). (1999). *Culture, power, place: Explorations in critical anthropology.* Durham, NC: Duke University Press.

Hammersley, M. (1999). Not bricolage, but boatbuilding: Exploring two metaphors for thinking about ethnography. *Journal of Contemporary Ethnography, 28,* 574–585.

Harrison, B. (2001). *Collaborative programs in indigenous communities: From fieldwork to practice.* Walnut Creek, CA: AltaMira.

Hurtado, A. (1996). *The color of privilege: Three blasphemies on race and feminism.* Ann Arbor: University of Michigan Press.

Lincoln, Y. S. (2001). Varieties of validity: Quality in qualitative research. In J. C. Smart (Ed.), *Higher education: Handbook of theory and research* (Vol. 16, pp. 25–72). New York: Agathon.

Lincoln, Y. S. (2004). From disdain to détente and back again [Review essay on the National Research Council's *Scientific research in education* and Mosteller and Boruch's *Evidence matters: Randomized trials in education research*]. *Academe, 90*(6).

Lincoln, Y. S., & Cannella, G. S. (2004a). Dangerous discourses: Methodological conservatism and governmental regimes of truth. *Qualitative Inquiry, 10,* 5–14.

Lincoln, Y. S., & Cannella, G. S. (2004b). Qualitative research, power, and the radical Right. *Qualitative Inquiry, 10,* 175–201.

Lincoln, Y. S., & Guba, E. G. (1989). Ethics: The failure of positivist science. *Review of Higher Education, 12,* 221–240.

Mieth, D. (1997). The basic norm of truthfulness: Its ethical justification and universality. In C. G. Christians & M. Traber (Eds.), *Communication ethics and universal values* (pp. 87–104). Thousand Oaks, CA: Sage.

Mohanty, C. T. (1988). Under Western eyes: Feminist scholarship and colonial discourses. *Feminist Review, 30,* 61–88.

Mosteller, F., & Boruch, R. (2002). Overview and new directions. In F. Mosteller & R. Boruch (Eds.), *Evidence matters: Randomized trials in education research* (pp. 1–14). Washington, DC: Brookings Institution Press.

National Research Council. (2002). *Scientific research in education.* Committee on Scientific Principles for Education Research (R. J. Shavelson & L. Towne, Eds.). Center for Education,

Division of Behavioral and Social Sciences and Education. Washington, DC: National Academy Press.

O'Hanlon, R. (1988). Recovering the subject: Subaltern studies and histories of resistance in colonial South Asia. *Modern Asian Studies, 22,* 189–224.

Parker, L., & Lynn, M. (2002). What's race got to do with it? Critical race theory's conflict with and connections to qualitative research methodology and epistemology. *Qualitative Inquiry, 8,* 7–22.

Ragin, C. C., Nagel, J., & White, P. (2004). *Workshop on scientific foundations of qualitative research.* Arlington, VA: National Science Foundation.

Ramos, A. R. (1998). *Indigenism: Ethnic politics in Brazil.* Madison: University of Wisconsin Press.

Reagan, T. (2005). *Non-Western educational traditions: Indigenous approaches to educational thought and practice* (3rd ed.). Mahwah, NJ: Lawrence Erlbaum.

Roth, P. A. (1990). Comment on "Is anthropology art or science?" *Current Anthropology, 31,* 275–276.

Said, E. (1979). *Orientalism.* New York: Pantheon.

Sandoval, C. (2000). *Methodology of the oppressed.* Minneapolis: University of Minnesota Press.

Scheurich, J. J. (Ed.). (2002). *Anti-racist scholarship: An advocacy.* Albany: State University of New York Press.

Smith, L. T. (1999). *Decolonizing methodologies: Research and indigenous peoples.* London: Zed.

Stanley, C. A., & Lincoln, Y. S. (2005, March-April). Cross-race faculty mentoring. *Change, 37*(2), 44–50.

Tillman, L. C. (2002). Culturally sensitive research approaches: An African-American perspective. *Educational Researcher, 31*(9), 3–12.

Wildavsky, A. (1975). *Speaking truth to power: The art and craft of policy analysis.* New Brunswick, NJ: Transaction.

Wing, A. K. (Ed.). (2000). *Global critical race feminism: An international reader.* New York: New York University Press.

Yúdice, G. (1996). *Testimonio* and postmodernism. In G. M. Gugelberger (Ed.), *The real thing: Testimonial discourse and Latin America* (pp. 42–52). Durham, NC: Duke University Press.

Zeni, J. (Ed.). (2001). *Ethical issues in practitioner research.* New York: Teachers College Press.

READER'S GUIDE

CHAPTER	SUMMARY	PRIMARY TOPICS	THEMATIC TOPICS
1.	Overview of Collection	Epistemology, Methodology	Paradigms, Resistances, Moments
2.	Social Science and Society	Sociology of Professions, Political Economy	Higher Education, Collaborative Research
3.	Critical Theorizing and Social Justice Studies	Compositional	Race, Class, Gender, Public Education
4.	Decolonizing Inquiry	Indigenous Rights	Corporate Layers of Research, Ethics
5.	Indigenous Knowledge	Kaupapa Māori Approach	Culturally Responsive Inquiry
6.	Ethics and Politics	Value-Free Experimentalism, IRBs	Social Ethics, Communitarian Model, Resistance Discourse
7.	IRBs	Methodological Conservatism, Evidence	Phenomenological Paradigm, Constraints on Inquiry
8.	Paradigm Controversies	Critical Issues, Axiology, Action	Voice, Praxis, Positivism, Postpositivism
9.	Critical Ethnography	Collaboration Policy Studies	Activist Anthropology and Sociology
10.	The Feminisms	Major Strands	Gendered, Decolonizing Discourse
11.	Critical Race Theory	Moral Activism	Ethical Epistemology, Multiple Consciousness
12.	Critical Theory	Critical Pedagogy	Critical Humility, Critical Hermeneutics
13.	Cultural Studies	Multiple Versions	Contextualism, Hermeneutics, Dialogic Validity
14.	Queer Theory	Critical Humanism	Critical Humanist Project
15.	Critical Reflexive Inquiry	Writing History	Resistant Texts, Discourses of Freedom
16.	Critical Ethnography	Regrounding Ethnography	Multisited Fieldwork, Para-Ethnography
17.	Eighth Moment	Writing the Future	History, Ethics, Politics, Performance-Based Studies

GLOSSARY

A

Action ethnography: Critical ethnography involving the ethnographer in collaborative, social justice projects. See also *Critical ethnography.*

Action research: Critical research dealing with real-life problems, involving collaboration, dialogue, mutual learning, and producing tangible results.

Advocacy: Arguing for action research projects that resist traditional forms of privilege, knowledge, and practice.

African American performance-based aesthetic: Using the tools of critical race consciousness to manipulate and criticize the tropes of minstrelsy that represent specific colonial racist practices.

Antifoundationalism: The refusal to adopt any permanent, unvarying, or foundational standards by which truth can be universally known.

Archaeology/genealogy: Textual and historical methods of interpretation, involving a complex set of concepts (savoir, connaissance, positivity, enunciation, discursive practice) associated with the work of Foucault; interpretive procedures showing how local practices and their subjected knowledges are brought into play, as in the history of sexuality.

Authenticity, validity as: Hallmarks of trustworthy, rigorous, valid constructivist inquiry; *Types:* fairness, ontological, educative, catalytic, tactical.

Autoethnography: Engaging ethnographical practice through personal, lived experience; writing the self into the ethnographic narrative.

Autohistory: Use of the autobiographical form to write life history or personal life stories and narratives.

Autopoiesis: A self (auto)-creation (poiesis) using the poetic and the historical to understand the current moment.

B

Belmont Report: Report issued in 1978 by the U.S. Commission for the Protection of Human Subjects. This report established three principles or moral standards (respect, beneficence, justice) for human subject research.

Biographical memory: A social process of looking back, as we find ourselves remembering our lives in terms of our experiences with others. Sociological introspection (C. Ellis) is a method for reconstructing biographical memory.

Black feminist thought: Critical race- and gender-based discourse linked to revolutionary black feminism; includes the work of June Jordan, Toni Morrison, and bell hooks.

Bricolage, bricoleur: A bricoleur is a person who uses bits and pieces and anything else to make do, to assemble a quilt, a montage, a performance, an interpretation, a bricolage, a new formation, like a jazz improvisation. The postmodern qualitative researcher is a bricoleur.

C

Care, ethic of: Carol Gilligan characterizes the female moral voice as an ethic of care, involving compassion and nurturance.

Catalytic authenticity: The ability of a given inquiry to prompt action on the part of research participants and the involvement of the researcher/evaluator in training participants in specific forms of social and political action if such training is desired by those participants.

Civic journalism: Journalism that shapes calls for a public ethnography and cultural criticism.

Cochrane Collaboration: An international group of clinicians, methodologists, and consumers formed to facilitate the collection, implementation, and dissemination of systematic reviews of multiple randomized clinical trials (RTCs).

Collaborative storytelling: An approach very similar to *testimonio,* in that it is the intention of the direct narrator (research participant) to use an interlocutor (the researcher) to bring his or her situation to the attention of an audience to which he or she would normally not have access because of his or her very condition of subalternity that the *testimonio* bears witness.

Communitarian model of ethics: A model of ethics calling for collaborative, trusting, nonoppressive relationships between researchers and those studied. It presumes a community that is ontologically and axiologically prior to the person. This community has common moral values, and research is rooted in concepts of care, shared governance, neighborliness, love, kindness, and the moral good.

Compassionate consciousness: An embodied way of being and knowing that is a nonaccountable, nondescribable way of knowing.

Compositional studies: Contextual, relational studies that are sensitive to the fluidity of social identities and that analyze public and private institutions, groups, and lives lodged in relation to key social and economic structures.

Constructivist grounded theory: Associated with the work of Charmaz, emphasizing constructionist, not objectivist, leanings; criteria include credibility, resonance, and usefulness.

Conversational interviewing: A style of interviewing focused on encouraging subject participation. Interviews can be conducted in an informal manner, and interviewers may share more personal information about themselves than conventional interviewers.

Creative analytic practices (CAP): Writers interpret as they write, so writing is a form of inquiry, a way of making sense of the world. Laurel Richardson and Elizabeth Adams St. Pierre (Volume 3, Chapter 15) explore new writing and interpretive styles that follow from the narrative literary turn in the social sciences. They call these different forms of writing CAP (creative analytical processes) ethnography.

Critical ethnography: Critical ethnographers, drawing from critical theory and the Frankfurt school, emphasize a reflexive focus on praxis, action, experience, subjectivity, reflexivity, and dialogical understanding. See also *Action research.*

Critical humanism: An approach to inquiry that focuses on the structure of experience and its daily lived nature and that acknowledges the political and social role of all inquiry.

Critical pedagogy: The critical reflexive ways in which cultural agents resist and undermine particular hegemonic ways of understanding.

Critical Race Theory (CRT): Patricia Hill Collins (1991), Mari Matsuda (1995), Gloria Ladson-Billings (2000), and Patricia Williams (1992) have crafted Critical Race Theory to speak explicitly back to the webbed relations of history, the political economy, and everyday lives of women and men of color.

D

Decolonization: Contesting colonial models of inquiry and domination, resisting hegemonic research protocols, and inventing new ways of knowing.

Diaspora identity: The identities of persons of color in the developing world who have been forced to move, to travel because of politics, economics, and other cultural forces.

Discourse analysis: The collection and analysis of spoken or written materials.

E

Ethnodrama: Popular theater consisting of ethnographically derived plays located within the tradition of epic theater.

Ethnographic gaze: The classic look of the white male ethnographer and the "other."

Ethnopoetics: Ethnopoetics could be labeled investigative poetry's immediate predecessor. It is an attempt to make poetry political by merging a critique of colonialism, soft anthropology, and a poetics of witnessing. The term *ethnopoetics* was coined in 1967 by Jerome Rothenberg, Dennis Tedlock, and their colleagues.

Evidence-based research: A new methodological conservatism stressing scientifically based educational research, research using the biomedical, random, clinical trial model.

F

Focus group as strategic articulation: Reconceptualizing focus groups as instruments for implementing critical pedagogy.

Freirian pedagogy: Pedagogy influenced by Paulo Freire in which the goal of education is to begin to name the world and to recognize that we are all "subjects" of our own lives and narratives, not "objects" in the stories of others.

G

Gaze: Poststructuralists and postmodernists have contributed to the understanding that there is no clear window into the life of an individual. Any gaze is always filtered through the lenses of language, gender, social class, race, and ethnicity. There are no objective observations, only observations that are socially situated in the worlds of the observer and observed.

Grounded theory: A largely inductive method of developing theory through close-up contact with the empirical world.

H

Habitus: Bourdieu used the concept of habitus to refer to a system of meanings and structures that generate and organize practices and representations that can be objectively adapted to their outcomes without presupposing a conscious aiming at ends or an express mastery of the operations necessary in order to attain them. Using a musical metaphor, they can be collectively orchestrated without being the product of the organizing action of a conductor.

Hip-hop movement: A gendered political, literary, and performance movement involving, in some instances, liberation work and a revolutionary call to resistance for African American and other marginalized communities. Some scholars and performers have made connections with the hip-hop generation and revolutionary black feminism.

Hybridity: Term that is characterized by literature and theory that focuses on the effects of mixture upon identity and culture.

I

Indigenous pedagogy: A pedagogy that privileges the language, meanings, stories, and personal identities of indigenous persons.

Indigenous theater: Indigenous theater nurtures a critical transnational yet historically specific critical race consciousness. It uses indigenous performance as means of political representation through the reflexive use of historical restagings and masquerade. This subversive theater undermines colonial racial ideologies.

Institutional ethnography: A form of ethnography focusing on power relations, systems of discourse, and ethnographic realities connected with the work of Dorothy Smith.

Interpretive sufficiency paradigm: Within a feminist communitarian model, paradigm seeks to open up the social world in all its dynamic dimensions. Ethnographic accounts should process sufficient depth, detail, emotionality, and nuance that will permit a critical consciousness to be formed. A discourse is authentically sufficient when it is multivocal, enhances moral discernment, and promotes social transformation.

J

Justice and investigative poetics: Fight for social justice through poems calling on scholars to become more active in their communities.

K

Kaupapa Māori research: In New Zealand, Māori scholars have coined a research approach as Kaupapa Māori or Dori research rather than employing the term *indigenist.* The struggle has been over the ability by Māoris as Māoris to name the world, to theorize the world. It is a particular approach that sets out to make a positive difference for Māoris that incorporates a model of social change or transformation and that privileges Māori knowledge and ways of being.

Knowledge economy: A term used by businesspeople to define the ways in which changes in technology such as the Internet, the removal of barriers to travel and trade, and the shift to a postindustrial economy have created conditions in which the knowledge content of all goods and services will underpin wealth creation and determine competitive advantage.

L

Layered texts: A textual strategy for putting oneself into one's text and putting one's text into the literatures and traditions of social science.

Liberation theology: A school of theology, especially prevalent in the Roman Catholic Church in Latin America, that finds in the Gospel a call to free people from political, social, and material oppression, which uses *testimonio* as a way of expression.

Local understandings: Ethnographic studies tend to focus on locally crafted meanings and the settings where social interaction takes place. Such studies consider the situated content of talk in relation to local meaning-making practices.

Ludic postmodernism: Postmodernist currents associated with Derrida, Foucault, Lyotard, Ebert, and others.

M

Method of instances: A method taking each instance of a phenomenon as an occurrence that evidences the operation of a set of cultural understandings currently available for use by cultural members.

Methodological fundamentalism: A return to a much discredited model of empirical inquiry wherein the "gold standard" for producing knowledge that is worthwhile is based on quantitative, experimental design studies.

Mixed-genre text: A text that crosses writing and interpretive formats (genres), including ethnography, history, fiction, poetry, prose, photography, and performance.

Moral/ethical epistemology: Epistemology that scholars of color have produced out of which critical theories emerged, where groups such as African Americans, Native Americans, Latinos, and Asian Americans have the experience of a racialized and postcolonial identity.

Mystory performance: Personal cultural texts that contextualize important personal experiences and problems within the institutional settings and historical moments in which the author finds himself or herself.

N

Narrative inquiry: A form of inquiry that analyzes narrative, in its many forms, and uses a narrative approach for interpretive purposes.

Naturalistic generalization: Generalizations made entirely from personal or vicarious experience.

Nonfiction, creative: A term suggesting no distinction between fiction and nonfiction because both are narrative. Thus, the difference between narrative writing and science writing is not one of fiction or nonfiction but the claim that the author makes for the text and how one's "truth claims" are evaluated.

O

Online ethnography: A form of ethnography acknowledging that computer-mediated construction of self, other, and social structure constitutes a unique phenomenon of study.

Ontological authenticity: A criterion for determining a raised level of awareness by individual research participants.

Organic intellectual: Educated citizenry to participate actively in democracy, knowing enough to "read the word and the world" (Freire, 1970); helping credentialed intellectuals do the reconstructive work.

Other, as research subject: It refers to those who are studied by action-oriented and clinically oriented qualitative researchers who create spaces for those "Others" to speak and making such voices heard.

P

Participatory action research: A movement in which researchers work with subordinated populations around the world to solve unique local problems with local funds of knowledge.

Patriarchal positivism: Control through rationality and separation that forms the dominant biomedical paradigm.

Performance ethnography: A critical and emancipatory discourse connecting critical pedagogy with new ways of writing and performing cultural politics in order to catalyze social change.

Performance methodology: A collectivized ensemble of precepts used by those committed to the communicative and pedagogical potential that knowledge—the process of attaining, sharing, and projecting knowing—can be accomplished through doing.

Performance of possibilities: A set of tenets offering both validity and direction for performance ethnography.

Performativity: The stylized repetition of communicative acts, linguistic and corporeal, that are socially validated and discursively established in the moment of the performance.

Poetics of place: Form of poetics in which, through the conveyance forms and content of language and story, we enter an analysis of places and the events that unfold in them.

Polyphonic interviewing: A method of interviewing in which the voices of the respondents are recorded with minimal influence from the researcher and are not collapsed together and reported as one through the interpretation of the researcher.

Postcolonial feminist thought: A mode of thought arguing that feminism takes many different forms depending on the context of contemporary nationalism. With attention to the invidious effects of "othering," it argues that Western feminist models are inappropriate for thinking of research with women in postcolonial sites.

Postmodern ethnography: Ethnography acknowledging that ethnographic practice is not apolitical or removed from ideology. Ethnographic practice hence has the capacity to be affected by or to affect social formations.

Poststructural feminism: Theory that emphasizes problems with the social text, its logic, and its inability ever to represent the world of lived experience fully. Poststructural feminists see the "communitarian dream" as politically disabling because of the suppression of gender differences and the exclusion of subaltern voices and marginalized groups whom community members are loath to engage.

Q

Quality, emerging criteria: Set of understandings in which the ethical intersects both the interpersonal and the epistemological.

Queer theory: The postmodernization of sexual and gender studies bringing a radical deconstruction of all conventional categories of sexuality and gender.

Quilt maker, qualitative researcher as: Texts where many different things are going on at the same time, different voices, different perspectives, points of views, and angles of vision.

R

Race, as social construction: A social constructionist conception of race refuses the notions of an essentialist or a biological ground for race, asserting, rather, that race is a linguistically and historically determined construct.

Racialized identity: Essentialized concepts of race imposed on specific individuals or groups.

Randomized clinical trial (RCT): Clinical methodology that offers a compelling critical analysis of the biomedical paradigms and currently is considered to be the best external evidence when considering medical interventions.

Reality, hyper: It is a way of characterizing the way the consciousness interacts with "reality," when a consciousness loses its ability to distinguish reality from fantasy, and when the nature of the hyperreal world is characterized by "enhancement" of reality.

Reflexivity, performative: A condition in which sociocultural groups, or their most perceptive members acting representatively, turn, bend, or reflect back on themselves (Turner, 1988).

Representation, crisis of: A moment of rupture in scholarship when texts began to become more reflexive, calling into question issues of gender, class, and race, and seeking new models of trough, method, and representation.

Rhizomatic validity: A form of behaving via relay, circuit, and multiple openings that counters authority with multiple sites.

S

Sacred epistemology: This epistemology places us in a noncompetitive, nonhierarchical relationship to the Earth, to nature, and to the larger world.

Safe spaces: Progressive social scientists have gained a foothold in the academy and have created safe spaces for themselves.

Scholars of color, moral epistemologies as activists: Seeking racial justice, scholars of color, using Critical Race Theory (CRT), enact critical and moral epistemologies (double consciousness, sovereignty, hybridity, postcolonialism).

Self-reflexive validity: A form of critical validity involving paying attention to one's place in the discourses and practices that are being analyzed.

Silences: Silences can reveal invisible social structures, as well as point to moral and ethical dilemmas and lack of awareness.

Social justice: A form of justice involving a moral commitment to social and economic reform and assistance to the poor; being an advocate for fairness and what is just.

Solidarity research: Research that empowers and promotes critical consciousness and acts of resistance.

Spirituality: A sense of the sacred, a sensuous and embodied form of being, including being in harmony with the universe.

Standpoint theory: Speaking and theorizing from a historically specific standpoint or position.

Subaltern: Colonized persons, made to feel inferior by virtue of class, color, gender, race, and ethnicity.

Subversive theater: A theater that unsettles official versions of reality and challenges racism and white privilege.

▣ T

Testimonio: A first-person text with political content, often reporting on torture, imprisonment, and other struggles for survival.

Textualism: The study of documents and social texts as the site for the representation of lived experience. The media and popular culture are sites where history and lived experience come together. Nothing, Derrida reminds us, stands outside the text.

Transformative action: Creative, political action that changes the world.

Truth: A contested term, given different meaning within positivist, postpositivist and postmodern, and other narrative epistemologies.

U

Uncertainty: The understanding that while social life is interdependent and displays regularities, the outcome of any given social event is uncertain and not fully predictable.

Unstructured interviewing: Open-ended interviewing involving an unstructured format, often used in oral history, participant observation, and PAR forms of inquiry.

Utopian performative: Performances that enact a politics of hope, liberation, and justice.

V

Validity, authenticity criteria: The hallmarks of authentic, trustworthy, rigorous constructivist inquiry include fairness and four types of authenticity: ontological, educative, catalytic, and tactical.

Validity, catalytic: The extent to which research moves those it studies to understand the world and then act to change the world.

Validity, transgressive: A subversive approach to validity, connected with deconstructionism and the work of Patti Lather. There are four subtypes: ironic, paralogical, rhizomatic, and voluptuous.

Verbatim theater: A form of realistic theater or ethnodrama that uses oral history, news accounts, and verbatim reports, thereby quoting history back to itself, bringing the immediate past into the present.

Virtue ethics of care model: An ethics that goes beyond utilitarianism to include feminist notions of care, love, and communitarianism.

Voice, paradigmatic issues: Hearing the other (and the author) speak in the text, presenting the other's self in the text.

W

Warranted assertion: A conclusion or assertion that is justified by a set of socially shaped reasons or judgments.

Wild places: Sacred places where meaning, self, and being dwell.

Women of color, as researcher: Women of color are urged to address, from within white patriarchy, culturally sensitive issues surrounding race, class, and gender.

Writing, as inquiry: Writing is a method of inquiry, writing is thinking, writing is analysis, and writing is a method of discovery.

Writing, performative: The kind of writing where the body and the spoken word come together. Performance writing shows and does not tell. It is writing that does what it says it is doing by doing it.

▣ X, Y, Z

Zombie research: According to Ken Plummer, a postgay humanist sociologist, in the postmodern moment, certain terms, such as *family,* and much of our research methodology language are obsolete. He calls them zombie categories. They are no longer needed. They are dead terms.

SUGGESTED READINGS

Chapter 3

Appadurai, A. (2002). Deep democracy: Urban governmentality and the horizon of politics. *Public Culture, 14*(1).

Appelbaum, R., & Robinson, W. (Eds.). (2005). *Critical globalization studies.* New York: Routledge.

Bhavnani, K., Foran, J., & Talcott, M. (2005). The red, the green, the black and the purple: Reclaiming development, resisting globalization. In R. P. Appelbaum & W. I. Robinson (Eds.), *Critical globalization studies.* London: Routledge.

Cahill, C. (2004). Defying gravity? Raising consciousness through collective research. *Children's Geographies, 2*(2), 273–286.

Fals-Borda, O. (1979). Investigating the reality in order to transform it: The Colombian experience. *Dialectical Anthropology, 4,* 33–55.

Fine, M., Roberts, R., Torre, M., Bloom, J., Chajet, L., Guishard, M., et al. (2004). *Echoes of* Brown: *Youth documenting and performing the legacy of* Brown v. Board of Education. New York: Teachers College Press.

Fine, M., Torre, M. E., Boudin, K., Bowen, I., Clark, J., Hylton, D., et al. (2003). Participatory action research: Within and beyond bars. In P. Camic, J. E. Rhodes, & L. Yardley (Eds.), *Qualitative research in psychology: Expanding perspectives in methodology and design.* Washington, DC: American Psychological Association.

Gordon, A. (1997). *Ghostly matters: Haunting and the sociological imagination.* Minneapolis: University of Minnesota Press.

Katz, C. (2001). On the grounds of globalization: A topography for feminist political engagement. *Signs: Journal of Women in Culture & Society,* 26(4), 1213–1228.

Katz, C. (2003). *Growing Up global.* Minneapolis: University of Minnesota Press.

Marcus, G. (1995). Ethnography in/of the world system: The emergency of multi-sited ethnography. *Annual Review of Anthropology, 24,* 95–117.

Marston, S. (2000). The social construction of scale. *Progress in Human Geography, 24,* 2, 219–242.

Oliver, M., & Shapiro, T. (1997). *Black wealth/white wealth: A new perspective on racial inequality.* New York: Routledge.

Painter, N. (1995). Soul murder and slavery: Toward a fully-loaded cost accounting. In L. K. Kerber, A. Kessler-Harris, & K. Kish Sklar (Eds.), *U.S. history as women's history: New feminist essays.* Chapel Hill: University of North Carolina Press.

Sassen, S. (2005). The many scales of the global: Implications for theory and politics. In R. Applebaum & W. Robinson (Eds.), *Critical globalization studies.* New York: Taylor & Francis.

Weis, L. (Ed.). (2008). *The way class works: Readings on school, family, culture and the economy.* New York. Routledge.

Weis, L., & Dimitriadis, G. (in press). Dueling banjos: Shifting economic and cultural contexts in the lives of youth. *Teachers College Record.*

Chapter 9

Field, L., & Fox, R. G. (Eds.). (2007). *Anthropology put to work.* Oxford, UK: Berg.

Lassiter, L. (2005). *The Chicago guide to collaborative ethnography.* Chicago: University of Chicago.

Chapter 10

Charmaz, K. (2006). *Constructing grounded theory: A practical guide through qualitative analysis.* Thousand Oaks, CA: Sage.

Clarke, A. (2005). *Situational analysis, grounded theory after the postmodern turn.* Thousand Oaks, CA: Sage.

Clarke, A. (2006). Feminisms, grounded theory and situational analysis. In S. Hesse-Biber (Ed.), *Handbook of feminist research, theory and praxis* (pp. 345–370). Thousand Oaks, CA: Sage.

Dankoski, M. E. (2000). What makes research feminist? *Journal of Family Therapy, 2*(1), 3–19.

Fonow, M. M., & Cook. J. A. (2005). Feminist methodology: New applications in the academy and public policy. *Signs: Journal of Women in Culture & Society, 30*(4), 2211–2237.

Guevarra, A. (2006). Managing 'vulnerabilities' and 'empowering' migrant Filipina workers: The Philippines' overseas employment program. *Social Identities: Journal for the Study of Race, Nation and Culture, 12*(5), 523–541.

Henwood, K., & Pidgeon, N. (1995). Remaking the link: Qualitative research and feminist standpoint theory. *Feminism and Psychology, 5*(1), 7–30.

Hesse-Biber, S. N. (Ed.). (2007). *Handbook of feminist research, theory, practice.* Thousand Oaks, CA: Sage.

Lather, P. (2006). *Getting lost: Feminist efforts toward a double(d) science.* Albany, NY: SUNY Press.

Maynard, M. (2004). Feminist issues in data analysis. In M. Hardy & A. Bryman (Eds.), *Handbook of data analysis* (pp. 131–146). Thousand Oaks, CA: Sage.

Sprague, J. (2005). *Feminist methodologies for critical researchers.* Walnut Creek, CA: Alta Mira.

Steinmetz, G. (2005). Introduction: Positivism and its others in the social sciences. In G. Steinmetiz (Ed.), *The politics of method in the human sciences: Positivism and its epistemological others* (pp. 1–56) Durham, NC: Duke University Press.

Steinmetz, G. (2005). Scientific authority and the transition to post-Fordism: The plausibility of positivism in U.S. sociology since 1945. In G. Steinmetz (Ed.), *The politics of method in the human sciences: Positivism and its epistemological others* (pp. 275–326). Durham, NC: Duke University Press.

AUTHOR INDEX

SUBJECT INDEX

ABOUT THE EDITORS

Norman K. Denzin is Distinguished Professor of Communications, College of Communications Scholar, and Research Professor of Communications, Sociology, and Humanities at the University of Illinois at Urbana-Champaign. He is the author of numerous books, including *Interpretive Ethnography: Ethnographic Practices for the 21st Century; The Cinematic Society: The Voyeur's Gaze; Images of Postmodern Society; The Research Act: A Theoretical Introduction to Sociological Methods; Interpretive Interactionism; Hollywood Shot by Shot; The Recovering Alcoholic;* and *The Alcoholic Self,* which won the Charles Cooley Award from the Society for the Study of Symbolic Interaction in 1988. In 1997, the Study of Symbolic Interaction presented him the George Herbert Award. He is the editor of the *Sociological Quarterly,* coeditor of *Qualitative Inquiry,* and editor of the book series *Cultural Studies: A Research Annual and Studies in Symbolic Interaction.*

Yvonna S. Lincoln is Ruth Harrington Chair of Educational Leadership and Distinguished Professor of Higher Education at Texas A&M University. In addition to this volume, she is coeditor of the first and second editions of the *Handbook of Qualitative Research,* the journal *Qualitative Inquiry* (with Norman K. Denzin), and the Teaching and Learning section of the *American Educational Research Journal* (with Bruce Thompson and Stephanie Knight). She is the coauthor, with Egon Guba, of *Naturalistic Inquiry, Effective Evaluation, and Fourth Generation Evaluation,* the editor of *Organizational Theory and Inquiry,* and the coeditor of several other books with William G. Tierney and with Norman Denzin. She is the recipient of numerous awards for research and has published journal articles, chapters, and conference papers on higher education, research university libraries, and alternative paradigm inquiry.

ABOUT THE CONTRIBUTORS

Zygmunt Bauman is Professor Emeritus at Leeds and also at the University of Warsaw. Before coming to Leeds in 1972, he was with the University of Warsaw and the University of Tel Aviv. Dr. Bauman has held several visiting professorships and is known throughout the world as one of the 20th century's great social theorists and foremost sociologist of postmodernity. He has published more than 20 books, including *Legislators and Interpreters* (1987), *Modernity and the Holocaust* (1989), *Modernity and Ambivalence* (1991), and *Postmodern Ethics* (1993). In 1990, the year of his retirement, he was awarded the Amalfi European Prize and, in 1998, the Adorno Prize.

Russell Bishop is foundation Professor and Assistant Dean for Māori Education in the School of Education at the University of Waikato, Hamilton, New Zealand. He has taught in secondary schools in New Zealand and the Cook Islands. Prior to his present appointment, he was a senior lecturer in Māori Education at the University of Otago and also Interim Director for Otago University's Teacher Education program. His research experience is in the area of collaborative storying in Māori contexts, having written a book *Collaborative Research Stories: Whakawhanaungatanga* and published internationally on this topic. His other research interests include strategies for implementing the Treaty of Waitangi in tertiary institutions, intercultural education, and collaborative storying as pedagogy. The latter area is the subject of a book, *Culture Counts: Changing Power Relationships in Classrooms* (coauthored with Ted Glynn, 1999), which demonstrates how the experiences developed from within kaupapa Māori settings, schooling, research, and policy development can be applied to mainstream educational settings. He is currently the project director for a New Zealand Ministry-of-Education-funded research/professional development project that seeks to improve the educational achievement of Māori students in mainstream classrooms.

Clifford G. Christians is Research Professor of Communications at the University of Illinois, Urbana-Champaign. He has been a visiting scholar in philosophical ethics at Princeton University and in social ethics at the University of Chicago, as well as a PEW Fellow in Ethics at Oxford University. He completed the third edition of Rivers and Schramm's *Responsibility in Mass Communication*, has coauthored *Jacques Ellul: Interpretive Essays* with Jay Van Hook, and has written *Teaching Ethics in Journalism Education* with Catherine Covert. He is also the coauthor, with John Ferre and Mark Fackler, of *Good News: Social Ethics and the Press* (1993). His *Media Ethics: Cases and Moral Reasoning* with Kim Rotzoll, Mark Fackler, and Kathy McKee is now in its seventh edition (2005). *Communication Ethics and Universal Values*, coauthored with Michael Traber, was published in 1997, and his book with Sharon Bracci, *Moral Engagement in Public Life: Theorists for Contemporary Ethics* appeared in 2002. He has lectured or given academic papers on ethics in Norway, Russia, Finland, France, Belgium, Italy, Netherlands, England, Switzerland, Singapore, Korea, Scotland, Philippines, Slovenia, Canada, Brazil, Mexico, Puerto Rico, Spain, Sweden, Hong Kong, and Taiwan.

Jamel Donnor is a Ph.D. candidate in the Department of Curriculum and Instruction at the University of Wisconsin–Madison, majoring in educational communications and technology. His research focuses on examining issues of access to and equity of technology for African American students, critical race theoretical applications to education, and the education of African American male student-athletes.

Michelle Fine is a Distinguished Professor of Psychology, Women's Studies, and Urban Education at the Graduate Center of the City University of New York. Committed to participatory action research in schools, prisons, and communities, her writings focus on theoretical questions of social injustice: how people think about unjust distributions of resources and social practices, when they resist, and how such inequities are legitimated. Interested in the combination of quantitative and qualitative methods as well as participatory action designs, her writings encompass questions of epistemology, methodology, and social change. Recent publications include *Echoes: Youth Documenting and Performing the Legacy of Brown v. Board of Education* (Fine, Roberts, Torre and Bloom, Burns, Chajet, and Guishard and Payne, 2004); *Working Method: Social Injustice and Social Research* (Weis and Fine, 2004); *Off White: Essays on Race, Power and Resistance* (Fine, Weis, Powell, Pruitt, and Burns, 2004); *Silenced Voices and Extraordinary Conversations* (Weis and Fine, 2003); *Construction Sites: Excavating Race, Class and Gender with Urban Youth* (Fine and Weis, 2001); *Speedbumps: A Student Friendly Guide to Qualitative Research* (edited with Lois Weis, 2000); and *Changing Minds: A Participatory Action Research Analysis of College in Prison* (2001, with Maria Elena Torre, Kathy Boudin, Iris Bowen, Judith Clark, Donna Hylton, Migdalia Martinez, "Missy," Rosemarie A. Roberts, Pamela Smart, and Deborah Upegui). She has offered expert testimony in a number of cases involving race, gender, and/or class discrimination.

Douglas Foley is Professor of Anthropology and of Education at the University of Texas at Austin. He specializes in the anthropology of education, American race relations, and ethnographic field methods. He also served for several years as coeditor of the *International Journal of Qualitative Studies in Education.* He is the author of numerous articles and several ethnographies, including *The Heartland Chronicles*, *Learning Capitalist Culture*, and *From Peones to Politics.*

Davydd J. Greenwood is the Goldwin Smith Professor of Anthropology and Director of the Institute for European Studies at Cornell University, where he has served as a faculty member since 1970. He has been elected a Corresponding Member of the Spanish Royal Academy of Moral and Political Sciences. He served as the John S. Knight Professor and Director of the Mario Einaudi Center for 10 years and was President of the Association of International Education Administrators. He also has served as a program evaluator for many universities and for the National Foreign Language Center. His work centers on action research, political economy, ethnic conflict, community and regional development, the Spanish Basque Country, Spain's La Mancha region, and the Finger Lakes region of upstate New York, where he carried out a 3-year action research and community development project with communities along the Erie Canal corridor. The author of seven books and numerous articles, his works include *Unrewarding Wealth: The Commercialization and Collapse of Agriculture in a Spanish Basque Town; Nature, Culture, and Human History; The Taming of Evolution: The Persistence of Nonevolutionary Views in the Study of Humans; Las culturas de Fagor; Industrial Democracy as Process: Participatory Action Research in the Fagor Cooperative Group of Mondragón;* a collaborative monograph with students, *Teaching Participatory Action Research in the University in Studies in Continuing Education;* and *Introduction to Action Research: Social Research for Social Change* (with Morten Levin). He has edited two books, *Democracy and Difference: A Comparative Study of the Impact of Legal-Administrative Structures on Identity in the United States and Spain* and *Action Research and Rhetoric: The Scandinavian Action Research Development Program.*

Egon G. Guba is Professor Emeritus of Education, Indiana University. He received his Ph.D. from the University of Chicago in quantitative inquiry (education) in 1952, and thereafter served on the faculties of the University of Chicago, the University of Kansas City, the Ohio State University, and Indiana University. For the past 20 years, he has studied paradigms alternative to the received view and has espoused a personal commitment to one of these: constructivism. He is the coauthor of *Effective Evaluation* (1981), *Naturalistic Inquiry* (1985), and *Fourth Generation Evaluation* (1989), all with Yvonna S. Lincoln, and he is editor of *The Paradigm Dialog* (1990), which explores the implications of alternative paradigms for social and educational inquiry. He is the author of more than 150 journal articles and more than 100 conference presentations, many of them concerned with elements of new-paradigm inquiry and methods.

Douglas R. Holmes teaches anthropology at Binghamton University. He has, over the last decade, written about the sociopolitical dynamics and cultural imperatives shaping advanced European integration. His current research examines the complex role of the European Central Bank in fostering economic integration across a rapidly expanding European Union. His collaborative work with George E. Marcus focuses on recasting ethnographic method to address the manifold challenges posed by anthropological research within cultures of expertise. He is the author of *Integral Europe: Fast-Capitalism, Multiculturalism, Neofascism* and *Cultural Disenchantmenets: Worker Peasantries in Northeast Italy*.

Joe L. Kincheloe is Professor of Education at City University of New York Graduate Center and Brooklyn College. He is Deputy Executive Officer of the Urban Education program at CUNY. He has written books and articles on research, cultural studies, critical education, and cognition, including *The Sign of the Burger: McDonald's and the Culture of Power* and *Kinderculture: The Corporate Construction of Childhood.*

Gloria Ladson-Billings is Professor in the Department of Curriculum and Instruction at the University of Wisconsin–Madison and a Senior Fellow in Urban Education of the Annenberg Institute for School Reform at Brown University. Her primary research interests are in the relationships between culture and school and critical race theory. She is author of *The Dreamkeepers: Successful Teachers of African-American Children* and is editor of the Teaching, Learning, and Human Development section of the *American Educational Research Journal.*

Morten Levin is Professor in the Department of Industrial Economics and Technology Management at the Norwegian University of Science and Technology in Trondheim, Norway. He holds graduate degrees in engineering and in sociology. Throughout his professional life, he has worked as an action researcher with particular focus on processes and structures of social change in the relationships between technology and organization. The action research has taken place in industrial contexts, in local communities, and in university teaching, where he has developed and been in charge of a number of Ph.D. programs in action research. He is author of a number of books and articles, including *Introduction to Action Research: Social Research for Social Change,* and he serves on the editorial boards of *Systems Practice and Action Research, Action Research International, Action Research, The Handbook of Qualitative Inquiry*, and *The Handbook of Action Research.*

George E. Marcus is Joseph Jamail Professor and Chair, Department of Anthropology, Rice University. He is coauthor of *Anthropology as Cultural Critique* and coeditor of *Writing Culture.* In 1998, he published *Ethnography Through Thick & Thin.* Through the 1990s, he created and edited the *Late Editions* series of annuals designed to document the fin-de-siecle in a number of arenas through ethnographic conversations. He is now at work on a memoir of his years supervising dissertations, which he views as a laboratory for the reinvention of anthropological method.

Peter McLaren is Professor, Division of Urban Schooling, Graduate School of Education and Information Studies, University of California, Los Angeles. Professor McLaren is the author and editor of over 40 books in a variety of areas that include the political sociology of education, critical pedagogy, and Marxist theory. His most recent books include *Capitalists and Conquerors: Teaching Against Global Capitalism and the New Imperialism* (with Ramin Farahmandpur) and *Red Seminars*. His writings have been published in 15 languages. Professor McLaren is the inaugural recipient of the Paulo Freire Social Justice Award, Chapman University.

Virginia L. Olesen, Emerita Professor of Sociology in the Department of Social and Behavioral Sciences at the University of California, continues to explore and write on critical issues in qualitative methods, women's health, feminist thought, sociology of emotions, and globalization. She is coeditor, with Sheryl Ruzek and Adele Clarke, of *Women's Health: Complexities and Diversities* (1997) and, with Adele Clarke, of *Revisioning Women, Health and Healing: Feminist, Cultural and Technoscience Perspectives* (1999). She is currently working on issues of skepticism in qualitative research and the problems of "the third voice" constituted between and among researchers.

Ken Plummer is Professor in Sociology at the University of Essex in the United Kingdom and is a regular visitor at the University of California at Santa Barbara. He has written or edited some ten books and a hundred articles including *Intimate Citizenship* (2003), *Documents of Life-2* (2001), *Telling Sexual Stories* (1995), and *Sexual Stigma* (1975). In 2001, he was the first recipient of the American Sociological Association Gagnon and Simon Award for outstanding contributions to the study of sexualities. He is the founding editor of the journal *Sexualities*.

Paula Saukko, Ph.D., is a Research Fellow at the ESRC-Centre for Genomics in Society (Egenis) in the School of Historical, Political, and Sociological Studies at the University of Exeter and an Honorary Research Fellow at the Peninsula Medical School, both in the United Kingdom. Her research interests are qualitative methodology and cultural studies of science and medicine, and her topical projects have focused on genetic testing for common illnesses and discourses of eating disorders. She is the author of *Doing Research in Cultural Studies: An Introduction to Classical and Contemporary Methodological Approaches* (Sage, 2003). She is also coeditor (with L. Reed) of *Governing the Female Body: Gender, Health, and Networks of Power* (forthcoming) and coeditor (with C. McCarthy et al.) of *Sound Identities* (1999). She is a member of the editorial boards of *Cultural Studies/Critical Methodologies* and *Kulttuuritutkimus* and is currently writing a book on lived social and historical dimensions of diagnostic discourses on anorexia.

Linda Tuhiwai Smith is Professor of Education at the University of Auckland. She is Joint Director of Nga Pae o te Maramatanga The National Institute for Research Excellence in Māori Development and Advancement, a center of research excellence hosted by the University of Auckland. Dr. Smith is a leading Māori and indigenous educationist and is well sought after as a speaker and commentator. Her work is recognized internationally through her book *Decolonising Methodologies: Research and Indigenous Peoples.* She has also published research on the history of Māori schools, Māori women and education, and other social justice themes.

Angela Valenzuela is Associate Professor in the Department of Curriculum and Instruction at the University of Texas at Austin and also the Center for Mexican American Studies. She is author of *Subtractive Schooling: U.S. Mexican Youth and the Politics of Caring,* winner of both the 2000 American Educational Research Association Outstanding Book Award and the 2001 Critics' Choice Award from the American Educational Studies Association. She is also the editor of *Leaving Children Behind: How Texas-Style Accountability Fails Latino Youth.* Her research interests are in the areas of urban education, race relations, high-stakes testing, and Latino education policy. Much of her current policy work stems from her position as Chair of the Education Committee for the Texas League of United Latin American Citizens (LULAC), the nation's oldest Mexican American civil rights organization.

Lois Weis is Professor of Sociology of Education at the University of Buffalo, State University of New York. She is the author or coauthor of numerous books and articles pertaining to social class, race, gender, and schooling in the United States. Her most recent books include *Class Reunion: The Remaking of the American White Working Class* (2004), *Working Method* (with Michelle Fine, 2004), and *Silenced Voices and Extraordinary Conversations: Re-Imagining Schools* (with Michelle Fine, 2003). She sits on numerous editorial boards and is the editor of the Power, Social Identity, and Education book series with SUNY Press.